Hans Keller (1919–1985)

Hans Keller 1919–1985: A musician in dialogue with his times is the first full biography of Hans Keller and the first appearance in print of many of his letters. Eight substantial chapters, integrating original documents with their historical context, show the development of Keller's ideas in response to the people and events that provoked them.

A musician of penetrating insight, Keller was also an exceptional writer and broadcaster, whose remarkable mind dominated British musical life for forty years after the Second World War. It was a vital time for music in Britain, fuelled by unprecedented public investment in the arts and education and the rapid development of recording and broadcasting. Keller was at the centre of all that was happening and his far-sighted analysis of the period is deeply resonant today.

Illustrated throughout by extracts from Keller's writings, diaries and correspondence with musicians including Arnold Schoenberg, Benjamin Britten and Yehudi Menuhin, this book vividly conveys the depth of his thought and the excitement of the times. Published for the centenary of Keller's birth, it is an illuminating celebration of his life and works for all those interested in the music and history of post-war Britain.

Alison Garnham was the initial archivist of the Hans Keller Archive when it was first established at Cambridge University Library in 1996. She is the author of *Hans Keller and the BBC* (2003) and *Hans Keller and Internment* (2011).

Susi Woodhouse is the current archivist of the Hans Keller Archive at Cambridge. She also works with the online Concert Programmes Project and the London Symphony Orchestra photograph archive.

'This is a detailed and revealing biography, rich in context and background, of one of the great musical thinkers, writers and broadcasters of our time. It casts a penetrating light on the post-war cultural scene and the passionate internal battles over music broadcasting on the BBC. Keller's many enthusiasms, from Schoenberg and Mendelssohn to Gershwin and the Beatles, shine through his fiercely communicative prose. And all are illuminated by the moving personal integrity of a man who, facing extinction by the Nazis in 1938, swore that if he survived "I'll never again be in a bad mood, whatever the circumstances of my life or death". Alison Garnham and Susi Woodhouse have written a vital chapter in the musical history of our times.'

Nicholas Kenyon

Hans Keller 1919–1985

A musician in dialogue with his times

Alison Garnham and Susi Woodhouse

with translations from the German by
Paul Fletcher

Routledge
Taylor & Francis Group

LONDON AND NEW YORK

First published 2019
by Routledge
2 Park Square, Milton Park, Abingdon, Oxon OX14 4RN

and by Routledge
52 Vanderbilt Avenue, New York, NY 10017

Routledge is an imprint of the Taylor & Francis Group, an informa business.

British Library Cataloguing-in-Publication Data
A catalogue record for this book is available from the British Library.

Library of Congress Cataloging-in-Publication Data
Names: Garnham, A. M. (Alison M.), 1964- author. | Woodhouse,
    Susi, author. | Container of (expression): Keller, Hans, 1919-1985.
    Correspondence. Selections.
Title: Hans Keller 1919-1985 : a musician in dialogue with his times / Alison
    Garnham and Susi Woodhouse ; with translations from the German by
    Paul Fletcher and music examples by Stephen Orton.
Description: Abingdon, Oxon ; New York, NY : Routledge, 2019. | Includes
    bibliographical references and index.
Identifiers: LCCN 2018038087| ISBN 9780754608981 (hardback) | ISBN
    9781138391048 (pbk.) | ISBN 9781315586175 (ebook)
Subjects: LCSH: Keller, Hans, 1919–1985—Correspondence. | Music
    critics—England—Correspondence. | Musical criticsim—England—
    Correspondence.
Classification: LCC ML423.K445 .G34 2018 | DDC 780.92—dc23
LC record available at https://lccn.loc.gov/2018038087

ISBN: 978-0-7546-0898-1 (hbk)
ISBN: 978-1-138-39104-8 (pbk)
ISBN: 978-1-315-58617-5 (ebk)

Typeset in Times New Roman
by Swales & Willis Ltd, Exeter, Devon, UK

Printed and bound in Great Britain by
TJ International Ltd, Padstow, Cornwall

This book is dedicated to the memory of
MILEIN COSMAN
who died as it was being written

and to
JULIAN HOGG
close friend and colleague of Hans and Milein

Sketch of Hans Keller by Milein Cosman in one of his notebooks, 1955 (CULHK).

Contents

Preface

> If there is any point in an anniversary at all (victimization by over-exposure apart), it is a momentary pause: we stop at the traffic lights to reflect, for a moment, upon where we are going. Or rather, we know where we're going, or think we know, but we think about what it means – perhaps even about what it means to have got that far.

The period of Hans Keller's active life as a British writer and broadcaster on music – and thus the main period covered by this book, 1945–85 – was one of the most vital and exciting times in this country's musical history. A combination of state patronage, massive investment in education, technological revolution and, above all, belief in the importance of music to the resurrection of national life after two devastating wars, created uniquely fertile ground. Into this came thousands of people who had fled what had been for two centuries the dominant musical culture of Europe, bringing their rich musical tradition into the new life of the former 'Land ohne Musik'.

Hans Keller, instinctive musician and compulsive writer, arrived from Vienna aged nineteen at the end of 1938. He was first drawn into writing about music by the impact of Britten's *Peter Grimes* in 1945 – both by the work itself and by its extraordinary reception. From then on he wrote continually and published prolifically, not only documenting but constantly interrogating what was happening around him. He was a born communicator, and it is not surprising that education and psychology should have been central to his thought, or that he should have become so intensely concerned with the new mass media.

These were the years when recording and broadcasting changed for ever how music was experienced, allowing the whole of society to hear what had previously been the preserve of a few. Composers and performers could now speak to millions, while all the time vast new repertoires were opening up, from the past and from radically different cultures. Music in the home became for most a passive rather than active experience, making the pace of change ever faster as the spread of musical innovation was no longer held back by the availability of performing skills. As all this bewildering change unfolded, discussion of music was taking place in the centre of the public sphere, rather than being confined to academia – which in any case was in its musical infancy in Britain at the start of this period. Keller was able to speak at a high level and in considerable detail to a broad public.

When Keller died, there were some who mourned that this brilliant mind had allowed itself to become so deeply drawn into what they saw as the ephemeral traffic of his day, his insights buried in literally thousands of letters, reviews and radio talks on events long since passed. And yet Keller was adamant that he wrote for the future, that objective truth was to be found through subjective experience, and that the issues with which he dealt would retain their importance: 'If the future recovers any of my articles from the wastepaper basket, they may not be interesting any more – but the subjects they discuss will, I insist, still be alive, or maybe more alive than when I discussed them.'[1]

This book is published on the centenary of Keller's birth. Its aim is to present – to the very different musical world in which we now live – the development of his principal ideas in the context of the events that provoked them. Short extracts from his letters, diaries, and published and unpublished writings are placed within the story of his life and times, together with a few of his intensely thought-provoking aphorisms. With so prolific a writer, there are many different paths that could have been taken through his vast oeuvre: this is offered as a start. The list overleaf of Keller's work now available in volume form, together with the full catalogue of his archive recently completed at Cambridge University Library, will allow others to take their own route.

As we pause at the traffic lights, the question Keller would ask (did ask, in the essay quoted above, to which the reader will come in due course) is not only where we are going, but why we are going where we are going – and what, ultimately, the purpose of the unique mode of thought we call music actually is.

---

1 'Today's Tomorrow', *MR* XXV/4 (November 1964): 343–4.

Key to Source Abbreviations

Archival Sources

Keller's archive is held in Cambridge University Library and all unpublished letters and manuscripts quoted in this book are there unless otherwise indicated. References to archives are abbreviated as follows:

CULHK   Hans Keller Archive, Cambridge University Library
WAC   BBC Written Archive Centre
ASC   Arnold Schönberg Center, Vienna
BPF   Britten–Pears Foundation
BLWG   William Glock papers, British Library
BLDM   Donald Mitchell papers, British Library
BLPH   Paul Hirsch papers, British Library
BLEC   Ernest Chapman papers, British Library
DSSA   Dartington Summer School Archive

Books

Frequent reference has been made to the volumes of and on Keller's work published both during his lifetime and after his death – abbreviated as follows:

1975   Keller, Hans. *1975 (1984 minus 9)*. London: Dobson, 1977.
BB1952   *Benjamin Britten: a Commentary by a Group of Specialists*, ed. Hans Keller and Donald Mitchell. London: Rockliff, 1952.
BB2013   Keller, Hans. *Britten: Essays, Letters and Opera Guides*, ed. Christopher Wintle and A.M. Garnham. London: Plumbago, 2013.
EOM   Keller, Hans. *Essays on Music,* ed. Christopher Wintle (with Bayan Northcott and Irene Samuel). Cambridge: CUP, 1994.
HKBBC Garnham, A.M. *Hans Keller and the BBC*. Aldershot: Ashgate, 2003.
HKC   Keller, Hans. *Criticism*, ed. Julian Hogg. London: Faber, 1987.
HKFA   Keller, Hans. *Functional Analysis: The Unity of Contrasting Themes* (Complete Edition of the Analytical Scores), ed. Gerold W. Gruber. Frankfurt: Peter Lang, 2001.
HKFM   Keller, Hans. *Film Music and Beyond*, ed. Christopher Wintle. London: Plumbago, 2006.

HKH	Keller, Hans. *The Great Haydn Quartets: Their Interpretation.* London: Dent, 1986.
HKI	Garnham, A.M. *Hans Keller and Internment.* London: Plumbago, 2011.
HKJD	Keller, Hans. *The Jerusalem Diary*, ed. Christopher Wintle and Fiona Williams. London: Plumbago, 2001.
HKKC	Keller, Hans. *The Keller Column*, ed. Robert Matthew-Walker. London: Lengnick, 1990.
HKM&P	Keller, Hans. *Music and Psychology: from Vienna to London*, ed. Christopher Wintle with Alison Garnham. London: Plumbago, 2003.
HKSMM	Keller, Hans, and Milein Cosman, *Stravinsky the Music-Maker*, ed. Martin Anderson. London: Toccata Press, 2010.
HKSym	'Hans Keller (1919–1985): A Memorial Symposium,' researched and compiled by Christopher Wintle, *Music Analysis* V/2–3 (July–October 1983): 342–440.

Periodicals

Frequently cited periodicals are abbreviated as follows:

LRB	*London Review of Books*
M&L	*Music & Letters*
M&M	*Music and Musicians*
MA	*Music Analysis*
MO	*Musical Opinion*
MQ	*The Musical Quarterly*
MR	*The Music Review*
MS	*Music Survey*
MT	*The Musical Times*
NR	*The New Review*
NS	*New Statesman*
RT	*Radio Times*

Acknowledgements

No work of this nature is possible without considerable help, and we are deeply indebted to all who have supported us. Our first thanks go to Hans Keller's Literary Executor, Christopher Wintle, the Cosman Keller Art and Music Trust, and the Syndics of Cambridge University Library for their kind permission to publish Keller's words and for all the support we have received during this project.

We owe much to Keller's friends and family members who have generously shared their memories with us over the years – and we thank in particular those who gave interviews quoted here: Martin Anderson, Leo Black, Peter Carter, Levon Chilingirian, Milein Cosman, Alexander Goehr, Stephen Hearst, Julian Hogg, Stephen Plaistow, Robert Ponsonby, Donald Rau, Lionel Salter and Inge Trott.

Without the expert knowledge of Sibelius software and the extraordinary patience and kindness of Stephen Orton, it would not have been possible to create the many fine music examples, and without the enviable technical skills of Francis Woodhouse it would not have been possible to group them together where necessary. Paul Fletcher translated many more letters than there was eventually room for and patiently answered all our linguistic queries. He and we also thank Barbara Schingnitz, who left no stone unturned giving scrupulous advice on the fine details.

To Laura Davey, Gillian and Barry Garnham, Julian Hogg, Chris Lord, Philip Rupprecht, Arnold Whittall and Christopher Wintle we are extremely grateful for their kindness in reading and commenting on chapters in draft, and we also thank Kathryn Puffett for her meticulous copy-editing. The further encouragement and advice of Michael and Marjolein Allen, Adie and Chris Batt, Bojan Bujić, Gerald Davidson, Jennifer Orton, Andrea Rauter, Evan Rothstein and David Wright have been much appreciated – as have been the happy times spent with David Ibbetson and the Cooke family during archival visits. Our Routledge editors, Heidi Bishop and Annie Vaughan, together with project manager Rosie Stewart, have been unfailingly supportive throughout this complex project, and we are grateful for their understanding and assistance through the twists and turns of the book as it evolved.

Special thanks are due to Julian Hogg and Jane Cassini for all their help with many illustrations and their preparation for publication. Milein Cosman's drawings and prints appear courtesy of the Cosman Keller Trust, and the images on pp. vi, 196, 213, 303, 305, 320 and 359 held in the Keller Archive by kind permission of both the Trust and the Syndics of Cambridge University Library. The cover portrait of Keller is reproduced by permission of the Trustees of the Lotte Meitner-Graf estate, Catherine Scudamore's photographs of Keller and colleagues at Dartington thanks to the Dartington Summer Arts Foundation, and the photograph of Keller at the Schoenberg centenary conference in Canada courtesy of McMaster University.

We are extremely grateful for all the help we have received from the staff of the British Library, the Britten–Pears Foundation and the BBC Written Archive Centre – especially the marvellous Jeff Walden. We also thank Jeremy Wilson for kindly inviting us into his home to see the Dartington Summer School Archive. The unfailing support of the Music Department at Cambridge University Library has been exceptional throughout the past three years – so to Anna Pensaert, Margaret Jones, Sarah Chapman, Justin Burrowes, Catherine Taylor and Kate Crane our deep and enduring gratitude.

BBC copyright content is reproduced courtesy of the British Broadcasting Corporation. We also thank the families and rights holders of Keller's correspondents for permitting the publication of extracts from private letters: the William Alwyn Foundation, the Britten–Pears Foundation, Theodora Boyd (acting on behalf of her brothers and sisters) and Jinny Blom (Eric Blom), Nicholas Bennett (John Carl Flugel), Jeremy Frankel and Dimitri Kennaway (Benjamin Frankel), Sebastian Balfour (William Glock), Peter and Nina Hamburger (Paul Hamburger), Anna Harvey (Jonathan Harvey), Michael Schuster and Desmond Hirsch (Paul Hirsch), Hugh Howes (Frank Howes), Guy Dammon (Arthur Jacobs), Mark and Deborah Kermode and Sharon Rubin at Peters, Fraser and Dunlop (Frank Kermode), Else Landon (H.C. Robbins Landon) and Mark Livingston (David Livingston and Donald Mitchell). Letters from William Mann are published with the kind permission of his daughters and that from Rudolph Reti thanks to Lucy Shevenell. Letters from Arnold Schoenberg are quoted by permission of Belmont Music Publishers, Los Angeles, the letter from Mátyás Seiber is published with the kind permission of Julia Seiber Boyd, and we are also grateful to David Lascelles for permission to quote Erwin Stein. Many thanks are also due to Bayan Northcott, Christopher Wintle and Hugh Wood for allowing the inclusion of extracts from their own letters.

We have made every effort to trace all rights holders and are indebted to Judy Lester for her generous help. We are also grateful for the advice of Christopher Scobie, Simon Wright, David Dymond, Heather Glen, Nicholas Clark and Margaret Jones.

Finally, to our respective family members we owe more than we can say – so to Francis and Joanna, Tony and Marie, Chris and Will, Mum and Dad, Frances, Nick, Ana and Alex: thank you all.

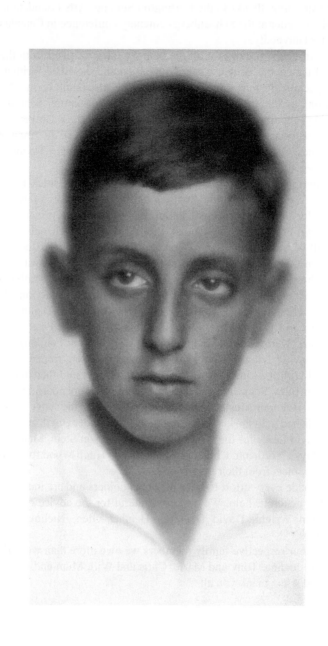

Out of Austria

Croydon airport, Tuesday 20 December 1938. A thin young man steps down onto the tarmac. It is hard to imagine his feelings. On the one hand, he is alive and he is free. But he buried his father two days ago. This morning, as he and his uncle waited at the airport in Vienna, his uncle was arrested and taken away. He himself was allowed to proceed to the departure gate, but as he went through passport control the officer stopped him: 'Keller, Keller. . . . . I know that name and I know that picture; there is something wrong with you.' He was taken to a side room and searched, knowing all the time that if the man remembered his instructions it would be the end. He has been running for his life for weeks now, able to be at home with his dying father only intermittently because of the warrant out for his arrest – indeed he has already been imprisoned once, beaten repeatedly, lined up ready for execution.

He scans the waiting faces. If his mother and sister are here to meet him, that means that his uncle has been released, phoned them, 'Hans is on the plane!' But there is no sign of them. He now feels sure that his uncle is on his way to Dachau.

~

Such was the nineteen-year-old Hans Keller's arrival in London. What does this do to a person? This was indeed the sort of question Keller would have asked. 'For a long time, I thought that if one happened to survive it all, it was important to have had this experience,' he said afterwards, 'because, otherwise, one would not really be aware of what human beings are capable of.' Examining this thought thirty-five years after his escape, however, he reached a different conclusion from his younger self:

> The trouble is that, psychologically, this realisation of what human beings are capable of at the most primitive level simply does not work in the long run. Today, although I know, purely intellectually, what I experienced, the emotional awareness of it has been repressed – or, to put it differently, I am just as incapable of appreciating this level of reality emotionally as I would have been if I had never experienced it. This type of repression is probably

the most dangerous obstacle along the road towards an ethical improvement of society. It's all very well to be intellectually aware of what people are capable of, but if you don't feel it in your bones, you are likely not to do enough about preventing recurrences of such sadistic climaxes.[1]

That was written in 1973, after a visit to Vienna during a difficult period in his life had drawn Keller's thoughts back to his early trauma. Back in 1938 what affected him most profoundly was not only the appalling depths of 'what human beings are capable of', but the moral and spiritual heights they could reach – especially those of whom the highly cultured Viennese society in which Keller was brought up took little note. Ten days after his arrival in London he sent a letter to the exiled German periodical *Das Neue Tagebuch* (now being published in Paris):

30 December 1938 – to the Editor of *Das Neue Tagebuch*
In German

Dear Sir,

As a Jewish refugee and former Schutzhaeftling[2] in a German holding camp I should like to permit myself to send you a few lines, the publication of which is all the closer to my heart because – after my own rather decisive experiences – I see in these lines a description of the feelings of a large section of Jewry. Furthermore I believe that I am doing the right thing in writing to you, because I assume that, even were you to disagree with me (which I consider very unlikely) you would not refuse publication of my letter for <u>that</u> reason. I am justified in this assumption by the standards of your paper, which are high not only in the intellectual sense.

Please do not fear that what follows is one of those reports of the sufferings of a Schutzhaeftling, already so much chewed-over; I want to say something quite different here:

During my imprisonment I had an opportunity to come to know the mass of Jewry, the majority, the much-maligned "Polische",[3] the orthodox Jews. The attitude adopted by these Jews in the face of the horrors meted out to them moved me to tears; I can say today that I am grateful to fate for having allowed me to experience the time of this imprisonment: just as I should not

---

1   'Vienna 1938', radio talk in the series *The Time of My Life*, BBC Radio 4, 3 February 1974. A recording is available in the British Library sound archive and the text is reprinted in *1975*, 28–48, and *HKI*, 17–28.

2   'Protective custody prisoner' – a term used for those whom the Nazi authorities arrested 'for their own protection' (this being the official defence for the rounding-up of Jews and political opponents without judicial warrant). 'Schutzhaeftling' is Keller's spelling: he did not use umlauts when typing.

3   *Polische* was a derogatory term used to denote the poorer East-European orthodox Jews in Vienna, as opposed to the cultivated assimilated German Jews of the Viennese middle classes.

have believed there could be such depth of evil as I was forced to experience in Germany, so I should never have thought there could be such high moral and spiritual qualities as I was able to witness during my imprisonment. There is only o n e equivalent in history for the hate- and revenge-free attitude of the tormented Jews: that is the attitude of Jesus Christ. It may seem paradoxical, but it is understandable to anyone who gives the matter thought: National Socialism, being the embodiment of the Antichrist, is faced by orthodox Jewry as the embodiment of Christ himself. I myself, having grown up in so-called "better" Jewish circles, am all the more entitled to stand up for eastern Jewry, which I am sorry to say is attacked often enough by Jews themselves; I have indeed often made use of this entitlement.

Never ever before did I have the opportunity (and I am unlikely ever to have it again either) to see the phrase "Lord, forgive them, for they know not what they do" come true in such a noble form as during the time of my imprisonment. I do not think that it is necessary to go into detail, or list examples: the impression would always remain fragmentary for those who did not live through it themselves. Therefore I shall only say one more thing: if it is permissible tentatively to speak of a "national characteristic", then I was able to observe a Jewish national characteristic; the Jew sees the future as black, because he has the opportunity to change it, to work on it. As soon as the future has become present and finally past, and he is therefore no longer in a position to change the facts, he tries to make something good out of all the evil, to catch a glimpse of light. In this way, I see something good in the persecution of Jews by today's German government: the spiritual refining and perfecting of the oppressed, as I had the good fortune to witness. The deeply moving fact that a large proportion of today's persecuted Jewry not only harbours no feelings of hate against its persecutors, but even meekly prays to God <u>for them</u> has, in my opinion, as yet received far too little attention.

Yours in sincere respect,

HK, London

The impression made on the nineteen-year-old Keller by this experience was all the stronger because it was the orthodox 'eastern' Jews – despised not only by Austrian Catholics but even by their fellow Jews – who were so Christ-like. In a short memoir of his family published in 1977, Keller described his fascination with orthodoxy as a child. Döbling, where Keller's family lived, was a long way from Leopoldstadt, the former Jewish ghetto (still known in the 1930s as *Mazzesinsel*), but Keller went there as often as possible from the age of nine, 'walking behind gesticulating orthodox Jews . . . trying to listen to what they were saying'. It was all so different from his own upbringing:

My father was a 'freethinker' whom it was difficult to recognize as a
Jew, psychologically or physically. . . . Our social context was that of the
Viennese cultural elite: Peter Altenberg and the composer Franz Schreker
had been in love with my mother, Mahler's wife her girl friend, and writers
like Alfred Polgar, Egon Fridell and Franz Theodor Csokor were regular
visitors to our house – which meant that while there were plenty of Jews
around, the atmosphere was typical of 'emancipated' Jewry which had left
the ghetto behind.[4]

Unlike his father, Keller did look Jewish, and his attraction to orthodoxy drew
strength not only from a degree of rebellion against his liberal assimilated parents, but
also from the anti-Semitic bullying he had experienced since his first days at school.
'Far from wishing to hide my Jewishness, I was intent on showing it wherever I
could' was his response, and he adopted a Jewish accent, attended synagogue, learnt
Yiddish, and became 'a fanatical supporter of the Jewish football club *Hakoah*'.

When, decades later, Keller recounted (for the first time since his *Neue Tagebuch*
letter) the events of his imprisonment in a radio broadcast, he described again the
extraordinary reaction of his orthodox fellow prisoners to their maltreatment, telling his listeners, 'I was stunned: this was one of the deepest experiences of my life.'

There they were, people who seemed quaint, curious figures in ordinary life,
now behaving in a detached manner which was far beyond the rest of us. I
remember a newspaper boy whom I had known because I always bought
my papers from him. He must have been about sixteen or seventeen. When
he came out at the other end of such a [beating], I literally didn't recognise
him; it took me minutes to discover who he was. But his behaviour was of
the orthodox kind, and when I asked him how it was possible for him to
behave like that, he laughed and answered, 'Well, we have had a few thousand years' training, haven't we? What difference does one more such incident make? These people haven't reached the stage where they know what
they're doing so you can't even blame them.' Then he told me a Jewish joke
which was appropriate to the occasion.[5]

Keller's letter seems to have particularly touched Leopold Schwarzchild, the
editor of *Das Neue Tagebuch*, who saw in it 'things which so obviously come
straight from the heart' that it demanded publication. A shortened version was
published anonymously in the next edition of the *Tagebuch*, framed by a brief
editorial introduction. Describing the impact the letter had had on him and his
colleagues, Schwarzchild concluded:

We felt obliged to allow this voice that wished to bear witness to speak. It
shows up a new, so far unknown aspect of this drama, which must move

4 'My Family, You and I', *NR* III/34–5 (January–February 1977): 13–23.
5 'Vienna, 1938', *The Time of My Life*, BBC Radio 4, 3 February 1974.

everybody: and which must give particular satisfaction to those Christian circles who have recently been dedicating themselves to charitable work on behalf of this suffering of strangers.[6]

~

Keller's mother and sister eventually found him at Croydon airport – to his tremendous relief, he discovered that their initial absence was merely the result of their having gone to the wrong door, and he was quickly reassured that his uncle had been released. 'Uncle Hans' (his mother's youngest brother, Hans Grotte, of whom Keller was particularly fond as a teenager, and who inspired his nephew's keen interest in the law) managed to get to London shortly afterwards, as did several more family members and friends. This was all thanks to the indefatigable efforts of Keller's English brother-in-law Roy Franey – 'without him the gas chamber would have been an absolute certainty.'[7]

Not many of Keller's letters survive from his earliest days in London. The following is one that does, written to his old schoolfriend Fritz Schönbach. Most of Keller's friends had been scattered to the four winds by now – Schönbach was then in Switzerland, but he soon came to England, whence he was deported as an internee to Australia before eventually joining his parents in Buenos Aires when the war was over. Other friends were making their way across Europe, some were already in England or America, some were still in Vienna, some had disappeared.

7 February 1939 – to Fritz Schönbach
In German

Dear Fritzi,

I've just received your letter of the 3rd.

I thank you for the only possible reaction: don't offer me condolences.

Mr Schönbach chooses to hold rather peculiar moral views: for a debtor to remember a long outstanding debt is "decent"?

My future plans are still rather vague; at the moment I have a few possibilities in view that I could take, – but as I have not, of all these useless possibilities, yet been able to discover the most useless – and therefore the most valuable to me personally – no decision has yet been arrived at. – At the moment, I am feeling fine, as always – all the more

6 *Das Neue Tagebuch*, 7 January 1939, 31. See *HKI*, 30–31.
7 'Hitler and History', *LRB* III/2 (5–18 February 1981): 14–15. Keller's sister, Gertrud, who married her English husband Roy Franey in 1934, was actually his half-sister from his mother's first marriage.

so because after that awful time (the time of my imprisonment) when I'd given up all hope of living, I'm now happy <u>to be alive</u>. But in spite of that I don't complain about what happened; if you ever get to see the Paris "Neue Tagebuch" of 7 January, you will find an article produced by my humble self (called ". . . . for they know not what they do") which sets out the reasons enabling me to derive some metaphysical benefit from the period of my detention, and persuading me to make the above statement.

I am v e r y glad to hear that you will probably come here, I hope soon!

What's the situation with the Reichsfluchtsteuer?[8] Or is it with your parents? Is that sorted out now?

Within the next week I shall have the pleasure of welcoming Georg Stroh. He is coming from Paris.

I can trust you (be proud, you are the only one who knows about it): I am writing a book at the moment – nebbich –.[9] Title: "On the Renaissance of Naivety within present-day intellectual Judaism". We'll see what comes of that. At the moment, I am gathering material and ideas. By far the most pleasant part of such work.

I am in correspondence with Kurti, for whom things do not seem to be going very well. Have you any idea what has happened to Kurti No. 2, larger edition, also called Rendilstein? That is to say, which coffee house is he sitting in now?

Apropos, apropos, apropos: this is a dreadful blow for me, a blow that struck me to the core: the lack of any coffee houses or any similar religious institution here. Yes, yes, it's bad. But I haven't yet given up on my quest for this wonderful Aura, Flora and Fauna. Every day, in this capital of the British Empire, you can see a crooked-nosed flat-footed Hebrew in search of an establishment at least vaguely similar to his temple. He might already have had some success: a Viennese fellow-sufferer has told him about a place that will supposedly suffice, given his reduced and very modest demands. He will find out for himself the truth of her advice as soon as possible.

Now then, we have exchanged enough Schmonzes,[10] my humblest respects, H.

P.S. You should receive the money by the same post.

---

8 Literally Reich Flight Tax. Originally a measure introduced by the Hindenburg government in 1931 to prevent too much capital moving overseas, it was used by the Nazi government to strip fleeing Jewish citizens of their assets.

9 *Nebbich* is a Yiddish word roughly meaning 'so what' in this context.

10 Yiddish, meaning 'idle talk'.

As Keller said to Schönbach, his future plans were vague – and at that time they could not be anything else. The visa Roy Franey had secured for him was only temporary, as the Home Office made very clear when it was issued: 'The visa has been authorized on the understanding that arrangements will eventually be made for your brother-in-law's emigration.'[11] Within months, however, war had broken out, bringing police registration, restrictions on movement and finally internment to 'enemy aliens' like Keller. By the time peace returned, six years later, it was to a different world.[12]

~

We are all made and unmade by the times in which we live, but Hans Keller had a mind exceptionally alive to everything happening around him. The shock of exile did quite literally unmake him, and so intense was his engagement with the new culture in which he was forced to reconstruct his life that both he and it were irrevocably altered by his creative, ever-questioning presence. For this reason, he is one of the most illuminating writers one could read on the musical life of Britain in the second half of the twentieth century. What kind of life he might have lived had he stayed in Vienna, had the Nazis and the war never come, is impossible to know. But it would have been very different – above all, it is quite possible that he would never have written on music at all.

From the surviving scraps of evidence of Keller's first nineteen years growing up in Vienna he appears to have been a compulsive writer from his earliest youth. But of the many subjects on which he wrote, the one that is conspicuous by its absence is music. He played and listened to music all the time ('I could live without words, if you could call it a life, but I would die without music') but he did not write about it. At the time of his emigration his intellectual interests centred around psychology and philosophy: in other letters to Schönbach he described himself writing things like 'a dissertation on the "Psychology and Logic of Wit"' and 'polemics against Schopenhauer', as well as studying logic – 'but this I find quite difficult, because it is hard to find logic among the English, particularly not in their logic books'.[13] A few weeks after the publication of his first letter to *Das Neue Tagebuch* he wrote again to its editor, this time disputing his interpretation of Hegel. Keller also had a keen interest in the law, and had circumstances been different it is possible to imagine him following his uncle Hans Grotte into the profession.

An image Keller often used to describe his relationship with music was that he needed it as a fish needs water. 'Music is not an "interest",' he later explained; 'to

11 N. Powell (Home Office) to Roy Franey, 4 July 1938, CULHK.

12 For a full account of Keller's wartime experiences and their effect on his intellectual maturation see *HKI*.

13 Keller to Schönbach, 10 October, 20 November, 2 December 1938, CULHK.

suggest to a musician that he is interested in music makes as much sense as suggesting to you that you are interested in liquid, food, or sleep.'[14] As a child, music simply pervaded his life, as a natural and necessary part of being a human being. Those visiting Vienna from Britain at that time often looked with longing on what seemed to them Vienna's native musicality, manifest not just in the consistently high standards of public performance, but in the secure place that music held throughout society. The chief critic of the London *Times*, H.C. Colles, for example, returning from the Schubert centenary celebrations in 1928, tried to explain to his readers how Schubert was to the Viennese no remote genius, but 'the man who gave them music for the Sunday Mass and part-songs for their holidays and convivial evenings'.[15] Despite the 'outstanding' performances he had been hearing during the festival from the Busch quartet and the Vienna Philharmonic, with their glorious tone, perfect phrasing and natural rhythm 'instinctive to every Viennese musician', the dominant impression Colles took home with him was 'rather Vienna itself and the way the Viennese take their music'. He was struck by how familiar Schubert was to the audiences, how his music was 'part of daily life, not the property of the concert room' – and of course how well funded and supported it all was, headed by 'the venerable Gesellschaft der Musikfreunde which spreads a maternal wing over innumerable agencies and activities of music making'. In short, the way music rested uncontested at the heart of Viennese life.

One disadvantage of such a strong tradition and secure establishment is a tendency towards conservatism – hence Schoenberg's famous *Verein für musikalische Privataufführungen*,[16] which was founded at the end of 1918 (a few months before Keller was born) and ran for three years, allowing its members to hear superbly prepared performances of a wide range of contemporary music that was otherwise ignored, attacked or poorly performed in Vienna at the time. Writing about it in the programme book of a London Sinfonietta series on inter-war Vienna in 1983, Keller linked Schoenberg's *Verein* with another private musical 'club' in Vienna which ran throughout the 1920s and 1930s, for which he also claimed 'historic' status and 'worldwide influence'. This was the regular private quartet session that took place every Saturday in Vienna's Neubaugasse:

> Schmidt was the cellist in the Neubaugasse; the leader was the greatest chamber-musician I have ever heard in my life, Schoenberg's lifelong friend and first teacher – Oskar Adler, with whom Schoenberg played quartets in his teens.[17]

In this most musical of cities, the composer Franz Schmidt was one of its most widely revered musicians in the inter-war period, both as composer and,

---

14 *1975*, 87.

15 'Vienna's Music', *The Times*, 1 December 1928, 10.

16 Society for Private Musical Performances. (Keller preferred to translate *Verein* as 'club' in this context.)

17 Keller, 'A Personal View of Vienna's 20's and 30's', in London Sinfonietta concert series programme book *Vienna: Reaction & Revolution*, 3–17 June 1983, 38–9.

in some eyes, the greatest cellist and pianist in Vienna. He was Rector of the Musikhochschule and the holder of many honours (the Order of Franz Josef, the title of Hofrat, honorary membership of the Vienna Philharmonic, an honorary doctorate from the University of Vienna and so on). Born the same year as Schoenberg, Schmidt's much more conservative style meant that he was in many ways Schoenberg's opposite. Nevertheless, they held each other in high esteem – as Keller put it, 'the polarity was rather like Brahms' and Wagner's, in that in private, there was a great deal of profound mutual admiration.' A four-handed piano transcription of Schmidt's Second Symphony was given at Schoenberg's *Verein* in 1919 and 1920, and Schmidt directed a fine performance of *Pierrot lunaire* with his students at the Musikhochschule in 1929, having been deeply moved by the work when Oskar Adler took him to Erwin Stein's performance at the *Verein* in 1921. Schmidt was apparently lost in admiration despite feeling that Schoenberg had gone beyond his comprehension in this work: afterwards he spoke to Adler about what he called Schoenberg's 'Weithörigkeit' – a word that is hard to translate but by which he seems to have meant 'the ability to hear into the distance'.[18]

Oskar Adler, the leader of Schmidt's Neubaugasse quartet, was a figure less publicly celebrated, but equally revered by those in the know. He was not a professional musician but a medical doctor who was also well known as an astrologer and philosopher. When Schoenberg met him at the beginning of the 1890s (when both were in their late teens) Adler was already a superb violinist and quartet leader, well read in poetry, philosophy and music theory. Schoenberg later called him 'my first teacher' and said that it was not until they met that his musical and literary education was able to get under way. Along with two other highly gifted friends, David Josef Bach and the slightly older Alexander Zemlinsky, Adler introduced Schoenberg to an artistic and intellectual world far above that of Schoenberg's lower-middle-class family (and his unfinished *Realschule* education) and helped convince him of his destiny as a musician.

Adler remained a close friend of Schoenberg and ardent admirer of his genius, though after Schoenberg left Vienna in 1926 they saw each other only once. Naturally Adler had been an active member of Schoenberg's *Verein*, in which he gave fourteen performances.[19] According to Adler's memory, he and Schmidt were first introduced around 1914, by one of Schmidt's pupils, Fritz Saphir, who was cellist in Adler's quartet at the time. Another of Adler's previous cellists had been Anton Webern (of whom Adler apparently complained 'you never quite knew when he had entered, there was no firm rhythmic articulation'),[20] but once Adler started playing with Schmidt, things moved to a new level. Writing to Schmidt's widow after his death, Adler described playing with Schmidt as 'like a service to God, a fact on which we wholly agreed without ever talking about it'. This spiritual quality of Schmidt's playing evoked for Adler memories of Schoenberg in their early days:

18 Adler to Schoenberg [c. July 1949], ASC.
19 Walter Szmolyan, 'Die Konzerte des Wiener Schoenberg-Vereins', *OMZ* 36/2 (1981): 82–104.
20 Quoted by Keller in 'A Personal View'.

Oskar Adler by Milein Cosman.

In my whole life there was only one man with whom I had as profound a friendship as with Franz Schmidt. That was in my youth, and the man was Schoenberg: at the time, we made our first steps into the field of chamber music. Our enthusiasm was great and powerful. Schoenberg didn't have much of an idea of how to play the cello: he was a total autodidact. Nevertheless, despite his defective technique, a similar spiritual power radiated from his playing as, later, from Schmidt's.[21]

In their later years of playing together (Schmidt died in February 1939, a few weeks after Adler's emigration), Schmidt wrote of the 'sheer joy' he experienced playing quartets with Adler, whom he described as 'one of the most important artistic figures I have encountered in my lifetime'.[22]

It was Adler's and Schmidt's partnership that made Saturdays in the Neubaugasse so remarkable. Sometimes they played as a violin and piano duo, but most of their time was spent exploring the string quartet repertoire. 'These quartet evenings turned into what can only be described as religious services,' recalled Adler:

We played at my surgery; the faithful listeners were next door in the waiting room. Usually, the ritual began with two Haydn quartets, which were followed by Beethoven, Brahms, Schumann, and Mendelssohn. Mendelssohn Schmidt loved above all other Romantics.[23]

The quartet had a regular viola player, Dr Strassberg – 'perhaps Vienna's best viola player' wrote Adler ('not perhaps', added Keller) – but the second violin seems to have been more variable, and Keller recalled that 'leading fiddlers queued up for this particular job':

It wasn't only the second fiddle for which you had to queue up: in order for you to be allowed just to listen, Adler and Schmidt had to be convinced of your outstanding musicality and musicianship, and many were the well-known musicians who found entrance to these quartet sessions as difficult as critics found it at [Schoenberg's *Verein*]. For what Adler and Schmidt insisted on was an almost active participation by the audience; they would maintain that any antagonism from a listener, however silent, would have an unfavourable influence on the quartet's imaginative powers.[24]

21 Letter from Adler to Schmidt's widow, quoted by Keller in 'Personal Recollections: Oskar Adler's and My Own', in *The Music of Franz Schmidt*, vol. 1, ed. Harold Truscott (London: Toccata, 1984), 7–17.

22 'Attestation', March 1934, written by Schmidt in support of Schoenberg's attempt to help Adler emigrate to America. Quoted in Amy Shapiro, *Oskar Adler: A Complete Man* (CreateSpace Independent Publishing, 2012).

23 Adler to Schmidt's widow, in 'Personal Recollections'. Keller added a footnote: 'Adler forgot to list Mozart, a more frequent component than Brahms.'

24 Keller, 'A Personal View'.

Among these privileged listeners during the 1930s was the teenage Hans Keller, and he even got to play second violin on rare occasions. It was a remarkable musical education – indeed Schmidt apparently called their sessions 'the real university for chamber music'. As well as the actual music, Keller reported that 'Adler and Schmidt used to exchange recollections from their respective musical pasts,' and their audience was full of other distinguished figures: 'I can't remember a single truly leading musician whom one did not meet at some of these Saturday afternoons.'

For the rest of his life, 'the full-blooded, passionate *Musikantentum*, the ever-spontaneous, ever-inspired, ever-varied and ever-new interpretations'[25] of the Adler Quartet remained the touchstone of Keller's understanding of music. In particular, those Saturdays in the Neubaugasse showed him what chamber music was for: a form in which musicians wrote and played for themselves, not an audience, and so could probe the most profound secrets of their art:

> The string quartet is 'between ourselves', a confidential communication from the composer to the players, and then between the players; the listener is the more or less welcome eavesdropper. . . . Improvisation is of the very nature of the string quartet's secret: the composer entrusts the player with part of the creative responsibility. An intimate communication, if it is to be successful, always involves active participation on the part of the addressee.[26]

'Adler and Schmidt were improvisers *par excellence*,' Keller remembered: 'their performances of quartets and sonatas evinced a revelational quality which, I felt, could be attributed to their readiness to submit, on the basis of their deep knowledge of any work they played, to inspirations of the moment.'[27] This improvisatory quality – a creative re-creation of the music – was something that Keller looked for subsequently in all performers, having been taught by Adler to see performance not as aspiring towards some 'objective' ideal, but rather as 'the tail end of composition'. A truly great performance was always unique:

> You may know a piece inside out, may have played it yourself, but in a great performance you hear it for the first time. The experience is as simple, as paradoxical as that.[28]

All his life Keller sought out and revered those few original geniuses capable of creating this kind of experience. The earliest of his surviving letters was written to one such – the violinist Bronisław Huberman, to whom Keller wrote an ardent fan letter in 1936. This letter was written during Keller's first trip to London as a schoolboy, visiting his sister and her new husband, Roy Franey. During the visit he went to hear Huberman playing at the Queen's Hall:

25 *MR* XII/2 (May 1951): 154–5.
26 'Rare Greatness', interval talk, BBC Radio 3, 14 May 1972.
27 'Natural Master', *Listener*, 25 October 1984: 34–5.
28 'The Art of Bronisław Huberman', *Music Weekly*, BBC Radio 3, 6 March 1983.

12 December 1936 – to Bronisław Huberman
In German

On the evening of your concert in London, 12 December 1936

I have just come back from your concert, and I feel the urge to write to you. I am only 16 years old – I just write this so that you won't attach too much importance to my letter. But I don't suppose that you will do that anyway. I only wanted to tell you how much I admire you, and how much I am in awe of your musical abilities. You probably receive many letters like this, and maybe mine won't even reach you, but that doesn't really matter, I shall feel a lot better just having written it. I am only here in London for a short while, am completely starved of music and was at your concert today. I'm sure that you weren't in the same spirits that you are in the Musikvereinssaal in Vienna (I believe it is tremendously presumptuous of me to say this), but you were Huberman and that is something so tremendous that one cannot express it in words at all. In your playing, one can sense your whole soul, which you have put into the violin, your opponents do not hear this. You are such an inconceivably higher being, that I am feeling very lucky to live at the same time as you and be able to listen to you. In my apartment in Vienna, I have records of you playing the Bach A minor Concerto and whenever I hear the following passages, which are played by you in such an inconceivable way, it sends shivers down my spine:

In the first movement:

In the third movement:

Tonight: I didn't like 2 pieces very much, maybe I'm still too young for them: 1. the Szymanowski, 2. one of your encores, it starts as if one were tuning the violin. – But the rest of the programme! – I thank you, many, many times for all the evenings past, and for the future ones too!!!

In deep adoration

Hans Keller, Vienna[29]

The comment at the end of this letter – about the two pieces Keller disliked – is telling. As a boy, Keller's musical repertoire was both conservative and confined to the Austro-German tradition. He enlarged it only slowly and cautiously, but setting aside rather than condemning that with which he couldn't engage ('maybe I'm still too young'). He was of course born too late to have experienced the wide range of new music from across Europe played in Schoenberg's *Verein*, and by the 1930s modernism in Vienna was in retreat. Schoenberg was gone and, despite Oskar Adler's earlier close association with him, there is no evidence that the music of the Second Viennese School ever featured in the Saturday sessions in the Neubaugasse, where Adler and Schmidt confined themselves instead to finding new things in an endless exploration and re-exploration of the masterpieces of the past. For the young Hans Keller, this was more than enough:

> I was never interested in music I couldn't understand, and the most advanced things I knew and loved as a boy were the late Beethoven quartets, which of course were more advanced than Brahms or Reger, and are more advanced than many things which appear nowadays. ... When one played the late Beethoven quartets, one felt one was alone – alone even inside oneself, for one part of one's mind fathomed the bottom of what the rest felt to be bottomless.[30]

As Keller grew older, his friendship with Adler became closer. Keller's parents, both very musical, kept open house for musicians, writers and artists, and Adler was often to be found playing chamber music there. Schmidt too came occasionally, and Keller's cousin recalled a particularly memorable performance of Schubert's 'Trout' Quintet.[31] Adler's friendship with the Kellers may have saved his life, for it was Roy Franey who secured British visas in 1938 for both Adler and his wife, after Schoenberg had been unsuccessful in efforts to get them

29 This letter was found among Huberman's correspondence after his death and printed in Ida Ibbeken, ed., *The Listener Speaks: 55 Letters from the Audience to Bronislaw Huberman* (Israel: Ramoth Hashawin, 1961). There is an inconsistency between the letter's date and Keller's statement that he was '16 years old' (he would have been 17 on 12 December 1936), but the date of Huberman's concert is confirmed by the *Times* review, 14 December 1936, 12.

30 'How I Got There', undated and unpublished article for *London Magazine* (proof copy, CULHK).

31 Inge Trott, oral communication, 29 March 2004: 'That was the first time I heard him and I was so impressed!'

to America. In England Keller played quartets with Adler more than ever, in London, in Huyton near Liverpool (where they were interned together), in the Lake District (where they went after their release), then back in London: 'Keller plays viola; he has developed as an excellent chamber musician,' Adler reported to Schoenberg in 1949.[32]

'Since conservative Vienna did not press the understanding of contemporary music upon me,' Keller later recalled, 'I grew up without it.' It was not only contemporary music that conservative Vienna did not press into Keller's ears, however, but any music outside the Austro-German tradition.[33] Reading Keller's recollections of his early musical life, one is given the impression of a highly developed yet closed society. It is as though what Stefan Zweig called 'das gold-ene Zeitalter der Sicherheit'[34] of Vienna before the First World War, with its settled social order and passionate reverence for the very highest artistic achieve-ment, lived on musically in those Saturdays in the Neubaugasse. Music, as Keller experienced it, may therefore have felt like a place apart, removed from the uncer-tainties of the inter-war world – an intense experience that he did not feel the need to analyse in words. Elsewhere there was much to write about in a changing world. The Vienna into which he was born in 1919 was a city reeling from its sud-den transformation from a great imperial capital to what was popularly described as a *Wasserkopf* – the swollen hydrocephalic head of a newly-shrivelled body. Its Jewish population also went from being one among many subgroups in a multina-tional empire to the only minority in a small German-speaking state, all the more visible for being disproportionately concentrated in Vienna itself. Keller's parents were well aware of the way the wind was blowing: his cousin remembered Grete Keller in 1934 saying of her daughter's marriage to an Englishman, 'We'll have a base in England if we should need one. . .'[35]

It is tempting to draw a parallel between the post-imperial Vienna into which Keller was born after the First World War and the London in which he found himself after the Second – another post-war city facing the dismantling of an empire of which it had long been the centre. But this is not a parallel that sheds much light on music. Amid the ruins of the Hapsburg Empire there was a strong sense that in the conservation of its glorious musical past Vienna could preserve the best of itself, whereas nobody in 1945 would have claimed that the greatest achievement of the old British Empire was its music. Instead, British musicians at the end of the war were looking forward, not back, conscious that their own

---

32 Adler to Schoenberg [c. July 1949], ASC.
33 In 'Personal Recollections' Keller wrote admiringly of how Schmidt 'knew, and remembered, *all music*' [our italics], and gave a revealing list of examples to show the breadth of Schmidt's knowl-edge: 'Whatever you raised, whether it was a point about a tricky passage in the Matthew Passion or John Passion, in a late Beethoven quartet, in any of the later Haydn symphonies, in a Bruckner symphony and, yes, in Schoenberg's *Transfigured Night* or *Gurrelieder*, he would jump up, wad-dle across to the piano, and play the passage in question in an instant perfect piano arrangement, stressing the inner part you happened to be talking about.'
34 'The golden age of security', in Zweig, *Die Welt von Gestern* (Stockholm: Berman Fischer, 1941), 8.
35 Inge Trott, oral communication, 12 April 2006.

musical heritage could scarcely compare with that of the nations they had vanquished, but convinced that now, at long last, their time had come.

~

In 1948, the innovative documentary film-maker (and founder of Mass Observation) Humphrey Jennings made a short film called *The Dim Little Island*. It was one of the last films he completed before his untimely death. Commissioned by the British government's Central Office of Information, it was intended to lift the spirits of a nation ground down by six years of war and still labouring under crushing post-war austerity, rationing and the coldest winter in living memory. The eleven-minute film Jennings produced consists of four meditations on the state of England, by four contrasting figures: the satirical cartoonist Osbert Lancaster, the naturalist James Fisher, the industrialist John Ormston and the composer Ralph Vaughan Williams. Although intended as propaganda, Jennings's film is not exactly upbeat – instead it has a gently elegiac tone and mixes a very British self-deprecation with a tentative hope for the future.

The original working title of Jennings's script was *Awful Old England?* – a line taken from Rudyard Kipling's 1903 poem 'Chant-Pagan', the song of a disillusioned returning soldier:

> Me that 'ave been what I've been –
> Me that 'ave gone where I've gone –
> Me that 'ave seen what I've seen –
> 'Ow can I ever take on
> With awful old England again . . .

The final title came from the opening of Osbert Lancaster's contribution:

> In ancient times the licensed fool was allowed to speak while the others held their peace, so perhaps I – as an avowedly comic artist – may be allowed to speak first. The comic artist is the guardian of reality: it is his privilege to remind the public what they really look like, and to destroy their happy illusions of dignity and beauty so sedulously built up by the advertising artist and the royal academician.
>
> But there are many other illusions: for instance, the illusion that, compared to the romance and mystery of high Tibet or the rolling prairies and limitless expanse of the golden West, Great Britain is rather a dim little island; the illusion that, compared to those talented Central Europeans, flogging the pianoforte for a very substantial remuneration, we are a hopeless dull musical nation; and of course that now, as always, the country is going to the dogs.

The section on music is the longest and most prominent of the film's four meditations, and Jennings seems to have paid particular attention to the details of his musical scenes and the planning of Vaughan Williams's material. He may have felt it was in music that the strongest refutation of the 'illusion' that 'the country is going to the dogs' was to be found. The resulting sequence is a classic example of the very powerful resurrection narrative that ran through British musical life in the immediate post-war years, built upon the earlier idea of the 'English Musical Renaissance'. Vaughan Williams's commentary includes tropes familiar from the Renaissance narrative, such as the primacy of English music during the Tudor period, and the location of national identity in folksong – 'those great tunes, which like our language, our customs, our laws, are the groundwork upon which everything must stand'. Overlaying these are new themes specific to the country's wartime experience, such as the portrayal of the newly knighted Malcolm Sargent (then famous for his 'Blitz tours' of bombed cities) as 'the apex' of the country's musical life, and a sequence intercutting footage of wartime fire-fighters with shots of Proms queues and crowds filling the Harringay stadium: 'during the late war, those who had never taken music seriously before began to crowd our concert halls from Kensington to Harringay to hear a symphony concert.' Vaughan Williams also projects a timely vision of national solidarity with his description of the 'great pyramid' of British musical life, linking together 'great virtuosi' and 'devoted musical practitioners' with 'that great mass of musical amateurs'. The film concludes with a stirring prophecy of the new life to come:

> So – the fire is ready to be kindled. It only requires a match to be lighted to set the whole ablaze. Some great upheaval of national consciousness and emotion. The Elizabethans experienced this; as a result they produced poetry and music that has never been surpassed. Have we not also experienced lately such a national upheaval? . . . Today our music, which so long had seemed without life, is being born again.

The feeling that something was stirring was shared by many musicians at that time and had been apparent well before the end of the war. Benjamin Britten, for example, felt strongly after his return from America in 1942 that there was '"something" in the air which heralds a renaissance. I feel terrifically conscious of it, so do Peter, & Clifford, & Michael Tippett & so many that I love & admire.'[36] At the end of the war, such feelings were accompanied by a very general determination that this precious flame must not be allowed to go out. 'Britain is at last recognized to be producing some of the greatest music of our time,' stated the Dartington Trust Arts Enquiry after an extensive survey of the nation's musical assets. 'And owing to the upheavals in Germany and Austria since 1933, London has a chance of becoming the musical centre of Europe.'[37] Sir George Dyson, Director of the Royal College of Music (the institutional embodiment of the 'English Musical Renaissance'), thought it already was:

---

36 Britten to Imogen Holst, 21 October 1943, in Britten, *Letters from a Life*, vol. 2 (London: Faber, 1991), 1161–2.
37 *Music: A Report on Musical Life in England* (London: PEP, 1949), 14.

> Our situation is not unlike that of Germany a century ago. Haydn, Mozart, Beethoven, Schubert, and Weber had all lived and died, but the fashionable European public still clung to the more Italian operas, Italian tunes, Italian players and singers. Schumann, Liszt, and Wagner tried to persuade their countrymen, often in vain, that the best music in the world had been and was being written on their own doorsteps. That is where we are now. Some of our fashionable public think that the centre of music is still in the centre of Europe. They are wrong. It is here and now.[38]

There was in this an inevitable element of post-war jingoism – perhaps a hope that, having defeated the Germans militarily (twice), Britain might now defeat them musically. Despite this, it must be stressed that British musical nationalism was built on what had been at base a very open musical society. The British had come late to the idea of a music of their own, music having been, until the later nineteenth century, regarded rather as something that foreigners did. It was common until well into the twentieth century for young British musicians to study in the conservatoires of Leipzig, Vienna or Paris, and equally common for French, German and Italian musicians to come to Britain to work – as the violinist and concert manager John Ella remarked in 1876, 'our cosmopolitan London orchestras are composed of the surplus talent of the continent.'[39] This constant movement across the Channel was due in large part to the comparative lack of musical infrastructure in Britain (in the shape of systematic musical education, permanent orchestras and secure funding). But this did leave the country distinctly hospitable to the music of other countries – even the author of *Das Land ohne Musik* conceded that 'perhaps more foreign music is performed in England than in any other country.'[40]

Therefore 'those talented Central Europeans' like Hans Keller who sought to make their home in Britain after 1945 were met by two opposing currents in the culture of their adopted country: a fundamental welcome and respect (even awe) overlaid by a strong but much more recent musical patriotism. This dual feeling produced psychological and social consequences that Keller observed with considerable interest. Vaughan Williams himself was a good example of the paradox. A deeply humane man, he worked tirelessly in support of refugee musicians during the war and afterwards became the patron of the pianist Ferdinand Rauter's Anglo-Austrian Music Society. But his personal sense of a uniquely English

---

38 Dyson, 'The Proms Should be Daring, Generous. . .', *RT* 96/1241 (25 July 1947): 5.

39 'Professor Ella's lecture on Spohr's "Jessonda"', *Orchestra* 19 (February 1876): 202.

40 'Das Land ohne Musik' (The Land Without Music) was supposedly a German description of Britain that the British took to heart. Its origins are unclear, but it appeared famously as the title of a book published just before the First World War by the German writer Oscar Schmitz. Schmitz claimed to have identified 'what distinguishes Englishmen from all other cultured races to quite an astonishing degree . . . the English are the only cultured race without a music of their own.' Schmitz, *Das Land ohne Musik* (Munich: Georg Müller, 1914), trans. H. Herzl (London: Jarrolds, 1926), 26.

music was profound and, as he wrote to Rauter, 'The great thing that frightens me in the late peaceful invasion of this country by Austria is that it will entirely devour the tender little flower of our English culture.'[41]

The BBC, which before the war had promoted a remarkably cosmopolitan music policy, wrestled in later years with the conflict between its vision of music as an 'international language' and its duty to musical Britishness. A wartime draft of future music policy by one very senior executive saw the duty of the *British Broadcasting Corporation* in this way:

> Music is an international 'language', which through the medium of broad-casting is heard and understood all over the world. . . . In spite of this rec-ognition of the international factor, the BBC regards it as a matter of first importance to develop a strong sense of pride in British music in order to exorcise the long-standing sense of inferiority in music and to rid music of its status as a foreign art.[42]

Some of the fuel for the nationalist narrative as it unfolded in Britain over sub-sequent years was undoubtedly economic. Osbert Lancaster's barbed comment in *The Dim Little Island* about the Central Europeans 'flogging the pianoforte for a very substantial remuneration' is an example of the feelings that led to such events as the extraordinary protest against the 1947 visit of the Vienna State Opera by the Musicians' Union, which tried to argue that British orchestral players should have been engaged to play in the pit – to which an exasperated Covent Garden Trust responded that it had 'not planned to engage a foreign orchestra to accompany the Viennese performances; it had merely set out to bring to London the Vienna State Opera *ensemble*.'[43] The argument was continually made that British organisations (particularly the increasingly influential BBC) should restrict the employment of for-eign musicians – and the playing and broadcasting of foreign contemporary music – until there was a comparable reception of British music and musicians overseas.

In truth, the opportunities available for musicians of all nationalities in Britain after 1945 were expanding exponentially, as music at all levels was publicly funded as never before. Money poured into music via the BBC, the new Arts Council and local municipal authorities, with the result that new festivals and orchestras mushroomed all over the country. The 1944 Education Act provided for universal secondary education and state support for university education, and this was supplemented musically by a new movement among local education authorities to set up their own music services, providing Saturday music centres, peripatetic teachers for schools, instrument hire schemes and a nationwide pro-liferation of county youth bands and orchestras, headed by the National Youth Orchestra of Great Britain (inaugurated in 1947). All this led to a voracious

---

41 Vaughan Williams to Rauter, 16 August [1942], in *The Letters of Ralph Vaughan Williams*, ed. Hugh Cobbe (Oxford: Oxford University Press, 2008), 344–45.

42 Basil Nicolls, 'BBC Music Policy', draft paper, 1 April 1942, WAC G28/42.

43 *The Times*, 8 September 1947, 7.

appetite for music among the post-war British public and a new sense of the importance of music to British public life. Russell Palmer, the editor of one of the many new musical surveys and directories published at this time, wrote excitedly that 'watching the great extent to which audiences to-day are drawing level with the music of our time, we are able to see the skill of British composers shining across the musical universe like a beam of light.' Ignoring the main reason for the recent arrival of so many European émigrés, he went on to address the 'foreign artists [who] have shown themselves anxious to reside in adopted brotherhood' with their British counterparts:

> We welcome these "permanent visitors," many of whom have taken our nationality, to join in the task of satisfying the British public's ever-growing appetite for music, even though they must regularly look to their merits if they are to keep pace with the superb artistry and virtuosity of British born and bred performers.'[44]

This was stretching it a bit. British performance standards in the 1940s were by no means the envy of the world – indeed the ragged playing of the BBC Symphony Orchestra during the 1946 Proms caused a crisis of confidence within the post-war BBC leading to a substantial financial investment in order to triple rehearsal time for the 1947 season. Performance standards were then of paramount importance to the BBC because September 1946 had seen the launch of its flagship Third Programme, the aim of which was (in the words of its founder, Director-General William Haley) 'to enable the intelligent public to hear the best that has been thought or said or composed in all the world'. Haley wanted this new service to be thoroughly international – especially in the 'international language' of music. George Barnes, whom Haley appointed to run the Third, was aware of the difficulties involved in implementing such a vision:

> English music has been cut off for so long from the Continent that one finds some complacency and at the same time a certain reluctance to face the comparison with European standards, which is inevitable now that two-way traffic between the Continent and this Country is again possible.[45]

Barnes's colleague, the pianist Etienne Amyot, responsible for the initial planning of the Third Programme, had a clear idea of the source of that reluctance – and why it was so important that the BBC should try to overcome it:

> I think it is very difficult for people here, no matter how deep their enjoyment of music and how keen their desire to hear contemporary works, to fix any adequate comparison of the degrees of performance if they have been

---

44 Palmer, *British Music* (London: Skelton Robinson, 1947), 11.
45 Barnes to Haley, 25 March 1947, WAC William Glock Talks File 1A.

denied any experience of hearing the great European performances between the last two wars. I know that when I was in Germany during this war I felt many a time that the standard of performance I heard in some small town was higher than that given at a highly publicised concert in London. As I said last night, I do believe it is a function of the Corporation, via the Third Programme, to attempt to raise the standard of performances in England. We do possess a group of composers who, in their way, are second to none anywhere else. But if the works of these brilliant young men are to be inadequately performed the influence they can bring to bear on this post-war generation, because of that inadequate performance, will obviously be greatly retarded. . . . I believe that, with the full cooperation of what Europe can offer us and with what we in turn can offer Europe, this country could truly come into its own again in the field of music.[46]

Amyot wrote this to a young music critic he had just met through the composer Michael Tippett. The critic's name was William Glock – the man who, with Hans Keller at his side, was to run BBC music during the 1960s, when the Corporation was at the height of its influence over the musical life of the country. When he and Amyot met in January 1947, Amyot was delighted to find an English musician with whom he felt 'able to talk quite freely and honestly of the present standard of musical performance in this country'. Glock and Amyot were both pianists who had studied in Berlin in the early 1930s (Amyot with Wilhelm Backhaus and Glock with Artur Schnabel) and their musical ideals were founded on that experience. Amyot had also spent the later part of the war in Germany, serving in the Allied Expeditionary Force's Psychological Warfare Division, and in 1945 he was involved in the planning of post-war broadcasting both in Germany and in Britain. He believed that the British at that time were greatly overestimating the deleterious effect of the Nazi regime on the general standard of musical performance in Germany, a belief with which Glock concurred:

A mere twelve years of Nazi rule could not break down the accumulated culture and knowledge of centuries, or the standards that went with them. Concert life would still be run with some responsibility towards the intellectual world; and the youngest science student would take more interest in music than many professionals over here.[47]

Amyot was keen to bring such standards to London, exploiting the fact that the terrible destruction wrought across Europe meant that the greatest artists were now looking for performance opportunities in Britain's relatively undamaged cities: 'That was the luck of the Third Programme. It came at a moment when you could have anybody. The very very greatest. They were only too eager to perform.'[48]

---

46 Amyot to Glock, 30 January 1947, WAC E2/348.
47 Glock, 'Music in Post-War Europe', BBC Third Programme, 8 July 1947.
48 Amyot, interviewed by Humphrey Carpenter, 3 May 1994, WAC R143/2/1.

In 1947 Amyot sent Glock on a tour of occupied Europe on behalf of the Third Programme, to bring back news (and evidence, in the shape of scores and recordings) of what had been going on musically since 1939. It was an eye-opening experience, from the terrible devastation of bombed cities ('we drove through empty, silent streets, amidst unbelievable ruins') to the musical wonders of the Vienna State Opera ('you have to see the musical spirit of the work penetrating every stitch of clothing and every floorboard') and the moving experience of witnessing Wilhelm Furtwängler's reunion with the Berlin Philharmonic after he was finally cleared by the denazification tribunals ('you could see that the players wanted to make this first concert memorable, that they loved Furtwängler, and had been waiting for the moment when he'd be cleared, and would conduct them again'). Glock took with him a suitcase of scores of recent British music and 'I found almost everywhere – in Munich, Prague, Berlin, Hamburg – the most intense interest in the works of our young English composers.' One composer in particular was already receiving considerable attention, and before he went home Glock was able to hear in Berlin the first German production of Benjamin Britten's new opera *Peter Grimes*.[49]

The astonishing success of *Peter Grimes*, when it reopened Sadler's Wells theatre only a month after VE day, became almost instantly a potent symbol of British musical resurrection – all the more powerful because unexpected. The history of opera in England – 'a record of dogged perseverance on the part of a few enthusiasts, amateurs and visionaries'[50] – had made it difficult even for those enthusiasts themselves to hope that a national version of this most foreign (and expensive) of musical forms could be established very soon. 'Even now, the prospect is not very inviting,' E.J. Dent (himself a pioneer of opera in English) had written in 1940. 'If a young English composer did succeed in making an immediate and sensational success at Sadler's Wells, where else can that opera be performed?'[51] Dent had thought that 'we must establish a whole network of British opera houses' before any British work in this form could have a chance of sustained life, but *Peter Grimes* was quickly taken up in Europe and America. It seemed almost too good to be true, and the expectations heaped on Benjamin Britten as a result left him in a slightly uneasy position for a homosexual pacifist whose wartime emigration was still a matter of resentment.

For Hans Keller in 1945 the experience of hearing *Peter Grimes* can only be described as an epiphany. It was the first time that music outside his own tradition had really meant anything to him, and it was the first contemporary work he felt

49 Glock, 'Music in Post-War Europe', BBC Third Programme, 3, 5, 7, 8 July 1947.
50 E.J. Dent, *Opera* (Harmondsworth: Penguin, 1940), 14.
51 *Ibid.*, 189.

he understood. It also brought him to start connecting his musical understanding with his studies and writing in other fields. Finally, the extraordinary reception of this opera and its composer by critics and audiences (both positive and negative) struck him forcefully. He began to think seriously about the musical society of the country in which – now that the war had ended and such decisions became possible – he and his family had chosen to make their home. Psychologically, what happened to Keller at this point might be described as the moment when music moved from his unconscious to his conscious mind, as he began to process the shock of his abrupt and traumatic move from a culture where music had a settled place into one which was much less sure of itself. Britain at that time seems to have been obsessed with its musical identity – of which fact an intelligent Austrian musician must have been sharply aware.

Musically, Keller had spent the war largely in émigré circles, having lessons from Max Rostal and playing chamber music with Oskar Adler and musicians he had met in the internment camps. He also did some orchestral playing – not an experience he much enjoyed – mainly with the orchestra founded by the German conductor Fritz Berend and the *Freier Deutscher Kulturbund*, which gave concerts in aid of the Red Cross. To some extent this wartime émigré life was imposed on Keller by the legal restrictions on refugees and his time in internment, which had intensified his sense of his own culture and forged new connections with other exiled musicians from his homeland. Of course, under wartime conditions it was difficult anyway to get much sense of normal life in Britain. Like everything else, music had been severely disrupted by the war – and this contributed to the general sense of excitement in 1945 when theatres reopened, the blackout was over, evacuated orchestras returned and musicians were released from the forces. Severe post-war rationing also limited what the general public could spend their money on – another reason for the huge spike in demand for the arts in the second half of the 1940s.

Keller had not been in search of new music when he went to *Peter Grimes* in 1945. On the contrary, his presence in the theatre that night was an accident: he thought he was about to hear *Così fan tutte*.[52] The 1945 summer season at Sadler's Wells presented *Peter Grimes* alongside five other operas – all fairly safe choices in box office terms, planned to counter potential losses on the new work (which in the end outperformed them all): *Così fan tutte, La Bohème, Madame Butterfly, Rigoletto* and *The Bartered Bride*. Keller noted in his diary the performance dates of each opera, but marked the dates of *Così* with special emphasis: instead of going once to hear each opera, he went to all the performances of the Mozart. At the end of the run, he got his dates mixed up, and instead of a seventh *Così* he found himself listening to something strange and new: the last performance of the season of *Peter Grimes*. He was stunned, regarded it immediately as a masterpiece and vowed to hear as much of Britten's music as he could. He had to wait until February 1946 for more performances of *Grimes*, but he wrote down the planned dates in his diary to make sure he would be there for every one. Meanwhile he gathered scores and recordings and watched the concert listings and the *Radio Times* for any mention of Britten's name.

52 See Alan Blyth, *Remembering Britten* (London: Hutchinson, 1981), 87.

One thing that helped *Peter Grimes* make such a profound impression on Keller that night was Peter Pears' performance in the title role. Keller had first encountered Pears' singing just a month beforehand, in the first of the Sadler's Wells performances of *Così fan tutte* on 22 June. It was an experience that stayed with him:

Peter Pears [extract]
Opera II/6 (May 1951): 287–92

Somewhere in the Wells gallery [. . .]. The Overture to *Così* has started. I am not yet a music critic; just a musician. I am lying on my back across three seats, with my mac as a pillow. I'm rather young and one production is as bad as another, so why should I see it? In any case the music will tell me more about the stage than the stage. As for singers, one is worse than another, particularly in England, particularly when you don't know it. So I haven't bought a programme. I wouldn't know the names, anyway. The opening trio is unfolding. The vocal triplets are pretty poor, but then they always are. Yet, do what I will, that tenor is not down to my decided expectations. Oh well, he'll soon make a mess of it all. Just wait for No. 3, the third trio with that marvellous start in, or from, the dominant, and the tenor's liberating opening in the tonic 'To my lady her fond lover such a banquet then will offer.' He won't sense the harmonic meaning of his entry. He won't get what is, comedy or no comedy, the heroic touch of the melody. He'll never recreate that jubilating tension in C major for which another composer would have needed one-and-a-half keys at the inside. He'll never . . . . but here, the third trio starts. It makes me, literally, sit up. The old Viennese axiom that apart from cellists the most unmusical people in the world are tenors vaporizes somewhere at the back of my mind. For once a singer who isn't a poor substitute for an instrumentalist! A voice of character which carries farther and deeper than any voice thrice as strong! A musician who knows, lives, what Mozart and he are doing, and who therefore knows how to define it. Within eleven bars, I have turned from a stern examiner into an admiring pupil. From now onwards the performance becomes – for me of all people – an impatient waiting for the tenor. I have started to watch him too. He does not merely act well. He instinctively acts the music. No movement, no fooling, that contradicts it. Plenty of humour, though. But beneath it, all that is required for an exhaustive characterization of Ferrando. All that puts Ferrando and Fiordiligi on a different level from Dorabella and Guglielmo. All that puts Ferrando himself on a different level from Fiordiligi. He is the most complicated and the deepest and yet the most charming character of the lot. His love making is not altogether a joke. It is in fact an involved business, based on two conflicting loves, one deeply disappointed, the other declared but not self-confessed. The *recitativo accompagnato* "Cruel one, wouldst thou fly me?" and the later, highly dramatic one "Gave thee my portrait! Oh perfidy!" show my singer in singularly full possession of the musico-dramatic facts. And when it comes to Ferrando's "While alas! thine absence mourning" in the A major duet, that unexpected and overpowering entry in the dominant minor (to which I find and feel only two parallels in Mozart's entire output, i.e. the tenor entry in *Don Giovanni*'s first duet with its similar psychological content and, likewise, the tenor entry in the *Requiem*'s "Tuba mirum"), the singer's expressiveness reaches such tense yet tender intensity, indeed such sublimity that as soon as the duet is over I ask the man behind me for his programme. "Shhhhhhh!" says he and everyone; thou shalt not disturb a *secco* recitative. However, he hands me the programme and I memorize the tenor's name. Just in case I should fail to accomplish it completely, there comes another reminder in the (second) finale – another of those dominant minor turns between heaven and earth that are not dreamt of in E.J. Dent's philosophy:[53] "What is this? A marriage contract?" It is only a matter of three bars, but it seals my allegiance. Musically speaking, I know now that this tenor can do everything.

Here was that same exceptional musical *life* that Keller had venerated in Bronisław Huberman, Oskar Adler and Franz Schmidt, which he recognised and responded to instantly – and which he had evidently never expected to find in an English tenor. It was not the quality of Pears' voice as an instrument that was so special – indeed Keller thought that Pears was a great singer 'because and in spite of his voice':

> It is unsensuous and unvoluminous enough to be absolutely dependent on musical expressiveness, on sharp delineation, subtle modulation, on intensive, individual shaping, on what Pears himself would call "characterisation" . . . I submit that *if he had been handicapped by a voice of greater physical "stature,"* he would have found it more difficult to achieve the pronounced character of his timbres, the powerful tensions of his phrasings (on whatever dynamic level), their decided formulations and forms, their dramatic force and lyrical flow. It is not easy to be the master of one's voice when it is easy to be its servant. Pears has been lucky enough not to have to face this temptation.

After this, Keller discovered Britten's own genius as performer as well as composer, and was struck by 'his deep-reaching capacity to feel himself into other

---

53 This production used Dent's translation of the libretto.

composers'. As the musical life of the country resumed after the war, Keller encountered more British performers whose special gifts he thought should be more widely known. He found the clarinettist Reginald Kell's performances 'strikingly similar to Huberman's in regard to the marked freedom with which he reads a work, and the impression of inevitable necessity that, all the same, his readings make'. He also thought 'it is deplorable that Ian Whyte, the conductor of the BBC Scottish Orchestra, is not given much wider scope.' A few months after *Peter Grimes* he drafted an article asserting that such gifted performers were 'not famous enough'.[54] He tried to show the importance of 'reproductive genius', contrasting its unrepeatable individuality with the current over-valuation of technical skill: 'the gramophone record disguised as a human being is very much in vogue nowadays.' He argued against the widespread contemporary notion that a performer's role was simply to realise as accurately as possible the composer's intentions: 'One cannot exactly relive one's own experiences, let alone those of others. And a performance suffers if at its root lies an attempt to realize an illusion.'

This article was never published. Until this point, Keller had not published anything on music – indeed he had scarcely written a word on the subject: he thought of himself primarily as a psychologist. During the war, he had written a great many (mostly unpublished) short essays and several longer papers (some highly technical) on various aspects of psychology, and in 1945 had been engaged for some time in an extensive research project on social groups, preparing a book (*The Psychology of Social Unity*) with an experienced sociologist twice his age. A few weeks after *Peter Grimes* he and his colleague presented a paper on 'The Psychological Significance of Some Sociological Conceptions of the Group' to the British Psychological Society, and an article by Keller examining 'Male Psychology' was accepted for publication by the *British Journal of Medical Psychology*.[55] By the time this article appeared, however, Keller had changed course completely.

Naturally Keller had brought none of his schoolboy writings out of Vienna in 1938, but a great deal of his unpublished work from 1939–45 has survived, revealing something of his wartime intellectual interests and his early development as a writer.[56] The first observation to be made is the change wrought in him by his time in internment from June 1940 until March 1941. Insofar as they can be accurately dated, Keller's writings from the pre-internment period show a compulsive writer still in search of his subject, writing on anything and everything and in a variety of forms. After internment, this experimentation was increasingly displaced by a new, almost obsessive, preoccupation with Freudian psychoanalysis. Although he brought no papers out of the camps, Keller's interest in Freud seems to have begun there, probably inspired by fellow internees. Willi Hoffer, whom Keller afterwards knew best of Freud's circle in London, was very impressed with the young Keller and arranged for him to be admitted to the library of the Institute of

---

54 'Not Famous Enough', undated typescript [1946], published in *HKM&P*, 192–6.
55 *British Journal of Medical Psychology* 20 (1946): 384–8, reprinted in *HKM&P*, 112–16.
56 Many of Keller's wartime writings are published in *HKM&P*.

Psychoanalysis, where Keller amassed a knowledge of psychoanalytic literature that Hoffer apparently considered 'unequalled'.

Keller was not a diffident young man, so was not shy of approaching the psychologists whose writings he read, and he was soon in correspondence with several eminent figures. Of the many potential mentors he met during the war, however, the one who was most important to his early development was not a Viennese psychoanalyst, but an English educationalist with strong interests in social psychology. When she first encountered Keller in 1942, Margaret Phillips was a lecturer in education at Stockwell College in Torquay, and she became Principal of Borthwick Training College in London in 1944.[57] She had published her first book, *The Education of the Emotions*, in 1937 and in 1942 began a long study of social groups, after observing the widespread disruption in society following the outbreak of war, which she thought afforded 'an opportunity for a social inquirer of much the same kind as the physical and mental damage of wartime offered to medicine'.[58] Phillips's research method involved assembling a large amount of primary material by means of questionnaires, diaries and interviews, and Keller first came across her when a duplicated copy of her initial questionnaire reached him in the second half of 1942.

This initiated an intense correspondence. Phillips was evidently intrigued by Keller and their letter-writing led to a formal collaboration as she drew him into her research project when she moved to London. They made a virtue of their methodological differences by adopting an alternating structure for their book, whereby each of Phillips's sociological chapters would be followed by one by Keller reviewing the same material from a Freudian perspective. At the same time Phillips was helping to shape Keller as an English writer. For example, her letter of 17 July 1943 (when she and Keller had still not met in person) contains what she called 'my third attack on your literary style':

> You have stonewalled me twice; I might if I had been a spot cleverer have noticed earlier that these were the only occasions on which I had been stonewalled. . . . What I want to ask you is; have you in the course of your self-analysis shed any light on the question of when you use each of your styles, and why? It is certainly not a matter of difficulty with English, because your other style is potentially a beautiful one, as I have said before. That style seems to me like the quality of your thinking when your whole personality is involved and not merely your intellect; then it is like the quality of Dr Adler's playing; properly speaking one would not speak of a style at all; it merely says what it has to say; the communication reaches one directly without the apparent intervention of an instrument or a person or a technique. So another way of putting the question is; when is the whole of your personality behind what you want to say and when only your intellect? And yet that

57 Borthwick was one of fifty-five emergency teacher-training colleges set up to avert an anticipated post-war shortage of teachers.

58 Phillips, *Small Social Groups in England* (London: Methuen, 1965), 3.

does not represent it either. Better say; what are the occasions on which you retreat to a pillbox and snipe at the enemy with words; which are those on which you exude clouds of sepia-coloured words into the water? (And what part does formal logic play in these tactics? Or is your passion for formal logic a separate one and if so what accounts for it?)

One of the ways in which Keller sought to hone his writing in English was by writing aphorisms. He had long been doing this in German,[59] and he now started writing them in English, as a way of playing with the language. *The Psychologist* published a number of his aphorisms on the theme of 'Maturity' – 'I do hope they won't go on for ever,' sighed Phillips after several sets of these: 'If they do I shall respectfully suggest (always supposing it matters) that one isn't mature till one has ceased to think or feel anything about the matter.'[60] Although she encouraged Keller's aphorism-writing – and gave him in 1944 a copy of the British philosopher F.H. Bradley's *Aphorisms* inscribed 'to Hans (another F.H.B!)' – she cautioned him against over-indulging his passion for paradox and verbal complication: 'The plays on words are all right in moderation and when they happen spontaneously but when they become a habitual mannerism –

> *Aphorisms are not valuable on account of their substance, but on account of their function. They transmit little truth, but they provoke the desire for it.*

a sort of compulsion – it is otherwise . . . if only you could take it all just a little more lightly & easily so that it need not be quite so clever!'[61]

She also questioned his earnest Freudianism: 'Even assuming Freud as the greatest genius ever, surely he need not have discovered the whole truth for all time? . . . Have you ever thought where your own passion for Freud has come from?' She was keen to tone down the Freudian technicalities in Keller's writing, in the interests of the readers of their book: 'Has it occurred to you – it has to me several times – that if only Freudian theory could be put in non-technical language – e.g. using 'conscience' instead of 'super ego' – it would be much more willingly accepted?'[62]

9 November 1944 – to Margaret Phillips [extract]

Dear Margaret,

Very many thanks for the letter & cheque – returning to London Thursday night. [. . .]

Readability: I shall try my best, or, maybe, my worst. What about the style of 'Male Psychology' (apart from the knowledge it pre-supposes?) Is that too "difficult?" [. . .]

---

59 See, for example, 'Schonend, weil in Kürze', *Zeitspiegl*, 26 October 1941.
60 Phillips to Keller, '24 August', CULHK.
61 Phillips to Keller, '24 May', CULHK.
62 Phillips to Keller [25 January 1945] and [November 1944], CULHK.

Substitution of Freudian terms by popular ones.

(1) General comment. I am not in favour of this. Freudian terms
were created out of a necessity, not out of pleasure at finding some
incomprehensible words. This necessity largely arose out of the
conception of the unconscious which is no popular conception yet,
however popular the word and its misinterpretations may be. This
conception, together with the recognition of the resistances and of
repression which it implies, as well as with realisation of the significance
of the Oedipus complex and of sexuality, is one which represents a very
bitter truth to the ego. For a long time to come, the latter will, more or
less deliberately, grasp at any opportunity to return, under the cover of
alleged progress, to pre-psycho-analytical outlooks. Two fine examples of
such reactionary processes are, of course, the teachings of [Alfred] Adler
and Jung. Now the proposed substitution would offer a unique occasion
for such reactionary activities, as indeed it has already done. The occasion
would be unique because the very substitution (unless popular terms are
endowed with new meanings, which in most cases is simply impossible
to achieve) would logically represent a reaction in the direction of pre-
Freudian thinking. New things can hardly be expressed in old words.
And if these newly found things are, on top of their novelty, extremely
unpleasant and therefore at first largely incomprehensible, the chance
that they will be properly understood vanishes, I should think not only
far-reachingly, but completely. According to the accepted meaning of the
old words, the substitution would objectively represent a major reaction.
Whatever there would remain of the Freudian sense would be drowned
in the subjective attitude towards the result of the substitution, so that
the reaction would become complete. [. . .]

(2) Super-ego and conscience. Conscience is a surface-conception,
super-ego isn't. Indeed there aren't many psychical processes which
are more conscious than, say, the pangs of conscience (under certain
circumstances), whereas there aren't many psychical processes which
are less penetrable by the conscious mind than the greater part of
the processes within the super-ego. [. . .] In order to arrive at an
understanding of the super-ego one has to consider its history and its
origin. The shortest description of the latter is that the ego creates the
super-ego out of the id. This may sound pretty mysterious; I shall explain
it presently. At this point I want to point out that as the super-ego is
created out of the id, it is likely to be less near to consciousness than the
ego – which in fact is the actual state of affairs.

Phillips was twice Keller's age, so it was natural that she should have been
a mentor to him during their early association – but it is striking how much she
evidently respected and admired him. 'I never know whether I ought to allow

anything for your youth,' she wrote to him once: 'You seem to me so – not mature, but timeless; but perhaps one ought.'[63] Throughout the time of their association, Keller was engaged in daily self-analysis (following Freud's own model), which he seems to have discussed with Phillips. This went on for five years, and Keller referred to it more than once in later years as having 'changed my life. At the end of it I knew far better who I was, and I could distribute my psychic energies far more economically.'[64] He claimed that he had turned to self-analysis only because he couldn't afford a formal training analysis, but some who knew him have expressed scepticism about whether the real reason was financial, and whether the fiercely independent Keller could ever have submitted himself to another analyst. It may be, however, that his association with Phillips at the same time meant that she fulfilled something of this role and so was as important as the actual self-analysis in helping Keller understand himself.

> *A truism is a truth stated without being re-discovered.*

Phillips also considered the question of what path Keller should follow after the war. As she wrote to him in 1943:

> My dear Hans, I have been doing a spot of rumination on the subject of 'you and work' – on the assumption that what you want to do is to practise psychology in this country after the war – though whether this is a correct assumption I don't know. You know I expect that this country is stiff with Viennese refugees all wanting to practise psycho-analysis – Austria has badly overdone her export of those . . . If you want to live by psychology you have to have either a medical or a psychological degree. The prejudice against ps-analysis is immensely diminished if you add to it a doctor's training – it becomes almost respectable then![65]

Keller was reluctant to embark on a medical degree. By 1945 he was already twenty-six years old, so a long course of study was uninviting, as was the prospect of undergraduate life: 'I do sympathise about the boringness for you of life with students,' agreed Phillips. On his release from internment he had taken an LRAM teaching diploma, so he may have been considering teaching music – perhaps combined with performance, though it seems unlikely that he would have been able to make enough of an income from his playing. From the scant details in his diaries, paid performances were few and far between and his cousin has stated later

---

63 Phillips to Keller, 15 July [1943], CULHK.
64 Mark Doran, ed., 'Hans Keller In Interview with Anton Weinberg', *Tempo* 195 (January 1996): 6–12. Keller's cousin Inge Trott has said his self-analysis also helped him rid himself of a stammer: 'Hans stuttered as a child, and right up to his twenties. He got rid of it himself.' Oral communication, 29 March 2004.
65 Phillips to Keller [August 1943], CULHK.

Hans Keller aged eighteen, on holiday at Kritzendorf in 1937, and in the Lake District after his release from internment in 1941.

that he never made much money that way.[66] Given that he also took three attempts to pass the LRAM practical examination, there is also the question of whether he would have been good enough.[67] This is hard to reconcile with Oskar Adler's high regard for his playing, but may be partly explicable by Adler's valuing musical understanding over technique. It is also possible that physical problems after Keller's two bouts of imprisonment played a part. He was released from internment on medical grounds and suffered ill health afterwards. Photographs dating from 1937 and 1941 show a marked deterioration in his appearance, confirming the statement by one of his uncles that Keller had suffered from 'very great nervous troubles and looks – although not yet 22 years old – like a 35 year old man'.[68]

---

66 Inge Trott, oral communication, 29 March 2004.

67 Three LRAM mark-sheets are preserved in CULHK, dated 9 September 1942, 15 December 1942 and 5 April 1943.

68 Rudolf Keller to the Under Secretary of State, Aliens Department, 27 January 1941, in support of Keller's application for release from internment, CULHK.

Although he may have considered teaching music and playing it, the idea of earning a living by writing about it seems never to have occurred to Keller until his *Peter Grimes* epiphany. Quite why this suddenly changed is an intriguing subject for speculation. One reason was evidently the psychological interest of Britten's opera – the complexity of Grimes's character made it a veritable gift for a psychoanalyst. From his many hours in the Institute of Psychoanalysis library, Keller discovered that the psychology of music as a subject was particularly underexplored: 'It is unfortunate that Freud was almost totally unmusical, otherwise he would have been in a position . . . to prove many of his discoveries by the analysis of musical mental processes which, to the non-psychoanalytical observer, represent a bewildering picture of psychic phenomena largely isolated from the rest of mental life.'[69]

Keller had made a few attempts in 1941–42 to link musical processes to those of the unconscious mind, and his archive contains some fragmentary manuscripts in both English and German, bearing titles like 'Manifestations of the Primary Process in Musical Composition', 'Dream-Work and Development in Sonata Form', 'Die abnormen Vorgänge in der Musik' (Abnormal Processes in Music) and 'Ansätze zur psychoanalytischen Musikbetrachtung' (Approaches to the Psychoanalytic Study of Music). But these were rather abstract general speculations – such as trying to show a parallel between the way dreams work on reality and the way in which the development section of a sonata form treats the thematic material of the exposition. Keller failed to get very far in this sort of investigation, and his drafts tended to break off after a few pages without going into the detail of specific works, leaving him to conclude that 'the psychology of music is the most difficult branch of applied psychology.'[70] He abandoned these attempts when he met Margaret Phillips, and music is scarcely mentioned in their long correspondence. But in 1945 Keller found in *Peter Grimes* a story of such intense psychological interest, and Britten's treatment of it so remarkable, that everything changed. Through his total absorption in this one work, Keller began to find a way into thinking and writing about the emotional meaning of music via its application to the drama – despite the fact that, as he wrote in his first psychoanalytical essay on the work, 'my whole emotional approach to music is not such as to make extra-musical associations particularly easy for me.'[71]

As soon as he could, he acquired copies of Montagu Slater's libretto and Erwin Stein's vocal score of the opera, and embarked on a psychological analysis of the work. He produced an impressive fifty-page typescript in three sections, examining in turn 'Grimes's Character' (which Keller diagnosed as 'anal'), 'Grimes and His Mother' (his ambivalent relationship with Ellen, his 'intra-uterine, death and rebirth fantasies', and the symbolic role of the sea), and 'Grimes and His Father' (his relationship with Balstrode, his attitude to the apprentices in a 'reversal of

---

69 'Studies in the Psycho-analysis of Music', undated fragment, CULHK.
70 'The Psychology of Film Music', *World Psychology* (1948): 23–6.
71 *HKM&P*, 128.

generations phantasy', and his Oedipal rebellion against the Borough society).[72] On the front cover of the manuscript there is a pencilled note for a potential fourth section on 'The Appeal of Peter Grimes. There are plenty of Grimeses.' This was a reference to the short article that Pears had written for *Radio Times* to accompany the broadcast of the opera on the BBC Third Programme on 13 March 1946 – concluding, 'There are plenty of Grimeses around still, I think!'

The internal psychology of the work itself was not the only thing that had caught Keller's psychologist's attention: the reaction of press and public also merited investigation. Keller loved a paradox, so was intrigued by a composer who was both unusually popular – 'Britten's popularity needs a special explanation' – *and* underestimated: 'In a way, a very definite way, his exceptional brilliance and cleverness are his bad luck. For the surety and sparkle of his workmanship tend to hide from many – even critics' – ears, the depth that lies beneath.'[73] During the second season of *Grimes* in 1946 Keller became very exercised by the critical reactions, taking particular exception to the opera critic Philip Hope-Wallace's negative review in *Time and Tide* (which criticised Pears for singing 'white' and sounding tired, and even suggested that the role should be sung by a baritone).[74] Keller immediately wrote a letter to the editor, defending Pears's 'unsurpassable' interpretation – the first example of what was to become one of his most passionate principles: the defence of great artists against the critics who misunderstood them. *Time and Tide* did not publish his letter, so Keller sent it to Pears and resolved to find somewhere else to publish his views. His decision to become a music critic had been made.

It was a perfect time and place. 'God how London is seething with intellectual & educational activity – so many new magazines, conferences, courses of every description,' wrote Margaret Phillips, contrasting post-war London with wartime Torquay. 'Talk about new growth – it's like the willow Herb on the bombed sites!'[75] Despite the fact that in the immediate post-war years 'paper is rationed more fiercely than meat,'[76] there was an extraordinary boom in the publication of new periodicals in the late 1940s. The editor of one such, writing in 1947, put the growth at 'thirty or forty' new journals being founded every *week* – most of which went swiftly out of business, consuming precious paper as they went.[77] One new magazine which began publication at the beginning of 1946 was *National Entertainment Monthly*. Aiming 'to cater for *every* member of the family and to encourage greater social activity', it provided for post-war Britons a guide to the wealth of new leisure activities now available to them. Listings and reviews

---

72 'Three Psychoanalytic Notes on *Peter Grimes*', published posthumously in *HKM&P*, 122–45.

73 'A Great English Composer', unpublished essay, *BB2013*, 1–6.

74 *Time and Tide*, 16 February 1946. Hope-Wallace was aware that the tone of his notice was 'ungrateful', but explained that this 'should be laid to a real fear that this near-masterpiece is not, after all, going to hold the stage. The thought of yet another hope of English opera going on the shelf is more than some of us can bear.'

75 Phillips to Keller [March 1947], CULHK.

76 *National Entertainment Monthly* I/2 (April 1946): 2.

77 Editorial, *Mandrake* I/5 (1947): 5–7.

of the latest films, books, plays and concerts sat alongside articles on gardening, fashion, sport and holidays, together with advice on housing, job prospects overseas and 'bringing-up baby'. 'Boredom', wrote its editor, is 'THE disease of the twentieth century', and his magazine had a mission to counter it. He may have hit a nerve: such was the demand for his little magazine that its first issue sold out immediately all over Britain and more than 1,000 letters from grateful readers were received.

This was the first English publication in which Hans Keller appeared as a writer on music, commissioned initially to produce a monthly survey of the nation's musical life – a time-consuming undertaking for which the magazine's 'painfully low' fees were scarcely adequate recompense. It was not only the low rate of pay that made writing for *National Entertainment* unsatisfactory:

4 May 1946 – to Peter Pears

Dear Mr. Pears,

Thank you so much for your letter. I'm very glad that you don't mind critics more than is emotionally inevitable.

The reason why I am writing again is that I'm unhappy about the enclosed review (National Entertainment Monthly, a new magazine), as it is printed. Not only did this idiot of a sub-editor (who is making a habit of distorting and vulgarizing my remarks) cut my detailed praise of your musical personality and your vocal capacities, but the sentence about your not being 'quite so vital on the first occasion' is all wrong. What I spoke of was the performance that was broadcast: this, I suggested, was not perhaps marked by the same vitality on your part as preceding and succeeding performances. I shall, of course, insist on a correction, and in order realistically to counterbalance the undue prominence thus given to a point of criticism of negligible importance, I shall add my conviction that you are among the most significant performers of our time, either in this country or elsewhere. (Today's performance, by the way – of which, unfortunately, I could only hear the first act and half of the second, whereafter I had to leave – was, to my mind, unsurpassed by you, and, to my imagination, unsurpassable by anyone else.)

For the rest, I can only hope you won't be too annoyed.

Here's another point: I'm working now on a psychoanalytic study of <u>Peter Grimes</u> (psychological research is one of my occupations; my second paper is just going to press in the British Journal of Medical Psychology). This article, tho' more extensive than yours in the Radio Times, can be regarded as a complement, on the psychological level, to what you expounded on the more sociological one. Do you think that Britten is at all interested in, or at any rate, not opposed to, the application to art of the psychoanalytic body of knowledge? Naturally I would only like to show him my paper when it is finished, if I knew that I wouldn't just waste his time.

Incidentally, why doesn't Sackville-West (<u>Peter Grimes</u> Wells Opera Book) mention the version of his example 5 that occurs in the storm interlude? Apart from the fact that each recurrence of this should, I think, be mentioned, its position and form in this interlude seems to be of outstanding psychological importance, since Peter's ambivalence is here inevitably impressed on the listener.

Kindly let me have the press cutting back, but please do not bother to reply if, as is probable, you have no time.

Throughout the rest of 1946 and 1947, Keller worked hard to find other outlets for his writing, and gradually his persistent efforts began to pay off. As he concentrated on breaking into music criticism, his psychological work with Margaret Phillips quickly dwindled and their book was never published. While most of what Keller was doing at this time was routine journalism, a great deal of profound thought was going on under the surface, as he worked out the implications of the epiphany he had experienced in his encounter with *Peter Grimes*, and what it was that he wanted to say. Phillips had been his primary mentor throughout his psychological research and the crucial wartime period of his self-analysis and the formation of his English literary style. But now, as he sought to bring his psychological knowledge to bear on his profound – but hitherto wordless – musical understanding, she could not help him. One who could, however, was a Viennese émigré musician of his own age he had met while interned on the Isle of Man: the pianist Paul Hamburger.

As well as being a remarkable pianist, later known for his sensitive accompaniment of lieder and his work as an operatic coach, Hamburger was highly intellectual and widely read in literature and philosophy, with a particularly keen insight into German, French and English poetry – something that made his lieder interpretations notably profound. His literary sensitivity was an important aspect of his special feeling for Britten's music, and Roger Vignoles, who studied with him in the 1960s, recalled that 'to hear his explanation of the poetry of W.H. Auden or Thomas Hardy (as in Britten's *On This Island* and *Winter Words*, respectively) was an illuminating experience.'[78] Hamburger was for Keller an ideal thinking partner at that time and their talks were frequent and evidently very fruitful – as Keller wrote later, 'Hamburger always inspires me.'[79]

Their earliest surviving letters date from November 1946, a particularly important time in the development of Keller's thought. Having completed the first three

78 'Paul Hamburger', *Independent*, 21 April 2004, 35.
79 Diary fragment, 12 October 1953, CULHK.

parts of his psychoanalytical study of *Peter Grimes*, Keller was beginning to expand his thoughts on the psychology of music beyond this one work of Britten's to other examples of what he called 'applied music'. By this term he meant music applied to a text or drama: thus opera, lieder, and also a new form that for a while became something of an obsession – film music.

The Psychology of Film Music [extract]
World Psychology (1948): 23–6, reprinted in *HKM&P*, 157–60

The psychology of music is the most difficult branch of applied psychology, but the psychology of what we might call applied (as distinct from absolute or pure) music offers a comparatively easy approach to the musico-psychologist. The reason, therefore, is clear. Whereas in pure music we encounter processes which, at any rate on the surface, bear little relation to such mental phenomena as have already been elucidated by psychological analysis, the processes that make up applied music, though in themselves as mysterious psychologically as those of pure music, are at least definitely related to extra-musical mental processes that have already been successfully subjected to scientific research. [. . .]

Of all branches of applied music, film music is the youngest. It has, indeed, been born into, and also out of, a psychological age, and for that reason alone it ought to be of particular interest to the psychologist, once he has noted its existence, which, so far, he has not. Film music, far more than many another art form, has a well-definable psychological function: while art in general aims primarily at representing the beautiful (which sometimes may be the ugly, not because the artist does not believe in beauty, but because he believes in the beauty of ugliness), film music aims to an unusual extent, indeed, often primarily, at suggesting psychological truth – thus an essential part of the psychological functions, or of the psychotechnics, of film music.

The development of the psychological, as distinct from the aesthetic aspect of music, has been going on for a long time; it indeed reached peaks before the advent of film music. Mozart was a unique figure in this as in many other respects, in that he succeeded in uniting, to the highest degree, an unsurpassed artistico-psychological insight with an unsurpassable aesthetic sense.

The reference here to Mozart is significant. Keller saw in Mozart's operas the same exceptional psychological insight that had drawn him to Britten, which led him to think deeply about what psychoanalysis could contribute to the understanding of these works he knew so well. Hamburger's knowledge of Mozart's operas was profound, and he and Keller went to all the performances then available. The late 1940s in London was an excellent time to be studying Mozart's operas, since there were then a great many productions being mounted (as the British made up for lost time) – including the visit of the Vienna State Opera in 1947, bringing magnificent productions of *Figaro*, *Così fan tutte* and *Don Giovanni* that set London ablaze.[80]

Since discovering *Peter Grimes*, Keller had been listening to as much of Britten's music as he could and was increasingly struck by similarities between Britten's creative character and that of Mozart. He described them both as 'classical' rather than 'romantic' in their 'restrained, yet explicit emotion' and their 'impeccable sense of form'. He was very clear, however, that this kind of 'restraint' did *not* mean inhibition: 'in this respect their exact contrary is Brahms.' Both were 'clever, supreme craftsmen', able to write on commission as though with total freedom, and their ideas were always conceived as pure sound: their compositions for orchestra 'are not orchestrated, but orchestral'. Their dramatic ability was extraordinary, but they were able to write in many other forms. Eclectic in their inspiration, their major stimulus nevertheless seemed to be primarily melodic – 'more materially, they are liable to be inspired by the human voice (as also by language, including foreign language), and indeed influenced by individual voices.' Finally, Keller was intrigued by parallels in the attitude of audiences and critics to both composers: 'Mozart and Britten are the only two composers I know who strongly and widely attract people who do not understand them,' he concluded, attributing this to the way in which 'their music is approachable on various levels, each seemingly giving a complete picture in itself.'[81]

He discussed all this with Paul Hamburger, and began to write a long essay on the subject in the autumn of 1946. The letters that survive between them show clearly that Hamburger was the ideal partner for this sort of exploration. He and Keller frequently showed each other what they were writing, encouraging and criticising each other's work. Keller's first draft of his essay on 'Britten and Mozart' drew from Hamburger twelve closely-written pages in response:

> Dear Keller,
>
> I have read your article with the greatest pleasure, and have, I think, learned quite a lot in the art of writing such articles by it. Form and presentation are absolutely excellent, conciseness so strong that one often wants your comment to it. The result is, unlike in my late effort, not heaviness and telescoped symbolism, but rather a kind of aloofness that carries the reader along quicker than he wishes to move, in fact you are demonstrating by your very style that remarkable "agility" of Mozart and Britten and many a reader

---

80 It was Etienne Amyot of the BBC who negotiated this visit, which he describes as 'the best thing we ever did', since it brought to London – and to the rest of the country via radio – a standard of performance most people had never heard before. 'It had very wide repercussions and not only in music but also in design . . . and from that moment everybody wanted to write an opera.' WAC R143/2/1.

81 All these quotations are from the essay 'Britten and Mozart' that Keller wrote towards the end of 1946 and published in 1948: *M&L* XXIX/1 (January 1948): 17–30. Reprinted in *HKM&P*, 164–76 and *HKI*, 234–47.

might be apt to stick to the surface and think he has understood your mani-
festum while he has barely scratched its skin.

. . . "restrained yet explicit emotion" I think is a bit too wide, it applies to
Bach, Purcell, Monteverdi and others as well. . . . The paradoxical element
in it is largely aphoristic. When the aphorism is dissolved the emotion shows
itself as mood and temperament, as a *source* of artistic creation whereas the
restraint is the process of creation. . . .

One of the things is M. or Br.'s queer attitude to compromise ("they don't
quarrel!"). Compromise between styles means for them not that they unite
contraries step by step by argument but rather that they negate contraries by
giving them each their right and place (dangerous for a minor composer). . . .

By the way: have you ever read that classical example of artistic comparison, Thomas Mann's "Goethe and Tolstoy" (and, implied, Schiller and
Dostoevsky)? One point he makes is that G. and Tolstoy have after long
struggle eliminated the antithesis of Nature and Spirit, whereas Schiller &
Dostojevsky are its proud champions throughout their life. Perhaps you
could mention that for Mozart and Br. this antithesis is crucial too, Mozart
by singular fortune having overcome it at such early age as his last style
in which Spirit becomes Nature, as in the 'Magic Flute'; Britain [*sic*] still
struggling to 'naturalise' Spirit. The choice of Donne as a poet still shows
the antithesis in full bloom. Both of them want to get away from it, that is to
become all 'Nature' whereas people like Schiller, Dostojevsky, Beethoven,
u.s.w. try to expel Nature and become all Spirit. . . .

For harmony I would mention that neither employs a set of graded dissonances (like Beethoven, Bach, the Romantics, V. Williams, even Walton),
in which chords and intervals of a higher degree of tension lean towards
lesser dissonances, those again towards lesser, till they are resolved. Mozart
and Britten are in favour (though not exclusively) of making sharp division
between the consonances and dissonances of their day. . . .[82]

These discussions on musical character received much stimulation at the end of
1946 from the publication in Britain of Alfred Einstein's *Mozart: His Character,
His Work*.[83] Hamburger discovered the book and sent it to Keller, who declared
himself 'quite extraordinarily gethrillt. What is more, it comes just at the right
time: I am now writing my article "Britten and Mozart", and already just briefly
flipping through it is giving me valuable material for this.'[84] Later, Keller told
Hamburger that he was adding 'a massive coda' to his essay 'in which I compare Einstein's comparison between Mozart and other composers with my own
Britten–Mozart comparison',[85] and he continued to draw on Einstein in subsequent essays.

---

82 Hamburger to Keller, 18 November 1946, CULHK.
83 (London: Cassell, 1946).
84 Keller to Hamburger, 6 November 1946, CULHK.
85 Keller to Hamburger, 7 July 1947, CULHK.

As well as their discussions on creative character, Keller and Hamburger were exploring thematic relationships and structural unity in Mozart's work. They exchanged a series of letters on this after attending the performance of *The Magic Flute* at Covent Garden on 20 March 1947. These letters are interesting both as an indication of the closeness of their thought – note the references to 'thought transference' – and for what they show of the seeds of Keller's later analytical methods.

Keller had started this exchange in a letter now lost, to which Hamburger replied:

> The "Zauberflöte" love-circle, by a strange coincidence, struck me at the performance, I meant to tell you about it but forgot; very queer to have you mention it suddenly! Do you think that Papagenos – Papagena "Viele kleine Kinder", or so, is the same?  (In the Duet)[86]

12 May 1947 – to Paul Hamburger

Dear Hamburger,

There is no doubt that the Papageno–Papagena sequence is the same. I haven't noticed this before. You, of course, have: '. . . . Welche Freude – wird das sein, wenn die Götter uns bedenken, uns'rer Liebe Kinder schenken, uns'rer Liebe Kinder schenken, so liebe kleine Kinderlein, Kinderlein, – ritardando – Kinderlein, Kinderlein, etc. <u>ad infinitum</u>, i.e. Sechslinge.[87]

I said to you, a few months ago, that I wouldn't talk any more about my supposed 'deep' relationship between identical or near-identical motives in different movements of the same work (your Erinnerungsfetzen)[88] until I could formulate at least some shadow of a proof. I think I can now.

Figaro: Trio, first act. Count has just appeared from behind the chair:

(1) Susanna:

---

86 Hamburger to Keller, 9 May 1947, CULHK.
87 'sextuplets' (*Magic Flute*, Act II, Scene 9).
88 'flash of memory'

(2) Last act Cavatina (Barbarina (die Nadel))

oh how   dread - ful   have I
Un - gluck - sel' -   ge   klein - e

lost - it
Na - del

[The two are] the same emotional and dramatic situation.

Now according to your most wegwerfend[89] theory, Mozart must have <u>remembered the future</u> here, for it is ex. I (not ex. 2) that <u>seems</u> to be an Erinnerungsfetzen (of ex. 2), as in ex. 2 the motive is the basis of the number. No, is it not much more plausible to suppose that the two examples have a common root? In the present instance there is not indeed anything mystical about this common Urbild[90] – the extra-musical associations make it easy for us to see it. But I'm quite sure the common Urgedanke[91] is equally present in an abstract piece, although I cannot, of course, directly <u>prove</u> it there. Still, the common formal* & textural functions** of the different manifestations of the hypothetical Urgedanke seem to be an indication of its existence. Mind you, I think the common Urgedanke is a far more extensive affair than these motifs – they're just symptoms. To me all this is really a question of Leitmotiv (or whatever you want to call it) von-innen-eraus, instead of von-aussen-erein.[92] And it is symptomatic (contrary to your opinion, I think) of unity. The Leitmotiv, or idée fixe, on the other hand, wants to show off unity, which may*** or may not**** be there. – Sorry, I have digressed from my 'proof' to (as it may seem) mere phantasy, but if you give me another 6 months, I might carry the matter further on a more rational level.

Ja, ich hoffe zu Sabata gehen zu können.[93]

Mit den ergebensten Empfahlgen am Papagena;[94] she needn't worry, you won't plan to commit suicide in a tragi-comic G minor – not even in F minor.

Yours

Keller

---

89 'dismissive'
90 'archetype'
91 'fundamental thought'
92 'from inside out instead of outside in'
93 'Yes, I hope to be able to go to [Victor de] Sabata.'
94 'With most sincere compliments to Papagena.' (This refers to the mezzo-soprano Esther Salaman, whom Hamburger was shortly to marry.)

* see for instance the Rückführungen[95] in the Linz Symphony

** fascinating once you start going into them

*** always in Mendelssohn, however superficial the whole thing may be

**** as sometimes in Wagner, however deep the whole thing may be

P.S. Love-circle: coincidence of your forgetting to tell me, my forgetting to tell you, and my writing you eventually: thought 'transference' (the term is misleading) can, nowadays, be considered proved. Have you read about the experiments?

20 May 1947 – to Paul Hamburger

Dear Hamburger,

This thought "transference"* business is becoming uncanny. Three or four days ago I wanted to write you a letter on the Prague Symphony part of which would have been downright identical with what you wrote me now. I was in town then, and actually turned towards the Leicester Sq. Post Office to get a letter card – but then bethought myself, for I should probably have needed 20 letter cards.

Yes, these relations are, I think, of great significance. May I add one or two points (I can't say everything I want to say about this – as you rightly say, superb – symphony, otherwise this would have to be an article).

The first recurrence of the violin figure (introduction) is not the (inverted) example you quote, but the (not yet inverted) fourth quaver of the Allegro's 6th bar (first violins):

The origin of this figure is to be found in the demi-semiquaver-"Roller" at the very beginning of the Adagio (cf. also the following triad, the piano on this common chord arpeggio, and the forte preceding and succeeding it).

Now so far we have four versions of this figure, but there are more. For instance, in the coda of the exposition:

95 'leadbacks'

As this is used in the development, Mozart introduces it shortly before, so as to drive us into it; in the recapitulation, on the other hand, it occurs just before the second subject! (which it doesn't in the exposition). At the same time the full significance of this version of the figure can, I think, only be understood, if the movement (as every great Mozart movement) is approached <u>outside time</u>, namely, (for instance) if the development is realized to be working out, not only the exposition, but also the recapitulation.

The choice of the motif for canonic treatment in the development is most typically Mozart. It is, seemingly, "unimportant" (cf. Traumverschiebung[96]), i.e. to the superficial ear it occurs just once, very "conventionally", as a one-bar extension of the first sentence. But to the Mozart ear it is nothing of the sort. It is first foreshadowed in bar 6/4 of the introduction (not the only thing that is foreshadowed there – see below); it comes out, a little less concealedly, in the descending chromatic sextuplets at the end of the introduction. (There are of course intermediary stages between these two versions). It has a quasi-cyclic significance in the introduction, it has a less quasi and more cyclic significance in the exposition where it occurs, "unimportantly", near the beginning and near the end, and it has a still more cyclic significance in the development, where it occurs at the beginning, and as Rueckfuehrung. This Rueckfuehrungsfunktion[97] is one of the reasons why it is so typically Mozart. For this function having been clearly established at the end of the Allegro's first sentence, the motive can be used for the development's chase towards the recapitulation, a chase whose speed is of course enhanced by canonic treatment. The development's unerring aiming at the recapitulation is something I find only in three composers: Mozart, Mendelssohn, Britten. Any connection with youthful maturity? If so, what?

The relations you note between the 2nd movement's first subject and the other movements may thus be supplemented:

96 'dream displacement'
97 'leadback function'

[...]

No really, I can't go on, otherwise I'll spend all afternoon over it.

* it is actually supposed that there is common (not transferred) thinking in certain only seemingly individual regions of the mind.

A further topic for discussion emerged shortly after this, when Hamburger's fiancée Esther Salaman met the eighty-six-year-old Max Schiller (widower of the famous French *diseuse* Yvette Guilbert). Though he lived in Paris, Schiller was very interested in Benjamin Britten as an opera composer. He drew Salaman's attention to the nineteenth-century Swiss writer Gottfried Keller, the first of whose *Seven Legends* ('Eugenia') he thought particularly suitable as the basis of a libretto for Britten. Hamburger spent some time translating it and sketching out a draft scenario, 'as an indication of the story's operatic possibilities'.[98]

Before approaching Britten himself with the idea, Hamburger sought Keller's advice.

23 October 1947 – to Paul Hamburger [extract]
In German

Dear Hamburger,

Although, as you so rightly say, all sorts of attractions for Britten lie in this potential text, <u>I personally</u> consider it quite out of the question that he will go ahead and tackle it. My opinion may be quite absurd, and you should please not attach too much significance to it, but I feel bound to express it. From an aesthetic point of view the story is perfectly suitable, psychologically, though, <u>completely wrong</u> for Britten. It strikes to the heart of the homosexual complexes; indeed the transvestism and the lesbian episode become the central point! Do you really believe that Britten can take such a detached view of his homosexuality, enough to treat its central complexes artistically? Yes, the complexes are exploited by him when it's a question of manifestations which either hide their origin or do not run up against the super-ego. For example, the mother fixation is given full expression in the previous three operas, as the super-ego can accept the emphasis on the mother figure. But you are suggesting just the opposite, the masculine woman as heroine. As I said, my own and possibly completely wrong view is that you haven't got the slightest chance of getting him to take that story. He would naturally rationalize his psychological disapproval aesthetically. [...]

Yours, Keller

---

98 See Hamburger to Britten, 11 November 1947, BPF.

In 1981, the Britten scholar and pioneer of lesbian and gay musicology Philip Brett credited Keller with being 'the first writer in England to my knowledge to deal openly and seriously with Britten's homosexuality as an element ("enormous creative advantage," he calls it) in his operatic character'.[99] It is all the more interesting, therefore, to see how penetrating Keller could be on the subject three decades earlier. It is also worth noting how widely known Britten's sexuality must have been in musical circles in the 1940s, easily visible to two (heterosexual) émigrés who scarcely knew him.

'It was not until I arrived in England, at the age of nineteen, that I learnt that homosexuality was a "problem",' wrote Keller in 1976. Growing up in Vienna, the issue had barely touched him. 'We had one or two homosexuals at school,' he remembered, but they neither bothered nor were bothered by their heterosexual colleagues: 'They were, in fact, tolerated better than we Jews, for while anti-Semitism preceded Hitler, anti-homosexuality didn't to anything like the same extent.'[100]

In Britain, the immediate post-war period was a time of increasing persecution of homosexual men – prosecutions in the late 1940s were already double pre-war levels, and were to increase five-fold by the time of the Coronation in 1953. This was an unspoken factor in some of the criticism that Britten encountered, including the negative reception of his coronation opera *Gloriana*, which was castigated for 'failing to recall the passionate, full-blooded vigour of the Elizabethan age', for lacking 'heartiness', and for the 'emotional aridity' of Britten's 'uneasily nervous, ungenerous music'.[101] The following year a campaign against 'vice in music' was launched by the former deputy administrator of Covent Garden, allegedly concerned about 'the influence of perverts in the world of music' – a concern that appears to have been primarily economic rather than moral: 'jobs for the boys'.[102]

In the end, Hamburger decided that he would send his 'Eugenia' translation and scenario to Britten after all. Britten's response is not recorded – but, as Keller had predicted, he did not use the idea.

~

At the same time as these intense exchanges with Hamburger, Keller was beginning to write regularly for film magazines. Again, it was a perfect time and place to address the question of film music, since most serious British composers were writing for the cinema in those days, and the quality of British film scores was far above most of what was being produced in Hollywood. The first magazine to publish

99   *Notes* 37/3 (March 1981): 579.
100 *HKC*, 129.
101 See [Frank Howes], *National and English Review* 141: 35, and *The Times*, 9 June 1953, 2; Richard Capell, *Telegraph*, 13 June 1953, 8, and Eric Blom, *Observer*, 14 June 1953, 11.
102 'Music Chief Leads Big Campaign Against Vice', *The People*, 24 July 1955, quoted in Richard Witts, *Artist Unknown* (London: Warner, 1998), 184.

Keller on film was the British Film Institute's quarterly *Sight and Sound*, for which he wrote from the winter of 1946–47. The second was *Contemporary Cinema*, the monthly journal of the newly formed Church of England Films Commission. At that time, no one else was writing specifically on film music – 'the most serious flaw about articles on film music is their scarcity'[103] – so Keller was creating a new genre of criticism. He thought this an important and indeed urgent task, for the popularity of cinema meant its music was likely to exert a substantial influence over the rest of musical life. The fact that so much film music was of poor quality meant this effect 'must become devastating if nothing is going to be done about it: film music is capable of becoming a weapon of musical mass destruction'.

In the autumn of 1947 the BFI commissioned Keller to write a series of 'Film Music Notes' on films as they were released, published anonymously in its *Monthly Film Bulletin*. These continued throughout 1948, by which time Keller was reviewing for more film magazines, most frequently *Film Monthly Review*. He tried to persuade non-film publications to take an interest in film music criticism, initially with limited success: most newspapers and magazines already had a film critic and a music critic, and it was hard to persuade them of the need for a separate category of film music criticism.

13 June 1947 – Letter to the Editor, *The Times*

Dear Sir,

Regular, competent newspaper criticism of incidental film music is urgently needed, (a) because most film music is bad, (b) because some film music is very good, and (c) because, good or bad, film music is heard by almost 20 million regular film-goers in Britain. [. . .]

Just over a hundred years ago, The Times established on its staff the first regular music critic to work for a daily. What if the greatest British newspaper once more took the lead?

Yours sincerely,

[Hans Keller]

The Times was not to be persuaded, but in October 1947 the BFI published a twenty-four-page pamphlet by Keller entitled *The Need for Competent Film Music Criticism. A pamphlet for those who care for FILM AS ART, with a final section for those who do not*.[104] To publicise this, Keller prepared a short summary of his argument:

---

103   'Film Music: Some Objections', *Sight and Sound* 15/60 (Winter 1946–47): 136. Antony Hopkins began a regular column in the same journal in 1950, to Keller's delight: 'Having pleaded the need for competent film music criticism for quite a time, I welcome the birth of a colleague: Mr. Antony Hopkins.' *MS* II/3 (Winter 1950): 189. Keller's collected writings on film music can be found in *HKFM*.
104   Full text in *HKFM*, 3–18.

THE NEED FOR COMPETENT FILM MUSIC CRITICISM

Lane: "I didn't think it polite to listen, sir."

Algernon: "I am sorry for that, for your sake. I don't play accurately – anyone can play accurately – but I play with wonderful expression."

Oscar Wilde, *The Importance of Being Earnest*

At the present time, film music criticism is perhaps more urgently needed than musical criticism proper. In the concert hall, almost everybody is his own music critic: in the cinema, almost nobody is. In fact, apart from music that forms part of the film's visual story, film music is perceived demisemi-consciously rather than consciously. Like Lane (if less humorously), even intelligent film-goers pretend a valid reason for their not caring to listen to background music: It wouldn't be polite, they say, to listen to something which just isn't meant to be listened to consciously. For is not film music but one element in the technique that produces the film as a whole? Why should we peep behind the scenes? Should we not be interested in results rather than in resources: in entities rather than in elements?

Now, quite apart from the fact that a film score may be an entire piece of art in itself, the serious art lover cannot legitimately disclaim his obligation to analytic contemplation. Just as it is his aesthetic duty to discover, say, the thematic relations between different movements of a symphony (Gustav Mahler was particularly keen on the listener's unearthing such relationships), so he will only understand a film completely if he takes the trouble to examine the "thematic relations" between the picture and its music. It falls to film music criticism to form (as Geoffrey Sharp said of ordinary music criticism) "the vanguard of public opinion", to stimulate qualified film-musical appreciation and depreciation.

More particularly, the film music critic is urgently needed to fight the mass of bad film music that influences the tastes of millions of film-goers (almost 20 million regulars in Britain alone) whose non-conscious listening attitudes render them pretty defenceless.

Film music may be bad in two ways. It may be defective by purely musical standards, and/or it may not be an integral part of the film as a whole. Like Algernon's playing, background music is often marked by "wonderful expression", but does not "play accurately," i.e, not in tune with the visual. As Alex Shaw (Producer of the educational film *Instruments of the Orchestra*, which is based on Britten's *Young Person's Guide to the Orchestra*) recently said of a film score: ". . . the music composer, dreaming of some other subject, has drenched the track with great waves of unnecessary sound." Expert criticism is required here, not only because film audiences do not bother to decide what is good and what is bad, but also because it would not always be easy for them to make this decision unaided; Film music being the youngest musical genre, standards of valuation – apart from those referring to purely musical principles – are as yet at a far more primitive stage of development than critical standards in any other field of applied or absolute music.

An important part of the film music critic's job must, to begin with, consist in criticising second-rate work by first-rank composers. Owing perhaps to the lack of criticism and of general attention paid to their scores, our best film composers do not always give of their best.

A word, finally, on good film music. Competent criticism must endeavour to throw light on, and interpret valuable film scores, especially where their value is of a subtle kind that tends to escape notice. Bernard Stevens' intriguing score to *The Upturned Glass*, for instance, whose tonal structure ingeniously corresponds to the film's psychological relations, definitely needs a critic's intervention if it is to be fully appraised.

The aim of all criticism is, ideally, the same as the aim of all teaching: to make itself unnecessary. Every pupil ought eventually to become his own teacher, every art-lover his own critic. Towards this end, film music audiences must themselves co-operate, and musicians and music-lovers among them should give the lead.

Outside his film work, Keller's success in finding outlets for his writing was still fairly limited in 1947. He managed to place a few individual pieces, but had not yet secured a regular column in any journal to replace his meagre income from *National Entertainment*. Then in May 1947 *New Life* took up his offer to review the first performance of *Albert Herring* in June, followed by the visit of Bruno Walter and the Vienna Philharmonic to the first Edinburgh Festival in September, where they were to perform *Das Lied von der Erde* with Peter Pears and Kathleen Ferrier.

New Life, which began publication in January 1947, described itself as 'a Jewish Pictorial Monthly' and was produced with a panache and lavish illustration unusual in post-war England – one contemporary review described it as 'exquisitely laid out and in style and appearance comparable with American magazines'.[105] Politically it was left-wing and internationally minded, publishing regular reports from a wide network of correspondents all over the world. Naturally it followed events in Palestine particularly keenly (the ending of the British Mandate, the establishment of the State of Israel and the ensuing Arab–Israeli war) and it published a special supplement on life in Palestine (including its music) in the summer

105 *AJR Information* (April 1947): 30.

of 1948. But it also published regular reports from America, Russia and all over Europe, including several from Austria, dealing with issues like denazification, the effects of currency devaluation, the resettlement of displaced persons and the return of Austrian Jews from emigration and internment. It painted a distressing picture of 'the precarious position in which the remnant of Austrian Jews and, especially, the Jewish D.P.'s in Austrian Camps, find themselves. They are placed in the midst of a population which is far from renouncing an old tradition of anti-Semitism, and which is even more impregnated with the poison of Nazism.'[106] There were sometimes more positive Austrian pieces – one issue featured the triumphant survival of Keller's old Jewish football club in Vienna ('Hakoah Lives on').[107] But any homesickness thus evoked was countered by painful reports like this, which appeared in the first issue to which Keller contributed:

> In a number of Vienna cinemas, particularly in the Staffa and Flottenkino, disgusting scenes broke out during the showing of the weekly news reel. When shots of the return of emigrants from Shanghai came on the scene, accompanied by the commentary ". . . .These are Jews returning to Austria to take part in the rebuilding of their homeland," a roar of laughter broke out among the audience, and hundreds of cries were heard of: "Gas them! Gas them!"[108]

In such a context, the magazine considered intellectual and artistic endeavour to be vital to building the 'new life' for which it hoped:

> Suffering humanity, especially the Jews, has just passed through the Valley of the Shadow of Death. What New Life awaits us? A life of security and freedom in which the innate capacity of our people can express itself in Music, Literature, Art, Science, Theatre, Cinema? A life in which the cultural heritage of the Jewish masses shall blossom forth into new and glorious flower? Or a continual struggle for survival, congested living in slums and camps, a restless refugee life, a mere existence?[109]

Considerable space was therefore devoted to the arts, and following his Britten and Edinburgh reviews, Keller was commissioned to write regular reports on the contribution of Jewish musicians to London concert life.

Securing a regular column in *New Life* was helpful (until it went out of business at the end of 1948), but it was its commission to review the first Edinburgh Festival that was for Keller a life-changing event. By the time he went, he had managed to obtain additional commissions for Festival reviews from *Tempo*, *Music Parade* and *Contemporary Cinema*, together with a press pass giving entry

---

106 *New Life* I/10 (November 1947): 8.
107 *Ibid.*, I/11 (December 1947): 9–10.
108 *Ibid.*, I/4 (May 1947): 6.
109 *Ibid.*, I/1 (January 1947): 1.

into all the concerts he wanted. But the most important feature of this trip was that he did not go alone.

New Life prided itself on the outstanding quality of its illustrations, both photographs and line drawings, and one of its most frequent contributing artists was a young German émigrée called Milein Cosman. The first issue of *New Life* featured a whole page of 'drawings from the sketchbook of MILEIN COSMAN' – marvellously evocative character sketches of 'East End Types' – and thereafter she frequently provided illustrations to articles and stories. Like Keller, Cosman was attempting to make a living from the post-war periodical boom, and at this date was doing so with rather more financial success than he was. She had published a number of sketches of dancers for magazines like *Ballet* and from the beginning of 1947 was a regular contributor to the BBC's weekly *Radio Times*. This was the golden age for line drawing in the *Radio Times* and Cosman became its specialist artist for portraits of musicians. In this role, she was soon as regular a presence at concerts and rehearsals as was Keller.

Cosman had come to London in 1939, to study at the Slade School of Art. War broke out almost immediately after her arrival, and she was evacuated with the rest of the Slade to Oxford, where she met the Viennese émigré composer Egon Wellesz, whose lectures inspired in her a deep love of Mahler. So when she heard in 1947 that the new Edinburgh Festival was bringing Bruno Walter and the Vienna Philharmonic to Scotland for two performances of *Das Lied von der Erde*, she was desperate to get there somehow. She managed to secure accommodation with a friend (no easy task in a packed Edinburgh that summer) and *New Life* agreed to publish her drawings from the Festival. The concerts were both sold out, however, so *New Life*'s editor suggested that she contact its music critic to see if he could help get her access.

Thus it was that Hans Keller met his future wife, on 30 August 1947 outside Goodge Street tube station. At the end of his life, he described his memory of that day:

> A Jewish quarterly wanted me to meet an artist whose drawings I had seen in the journal. I had seen 'Milein Cosman', and I thought to myself this would probably be an old Jew with a long beard: the drawings looked to me like work by a mature artist. So can you describe my surprise when we met outside Goodge St. tube station – and along came a girl? I think we 'clicked' immediately – I have that suspicion: you'll have to ask her if she confirms it! We then went together to Edinburgh, to the Festival, and we've never parted since.[110]

According to Hugh Wood, Cosman's first impression of her future husband was 'He looked like a very thin Indian who had forgotten his turban. I remember

110   'Hans Keller in Interview with Anton Weinberg', *Tempo* 195 (January 1996): 6–12.

Milein Cosman and Hans Keller in Piccadilly in the 1940s.

thinking "I'd really like to draw that man!"'[111] Over the next four decades she did so hundreds of times.

While Keller was in Edinburgh with Cosman, Paul Hamburger and Esther Salaman were getting married back in London. Keller wrote from Edinburgh to congratulate his friend – and to give him an excited account of the 'first-class life' he was enjoying:

10 September 1947 – to Paul Hamburger
In German.

My dear Director,

I offer my most respectful congratulations and thank you also for your meschuggenes[112] telegram. And if you leave E flat major again from time to time over the years, then think of this: who doesn't, apart from an Austrian composer whose name now escapes me but who does not manage to get out of C major in his violin sonata. Which reminds me of the story of another composer, a friend of Brahms whose name likewise escapes me. One evening this person did not appear at the local and when people asked where he was, Brahms opined, 'He is composing a piano sonata at the moment, and today he went <u>suddenly</u> from C major to G major and for the time being can't find his way back.' Probably a Lotzelach[113] you knew already anyway.

I live a first-class life here; if you either have a lot of money or are a member of the press, life is made a bed of roses for you – only not by Bruno Walter who doesn't allow people into rehearsals. (Lied v d Erde, Pears, Ferrier, Vienna Philharm.) But I have telephoned Pears and 'he'll fix it with Mr Wolter'.[114] I'm shmoozing the members of the Vienna Philharmonic a lot, which is very interesting as long as they don't talk about music. Buxbaum, who was warmly embraced by all his colleagues on his arrival here, sits on the first desk; Schneiderhan, a former party member and (speaking from memory) overrated as a violinist, is concertmaster.

The Figaro here is not bad (apart from one or two lapses of taste in the accompaniments to recitatives for which Süsskind is apparently responsible). We have a Count here who is idiotically underrated: whatever his failings, he sings in the ensembles not only with deadly accurate and suggestive intonation, but also with a phrasing that flashes from here to Glasgow. At the same time he's a dull dog – that's why

111 *HKSMM*, 12.
112 Yiddish, 'crazy'.
113 Yiddish, 'an old joke'.
114 Keller writes Pears's words in English (with his anglicised pronunciation of 'Walter').

he is underrated.[115] During the march they do the scene changes and
the arseholes in the audience think it's the interval and talk through
the march, which Süsskind builds up splendidly – from the mysterious
into open anticipation, not forgetting the gloomy-dramatic implications
(count/countess). But when I applaud in solitary fashion after the trio the
indignant cultured music-lovers go "Shhh!"

I'm coming back on Sunday and after I've written up all my stuff I'll ring
you up, tho' I don't know where. Will you convey to Mrs Hamburger my
deep sympathy – tho' to some extent she walked into the abyss.[116]

Keller

The Vienna Philharmonic's visit to Edinburgh marked the first time its
renowned principal cellist, Friedrich Buxbaum, had returned to his seat since his
dismissal by the Nazis nearly a decade before (though it was not to be a permanent
reunion and he died the following year). Bruno Walter likewise was conducting
the orchestra for the first time since the *Anschluss*:

The Edinburgh Festival [extract]
New Life I/9 (October 1947): 29

Musical considerations apart, it was fitting that Walter should celebrate
his post-Hitlerean reunion with the Vienna Philharmonic by conducting
the greatest work of an Austrian Jew.

Mahler wrote to Walter in 1908: "My dear friend . . . I have been very
diligent. . . . I don't know myself what name could be given to the
whole thing. . . . I have had a beautiful time, and I daresay it (the *Song
of the Earth*) is the most personal I have so far done." In 1911, Walter
conducted its first performance. But the 1947 performances seemed
"first ones," too, not only because the majority of the Edinburgh
audiences had not, apparently, heard the work before, but also because
Walter re-created it with the same youthful enthusiasm, if probably
with yet a greater maturity of insight, than I assume him to have brought
to the premiere. Assisted by Kathleen Ferrier and Peter Pears, better
interpreters than whom he could not have found among contemporary
singers, and by the high-spirited Vienna Philharmonic (whose 'celli
were led by their former – Jewish – principal, Prof. Buxbaum), he
gave what would have been a well-nigh perfect rendering had not the
celesta (introduced in the last piece, the *Abschied*) been lavishly off the

115 John Brownlee.
116 The final paragraph of this letter is in English.

Drawings by Milein Cosman at the 1947 Edinburgh Festival: Peter Pears; Kathleen Ferrier;
Bruno Walter and Kathleen Ferrier in recital.

orchestra's pitch. One or two smaller blemishes elsewhere did not reduce our enjoyment of this master-conductor's finished conception of the masterpiece he perhaps loves most and understands best.

Regular reviewing of concerts and films was enjoyable and (a little) remunerative, but Keller also wanted to write more seriously for musicians – and to publish his work in music periodicals. He wanted an outlet for the sort of thinking he had been doing with Paul Hamburger – and specifically for his essay on 'Britten and Mozart'. He first tried *The Musical Times*, whose editor, William McNaught, was interested in the article and evidently suspected that this unknown new writer might be going somewhere. But he found Keller's style too much of an obstacle:

> I don't like joining the wrong queue; but I must follow my opinion. I have respect for the observation, thought and critical faculty that produced the matter at the core of the article (is that wide and narrow enough?); but I find no merit in the way it is expressed. The use of language is awkward and often obscure in its junctions, implications and allusions.[117]

It took another year for 'Britten and Mozart' to see the light of day and it was read by the editors of several journals before one finally accepted it. This was not altogether a bad thing, since it aroused interest even in those who decided not to publish it, and it helped to establish 'Hans Keller' as a potentially interesting new name.

The first person to read it – after Hamburger – was Britten himself.

25 November 1946 – to Benjamin Britten and Peter Pears
BPF

Dear Mr. Britten and Mr. Pears,

I should be very grateful to you for a word or two of criticism – favourable or otherwise – on the enclosed MS. But I shall <u>perfectly understand</u> if you will return the article without having had the time to read it or to comment on it.

Yours very sincerely,

Hans Keller

The following month a letter came from Britten's publisher: 'Benjamin Britten gave me your article which he had read and liked very much,' wrote Erwin

---

117   McNaught to Keller, 14 February 1947, CULHK.

Stein – adding, encouragingly, 'I completely agree with you and would very much like to see you some time.'[118] Stein was also a Viennese émigré – one of Schoenberg's earliest pupils and a close friend of Berg, Webern and Zemlinsky. He had been director of performances in Schoenberg's *Verein für musikalische Privataufführungen*, after which he joined Universal Edition as its artistic advisor and editor of its journal *Pult und Taktstock*. Forced out of Vienna by the arrival of the Nazis in 1938, he quickly re-established himself in London thanks to the entrepreneurial Ralph Hawkes. Hawkes was a man of tremendous energy and commercial acumen, whose firm became a leading force in British music after the Second World War. After completing the merger of Hawkes & Sons with Boosey & Company in 1930, Hawkes was struck by the impressive list of contemporary composers published by Universal Edition in Vienna. He negotiated a role for Boosey & Hawkes as Universal's British agent, which meant that when the Nazis arrived he was well placed to arrange a swift transfer to his firm of some of its most significant executive talent. Hans Heinsheimer took charge of Boosey & Hawkes' New York office, while Erwin Stein and Ernst Roth brought added musical authority and publishing experience to the head office in London. Composers soon followed. Béla Bartók was one of the first to transfer from the nazified Universal Edition, and soon Boosey & Hawkes was promoting an impressive list of international names, including Stravinsky, Strauss, Mahler, Kodaly, Copland, Prokofiev and Rachmaninov.

One important new venture that Stein managed for Boosey & Hawkes was their new concert series that began at the Wigmore Hall in 1941. To embark on this in the middle of the war was a risky enterprise, but the timing turned out to be most fortuitous when the first season opened shortly after London's principal concert hall, the Queen's Hall in Langham Place, was destroyed by bombing. The new concerts presented blitzed Londoners with a rich array of contemporary music, much of which they had never heard before. Stein himself conducted a memorable performance of *Pierrot lunaire* in 1942 and made a new English translation of the text of Mahler's *Lied von der Erde* for a 1943 performance of Schoenberg's arrangement of the work. Concerts like these were 'like manna in the wilderness to the people who are really interested in modern music', said Leslie Boosey, 'as there is nothing else of the kind available to them.'[119]

Stein had first met Britten well before the war, during the brief visit Britten paid to Vienna in 1934 at the age of twenty-one – the year before Hawkes tempted him away from his previous publisher, Oxford University Press. When Britten came back from America in 1942 he was delighted to find Stein installed with his new publisher, and he and Pears quickly became very close to Stein and his family. Indeed, when Keller started sending his writings to Britten, the Steins were sharing a house with Britten and Pears (their own flat having been damaged by fire). *The Rape of Lucretia* was written while they were living together and Britten dedicated it to Stein.

118 Stein to Keller, 31 December 1946, BPF.
119 Quoted in Wallace, *Boosey & Hawkes: The Publishing Story* (London: Boosey & Hawkes, 2007), 33.

Boosey & Hawkes's journal, *Tempo*, had ceased publication during the war, and Stein helped restart it in 1944, while its editor, Ernest Chapman, was still in the forces. Stein sent 'Britten and Mozart' to Chapman in January 1947, telling him 'I think it very interesting but in reading it again I have some doubts about the English. Do you think the man can be employed?'[120] Chapman decided not to publish this particular essay – 'I got it into my head that it would require a lot of alteration' (a view he subsequently changed)[121] – but he did think Keller worth employing, and commissioned him to write something on Britten's Second Quartet, which Boosey & Hawkes had published a few months earlier. All did not go smoothly, however. When Chapman received Keller's first draft, he found it 'indigestible in its wealth of detail', so asked Keller to rewrite it in simpler terms and discuss it again with Stein. Stein too began to have doubts:

> Keller is doing some alterations which I suggested but is sending it tonight, so you will receive it, I hope, in the morning. I am by no means sure of this article. The man is a bit of a disappointment. He has some imagination but is not clear and likes to stress minor points. See what you can do with the English. I think some expressions are not very clear, but you will find the meaning.[122]

One part that ended up being deleted was Keller's opening, which took aim at the 'lukewarm press' the work had received. 'I would prefer a less polemical tone in references to critics with whom you happen to disagree – it does not help anyone, least of all yourself,' Chapman told him. English critical conventions were different from those in Vienna, he explained: 'It's more or less a tradition here that critics shall not criticize critics.'[123] Stein too tried repeatedly to explain to Keller that the English would not take well to being told they were wrong: 'They call it "wanting to be clever". I know it is only being clever. But Schoenberg once said: I know many things I do not tell.'[124]

Chapman and Stein both worked closely with Keller on the text of this article – multiple drafts with comments from both survive in Keller's and Chapman's archives, showing that Keller tried hard to produce a version they would accept. To make matters worse, it gradually became clear that Chapman and Stein were not in agreement with each other – 'Small wonder that at the time I felt compelled mir die Haare einzeln auszuraufen trying to serve two bosses,' wrote Keller afterwards.[125] A huge row finally erupted over an innocuous reference to William Walton, which Stein deleted and Chapman reinserted. Although the bewildered Keller had no idea what was going on, the question of whether Walton (*not* published by Boosey & Hawkes) could be mentioned in an article about Britten (Boosey & Hawkes's star composer) lit the fuse of a long-running argument over

120   Stein to Chapman, 16 January 1947, BLEC, Add.62948.
121   Chapman to Keller, 21 June 1947, BLEC, Add.62948.
122   Stein to Chapman, 10 February 1947, BLEC, Add.62948.
123   Chapman to Keller, 7 February and 21 June 1947, CULHK and BLEC, Add.62948.
124   Stein to Keller, 12 August [1953], CULHK.
125   'to pull my hair out one by one'. Keller to Stein, 5 July 1947, CULHK.

Tempo's impartiality and Britten's increasing dominance over the firm, which afterwards cost Chapman his job.

This was something of a baptism of fire for Keller, though he was consoled a few months later by a commission from another of Stein's colleagues at Boosey & Hawkes, Anthony Gishford (a cousin of Hawkes and friend of Britten who took over the editorship of *Tempo* from Chapman) for a short booklet about Britten's two new operas, *Lucretia* and *Herring*. 'It is really a question of reducing complex ideas and thoughts to their underlying essentials,' Gishford told Keller, adding gratifyingly, 'From what I have read of your work I feel that you should be particularly well qualified to do this.'[126] Even better news arrived in a letter from the editor of the prestigious musicological journal *Music & Letters* offering to publish 'Britten & Mozart'. 'I was never so happy so far about the publication of any of my stuff,' wrote a joyful Keller to Stein. 'I am writing to Britten by the same post.'[127]

It was probably during the writing of his article on Britten's Second Quartet that Keller first met the composer in person. Asked in an interview years later when he had first met Britten, Keller recalled that the meeting had been arranged by Erwin Stein and that it consisted of 'a long discussion about sonata structure'.[128] Britten's approach to sonata form was what interested Keller most about the new quartet, and the first draft of his article confined itself entirely to a study of its first movement. Even after Chapman had insisted the article should cover the whole work, Keller still focused on Britten's solution of what he called 'the modern sonata problem', defined as 'how unity is achieved within an extended polythematic ternary circle'.[129] He was particularly interested in the relatively loosely organised development section and the displacement of some of its functions into the extended exposition: 'Having left the more formal aspects of 'development' to the second part of the exposition, the development proper is free to fantasize.'[130]

Among the many other reviews of Britten's quartet Keller read while writing his own contribution for *Tempo* was a piece in *The Times* by its chief music critic, Frank Howes, examining the question of chamber music from a nationalist perspective:

> Among the various strands of English music we are apt to overlook that of chamber music. We think of our continuous tradition of choral music, we remember that there is a parallel tradition of solo song of almost equal achievement, we pass apologetically and quickly over the fragments of an operatic tradition, and comfort ourselves that in church music at any rate the tradition was interrupted only once, at the Commonwealth and then briefly. We confess frankly that we have been backward in orchestral composition and did nothing effective till Elgar, but when we think of chamber music we have in mind not a school of composition at all but a picture of amateurs cultivating the Viennese classics.[131]

---

126 Gishford to Keller, 11 September 1947, CULHK.
127 Keller to Stein, 5 July 1947, CULHK.
128 Alan Blyth, *Remembering Britten* (London: Hutchinson, 1981), 87.
129 From an early draft of the article, CULHK.
130 'Benjamin Britten's Second Quartet', *Tempo* 3 (March 1947): 6–9. Reprinted in *BB2013*, 12–17.
131 Frank Howes, 'English Chamber Music', *The Times*, 17 January 1947, 6.

Howes went on to assert that the natural form of English music was 'essentially monothematic' and that 'English composers have never taken naturally to sonata form, which is for all its universal validity an essentially Austrian way of thinking in music.' Keller was fascinated: 'My knowledge of English music is not yet nearly wide enough to allow my discussing this interesting suggestion,' he wrote in his article, but this question surely featured in his talks with Britten and Stein. In his article Keller had been quick to assert that Britten had risen to the challenge of writing a modern sonata form 'with perfect ease' – though in his private conversation with Britten he ventured the opinion that he had 'not altogether solved the problem of development'.[132] A long discussion apparently ensued in which they tried to define the essential nature of sonata form – and specifically whether the most important contrast was thematic or tonal. Keller asserted that more vital than either of these was the contrast between statement and development:

> I pointed out that successive analytic fashions, highlighting thematic contrast and tonal contrast, had not hit the very heart of the sonata's matter, which was *the contrast between statement and development, and its integration* – statement meaning stability, and development (continual modulation in tonal music) a labile structure which was not confined, of course, to the official development section.
>
> A long pause punctuated the end of our conversation, and then Britten said, 'One day, I'll write a string quartet for you.'[133]

132 Blyth, *Remembering Britten*, 87.
133 'Britten's Last Masterpiece', *Spectator* 242/7872 (2 June 1979): 27–8. Reprinted in *BB2013*, 170–73.

Critics and Musicologists

Keller began his writing life in Britain amid a rapidly expanding musical press. *Tempo*, the journal to which his writing about Britten first led him, had been founded in 1939 as *The Boosey & Hawkes Newsletter*, and thus started life within an old tradition of music journals owned by publishing houses. Britain's longest-running music periodicals of the time had similar roots, *The Musical Times* having been published by Novello since 1844, and *Monthly Musical Record* by Augener since 1871. A younger example was *The Chesterian*, founded by J.&W. Chester in 1915. Other long-established periodicals were similarly embedded in various branches of the music trade, such as *Musical Opinion and Music Trade Review* (founded in 1877), *The Strad* (founded in 1890) and – responding to the opportunities opened up by new technology – *The Gramophone* (founded in 1920).

The landscape after 1945 was very different. The post-war public funding of music and the new opportunities to hear it via broadcasting and recording meant that Britain's previously precarious musical economy was undergoing a fundamental change. The growth in the public interested in serious music seemed at that time to be exponential, and it was clear that as soon as wartime restrictions on paper started to ease, there would be a big market for new musical publications. Ernest Chapman was very conscious of the limitations imposed on *Tempo* by its status as a publisher's 'house organ', and he was keen to give it a broader identity to preserve the journal from competition in the new post-war world. Since Boosey & Hawkes's links with Universal Edition meant that it now published an impressive array of prominent modern composers, *Tempo* was well placed to become England's principal journal of modern music – provided it was not seen to be too partial. But there was no room for complacency, as Chapman was well aware: 'The paper situation over here is improving with regard to the allocation for periodicals', he wrote in December 1945 to Hawkes (then in New York looking after the firm's substantial American interests). 'There are signs of possible serious competition which give me slight jitters. William Glock – who has lost his job on the "Observer" – told Stein that he would like to start a magazine independent of any publishers. . . . If I may state frankly my personal feelings, they are that TEMPO is at present a first class <u>house-organ</u> of a propagandist nature, but that its standing, influence and sales could be enormously enlarged if it were allowed to become much more independent and impartial.' A year later, he warned Hawkes that 'no less than <u>five</u> new music-papers are scheduled to appear here!'[1]

Glock's wartime column in *The Observer* had earned him a serious reputation among musicians as a critic of unusual perception across a wide range of repertoire. 'Only Newman in recent years has had a following comparable with mine', he told his editor, Ivor Brown, whose more conservative tastes had become increasingly irritated by Glock's writing about modern composers.[2] The composers themselves did not share Brown's views: 'May I say how tremendously happy your Observer articles have made me?' (Britten); 'The more I read your last Observer article, the more pleased I am about it' (Tippett); 'I want to thank you for your article on Schönberg, not only as a friend and former pupil of Schönberg, but as a musician who tries to keep alive the spirit of the Viennese tradition' (Wellesz).[3] Although Glock was, in the words of Lennox Berkeley, 'a terrifyingly severe critic', even this was considered a good thing:

> It really means something with him. He's got a standard which is a real one,
> and he knows about music – I mean knows what it's about, and is able to detect
> at once anything 'extra-musical' – i.e. having nothing to do with music.'[4]

The final straw for Brown had been Glock's obituary for Bartók in 1945, but modern music was not the only issue. During the war Brown had been Director of Drama for the Council for the Encouragement of Music and the Arts and he was proud of the work that CEMA had done, not only in keeping the arts alive but in creating a huge new public for them. He now thought his music critic should be catering primarily for the people CEMA had introduced to music – as Glock told his sister after his sacking, 'It was part of IB's argument that I didn't play up or down enough to the New Audience.'[5] But Glock was unwilling to squander his few column inches on elementary observations about standard repertoire: 'I have had to look upon every article as a precious thing not to be wasted on subjects only too well covered by others,' he told Brown. 'There are thousands of people, to my knowledge alone, who look upon my column as the only one on music in a national newspaper that has unfailing integrity and seriousness.'[6]

Glock's new journal, *The Score*, did not make its appearance until the summer of 1949, and when it did it aimed clearly at the musical and intellectual high ground – true to what another critic called his 'intransigent standards of excellence'.[7] One model was Minna Lederman's New York journal *Modern*

---

1   Chapman to Hawkes, 29 December 1945 and 19 December 1946, BLEC Add.62948.
2   Glock to Brown, 28 October 1945, BLWG MS Mus.953. Brown was chief drama critic on *The Observer* 1929–54, and editor of the paper 1942–48. Ernest Newman was in 1945 the Grand Old Man of British music criticism, then nearly eighty years old but still writing for *The Sunday Times*.
3   Britten to Glock, 25 January 1943; Tippett to Glock, undated; Wellesz to Glock 16 September 1945, BLWG MS Mus.957–9.
4   Berkeley to Britten, 5 January 1940, in *Britten: Letters from a Life*, vol. 2: 1939–45, 1991.
5   Glock to Marjorie Glock, 1 November 1945, BLWG MS Mus.953.
6   Glock to Brown, 28 October 1945, BLWG MS Mus.953.
7   Martin Cooper, 'Music,' *Spectator* 6477 (15 August 1952): 216.

Music, which had ceased publication in 1946 after twenty years, leaving a gap in the American market that Glock's journal did something to fill. But although *The Score* sold more copies in America than at home, there was clearly a British market for such a periodical in the late 1940s, and the musical high ground began to become more crowded. This was quite a change from the situation before the war, when the only serious musicological journal had been *Music & Letters*, founded in 1920 by Glock's predecessor and mentor at the *Observer*, Arthur Fox Strangways. 'Mr. Fox-Strangways saw an obvious opening', according to *The Times*, for 'there was then no journal for the discussion of music apart from the news values of current events and the interests of the publishing houses.'[8]

Music & Letters had reigned supreme as Britain's chief journal of serious musicology for twenty years. Fox Strangways owned and edited it until 1937, when his money ran out – as his critical colleague Frank Howes put it, 'he lived longer than he had budgeted for.'[9] Ownership of the journal then passed to his friend Richard Capell, music critic of the *Daily Telegraph*, who asked Eric Blom, music critic of the *Birmingham Post*, to edit it. Blom was an interesting and important figure in British musical life, and a significant early stimulus to Hans Keller. Keller first encountered him as the editor of *Music & Letters*, when he published 'Britten and Mozart', but they soon crossed paths more frequently after Blom returned to London to become music critic of *The Observer* and editor of the fifth edition of *Grove's Dictionary of Music and Musicians*.

As the editor of *Grove*, of *Music & Letters*, and of the popular *Everyman's Dictionary of Music* and the *Master Musicians* series (in which his own 1935 book on Mozart was particularly successful), the author of many other books on music, and also a prominent critic writing for a national paper, Blom was a very well known figure in the British musicological Establishment. He was an extremely diligent scholar, whose new edition of *Grove* represented the most comprehensive revision since the dictionary's inception, almost doubling its size and rewriting much of its contents. Right up until his death in April 1959 he was hard at work on a supplementary volume of *Grove* and still writing his *Observer* column.

Blom never held a position in a university (though Birmingham honoured him with a D.Litt. in 1955) and indeed had never attended one. This was not unusual at that time, when most British musical scholarship took place outside the universities and most musicians, if they took degrees, studied something other than music. The Arts Enquiry's 1949 report on musical life in England described the situation then as follows:

> Musicology in England has largely been carried out by individual musicians who have worked for the love of it, for the most part in isolation. . . . Some scholars have held teaching appointments in universities, and there they have had opportunities of trying out the music they are interested in. The scholarly productions of early opera at Oxford and Cambridge have already

8 'Musical Reviews', *Times*, 8 March 1941, 6.
9 *M&L*, XL/3: 205.

been mentioned. But until recently the universities themselves have done little to encourage musical scholarship and provide facilities for it.

The same report lamented that 'a great opportunity was lost before the war when the services of more refugee German and Austrian scholars might have been secured for music in this country. Many of them went to America, which is already beginning to reap the benefit of their work.' Two Austrian musicians who did find posts in British universities were Hans Gál, whom Donald Tovey invited to Edinburgh, and Egon Wellesz, who became a fellow of Lincoln College, Oxford. When Wellesz arrived in Oxford in 1938, however, he was to find himself in the History Faculty, there being at that time no Faculty of Music or programme of undergraduate study in music (the same was true in Cambridge). Although the post of Professor of Music was centuries old, it was generally held as a part-time appointment – indeed Sir Hugh Allen (the incumbent when Wellesz arrived) was, during two of his three decades at the university, Director of the Royal College of Music at the same time.

The editorial office of *Music & Letters* sits nowadays within the Faculty of Music at Cambridge, and its editorial board consists of full-time academics at universities all over Britain. Such was the revolution in British music education during the second half of the twentieth century that it is hard now to appreciate the fragmentary nature of the musicological world that Hans Keller found on his arrival in this country. Even in Oxford, as Bojan Bujić has written, there was in music 'no research work other than as a private pursuit of a few interested individuals', and Wellesz, when he started to give tutorials in music history, was appalled at the 'unbelievable ignorance' of his students.[10]

His English students' education hitherto would largely have concentrated on the practical study of performance and composition, the latter through writing pastiches of the classics. Many of those in Wellesz's classes would have been organ scholars, with English church music at the centre of their repertoire. Although the recent arrival of radio and the gramophone was starting to open up new opportunities, their musical knowledge would still have been limited by the availability of good performances: Frank Howes, chief music critic of *The Times*, described suffering from this problem himself during his undergraduate days, when 'I did not often hear an orchestra'; he attributed his own education in orchestral music largely to his later attendance at the Henry Wood Promenade Concerts:

> A single season of Promenade Concerts . . . served to teach one the outline
> of the orchestral repertory and after a few such seasons one had one's Bach,
> Mozart, Beethoven, Brahms taped, with much also of the nineteenth century.[11]

---

10 Bujić, 'Shipwrecked on the Island of the Blessed: Egon Wellesz's New Beginnings in Wartime Oxford', in *Ark of Civilization*, ed. Sally Crawford, Katharina Ulmschneider and Jaś Elsner (Oxford: Oxford University Press, 2017), 313–26.

11 Frank Howes, 'From Our Music Critic: an Autobiography' (1972), 258–9. Unpublished manuscript, BL MS Mus.283.

English writing on music was dominated by a concern for literary style and a connoisseur-inspired interest in the development of taste, rather than by any systematic investigation of historical evidence or exploration of harmonic theory. It was also heavily influenced by the model of the narrative programme note, which Donald Tovey had taken to a high level of sophistication. Eric Blom (who had begun his career producing programme notes for the Proms) had a great concern for literary style, and for the preservation of a distinctively English manner of writing about music. 'So much musical literature nowadays which at first sight appears to be English turns out to use a language that can only be called Musicologese,' he complained in his preface to *Grove*, where he made a point of preserving English musical terms from German–American neologisms.[12] He was by no means alone in giving a high place to literary quality in writing about music: among British critics this was seen as a national virtue. Indeed, it may be said that the mere title of *Music & Letters* is indicative.

Hans Keller found in Britain an intellectual world which, while very different from that of Vienna, nevertheless presented many opportunities for an aspiring young critic like him. In the absence of a highly institutionalized study of music, freelance musical journalism could be very influential, and there were many points of entry. The individualism of the profession would have suited him well, and in the presence of so much self-education, his own disrupted education was not a problem. His opportunity to make both a living and a mark came in the appetite for change that followed the end of the war and the remarkable growth of new periodicals. Not only was there now a multitude of publications needing music critics, but some of them (like Glock's *Score*) sought to be a serious forum for musical thought, and to open what their editors perceived to be an old-fashioned and parochial British culture to the wider world. *The Score* was not the first on the scene: in fact, the main rival to *Music & Letters* had already appeared during the war, when Geoffrey Sharp started publishing *The Music Review* in Cambridge in February 1940. When the war was over, it was to be Sharp who gave Keller his first real break as a serious music critic. Although Blom provided significant early encouragement with the publication of 'Britten and Mozart' in *Music & Letters*, it was in the pages of *The Music Review* that Keller began to make his name.

'War babies are sometimes difficult to handle: but the life of this one, however short, will be as full as we can make it,' wrote Sharp in his first editorial, acknowledging that 1940 was an inauspicious time to launch a new periodical. Looked at another way, the uncertain times gave him a unique opportunity in the shape of the arrival in his home town of displaced continental scholars.

12 Blom, preface to the fifth edition of *Grove* (London: Macmillan, 1954), vol. 1, vi.

Right from its foundation, *The Music Review* became 'the home of Continental criticism dispossessed'.[13] That Sharp was able to do this owed a great deal not only to his own character, but also to that of Edward Dent, who was both Sharp's musical inspiration and the reason why Cambridge became something of a centre for émigré musicologists.

Sharp, who turned twenty-six in 1940, had been brought up in Cambridge. He read engineering at Trinity College in the early 1930s, before spending a few years in London studying acoustics and amplification with a prominent radio manufacturer, and music history at the Royal College of Music.[14] As was the case with so many students who passed through Cambridge in the first half of the twentieth century, the development of his musical interests was primarily the result of his friendship with Edward Dent. Dent was a unique figure in British musical life – as Cambridge's Professor of Music he was 'the first scholar to hold the post' (strange as that now sounds) and 'one of the very few figures in British music who carry even greater weight abroad than at home'.[15] After 1918 he had worked tirelessly to re-establish links between musicians in different countries, founding with Rudolph Reti and Egon Wellesz the International Society for Contemporary Music, of which he was unanimously elected the first President. Later he also became President of the International Society for Musicology, the only individual ever to hold both positions.

Although his fluency in languages, extensive knowledge of European culture and high standing as a scholar were crucial to Dent's success in establishing international relations after the war, just as vital were his warm hospitality and personal kindness, his subtle and persuasive advocacy, his wide interests and engaging wit. These characteristics were also what made him such a strong influence on younger generations at Cambridge. Even in his earlier days there, during the years when his first temporary fellowship at King's had lapsed and he was an isolated figure with no official position, 'for nearly all of us younger men it was Dent, more than anyone else, who kindled our enthusiasm and held our allegiance.'[16] (It may be noted here that even Dent, the most prominent English musicologist who *did* work within a university, spent nearly two decades on the outside.)

Another reason for his popularity with subsequent generations was his irreverent and anti-Establishment views. Not only were his opinions frequently unorthodox, but over the years they tended to change to oppose the current consensus, which meant that he continued to be a fresh and invigorating stimulus to the young over several decades. For example, Philip Brett has suggested that Dent's important early work on Scarlatti was a reaction to 'the still-prevalent Handel-worship in England', given his later esteem for Handel.[17] And indeed

---

13 *The Times*, 27 February 1942, 6.

14 'Obituary: Mr Geoffrey Sharp', *The Times,* 10 April 1974, 20.

15 Winton Dean, 'Edward J. Dent: a Centenary Tribute', *M&L* LVII/4 (October 1976): 323–61; Francis Toye, *For what we have received* (London: Heineman, 1950), 64.

16 Toye, 65.

17 Brett also attributes Dent's 'protest against orthodoxy' in part to his homosexuality – the closet 'not so much confining as defining lives like his'. 'Musicology and Sexuality: the example of Edward J. Dent', in *Queer Episodes in Music and Modern Identity*, ed. Sophie Fuller and Lloyd Whitesell (Urbana, IL: University of Illinois Press, 2002), 177–88.

Dent's former student Philip Radcliffe recalled that Dent once told him that 'in the days when Handel was more popular than Bach he preferred Bach, but now, when Bach was so much more popular, he found that he preferred Handel'.[18] This side of Dent's character would have appealed to Geoffrey Sharp, who had a strong anti-Establishment streak in his own personality – one of the reasons why he was later to welcome and enjoy Hans Keller's polemics.

The émigré musician who was most important to *The Music Review* in its early days was Paul Hirsch, the great bibliophile and collector of 'one of the finest general collections of printed music and musical literature amassed anywhere in the twentieth century'.[19] By 1936 the political situation in Germany had made it impossible for Hirsch to stay any longer at home in Frankfurt, and he appealed to Dent for help in bringing himself, his family and his precious library to Britain. Dent responded swiftly, and by the autumn of that year Hirsch and his family were safely settled in Cambridge, with his music library housed in the new University Library building on West Road, 'where it occupied nearly 1,000 linear feet on the fifth floor'.[20]

The twenty-three-year-old Geoffrey Sharp had his first sight of the famous library on 22 January 1938 and quickly returned. Soon he was regularly consulting Hirsch's scores, showing Hirsch articles he was writing and inviting him to hear his latest gramophone equipment.[21] When Sharp decided to start a new periodical the following year, Hirsch was one of those to whom he turned for help:

> I am trying to start a new musical quarterly with the title (probably) of 'The Dulcimer'. I hope it will be rather more progressive & less archaic than 'Music and Letters' & not as precious as the old 'Sackbut'.
>
> I have not yet got a publisher – the Oxford Press & Messrs. Faber have refused, but the Cambridge Univ. Press are vaguely interested & want full details of the paper's aims, objects etc & a list of contributors. May I give them your name as a prospective contributor? I should be very glad indeed to have any article on music from you that you have the time & inclination to write.[22]

Hirsch approved of Sharp's plans, and wrote for the first issue of *The Music Review* (as it was rechristened) an article on 'Some Early Mozart Editions'. He also helped put Sharp in touch with the Schubert scholar Otto Erich Deutsch, who had just arrived in Cambridge as a refugee from Hitler's annexation of his native Vienna. Deutsch's article on 'The Riddle of Schubert's Unfinished Symphony'

---

18 Philip Radcliffe, *E.J. Dent: A Centenary Memoir* (Rickmansworth: Triad Press, 1976), 6.

19 Alec Hyatt King, 'Paul Hirsch and his Music Library', *British Library Journal*, vol. 7, no.1 (Spring 1981): 1–11.

20 *Ibid.*

21 Judging from his article 'The Gramophone in Musical Education', *M&L* XX/3: 199–202, the ex-engineer Sharp owned some very superior equipment.

22 Sharp to Hirsch, 14 April 1939, BLPH. *The Sackbut* was a monthly periodical of small circulation founded by Peter Warlock and Cecil Gray, which ran from 1920 until 1934. Gray contributed to the opening issue of *The Music Review* and several issues thereafter.

appeared in Sharp's first issue and was followed in the next two issues by 'The First Editions of Brahms' – 'the first time that an attempt has been made to determine the first editions of all the works of a great master'.[23] A third eminent émigré who contributed to Sharp's opening issue was Egon Wellesz, whose essay on 'The Symphonies of Gustav Mahler' appeared in pride of place, illustrated with copious engraved music examples and handsomely reproduced plates showing a photograph of Mahler and a facsimile of a letter from Mahler to Wellesz. Sharp would have known Wellesz through Dent, who had been instrumental in Wellesz's flight to Britain and had invited him to lecture in Cambridge on his arrival.

After that first issue, Hirsch's own articles for *The Music Review* were infrequent, but he was an active supporter in other ways, and undoubtedly *The Music Review* would not have been able to become 'the home of Continental criticism dispossessed' quite as quickly without him. One of his most important early contributions was to facilitate the publication in *The Music Review* of 'Mozartiana und Köcheliana', Alfred Einstein's supplement to his third edition of the Köchel Mozart catalogue. The third edition of Köchel had been published by Breitkopf & Härtel in Leipzig in 1937, but Einstein never regarded it as finished and even before it was out was already revising it. Hirsch knew from Richard Capell, the new owner of *Music & Letters*, that he and Blom were hoping to publish Einstein's supplement in their journal 'if it can be done without my entirely ruining myself!'[24] It was probably the outbreak of war that put paid to that project, and Hirsch then realised an opportunity for both Einstein and Sharp (for whom money appears to have been less of a problem[25]). It was a substantial coup for *The Music Review* in its first year, since libraries would have to buy the journal for the sake of having Einstein's work complete, which must have meant many sales in America as well as Britain and useful publicity in the academic world. As for Einstein himself, he was overcome by Sharp's generosity, knowing what an expensive undertaking such a large and complex work would be for a new periodical: 'I shall never forget this and shall never be in a position to reciprocate.'[26]

Another reason for the failure of the *Music & Letters* plan may have been the question of language. Naturally Einstein's work on Köchel had been in German, and it would have seemed most peculiar to publish a supplement in a different language from that of the original work. Translation would also have caused innumerable bibliographical complications, because Einstein would not have been able to use the same abbreviations and references. However, one wonders whether

---

23 This was published in two parts in the second and third issues of *The Music Review*, diplomatically subtitled 'To commemorate the Cambridge degree offered to Brahms in 1876 and 1892'.

24 Capell to Hirsch, 17 October 1938, BLPH.

25 Sharp had a comfortable private income, which allowed him to subsidise his journal and devote his time to it. His family owned Fulbourn Manor, where he lived until his marriage, after which he and his wife moved to Takely, Essex, where they lived in 'up-market style', according to the memoirs of one of their neighbours, the novelist Barbara Kaye – see *The Company We Kept* (London: Werner Shaw, 1986), 85.

26 Einstein to Sharp, translated by Hirsch, 16 January 1940, BLPH.

Eric Blom would have been completely happy to print in German in *Music & Letters*, especially in 1940, when Hitler was threatening Britain with invasion and anti-German sentiment was at its height – and when people like Hirsch, Deutsch and Wellesz (and Hans Keller) were interned as 'enemy aliens' (a fate avoided by Einstein himself by refusing the offer of a post at Cambridge in favour of America). Geoffrey Sharp's courage in publishing in German at such a time was remarkable, and certainly appreciated by Einstein, who wrote to Sharp to express his hope that it would 'not cause *you* any inconvenience'. It could well have done: association with 'enemy aliens' was viewed with suspicion (Hans Keller's brother-in-law was taken in for questioning at Brixton police station about the Austrians in his house). Sharp was also a pacifist, and at the very time when 'Mozartiana und Köcheliana' was going to press, he was in London appearing at his Conscientious Objector Appeal hearing.[27]

~

Hans Keller's relationship with Geoffrey Sharp did not get off to the best of starts. Sharp was one of the editors who had rejected the manuscript of 'Britten and Mozart' – but while others had made positive comments (Cyril Connolly of *Horizon*, for example, read it 'with great interest' before 'regretfully' turning it down),[28] Sharp's response seems to have been more bluntly negative. His original letter to Keller is lost, but a flavour of its contents can be surmised from Keller's reply:

18 January 1947 – to Geoffrey Sharp

Dear Mr. Sharp,

Thank you for your frank comments on my article BRITTEN AND MOZART. I do not propose to discuss your whole letter, if only because I am sure that you would not welcome my full-length reply.

There is, however, one point you make which I cannot let pass without comment: "And your final paragraph, with its impertinent backhander at Haydn's expense, is one of several little pinpricks . . ." What I say at that point is simply that in a future musical characterology Haydn and Mozart won't be grouped together. As all readers of the MS except for yourself recognized, there is not the faintest suggestion in this of an "impertinent

27 See Sharp to Hirsch, 29 September and 8 October 1940, BLPH.
28 Connolly to Keller, 18 December 1946, CULHK.

backhander at Haydn's expense"; if there is an aggressive element involved in my final paragraph, it is directed against those text-book minds who class Haydn and Mozart together. In other words, you are mistaking my characterological classification for what you wrongly infer to be my aesthetic valuation. While I should agree with you that anyone capable of an impertinence towards Haydn is not worth being listened to, it seems to me that an accusation of impertinence should only be voiced if one is quite certain that it is justified.

But then your whole reaction appears to be somewhat emotional, and as such is not open to argument. This observation is not intended as an offence; with all of us some particular brand of reactions tends to be affective rather than effective.

For the rest, my principal aim as a writer is to be as straightforward and frank as you are in your letter, and it may thus be that at a future date some part of my work that is a little more in your line will prove to you that it merits what you call "more careful consideration".

Sharp heartily disliked Britten's music, and the more others praised it the more he seemed determined not to agree. Writing to Hirsch to explain his absence from the premiere of *Peter Grimes* ('for the very good reason that the management did not send us tickets!'), he told him:

> I have heard nothing of Britten's so far to make me believe that he is (or ever will be) more than a fair craftsman – though I think his Variations on a Theme of Frank Bridge & the Michelangelo Sonnets are good sound stuff. Then of course there is the out-&-out rubbish like the Piano Concerto & the sickly, mawkish Serenade for Tenor, horn & strings! No, I shall be astounded if Peter Grimes is a masterpiece.[29]

Despite Hirsch's pleas to him to 'go un-biased' and Sharp's promise to 'do my best to be objective',[30] his eventual review was extremely negative, describing the music as 'poverty-stricken' and 'virtually without melody', and most of the singers as 'no more than marionettes' (he didn't mention Pears at all).

> Britten's score is arid and "devilish smart". He seems afraid to develop a lyrical vein and reluctant to express in his music any emotional conflict, or other sign of a strong and vigorous personality.[31]

29 Sharp to Hirsch, 17 June 1945, BLPH.
30 Hirsch to Sharp, 19 June 1945; Sharp to Hirsch, 20 June 1945, BLPH.
31 *MR* VI/3 (August 1945): 187–8.

Paul Hamburger encouraged Keller to try Sharp again with something different. Their many discussions about thematic relationships and Einstein's *Mozart* had stimulated Keller to write more about Mozart, developing his ideas on musical character and applying psychological and biographical points to the study of thematic relationships and musical structure. His next substantial article was inspired by what Einstein had written about Mozart's return to quintet writing in his last years and its possible relationship to Boccherini (who was particularly celebrated as a composer of quintets). Speculating on the reasons for Mozart taking up quintet writing at that point, Einstein had suggested that

> An external inducement was perhaps the death of Frederick the Great and the accession to the throne in Berlin of a violincello-playing dilettante. On 21 January 1786 Boccherini had received the title of Prussian Court composer, and Mozart habitually took careful note of lucrative appointments of that sort.[32]

In view of this, Keller thought it odd that Einstein had made 'no mention of the intimate relation between the last movement from one string quintet in C of Boccherini and movements from at least three of Mozart's major works'. After all, Einstein had examined the issue of Mozart's quotations in some detail and cited various relationships with Boccherini that Keller thought to be of slighter significance.

Perhaps reluctant to try Sharp again after the 'Britten and Mozart' rebuff, Keller first sent 'Mozart and Boccherini' to William McNaught at *The Musical Times* and Eric Blom at *Music & Letters*, both of whom admired it. The trouble with these long-established journals, however, was that they were in receipt of considerably more good material than they could print.

28 June 1947 – to Paul Hamburger [extract]
in German

> The story of the Mozart-Boccherini article will interest you: it came back from the Musical Times with the observation they would take it (!) but it would have to wait at least a year until publication. That's why they gave me free rein to get it accepted somewhere else. Whereupon I sent it to <u>Music and Letters</u> (Blom). Blom sent it back with much praise and said, as it was already accepted by the Musical Times anyway, he (Blom) would rather have the Britten–Mozart article (which I had mentioned in my letter); he wouldn't dare accept two articles from the same writer at the moment: he had a long queue. He could not blindly promise me to take the Britten–Mozart article, 'but from what I have seen from

---

32 Alfred Einstein, *Mozart: His Character, His Work* (London: Cassell, 1946), 190.

you it is more than likely that it will be what I want.' In conclusion he advised me to try the Music Review before sending it back to the Musical Times. Following his (and your) advice, I sent the thing to my bosom pal G. Sharp. And lo and behold! – he accepted by return of post and with pleasure – the music examples are already going to print. Mind you, he sent me my nice family tree back with the request I produce a tidier copy which the printer could use.

'Mozart and Boccherini' appeared as the opening article of the November 1947 issue of *The Music Review*, with the 'family tree' (a diagram showing the relationships between the Mozart and Boccherini works concerned) expensively printed as a two-colour plate. It was read carefully and with interest by *The Music Review*'s readers and fellow contributors, and a three-way debate between Keller, Alec Hyatt King and Hans F. Redlich ran in the correspondence columns for months. After 'Mozart and Boccherini' Keller appeared in every issue of *The Music Review*, and quickly became one of its most regular reviewers. Whereas *Music & Letters* confined its reviews section to books and published scores (Eric Blom's view being that 'A quarterly cannot deal with topical matters'[33]), Geoffrey Sharp took a broader view, and his journal covered concerts, opera, festivals and broadcasts, together with gramophone records and occasional articles by the editor on the latest technology. Sharp was very open to suggestions, and Keller, omnivorously devouring all he could of the expanding musical life around him, was full of ideas.

Sharp allowed considerable flexibility in the format and length of reviews – Keller's piece on the 1948 Edinburgh Festival is one example of combining a topical review with analytical detail, continuing his Einstein-inspired exploration of the structural and psychological significance of thematic connections and borrowings. Discussing the problems of the Glyndebourne production of *Così fan tutte* at Edinburgh, he advised the conductor and singers to 'look up Ex. I*b* [Tamino's E♭ aria in *Die Zauberflöte*] which would give them an idea of what Ex. I*a* [the recitative leading up to Ferrando's B♭ aria] is about. (Ex. I*a–b* is a clear case of an inter-operatic *Leitmotiv*; it does not, to my knowledge, recur anywhere else in Mozart.)' His lengthy digressions (and copious music examples) were required, he wrote, to justify his negative opinion of a production likely to be praised elsewhere: 'Well aware that I may be the only critic who holds this view, I can only say that I should be prepared to substantiate it in full detail.'[34] At the same time, Keller was also capable of writing very concisely. His ability to be brief while making points of real interest made him a valued contributor for a journal whose quarterly publication meant that its concert reviews had to cover a huge range.

Ironically, Keller's first review for Sharp was on Britten: the new Covent Garden production of *Peter Grimes*, on which he was quick to observe that 'while Tyrone Guthrie's new production has widely been commented upon, the

33 Blom to Keller, 25 October 1947, CULHK.
34 *MR* X/4 (November 1948): 295–300.

alterations in the work itself have gone entirely unnoticed.' He made a related point in his review of *Così fan tutte* at Sadler's Wells: 'Why do the cuts in opera productions escape criticism, whereas interpretational mishaps, which vary from performance to performance, don't?' One possible answer was that some critics might not have known the works thoroughly enough to notice all the cuts and changes. Among British critics, this would have been particularly the case in opera, as Dent observed in an article reflecting on the Vienna State Opera's 1947 visit:

> Opera in England carries on its existence in such precarious conditions that our critics, both amateur and professional, seem never to have acquired adequate standards by which to form their judgements on it. . . . They have . . . little or no experience of routine opera, as the foreign critics have, and little knowledge of its historical background. The result is that they seldom seem to see an opera as a complete whole, whether it be a new opera or an old one.[35]

Certainly Keller's reviews stood out for their thorough knowledge of the score and his ability to relate tiny musical details to the structure of the work as a whole (with ostentatiously precise references, bar-numbers and all). Even in music new to him, his acute ear, perfect pitch, and impressive musical memory meant that he was still able to make very precise observations on one hearing. Nevertheless he seized every effort to hear works on which he was writing multiple times – even those he already knew intimately:

November 1947 – to Miss Kay Martin, Cambridge Theatre

Dear Miss Martin,

I am working on a series of supplementary articles to Einstein's recent book on Mozart. The first two of these are finished; they are going to press in *The Music Review* and *Music and Letters* respectively. In connection with my studies, I should very much like to attend as many DON GIOVANNI performances as possible. As critic, I presume I am only entitled to press tickets for a single occasion, but would it be possible, in view of the nature of my work, to grant me access to a number of performances? Any odd place in the theatre would do (behind the stage, for instance); I don't want to see anything.

I am fully aware that this is a somewhat unusual request; please do not hesitate to decline it if there is any difficulty.

Yours sincerely

Hans Keller

35 'Lessons from Vienna', *MR* VIII/4 (November 1947): 274–81.

When reviewing new works in particular, he went continually to rehearsals if he could. He obtained scores where possible, and his torch on a score in the corner of a darkened opera house became a familiar sight. The importance Keller laid on thorough knowledge of every detail of the music was in stark contrast to the critical philosophy of Frank Howes, chief music critic of *The Times*, who made it a positive principle to 'avoid rehearsals and most forms of preliminary study', preferring to follow Forster's dictum that one should approach a work of art 'eternally virgin':

> I prefer not to follow a new work with a score. I stay away from rehearsals and I prefer to do my homework after, not before, I have heard a work. The reason for this is that more important than any of these things, valuable as they may be, is the immediate impact of the work as a whole. . . . One should not spoil the impact of a symphony by the stops and starts of rehearsal, by listening to an opera in a dead cold theatre, and for me by the shift of interest away from the aesthetic towards the technical in following with a score.[36]

Geoffrey Sharp's confidence in Keller's musical judgement grew rapidly – although they never agreed about Britten, and Sharp was not uncritical of Keller's literary style. Still, Keller recalled with gratitude the way that Sharp had given him 'total freedom' in *The Music Review* in those early years. This was partly due to the considerable overlap in their musical interests and repertoire. Neither was much interested in early music, for example, and Sharp was also more aligned with the German than the French musical tradition. Britten was one major area of disagreement, but they were united in their lack of enthusiasm for Vaughan Williams. Keller was also good at persuading Sharp into new areas: after getting his first film music piece in as an 'exceptional case' he quickly turned it into a regular film music column. But above all, he and Sharp were drawn together by their naturally anti-Establishment temperaments, and their keen desire to reform the way music was written about in Britain.

Sharp was quite happy to break what Ernest Chapman had told Keller was the 'tradition here that critics shall not criticize critics'. One prominent target was Frank Howes, whom Sharp considered 'among the worst offenders',[37] and who was to be a recurring figure in Keller's later anti-critical campaigns. He and Eric Blom were perhaps the two chief representatives for Keller of British 'Establishment' critical opinion in the 1940s and 50s. Blom was the more open and cosmopolitan figure of the two (born in Switzerland of Danish descent, educated privately abroad and an excellent linguist). Howes, on the other hand, was thoroughly English and his musical interests notably so: a significant early study of William Byrd was followed by books on Vaughan Williams and Walton and a history of the English Musical Renaissance. Born in Oxford (where he read

36 Howes, 'Autobiography', 300, BL MS Mus.283. (Reference to E.M. Forster, *Two Cheers for Democracy* (London: Edward Arnold, 1951), 126.)
37 Sharp to Hirsch, 15 November 1949, BLPH.

Classics), Howes did not travel abroad until he was thirty-three, by which time he was already writing for *The Times*. He had encountered Hugh Allen at Oxford, but had little formal music education until he went as a mature student to the Royal College of Music a decade later: 'I decided that I must, despite my age, become a music student in order to insert some foundations beneath my active music-making, which meant making further serious attempt upon the harmony that I had begun by correspondence in 1915.'[38] Despite his Classical education, Howes was not a natural linguist, having drawn more from the literary and historical elements of his studies, which he described as giving him a 'life-long concern with words, ... history, archaeology and aesthetics'. At the RCM he was similarly less interested in the grammar and syntax of his harmony lessons than in the music appreciation and criticism classes run by

> 'The appreciation of music'
> makes as much sense to me as
> 'the appreciation of God'.

H.C. Colles, then chief music critic of *The Times*. Colles liked his lively writing and invited him to join *The Times* in 1923, where he remained for the rest of his career, succeeding his mentor as chief critic in 1943.

The Times's position as Britain's principal newspaper of record gave its critics a particular status. Although they wrote anonymously (a tradition that Keller thought endowed them with a spurious authority), it was well known who they were, and they usually occupied other posts of musical importance. Longevity in the post was a feature of successive holders of the 'Our Music Critic' title, which made for stability (and conservatism) in a changing world: Howes and his predecessor, Colles, wrote for *The Times* for thirty-seven years each. Colles's predecessor, J.A. Fuller Maitland (chief critic for twenty-two years) had been Sir George Grove's assistant editor on the first edition of his great Dictionary. Having edited the second edition himself, Fuller Maitland passed the editorship to Colles, who produced the third and fourth editions in 1927 and 1940. This association of *The Times* and *Grove* naturally further enhanced the standing of 'Our Music Critic' as a fount of musical knowledge, though the publisher Macmillan broke tradition in 1954, giving the editorship of the fifth edition of *Grove* to Blom rather than Howes. Still, Howes held plenty of other posts of importance in the musical world. He served as President of the Royal Musical Association and Chairman of (*inter alia*) the BBC Central Music Advisory Committee, the Musicians' Benevolent Fund, the English Folk Dance & Song Society and the Critics' Circle, as well as sitting on the music panels of both the Arts Council and the British Council, teaching at the Royal College of Music and examining for the Associated Board.

One of Howes's interests was psychology, and his first published book was *The Borderland of Music and Psychology*, which appeared in 1926. In 1948 he attracted Keller's attention with *Man, Mind and Music: Studies in the Philosophy of Music and in the Relations of the Art to Anthropology, Psychology, and Sociology*: 'The truths here conveyed could have been set forth in half the number

---

38 Howes, 'Autobiography', 121.

of pages, while the subject as indicated by the title could not possibly be developed in a book of less than twice the present size,' wrote Keller in his review. 'And to extricate the author's verifiable truths from his verifiable untruths would, in all conscience, take a book itself,' he continued, deploring Howes's apparent lack of knowledge of, or interest in, Schopenhauer and Freud.[39] Robert Simpson, reviewing the same book, gave this explanation of Howes's appeal as a writer despite his weaknesses as a musician:

> The book shows clearly the reasons for the author's eminence as a musical journalist, for he has developed a rare power of relating, in readable terms, his very extensive general knowledge to his feelings about music. To the layman, such writing must prove exciting and plausible: for the musician everything depends on how far he can agree with Howes' views on music; if he finds these unsound the rest of the matter will naturally become suspect. So often does this seem to me the case that any judgment must needs be as completely subjective as the book itself.[40]

Keller's first attack on Howes as a music critic came when they both reviewed the first performance in England of Bruckner's Seventh Symphony in May 1948. Howes used his review to explain why Bruckner – and indeed all recent Austrian composers – was part of a 'dying tradition' that could not appeal to the English: 'We have no patience for Bruckner, we think Mahler a *petit maître* who obstinately uses grandiose forms too big for him, and Schönberg we consign to America and his works to the devil.'[41] In return, Keller used his review to attack Howes – prefacing his article with a pointed quotation from the Talmud: '*Teach thy tongue to say, "I do not know"*.'[42]

What is interesting about Keller's reaction to Howes on this occasion is that he was only a very recent convert to Bruckner's music himself. Looking back years later, he recalled how long it had taken him to overcome his original antipathy. Despite his father's love of Bruckner, he wrote, 'it was only in this country that the truth about this towering genius gradually dawned on me – though it was a difficult dawn, since at the time performances were few, bad, and far between, Bruckner being considered an unexportable Austrian provincial, like Mahler.'[43] Mahler too had not been especially beloved of the young Keller ('it was only after I had acquired British nationality, musically as well as legally, that I really came to understand at any rate some of this master's symphonies'[44]); and as for Schoenberg, Keller was at this date still avoiding his music as assiduously as was Howes. It almost seems as though the opposition of the English 'Establishment' to the recent music of his homeland was partly responsible for driving Keller to re-examine it.

39 *MS* I/6 (1949): 201–2.
40 *MR* X/1 (February 1949): 52–3.
41 'Bruckner's Music: a Dying Tradition', *The Times*, 21 May 1948, 7.
42 *MR* IX/3 (August 1948): 187–8.
43 'My Family, You and I', *NR* III/34–5 (January–February 1977): 13–23.
44 'National Frontiers in Music', *Tempo* 33 (September 1954): 23–30. Keller told Donald Mitchell that he 'found Mahler banal' as a child (Keller to Mitchell, 24 February 1958, CULHK).

In keeping with his professional anonymity, Frank Howes did not respond to Keller's reproaches, nor did Keller ever succeed in altering his views. Eric Blom, on the other hand, enjoyed debate, and engaged keenly, both in private and in print, with all the many issues Keller raised. 'You must be quite the nicest person I've never met,' wrote Keller after one of their wrangles – and indeed Blom does seem to have been unusually patient and modestly immune to offence. Their earliest recorded argument was over the amateur City Opera Club's 1949 performance of *La clemenza di Tito*, which Blom had welcomed as 'an interesting and enjoyable venture in many ways' and 'a welcome opportunity to put "La clemenza di Tito" in its place once more'.[45] Keller's review, on the other hand, was scathing about the Club's 'unmentionably inept rendering in which hardly a single orchestral bar is as much as bearable', and criticised both the Arts Council for supporting it ('instead of encouraging everybody to do everything, one ought to teach Everybody what to leave alone') and also 'certain irresponsible notices in responsible newspapers' – a clear reference to Blom's mild praise.[46] At the same time as this public attack, Keller was trying to persuade Blom to publish his aphorisms in *Music & Letters*, an irony not lost on Blom:

Dear Dr. Keller (apologies for "mistering" you before),

Many thanks, but I think I had better not embark on your aphorisms, though most of them are much to the point. The difficulty is that, once started, they would be difficult to stop, and there is no knowing whether you could keep up the quality, or what you might ask me to put in later. And you know you and I don't always agree.

You made no bones about that in the M.R. (By the way, why doesn't Sharp publish these sparks of yours, since you are one of his boys?) It is obvious that I am the guilty party in the matter of the 'Clemenza di Tito' performance. But aren't we all interested in <u>music</u>? Or are performances and personalities more important? Our fundamental difference is that I would rather hear a bad performance of 'Titus' than none at all, and you not. And another, I suspect, that you want to apply the same standards to everything, as though it mattered as much what happens in any hole-and-corner place as what they do at Covent Garden.[47]

11 August 1949 – to Eric Blom

Dear Mr Blom,

You were quite right in mistering me; people are wrongly "doctoring" me.

I did not send the aphorisms to Sharp because I didn't want Keller to overcrowd the M.R.

---

45 'Mozart's "Titus"', *Observer*, 1 May 1949, 6.
46 *MR* 10/3 (August 1949): 220.
47 Blom to Keller, 10 August 1949, CULHK.

". . . aren't we all interested in <u>music</u>? Or are performances and personalities more important?" There is no music without an understanding performance. This is where you misunderstand me. What I want is a performance that lives on re-creative understanding instead of dying of sentimentalized or intellectualized ignorance or of badly tinned feelings. (All tinned feelings are badly tinned.) I am not hankering after perfection. A technically defective rendering into which the interpreter puts his whole and wholly understanding mind will overwhelm me; a technically perfect execution which does not develop out of both a plastic idea of the whole and an ever-spontaneous experience of what the whole makes of its parts will bore me to death; it will sicken me to death when the utmost technical brilliance and a superficial musical respectability are paired with a complete lack of inspiration and of musical development (not in the technical sense), as in the case of Toscanini's Beethoven or Brahms. Beneath a certain technical standard on the part of orchestra and singers there is of course nothing a conductor can do; the 'Titus' production was doomed to failure. What I was furious about was the lack of artistic conscience that made the venture possible, and the Arts Council's customary practice of supporting every idiocy as long as it sounds vaguely "cultural". Don't you see the harm of such performances? How many music lovers know 'Titus'? And how is the novice to understand a work if the performance does not make its musical logic clear, not to speak of such insults to the senses as must send many a sensitive person to the lavatory? You should have heard some of the newcomers' comments on the <u>work</u>! On the acoustic level our basic difference is simply that I am more sensitive, or if you like more hysterical than you; when I hear a performance like this I start to sweat until I'm wet all over, I get a terrible headache, in fact I get so much worked up that I'm literally near despair. But I should never have written my review on the basis of bad sound, bad intonation etc. alone. Indeed I prefer Welitsch's wrong notes to the right ones of any other Donna Anna I know, though I don't consider Welitsch the right Donna Anna.

You misunderstand me once more when you say that I want to apply the same standards to everything. On the contrary, before starting on any review, I conscientiously work out the standards I have to apply, taking into account both the potentialities of the composer or the performer or the venture concerned, and his or its actual and possible, positive and negative effects on musical culture as a whole. Take the last M.R., p. 221. Had I judged Winifred Heidt's Carmen by the same standards as Schwarzkopf's Mimi, I should have said that the former was impossible. And had I judged Schwarzkopf's Mimi by the same standards of musicianship as Pears' evangelist (p. 214 f.), I should have found more than a single fault in her interpretation, even though Mimi is a thousand times easier musically than the Evangelist. My only constant rule is that a performance that does not convey musical understanding is worse than none. And there is no musical understanding without an emotionally inspired conception of form, i.e., the very thing which is absent in most performances nowadays. Which is one of the reasons why music is becoming more and more an emotional or intellectual amenity, or else a medical requirement, instead of a spiritual necessity. I am fighting a lonely battle against this develop- (envelop-) -ment, and you mustn't be offended if I don't apply the same standards to Eric Blom and Bill Brown, and therefore attack the former as vehemently as possible when he lends his countenance to decline of music.

A couple of months later, Keller took issue with another of Blom's *Observer* reviews, this time of the new Sadler's Wells production of *Don Giovanni*, of which Blom had written:

> Whenever any opera house ventures on this greatest and most difficult of all tasks, one is called upon to be indulgent. Yet so far as one's own inclinations go, one is apt to be exacting to the point of unreason. Judgments of any performance are thus bound to waver, and to keep them tolerably steady one can only measure it by sincerity of endeavour.[48]

This time Keller tried a different approach:

[November 1949] – to Eric Blom

Dear Mr. Blom,

Would you be prepared to consider an article on ERIC BLOM AND 'DON GIOVANNI' : SOME ULTIMATE PROBLEMS OF CRITICISM ?

No – unless I hear from you.

Yours sincerely,

[Hans Keller]

'I wish I knew exactly what you mean,' sighed Blom. 'Is it a joke – or what? I know you disapprove of me on the whole, but I should of course be very curious to see what your objections are this time.'[49]

48 'Don Giovanni', *Observer*, 30 October 1949, 6.
49 Blom to Keller, 5 November 1949, CULHK.

8 November 1949 – to Eric Blom

Dear Mr. Blom,

No joke. I should start from your premise, ". . . to keep judgments of any performance tolerably steady one can only measure it by sincerity of endeavour", discuss its applicability as a critical principle; show how the all too extensive and exclusive use you make of it misleads you – a man who would otherwise have arrived at an exceptionally balanced judgment – into misleading criticism; and finally demonstrate the importance (no matter whether you or I or both of us are wrong) of fundamental critical principles, and of the writer's and reader's awareness of the principle(s) applied in any particular instance. On this last point, I believe we agree. The whole thing is intended as a contribution to the theory of criticism, and if it succeeds in showing the complicated situation in which we (the critics) are, and in delineating the many important complications, it will be worth while. [. . .]

The reason why I wish to base the article on your 'Don Giovanni' notice is exactly the opposite of what you think: I do not "disapprove of you on the whole." For obvious reasons, whenever I have to criticize a widely accepted artistic or critical attitude, I always try to find its worthiest representative; my 'Kyla Greenbaum and the Psychology of the Modern Artist' in the forthcoming issue of MR shows the same approach in another field. If you will have a look at this issue, you will, incidentally, see why I hesitate to submit my idea to Sharp: he may not altogether welcome the thought of the 'Music Review' becoming something of Keller's house organ. [. . .]

Already the letter you wrote me upon my 'Titus' notice in MR seemed to show that your picture of my picture of you was wrong. This is not surprising; since our profession is, to an alarming extent, composed of ignorant impostors and, on the other hand, cowardly cognoscenti, you probably have not often been attacked by someone who knew what he and you were talking about.

Half an hour's talk might clear up a lot of misunderstandings.

'It's good to know that we are not at loggerheads altogether,' replied Blom, who nevertheless felt that 'I can't publish an article in which I am made to figure, though it would be fun to see it printed somewhere.'[50]

Keller's principle of directing his attacks at 'the worthiest representatives' of any widely accepted attitude he deplored naturally led him in the direction of many sacred cows. This, together with his polemical style and ostentatious erudition – and

50 Blom to Keller, 12 November 1949, CULHK.

his seemingly limitless self-confidence – began to grate on some of *The Music Review*'s readers. Unfortunately for Sharp, one particularly irritated reader was his old mentor Paul Hirsch. Hirsch's copies of *The Music Review* are preserved in the British Library and his occasional marginalia bear testimony to his frustration with Hans Keller. The final straw was this review of the Busch Quartet playing Haydn, Mozart and Beethoven in Chelsea Town Hall in May 1949:

Busch Quartet: Haydn, Mozart and Beethoven
MR X/3 (August 1949): 219–20

I attended the first two of the four recitals which comprised the four last quartets of the classical masters. As good a programme as any, according to a leading critic. A bad plan, I suggest, for it necessitated the performance of the only work of the grown-up Haydn which is not fit for performance, *i.e.* the last Quartet, Op. 103. But I should like to point out that the second movement (which the Buschs did not play) is the first Minuet not to be in the tonic. Unfortunately Haydn's intentions cannot be fully appreciated because the Quartet is incomplete and because the two complete movements are not finished.

Another wrong choice was that of Haydn, Op. 76, No. 6, as first quartet. The Buschs should know that sound is not their strength, and hence should not start off in E flat. But then, as far as Haydn and Mozart are concerned, they know absolutely nothing. It is, quite seriously, a mystery to me how a musician of Busch's stature can play these composers without realizing that he does not understand them. To give one example of his blatant misinterpretations, the trio of the just-mentioned E flat Quartet was played with a heavy accent on each minim. While the tune derives from bars 5–6 of the minuet, in which the minims *are* accented, one of the trio's main points is its contrast to the minuet, expressed in the spacious, unburdened, dreamy, yet directive flow of the E flat major scale whose accents must be imperceptible and imperceptibly shaded. Once the scale becomes aimless the whole thing seems baseless. Busch's leadership gone, the others' limitations shone. Bruno Straumann (2nd violin) appeared unhappy that he could not play Paganini, while Hugo Gottesmann (viola) did not seem to care much whether or what he played. Hermann Busch's uncertain intonation was of course most devastating in Haydn's basses. Not that there was any merit in the rendering of Mozart K.575 and 589. Indeed it was tragicomic to hear, for once, Einstein's *Authentic Edition* being heeded, in performances in which, for once, truth to the letter did not matter.

But Busch's Beethoven! Here was musical life. Only very few things were downright wrong, such as the jumpy semiquaver in the opening

motif of the *Alla danza tedesca*. Tragicomic, once more, to witness how
Beethoven's endeavours to tell the performer precisely what to do
result, again and again, in the performer's doing precisely the wrong thing.
What Beethoven tried to indicate here was that the motif should float to
and (especially) fro, not that it should vanish like a snapped elastic. All the
same, the B flat major compelled attention throughout and the C sharp
minor through and through. The mishaps in the latter's *Presto* (no need
to say where!) did not matter at all, for once a Beethoven performance
lives it is difficult to kill it, and while the viola in No. 6 was unworthy in
its earthly expression, Busch's entry with the theme meant sublimity. If
performances of late Beethoven always leave some dissatisfaction, this
is his awing fault. There is only one way of playing these works, and that
one is wrong. Or it comes out wrong, anyway. For none of us is yet near
enough to where Beethoven was then to make what he thought, real.

When the review appeared, Hirsch wrote to Sharp:

> You know that I am one of the oldest friends of your MUSIC REVIEW, and
> I have told you again and again how much I appreciate its high standard. This
> standard also applies to the August number, with one exception, and I do hope,
> you will excuse me if I tell you frankly what this exception is: Mr. "H.K." (whom
> I don't know, and of whom I don't know where he comes from) is beginning to
> go "on my nerves!" . . . Adolf Busch is a wonderful artist and a strong personal-
> ity – but who is Mr. Keller?? There are other instances where H.K. has been
> offensive in his critiques and reviews, but this one is no doubt the worst.
>
> Forgive me, dear Geoffrey, if I am outspoken too, but I really got quite
> furious when I read this passage.[51]

Sharp showed Hirsch's letter to Keller: 'I think he has overstated his case but
perhaps we should not have printed the passage of which he complains.'[52] Keller
was unrepentant:

30 August 1949 – to Paul Hirsch

Dear Mr. Hirsch,

'The whole musical world' is not musical and therefore usually wrong;
and where it is right it is so for the wrong reasons. Its worship of Busch
illustrates my point. That people's admiration for his undoubtedly
great achievements cannot be based on real musical understanding is

51 Hirsch to Sharp, 26 August 1949, BLPH.
52 Sharp to Keller, 27 August 1949, CULHK.

for me proved by the fact that they do not see his limitations. It was for this reason that I was aggressive: Everyone knows the good Busch has done; few realize the harm he is doing through his sanctified but un-understanding renderings of Haydn and Mozart. My judgment cannot, as you say, be 'proved'. But it can be substantiated. If I cited only one example of what I meant, this was solely due to lack of space. Were you highly interested in my standpoint, I should willingly explain it to you on the basis of the scores, and in great detail. Since, obviously, you are not, I can only add that I at least strengthened my statement by one representative piece of concrete observation, whereas all you have to say in support of your impression that my statement is sheer nonsense, is that the whole musical world would disagree with me. I do not propose to be taught by the whole musical world what to teach them.

'I for one,' wrote Hirsch indignantly to Sharp when he received this, 'have no desire to be taught by him.'[53] The ensuing correspondence produced more heat than light over the next few months, but it is notable that Sharp (who was perfectly capable of putting his foot down) was not in this instance persuaded even by such an important friend to curb Keller in any way.

In the November 1948 issue of *The Music Review*, Keller began a new column, entitled 'First Performances'. By way of announcing his intentions, the column was headed by a quotation, in bold and italic type, from Alan Bush's report on the Second International Congress of Composers and Music Critics:

> There was general agreement that the standard of musical criticism, especially when dealing with new works, was low. Critics contented themselves with unprincipled methods of evaluation, or vague descriptions of the new works. Usually their mere emotional reactions were wrapped up in pretentious verbiage, so as to give them a pseudo-scientific verisimilitude.[54]

The sub-headings Keller sometimes added to the 'First Performances' title in later issues were along the same lines: 'First Performances and their Reviews', 'First Performances and how they are reported', 'First Performances: their pre- and reviews' etc. Despite this, his column primarily discussed the music, and was remarkable less for attacks on critics than for the amount of interesting musical detail that Keller managed to include, in his inimitable aphoristic style. It gives

If you want to live successfully you have to understate your feelings. If you want to write successfully you have to overstate them.

53 Hirsch to Sharp, 14 September 1949, BLPH.
54 *MT* 89/1267 (September 1948): 280–81.

a lively sense of concert life at the time, and shows Keller's deep engagement both with the works themselves and the way in which they were performed and discussed. In the February 1950 column, however, in which he reviewed the first British performance of Schoenberg's String Trio, Keller could not resist discussing the critical reaction at length, admitting that 'in recording these gems of "musical" criticism in a musicological journal, I have a secret hope of preserving them for succeeding generations.'

The following issue of *Musical Opinion* took extensive revenge in its editorial:

> We were . . . astonished at the tone of an article entitled 'Concerts and Recitals: First performances and How They are Reported' which appeared in the February issue of *The Music Review*.
>
> As far as we can gather from its extremely turgid English, the main purpose of the author, a Mr. Hans Keller, was to ridicule the criticisms already published by Bonavia of *The Daily Telegraph*, Scott Goddard of *The News Chronicle*, Frank Howes of *The Times*, and of our own contributor, C. G.-F. . . . Of the scholarship and antecedents of Messrs. Bonavia, Scott Goddard and Howes we have no doubt. We are not so well informed about those of Mr. Keller. According to our scanty information, he came to this country as a refugee from Vienna in 1938, since when he would appear to have spent the major portion of his time in memorising strings of polysyllables from the English dictionary and seeking opportunities to use them.[55]

'Mr. Keller's attacks on his fellow critics prompted us to look through some of his own writings,' continued the leader writer, who proceeded to give several quotations as examples of the sins to which he was objecting: over-complication, incomprehensible vocabulary, too many references (including 'to his *own* writings'), psychoanalytical jargon, 'microscopic investigations' and – above all – immodesty.

> As to his denigration (we got that one from him, too) of his fellow critics, we would remind Mr. Keller, who, by the way, has only lately been elected a member of the Critics' Circle, that those who claim the right of asylum have also a duty of courtesy towards their hosts. His error is common to many of his race, in mistaking garrulous verbosity for erudition . . . The reader will observe that with all his study of the English dictionary, there is one word that Mr. Keller appears to have overlooked – *modesty.*

Unsurprisingly, Keller had faced some difficulty in getting elected to the Critics' Circle. George Dannatt, elected the previous year, was at the meeting at which Keller was first proposed:

---

55 'Musical Criticism and How It Is Done', *MO* 73/871 (April 1950): 390.

You had to be put up by two sponsors who checked your credentials. After being elected a member I did attend a few meetings where people were considered for membership and the criteria were pretty tough. For instance I remember that Hans Keller was initially turned down for membership, with Martin Cooper reading out some reviews and stating that we could not have someone writing like that![56]

Even after Keller was successfully elected in 1950, his fellow members were still raising objections. 'Fisk complained about your stuff in MR at considerable length,' Geoffrey Sharp told him after one meeting Keller missed. 'An entry was to be made in the minute book expressing the hope that you would take an early opportunity of explaining your hostile attitude to your fellow critics.'[57]

There were, however, several younger critics who were very excited by Keller's new style of reviewing – so much so that Keller was led to hope for 'the emergence of a new school of criticism under my influence'.[58] One of those who was most impressed was Donald Mitchell, the young editor of another new journal, *Music-Survey*. This is how he recalled the first time he read a Keller review:

I was knocked out by it, by its precision, its confidence and all the very specific points it made, whether adverse or positive. Gone were all those boring generalities and tedious descriptions, stuffed with modifiers and qualifiers – our Sunday-paper review sections are still littered with them – and in their place, detailed observations on rhythm, pitch, tonality, modulation, dynamics, nuances of expression, which left one in no doubt that here was a critic who knew what he was talking about. And even more amazing, knew the work he was talking about, from the inside outwards, as Hans himself might have said. Moreover, I seem to remember that, lest anyone might think that this critic had not done his homework, there were footnotes in which he laid out his sources. It was an astonishing performance – and there were many others of a like kind – which punched a big hole in the facade of English music criticism as it was practised in the 1940s and 1950s. It has never been – or looked – quite the same since.[59]

Above all, it was Keller's sheer musicality that most struck Mitchell, and the way in which his committed attention to what the composer was saying transcended style, ideology and historical period. As in his Britten and Mozart parallel, Keller approached composers of widely differing periods or styles in the same spirit, with perceptive results. For Keller, thought Mitchell,

56 Dannatt, 'Memories', in William Russell and Peter Cargin, *A Critical Century* (London: Critics' Circle, 2013), 61–3.

57 Sharp to Keller, 13 June 1950, CULHK. 'Fisk' was Clinton Gray–Fisk of *Musical Opinion*.

58 'Hans Keller's Reply', *Hallé* 21 (February 1950): 13–15. (Naturally this statement was cited by *Musical Opinion* as another example of Keller's arrogance.)

59 'Donald Mitchell remembers Hans Keller', *LRB* IX/15 (3 September 1987): 8–11, reprinted as 'Remembering Hans Keller' in Mitchell, *Cradles of the New* (London: Faber, 1995), 461–80.

A quartet of Haydn's . . . or an opera of Mozart's was as *immediate* as if it had been composed only yesterday. It was that extraordinary capacity to enter the past and to experience it as the present, that made Hans's insights so fresh and original, so close to the music. He erased history, as a writer.[60]

~

Donald Mitchell was six years younger than Hans Keller and eleven years younger than Geoffrey Sharp. He had been a schoolboy at Dulwich College when war broke out, and when he reached conscription age in 1943 he registered as a conscientious objector, spending the rest of the war in the Non-Combatant Corps. During his time in the NCC he suffered the death of his mother, his most important early musical influence. A highly talented singer (who broadcast several times for the BBC in the late 1920s), Kathleen Mitchell had been born and brought up in Switzerland, and studied at the Leipzig Conservatoire. She had remained in Leipzig throughout the First World War, staying with a Jewish family, whom she and her English husband helped flee Leipzig in the 1930s. Under her influence, the young Donald grew up with a much more European musical outlook than most Englishmen of his age:

> As a result of this, and my mother's musical education – Nikisch for her was still a living memory! – I was in contact as a boy with all kinds of music that I think would not have been much of a domestic presence in England at the time, for example songs by Pfitzner, Reger and Schoenberg – it was my mother's voice that first introduced me to the *Gurrelieder*![61]

Mitchell's very first publication was 'Elegy in Memory of My Mother', written in August 1944 when he was nineteen and printed the following year in a slim volume of poetry in her memory, alongside sonnets by three of her friends.[62] One of the contributors to this volume was the eccentric poet and writer E.H.W. Meyerstein, then in his mid-fifties and living in his old college at Oxford to escape the London bombing. Meyerstein disliked Oxford and what he called its 'academic malignity' and liked to get away when he could. But he made it difficult for himself by refusing ever to stay in hotels and sometimes trying the patience of those of his friends who were able or willing to put him up. From the spring of 1941, however, he made regular visits to the village of Takeley in Essex, to stay with the antiquarian bookseller Percy Muir and his novelist wife Barbara Kaye

---

60 Address by Mitchell at Keller's funeral, 13 November 1985, reprinted in *Tempo* 156 (March 1986): 2–3, and in *Cradles of the New*, 457–60.

61 Mitchell, interviewed by Christopher Wintle in 2001, *HKI*, 266–7.

62 Donald Mitchell, *et al.*, *Justa Catharinae Mitchell a quatuor moerentibus, amoris & recordationis causa*, etc. (London: (pub. not identified), 1945).

(who has given in her memoirs a vivid portrait of 'the strangest man I have ever known'[63]). Meyerstein was highly musical, and was delighted when the Muirs introduced him to neighbours who had recently moved into the village: Geoffrey and Mary Sharp. He struck up a friendship with Sharp (staying with the Sharps after he fell out with the Muirs), and his reviews and poetry became a regular feature of *The Music Review* from May 1941.

In the years after Kathleen Mitchell's death, Meyerstein was an encouragement to her son's literary ambitions, and he was probably instrumental in the publication of Mitchell's first article – in *Mandrake,* a new journal of poetry and prose that another of Meyerstein's young friends, the poet and novelist John Wain, started in Oxford after the war.[64] Mitchell's article on the life and music of Max Reger appeared in the second issue of this journal (February 1946), at a time when Reger was almost completely unknown to British audiences. It seems to have attracted some attention, for shortly afterwards Mitchell was invited by the BBC to give a broadcast talk on Reger, which his friend Harold Truscott illustrated at the piano.[65] This led to more work for the BBC: an interval talk on Brahms at the end of 1946 plus script research and translation for the Light Programme's musical feature *Fantasia.*[66] This early success apart, Mitchell recalled that 'I didn't expect to find much of a market for my particular interests', and indeed doesn't seem to have published anything else until he set up his own journal the following year. It is not known whether Meyerstein introduced him to Geoffrey Sharp at this stage, but if he did nothing came of it until 1948.

Mitchell was, however, a keen reader of *The Music Review*, for which another of his friends, the composer Robert Simpson, was now writing. He and Simpson had met during the war, while Simpson was also doing non-combatant service alongside his musical studies with Herbert Howells. Mitchell, with Harold Truscott and Harry Newstone (another Howells pupil), would meet regularly at Simpson's home in south London to share their enthusiasm for composers like Bruckner, Mahler, Reger and Pfitzner, whom most British musicians ignored:

> During the times of blackout and air raids we would listen to those great unknowns, Bruckner (Bob's favourite) and Mahler (mine), surrounded by towering stacks of shellac 78 rpm discs, with thorn needles and needle sharpener to hand. Bob too was an implacable pacifist and undoubtedly influenced me. I certainly respected the strength of his views, musical and political, and perhaps envied the total certainty with which he held them.[67]

63 Kaye, *The Company We Kept*, 132.
64 The Meyerstein collection of manuscripts in Hull University archives includes around 200 letters and postcards from Meyerstein to Donald Mitchell dating from 1944–49. Meyerstein was a contributor to the first issue of *Mandrake* (Wain and the other contributors were current or recent undergraduates). Mitchell's article appeared in the second issue, February 1946.
65 In the series *Music-Lovers' Diary*, BBC Home Service, 7 July 1946.
66 See WAC, Donald Mitchell contributor file.
67 Mitchell, interviewed by Christopher Wintle, *HKI*, 269.

After the war was over, Simpson founded the Exploratory Concerts Society, which began putting on recitals and lectures in 1947, to promote the music of such neglected composers (who at this date also included Haydn). Perhaps a similar impulse lay behind Mitchell's founding of *Music Survey* at the same time. Lacking much outlet for his writings elsewhere, the twenty-two-year-old Mitchell felt that 'the solution was to start a periodical of my own which could put forward reasoned arguments for those composers about whom I felt passionately at the time.' Simpson, Truscott and Newstone all contributed to the early issues, and Meyerstein wrote for every one. Meyerstein's old friend Oliver Gotch contributed too, as did Cyril Stepan, another of the poets who had written for the memorial volume for Mitchell's mother (he also became *Music Survey*'s assistant editor). Printing was handled by 'a very small firm in the south of London, a family business I'd known since my childhood', Mitchell remembered. 'I think the type was virtually set by hand on antiquated machinery, while the average age of the printers must have been well over seventy.'[68] Financial support for the venture was generously provided by William and Kathleen Livingston, who ran Oakfield School in Dulwich, the prep school where Mitchell secured a teaching post after his discharge from the NCC.

Mitchell modelled his paper to some extent on *The Music Review*, combining essays on a variety of subjects with a reviews section covering books, published music, concerts, opera, gramophone records, broadcasts (and, once Hans Keller started contributing, film music). However, the balance of the magazine was weighted towards the topical reviews section, with fewer substantial essays and hardly any historical musicology. It was a slighter publication than *The Music Review*, produced and sold considerably more cheaply. (As a guide, the respective prices of the two publications were two shillings and sixpence versus seven shillings, with production quality to match. Glock, when he finally got *The Score* off the ground in 1949, took the opposite route to Mitchell, concentrating on substantial essays and almost no reviews, with high-quality production and a price of five shillings.)

Mitchell was just getting his fourth issue of *Music Survey* to the printer when the August 1948 edition of *The Music Review* came out. No doubt he would have read it keenly, to see the latest from Hans Keller (this was the issue in which Keller took Frank Howes to task about Bruckner) and from his friends Meyerstein and Simpson (who also castigated *The Times* for an incompetent review of Artur Schnabel's first symphony), as well as the report of Simpson's latest 'exploratory concert'. He would probably also have turned eagerly to page 196, on which his own first piece for *The Music Review* (a review of *Boris Godunov* at Covent Garden) was printed. Then, 'when I was idly turning over the pages of the correspondence at the back', he noticed a letter from the same Hans Keller he so admired. It was not the contents that struck him so forcefully on this

68   Mitchell, interviewed by Patrick Carnegy, in *Music Survey: New Series* (London: Faber, 1981), preface.

occasion (it was part of Keller's ongoing debate with Redlich and Hyatt-King), but the address:

> To my utter astonishment I found that he was living at . . . Herne Hill which was just down the other end of the street in south London, very, very near to me. And I thought, good heavens, I simply must get in touch with this chap, and wrote him a letter.[69]

Keller responded, and they spoke on the phone, arranging to meet on 17 November 1948, at a concert at the Central Hall, Westminster (where Keller was reviewing Gordon Jacob's Second Symphony for his 'First Performances' column in *The Music Review*). They discussed how they would recognise each other: Keller's diary for that date notes 'Mitchell top of staircase (buffet) *MR* in his hand, red shirt & tie'. Mitchell says he was 'rather bewildered' by Keller's self-description, which 'not only included sensible references to his prominent moustache but, rather more mysteriously, signals about his "big" nose'.

> I must have been rather a naïve young man, but it was some time before the penny dropped: this was Hans's coded way of conveying to a stranger that he was a Jew. It pains me still to think of it, pains me above all to think that Hans should have thought it necessary to give me, in some sense, advance 'warning'.[70]

This was not a subject to which Mitchell had previously given much thought, but as he got to know Keller better, he realised 'how profoundly conscious he was of his Jewishness . . . and how deeply he had been affected by his fearful experiences in Vienna pre-war'. As they worked together, it was borne in upon Mitchell repeatedly that the opposition Keller encountered was not just a result of his own combative style, but tainted by darker inflections – as the references in the afore-mentioned *Musical Opinion* editorial to Keller's 'antecedents' and 'race' show clearly to modern eyes. The late 1940s were years of particular tension, with the end of the British mandate in Palestine in 1948 and the return of Oswald Mosley to politics the same year. 1948 was also when the majority of naturalisation appli-cations from continental refugees were finally granted – Keller himself became a British citizen in August that year.

Keller later made reference to having acquired British nationality 'musically as well as legally' at this time, and Donald Mitchell played a significant role in this musical naturalisation. Although the process had begun with *Peter Grimes* three years earlier, most of Keller's practical music-making was still confined within émigré circles and his principal musical 'thinking partner' until this point was Paul Hamburger. Paradoxically, what Keller seems to have meant by gaining

---

69 *HKI,* 265.
70 Mitchell, 'Remembering Hans Keller'.

British nationality 'musically' was partly to do with the new understanding of Austrian music he achieved by viewing it through British eyes – in the essay in which he discussed this, he cited in particular the importance of Britten's music to his understanding of Mahler. Donald Mitchell's eager exploration of recent Austrian and German music thus gave Keller an ideal partner with whom to re-explore it himself through an English lens – a *positive* lens, moreover, which could counter the opposition of Howes and Blom.

Keller took his new friend to his home in Herne Hill, where he and his mother lived next door to his sister's family, and the great Oskar Adler held court.[71] Mitchell was entranced: here was a living pocket of the European musical culture that so fascinated him (as well as, perhaps, something of the family life he had lost after his mother's death). Mitchell once said of Benjamin Britten's friendship with Erwin Stein that it had given Britten a vital experience of musical Vienna –'I've often thought that Erwin in a very real and musically rich way provided Ben with that experience of Vienna that he had been denied earlier, when his plans to study with Berg had been scotched.'[72] It might be suggested that Mitchell's friendship with Hans Keller played a similar role in his own development.

> Hans might have scorned my thinking of him as 'Viennese': but he could be conspicuously Viennese when there was a part of that culture with which he could whole-heartedly identify himself. I remember very well when that wonderful old Decca set of *Die Fledermaus* first appeared (1951), with Julius Patzak (one of Hans's heroes), Hilde Gueden, and the rest. The discs were transported to the house next door, where Hans's half-sister lived with her English doctor husband, and were played over and over again with the entire Keller family as audience – and no one enjoyed every inflexion of the performance more than Hans and his mother. I got a sense then of the Vienna in which they had been steeped and which still meant so much to them, despite their brutal ejection.[73]

Living round the corner, Mitchell became a regular member of the music-making in the Keller–Franey family circle, as well as attending frequent concerts with Hans. When he was asked years later what he and Hans talked about during their earliest encounters, Mitchell said 'I recall babbling on about Mahler and the books I wanted to write about him and was somewhat taken aback when Hans halted the flow by declaring that the book that *really* needed

---

71 Keller's mother lived at 30 Herne Hill and the Franeys at 32 Herne Hill (a house designed for them by Keller's father and cousin).

72 Mitchell, quoted in Carpenter, *Benjamin Britten* (London: Faber, 1992), 216–17.

73 Mitchell, 'Remembering Hans Keller.'

Hans Keller playing viola in an unidentified string quartet. Drawing by Milein Cosman.

to be written was one about Franz Schmidt.'[74] Mitchell had 'barely heard' of Schmidt at that time, but later reflected that it was 'a revealing choice – very Viennese, traditional and conservative'.[75] This was an aspect of Keller's musical character that confused Mitchell, and he struggled to reconcile this 'unexpected vein of conservatism' in a personality 'so plainly sceptical, radical and innovative'.

In particular, he remembered the surprise he felt when Keller described his difficulties with Schoenberg, with whose music Mitchell had been familiar from childhood, courtesy of his mother's voice: 'She used to sing "So tanzen die Engel" from the *Gurrelieder* and it cast a spell on me.' As he grew up, Mitchell listened to as much Schoenberg as he could find in wartime England, so had developed an understanding of this music far in excess of Keller's, whose only concrete childhood memory of it was his own incomprehension at the performance of the Fourth Quartet, which he had heard as a seventeen-year-old in Vienna shortly before the *Anschluss*. Mitchell, on the other hand, when discussing with Keller

74 *HKI*, 271.
75 Mitchell, 'Remembering Hans Keller'.

post-war performances of *Pierrot lunaire*, was able to compare them with 'the strongest memories of Stein's very loving performance' in the Boosey & Hawkes concert he had heard when he was seventeen in 1942.[76] 'It amuses me now to find that in one respect I was actually ahead of Hans! I enjoyed listening to Schoenberg, while Hans at the time, when he overheard a broadcast of *Pierrot*, in his own words, was "looking round for something to throw at the radio to stop this awful noise".'[77]

That was about to change.

---

76 Mitchell to Keller [c. February 1952], CULHK.
77 *HKI*, 271.

Music Survey

Before I came to understand – or, to put it more truthfully and modestly, to divine – Schoenberg, I knew that great music had to come from, and go to, another world, but it never occurred to me that music could encompass three other worlds – God, the remotest thinkable future, and the remotest feelable past. But then, it is of the essence of genius that he not only *says* for the first time, but also *is* for the first time. Every genius is the first genius; he destroys all previous conceptions and definitions of "genius". Thus, while every talent has to put up with *wrong criticisms from the ignorant*, it is the tragedy of genius alone that he is greeted with *irrelevant criticisms from the knowledgeable*. I well remember the none too distant time when I used my professional knowledge for the reassuring purpose of rationalizing my acute aversion to – or, as I now realize, my deep-rooted fear of – Schoenberg. I kept these thoughts to myself, not only because of my intellectual and musico-technical respect for Schoenberg's mind, but above all because I guiltily, if dimly, suspected that something was going on there which I considered basically weak because I was too weak – artistically too neurotic, too past-bound, group-bound – to dare open myself up to it. In sober words, I knew that I didn't know what I was being knowledgeable about.

This passage comes from a draft of one of Keller's 'First Performances' columns for *The Music Review*, and shows the magnitude of what happened to him on 15 November 1948, as he listened for the first time to Schoenberg's Second Chamber Symphony on the radio.[1] Keller's dawning comprehension of Schoenberg represented a tectonic shift in his musical understanding – 'the door was now open not only to the understanding of Schoenberg's atonal and twelve-tone music, but to contemporary music in general'[2] – and it happened two days before his first meeting with Donald Mitchell, who played a crucial part in the new thoughts it set in

1 *MR* XI1/3 (August 1951): 225–7. The second half of this extract does not appear in the published version.
2 'How I got there', undated proof, marked in Keller's hand 'unpublished because I refused to change', CULHK.

train. Keller described this moment as a 'revelation', and it was as significant an event in his musical development as his first hearing of *Peter Grimes*. But while his *Grimes* epiphany had opened a way into the contemporary English musical culture in which he found himself (and enabled him to apply his recent psycho-analytical learning to its interpretation), this new understanding of Schoenberg resolved a disjunction with his Austrian past. 'I was never interested in music I couldn't understand,' wrote Keller of his youth, and throughout his life he continued to avoid music that he could not connect with his own tradition. But while it was relatively easy to set aside early music and non-European music (and even to a large extent French and Scandinavian music), to refuse to engage with composers like Bruckner, Mahler and Schoenberg was a problem. They *were* part of his own tradition – and, in the love of his father for Bruckner and Oskar Adler for Schoenberg, part of his own childhood.

Keller had gone to *Peter Grimes* by accident, unaware of what he was about to hear. Similarly, the beginning of his understanding of Schoenberg was facilitated by the fact that he didn't know whose music he was listening to. Years later, he described how it happened:

> One night I twiddled about on my [radio] set and got into the middle of a fascinating piece, transmitted from somewhere abroad. My excitement mounted as the music developed. The more complex it got, the clearer it seemed – an experience which doesn't happen to you every day. Whoever the composer was, he was a neglected genius: as the work ended, I had come to feel quite protective and pioneering about him.[3]

As a late reworking of an earlier tonal piece, the Second Chamber Symphony was an ideal introduction to Schoenberg's mature atonal style 'which here, as it were, expressed itself tonally'.

> In a flash – well, in about quarter of an hour, anyway – I got the hang of his thought, and once the thought, with the feeling inside it, had impressed itself on me, the style didn't matter so much any more. . . . I familiarised myself with a great deal of Schoenberg's music before I started bothering about twelve-tone technique as such. With me, the emotional click must always come first, and the intellectualization, which my mind does ultimately require, has to be spurred on by emotional understanding, or rather, by understanding emotion.

Keller's exploration of Schoenberg's music was necessarily slower than of Britten's, because of the relative scarcity of performances. However, Schoenberg's 75th birthday in September 1949 brought a few more opportunities to hear his works. The London Contemporary Music Centre's birthday concert on 8th November featured the Op. 11 and Op. 19 piano pieces and the first

3 *Ibid.*

British concert performance of *Pierrot lunaire* since Erwin Stein's in 1942. The BBC broadcast this performance of *Pierrot* (twice) on its Third Programme and marked Schoenberg's birthday with several more programmes: a recital of his piano music on the day itself was followed by the Piano Concerto, the Violin Concerto and the Variations for Orchestra, plus broadcast talks and articles in the *Radio Times*. Of particular interest to Keller was the first British performance of the 1946 String Trio, broadcast on 14 January 1950 after repeated delays resulting from the difficulty of finding performers prepared to undertake it.[4] The London String Trio's performance was generally thought to be excellent – though Keller, while acknowledging it was 'technically superb', detected a certain lack of understanding: 'it was a bad sign, at any rate, that upon one's first hearing of this difficult work one often noticed decidedly wrong phrasings: would-be passionate scannings which scorned the thematic structures.' Nevertheless he conceded the performance had created an 'immensely powerful impression', agreeing with Edward Clark that 'no one present could doubt, even at a first hearing, that here was one of the masterpieces of contemporary chamber music.'[5] Still, the London critics did their best, with the *Telegraph* decrying the work as 'futile' and the *News Chronicle* comparing it to 'an assortment of statistics'. Keller ridiculed such comments with glee in his 'First Performances' column: 'I propose that we – musicians, musicologists, critics – offer this belated birthday present to Schönberg: to shut up in future unless insight bids us speak.'[6]

~

In addition to his regular work for *The Music Review*, Keller now joined Mitchell's team of reviewers, attending his first concert for *Music Survey* little over a week after their first meeting. The issue in which he first appeared (No. 5) also contained the first part of a substantial article by one of Schoenberg's American pupils, Dika Newlin, on 'Schönberg in America'. Ernest Chapman had given Keller her 1947 book *Bruckner, Mahler, Schoenberg*[7] to review for *Tempo*, but the article Keller had then written had been concerned more with her 'disturbing' omission of Franz Schmidt than with any of the title figures.[8] Now, on the other side of his Schoenberg epiphany, Keller read her new article with considerable interest, noting particularly her discussion of Schoenberg's idea of tonal 'regions', her insistence on his term 'pantonality' and 'the fact that the method

---

4 See correspondence between Kenneth Wright and Bomart Music Publications, 1949–50, WAC Schoenberg composer file 1.

5 Clark, 'Recent Schoenberg Performances', *MS* II/3 (Winter 1950): 181–2.

6 *MR* XI/1 (February 1950): 38–40.

7 (New York: King's Crown Press, 1947).

8 *Tempo* 9 (Autumn 1948): 28–9.

of composition with twelve tones does not exclude tonalities'.[9] Keller was and remained particularly interested in the relationship between dodecaphony and tonality, writing many years later that 'it is my submission that Schoenberg's plunge into atonality and its development into dodecaphony meant the banishment of tonal harmony – not, as he consciously thought, from his music, but from its foreground into its background.'[10]

Mitchell's next issue of *Music Survey* contained seven reviews by Keller, including a lengthy 'experiment in concrete criticism' on the February 1949 production of *Figaro* at Covent Garden: 'The following selection of criticisms will not always deal with what is most important, but rather with what has little chance of being discussed elsewhere,' he explained. 'And now, dear reader, open your score, and follow me right through the opera, particularly if you are engaged at Covent Garden.' In this issue, Keller's name was listed as a member of *Music Survey*'s editorial board. By the time that it went to press, however, things had moved on, as Keller told Sharp in his next letter:

21 February 1949 – to Geoffrey Sharp

Dear Sharp,

Many thanks for yours of the 11th. I was looking forward to your radio talk, but unfortunately I couldn't listen. Thanks for the tickets. Enclosed please find 1st instalment for May issue. Strawinsky's Orpheus will be included in the note on FIRST PERFORMANCES; may I also include the Mass (1st perf. in Engl.) again? I have heard all three broadcasts, and I'd like to criticize the performances, particularly since everybody approved of them. Also heard the Wellesz symphony, which is a very fine work: should be delighted to write it up. Shall I go to Wozzeck? Don't reply if not. I went to one of the Lunch Hour Concerts at the Wigmore Hall; the works first performed there were bad, so I wrote them up for Mitchell. Elsie Hall and Herman Salomon not worth space. Rang up Ibbs & Tillett today, re Press Tickets Bernac-Poulenc to-night. "Sorry, Press very restricted tonight." Should have liked to kick up a row, but didn't dare to, without your authority. But I'd like to say a few words on this incident in FIRST PERFORMANCES; one could then send them a copy – they ought to see MR once, anyway. <u>Carmen</u>: Curtthoys sent me tickets without my asking him; shall go & report. Payment: Yes, I quite understand.

Mitchell has asked me to co-edit MUSIC SURVEY with him. I consented on condition that my work for MR remains unaffected. Thus for instance, if I go to E'burgh & you don't, I'll do it for MR, not for MS. (In my

---

9 These passages are marked in Keller's copies of *Music Survey*.

10 'Schoenberg's Return to Tonality', *Journal of the Arnold Schoenberg Institute* V/1 (June 1981): 2–21.

forthcoming Film Music note in MS I'm referring the reader to MR as
often as possible.) And now for my first editorial request. For the first
number under the new regime (No. 7, Summer Issue, i.e. the one after
the next) we are planning a symposium on Britten. Against: Sharp; For:
Keller. We aren't very hopeful that you'll do it, but I think it would be
great fun. If you like the idea at all, I suggest that you first attack Britten's
work, and that I defend it. Thought this might suit you best; don't mind
doing it the other way round. For the rest – NO, unless I hear from you.

In the end, *Music Survey*'s 'symposium on Britten' was not published until the
spring of 1950, in the fourth issue to appear under the joint editorship of Mitchell
and Keller. Unsurprisingly, Sharp decided not to offer his views for dissection by
Keller, but the relationship between *The Music Review* and *Music Survey* was nevertheless a warm one. There were, however, clear differences in editorial policy
and character. *Music Survey* in its new incarnation was a journal with a mission:
'defence of great or substantial composers whom our musical world neglected'.[11]
As is shown in Keller's 'first editorial request' to Sharp, this defence was to be
couched in deliberately polemical terms. Both the mission and the polemical style
were Keller's. Although Mitchell had felt frustrated by what he called 'the awful
parochialism of English musical life, the complacent provinciality of the opinion-
makers', this had not hitherto coalesced into any explicit vocation for his journal –
indeed he confessed himself 'nonplussed if anybody asked me why in fact I
started the paper'.[12] Still, Mitchell's un-English taste in music had already begun
to give his journal a certain character: there were not many places in which one
could read an interesting article on Pfitzner at that date, or the unpublished letters
of Max Reger.

Another new feature after Keller's arrival was the ferocious editing, footnoting –
and often re-drafting – of its contributors' work. Although it was an editorial principle that writers should be chosen for their musical understanding above their
literary ability, Keller was still uncompromising about the writing, and where a
piece was deficient he and Mitchell simply rewrote it. The resulting style was
very different from the urbane elegance of *Music & Letters*, but it had a distinct
character of its own: a contemporary review described it as 'vivacious, sinewy and
free from waste. Undoubtedly one wants to read *Music Survey*, for its *bravura*, its
ungoverned cleverness, and (let us, too, be just) the large amount of scholarly and
musicianly comment that fills the spaces in between.'[13] Even Frank Howes was
indulgent, commending the lively style of its reviewing – though he also informed
its editors that while 'fine controversial frenzy' might be 'healthy for aesthetic
discussion', 'the same sort of treatment applied to reviewing transgresses the generally observed maxim that dog does not eat dog'.[14] Mitchell was fascinated by

11 *Music Survey: New Series*, preface.
12 *Ibid.*
13 'Notes and News: The Quarterlies', *MT* 92/1295 (January 1951): 38–40.
14 'Musical Journals: Some Newcomers', *The Times,* 3 March 1950, 7.

the way in which Keller's 'astonishing linguistic ability enabled him to look at English from the outside and perceive potentialities not immediately apparent to those whose mother-tongue English is'. Furthermore, 'everything had to be considered at the deepest level, from the content of a contribution to the distinction between commas Roman and italicized.'[15] There is an echo of Karl Kraus in the way that Keller's passion for ruthless accuracy even in the smallest of grammatical details acquired a kind of moral importance – it was part of his search for the truth. It was also part of the polemics: another stick with which to beat any opponent.

A classic example of this is his 1951 exchange with William Mann, a young critic who had been writing for *The Times* since 1948 (and who later succeeded Howes as 'Our Music Critic'). Mann had rather unwisely sought to take Keller to task for what he saw as *Music Survey*'s carelessness with the *Umlaut*, as follows:[16]

SIRS, – I write to you, as a writer in and reader of your periodical, about a point of typography. This is the *ummlaut* which you are so assiduously trying to eliminate.

The *ummlaut* is an honoured member of the German vocabularic family. Its ancestry, like that of the French circumflex accent, is irreproachable and its use invaluable. Sirs, you are now making away with it. Schönberg may well become Schoenberg – he himself, I believe, has now adopted this Americanized spelling. But another musician whose name frequently appears in your columns, Dr. Furtwängler, is to be spelt, by your decision, Furtwaengler. And the passage that leads from the development to the recapitulation of a movement in sonata form is spelt by your magazine, not *Rückführung*, but *Rueckfuehrung*.

This ugly typographical periphrasis cannot be caused by the want, in your typesetter's armoury, of a's and o's with ummlauts on top. In your last issue but two, Schütz was spelt as I write him here, in one notice, and, in another, according to your own quaint prejudice – Schuetz.

Sirs, the two spellings are not symphonious ; the symbol ü is acceptably, if not exactly, pronounced like a stopped *ee*, but *ue* must be pronounced *oo-e* in so explicit an alphabet as German.

What is the more important is that such spellings as *Muehlenraeder* and *Luenebuerger* look *unsightly*. Your magazine is designed to be *read*; let it not be an offence to the eye.

I am, Sirs,

Yours faithfully,

WILLIAM S. MANN

P.S. – What do you do about *Häuser*?

---

15 *Music Survey: New Series,* preface.

16 *MS* IV/1 (October 1951): 381–2. Mann's misspelling of *Umlaut* was an uncharacteristic error, in view of his excellent German.

2 July 1951 – to William Mann

Our respected contributor's attempt to write more than 250 words about nothing is completely successful ; less so his touching endeavour to teach me my mother-tongue. His observations on the *Umlaut* are in fact almost as well-founded as his spelling of the word itself. This was originally formed by Klopstock, and confined to its present meaning by J. Grimm in 1819. In any case, it means (as it says itself) sounds, not dots. There are three ways of spelling the *Umlaut:* (I) 2 dots, (II) a tiny "e" over, (III) an "e" after, the *umgelautet* vowel. Nowadays, No.III is admittedly *Ersatz* (used, for example, in telegrams) whose general recognition derives, however, from its more honourable history : it actually antedates No.I in nouns with initial *Umlaut*, and most persistently in such foreign (Latin and Greek) words as *Aedification, Aegide, Aera, Oeconomie, Oedem, Oenomanie, Oesophag*, etc. To suggest that "the two spellings are not symphonious" would therefore be inaccurate, even if Mr. Mann had chosen the right English word for what he wrongly means, namely, "homophonous." The German Latinist spontaneously speaks "*Caelius mons*," "*Asa foetida*," "*aegri deliria somni*" (never, of course, printed with ligatures) with *Umlauten*. The tendency to pronounce "ae," "oe" and even "eu" as *Umlaute* is wellnigh all-pervading, affecting as it does two-syllabled vowel sounds. Thus, although in 1915 *Duden* declares all No.III's to have been replaced by No.I's, and therefore spells the quadrisyllabic "*Aeronaut*" without the diaeresis (*Trennpunkte*) which Kiesewetter, in 1888, had applied, as a matter of course, to this word as well as to "*Lues*," both Schlessing-Wehrle and Brockhaus revert ruefully to "*Aêronaut*" in 1927 and 1935 respectively. Brockhaus adds "*Aêroplan*," but while the diaeresis distrusts Mr. Mann, the spoken language mistrusts both him and the dictionaries at variance with him : today, true to Duden, nobody writes or prints "*Aêroplan*," but, in defiance of Duden, everybody says "Äroplan;" the only person from whose throat I ever heard an *Aêroplan* emerge was a Hungarian.

The discrepancies in our typography are due to the recent enrichment of our printer's armoury : our remaining No.III's had previously been set up in type. I feel the only words wherein No.III could conceivably offend are proper names.[17]

ED.(H.K.)

---

17 Writing Schoenberg's name, Keller consistently used Schoenberg's own American spelling, as did *Music Survey* after he became co-editor. This was unusual in Britain at the time: the editors of most other journals and newspapers (including Geoffrey Sharp in *The Music Review*) imposed the spelling 'Schönberg' until the 1960s. (Quotations from printed sources in this book are given as originally published.)

P.S.– Previously we should have printed *Haeuser;* nowadays we put your two dots in the right place.

REFERENCES :– Brockhaus, F. A. (publ. & ed.), *Der Sprach-Brockhaus,* Leipzig, 1935. Duden, *Rechtschreibung der deutschen Sprache und der Fremdwörter,* 9th ed. (Wülfling, E., & Schmidt, A. C.), Bibliographisches Institut, Leipzig and Vienna, 1915. Kiesewetter, K. (ed.), *Fremdwörterbuch,* 7th ed. (Scholtz, A.), Glogau, 1888. Schlessing-Wehrle, *Deutscher Wortschatz,* 6th ed., Stuttgart, 1927.

The fact that Mann was also a contributor to *Music Survey* made no difference to Keller's reply, and there are frequent examples throughout the journal of public disagreement with its own writers. Even Geoffrey Sharp was not spared: having reviewed the Salzburg and Bayreuth Festivals for Mitchell and Keller, he found the printed version spattered with square-bracketed editorial inserts signed 'HK', taking issue with various things he had written.[18] 'PLEASE let Editorial footnotes to other people's contributions stop with the present issue,' wrote an exasperated Ernest Chapman – in a letter which was duly footnoted when printed in *Music Survey*: 'Editorial footnotes are either right or wrong – EDS.'[19]

The Editors (accompanied sometimes by their Editorial Board) also wrote letters of protest and correction to the editors of other journals – one particularly protracted correspondence was with Clinton Gray-Fisk of *Musical Opinion* over his review of the London Contemporary Music Centre's Schoenberg birthday concert: 'Our attention has been drawn to your critic's denigration of one of our age's most influential minds.' Amid a sweeping attack on Schoenberg's 'unintelligible' idiom (unpleasantly recycling Bax's 1943 comment about 'morbid growths emanating from the brains, rather than the imaginations, of a few decadent Central European Jews'), Gray-Fisk had described *Pierrot lunaire* as '612 bars of etiolated and emasculated shreds of sound represent[ing] the nadir of decadence'.[20] Gray-Fisk's readers had on this occasion ample opportunity to form their own opinion, for not only was the concert

> *What seems morbid music frees the feelings our morbidity makes us fear.*

---

18 See *MS* IV/2 (February 1952): 426–30 and Mitchell to Keller, 24 February 1952, CULHK.

19 *MS* II/4 (Spring 1950): 282. Chapman also took issue with the editors' policy of tolerating American usage: 'The next time that I read that a piece of music "totalizes seventy-two measures" I shall come round to Oakfield School with a loaded revolver, and if I die as well as you it will be well worth while.' Keller and Mitchell's policy on American language was set out in a note accompanying Konrad Wolff's obituary for Artur Schnabel (*MS* IV/2 (February 1952): 409: 'We have not anglicized this article because we do not think that American is just bad English.'

20 'London Contemporary Music Centre', *MO* (December 1949): 167–8, quoting Bax, *Farewell My Youth* (London: Longman, 1943), 21. Keller and Mitchell challenged Gray-Fisk to name 'a single Central European Jew, Schoenberg apart, who has taken a leading part in the development of twelve-tone music.' When Gray-Fisk responded with Berg, Webern and Krenek, he was duly informed by Keller and Mitchell that none of them was Jewish.

transmitted twice on the Third Programme, but a few days later the BBC broadcast of Schoenberg's own gramophone recording of *Pierrot*. Listeners thus had three opportunities to hear the work – their first since 1946, when the Third Programme in its opening weeks had included a late-night broadcast of the same recording.

Keller remembered very vividly that previous 1946 gramophone broadcast – and his own 'hostile' reaction to it. It was the first time he had ever heard the work, and he had then found it just as incomprehensible as did Gray-Fisk:

> The simultaneous absence of key and (in the 'speaking voice') of pitch was more than I could bear; both my sense of harmony and of true intonation were deeply offended. I remember wanting to smash the wireless set.[21]

The difference between his reaction then and Gray-Fisk's three years later, Keller would have said, is that Keller kept his to himself. The importance of – and difficulty of – knowing when you understand a piece of music (and not speaking publicly about it unless you do) was the subject of Keller's first editorial for the new *Music Survey*:

On Musical Understanding [extract]
MS II/1 (1949): 6–8, reprinted in *HKI*

To describe musical understanding to the musical is unnecessary; to explain it to the unmusical is impossible. [. . .]

How are we to know if and when we belong to the few who really understand? If and when we belong, we know. But we do not always know if and when we don't belong. An example from my own experience: I had been passionately in love with *Figaro* since my childhood. I had always been delighted with, indeed intensely moved by the sextet. I had every wrong reason to believe that I understood this piece completely, for I knew it inside out. Until one day I discovered that what I had known inside out was not much more than its outside. It had been an exhausting day; I arrived at the opera later in the evening, and on the verge of going to sleep. When I entered, the sextet was just starting, and now, for the first time, I heard everything it revealed and concealed. Its cogency, its universality, the heavenly resignation underlying this understatement of all that moves, divides and unites the world, the easy victory over deep tragedy that is its humour – it all overwhelmed me and, to be frank, I cried. From then onwards, I was convinced that the sextet was *Figaro*'s best number, and when some time later I read that Mozart himself thought so, my belief that I understood Mozart received a confirmation it did not need.

---

21 'How I got there'.

Now it is my understanding of, for instance, Mozart, which gives me a standard by which I judge what I understand and what I don't. I think that nobody should talk or write about music unless he has developed such a standard. That there is no further standard by which one can objectively ascertain the existence of one's criterion of understanding is unfortunate, but does not get us round the need for it. Doubtless the composer(s) on whose understanding our standard is based must be part of our lives. One trouble here is that one meets and reads people who have made a composer part of their lives while showing a none too exhaustive understanding of his music.

The other trouble is that once you have lived yourself into the music of one composer, your understanding of other composers may suffer, especially of those whose artistic tendencies are in some way opposed to the individual traits of your favourite. This risk does not simply stand in inverse relation to your musicality, but depends to a great extent on your character. The strongly original and revolutionary genius shows less broad an understanding for other composers than the more conservative and eclectic genius; otherwise, indeed, the former could not be revolutionary, nor the latter eclectic. Similar with the listener, according to whether or how far he tends to be single- or many-minded.

True understanding, therefore, is extremely rare. And true understanding of one thing is not a guarantee of understanding something else: as Keller put it elsewhere in this editorial, a major 'obstacle in the way of our understanding something is our understanding of something else'. The most musical of critics, therefore, could still be wrong – and, again, friends were not immune from being publicly admonished:

21 March 1950 – Letter to the Editor, *The Music Review*
MR XI/2 (May 1950): 168

Sir,

Obviously Mr. Robert Simpson's review of Schoenberg's Theme and Variations Op. 43a (MR XI/1/50, p. 67) is "the result of his failure to grasp Schoenberg's artistic aims." What to Mr. Simpson's ears are "arbitrary note-patterns" is music to ours. The proposition that Schoenberg's methods of composition "defy the acoustic relationships of sound" is strictly and provably meaningless. We fail to understand how one of this country's most capable writers on music, and indeed one of our own most valued contributors, can consider himself competent to review music which, on his own admission, he does not understand,

and how you, Sir, could see your way clear to print the outcome of his bewilderment.

Yours faithfully,

Donald Mitchell,
Hans Keller,
   Editors.
Robert Donington,
   Editorial Board.

When Geoffrey Sharp printed this in *The Music Review* he appended his own editorial footnote: 'Contributors to MR do not necessarily have to be, nor even to masquerade as knowalls. (ED.)'

~

Keller always said that behind all the polemic and belligerence of *Music Survey* was 'something which had nothing to do with aggression, which was sheer enthusiasm, musical enthusiasm for composers who were not yet recognized as being great'.[22] But it must be admitted that there was also sheer enthusiasm for the polemic itself. Controversy was a good way of getting the journal noticed and its arguments heard, as Keller was well aware. This was

> *Nothing is further from the truth of music than its partial understanding.*

a new policy to Mitchell, who had previously 'pursued a polite English tradition of not attacking colleagues'. But he now saw how effective provocation could be: 'Hans had taught me how to be usefully and legitimately impolite.'[23]

Keller's initial idea of a polemical 'Britten issue' was postponed when, in the first flush of his conversion to Schoenberg, another topical controversy caught his eye. Thomas Mann had published his novel *Doctor Faustus* in 1947, offending Schoenberg by his portrayal of the central character, Adrian Leverkühn, as the inventor of the twelve-tone method. Schoenberg wrote an aggrieved letter to the American *Saturday Review of Literature*, which was published, with a reply from Mann, on 1 January 1949. Keller was alerted to the dispute when both letters were reprinted in German in Melvyn Lasky's new American-German journal *Der Monat* in March – at which time Keller was preparing with Mitchell their first jointly edited *Music Survey*, which was to include an essay by Paul Hamburger on

22 *Music Survey: New Series,* preface.
23 *HKI,* 271.

Mann's novel: 'Thomas Mann's "Dr. Faustus" : A Contribution to the Philosophy of Music'. It made sense to follow this with something on the current controversy between Mann and Schoenberg.

One person with whom Keller would certainly have discussed all this was his old mentor, Oskar Adler, whose memories of Schoenberg in their youth now held a new immediacy. For years Keller had been hearing Adler talk about his great friend, but it was not until his own conversion to Schoenberg's music that he started paying proper attention:

> From the outset Adler told me a great deal about Schoenberg's early years, but since as a boy I did not understand Schoenberg's music, I was not particularly interested in his history, and did not listen very attentively. However, at later stages I tried to fill in the gaps in my knowledge, and, from his deathbed, Adler dictated (and sang) to me what one might call a shorter history of Schoenberg's youth.[24]

Adler had not seen Schoenberg since 1933 and although they had continued to correspond during the 1930s, they had lost touch during the war. In the spring of 1949, it was rumoured that Schoenberg was intending to visit Europe, having received all sorts of invitations for his 75th year, and Adler was delighted at the thought that he might see his old friend again.

Among the many European invitations Schoenberg received that year – from Germany, France and his native Vienna – was one from England: William Glock approached him to ask whether he would consider lecturing at the new Summer School of Music he was running at Bryanston in Dorset. The original idea for this Summer School had emerged during the first Edinburgh Festival in 1947, when the pianist Artur Schnabel had suggested 'a Summer School in which audiences could not only hear outstanding performances but also attend classes and lectures in order to deepen their understanding of music' – thinking, perhaps, of Salzburg's Internationale Sommer-Akademie, or his own summer master-classes at Tremezzo before the war. It was also Schnabel's suggestion that his former pupil Glock would be just the man to run it. After five years, the School transferred to Dartington, where for a while it was the most exciting and imaginative musical institution in Britain, the seed of the radical policies that Glock was later to pursue on the vast canvas of the BBC. In its first year at Bryanston in 1948, composition had been taught by Paul Hindemith and Nadia Boulanger. Hearing that Schoenberg was contemplating a visit to Europe in 1949, Glock wrote to see if he would teach at the second Summer School. Schoenberg seems to have taken the idea seriously, telling Glock as late as May that 'I hoped, until about a week [ago], that I can come and do this,' before reluctantly concluding that 'my health is not in such a state that I can dare to undertake such a trip.'[25]

---

24 'Schoenberg and the String Quartet', *Listener* 63/1621 (21 April 1960): 731. Adler died on 15 May 1955. The dictated history of Schoenberg's youth has not survived.

25 Schoenberg to Glock, 9 May 1949, ASC.

Keller first wrote to Schoenberg in April 1949, when it was still thought the composer would be coming over. Although his ostensible reason for writing was to ask permission to reprint Schoenberg's letter to Thomas Mann, an underlying motivation was to re-establish contact between Schoenberg and Adler:

25 April 1949 – to Arnold Schoenberg
In German. ASC

Dear Mr. Schoenberg,

I have read the controversy between you and Mann in 'Der Monat' and would like to reproduce it without comment in this magazine of which I have just become co-editor. May I therefore ask you for permission to publish your letter to the 'Saturday Review of Literature' again? And may I also venture to invite you to reply on your own behalf to Mann's answer to the Saturday Review? German or English as you wish; if you were to write in German, I would translate the letter and submit it to you for authorisation. I would hardly have dared to make this suggestion but Oskar Adler encouraged me although it didn't seem likely to him either that you would agree to it.

This brings me to the private part of my letter. Would it be possible for you to write a few lines to Oskar Adler? I think he would be incredibly pleased. He is himself contemplating the idea of writing to you, but knowing him as a letter-writer it would take an eternity for anything to happen, especially in view of the importance of the letter. On the other hand, a letter from you would make him very happy and give rise to a speedy reply. (As a musician I grew up in Adler's care and am a close friend of his.) His address is 11 St Matthew's Rd, Brixton, London, S.W.2. You could perhaps mention that I had given you his address in the letter in which I asked you for permission to publish the controversy.

And now another thing: could you possibly arrange for Adler to receive a copy of your String Trio Op 45? I gather from Dika Newlin's article in this magazine that it is not yet published; meanwhile perhaps there is a spare copy or perhaps in the interim it has already been published? We could then study it (I am Adler's violist) and perhaps perform it.

I thank you in advance for a speedy reply and remain with respectful greetings

Your Hans Keller

(the son of Grete Keller if you remember her)

His letter received a swift and positive reply. Schoenberg expressed himself 'particularly grateful that you have news of my friend Oskar Adler whose address I have sought in vain to find'.[26] He wrote to Adler ('My dear good old friend, I have not had an address for you for so long, and now at last I have a chance to write to you'), and Adler's delight was just as Keller had predicted: 'My dear, dear old friend, I am so profoundly happy to have a letter from you in my hands after so long.'[27] The minds of both men naturally turned to the past: in his long, affectionate letter to his old friend, Adler told him how much he was still in his mind:

> It is a sign of old age that memories of youth and our common adventures of that time are becoming so vivid. Recently I have been talking a lot about you and your life's work, and have told many anecdotes from the times of the cello and Polyhymnia and afterwards – so much so that it has repeatedly been suggested that I should put down some of these memories in writing. Now that I am in my 75th year, I am beginning to understand much of what I was unable to understand in the past.

This prompted Schoenberg to set down his own memories in writing, the result being his article 'My Evolution', in which he paid tribute to Adler, 'whose talent as a musician was as great as his capabilities in science. Through him I learned of the existence of a theory of music, and he directed my first steps therein. . . . All my acquaintance with classical music derived from playing quartets with him, for even then he was an excellent first violinist.'[28]

Schoenberg erroneously thought that he remembered Keller from the time of his residence in the Viennese suburb of Hietzing (where Schoenberg lived in 1910–11 in a flat belonging to Keller's mother), but it was in fact Keller's father whom he had met.[29] As to Keller's request to reprint the controversy with Thomas Mann in *Music Survey*, Schoenberg was more than happy to see his letter reprinted – indeed he had now been irritated further by Mann's publication of *Die Entstehung des Doktor Faustus* (especially its tribute to Theodor Adorno).[30] 'He now publishes this "Story of a Novel" and continues his unfair behaviour,' complained Schoenberg in a new article setting out his grievances, which he now sent to Keller for *Music Survey*. Keller's delight at this opportunity to publish a new piece of writing by Schoenberg was not unmixed with anxiety:

---

26 Schoenberg to Keller, 2 May 1949, ASC.
27 Schoenberg to Adler, 2 July 1949; Adler's reply is undated, ASC.
28 'My Evolution' was originally written in English; manuscript dated 2 August 1949. First publication in German was in the September 1949 editions of both the Berlin journal *Stimmen* and the Viennese *Oesterreichische Musikzeitschrift*. Schoenberg offered the English version to William Glock for *The Score* (Schoenberg to Glock 7 September 1949, ASC) but Glock did not publish it. Its first publication in English was in 1952, *MQ* XXXVIII/4 (October 1952): 517–27. Reprinted in *Style and Idea* (London: Faber, 1975), 79–92.
29 Keller's mother owned a house at 113 Hietzinger-Hauptstrasse, Vienna XIII, part of which comprised the apartment in which Schoenberg lived from 1910 until he moved to Berlin in the summer of 1911. See *MS* IV/3 (June 1952): 450.
30 Mann, *Die Entstehung des Doktor Faustus; Roman eines Romans* (Amsterdam: Bermann-Fischer, 1949). Adorno had been Mann's musical adviser during the writing of the novel.

I was really frightened to begin with. Schoenberg had written the article in German and I translated it. Some of it, however, was clearly libellous. So I had to rewrite little bits in order to keep just within the law of libel and, knowing Schoenberg's personality, I expected an outburst.[31]

Mitchell recalled that some of the phrases Keller had to ease out of the article were Schoenberg's description of Mann as a mere 'Tagschreiber' (journalist), and of his sentences as 'tapeworms'. On the other hand, Schoenberg's description of the Austrian musicologist Professor Richard Wallaschek as an 'idiot' was left in, once Keller had established that Wallaschek was no longer alive (so could no longer sue for libel).

26 June 1949 – to Arnold Schoenberg
In German. ASC

Dear Mr. Schoenberg,

Excuse the slight delay; I have literally had to work day and night of late. No, it wasn't me you remembered but my late father. I was only a little lad when you left Vienna; I am now 30.

You can hardly imagine my joy at the material you were good enough to send me. In order to be able to publish your observations in full now, I must give up my original plan to print the complete correspondence through lack of space. This doesn't matter, though; as you see, I have provided your report with some explanatory notes, and also the business has been talked about so much that the reader of a music magazine will be prepared for your additional observations. I have taken the liberty of deleting one or two words which could drag you and ourselves into a libel case. And if the idiot Wallaschek is not yet dead, we should regrettably also have to leave out this honorary title. I should be extraordinarily grateful to you if you could send me your approval of the translation very soon so that we can put your thoughts in the next number.

Your pupil was at Adler's yesterday but I still haven't spoken to Adler alone since then; so I only know that there would be a lot to relate. By the way, Adler is very much in agreement with my few introductory words to your observations; I hope you will be too. He will now write something for us about "Music and Geometry", comparing conic sections and musical forms. We can't wait for your trio; I hope it will arrive soon. For a while now we've been hearing that you're coming over here. Adler has already been looking forward to this very much: "And when

31 *Music Survey: New Series*, preface.

Schoenberg comes, we'll play the quartet which we started on when we were young, the early Mozart in G major." But I hear you're not coming, so for the time being I'll miss out on the opportunity to play quartets with Schoenberg.

A single hearing of the Second Chamber Symphony and the variations for organ made the most powerful impression imaginable on me; my 24-year-old colleague, Mitchell, the other joint editor of Music Survey, was also quite overwhelmed by the latter work. (He has not yet heard the Chamber Symphony.)

You wouldn't consider writing a few lines for our magazine once every quarter?* The reason I venture to make this suggestion is simply that if masters of music are rare, masters of music who can express themselves outside music in a masterly way are rarer still; this is why one must summon up courage to "tackle" such a one. At the same time, however, I know very well that you will most probably say "no", so please don't trouble to answer unless you contemplate doing it. Or one could do something like "Letter conversations with Arnold Schoenberg" in which you react briefly to various points I put to you, to the extent you find them worthy of comment. . . . . But, as I said, I am almost certain that you have neither the time nor the inclination for such things.

And if you do not have any time, please do not answer this letter at all but simply send me the translation back without comment – provided that you find it satisfactory.

With the most respectful good wishes,

Your

Hans Keller

*Or just once

Schoenberg sent back the translation immediately with a postcard, 'Okay, fine', and the article 'Further to the Schoenberg–Mann Controversy by Arnold Schoenberg' appeared in Keller & Mitchell's second issue of *Music Survey*. Mitchell was delighted with it: 'The more I read it the more I laugh,' he told Keller. 'It's a very comic piece. Excellent. I wish he'd write more some time. Don't forget to post a copy off to Thomas Mann. . . .'[32]

32 Mitchell to Keller, November 1949. Keller did send a copy to Mann: 'Would you believe', wrote Mann to Adorno, 'that Schoenberg has fired still another broadside at the book and at you and me?' Nevertheless, it prompted Mann to write again to Schoenberg, who finally buried his hatchet: 'Let us make do with this peace: you have reconciled me.' Schoenberg to Mann, 2/9 January 1950. Schoenberg, *Letters*, ed. Stein, trans. Eithne Wilkins and Ernst Kaiser (London: Faber and Faber, 1964), 278.

Keller and Mitchell's third *Music Survey* published the letter Schoenberg
had sent to his friends on the occasion of his 75th birthday, together with a survey of recent performances by Edward Clark, the Schoenberg pupil referred to
in Keller's letter above. Clark had been an extremely significant figure in the
reception of contemporary music in Britain in the inter-war years, doing more
than anyone in the country to promote Schoenberg's music hitherto. Born in
Newcastle, he had studied widely on the continent (including with Schoenberg
from 1910 until the outbreak of war), and as a result had a formidable network
of friendships with musicians all over Europe. In 1924 he joined the new British
Broadcasting Company, where his uniquely imaginative programming and profound knowledge of contemporary music was to have a defining effect on the role
of radio in British musical life. As time went on, however, and the BBC grew
into a more bureaucratic organisation, it became increasingly difficult to accom-
modate Clark's anarchic personality, and he left its staff in 1936, to his own regret
and the detriment of BBC music. By the time Keller met him, he was a somewhat
isolated figure, though still making significant, if only occasional, contributions
to radio programming, such as his Third Programme series 'Turning-Points in
Twentieth-Century Music', which ran from January to March 1948.[33]

19 November 1949 – to Arnold Schoenberg
In German. ASC

Honoured master,

Would you have anything against our publishing the letter to your friends
in the above magazine? I am not just thinking of the English translation
but also, if possible, a copy of the facsimile. If you have no objection could
you let me have your consent by return? Don't bother with a letter; an
air postcard – "OK" – will suffice.

As Adler has informed you, I spoke to the publisher Denis Dobson about
your new book.[34] He said he would write to you at once; you should
therefore have received his letter already.

By the way, Adler will probably be writing for the next number (in
which I so very much want to include your letter) about the twelve-tone
forum in "Music Today" to which you have also contributed. In the same
number we are publishing an article by Leibowitz on André Casanova.

Your very respectful

Hans Keller
(Joint Editor)

---

33 See Jennifer R. Doctor, *The BBC and Ultra-Modern Music, 1922–1936* (Cambridge: Cambridge
University Press, 1999) for details of Clark's BBC career.
34 *Style and Idea* (New York: Philosophical Library, 1950). In the event, its British publisher was
Williams & Norgate.

What caused the change in Keller's mode of address to Schoenberg (from 'Sehr geehrter Herr Schoenberg' to 'Verehrter Meister') is not known: perhaps his increasing familiarity with the circle of Schoenberg's friends was making him more aware of the composer's extreme sensitivity. Or perhaps it was a sign of special commitment to this remarkable genius; the next edition of *Music Survey*, in the spring of 1950, announced in no uncertain terms its future dedication to Schoenberg's work:

Schoenberg

As long as any great music needs partisanship we shall be found to be partisans. From now on, every issue of this journal will reserve space for the special subject of Schoenberg until, with our help or without, he has ceased to be a special subject. If we are the first who, while not members of the Schoenberg school, decide upon such constant support, this is Schoenberg's merit as well as a reminder of history at which we are ourselves, as it were, surprised. – EDS.

By now Keller was well in harness as co-editor – indeed he was from the start fully engaged with every aspect of the journal's production, partly because Mitchell was away from London for long periods during the first year of their collaboration. As a result, Keller was working furiously hard. 'Do *please* take care of yourself and don't work too hard. Let Music-Survey go to the devil. I'm sorry now that I left you so much to do,' wrote Mitchell guiltily from Switzerland as their second issue was being prepared back in London.[35] When he got back, Mitchell began a year's study at Durham University, which meant a lot of editing by correspondence:

November 1949 – to Donald Mitchell

Dear Don,

Thanks for yours of the 16th. You are an optimist. We'll never have everything in by Dec. 1st. Redlich, for instance, is just asking for more time, and I originally told him – early Dec. Nor do I want to rush him too much, as he does it for nothing (I wouldn't). But why should the

---

35 Mitchell to Keller, 5 September 1949, CULHK.

printer take 2 months? And what's the hurry, anyway? As far as I can see, the only publication-date which ought to be as early as possible is the summer one, and there is plenty of time for adjustment till then. For me personally, time is a problem too at the moment. And we want a bit of time for revising; quite a lot of the stuff coming in is badly written.

I'm furious about the "D" instead of "D flat" on p.102, l.14 of the new issue. The page proof has "D flat"! The "flat" (symbol) was apparently set, but didn't come out on this (as distinct from the page proofs') paper. If the passage made nonsense now, I wouldn't mind so much, but it makes bad sense. I shall try, in vain no doubt, to get a correction slip in, at the printer's expense; otherwise a corrigendum in the next issue, pointing out that the misprint was beyond editorial correction. That might teach him.

No reply yet from Philharmonia; I suppose I shall have to write again soon.

I have asked Milein to write about the sets of Salome; we shall see what she turns out.

Did I mention that Redlich will also write about the Beethoven (Pelican Symphony)?

At the moment I'm re-editing the Leibowitz; wonder what to do about the music exx. I think one could cut them out with a music ex. on front and back of each slip; could they be photographed that way? I'll try to do that & to touch them up where necessary; have a look at them then & tell me what you think? Have you anyone for copying music exx. (Simpson apart)?

I'm thinking of doing all my Covent Garden reviews tog. in a bunch, in order to save space.

No reply from Benjamin yet.

Britten issue: Milein made what I think is a marvellous drawing of Britten FROM BEHIND (conducting); Radio Times wouldn't have it because of unconventional position. Would it cost too much to have it as end piece, i.e. about half-page (as Milein suggests), and to have another of her Britten drawings as whole page? You won't hesitate to decline, of course.

Speaking of declining, a Cambridge College invited me to talk on any subject I liked – travel expenses only. I said no. Was I wrong?

Hope Adler will write his thing in spite of illness; I'll ask him tomorrow. Schoenberg, incidentally, has written about him in a German musical journal. Haven't seen it yet.

Basler Nachrichten sent me something over 3£ for all my articles so far! My financial situation is, for a change, desperate. This isn't an appeal – I can always borrow from my sister.

For the rest I'm not down. Shall write again soon.

As ever

[Hans]

Most of this refers to Keller and Mitchell's third joint issue in January 1950, though evidently the following two issues were also well under way. Redlich on Beethoven was part of a 'Symposium on a Symposium', an extensive joint review by fourteen different writers of the new multi-authored Penguin book on *The Symphony*, edited by Ralph Hill. This was intended for the Summer 1950 issue, before which was to come the long-planned symposium on Britten. Mitchell very much liked Cosman's drawing of Britten from behind, but in the end a side view of his conducting was used as the frontispiece – to much acclaim, according to Mitchell: 'I hear everyone cuts her drawing of Britten out and sticks it on their walls – there's fame for you.'[36] As well as asking some of their regular contributors (Paul Hamburger, Hans Redlich and Harold Truscott) to write on Britten, they sought contributions from some of Britten's close associates. Eric Crozier was approached for an article on the English Opera Group and E.M. Forster for something about *Billy Budd*, both of whom declined (Crozier felt he was 'too much of a fond parent'). 'Two months of pressure' from Keller eventually extracted a short note on the *Spring Symphony* from Britten himself, though when it came it was a disappointment: 'it was vapid. I think he felt in some way guilty about verbalising.'[37] 'Much better than nothing,' thought Mitchell; 'for advertising and general commercial policy it's a good thing that we have something of Britten's to put in.'[38]

The symposium was headed by substantial articles from both editors. Mitchell, discussing Britten's style in the context of his *St Nicolas* cantata, took as his starting point the Australian critic Stephen Williams's assertion that 'the world is still waiting for him to produce a genuine masterpiece, that will appeal to the heart as much as to the brain.' Keller's piece was also a defence of Britten against his critics – not arguing with specific examples this time, but exploring their possible psychological motivation.

Resistances to Britten's Music: Their Psychology [extract]
MS II/4 (Spring 1950): 227–236, reprinted in *EOM*,10–17 and *BB2013*, 34–44

This article is unfair. It attempts to explain hostility towards Britten's music on the assumption that from an intra-musical standpoint his

---

36 Mitchell to Keller, 6 May 1950, CULHK.
37 Quoted in Alan Blyth, *Remembering Britten* (London: Hutchinson, 1981), 88.
38 Mitchell to Keller, 27 February 1950, CULHK.

major works are largely unassailable. Thereby many a respected colleague's unfavourable opinion of Britten is countered below the musical belt. Since, however, for me there is no doubt about Britten's greatness which indeed I tried to imply in a previous study ('Britten and Mozart'), I have no honest choice for my line of intellectual action. [. . .]

II. INDIVIDUAL PSYCHOLOGY : THE POLYCRATES COMPLEX
Timeo Danaos et dona ferentes. Virgil, Aeneis II, 49.

The term "individual psychology" is here used not in its factious sense, *i.e.* as denoting the theories of Alfred Adler in opposition to those of Freud (psychoanalysis) on the one hand and Jung (Analytical Psychology) on the other, but simply as distinct from "social" or "group" psychology. Under the present heading, then, we have to consider which mental forces, other than those determined by its sociological and historio-geographical context, are likely to oppose Britten's music. [. . .]

Now what are the reasons why even many otherwise understanding musicians refuse to be drawn into Britten's net, why they regard not only his lucky stardom, but even the most immediately striking of his musical endowments and attainments – his effortless ease and productiveness, his supreme craftsmanship, brilliance, virtuosity, his spontaneity, inventiveness, cleverness, agility, versatility, not to speak of his so-called "eclecticism" (always demonstrably individual) – with the gravest suspicion, as if these qualities were in themselves defects and went to prove an absence of the inner, the deep, the lasting? [. . .]

Britten's most obvious qualities all imply an overmeasure of good and easy artistic fortune – partly really, partly seemingly. From the extra-musical (psychological as well as merely material) gains which he derives from his talent for popularity, to the intra-musical comfort (fearfully overestimated by the outsider) of his "taking the gifts of his epoch, intact, and as self-evident matter, utilizing them at his will," of "shuffling [them] like a pack of cards" (as Lang says of Mozart), of his "yielding to an influence quite ingenuously, quite in the feminine fashion" (as Einstein says of Mozart), Britten's gifts convey the exceptional impression of being gifts: of his not having to pay for them.

Surprisingly perhaps, Britten's own reactions to his exalted position do not in psychological essence appear to differ greatly from those of his detractors: he does not seem altogether alive to his genius – he clearly has ideas below his station. Bach could be unaware of his genius; Mozart stood at the border of genius's self-knowledge; Beethoven, with his character behind him and 19th century history before him, ruthlessly invaded the realm of self-cognition. At the present, over-conscious stage of our culture it is not easily possible for talent or genius not to be fully conscious of itself and its significance, unless strong endopsychic resistances put a stop to self-recognition. That Britten's mind would seem to harbour these can be gathered not only from his extreme modesty, but also from the fact that just as his depreciators minimize the value of his various "lucky" qualities, so he minimizes the part they play in his art and doubtless overestimates the contribution of his hard and regular work.

[...]

The human "need for punishment" (*Strafbeduerfnis*) was discovered by Freud, who showed it to be the result of tensions between ego and superego. [...] To Prof. Flugel we owe the delineation and delimitation of the whole complex that roots in the need for punishment, and also a telling and colourful label – quite in the psychoanalytic tradition:–

> If we do not experience sufficient pain, if things go too well with us and we have too much luck, we begin to feel uneasy because our need for punishment has not been met. Hence at bottom the fear of Hubris, of arrogance or 'uppishness,' which the ancient Greeks, themselves a relatively guilt-free people, were yet able to discern as a fundamental trait [...] I would suggest that it be called the Polycrates complex, after Polycrates the tyrant of Samos. . . .

It was for instance, I believe, the Polycrates complex which was responsible for Oscar Wilde's fate: unable to tolerate his easy and complete success on the one hand and his amoralistic philosophy on the other, it drove him by every available means – *i.e.* both through his offences and his subsequent behaviour – into one of the most savage forms of self-punishment great talent has ever meted out to itself. [...]

III. SOCIAL PSYCHOLOGY : GROUP SELF-CONTEMPT
Paepstlicher als der Papst sein. (German saying)

Britten's work meets with far more understanding and far less resistance abroad than in his own country. The proverb "*Nemo propheta in patria*" springs to mind [...]

In the investigations which Margaret Phillips and I have undertaken into the psychology of small social groups (and on which each of us has so far given only a preliminary report) I encountered, in the diary of an Auxiliary Fire Brigade's group life during the war, a social psychological attitude to which I have given the somewhat unprecise name of "group self-contempt", and which seems to me to make its invariable appearance in any group as soon as certain clearly definable conditions are fulfilled. [...]

A group is dominated by another group in superior position: women by men, Jews by Gentiles, prostitutes by society and so on. Since the dominated group inevitably feels the dominating group to be *in loco parentis*, the former's members project part of what might loosely be called their common superego on to the dominating group, with the result that they turn part of the aggression which they would but can't release towards the dominating group back against their own group. [. . .]

British anti-Brittenism is, I submit, a prominent aspect of British musical group self-contempt, though in this case the dominating group which, together with the contempt it displays, ("Das Land ohne Musik"), serves as a model for the group-self-contemptuous attitude, has its centre — the bulk of the Austro-German tradition's exponents and followers — in the past and only its periphery — the Adornos — in the present. But while this self-contempt can be heard at work in many English compositions themselves, it does not readily direct itself against the more exclusively English composers who have developed at a safe distance from Austro-German techniques, so that they are not so easily felt to offend against them.

Having developed the notion of 'group self-contempt' during the war, what prompted Keller to apply it now to British musicians was the press reaction to the premiere of Britten's *Spring Symphony* – specifically two articles in the *Listener*: one previewing the broadcast and one reviewing it. He thought it significant that Scott Goddard's preview had chosen to concentrate on 'Britten as an Instrumental Composer', tracing his progress from the 'seed' of the early Sinfonietta, to Sinfonia (da Requiem) and Symphony. The *Spring Symphony*, thought Goddard, 'sounds as though it may be the kind of work that would call forth the composer's finest style of orchestral writing. It is rumoured that as well as the vocal numbers this new symphony contains a number of purely orchestral movements.' It seemed clear to Keller that such 'rumours' were fuelled by a deep desire for the work to be a 'proper' symphony – a theory confirmed by Dyneley Hussey's review two weeks later, expressing 'disappointment that Britten has not given us the true symphony which his extraordinary musical gifts should enable him to produce'.[39]

This kind of writing led Keller to reflect on the significance for British musicians of 'the Austrian honorary degree "Symphony"'. The form was seen as the supreme achievement of the Austro-German tradition, and conquering it of paramount importance in laying to rest the ghost of 'das Land ohne Musik'. (One might note in this context the increasingly symphonic nature of post-war British concert programmes and the large number of symphonies composed by mid-century British composers.) A symphony by Benjamin Britten would have had particular resonance: he was already the conqueror of another 'foreign-owned'

39 Goddard, 'Britten as an Instrumental Composer', *Listener*, 7 July 1949, 40; Hussey, 'Broadcast Music: Song-Cycles', *Listener*, 21 July 1949, 123–4.

form – opera – so it is not surprising there were half-conscious hopes that the *Spring Symphony* might be another *Peter Grimes*.

In the event, the disappointment that the work had, in this sense, not lived up to the promise of its name led in a curious way to a more positive press than might otherwise have been the case, thought Keller, who suspected that Britten's critics were determined to find fault one way or another with his presumption. Had their group self-contempt *not* been able to deny the work the title of 'symphony', Britten's consequent success would have been unbearable: the Polycrates complex would then have required there to be something else wrong with the work. As it was, the critics' praise of everything except its title was revealing: 'The reactions to the "Spring Symphony",' wrote Keller, 'offer some insight into the possible interaction of the individual and social psychology of resistances to Britten: group self-contempt having ascertained beyond doubt that not all is well with the work, the Polycrates complex is appeased.'

Towards the end of his article, Keller speculated briefly on what the future might hold. Noting that British musical self-contempt 'takes its orders from Vienna's past' rather than the present, he thought he detected 'subtle signs that British musical developments are about to exert a powerful influence on Vienna, so that in the not too distant future we may get the reverse spectacle: Austrian group self-contempt with the renascent English tradition as dominating group'. Of course at this date Keller's view of Austrian psychology was necessarily conditioned by the fact that he – and all the Austrian musicians he knew – had by now been away from Austria for more than a decade.

After Keller became a British citizen in 1948 the possibility of international travel became open to him again. He did not immediately apply for his passport, however, and although the rest of his family had a continental holiday in 1949, he did not accompany them. Milein Cosman also travelled abroad twice in 1949. Her first trip was in June, through Germany to Vienna, where her brother Cornelius had settled with his family. She went with a commission from the Viennese émigré George Weidenfeld for his new magazine *Contact*, to make a pictorial record of the devastated German cities through which she travelled – not an easy assignment for Cosman's first visit back to her home country. On her return to Britain, she joined Keller at the Edinburgh Festival, on which he was reporting for *The Music Review* and she was drawing for *Heute*, the US-sponsored German illustrated magazine. The following month she was back in Germany with another commission from *Heute* for portraits of the members of the first post-war government of the Federal Republic in Bonn.[40]

40 'Skizzen aus Bonn', *Heute*, 9 November 1949.

According to Cosman's biographer, Ines Schlenker, she toyed at that time with the idea of seeking more work outside England. She also 'relished her continuing pre-war friendships,' and the question of whether to go back to Germany must have occurred to her, especially after her parents decided in 1949 to return to Dusseldorf. But she did not seriously consider it, because of 'Hans's adamant opposition to going back to his own country' – this, says Schlenker, 'put an end to all thoughts of leaving England.'[41] At first Keller did not seem eager even to pay a visit – particularly not to Vienna itself. And so while his family, and Cosman, and close associates like Donald Mitchell and Geoffrey Sharp all travelled to the continent in 1949, Keller remained at home.

In February 1950, however, he received a letter from Guido Gatti, editor of the Italian journal *La Rassegna Musicale*, manager of Lux Films and secretary-general of the Maggio Musicale Fiorentino, the festival of music held in Florence each May. Gatti wanted advice about the congress on 'Music and the Cinema' being held as part of the festival, for which preparations were woefully behindhand. According to a review of the festival in *The Spectator*'s June issue, 'it was not until last February that the Comune of Florence knew definitely that the State would, as usual, provide half the financial backing for the Maggio Musicale, and consequently the festival this year has a certain haphazard air.' Time was short, and Gatti needed help in assembling a suitably prestigious international body of delegates.

He could scarcely have found a better guide than Keller to the world of British film music, nor a more stimulating source of ideas. Gatti wanted to know what 'you would want a Congress on Film Music to discuss, and who, among the invited, could best deal with it'. But first, there was the question of whom to invite:

> Among British musical men, I thought of inviting the following composers: W. Walton, A. Bliss, and Anthony Hopkins; the director David Lean; and the conductor M. Mathieson. Should these men accept the invitation to the Congress, do you think that British film music would be adequately represented? Or are there other important and dynamic names that should be included?[42]

Keller supplied a list of potential personnel to supplement Gatti's:

February 1950 – to Guido Gatti [extract]

BENJAMIN FRANKEL	brilliant at conferences
ALAN RAWSTHORNE	a pessimist as to the possibilities of film music; may therefore be able to contribute stimulating criticism.

---

41 Schlenker, *Milein Cosman: Capturing Time* (London: Prestel, forthcoming).
42 Gatti to Keller, 6 February 1950, CULHK.

VAUGHAN WILLIAMS	should be invited tho' he won't come
BERNARD STEVENS	very articulate
MATYAS SEIBER	" "
WILLIAM ALWYN	enormous film-musical experience
CONSTANT LAMBERT	thoughtful
Further possibilities:	Arthur Benjamin, Richard Arnell, Clifton Parker, Arnold Bax, Lennox Berkeley, Norman del Mar (has written music for short films; deeply cultured musician, brilliant talker. Conductor by profession), Brian Easdale, Alan Gray – all of whom would make valuable contributions.

I suggest you write to the first seven whether (a) they would like to submit suggestions for papers they would care to read; (b) whether they would be willing to do a paper on a subject suggested by the Congress. (For possible subjects, see my SUBJECT LIST which I shall send anon.)

(b) Film-musical Directors

ERNEST IRVING	the Ealing counterpart to Mathieson
HUBERT CLIFFORD	Korda Group

(c) Director

PAUL ROTHA	Documentary director with special interest in film music

(d) Musicologist

WILFRID MELLERS	Composer and researcher with special interest in film music. Exceptionally perspicacious. He will be responsible for the article AMERICAN AND CONTINENTAL FILM MUSIC in the forthcoming (5th) edition of Grove's Dictionary (while I shall be doing the article on BRITISH FILM MUSIC). A paper from him might be more valuable than from many a composer.
HUNGARY: LASZLO LAJTHA	An absolute necessity. Not only a first-rate film composer, but an original thinker on the aesthetics of film music.

AMERICA: ROZSA: I don't see much point in inviting him. Except for a few ideas (e.g. in "Spellbound") which show what he might have become, he seems to produce nothing but hack. You might in fact just as well invite Max Steiner. There wouldn't be much common ground between such people and the musicians you have in mind. Why not rather invite:

(a) HANNS EISLER, author of <u>Composing for the Films</u> (New York, 1947), and

(b) ERNEST TOCH?

FREDERICK W. STERNFELD,   an able writer on film music should I think also be invited

RUSSIA: PROKOFIEV

ITALY: RENZO ROSSELINI,   Roberto Rosselini's brother, will, I hope, be able to attend. I don't know all his (88) film scores, but I have found his approach remarkable in more than one case.

A couple of days later, Keller followed this letter with a lengthy list of subject suggestions, including 'Film music and its audiences', 'Film music criticism', 'Possibilities of new forms and textures of dramatic music' and 'Problems of harmony and tonality'. He particularly urged Gatti not to neglect the latter: '<u>Problems of Harmony and Tonality</u> are very widely neglected, both practically and theoretically. Diatonicism & chromaticism, monotonality – extended tonality – pantonality, the relation between tonal and dramatic structures, the integration between dramatic relations and key-relations, the use of what I have called "Leitkeys" and "Leitmodulations", the question of when to use concentric and when progressive tonality (there's a lot of arbitrary progressive tonality in film music, even in otherwise responsible scores) are among the many aspects which require examination.'

Gatti also asked Keller's advice on 'any British films that might be interesting from a musical point of view, whether for their artistic or technical achievements', to which Keller responded with another detailed list, giving his reasons for the selection of each film. In Walton's 1948 score for *Hamlet*, for example, he recommended the Players' Scene for the way in which its 'alternation, within one and the same piece of music, of realistic period music with "background" music points the way to new forms of dramatic music'. He also thought the 'Fugato introduction and background to soliloquy "Oh that this too too solid flesh" is a model of melodramatic texture. Speech entry is felt as logical element in unfolding of texture, and the music preceding this entry makes it possible for the listener to take in the succeeding background music in spite of the speech, since the background entries offer him known quantities.' He recommended Alwyn's *The Rocking*

Horse Winner (1950) for the 'excellent thematic treatment of the rhythm of the most important sentence in the dialogue', Bernard Stevens's *The Upturned Glass* (1947) for its 'tonal build-up' and its 'key-relations mirroring relations between protagonists' and Benjamin Frankel's *London Belongs to Me* (1948) for its 'skilful construction and manipulation of Leitmotivs (cf. combination of landlady- and fake-motifs)', noting also the 'integration of hero's whistling of theme song with background music (a device of which Frankel is fond)'.

Gatti was delighted to receive such a thorough response and immediately added Keller to the list of speakers to be invited, suggesting that he speak on 'Featured Music: Classical Quotations'. Thus it turned out that Keller's first trip abroad after the war was to Florence. Cosman travelled there ahead of him: they had both secured commissions from various journals, including a joint one for an illustrated piece on the city and its festival: 'Florence the Fabulous'.[43] The British delegation to the conference, as it was finally constituted, comprised the composers Alan Rawsthorne, Benjamin Frankel and Antony Hopkins, director Jack Lee and critics Wilfrid Mellers and Keller himself. (Mellers was unfortunately prevented from travelling at the last moment, and his paper was read for him by Hopkins.)

As agreed, Keller's paper examined 'Featured Music', which he defined as 'any piece, complete or interrupted, which is not only perceived as accompaniment, but identified as something else. It may be recognized as quotation, imitation, pasticcio, caricature, or on the other hand so-called "realistic" or "stage" music, by which the sound track lets you hear what you [see].' Taking issue with the film historian John Huntley's definition of featured music as music which is 'not an integral part of the film itself, but which emerges as a unit of its own', Keller insisted that integration was aesthetically essential, and took his audience through

At the 'Music and the Cinema' international congress in Florence, 1950.
L to R: Hans Keller, Benjamin Frankel, Alan Rawsthorne.

43 *Illustrated*, 15 July 1950, 40–43.

a series of positive and negative examples, from William Walton's successful period music in *Hamlet* to Lionel Newman's painful use of Mozart's Clarinet Quintet in *Apartment for Peggy*.[44]

At the end of his lecture Keller turned unexpectedly to Mozart's Quartet in C, K.465 for a supreme example of the kind of integration he was looking for:

Featured Music [extract]

A great deal remains to be learnt from Mozart in the handling of featured music. I am not merely thinking of his realistic stage music, but also of his use of cliché. For a cliché, a familiar quotation without quotation marks, a phrase which is not only perceived as phrase but identified as time-honoured formula, can be considered a similarly special case of "featured music" as a quotation itself. We all know this galant cliché which dates from the time of Christian Bach: –

In 1785, about five years after the galant half-century had drawn to its close, when every musician must have recognized the cliché as such, Mozart "featured" it most prominently at the end of the second subject stage of the C major quartet's finale:

Mozart K.465 finale, 85–95

---

44 Keller's talk covered some of the same ground as his first film music article for *Music Survey*, 'The Question of Quotation', *MS* II/1 (1949): 25–7, reprinted in *HKFM*.

We feel that nothing could be further from a cliché than this cliché as it is here utilized. Thematically it grows necessarily, yet surprisingly, out of the preceding semi-quaver passage; texturally, it takes an – I think – unprecedented single-line course, in order to form a transition, without modulation, from G major to E flat major, thereby assuming an undreamt-of harmonic function. Over the tight-rope of a cliché Mozart dances to the flat submediant. He avails himself of the very fact of the cliché for integrating it in the most original manner. For only on the basis of its familiarity could he invest this phrase with a formal significance so overpoweringly unfamiliar; only in view of the fact that a cliché is potentially unorganic, hostile to unity, could he make it so astoundingly organic. Mr. President, I submit that here is – en miniature and in bare aesthetic principle – an ideal for the integration of any music which runs the risk (to revert to Huntley's words) of 'not being an integral part of the film itself.'

> Art arises where the arbitrary and the predictable are superseded by unpredictable inevitability.

Keller's paper was followed by the appearance of the sole representative of Hollywood, Daniele Amfitheatrof, a Russian-born Italian composer who had been resident in America since 1937, producing music for a large number of films. According to Keller, he presented 'a collection of excerpts from Hollywood sound hacks which – with the exception of Aaron Copland's excellent score for "Of Mice and Men" – couldn't have been worse'. 'Reactions threatened to be polite,' until Benjamin Frankel stood up and 'delivered *ex abrupto* fireworks on Amfitheatrof's excerpts in particular and Hollywood music and orchestration in general' – much to the delight of both Keller (who had long been a scourge of Hollywood music) and the majority of the conference. 'Great excitement: practically all European delegates took Ben's side,' Keller noted with satisfaction. Still, this episode provided the sole flurry of controversy at a Congress that in Keller's opinion 'suffered almost throughout from soliloquies that, however worthy in themselves, didn't need a Congress: they could have been published at lesser cost'.[45]

Although Keller felt that he might just as well have read the Congress papers at home, his trip to Florence had other compensations, the 'most rewarding' being the first stage performance of Luigi Dallapiccola's opera *Il Prigionero*. From what he had heard of his music in London, Keller already thought Dallapiccola 'an astounding genius',[46] and the new work did not disappoint him.

---

45 See Keller's accounts of the conference: 'XIII Maggio Musicale Fiorentino', *MR* XI/3 (1950): 210–12, and 'The First Film Music Congress', unpublished draft, CULHK. For an example of Keller's opposition to Hollywood music, see 'Hollywood Music: Another View', *Sight and Sound* 16/64 (Winter 1947–48): 168–9, reprinted in *HKFM*, 36–41.

46 *MR* X/1 (February 1949): 40–42.

XIII Maggio Musicale Fiorentino
MR XI/3 (August 1950): 210–12

The dodecaphonic *Il Prigionero* was composed between 1944 and 1948. Its marked individuality makes the study of certain general contemporary tendencies manifesting themselves in it an all the more fascinating task. First of all, it strongly draws upon sado-masochistic energies just as – to take one of its extreme opposites in well-nigh every other respect – the Stravinsky *Mass*. Indeed the story itself – a prisoner of the Spanish Inquisition is tortured, before his execution, with the illusion of liberty – could not more fairly equilibrate intense sadism and masochism. Secondly, the twelve-tonal structure not only gives prominence to common chords, but in fact employs a well-defined diatonic ingredient as prominent means of unification. Thirdly, this diatonic element corresponds to what, as I have often pointed out, is one of the strongest and most widely active tendencies in contemporary tonal music: the semitonal shifting of keys. In the first of the three scenes which succeed the prisoner's mother's prologue, the transition, not always immediate, between the B minor and C minor chords appears as the first episode's binding factor, both triads being repeatedly sustained; and it soon becomes clear that we are here confronted with a central motto- and Leit-progression and -modulation, though not of course always on the same degrees: before the end of the first scene, for instance, where the prisoner escapes from his cell, we get an F minor – F sharp minor transition. The succeeding, and only orchestral interlude develops the motto-progression with considerable insistence, while in the short third scene (just over 5 minutes), where the prisoner has escaped into a garden and his hopes reach their zenith, the motto plays its role at first more unobtrusively than at any previous stage; it is only when the Great Inquisitor appears, "embracing" and recapturing the prisoner, that it emerges again into the foreground. And just before the tragic end, the solo violin gives a linear version of the motto: C– D♭–C–D♭. The opera does not end diatonically, though there is a vague allusion to the orientation of F. Incidentally, the very end is least convincing; one has the suspicion that the composer did not know how to finish. The intermezzos between prologue and first scene and between the second and third scenes are choral; the third scene is the only one within and throughout which the chorus (always invisible) is used. The greatest part of the work is immensely expressive and impressive as long as you don't look at the stage, for if you look you don't see what you hear: the "action" chiefly consists of the drama of the prisoner's inner life. I have not met a musician who did not object to the untheatrical character of the piece. The composer is said to have declared in defence that the future of opera lies in the subjective drama. This notion has been ridiculed. Both sides are, I think, right and wrong. The subjective drama probably has a future in opera. But the endopsychic conflicts must be sufficiently projected into, and personified in the outside world of the stage to make a visible story. It will at the same time be realized that *Il Prigionero* would be ideally suited for the Third Programme.

In Florence Keller met Dallapiccola, who offered him a recent article he had written on the finale of *Don Giovanni* – in which he located 'the first example of expressionism in opera' in the Statue Scene. The piece had just appeared in *Rassegna Musicale*, but Keller swiftly secured Gatti's agreement to its republication, and Deryck Cooke translated it for *Music Survey*. Dallapiccola had been prompted to write on *Don Giovanni* after coming across an observation by Heinrich Jalowetz about the series of ten different notes at the beginning of the development section of Mozart's G minor symphony.[47] 'Of course, it did not need Jalowetz's acute observation to convince me of the audacity of Mozart's genius,' he wrote, but it had stimulated him to think more about Mozart's anticipation of the modern – an idea that chimed very much with Keller's own thinking, although he considered Dallapiccola wrong to speak of the G minor symphony passage as a 'series of ten notes'. What was important about this passage, as Keller later described it, was not the tonal (and rhythmic) disintegration that these ten different notes in succession produced, but the *re-integration* of the structure by means of the strict serial use of a three-note row (diminished fourth and diminished seventh).[48]

~

Donald Mitchell greeted Keller's return from Florence with a long letter from Durham detailing all the work still needed on the summer issue of *Music Survey* – and how urgent it all was – in six pages of his best illegible scrawl ('I'm sure you detest long letters').[49] To make matters worse, Keller found when he got back to Herne Hill that his mother had taken the opportunity of his absence to do a little spring cleaning:

8 June 1950 – to Donald Mitchell

Mostly dear and partly definitely damned Joint,

Your letter caused the expected heart attack, but since I do not wish to waste time over formalities, I shall not enlarge upon the route by which

---

47 Jalowetz, 'On the Spontaneity of Schoenberg's Music', *MQ* XXIX/4 (October 1944): 385–408.
48 See 'Strict Serial Technique in Classical Music', *Tempo* 37 (September 1955): 12–24, reprinted in *EOM*, 169–78.
49 Mitchell to Keller, 5 June 1950, CULHK.

you may go to hell. Take my mother with you, though: with the best of intentions, she cleaned and "cleared" my rooms. They're very pleasant in that I can move and sit at my desk and so on, but despite (because) her organisation I CAN'T FIND A THING. I literally spent hours to find Dickinson, for instance; same with Symposium.

To your beloved points. I hope Goldbeck will send his promised Florence report in time, but I wouldn't rely on it. If the stuff doesn't arrive, I'll do something, damn it and everything. Dickinson enclosed. Chased Hamburger. I wrote to Reich from Florence but since he didn't reply (he always does) I fear he never got my letter. The Italian post is moody: I never received the present issue of MS which Kath sent by air mail, and another chap at the Congress got an important (and, I believe, registered) letter of his lost too. Yes please drop Redlich a note re Ariadne. Perhaps it's good even that we save up Reich for something else, maybe Schoenberg (section). Which brings me to (a) my having lost or mislaid Amis's Verklaerte Nacht rubbish (rang him & asked him for copy so that I may attack him; he can't find one at the moment; shall write Tribune); (b) my not knowing that chap Nachod's (the Gurrelieder man's) address or number; Dobson knows it but I just hear he's still in Italy; my mother knows it too maybe but she's in Oxford at the moment. Who's got the letter we sent to N.S. & N., you or I or both? I have the corrected Symposium proofs, or most of them anyway. Shall check anon what's missing. Truscott on Schumann reached me (enclosed); Wood on Sibelius not. No report from Germany so far, I hear the "Stimmen" are giving up, which is probable, since they were so good. Aldeburgh: Don't know, don't think I'll have time. In fact I have doubts about Cheltenham too. It's absurd: one is a music critic and hears everything except the things one wants to hear. Yes, we'll certainly add a footnote to the Symposium, as suggested by Denis. Don't be annoyed with Capell: do you expect him not to be? And while his tendentious "summary" of my article is terribly misleading, even an objective one would be, within that space. Yes, Searle on Webern. Extremely sorry about dentist. I know what it's like. But then we're toughs, says the cretin. Esther's letter (v. good) appeared in MO. And once again they touched the matter (& her in particular) in their editorial. Enclosed please find one thing or the other. Didn't tell you about Dallapiccola article yet: I'm v. glad, aren't you? I talked with him & then wrote to Gatti. I suppose we've got the relevant number of Rassegna?

The rest of this letter is missing, but this fragment gives a good picture of the hectic life of a *Music Survey* editor. Mitchell was not due back from Durham until 21 June – 'tell your mother to have coffee ready on the 22nd' – after which there would be a very short time to get the journal out before the holiday season. Keller's 1950 holiday was to be a significant trip: his first visit to Austria since the war. He went to Salzburg, to review the Festival – but despite staying in Austria for five weeks did not go back to Vienna. Over the next few years he went regularly to Austria, but only to Salzburg in the summer and Tyrolean ski resorts in the winter. Given Cosman's brother's residence in Vienna, this does appear to have been a deliberate – and most understandable – avoidance of his old home.

A few weeks before he left for Salzburg, Keller received a letter from Professor John Carl Flugel, the inventor of the Polycrates complex, who had 'read with much interest your most suggestive article on Britten's music':

> I was particularly struck by the relationship you tried to establish between 'Group Self Contempt' and the Polycrates Complex, and am very glad you have been able to make such profitable use of this latter concept of mine. . . . Your own concept of 'Group Self Contempt' is certainly a very illuminating one in the whole domain of group psychology and I look forward to further contributions from you on this important subject. . . . It occurs to me that if you are prepared to develop this last mentioned theme at some greater length, it might be an interesting subject to discuss at some future meeting of the Social Psychology Section of the B.P.S.[50]

This was followed by an invitation from the British Psychological Society to lecture on Musical Self-Contempt in Britain on 4 November. One of Keller's tasks during his Austrian visit, therefore, was to develop his ideas on the relationship between Austrian and British musicians by observing it from the Austrian side.

> *The relation between art and psychology is not without friction: the psychologist envies the artist; the artist fears the psychologist.*

Keller had been thinking more about British musical group self-contempt while he was in Florence, having spent time at the conference with Alan Rawsthorne – a composer whose music 'seems to be quite un-English, not to say anti-English', and in whom, Keller thought, group self-contempt had actually been a positive force. Another composer whose group self-contempt had served his creativity well was Elgar, whose unusual position in the history of English music Keller had been prompted to consider by an intriguing remark of Wilfrid Mellers, the 'exceptionally perspicacious' critic he had recommended to Gatti.[51]

Musical Self-Contempt in Britain [extract]
BPS lecture, 4 November 1950, reprinted in *HKM&P*

> By the time of the beginning of the national <u>renaissance</u> group self-contempt was, we may suppose, in full swing. And here we suddenly find ourselves able to contribute towards the explanation of a strange case in English musical history that, to my knowledge, has so far defied any

---

50　Flugel to Keller, 22 June 1950, CULHK.
51　See 'Alan Rawsthorne and the Baroque', *Tempo* 14 (14 March 1946): 2–5.

scientific elucidation whatsoever. I mean the case of Edward Elgar. In 1946, Wilfrid Mellers wrote a paper on "Alan Rawsthorne and the Baroque" wherein the problem of Elgar, which many do not even see, is clearly defined, though nowise explained. Mellers says:– "The great social-dramatic phase of instrumental evolution we simply by-passed, so that it is hardly surprising that when Holst and Vaughan Williams came to work towards the renaissance of our musical culture they should have returned to the great days – to Tudor polyphony and, behind that, folk-song and hence to a fundamentally vocal conception of their art. The unique case of Elgar, whose magnificently ripe symphonies are as it were THE CULMINATION OF A SYMPHONIC TRADITION THAT HAD NEVER HAPPENED, we may legitimately regard as a 'sport' in our musical history."

Ladies and Gentlemen, I have the greatest respect for my colleague, whom I consider, in fact, to be one of our age's leading musicologists, but I suggest that before one "legitimately regards" a phenomenon as a "sport in history", one might yet more legitimately not regard it as anything at all. However, Mellers' paradoxical observation that Elgar's symphonies are the culmination of a symphonic tradition that had never happened is a penetrating epitome of the problem. Now depth psychology leaves us in no doubt as to how to regard such manifestations of mental life as seem to be the result of something that has never happened. The answer to the problem is that this something has happened, not in factual reality, but in psychical reality. As Freud says: "It would not be right to underestimate this psychical reality in comparison with factual reality. Its consequences are important enough." Well, on the assumption that group self-contempt played an active part in Elgar's musico-mental make-up – an assumption heavily supported by his own music – the psychical reality, in his own mind, of the symphonic tradition that never happened in factual reality, follows as a mere corollary. Elgar's deep-seated wish for, and unconscious phantasies of, a symphonic tradition whose factual absence we have recognised as one of the chief causes of group self-contempt, must in that case have been so powerful that he embarked upon the task of crowning, and thus proving the existence of, this non-existent British symphonic tradition: his was, if I may say so, a supremely successful flight into reality. His genius enabled him to realise what early psychoanalysis called the infantile "omnipotence of thought" to an extreme degree which even the most imaginative critic would have been unable to foresee. The British symphonic tradition became, a posteriori, so much of a reality that we can say for certain that Wilfrid Mellers would have taken its existence for granted if he hadn't known that it wasn't there.

Britten's *Rape of Lucretia* was given its first Austrian production at Salzburg that year and Keller was deeply disappointed by how little the great Austrian musicians performing it seemed to understand it. The Male Chorus was sung by Julius Patzak, whom Keller revered – but he sang Britten's music 'with little understanding, the phrasing clinging to the meaning of the words rather than to the logic of the melodic line'. Backstage, Patzak explained to Keller his dislike of the music by saying, 'The man hasn't *learnt* enough; it's badly written.' Keller was astounded: 'I am professionally bound to believe my ears, but this time I couldn't. Whatever you want to find wrong with Britten, it is provable nonsense to consider his technique defective.'

There must, Keller thought, be more than musical reasons behind such wilful misunderstanding: 'his untenable criticisms would appear to show how drastically sociological and musico-historical forces can distort even a perspicacious Austrian's picture of contemporary English music.' But at least Patzak's resistance to the work was conscious. In the case of the conductor, Josef Krips, who outwardly expressed enthusiasm for the work, Keller diagnosed unconscious resistance, through some of the oddities in his interpretation – one example being at the beginning of the second Act, where 'Prof. Krips surprised us (the small British colony) by the neck-breaking speed with which he chased through the lullaby.' Although this turned out to have been the result of Krips misreading the metronome mark, 'we know from the researches of Freud and his school that such mistakes are likely to have an unconscious meaning.'[52]

Keller also found food for thought in the modern German and Austrian operas performed at Salzburg that year – in both the works themselves and the audience reaction. The opera that was paired in performance with Britten's, Blacher's *Romeo und Julia*, was received with what Keller found incomprehensible enthusiasm by its Austrian audience:

First Performances : Boris Blacher's *Romeo und Julia*
MR XI/4 (November 1950): 323

The first stage performance at the Salzburg Festival of Boris Blacher's so-called Chamber Opera *Romeo und Julia* (after Shakespeare) reduced me to well-sighted rage. The work can be described in one word – castrated. I suggest to all composers and music lovers who still have so much pseudo-post-romanticism in their bones that they are forced to react violently against it, to let themselves be psycho-analyzed, instead of producing and applauding the enthusiastically empty and purely negative symptoms of their neuroses. Indeed, it is not Tchaikovsky or Wagner or Mahler or Berg or Schönberg who are (as so many simple-minded critics think) "morbid"; the real morbidity

---

52 'England in the Austrian Mind', *Colophon* I/8 (October 1950): 27–30.

of our artistic age (at the moment perhaps particularly in Germany) lies in its sham hygiene. Mr. Blacher appears and says, "I've just come to tell you that I don't want to tell you anything" and walks out again, whereupon the audience clap their hands off, confronted as they are with so much sanity, all in a nutshell. The music is just worked well enough to deceive psychopaths and blockheads in the way in which any fourth-hand late-Stravinsky would, and there is such a complete absence of any sort of relationship, positive or negative, between stage and score that the unthrillable are thrilled to bits. Stravinsky's reaction against romanticism has produced telling results; but that the post-Stravinskyans' reactions against post-romanticism will ever produce anything at all is highly improbable.

Strauss's late masterpiece *Capriccio* had fallen on deaf ears in Salzburg – another symptom of the neurotic version of anti-romanticism that developed in Germany and Austria in the post-war years, as their populations struggled with the unbearable taint now staining their glorious musical heritage, which the denazification tribunals only served to emphasise.

"YES, THE WORLD IS FULL OF PEOPLE"
("Ja, die Welt is voller Leute." – Wilhelm Busch.)
MR XI/4 (November 1950): 312

Furtwängler aside, there was one outstanding event in the operatic field: Strauss' last, chamber-stylish opera *Capriccio* which, in view of most of the master's late works, I approached with unfavourable prejudices, only to be completely converted. For once I agree with W. R. Anderson (*Musical Times*, September, 1950) that "the old man's skill in keeping the thing in the air during one act lasting two and a quarter hours" is unique among contemporary efforts, though I personally would not adopt that kind of language for the description of this consummate, uncannily ingenious structural arch with its complex series of gradually tensioning, constituent curves, its liberating abundance of naturally extensive melody, its end at the exact and only point in mid-air where an end is possible. The reception was cool, polite, bored, and partly, if not overtly, hostile: Germany and Austria are at a yet earlier stage of anti-romantic childishness than we. Besides, the musical world, let alone the festival hell, is full of people; as Strauss wrote to Krauss, the librettist, in 1941 (see Willi Schuh's *Über Opern von Richard Strauss*, Zürich, 1947, which gives all the necessary information about the work), "*Capriccio* is not a piece for the public, at any rate not for an audience of 1,800 per evening. Perhaps a morsel for cultural epicures". Indeed, the opera's esotericism is of an unusual kind; its secret is neither depth nor advancedness, but solely subtlety (*i.e.* "decadence" for the decadent).

~

Just before Keller had travelled to the Salzburg Festival, he had received an unexpected package. To his delight, it contained a copy of Dika Newlin's newly-published edition of Schoenberg's writings, *Style and Idea*, sent from Schoenberg himself with a handwritten dedication on the flyleaf. It was 'the first sign that he had taken note of my writings.'

25 July 1950 – to Arnold Schoenberg
In German

Honoured master,

Just before my departure for Salzburg I received your book <u>Style and Idea</u> with its dedication which moved me deeply. Now, from the ship, my profuse thanks – and also for the fact that you can imagine my joy.

I am reading the book now and will write again after my return to London.

In the meantime, renewed thanks from one who knows why he is devoted to you.

Hans Keller

On his return, Keller found among the pile of *Music Survey* articles awaiting editing a report from Christina Thoresby on the ISCM Festival in Venice, describing the performance given on Schoenberg's 76th birthday of *A Survivor from Warsaw*. This was a work that Keller was anxious to hear, having read René Leibowitz's account in *Horizon*: 'when shall we hear the *Survivor from Warsaw* (1947) in this country?' he had asked in the Spring 1950 *Music Survey*. 'France has no Third Programme, but the Paris radio broadcast the work in December, 1948.' Thoresby's account of an initially hostile audience being won over to the extent of demanding an immediate repeat performance struck Keller forcibly, and he hastened to congratulate the composer:

18 September 1950 – telegram to Arnold Schoenberg
ASC

JUST HEARD OF SURVIVORS OVERWHELMING SUCCESS AT VENICE EVERYTHING COMES IN THE END EVEN THE FUTURE

HANS KELLER

Keller had assumed that he would be reviewing *Style and Idea* for *The Music Review*, but when Sharp commissioned a review, Keller found, to his astonishment – and annoyance – that it was not from him. Quite incomprehensibly, he thought, Sharp had given *Style and Idea* not to a musician, but to a poet.

But when he read Meyerstein's review, he changed his mind:

Response to E.H.W. Meyerstein's review of *Style and Idea* [extract]
MS IV/2 (February 1952): 435–6.

E. H. W. Meyerstein says the rightest thing in the simplest words when, in his notice on *Style and Idea*, sensitively entitled A MASTER'S TESTAMENT, he explains that "the book, in a sense, is a justification of cerebrality, showing at every point that, granted the inspiration, no amount of logical thinking is unnecessary." Granted the inspiration. Dr. Redlich's phrase does not grant it and therefore misleads.[53] Meyerstein's own review, however, is a masterpiece: one of the most exhaustively understanding and most beautiful pieces of appreciation that have ever been written. When I heard that MR's editor had given *Style and Idea* to a reviewer who was not, in my opinion, qualified for this particular task, I was furious. Now I repent. I should have thought of Schoenberg's own observation on the layman – on certain laymen (my trans.) :

> And what, then, about the layman, who knows nothing of the tablature? Schopenhauer explains mediocrity's respect for the work of art as belief in authority. This is doubtless true of the broad masses. But among laymen I have found individuals whose organs of perception are far sharper than those of most experts, specialists and professionals (*als die der moisten Fachleute*). And I know for certain that there are musicians who are more receptive to painting than many painters ; and painters who are more receptive to music than most musicians. (*Harmonielehre.*)

And poets. But it remains the exceptional merit of Meyerstein the poet that he fully recognizes Schoenberg the musical genius in Schoenberg the writer.

In the meantime, the book had received many other reviews – some distinctly hostile. Keller had actually been 'looking forward to the more aggressively critical reviews, because there are one or two points in what I otherwise consider the masterly analytical part of the book which are open to criticism & could arouse fruitful discussion. I was severely disappointed, for by & large the critics concentrated on expounding their view that Schoenberg was not so great as they thought

---

53 Keller was objecting to the description of Schoenberg as 'the veteran champion of the boldest cerebral experimentalism in music' in Redlich's letter to the editor of *The Music Review* – a letter intended for the May 1952 issue, but not in the end published.

he thought he was, and did not for the rest furnish much proof of really having studied the analytical suggestions of the book.'[54]

Worst was Winton Dean in *Music & Letters,* whose flippant opening sentence – 'Schoenberg's latest work is written in the twenty-six letter system' – set the tone.[55] Keller was appalled when he read it, and did not let the fact that Dean was 'a valued contributor to this journal upon other subjects' stop him deciding to make the 'staggering ignorance' of the review, rather than the book itself, the major subject of his own review for *Music Survey.*

His resolve was strengthened when he received a letter from Schoenberg himself:

> Dear Mr. Keller, you have my book and I assume you know, what is its value – or not?
>
> Enclosed you find a very unpleasant review, written by one of these non-musicians, who look in my music only for the twelve notes – not realizing in the least its musical contents, expression and merits. He is very stupid and insolent and would deserve a treatment like that you can give him.[56]
>
> I hope you are interested! Now sharpen your pen.
> Cordially yours,
> Arnold Schoenberg

January 1951 – Telegram to Arnold Schoenberg

PEN SHARPENED

HANS KELLER

The timing could not have been better, for Schoenberg's letter arrived just as Keller was completing his criticism of Dean:

Schoenberg and the Men of the Press [extract]
MS III/3 (March 1951): 160–67

The decisive happens despite.

NIETZSCHE.

The critic stumbles along behind the artist.

J. ISAACS.

---

54 Note in a 1952 notebook, CULHK. Keller's letter to Stein of 12 December 1950 gives an indication of what his criticisms of Schoenberg might have been: 'Against all harmonic sense he regards the chromatic connective in the 7th bar of the Brahms A minor quartet's slow movement theme as a possible derivative of the initial interval of a second; or because he seriously considers the possibility that the 2nd phrase of his Mozart quotation on p. 95 of <u>Style and Idea</u> starts on the fourth beat of bar 2'.
55 Dean, 'Schoenberg's Ideas', *M&L* XXXI/4 (October 1950): 295–304.
56 Probably Richard S. Hill in *Notes* VIII/1 (December 1950): 167–8.

We gather that Schoenberg's new book *Style and Idea* will very shortly be published in this country (Williams & Norgate). This seems the moment, then, for dispelling some of the prejudices which may have been aroused against the work by certain reviews of its American edition (1950), immoral at their worst and ignorant at their best. With Richard Capell's *Daily Telegraph* review, entitled *Schoenberg's Ideas*, I have dealt in an article (under my present title) in the February issue of *Colophon*, where I have also examined John Amis's (*Tribune*) and Frank Howes's (*The Times*) latest verdicts on Schoenberg's music. Richard Capell himself bequeathed this subtly ironical title to Winton Dean, inviting him to produce what turned out to be an extended tirade on the book in *Music & Letters*, and it is against this article-review as well as against Richard S. Hill's review in *Notes* (Washington) and Professor Gerald Abraham's emissions *ex cathedra* Monthly Musical *opinionis* that I here propose to defend the composer.

Nothing is easier, and nothing more convincing to the ignorant, than to sweep over the deep. Nothing is more relieving than to talk about what one doesn't know, for it's the easiest thing to be done about it; besides, it promotes solidarity among the light-minded, promotes that jolly good highbrow fellowship which keeps the music critic's conscience ever supple and easy. Artistic stupidity hides behind anti-artistic intelligence which takes everything into humorous account except genius. Genius tends to be a disturbing phenomenon for the critic, for its recognition depends upon the creation of new standards of evaluation. Music criticism justifies itself where an inspired vision of the future supersedes all acquired illusions of the past. Otherwise, it merely judges itself: perhaps it is because the critic criticizes himself that he doesn't want to be criticized by anybody else. Or perhaps it is because he feels more certain than secure. In any case, one has to grant him that his certainty is based upon his professional knowledge; but, alas, most professionals who construct this body of knowledge are amateurs without the imagination of amateurs. They know enough to judge the past by its future, but when it comes to the present they judge it by its past. As for the future – that, they say, can look after itself. "Can" and "must," however, have no future tense, and what can and must be known and said, can and must be said now.

This article had a curious history. The version quoted above, which Keller was finishing as Schoenberg's letter arrived in January, was not the first piece he had written under that title. A previous – rather different – version had been the subject of months of controversy within the ranks of *Music Survey*'s editorial board, a controversy heated enough to involve an appeal to the journal's owners, the Livingstons:

21 October 1950 – to Kathleen and David Livingston[57]

Dear Kath and David:

As a matter of both artistic and editorial principle it is quite out of the question for me to agree to withdrawing my article on SCHOENBERG AND THE MEN OF THE PRESS. In short, either we go ahead with it or I resign completely from MUSIC SURVEY to which I shall not, in that case, contribute in the future.

As I will prove to you when we next meet, there is no personal ill-feeling at all involved in my part; I understand you and you don't understand me and that is all.

David Livingston replied that he had tried hard to follow a policy of non-intervention 'and having read through the article I see no reason for intervening now':

> Mr. Hans Keller is a scholar and a musician of taste and discernment; his articles and criticism command respect in any journal; his contribution to the high esteem in which Music Survey is held cannot be measured.[58]

Nevertheless, he did reveal some reservations:

> I accept wholeheartedly the view of the Editors that the subject is one of importance. I am in agreement with the policy of exposing ill-informed or irresponsible criticism; by all means name the offender and quote his offence; hit, and hit hard. But, gentlemen, do not, I beg of you, use the language of the gutter press. I cannot accept the argument that only by so doing can you bring home to the bad critic the enormity of his crime. You alienate him – not educate him, and you offend the true music lover for whom you write.

20 November 1950 – to David Livingston [extract]

The Director's policy of non-intervention is greatly appreciated, and his criticisms have been seriously considered.

I, too, am against using the language of the gutter press. But language is not merely used, it is formed or deformed by its use, and a word which belongs to the gutter press in one context doesn't in another. In short, when I use mud, I mean mud. And when I mean mud, it isn't only I who means it, but all those who serve the art I serve. True, they don't write "mud", tho' they may say it. That is because they have taste. I am a

---

57 W.W. Livingston was known as 'David'.
58 Livingston to Keller and Mitchell, 12 November 1950, CULHK.

confirmed enemy of established taste. Every great advance in science as well as in art has been tasteless, though it has contributed towards new standards of taste, to be exploited by those who can't do anything else. In musical criticism, taste has all but buried veracity. I don't like mud, but if someone slings it at art it is my duty to say that he does so. In consequence, I seem to be tasteless but am truthful, whereas he seems to be tasteful but is tasteless in the only constantly valid sense of the term, namely, the moral sense. I agree that I alienate the bad critic and that I do not educate him. This is precisely what I want to do. Good critics are born, not made; bad critics have to be made afraid. They hold a certain amount of aggression in store against Schoenberg's advance, and the sooner their fear makes them release it the better. One can only educate where there is something educible.

[...]

I perfectly understand and respect the feelings which have prompted you to your criticisms. And I really thank you for your wishing us good luck, tho' we don't need it. They need luck; we are right.

HK

These letters between Keller and Livingston went into considerable detail about the article, from which it is clear that what they were discussing is not the version published in *Music Survey* the following March. The first version, whose allegedly 'gutter press' style caused all the problems with his colleagues, Keller seems to have sent to *Colophon*. It is now lost, for the February issue never appeared and *Colophon* collapsed soon afterwards, owing Keller much-needed fees. In Keller's archive, however, there is a single page which may be its opening:

Schoenberg and the Men of the Press – I
Manuscript fragment

It is morally and logically necessary to begin this article with a humourless, personal statement. During this past year it has been increasingly borne in upon me, by rumour, by letters, by the musical and even by the daily press, that those of my writings which resemble this article in tone or content are being monotonously misunderstood by a section of my colleagues and readers. Above all, I am reproached with what is considered my aggressive and arrogant attitude towards fellow critics. I do not propose to split many hairs about what they call aggression and arrogance and what I don't. But this must be said: that none of my critics, while suggesting variously that I should remove myself to Austria or to Israel, has yet bothered to discover that each manifestation . . .

The manuscript breaks off at this point and the other pages are missing. Its tone is strikingly personal – an indication, perhaps, that the opposition Keller had been so cheerfully stoking with his own polemics might have begun to affect him. In this context it should be noted that during the autumn of 1950 Keller was very unwell. He had had more than one bout of ill health that year and after his return from Salzburg was ill for a considerable time with a punctured lung. Among other things, this prevented his attendance at the British Psychological Society's meeting in November to deliver his paper on 'Musical Self-contempt in Britain', which had to be read for him.[59]

The first version of 'Schoenberg and the Men of the Press' must have been written during Keller's illness. According to Livingston, it included the statement that 1950 had been 'a rotten year' for Schoenberg's music, 'started off' by the journal *Musical Opinion* – this refers to Clinton Gray-Fisk's review of the LCMC Schoenberg birthday concert. At the same time as Gray-Fisk was attacking Schoenberg, *Musical Opinion*'s editor, Laurence Swinyard, was attacking Keller in his editorials, and the two controversies ran in parallel throughout the spring and summer of 1950. Readers conflated the two disputes: in one letter to the editor headed 'Schoenberg', the composer Alec Rowley opined that the trouble was that 'these gentlemen who arrived in this country just before the last war cannot know that the subject [of Schoenberg] is out of date.' As 'guests of this island,' he went on, 'they should learn the elements of decency, and remember that a code of behaviour, plus a modicum of gratitude towards our critics and composers, is expected of them. Otherwise, I respectfully suggest that they return to their own country.'[60]

All this may have caused Keller to feel an extra emotional identification with the embattled Schoenberg. As he defended Schoenberg from 'these non-musicians, who look in my music only for the twelve notes', he found that his own critics were also engaging less with what he was actually saying than with the manner in which he said it. The common British view of Schoenberg as a cold, intellectual constructor was extremely frustrating

> *Intellectual music is emotional music we do not understand.*

to Keller, whose own response to his music was primarily an emotional one. In response to Richard Capell's dismissal of Schoenberg's admirers as 'a small band of young intellectuals', Keller declared 'I myself, at any rate, am a musical "emotional" whose intellect happens to be as strong as his feelings.'[61]

Keller's acute awareness of the difficulty of applying the intellect to a musical language so new – and the dangers of theorising with insufficiently developed concepts to an audience to whom this musical language had yet to speak – is

---

59 See Flugel to Keller, 7 November 1950, CULHK.
60 *MO* (May 1950): 475.
61 See Keller to Livingston, 20 November 1950, CULHK.

very clear from his account of his (long-awaited) first hearing of *A Survivor from Warsaw*:

A Survivor From Warsaw [extract]
MS III/4 (June 1951): 277–80, reprinted in *EOM*, 80–82.

It is inexplicable why the Third gave only a single presentation of this short and extremely difficult work which, in New York as well as in Venice last year, had to be immediately repeated upon the audiences' request.

Severely enervated by the interference of a motor which completely extinguished one third of the broadcast and reduced the rest often to the almost indistinguishable, I was yet so overcome by what I could hear that I am driven to set down my impressions which, unaided as they were by a score or a previous hearing, may not be altogether reliable.

Much is being said for and against the drastic newness of Schoenberg's technique which is here applied in strict fashion, but I think we do not sufficiently realise how new to music, indeed to our conscious minds, are the psychic regions from which this way of composing has emerged and which it explores.

Every honest and musical writer on music knows the paralysing state of "having something to say," for whenever we really have something to say about a musical content, we find that we can't say it: unfortunately one cannot express music criticism in terms of music.* Hence we escape, with full justification, into technical language, for though technical descriptions are far from expressing the whole truth, they have the advantage over metaphorical descriptions of denoting nothing but the truth. Their representational value, however, stands in direct relation to the reader's knowledge of the compositional processes from which they have been abstracted; for instance, when I suggest that the first movements of Beethoven's Op. 59, No. 1, and of Prokofieff's 5th Symphony form a bridge between the potential repeats of their expositions and their actual developments by starting off the latter with the first subjects in the tonic, you know what I mean because many classical sonata arches are part of your experience.

In the case of the *Survivor*, however, a technical description would be of the most limited avail, partly because the compositional processes from which twelve-tone-technical descriptions are abstracted are so widely unknown, and partly also because with this new music the process of analytical abstraction itself has not, to date, progressed very far: the completest technical description of the *Survivor*, from specialist to specialist, would be more incomplete than a popular description of

Mozart's G minor Symphony from music critic to Promenader. Thus,
while the *Survivor* reveals a new world of possible expressibles, I feel
more paralysed than ever. One overriding impression however, I can
formulate: Schoenberg has succeeded where psychology (despite Jung)
has so far failed, i.e. in establishing the link between two kinds of depth –
psychological depth, which is the primitive, the elemental, the instinctual,
and artistic depth, which is the sublime, the supernatural. The Romans
seem to have known after all what they were talking about when they
said *altus* and meant either "high" or "deep": the *Survivor* shows hell and
heaven to be contiguous. [. . .]

* Except for certain forms of unfavourable (including also corrective) criticism.
Mozart's *Musikalischer Spass* is a piece of music criticism expressed in music.

Six months later, the BBC and the LCMC collaborated in the first live performance in Britain of *A Survivor from Warsaw* – a performance that Keller
described in the following issue of *Music Survey* as 'an unrecognised *débacle*'.
The trouble with such new and unknown music, he thought, was that it quickly
fell into a vicious circle of bad performances leading to misunderstanding and
rejection, leading in turn to fewer and worse performances. Eventually a point
is reached 'where every inadequate Schoenberg interpretation is disastrous, i.e.,
worse than none, because it does everything against and nothing for the so far
uncomprehended work. There are too many Schoenberg performances because
there are too few.'[62]
    And indeed, this performance did not advance Schoenberg's cause at all. The
reviews were largely uncomprehending – and even BBC's Leonard Isaacs (who,
as Third Programme Music Organiser, was partly responsible for the concert)
described *A Survivor from Warsaw* afterwards as 'a pernicious piece of horror':

> I can find no saving grace in it anywhere. That Schoenberg was deeply moved
> by the story which he relates is unquestionable, but he relates it accompanied
> by such indescribably weird and horrible sounds, and continues these even
> through the chanting of the Shema Yisroel, that he defeats his own purpose.
> In any case this is a documentary and not a piece of music.[63]

    The first German performance of the work, as Humphrey Searle reported for
Music Survey, had been given at the Darmstadt International Summer School on
20 August 1950, a few weeks before the triumphant occasion in Venice. Searle – a
former BBC producer – was also reporting for the BBC on events at Darmstadt
that year, and it may have been his insistence that this 'most exciting work of
Schoenberg that I have heard . . . really must be done over here' that led to the
BBC's production.[64] The following year it was rumoured that Darmstadt director

62 'Schoenberg: the Problem of Interpretation', *MS* IV/1 (October 1951): 343–5.
63 Isaacs to Herbert Murrill, 21 June 1951, WAC R27/157/1.
64 Searle, report on Darmstadt 1950, WAC R27/225/2.

Wolfgang Steinecke had finally succeeded in getting Schoenberg to agree to teach there, and there was much excitement at the news.

25 May 1951 – Telegram to Arnold Schoenberg
ASC

NEWSPAPER SAYS YOU WILL LECTURE AT DARMSTADT IS THIS TRUE I WOULD TRY MY UTMOST TO COME

HANS KELLER

But, as in 1949, Keller's hopes of actually meeting Schoenberg were dashed – this time permanently. Schoenberg died on 13 July.

~

Hans Keller takes the ski-lift at Kitzbühel during one of his annual skiing holidays with Cosman in the 1950s.

Following his first trip back to Austria in 1950, Keller returned twice in 1951 – skiing at Easter and attending the Salzburg Festival in August. Once again he avoided Vienna, despite the inauguration of the new Wiener Festwochen that year, under the auspices of the allied occupying powers – a significant effort at post-war regeneration. Another noteworthy event Keller might have attended, but didn't, was the premiere of Stravinsky's *Rake's Progress* in Venice on 11 September 1951. Milein Cosman – keen to see Venice again – went straight there from Salzburg, with a commission from *Opera* magazine for sketches of the performance, but Keller pleaded pressure of work and hurried back to London. For Cosman, this was the start of a veritable 'obsession' with drawing Stravinsky – 'one of the strongest visual impressions of my life'.[65] For Keller, listening at home on the Third Programme, the impression made was much slighter: *The Rake's Progress* struck him as a 'sham creation' whose models (principally *Così fan tutte*) he thought 'easily recognisable'[66] – a disappointment after his admiration for the Mass, the Symphony of Psalms and the Symphony in Three Movements. It is perhaps noteworthy that Keller didn't include a review of the *The Rake's Progress* in *Music Survey*, despite arranging for one to appear in *The Music Review*. In any case, he had a multitude of other things to think about, not least of which was the first Salzburg production of *Wozzeck* – a far more interesting operatic experience to Keller than the *Rake*, and a work whose relationship to its models and influences he was eager to study.

6 September 1951 – to Geoffrey Sharp

Dear Geoffrey,

Just back and in the thick of every bloody thing. Many thanks for your card of Aug. 15 from Bayreuth. Looking forward to your review. Looking definitely backward to Redlich's irresponsible Profile of Stevens in Aug. MR. Why, he doesn't even know the most important Stevens, e.g. the Quartet. Which reminds me: what happened to my review of this score? You sent me the proof together with my proofs for May '51 MR, & I returned it tog. with them, but as far as I remember it hasn't appeared yet. Have you changed your mind about it? If so, please let me know, so that I can publish it elsewhere.

Hans Rutz, chief of the Music Section of Rot-Weiss-Rot radio whom you may remember as contrib. to MR, is covering the Stravinsky in Venice. He is anxious to get British assignments, as he will need every £ he can get when he comes to London later in the autumn to cover BILLY BUDD. Do you want something on the Stravinsky? Please let me know at once. I should be prepared to translate the piece.

65 *HKSMM*, 173–4.
66 *BB1952*, 335.

Among the books for review I received while in Salzburg there are at least two which may interest you: (1) Anton Bruckner, VORLESUNGEN UBER HARMONIELEHRE UND KONTRAPUNKT (Ed. Ernst Schwanzara), Oesterreichischer Bundesverlag – i.e. the first publication of the complete text of Bruckner's lectures at Vienna University (1891–4), music exx. included, by a chap who took it all down in shorthand. (2) H.H. Stuckenschmidt, ARNOLD SCHOENBERG, Atlantic Velag Zürich, just out, same sort of thing as Willi Schuh's UBER OPERN VON RICHARD STRAUSS, E.W. White's BRITTEN, or Krenek's AUTOBIOGRAPHY in the same series. Please let me know if you want me to review them for MR (Feb. '52 if poss.), in which case I shall get someone else for MS.

Furtwängler contacted me on my (and his) last day in Salzburg: he read a lot of my stuff & wanted to know me. We arranged a big Schoenberg discussion for Oct. when he will be in London for a few days to conduct the Philharmonia Orch. with Myra Hess. (I attacked him very heatedly, both over the radio and in the press, over certain remarks he made about Schoenberg in an otherwise magnificent lecture on BEETHOVEN UND WIR: BEMERKUNGEN AMLAESSLICH DES 1. SATZES DER 5. SINFONIE: would you incidentally be interested in a report on this for Nov. MR?) His secretary says he would have no objection to having the text of this discussion published. Any interest? No immediate reply needed in this instance.

Curiously enough, Furtwängler doesn't know much of my stuff on him. If you wish to rectify his opinion that MS "is the only musical journal" – he doesn't seem to know MR – I shall be delighted, for you'll save me 17s: I promised his secretary to send him the Nov.'49 & Nov.'50 issues of MR, one containing my review of his Gespräche über Musik (pp. 303 ff.), the other my article on SALZBURG: FURTWAENGLER'S GENIUS. If you can spare these, please have them sent to Fra Dr. Tiedmann, Sec. to Furtwängler, Konradstrasse 12, Munich, & have my pieces marked on the covers, particularly the book review, which isn't easy to find. If you can't spare these copies, please let me know at once.

I spent 3 highly enjoyable days with Klemperer, who had become interested in me when reading my article on SCHOENBERG AND THE MEN OF THE PRESS. I'm vaguely thinking of writing something like TALKS WITH OTTO KLEMPERER, but not just yet.

If you have no objection, I shall include Salzbg's Wozzeck in FIRST PERF'S, among other things because I consider it scandalous that the first Salzburg perf. of the work sh'd have taken place as late as this, and that yet, at this time of the day, it sh'd have encountered resistances from press, Landtag (Salzburg diet) and public (poor box office returns). At the same time I'd

like to make some new observations on the work, particularly on what
I regard as its extreme, if often hidden, eclecticism, which to me seems
to be the explanation of its success with people who do not otherwise
like an advanced idiom. For this purpose, I sh'd be glad to be allowed a
few music exx., say, one showing a translation of a Beethoven theme, one
consisting even of a bit of Puccini, one Mendelssohnian, one Mahlerian,
one Straussian, one Schoenbergian. . . . as many or as few as you like.
I have studied the score pretty thoroughly. The subject is of topical
interest in view of the Covent Garden production of WOZZECK next
Jan. (which, incidentally, will probably be better than the Salzburg effort).

Do you want anything on Furtwängler's (a) BRUCKNER V and (b)
Beethoven IX? Both performances were overwhelming. In the case of the
Bruckner, I should again like a music exx. (tho' I'm sure you can't spare
the space), i.e. of the only weak spot in the whole work (original score).

Kindly let me know (a) desirable, (b) latest press date for Nov. stuff.

What happened to your record review for MS? Changed your mind or
something?

Milein is in Venice; I couldn't spare the time. Regards to Mary. When
she was at a safe distance from Salzburg, I started gambling in a big way,
alternatively losing everything I had won and winning everything I had
lost. Apart from sleeping, it is the only moral occupation I know, for the
only person it can possibly harm is oneself. After Mary has written her
chapter ON GAMBLING I shall add one on GAMBLING ON.

Yours,

Hans

   This letter to Sharp makes clear how hugely stimulating this 1951 Salzburg
trip was for Keller. One of his greatest pleasures was evidently the interest in
Music Survey shown by eminent performers: it was not only in Britain that it was
causing a stir. Keller also made his first radio appearance while in Salzburg in
1951. He had previously sent a couple of talks suggestions to the BBC, but had
not pursued the idea of broadcasting with much vigour (unlike Geoffrey Sharp,
who was extremely keen to get on the radio). On Rot-Weiss-Rot (the American-
controlled Austrian radio station that operated until 1955), Keller not only
attacked Furtwängler's views on Schoenberg, but also 'raised hell' about the fact
that in Austria this first Salzburg production of *Wozzeck* should still be considered
'courageous'. Comparing the situation with Britain – 'even our oldest fogeys over
here acclaim *Wozzeck*' – he told the Austrians they had 'got stuck at Bruckner' (as
indeed he himself had been during his Viennese years).[67]

67 *MR* XIII/4 (November 1951): 311.

Austrian conservatism meant that Keller's own first opportunity to hear *Wozzeck* had not come until March 1949, when the BBC broadcast a concert performance from the Royal Albert Hall. The BBC had been a strong advocate for Berg's opera well before the war, mounting the first complete British performance at huge expense in March 1934 – a landmark in the reception of musical modernism in Britain. One listener who remembered it vividly was Humphrey Searle, who afterwards was one of the first in Britain to embrace serial composition.[68] 'It was to change the whole course of my musical life,' he wrote later; 'I was utterly shaken by the power of the music.'[69] Encouraged by the enormous success of this broadcast – and Berg's own sadness that 'this immense amount of work, perseverance, talent and genius . . . was put together only for this *one* performance'[70] – the BBC tried hard to collaborate with Covent Garden on a fully staged performance for 1935. But there was neither the will nor the money at Covent Garden to invest in such a project at that (pre-Arts Council) date, so it was not until 1952 that British audiences – including Hans Keller – finally got to see *Wozzeck* on the stage.

Contrasting the Salzburg and London audiences and critics, Keller was struck by the British enthusiasm for *Wozzeck*, and wondered why 'even our oldest fogeys' were so enamoured of it. Although he suspected that acclaim for *Wozzeck* was sometimes used 'as a stick with which to beat Schönberg', he nevertheless recognised the acclaim as genuine, and began to turn over in his mind 'how *Wozzeck* achieved its international popularity'.

The Eclecticism of Wozzeck [extract]
MR XII/4 (November 1951): 309–15 and XIII/2 (May 1952): 133–7.

I submit that the strongest cause of Berg's popularity is his eclecticism. Once one has felt oneself fairly thoroughly into *Wozzeck*, one realizes that there is hardly an untraditional bar, the (mostly legitimate) derivativism extending not only over the language, but also straight into the content, the musical thoughts. In other words, the atonal aspect of the work is just as eclectic as the tonal one, sometimes even more so: the tonal style of one section may be relatively untraditional, whereas the atonal ideas of another section may derive straight from Beethoven. Let us look at two cornerstones, the (*quasi-*) prologue and the epilogue. The prelude of the 1st scene (which is composed as a character-piece on the Captain in the form of a continuous suite), that is to say, has for its theme – Ex. I*a*, recurring later in identical (untransposed) form at the beginning of the phantasy (act II/2) that introduces the triple fugue and, of

68 Another was Elisabeth Lutyens, whose second husband was Edward Clark.

69 Searle 'Quadrille with a Raven', http://www.musicweb-international.com/searle/you.htm (accessed 21 March 2017).

70 Berg to Adrian Boult, 15 March 1934, quoted in Doctor, *The BBC and Ultra-Modern Music*, 275.

course, as first subject of the fugue itself – a derivative from the equally opening theme of Beethoven's Sixth (Ex. 1*b*), as unashamed in rhythmic structure and melodic outline as it is transmuted in matters emotional and idiomatic.

Ex. 1a Wozzeck, bar 4   **Ex. 1b** Beethoven, 6th Symphony, bars 1 f.

Ex. 2 Wozzeck, epilogue

At the same time, its pull to B (Beethoven's dominant has become Berg's un-dominating tonic) will be clearer here, in harmonically uncontradicted isolation, than in the opera house. [. . .] There is nothing hidden, on the other hand, of the epilogue's tonality; in fact, D minor is, as it were, what the piece "is about". Its tonal language has often been called Mahlerian, but its modes of harmonic expression are in fact highly original, unmistakably Berg; that they owe certain general traits to Mahler is as inevitable and self-evident as it is uninteresting. What is less evident and far more interesting is that the theme (Ex. 2) starts out, even in mood, from the Nocturne of Mendelssohn's *Midsummer Night's Dream,* but is prevented from running an epigonic course, and deflected from too peaceful an emotional atmosphere, by following up the quartal implications with which its previous occurrences (e.g. Ex. 4*a*–*b*) have invested its upbeat, only to arrive, in a context that has meanwhile become completely Bergian, at a completely Puccinian phrase and texture (Ex. 2, bars 3/2*f.*): about the last influence one would have suspected in Berg, indicative at the same time of the extreme width of his eclecticism.

Pedal on G–D (W.W.,Str.) in bass

Ex. 3a Wozzeck, bars 657 f.

Ex. 3b Siegfried Idyll, bars 86 f.

Ex. 4a Wozzeck, bars 248 f.   **Ex. 4b** Wozzeck, bar 395

Ex. 4c Schoenberg, 1st Chamber Symphony, bars 5 f.

More frequent, and less surprising, are his references to Wagner's
thematic shapes, Ex. 3*a*, for instance, having arrived from the *Siegfried
Idyll* (Ex. 3*b*) via the *Verklärte Nacht* in a *subordinate part* of the first act's
five character-pieces, *i.e.* the one on the Tambourmajor. Perhaps most
frequently, Berg draws on Schönberg. This greatly surprised me, in that
when I heard *Wozzeck* years ago I was not sufficiently well acquainted
with Schönberg to realize that his architectural and thematic influence
on the opera was as strong as, if not indeed stronger than, his
idiomatic influence. In particular, Schönberg's first chamber Symphony
must have been deeply active in Berg's mind. Most obviously, there is
the exact scoring of Schönberg's chamber orchestra in the separate
orchestra of the *largo* that forms the slow movement of the opera's
central symphony (act II). Also, like Schönberg's, this symphony is in
five continuous movements (of which the above-mentioned phantasy
and fugue is the second); their structural relation to the chamber

Symphony I hope to show on a future occasion. In the present limited space, I am confining myself to two important thematic invasions of the chamber Symphony into *Wozzeck*. The first makes Schönberg's basic phrase (Ex. 4c) into one of the opera's principal themes, the earlier occurrence of Ex. 4*a* (in the character-piece on Andres) being less directly related to the Schönberg (and more directly to Ex. 2) than the later occurrence of Ex. 4*b* (in Marie's lullaby, which is part of her own character-piece). Incidentally, the way from Beckmesser's lute is long but straight.

Han-sel spann Dei-ne sechs Schim-mel an,

Ex. 5a Wozzeck, bars 388 f. [Marie]

Ex. 5b(i) Wozzeck, Act II bars 151 f.

Ex. 5b(ii) Wozzeck, Act II bars 155 f.

Ex. 5b(iii) Wozzeck, Act II bar 158

Ex. 5b(iv) Wozzeck, Act II bar 159

Ex. 5b(v) Wozzeck, Act II bar 160

Ex. 5c Schoenberg, 1st chamber Symphony, bars 9 ff.

The second invasion conquers the B♭ minor phrase (Ex. 5*a*) of the berceuse itself, divests it of its siciliana character by changing round the dotted rhythm, infuses it with the character of Schönberg's first subject's first theme's (Ex. 5*c*'s) principal motif, assigns it *the same structural position* in the symphony's (*i.e.* act II's) first (sonata) movement, and finally, in the subordinate parts of the latter's *coda* (see Ex. 5*b* (i)–(v)), almost replaces it by the Schönberg motif. While an inspection (or, better still, audition) of all the relevant sections in both the chamber Symphony and *Wozzeck* is absolutely necessary for a full appreciation of the latter invasion, it will perhaps already be realized that as in the case of the quartal theme (see Ex. 4), Schönberg's influence is again as it were gradually uncovered by Berg, not being discoverable yet in Ex. 5*a* which, nevertheless, must have been composed in view of what was to happen to it in the course of symphonic events. With Ex. 5, this intramusical progress *cum* historical (and psychological) regress is not only observable in the very long run, but also in the short run of the symphony's *coda* where, as the successive examples 5*b* (i)–(v) partly show, *the development of and to the model* (as I should like to call this tendency) makes itself felt within the smallest possible musical space. [. . .] How far now is Berg's own eclecticism open to criticism? As far as he does not say something new; and he says something new almost all the way through. Perhaps one case in question is the symphony's scherzo movement (act II, scene 4) which, proceeding from Mahler (bars 412–429) to Richard Strauss (bar 429 *ff.*), almost loses Berg on the way. A *pastiche* is of course dramatically needed at this point, but not one on Mahler and Strauss. *Peter Grimes*, though in its turn drawing on *Wozzeck* in a great variety of ways, solves the parallel problem with far more originality. In Berg's case, the Ländler is nowadays beginning to sound "delightful", which it shouldn't – but that is the fate of every good *pastiche* that lacks personality. The rest of Mahler's influence – including even bars 5 *ff.* of *Wozzeck*'s drinking song in act III, *i.e.* the phrases to "*Mein Wein is gut, mein Bier is klar*" . . .etc., which come as straight as creatively possible from "*Der Lenz ist da, sei kommen über Nacht*" (*Lied von der Erde*, V: "*Der Trunkene* (!) *im Frühling*) – is above criticism. Not so, however, all the unofficial Schönberg quotations (which are not, of course, confined to the chamber Symphony: at the end of the invention on the continuous pedal of B (act III, scene 2), for instance, Marie dies to the basic motif of Schönberg's piano pieces, Op. 11); sometimes Schönberg's influence seems too new and powerful to allow sufficient amalgamation in Berg's mind. Thus, paradoxically, the most epigonic part of *Wozzeck*'s eclecticism (Ländler apart) consists of some of its most modern sections. Where, on the other hand, Berg avails himself of Schönberg's techniques rather than themes, his inventiveness often flows most freely and individually.

To Eric Blom, this kind of writing was 'a musical game not unlike the hunting of the Snark' and he had some fun at Keller's expense in his *Observer* column.[71] This was the first of many such sallies from Blom, and Keller rarely let them lie when he felt they were propagating inaccuracies – in this case the implication that he was accusing Berg of plagiarism. But his protests (even if printed) rarely elicited the desired response. 'It is very naïve and amateurish of Mr. Keller to think that any reference to him made in public requires an answer,' wrote Blom (much as he personally enjoyed their disputes), 'for he must have discovered by this time that newspapers just can't be bothered with our arguments.'[72]

In the run-up to the Covent Garden production of *Wozzeck*, Keller was, as usual, assiduously attending rehearsals. The first performance took place on 22 January 1952, and one of Keller's diary fragments survives from the week beforehand. It gives a vivid glimpse of his daily life – including not only the *Wozzeck* preparations, but also how much time he was still spending in the cinema.

January 1952 – diary fragment

15.1.52

Morning: Wrote cards to Bubtschi, Stein (warning him not to let Mewton-Wood do Schoenberg's George Songs and pointing out to him the English Opera Group's idiocy in performing a Mozart piano c'to with string quintet), Harewood (inviting him to apply for membership of the Critics' Circle), Dallapiccola (telling him that I can't arrange a recital for him over here and that Seiber is going to have a Dallapiccola song done in his Third Programme lecture – in the Schoenberg series – on 12-tone music).

Saw Press Show of Carol Reed's self-consciously 'good' Outcast of The Islands with music, needless to say (see Black Narcissus) by Brian Easdale. Alas, since I know the first 10 mins. of his opera The Sleeping Children (into which Paul Hamburger's creative mind read value: that's what I call creative criticism!), his deficiencies irritate me even in the cinema, where they always pose as, and sometimes are, virtues: his lack of melodic invention, development, breath – his inability to conceive on any mentionable scale. But he is not pretentious – a fact which shows from his concentric tonalities (D major in this instance) up- and sidewards.

Afternoon: Press Show of Royal Journey (Elisabeth and Philip in Canada), with cheap (unnamed) music & inane commentary. (National Film board

---

71 'Beg, Borrow or Steal', *Observer*, 2 March 1952, 6, and 'Critics Criticised', 16 March 1952, 6.
72 Blom to Mitchell, 13 January 1953, CULHK.

of Canada, "photographed in breath-taking Ekta Colour".) Psychologically convinced monarchist as one is, one's patience is stretched to the utmost by a commentary which treats these exalted parent figures as ordinary, oh so beautifully ordinary, tourists. How can one suppress one's disgust if the naivest spectator is thus asked to lie to himself, to take the as-such-known illusion in front of reality more seriously than that of a novel? To regress beyond the point of sanity by really replacing conscious reality by phantasy?

I lost my gloves and edited part of Hamburger's chapter on the <u>Chamber Music</u> for our Britten Symposium. What a job, with his graphs, his Germanisms, his private style. Yet, what a chapter!

The boil on my back at last opened – a terrific flow – and I am beginning to feel myself again. A good boil plaster: <u>Elastikon</u>.

Mutti phone call: – It turned out that I did not lose my leather gloves after all, but that Mitchell took them by mistake! Sent something to <u>Statesman's This England</u>, from <u>Holiday Fanfare</u> (News Chronicle Publication): 'Salzburg and the Salzkammergut. . . . may well be described as the Lake District of the country.' Bought Suschitsky tickets for 3rd <u>Wozzeck</u> performance when I was at CG in the morning; since they cost 30s each, I wrote him a card in the evening offering to dispose of them elsewhere if he liked.

Reflected that: (1) to waste time on nothing is better than to waste time on something; (2) many people are anxious about their development when they ought to be busy trying to stay where they got to; (3) I am so un-natural that I am shy about my appreciation of bleakly sunny Hyde Park.

5 o'clock: lesson to Stephen: he is ill with tonsillitis, & I gave him new home-work and took his dictionary a stage further; then left. Quickly back to Milein, who had had a wisdom tooth out (one hour; Penicillin injection), developed an enormous cheek and felt rotten. Soon went to bed with her to make her sleep, but got up again around 9.30 for a meal.

16.1.[52]

a.m.

Lost another glove in tube! Something going on in the way of guilt, what with a burnt finger and the boil on my back. – Wozzeck rehearsal, last act. Promises to be better than the Salzburg production – which, true, isn't saying much. Kleiber lost his temper for the first time because Mr. [Eric] Mitchell substituted in the second run-through for Mr John Gardner at the stage piano and ran away at an impossible speed (not having rehearsed the section with Kleiber before). 'Absolutely impossible', sweating Kleiber shouted to Reginald Goodall who apparently is responsible for the musical sub-management. I was sitting with Goodall and had a good view at full score & stage. The tonal scheme — for such there is — is becoming clear to me: a lot is related to the D minor of the Epilogue, but that final bitonal effect, supported no doubt by the instrumentation (strings for the eventual, surprising G major chord) must be further gone into. Why such pacifying liberation at the turn from implied E major (or is it also implied A major) to the overpowering (outweighing) G major? Was there perhaps E minor feeling in spite of the C♯ in the wood, so that G major is felt as resolving relative major?

Milein Cosman and Hans Keller at home at 50 Willow Road, where they lived from 1954 until 1967.

P.M.

Walked 2 hours in Hyde Park which did me a lot of good. Apparently I'm not used to so much <u>fresh</u> air, for I felt like after a holiday.

∼

Wozzeck followed hard on the heels of another major operatic event: the premiere of Britten's *Billy Budd*, which marked the end of the 1951 Festival of Britain – and Britten's return to the London stage after what was seen in some quarters as a disappointing retreat to the provinces and the continent since the remarkable success of *Peter Grimes*. The occasion might therefore have been expected to call forth in full the various psychological 'resistances' Keller had identified after the premiere of the *Spring Symphony* – and indeed one critic confessed that 'many of us entered Covent Garden on Saturday (when the composer conducted the first performance) with a mean, sneaking hope that we might be able to flesh our fangs on it.'[73] Donald Mitchell thought his critical colleagues' reaction so misconceived as to warrant a treatment similar to that meted out by Keller to Schoenberg's critics, and he fleshed his own fangs with relish on his fellow critics in the February 1952 *Music Survey*.

During the heated arguments within *Music Survey*'s Editorial Board over 'Schoenberg and the Men of the Press' in 1950, one Board member, Denis Stevens, had apparently told Mitchell that he and several others would resign if the article appeared. In the event none did so (apart from Hans Redlich over an unrelated matter[74]) and the Board seems to have recovered its equanimity. Mitchell's new article 'More Off than On "Billy Budd"' threatened to be just as controversial: 'I've had numerous 'phone calls, post cards, letters and conversations about the <u>Budd</u> piece with friends, foes and complete strangers,' he told Keller, adding happily that 'the issue seems to be selling pretty vigorously so far.' (Felix Aprahamian was raising sales by asking fellow critics whether they had seen what had been said about them in *Music Survey*: 'And off the <u>Budd</u> critic runs, poor chap, to try and find a copy. Pity it's so difficult to get hold of. I'm told

---

73 Stephen Williams, *Evening News*, 3 December 1951.

74 Ironically it was one of Stevens's own reviews that caused Redlich's resignation from the Board (which he had only just joined): the review of the Oxford University Opera Club's production of Berlioz's *Les Troyens,* which appeared in the March 1951 issue of *Music Survey*. Given Professor Westrup's increasingly ambitious activities as an opera conductor, wrote Stevens, 'I wonder whether music students now receive any supervision at all.' A letter from Westrup's lawyers produced an editorial apology in the next issue.

Hope-Wallace spent a vain hour searching in the Charing X Rd!')[75] Although no correspondence with Board members over Mitchell's article survives, it may be significant that the issue in which it appeared showed two names missing from the Editorial Board, and in the following issue there was no trace of an Editorial Board at all.

That issue – June 1952 – was to be its last. The journal's demise was not planned or even foreseen: it appears rather to have wilted under the pressure of its editors' changing and expanding lives. One major development was the commission they secured in March 1951 for a book on Britten; this became *Benjamin Britten: A Commentary on his works from a group of specialists*,[76] which was published at the end of 1952, bringing considerable attention to Keller and Mitchell – and their subject – not all of which was entirely welcome. Other commissions followed; the same publisher took up their suggestion of a book of essays by Erwin Stein, which Keller edited and translated, and which turned out to be a lot of work: weeks of research in Austria tracking down copies of long-lost periodicals containing Stein's early articles, as well as what Stein called his 'magnificent . . . accurate, critical & almost self-effacing translation'.[77] With so much other work on hand, it became impossible to produce the autumn issue of *Music Survey* on time – or indeed at all. A more serious problem was the break-up of the marriage of David and Kathleen Livingston, who had been funding *Music Survey* since its inception. Kathleen had become very involved with the journal's organisation, fell in love with Donald Mitchell and eventually left her husband for him. It would not be surprising if the journal's funding had ceased as a result.

And so the two '*enfants terribles* of music criticism' (as one reviewer of their Britten *Commentary* called them[78]) came to the end of their partnership and – though they remained very good friends – began to go their separate ways.

It had been a memorable three years.

75 Mitchell to Keller, 24 February and 1 March 1952, CULHK.
76 (London: Rockliff, 1952)
77 *Orpheus in New Guises* (London: Rockliff, 1953). Stein to Keller, 11 July [1953].
78 'P.J.I.' in *Apollo*, March 1953.

Dodecaphoneys

Everyone dies too soon for someone, but not even every genius dies too soon for art, early though he may die for his years. Musically speaking, for example, Mendelssohn died almost too late, whereas not only Schubert, but also Beethoven died earlier than Mozart. It is not alone a question of development attained, but also of development attainable. Beethoven travelled unfathomably far, but as we begin to understand his latest works we fathom that he could have travelled far further. With Schoenberg it seems exactly the same. But in addition, he was born too early. It was really his premature birth which the newspaper obituaries, unintentionally, mourned.

Psychologically speaking, mourning is unconscious guilt. Morally speaking, mourning is conscious duty. We have not done enough for him; we who feel and think, bear the responsibility for the many who don't. In the end, however, when all is said about, and little done for, the real, the real does itself. Meanwhile, we shall continue to say that a dying culture can, if it will, see the light beyond its grave. Will it? There is nothing so painfully morbid as health to the moribund. Otherwise it would by now be common knowledge that Einstein, Freud and Schoenberg are the discoverers of the future.

Schoenberg died on 13 July 1951 and this is the obituary Keller wrote for him in *Music Survey*. It was printed in the October 1951 issue, as part of a symposium of nine short tributes, followed by an article from Luigi Dallapiccola on his own experience as a serial composer: 'On the Twelve-Note Road'. *Music & Letters* also opened its October 1951 issue with an obituary symposium, albeit on a larger scale with twenty-five contributors. Placing the two symposia side by side gives a fair summary of Schoenberg's reputation in Britain at the time of his death. *Music Survey*, the new smaller upstart journal, showed the interest in Schoenberg among some younger British musicians, influenced by the recent arrival of wartime continental émigrés, among whom numbered several of Schoenberg's pupils and associates. The more venerable *Music & Letters*, on the other hand, represented the bulk of the British Establishment, headed by composers of the older generation (Vaughan Williams, Dyson, Bax, Bliss and Howells, all of whom expressed themselves antipathetic to Schoenberg's music) and including only one Schoenberg pupil (Egon Wellesz). By contrast, *Music Survey*'s symposium was headed by Oskar Adler, Erwin Stein and Karl Rankl and was uniformly laudatory.

The only person to contribute to both journals was the composer Humphrey Searle, whose insistence in *Music & Letters* on the importance of Schoenberg as *composer*, rather than as theorist or teacher, went against the general tenor of his fellow contributors, many of whom, while admitting the force of Schoenberg's influence, regarded him as 'a greater teacher than composer' (William Mann) and compared his music unfavourably with Berg's. Keller was right that, for the British, Berg was 'a stick with which to beat Schönberg', and Herbert Howells spoke for many in the symposium when he wrote that 'Schönberg's death has somehow fixed my mind more upon Berg than upon himself.' Searle was also one of the few in *Music & Letters* to praise Schoenberg's late works: most contributors, even if they confessed admiration for works like *Verklärte Nacht* or *Gurrelieder*, could go no further: 'From the Three Piano Pieces onwards Schönberg never seemed to wait upon my sluggish understanding,' wrote Scott Goddard, 'and when I notice a person listening to it with mistrust on his countenance and fear in his eyes I know

> Schoenberg dies; the horde falls upon the father and devours him.

what he is going through.' 'I thought the String Trio a perfectly horrible piece of music,' wrote Felix Aprahamian, adding 'I suppose, for Hans Keller's sake, I shall have to get a score and try again.' Reading all this, Frank Howes noted complacently that 'the consensus of opinion agrees with that expressed in *The Times* . . . that Schönberg is a great musician but not a composer at all.'[1]

In *Music Survey*, Searle put his trust in 'the voice of youth' to articulate a proper understanding of Schoenberg's music, and indeed new voices were beginning to emerge. A twenty-one-year-old undergraduate at Cambridge called David Drew contacted Keller and Mitchell in the autumn of 1951 and his 'humble petition and advice to English critics' (addressed principally to Eric Blom) was published – 'sympathetically edited by Keller' – in the next *Music Survey*.[2] Drew's interest in modern music had been encouraged by his Classics master at school, who supplied him liberally with scores of Stravinsky and Schoenberg, together with accounts of Hindemith's teaching at Glock's first Bryanston Summer School. At Cambridge Drew fell under the influence of F.R. Leavis and Wilfrid Mellers (a close associate of Leavis and music critic of his journal *Scrutiny*) while having composition lessons from Roberto Gerhard – another significant émigré musician (and Schoenberg pupil) who had found a home in Cambridge.

---

1 *The Times*, 5 October 1952, 8.
2 'Schoenberg', *MS* IV/2 (February 1952): 438–9. Drew's account of his early years can be found on http://www.singscript.plus.com/daviddrewmusic/ar1950-53.htm (accessed 13.4.17). Blom's reponse appeared in *The Observer* on 8 June 1952, 6. Keller's subsequent letter to the editor was not published.

Another new voice appeared in the January 1952 edition of *Music & Letters*. This was the twenty-eight-year-old Oliver Neighbour, who had just joined Alec Hyatt-King at the British Museum. When Schoenberg died, Neighbour was already immersed in an extensive study of his works, the results of which were now published in *Music & Letters* under the title 'In Defence of Schönberg'. This title, together with its appearance in the issue immediately following the obituary symposium, gave the impression that Neighbour's article was a direct response – although, as he made clear in his preface, it had been completed long beforehand.

Donald Mitchell met Neighbour a few weeks later at a London Contemporary Music Centre concert, where he had gone to hear a rare performance of Schoenberg's String Trio. Reporting afterwards to Keller (who was away skiing), Mitchell gave his first impressions:

> The Schoenberg trio was splendid – rather roughly played, but not unmusi-cally. Even The Times (see att'd) was impressed. By the way at that con-cert I met that fellow who wrote the M&L article (post-symposium) on Schoenberg – O.W. Neighbour. That is his name too. He works in the music dept. at the British Museum. Quite young, very shy, wayward, but certainly seems to have made a very thorough and honest study of Schoenberg. I talked a lot with him. He half approves–disapproves of our Schoenberg line. Indeed he actually thought of having a minor attack on us in his piece. Needless to say he's a devoted reader of MS (as are most of his friends and acquaintances). It took him a year (!) to write that piece – it was started long before Schoenberg's death and its publication after the symposium was really accidental. He merely changed his 1st para. accordingly.[3]

Despite his half-disapproval of *Music Survey*'s aggressive stance on Schoenberg, Neighbour consented to become a contributor, and his short piece on the String Trio appeared in the last issue of the journal in June 1952. Keller and Mitchell planned this as a special 'Schoenberg issue' – analogous to their earlier 'Britten issue' – originally intended to contain reviews of the Schoenberg concerts, books, records and broadcasts that were proliferating after his death. But their plans changed, and all but one of these reviews were dropped in favour of a series of Schoenberg's letters, published both in German and in (Keller's) English translation (with some in facsimile as well). The letters were collected from a num-ber of different recipients, including Oskar Adler, Erwin Stein, Humphrey Searle and Keller himself, and date mostly from Schoenberg's American period. These later letters were supplemented by a collection of much earlier ones, to the pianist Marietta Werndorff, née Jonasz – the sister of Keller's mother's first husband.

Keller and Mitchell were keen to publish original documents by Schoenberg, and around this time a visit was paid to his widow on their behalf which might have opened up more opportunities to do so. The following account comes from a tan-talising fragment of a letter found in Keller's archive, written to Donald Mitchell

---

3 Mitchell to Keller, 1 March [1952], CULHK.

and sent on by him to Keller. There is no indication as to who the writer was, but it was clearly someone closely associated with *Music Survey*: a strong possibility is Kathleen Livingston. The writer evidently felt a little nervous approaching the widow of the great man – 'Now yesterday I took my courage in both hands and rang Arizona 35077 and spoke to Mrs. Schonberg' – but Gertrud Schoenberg was extremely welcoming. According to the letter fragment,

> Music Survey is held in high esteem in that house, and Schonberg thought it a wonderful paper. She told me how her husband spent his life making bitter mistakes in everything but his music – all the ironic misunderstandings with authorities and peoples, but complete faith and happiness in his work. They are waiting very anxiously for the Schonberg issue to appear, and she would like to write a "reply" on some aspect of his life and work that is bound to evoke a response in her when she reads the issue. Her great point is that she doesn't want to justify and recriminate, but wants the music to grow in its own time. She fears the cliques that seem to be forming within the Schonberg ranks, and suspects that only one thing will be harmed in the end, and that is the music, if too many people claim an esoteric knowledge and an exclusive understanding. Hoffman, an ex-pupil of Schonberg's is living in the house, and looking after the papers and so on, and he mentions 150 articles of varying length that he would like to have published. There is the question of copyright to be settled if an English periodical publishes these, or some of them, first, but they both felt that it would be a good thing if M.S. had a chance to print some articles in instalments. So if Hans would write, I think something on these lines might be forthcoming. Another thing, she had 6 death masks cast, and I saw one. It is a most beautiful face. She would like one to come to England, if it is wanted, and I said you and Hans would find out where would be best. One has been sent to Germany, one is here, one to France; she doesn't want it to come to England uncherished. I wish I could have changed places with you and Hans when she took me to Schonberg's room, which has been left just as he worked in it. . . .
>
> I have the feeling that you could get whatever material you wanted and full cooperation from Mrs. S. She is primarily concerned with the music, and the growth of understanding, hates the critics who cavil at every performance and put their hands deep into their pockets and do nothing about it. She doesn't put Hans in that class as he sharpens his pen to some purpose. . . .
>
> Altogether, I think it was a worth while visit of good will. I feel very acutely inadequate on these occasions; it's no good pretending to a knowledge and understanding I haven't got, but I go on wishing I had some. Nevertheless, I'm sure you and Hans could go right ahead with any sort of proposition about the articles (Hoffman would give you a list of subjects and probably send you some to read) and I think her contribution next time might be very interesting.

This visit took place in the spring or early summer of 1952, shortly before the publication of the Schoenberg issue of *Music Survey*, which Mrs Schoenberg clearly knew about. Strangely, however, she seems not to have known in advance about the inclusion in it of the Schoenberg letters – and even more strangely it doesn't seem to have occurred to Keller and Mitchell that they should have asked her permission. (Odd that the legally-minded Keller should have got his copyright law wrong on this point!) The letter she wrote when she received her copy has not survived, but she probably objected most to the inclusion of the third of the Werndorff letters (Schoenberg's comic apology for missing an appointment), whose 'childishness' when spread over 5 pages (plus facsimile) she may have thought added little to his reputation.

Keller was in Austria from June to September that year (attending the Salzburg Festival and working on Erwin Stein's book), so her letter took some time to reach him. Once he received it, his reply was prompt, but remarkably undiplomatic. Gertrud Schoenberg's response is not recorded.

21 September 1952 – to Gertrud Schoenberg

Dear Mrs. Schoenberg:

Erwin Stein has forwarded me your letter to Austria (I shall return to London by the end of the month). Here is my reply. As you may or may not know, I am neither tactful nor tactical; on the other hand, I am truthful. You of all people, I should imagine, will appreciate this. My reaction is, of course, private and personal. The publication of the Schoenberg letters was a joint decision of Donald Mitchell and myself, so (since I cannot talk for him) if you want Music Survey's reply, i.e. an 'official', joint reaction, you will have to wait until I am back in London.

If I had had the very slightest idea that you could possibly object to the printing of these letters, I should not of course have dreamt of doing so. (At the same time, I was not aware that "private letters are not to be published without the consent of the author or his heir": on the contrary, I was informed that letters were the sole property of their addressees. My information may be wrong, but in any case I vehemently resent your implied suggestion that I was aware of doing something 'behind your back.') Thus far I am deeply sorry, but no further.

You are "at a loss what purpose these letters should accomplish." The purpose of truth, of documentary evidence, however slight in any particular instance. A letter expresses some fraction of the personality of its author, expresses it when he lies or pretends, expresses it with particular force in the case of a letter-writer like Schoenberg (or Beethoven) who always writes the truth even when he jokes or when he has the courage to be childish (every truthful personality has to have the courage to be childish, because there is no personality without childishness). The letters, many of which would probably have been lost without my publishing them (and the rest badly translated at a later stage), certainly do not "give a clear picture of Arnold Schoenberg's life and character"; only an idiot would assume that they could, and Music Survey is not published for idiots. But the publication of these documents is a modest contribution towards such a picture which itself can only be given in the distant future.

Of course, even this picture will be of infinitesimal importance when compared with Schoenberg's music, but who are we (musicians) to decide what precise significance our knowledge of the character of genius may assume? We (thinking beings) have to serve the 'cause' of truth and God will supply the reason why.

The BBC, which before the war had been the most significant promoter of Schoenberg's music in Britain, took its time to decide on a suitable commemoration. In December it was announced that 'in the first three months of 1952 the Third Programme is to attempt an original kind of obituary. An extensive selection of Schoenberg's works will be played, set in a framework of talks and comment designed to show their technical, social, and philosophic significance.'[4] This was no easy undertaking: Edward Clark and Humphrey Searle had left the BBC's staff by this time, so Schoenberg's music no longer had an understanding advocate within the Corporation's own music department. Outside advice was going to be needed, and Erwin Stein wrote to offer help: 'I feel that as his oldest pupil alive (Berg and Webern were my colleagues) I should offer to the B.B.C. my advice.'[5]

Herbert Murrill was Director of Music at the time, with Leonard Isaacs responsible for music in the Third Programme: they both agreed that the BBC should steer clear of what they saw as 'the small group of fanatical apostles of Schönberg' – of whom Stein was presumably one.[6] For the same reason, they decided against importing continental performers, Isaacs considering it 'much better for the Schoenberg works to be undertaken by our own regular conductors in the course of their normal programmes. The other thing merely serves to perpetuate the charmed circle.'[7] Unfortunately, 'our own regular conductors' were not all thrilled to have Schoenberg inserted into their programmes.

4 *RT*, 28 December 1951, 17.
5 Stein to Murrill, 28 August [1951], WAC Schoenberg, composer file 1.
6 Isaacs to Murrill, 11 September 1951, WAC R27/500/6.
7 Isaacs to Tippett, 4 December 1951, WAC RCONT1, Tippett Artist File 1.

Chief Conductor Malcolm Sargent was dismayed to find the Five Orchestral Pieces in one of his concerts, even going so far as to request that the announcer make clear that its inclusion 'is due to the existence of a Schoenberg scheme and not to his own liking of the work'.[8] Despite the fact that it had been Sargent's predecessor at the Proms, Henry Wood, who had given the premiere of the Five Pieces forty years earlier, Sargent decided he could not face them and was indisposed on the day of the concert.

The wish to avoid 'the charmed circle' was one of the reasons behind the choice of Michael Tippett as Series Editor for the Schoenberg commemoration. Another reason was Tippett's importance as a broadcaster in the early years of the Third Programme. Etienne Amyot had met Tippett before the war and been much impressed by his fertile mind. Later, Tippett's ground-breaking work as Music Director of Morley College showed his effectiveness as an innovator and communicator of new musical ideas. William Glock, who first met him in 1943 (when Tippett brought his Morley singers to Stafford, where Glock was stationed with the RAF), was fascinated both by his eclectic exploration of widely differing kinds of music 'from Pérotin to Hindemith and from plainsong to jazz and negro spirituals', and by his infectious enthusiasm: 'he sings, talks, dreams and gesticulates music. I would not have exchanged [his concert] for a hundred Tschaikowsky programmes.'[9] They met again in London, and soon Glock was enjoying countless 'animated discussions held in the underground, on the street, at my flat in Hampstead, in his house at Oxted, and from which I learnt so much'.[10] When the Third Programme started, Tippett introduced Glock to Amyot and the discussions continued around the tremendous possibilities opened up by the BBC's exciting new service. As has been seen, Amyot used Glock to tour Europe on behalf of the Third in 1947. Tippett he used to help overcome the resistance of the network's Head, George Barnes, to contemporary music: 'I introduced Tippett to George and they got on awfully well. . . . [George] said to me, "I think I'll learn a lot about avant garde music through this chap Tippett and he ought to do a lot of talks." And Tippett did do a lot of talks.'[11]

Tippett was excited by radio as a medium, and thought the flexible and cross-disciplinary planning of the Third Programme was the way to make the most of it – in contrast to what he saw as the 'entrenched' Music Department of the early 1950s 'which rarely rose above the general reproduction of music in concert form'. Writing in 1959, he recalled being asked to do the Schoenberg series 'not at all because I was a Schoenbergian in the musical sense, but because I was passionately interested in the possibilities of Third Programme broadcasting'.

> I proposed that we should treat Schönberg's life as symbolical of all the artistic problems, in the widest possible sense, of the first fifty years of

8 Isaacs to Rutland, 2 January 1952, WAC Schoenberg, composer file 1.
9 *Observer*, 25 April 1943, 2, and 19 December 1943, 2.
10 Glock, *Notes in Advance* (Oxford: Oxford University Press, 1991), 47.
11 Amyot, interviewed by Humphrey Carpenter, 3 May 1994, WAC R143/2/1.

this century. The unusual quality of this approach is that we rarely use a composer's life in this way, where we may more often see a poet's. But it is quite certain that Schönberg himself, composer, writer and painter, was a true figure to be made into such a symbol.[12]

Tippett wanted the series to 'give the feel of intellectual Europe before the Nazis', placing Schoenberg among a host of other artists and thinkers and ranging across literature, psychology, mysticism and astrology. With such wide-ranging extra-musical ideas – and, it must be admitted, a lack of sympathy with Schoenberg's musical language on the part of both Tippett and Isaacs – it is unsurprising that some of the practical arrangements for the concerts were not ideal, and that the talks loomed larger in the Editor's mind than the actual music. It is symptomatic that the talks in the series were all accorded a repeat (and in some cases a *Listener* reprint), but most of the concerts were not. The determination to avoid 'apostles of Schönberg' also meant that the BBC deprived itself of much useful expertise. Indeed, the series was already on air when Isaacs remembered that one of the foremost British experts on Schoenberg's music was a former colleague – it seems extraordinary the BBC should have forgotten this. He wrote rather desperately to Tippett:

> A rather horrid thought struck me a few minutes ago, which is that we have not found a place anywhere in the Schoenberg series for Edward Clark to speak. I should have thought of this long ago, but I did not, and no-one drew my attention to the omission. Both because he is the President of the I.S.C.M. and the L.C.M.C., and because he would indeed be the spokesman for all the enthusiasts, and because I suppose he has done more than any one man in this country for Schoenberg's music, I feel certain that a place ought to be found for him somewhere to speak on some aspect of Schoenberg's work. I am sorry if this appears to be a spanner in the works, but despite all I have said about keeping away from the partisan spirit, I feel his omission would cause quite unnecessary offence and would be taken to be deliberate by all those who did not know that it was accidental.[13]

Keller therefore may have had some justification for his view of the BBC's series as 'a protracted amateur performance in the worst sense', though it did produce some broadcasts for which he was grateful – one was Mátyás Seiber's talk on 'Composing with Twelve Notes', which he and Mitchell reprinted in *Music Survey*. Overall, however, Keller did not think the series had done Schoenberg many favours:

---

12 Tippett, *Moving into Aquarius* (St Albans: Paladin, 1974), 28–9.
13 Isaacs to Tippett, 2 January 1952, WAC RCONT1 Tippett Artist file 1B, 1952–55.

The BBC's Victory over Schönberg [extract]
MR XIII/2 (May 1952): 130–31

It immediately emerges that the series is a child of ambivalence rather than of unmixed love. It emerges from the choice of the editor, of the speakers, of the performers, it emerges from the general disorganization which includes the provision of disastrously short rehearsal times in at least three important instances. Nevertheless, the series comes to include events for which the artistic listener has to be unqualifiedly grateful. In fact, the listener too is forced into a position of ambivalence.

(1) The *General Editor* is Michael Tippett, who approaches his task unprejudiced by any digested knowledge. It is at once apparent that the Third has chosen the "objective approach" – a wonderful rationalization of ambivalence which conveniently forgets that, applied to an as yet esoteric composer, objectivity must needs mean ignorance. [. . .] I have the greatest respect for Tippett the composer and Tippett the thinker, but none for his accepting this job: it is as if I were to accept the general editorship of a Sibelius or Delius series.

(2) *Of the other speakers*, three are outstanding: Seiber on Schönberg's technique, Clark on the Berlin, and Kolisch on the American years: islands of facts in a sea of unoriginal and irrelevant phantasies. Wellesz is another of those wonderfully ambivalent, "objective" selections: the only Schönberg pupil who has turned away from Schönberg. He makes an honest job of his talk and tries indeed to be objective, but that is not enough, for his waning interest in Schönberg renders him incompetent, in fact ignorant, as far as the composer's later works and theoretical concepts are concerned. It is sad to get from the first and enthusiastic Schönberg biographer such doubly wrong information as that "from now on" (*i.e.* after *Pierrot Lunaire*) Schönberg used as the basis for every (*sic*) composition a theme (*sic*) consisting of all the notes of the chromatic scale, or that Schönberg rejected "atonal" in favour of "atonical", which was true enough at the time, but meanwhile the composer, in his as yet unpublished book on *Structural Functions of Harmony*, had (without Wellesz' knowledge) developed the concept of "pantonality" instead. Besides, Wellesz mistranslates a crucial passage in Schönberg's manifesto-like programme note for the "George" Songs, putting "craftsmanship" for "Sicherheit". The motley array of speakers includes Alan Price-Jones who isn't even a musician and fortunately knows absolutely nothing about Schönberg so that he is compelled to confine himself to irrelevant remarks on "The Background of Old Vienna" (Schönberg should have listened to that one!), and Alfred Polgar, whom to interview the BBC apparently pays Tippett a journey

to Switzerland, the yield being of course nil, for Polgar (a first-class essayist, literary and dramatic critic and with Freud the best German stylist since Schopenhauer) knows as much about Schönberg as any old Viennese intellectual.

(3) In the *selection of performers* too, an ambivalent attitude, or/and an abysmal ignorance is apparent, in that there is a definite tendency to choose well qualified musicians for the one job for which they aren't. The second Quartet is given to the New London, whose highly promising young leader hasn't the first idea about this music (already the *tempo* of the opening finishes everything) and to Patricia Neway (somewhat better in *Erwartung*) whose approach could not be wronger; the best possible, because practical criticism of her performance is unintentionally given by Wellesz when he plays the opening of the fourth movement on a record of an excellent performance: suddenly the virginal listener understands what the music means. Perhaps the most amusing case is that of the "George" Songs which are given, at outrageously short notice, to Esther Salaman and Paul Hamburger. Musical musicians, and unprejudicedly adventurous ones too, in all conscience, but the trouble is that Schönberg did not write the work for mezzo (a fact which the BBC, with its thorough objectivity, does not find out), so that Miss Salaman has to transpose some of the Songs and thereby eliminate the harmonic structure from the performance. Literally opposite Broadcasting House sits Erwin Stein, Schönberg's oldest pupil, the first exponent of the twelve-tone method, and the first coach of the "George" Songs.

The series has not finished at the time of writing, but the BBC's score over Schönberg is so high that victory is certain.

But there was worse to come. Tippett's final talk, entitled 'Air from Another Planet' broadcast on 21 March, contained an error relating to Schoenberg's famous fear of the number thirteen that was particularly upsetting:

21 March – telegram to Michael Tippett

OSKAR ADLER NEVER WARNED SCHOENBERG OF ANYTHING WHATSOEVER DID NOT WRITE ALLEGED LETTER DOES NOT BELIEVE IN NUMEROLOGY YOU MUST CHANGE INCRIMINATING END OF YOUR TALK IN SUNDAYS REPEAT LETTER FOLLOWING

HANS KELLER

A letter did follow, posted the same day and couched in the most dramatic terms: 'Fortunately Dr. Adler's wireless is out of order, so that he will not have heard your talk. But he may hear the repeat on Sunday, and if the concluding section remains unchanged, its groundless accusation may kill him.'[14]

The nature of the accusation was spelled out in a letter to *The Listener* the following week:

27 March 1952 – to the editor of *The Listener*

Sir, – I write on a serious matter, not to criticise, but factually to rectify the concluding section of Michael Tippett's 'Air from Other Planets', which talk was the last event in the Third Programme's Schönberg series. Mr. Tippett referred anonymously to what he did not realise was a wrong report in the *Musical Quarterly*, New York, October 1951, according to which Schönberg had, on the occasion of his seventy-sixth birthday, received a letter from his friend Oskar Adler warning him that the coming year was critical because seven and six add up to thirteen.

Schönberg died on July 13, 1951, at the age of seventy-six, and the report implied, however unintentionally, that Dr. Adler's alleged letter contributed indirectly to Schönberg's death. Mr. Tippett made this implication yet more explicit by adding, in an atmosphere which he had charged with emotion: 'Poor Schönberg! What a strange friend!'

With the full authority of Dr. Adler (who is of Schönberg's age and is at present recovering from a serious illness), I wish to state emphatically that (1) he never wrote the alleged letter; (2) he never, on this or any occasion, warned Schönberg of anything whatsoever; (3) he does not, in fact, believe in numerological superstitions.

Yours, etc.,

HANS KELLER

Tippett clearly thought Keller was over-reacting: 'Don't let us get it out of proportion. I mentioned neither Adler's name nor the Musical Quarterly, so it can only be such people (very few indeed) who have seen the M.Q. in this country, who will know to whom by implication I referred.'[15] The strength of Keller's reaction may be attributed to the fact that he had already been trying for months to get *The Musical Quarterly* to publish a retraction of the original wrong report on which Tippett's story was based – as well his concern for Adler, who had recently suffered several bouts of severe illness. To Keller the issue was simple: a damaging wrong fact had been published, which should be corrected before it spread any further. But the author of the article, Walter Rubsamen, had been upset by what he

14 Keller to Tippett, 21 March 1952, CULHK.
15 Tippett to Keller, 22 March 1952, WAC RCONT1 Tippett Artist file 1B.

saw as Keller's 'contentious tone', and took some time to admit his mistake and its unfortunate implication. Even when he did, he did not seem to think that it was possible to do anything about it in *The Musical Quarterly*.[16]

16 April 1952 – to Paul Henry Lang, editor of *The Musical Quarterly*

Dear Dr. Lang,

Enclosed please find a copy of a letter to which Prof. Rubsamen has added the following note: – "I suggest that this be published in The Music Review. The Musical Quarterly has never made a practice of printing material of this sort. – W.R."

I was stunned and had to call in a colleague in order to believe my eyes. He observed – very acutely, I think – that this note completed a chain of reactions that might go straight into a Kafka novel.

The Musical Quarterly publishes a piece of wrong and incriminating information. My correction is not published, but referred to the author of the article in question. The author does not hasten to send a correction to the Musical Quarterly, but sends me an evasive letter which does not admit the misinformation, states that my personal feeling was responsible for my impression that he was implicating someone, suggests that editorial cuts must have contributed to this feeling (surely a suggestion which, if there is <u>any</u> point in it at all, ought to be submitted in public print), and actually reproaches me with the "tone" of my letter. At this stage in the proceedings I appear as an ill-mannered busy-body.

Meanwhile his misinformation, whose implications I am supposed to have more or less invented, is passed on, via the British Broadcasting Corporation, to millions, and the implications are made as explicit as (legally) possible. But it is only after (a) a renewed and detailed remonstrance, (b) my pointing out to him the public consequences of his misinformation, and (c) my sending him a cutting from the BBC's publication "The Listener" containing my emphatic denial of the information and implications in question, that the author finds it necessary to admit that his information was wrong. He does not, however, correct it in the journal where he published it, but suggests that I should walk up to the Editor of The Music Review and say: "Please devote a bit of your space (i.e. money) to a correction of, and apology for, a mistake made by another journal in another country." And the readers of The Musical Quarterly shall, apparently, remain misinformed.

16 Rubsamen's original article was 'Schoenberg in America', *MQ* XXXVII/4 (October 1951): 469–89.

My original request stands, but this is my last long letter substantiating it. There is little pleasure for one who lives by his pen in spending time and money on this kind of correspondence. It is yet less pleasurable for a young musicologist to pick a quarrel with the Musical Quarterly and its highly distinguished Editor. But if you know me at all, you will realize that there is only one course of action open to me. If – as I cannot bring myself to believe – it is the "practice" of the Musical Quarterly not to correct its errors and not to apologize for damaging implications arising therefrom, if, in short, my original request is not acceded to, I shall raise hell.

I shall be most grateful for your immediate reply.

This letter had the desired effect. Lang assured Keller 'I can fully understand your indignation' and Rubsamen's retraction was published in *The Musical Quarterly* at last.[17]

A picture of British reactions to the death of Schoenberg would be incomplete without looking at the May 1952 issue of William Glock's journal *The Score*. *The Score* was an exact contemporary of Keller and Mitchell's 'New Series' of *Music Survey* (having also made its appearance in the summer of 1949), but the two journals were very different. *The Score* appeared much less frequently, was not intended to be topical, and initially contained no reviews. It was also notable for its interest in early music (something that never much concerned Keller) and its lack of interest in the nineteenth century. Stravinsky apart, there was not a vast amount in its pages about twentieth-century music – until the Schoenberg issue, which seems to have marked a turning-point in more ways than one. It is important to make this point, since Glock's later association with the avant garde has led some to portray *The Score* as a specifically contemporary magazine from the start, or to assume that since Glock had studied in Berlin when Schoenberg was teaching there, he had become a Schoenbergian in the early 1930s.[18] But it was Hindemith and Bartók to whom Glock was initially drawn, followed by Stravinsky, who became his main focus after the war. Of Schoenberg's works, the

---

17 *MQ* XXXVII/3 (July 1952): 501.
18 See for example Neil Edmunds, 'William Glock and the British Broadcasting Corporation's Music Policy', *Contemporary British History* 20/2 (June 2006): 233–61. However, it was performance, rather than composition, that was Glock's main focus in Berlin; and if he had any composition lessons, they would have been with Hindemith, not Schoenberg (see Glock's letters home to his family, BLWG MS Mus.935).

only one on which Glock wrote before the 1950s was the Piano Concerto, given at the Proms in 1945. His view was then – and remained – that 'Schönberg is, above all, an anti-modernist. What he discovered was a technique which would allow him to continue writing in the great Viennese tradition.' As to the twelve-tone technique itself, Glock doubted at this point that it could have any universal application and thought it 'only valid for Schönberg and for those in the same spiritual situation'.[19]

After this, Glock largely left Schoenberg to one side until 1952 – despite the composer having offered him two of his essays for *The Score*'s first issues.[20] Although he did (unsuccessfully) invite Schoenberg to lecture at his Bryanston Summer School in 1949, Glock did not feature any of his music (or Berg's or Webern's) in the concerts there – neither that year, nor throughout the five years of the School's Bryanston period – an omission he himself later admitted was 'strange'. For Glock, it was Stravinsky, not Schoenberg, who was the cornerstone of his understanding of contemporary music – a fundamental difference between him and Hans Keller. As Glock described it, 'we set out in twentieth-century music from different points of the compass':

> For Keller, the Schoenbergian attempt to preserve a continuous development from the Viennese classics to the present day seemed natural and inevitable. For myself, on the other hand, both through temperament and artistic incli-nation, the path followed by Stravinsky lay much closer.[21]

It seems to have been the *Music & Letters* obituary symposium that prompted Glock's decision to make Schoenberg the main subject of his next issue. He now embarked on a serious study of Schoenberg, and his diary is peppered with lists of the scores and records he was acquiring and notes of talks with Schoenberg pupils Erwin Stein, Karl Rankl, Max Deutsch and Edward Clark (plus a note to ask Oskar Adler if he might write 'something on S's early days'). He also approached Roberto Gerhard, Roger Sessions and Mátyás Seiber for articles, and translated Frank Martin's 'Schönberg et nous'. He went down to Wadhurst with Tippett and spent time discussing their respective Schoenberg projects, jotting down notes in his diary afterwards:

> What kind of human being are we trying to express? . . . Can anyone describe in metaphor or otherwise their understanding of atonal music? S's own writings are v. muddled. . . . Consider the 'old' rhythms (and textures) of S. . . . The waltzes! . . . Has the 20th C discovered any new forms? Does this matter?[22]

---

19 'Music,' *The Observer*, 16 September 1945, 2.
20 See Schoenberg to Glock, 2 August and 7 September 1949, ASC.
21 Glock, *Notes in Advance*: 103.
22 Diary entries for 20–21 November 1951, BLWG MS Mus.972.

His reading at the time included Stuckenschmidt's new biography of Schoenberg and several foreign journals, including the 1924 and 1934 issues of *Anbruch* and the French journal *Contrepoints*, where he first read the writings of Pierre Boulez. At the same time, he read in Virgil Thomson's new essay collection *Music Right and Left* Thomson's account of what was going on in Paris and how 'its most intelligent critic, in my judgment, is Pierre Boulez, also a composer of phenomenal gifts.'[23] Glock was intrigued:

> S[choenberg] & B[erg] condemned for compromising between 12-tone technique and tonality; also for using old forms. Thus S & B at once wrote works as grandiose as any of the preceding period, while W[ebern] avoided these signs of transition. What is the form of 12-tone music?? W's 'rigorous purity & tactical modesty'. The actual impact of the music must not be forgotten; nor the physical basis, or lack of basis. Boulez accuses S. of presumption (in casting his music at once in large forms) and of timidity (in calling on sonata form, rondo, passacaglia etc). W → a new 'être musical'.[24]

Glock approached Boulez about a Schoenberg article – 'just wrote on the off-chance to Paris and said "Would you like to contribute?"'[25] – and in December a manuscript arrived, in Boulez's characteristically microscopic script. It proved 'a terror to translate' and Glock asked Clare Sheppard to work on it. After she produced a first draft, they spent the day on 19 December struggling with it together – 'I wondered sometimes during our long session whether it's worth all the trouble.' Even after that it needed considerably more work: his diary shows him 'still working on Boulez's article' a month later.[26]

It was worth the trouble, for when it appeared this article became the most famous piece of writing *The Score* ever published and it marked the start of what was to become an important association between Glock and Boulez. Translation into English brought Boulez's radical views to a wider international audience in the same year as several notable performances of his music. The month the article appeared, Boulez and Messiaen performed his revolutionary essay in total serialism *Structures I* during the 1952 Paris festival, and a few weeks later *Le soleil des eaux* was given at the ISCM Festival in Salzburg. Then in July came Boulez's first appearance at Darmstadt and the long-awaited performance there of his Second Piano Sonata.

Still, in 1952 the new avant garde, of which Boulez was to become the leading light, was as yet only a tiny pin-prick on the musical horizon, especially in

23 'On Atonality', *Music Right and Left* (New York: Henry Holt, 1951), 181. Thomson had lived in Paris for many years between the wars and maintained close contacts there after he moved to New York in 1940.

24 Diary entry, 25 November 1951, on Boulez, 'Moment de J.- S. Bach', *Contrepoints* 7 (1951): 71–86.

25 Glock, interviewed for Barry Gavin's film on the Summer School, *A few yards out to sea* (1988).

26 See diary entries 29 November, 7 & 19 December 1951 and 18 January 1952, BLWG MS Mus.972–3

Britain, where the idea that there could be something even *more* radical than Schoenberg was scarcely conceivable. Eric Blom and Richard Capell had come across Boulez's 'brilliant and penetrating' writings in *Contrepoints* in 1950, but had not heard any of his music – 'when we do, shall we find him entertaining?'[27] The score of the Second Piano Concerto reached the BBC in 1950: 'Look at it – oh lor!' wrote Leonard Isaacs to Herbert Murrill, who responded 'I have looked at it and can hardly believe my eyes. Home Service listeners wd hardly be able to believe their ears.' Two years later, *Le soleil des eaux* was actually approved for broadcasting by the BBC's score-reading panel, and the honest struggles of its three assessors make interesting reading.[28] But otherwise there was little sense in Britain that another revolution was on the horizon. Most critics seem to have felt that (as William Mann put it in *Tempo*) 'the age of experimentation that succeeded the revolt from tonality would seem to be over,' and modernism was now (to quote *The Times*) both 'hopelessly dated' and an unfortunate *cul-de-sac* from which continental Europeans were still struggling to extricate themselves. 'Ours has become a time', thought Mann, 'to sit back and thrash the whole business out.'[29] Keller too thought then that 'the emergence of new schools of composition is unlikely, now that the musical world has more or less settled down between the poles of Schoenberg and Stravinsky.'[30]

~

In 1952, Glock and Keller had still not met – though they were very much aware of each other: Glock remembered Keller as 'a prominent member of many concert audiences, animated and note-scribbling'.[31] Keller's copy of *The Score*'s Schoenberg issue survives, and it is interesting to see his reaction to its contents. He clearly read it carefully, and frequent annotations appear in the margins of his copy.

May 1952 – to William Glock

Your Schoenberg issue. Could have been worse, could have been better.

Hans Keller

27 See Capell, 'Review of Periodicals', *M&L* XXXI/2 (April 1950): 177–82, and Blom, 'Music, Letters and Things', *Observer*, 2 April 1950, 10.
28 The readers were Benjamin Frankel, Clarence Raybould and Gordon Jacob, WAC R27/553. It was not broadcast for another decade.
29 See William Mann's review of the first (and only) issue of the new ISCM journal 'Music Today' in *Tempo* 15 (Spring 1950): 35–6. Also see *The Times* reviews of the first concert of Humphrey Searle's new 'Society for Twentieth-Century Music', 29 January 1952, 7, and the 1952 ISCM Festival, 16 July 1952, 5.
30 'The 26th I.S.C.M. Festival at Salzburg', *Tempo* 24 (Summer 1952): 14, 31–3.
31 Glock, *Notes in Advance*, 103.

According to Glock's recollection, this postcard was his first ever communication from Keller, and 'a brief period of correspondence' followed – Glock's diary notes letters between them on 17 May, and on 9, 11 and 17 June. None of these has survived, though it is safe to assume that Keller was almost certainly taking vehement issue with the contents of *The Score*. Glock remembered his early letters from Keller as being 'invariably aggressive' – indeed the one that arrived on 17 June is marked with three exclamation marks in his diary.

Glock had opened his Schoenberg issue with an editorial in which he contrasted the international adoption of Schoenbergian dodecaphony with the 'isolated genius' of Stravinsky. Judging by his marginalia, Keller questioned Glock's contention that no younger composers were following Stravinsky ('What about Stravinskyism (ostinati, staticism etc)') and disputed the description of Schoenberg's rhythms as 'stale'. But he marked with approval the idea that 'the subtle interrelation between horizontal and vertical . . . may well be one of Schönberg's most profound suggestions, one of his greatest contributions to musical thought.'

In Boulez's article, Keller must have recognised a polemicist as pugnacious as himself. Its mere title – 'Schönberg is Dead' – was startling. 'The title was aggressive, yes,' Boulez admitted, though he insisted the content was not.[32] Writing to John Cage at the time, Boulez justified his polemical stance as 'indispensable in order to be able to separate me from the dodecaphonic academicians'.[33] In the early 1950s Keller too was getting fed up with a new dodecaphonic orthodoxy he found emerging in the new-music scene, just as irksome as the anti-dodecaphonic orthodoxy of the old British Establishment. Reporting on the 1952 ISCM Festival, he complained that 'The new Certificate is TWELVE-TONE. In the programme notes you could read that X had come to terms with the twelve-tone technique, that Y was just going through the critical period of coming to terms with the twelve-tone technique, and that Z had definitely promised to come to terms with the twelve-tone technique the day after tomorrow. . .'[34]

Boulez's proposition was that although Schoenberg had 'brought about one of the greatest revolutions that has ever taken place in music', he had failed to see the 'true nature' of his own method. As Boulez saw it, Schoenberg seemed to want only 'to construct works of the same kind as those of the tonal world he had just abandoned' rather than explore potential new structures specific to twelve-tone composition. To Boulez, such compromise with the past was impossible, since 'a contradiction arises between the forms dictated by tonality and a language of which the laws of organization are still only dimly perceived.' Only Webern had composed works 'whose form arises inevitably from the given material', while Schoenberg's music was full of 'reminiscences of a discarded world':

---

32 Boulez, interviewed for *A few yards out to sea* (1988).

33 Boulez to John Cage, December 1951, in *The Boulez–Cage Correspondence*, ed. Jean-Jacques Nattiez (Cambridge: Cambridge University Press, 1993), 118.

34 '26th ISCM Festival and Third Twelve-tone Congress', *MR* XIII/4 (November 1952): 298–9.

> Let us then, without any wish to provoke indignation, but also without shame or hypocrisy, or any melancholy sense of frustration, admit the fact that SCHÖNBERG IS DEAD.

Keller – for whom Schoenberg's reintegration of tonality and 'simultaneous structural functionality for dodecaphony and tonality' made complete sense[35] – would have disagreed with much of this, and in a marginal note on Glock's preface he wrote that 'Schoenberg found a new-fashioned way of constructing those traditional forms which remain traditional because they are eternal.' In the margins of Boulez's essay he took issue with his opening statement that Schönberg's work is 'essentially experimental', probably because the picture of Schoenberg as a technical experimenter rather than expressive artist was one that Keller was used to countering – and indeed had just done so again while reading Virgil Thomson's *Score* essay in the same issue. Thomson had claimed that it was 'the designing and perfecting of [his] mechanism' that was 'the guiding preoccupation of Schönberg's career'. 'The works themselves,' he went on, 'are all secondary to a theory; they do not lead independent lives.' ('Idiot', thought Keller.)

The *Score* article that most impressed Keller was Roger Sessions's 'Notes on Schönberg and the "Method of Composing with Twelve Tones"', which bears several marginal notes of praise. Glock too had been particularly pleased with this, considering it 'one of the best things in No. 6'.[36] Keller thought Sessions's history of the chromatic impulse 'very good' and particularly liked his definition of a musical problem as being 'an *expressive* crisis' not a technical one: 'The concept of technique,' Sessions wrote (and Keller underlined this) 'has to do with solutions, not with crises or problems as such.' His whole article was an argument against taking technical ideas out of context: Schonberg's music 'is greater than any system or technique'. Keller also approved of Sessions' criticism of the 'kind of orthodoxy' that had developed around dodecaphony – 'a convenience since orthodoxy offers both a safe refuge and an easy point of attack' – which must be false because dodecaphony is constantly in development: 'precisely because it is a living process and not a dogma, it means something different, and shows a different aspect, in every individual personality.'

Unfortunately Glock and Keller did not manage to bring their epistolary discussions to any measure of agreement (or agreement to differ) at this stage, since Keller left for an extended stay in Austria just at the point when Glock had taken offence at his letter of 17 June. Glock wrote straight back to Keller the same day, in terms which may perhaps be guessed from the following:

---

35 For the rest of his life, Keller remained intensely interested in the repressed tonal background of Schoenberg's atonal harmony. See his review of Kenneth Hicken's book on Schoenberg's Op. 19 (*Tempo* 151 (December 1984): 37–8), whose 'minutely specific investigations into the harmonic aspect of Schoenberg's post-tonal music belong to our century's most illuminating analytic endeavours' and subsequent correspondence with Alexander Goehr, CULHK.

36 Diary, 5 March 1951, BLWG, MS Mus.972.

2 December 1952 – to William Glock
BLWG MS Mus.954

Dear Mr. Glock:

I am replying to your letter of June 17 which reached me half an hour before I left for a 4 months' stay in Austria.

Why do people always start to teach you as soon as they feel offended? I have a horrible suspicion that teaching is a chronic state of offendedness.

What you call my arrogance is the orchestration of my frankness and, like all good orchestration, a means of economy.

In point of fact I am extremely humble, in that I feel too ignorant to talk about certain things (say, Sibelius) about which I know more than many who write about them in the most self-assured manner.[37] Years back, John Amis told me that my attitude reminded him of yours, that you and I ought to meet, and that we should probably get on very well with each other. That's why I was abrupt. I simply dropped preliminaries.

I know when I know and shut up when I don't. Just as the latter attitude isn't self-abasing, the former isn't overbearing. In fact, they're both the same: realistic.

In a word, it seems improbable that I'll have changed – in this respect – by 1960.

I did not want to offend you: I respect you too much. I did not intend to seem what I am not (arrogant): I respect myself too much.

Yours sincerely,

Hans Keller

P.S. Despite our row, you will perhaps agree with my Editorial in MS IV/3 (enclosed).

Thus Keller got off on the wrong foot with the man who was to be his most important future collaborator. David Drew, who was soon to know both men well, was under the impression that the Schoenberg issue of *The Score* 'precipitated a state of war between *The Score* and *Music Survey*'. This may be an overstatement,

---

37 Two years later, Keller broke his resolution not to talk about Sibelius in a detailed appreciation (probably on one hearing and without seeing the score) of his incidental music for Hofmannsthal's *Jedermann*, Op. 83, provoked by Scott Goddard's dismissal of its 'slender contribution to the drama', *MR* XVI/2 (May 1955): 141–5. Another Sibelius piece he liked was the Violin Concerto: 'Those who really understand Sibelius tell me that it's one of his more primitive works, which is no doubt why I understand it and love it.' Keller to Bayan Northcott, 20 October 1978, CULHK.

but Drew was probably right when he went on to say that it was not only the Schoenberg articles that had provoked Keller:

> Hans Keller's sense of personal and public affront was not, perhaps, unaffected by the fact that in the same issue [Glock] had also dared to publish Anthony Milner's hostile review of *Billy Budd* (balanced though it was by Peter Gellhorn's favourable one) and, worse still, Herbert Murrill's endorsement of *The Rake's Progress*, a masterpiece that Hans at that time held in the deepest contempt.[38]

Any 'state of war' between the two journals could not have lasted very long, as *Music Survey* stopped publishing at this point. However its spirit (in the sense both of Keller and Mitchell's partnership and of its distinctive polemical defensive voice) was prolonged into 1953 by the publication of their book *Benjamin Britten: A Commentary on His Works from a Group of Specialists* in December 1952 and the ensuing critical fall-out. Glock reviewed the book in a half-hour talk on the Third Programme at the end of January 1953, in terms that made very clear the differences between him and Keller over Britten and Stravinsky.

The appearance of such a substantial and serious book about a composer who was not yet forty caused quite a stir, and it was very widely reviewed – copies of over a hundred reviews are preserved in the Britten–Pears library, and Ernest Newman, for example, twice devoted his *Sunday Times* column to it.[39] While there was much admiration for its conscientious scholarship, it was thought by many to be marred by an over-defensive and 'reverential' attitude to its subject – who, as Winton Dean pointed out, 'is too potent a figure to require a bodyguard'.[40] Glock, whose early admiration for Britten when he was writing for the *Observer* in the 1940s[41] had now moderated, also found in it 'a somewhat monotonous chanting of the 150th Psalm'. The presence of some of Britten's close associates like Peter Pears, Erwin Stein, Imogen Holst and the Earl of Harewood among the list of twenty contributors strengthened the impression of a lack of objectivity and led some critics (including Eric Blom) to allege that this was less a group of specialists than a group of friends.[42]

Predictably, Blom's review led to another exchange of letters between him and Keller, after Keller and Mitchell's insistence that 'we are neither friends nor even personal acquaintances of Benjamin Britten' was met by Blom's retort that 'they write as if they were, and one is justified in drawing the obvious conclusion from the fact that the symposium they edit contains contributions from so many people

---

38 Drew, 'An open letter to Sir William Glock on the occasion of his 80th birthday', *Tempo* (December 1988): 21–3.

39 On 4 and 18 January 1953.

40 *MT* 94/1322 (April 1953): 165–7.

41 See, for example, his lyrical review of the premiere of the Serenade for Tenor, Horn and Strings (*Observer*, 24 October 1943).

42 Blom, 'Bouquet for Britten', *Observer*, 21 December 1952, 6.

who <u>are</u> friends and acquaintances; also from the other fact that Mr. M. and Mr. K. rise in arms the moment someone expresses disapproval or even a doubt of anything Mr. Britten has done.'[43] Still, it was true that Keller hardly knew Britten at this date (the meeting arranged by Stein had not been followed up by closer acquaintance) and Mitchell hadn't met him at all. But when the *Commentary* was published, Britten wrote to them both: 'I don't see why we should continue to please our detractors by remaining strangers – can't we really meet and have a good talk, someday when this opera is finished and we can all be in London?'[44]

Keller's own contribution to the book was a new essay on *Peter Grimes* and a long final chapter entitled 'The Musical Character' – and it was this final chapter which elicited the strongest reactions. Its first half consisted of a reprint of his 'Britten and Mozart' essay; the second was a lengthy disquisition on 'The Crisis of Beauty and Melody' in twentieth-century music.[45] Here is an extract from the latter's section on new music's move 'From Beauty to Truth':

From Beauty to Truth [extract]

(i) The General Cultural Situation

More sexual than aggressive energies are needed for the creation of beauty; more aggressive than sexual energies are needed for the discovery of truth. Recent times have brought greater sexual freedom and perhaps unprecedented frustration of aggressive tendencies, so that from the standpoint of social psychology alone the development from beauty to truth must be considered inevitable. That far more people are being killed and tortured today than in previous times when there was less talk about humanity does not of course mean anything in terms of psychic economy: it all depends on how you kill them. Our technical advances have unfortunately made it possible for us to kill a maximal number of people at the minimal level of psychic expenditure, whereas formerly even small-scale killings involved the release of powerful amounts of aggression, with the emergence of correspondingly powerful guilts afterwards. In addition, while opportunities for the discharge of aggression are steadily decreasing, aggressive urges themselves are actually on the increase, not only because unreleased aggression makes for further aggression (whether turned against the self or outward), but also because our comparative freedom from sexual restraint increases our intra-psychic inhibitions and anxieties; owing to the infantile Oedipus situation we tend to fight for a freedom we cannot bear – all the less since the loss of religion (no matter whether this means, objectively,

43 Blom to Mitchell, 13 January 1953, CULHK.
44 Britten to Keller and Mitchell, 21 January 1953, BPF.
45 Reprinted in *BB2013*.

the loss of truth, or of illusion, or of both), itself partly the effect
and partly the cause of increased aggression, has robbed us of our
security which the new and often equally emotional religions, whether
Sciences or States, can only very partly restore. Hence unprecedented
frustration, hence unprecedented neurosis and aggressiveness. From the
concentration camp to the sado-masochistic, percussive double stoppings
on what was once the 'singing' instrument of the violin, sadism is liable to
manifest itself on every level of barbarity or sublimation. [. . .]

(ii) The Artistic and Musical Situation

One of the reasons why we tend to consider Mozart's truths beautiful,
and Bartók's full of many other things beside and above and opposed
to beauty, is that by this late time in our culture most pleasant truths
have been discovered and it remains the unpleasant task of our
geniuses to unearth repressed material which the conscious mind
duly regards as ugly. It needs more courage today than ever to be a
good artist, and more cowardice than ever to be a bad artist; nor is it
surprising that there are so few people left who have the courage not
to be artists at all.

The time of the simply beautiful feeling as well as of the simple tragedy
is over because we know all about them; the rest is either silence or
Hollywood or the Soviet Symphony. At the same time, Soviet 'social
realism', Picasso's 'grasping of the world' and Schoenbergian 'truthfulness'
and 'factuality' all assert that truth is better than fiction; again, the same
idea or pretext inspires the furthest opposites.

From Strawinsky's rediscovery of the past (a testimony of our culture's
years; History is a sign of old age) to Schoenberg's discovery of the
future, from Hindemith's utility to Britten's social conscience, from
Schoenberg's inspired thematicism (to thine own theme be true) to
an uninspired remark in the *Oxford Harmony*, vol. 2, which condemns
coloratura and suggests that nowadays composers want, and ought, to
get on with the job, from Bartók's aggressiveness to Strawinsky's sado-
masochism, from Webern's asceticism to Boulez's aggressive narcissism,
from the historical reality behind *Wozzeck* to the spiritual topicality of
Il Prigionero (likewise based on a true story), from the Contemporary
Composer's uninspired compositions to his searching programme notes
on what he thinks are his compositions, the fight for one or the other
aspect of truth and reality is in full if asymmetric swing, criss-crossing and
ploughing the field of new music without much regard for the beauties it
might, and sometimes still does, yield. At its worst, beauty has become a
waste product, at its best a by-product. It is a largely desexualized fight,
then, and perhaps Schoenberg is the only one who has begun, despite

and in conjunction with his powerful aggression, to resexualize music. But then, Schoenberg is of the future, of a new culture.

This kind of writing annoyed a lot of readers – but they also found it highly stimulating, and in many critics the two reactions could be found side by side: 'Hans Keller's pages on "The Musical Character" are an astonishing amalgam of penetration and irrelevance, close argument and arrant swashbuckling,' wrote one; 'Mr. Keller seems at pains to obscure a real gift for musical discourse by indulgence in psychological jargon.'[46] Another confessed himself 'strongly tempted on first reading it to throw the book into the nearest convenient receptacle; but the thing has an odd fascination, and on re-reading it a lot of wheat appears among the tares. One certainly cannot ignore Mr Keller, a fact of which he is probably well aware.'[47] Glock seems to have had a similar reaction, when of all the chapters in the book he found himself simultaneously most irritated by yet most interested in Keller's, on which he focused much of his review. 'Amidst all this nonsense and perversity there are gleams of penetration and of great intelligence: the most annoying chapters are the best.'

It was Keller's reference to Stravinsky's lack of melodic originality – and specifically his statement that 'underlying the melodies of *The Rake's Progress* the listener senses a process less allied to composition than to stamp-collecting' – that Glock found intolerable, and he therefore made Stravinsky as much the subject of his radio talk as Britten. 'It is obvious that we trod on Mr. Glock's Strawinskian toe,' wrote Keller and Mitchell afterwards.[48] 'In retrospect,' Mitchell conceded many years later, 'I'm not at all sure that Glock did not have a point':

> When the *Commentary* came to be re-issued in 1971, I tried to persuade Hans to revise or at least acknowledge what I felt to be an inadequacy – to put it mildly – but without success. However, it led to a truly vintage riposte from the Hans Keller of 1971, who believed he had no right, as he put it, 'to criticize the Hans Keller of 18 years ago: the latter is not around to defend himself'.[49]

As might be imagined, Glock and Keller's relationship did not make any progress for some time after this. The ice was finally broken by David Drew, who shared Keller's love of the cinema and proposed to Glock that the special edition of *The Score* he was planning on American music in 1955 should contain something on Leonard Bernstein's film music – and that Keller should write it. Glock eventually 'allowed me to tempt the still belligerent Keller into the enclaves of *The Score*,' recalled Drew. Glock recorded in his diary: 'Have taken the plunge, and told D. Drew to go ahead.' All went well: Glock thought Keller's piece 'excellent'

---

46 Dean, *MT* 94/1322 (April 1953): 165–7.
47 Alec Robertson, *Time and Tide*, 21 March 1953.
48 Unpublished letter from Keller and Mitchell to the editor of *The Listener*, BPF.
49 *HKI*, 275.

and went on to commission from him an article on Skalkottas: 'take your time; it should be a major affair, and I'm sure it will be.'[50]

That article was never written, probably because of the difficulty of getting access to enough scores and performances of Skalkottas's works in the years after his death. Keller had already written one short piece on Skalkottas – a preview for *The Listener* of a Third Programme broadcast of the Second Piano Concerto – for which he had had to 'rely on my acoustic experience of the recording to be broadcast on Monday: the single score and the two piano reductions in official existence appear to be at Athens'. Still, from what he had so far managed to hear, Keller felt sure that Skalkottas was extraordinary: 'the first real and great twelve-note composer since Schoenberg: Berg was not really a twelve-note composer at all, and Webern was a master of unreality'.[51]

Keller's next article for Glock was – ironically – on Stravinsky, whom he paired – surprisingly – with Gershwin. Discussing the difference between erotic syncopation (Gershwin) and aggressive syncopation (Stravinsky), Keller painted a vivid picture of Stravinsky's rhythm 'swimming upstream', a symptom of the composer's 'creative sado-masochism' investing his music with its 'unique, tense, meaning-laden suppressionism'. He argued against Adorno's view that such anti-expressiveness must mean emptiness, saying instead that it results in 'fullness fully opposed, in a state of statically intense tension which, on the deepest level, is achieved through his opposing the flow of rhythm by rhythm itself'. Gershwin, on the other hand, 'never moves up-stream, never suspends time':

> His syncopations are either anticipations or anticipatory suspensions: when he stems the flow, the effect is that of a floodgate, in that an all the intenser forward-motion is anticipated. . . . Nowhere is this fundamental character difference between him and Stravinsky more striking than where Stravinsky might be thought to meet him on his own ground, in the *Ebony Concerto*, whose every upbeat serves its own opposition, serves to be beaten back or beat itself back.[52]

Keller's interest in Gershwin had been stimulated by the first London production of *Porgy and Bess*, which opened at the Stoll Theatre in Aldwych in October 1952. Once again it was the critical reaction to the work, as much as the work itself, that made him put pen to paper: 'I've been rather annoyed at the high-handed way in which the work has been reviewed,' he wrote to Geoffrey Sharp, telling him he wanted to include it in his next 'First Performances' column. 'The point is that here is a full-blooded musician with plenty of creative imagination – and this is the last thing which these people notice, no matter whether it's Schoenberg or Gershwin.'[53]

---

50 Glock to Keller, 19 April 1956, CULHK.
51 'Nicos Skalkottas: An Original Genius', *Listener* 52/1345 (9 December 1954): 1041.
52 'Rhythm: Gershwin and Stravinsky,' *The Score* 20 (June 1957): 19–31, reprinted in *EOM*, 201–11.
53 Keller to Sharp, 2 December 1952, CULHK.

Leontyne Price as Bess, drawn by Milein Cosman at the London premiere of Porgy and Bess *in 1952. Price signed the portrait 'thank you' because Cosman was 'the first artist who hasn't blacked in our faces'.*

'I find your Porgy & Bess stuff ingenious and interesting,' wrote Sharp when he received Keller's draft in January, 'but I am convinced that Gershwin himself never had the slightest idea of the subtleties you claim to have discovered!' 'Is this supposed to invalidate anything?' asked Keller; 'The things of which a composer usually is aware are so obvious that they need not be analysed.'[54] What Keller wanted to analyse in this particular case was the surprisingly rapid turn to the relative minor's tonic major at the end of the (unrepeated) first line of 'I got plenty o' nuttin'', and the way in which Gershwin used phrase extensions in order to balance excisions of expected symmetry. He proposed 'a new critical principle' that 'in music composed' (as Gershwin's was) 'against a symmetrical rhythmic scheme, every manifest rhythmic irregularity based on an extension will – if it is not arbitrary – be found to counterbalance a latent irregularity based on an abridgment.' This principle he also applied to the passage in Mozart's G minor Piano Quartet K.478, whose rhythmic structure Schoenberg had described as 'an enigma', but which Keller thought 'no longer presents enigmatic syntax if one analyses it with the help of my principle (though there matters are far more complicated than in Gershwin's banjo song, for Mozart composed the passage against *two different* metric background schemes and levels)'.[55]

Keller described Gershwin as 'a major master of minor forms' – a description he also used of Webern, the difference being that 'while Webern was, essentially, a simple-minded master whose language made his miniatures sound complex, Gershwin's was, essentially, a complex genius whose language made his miniatures sound simple.' This comparison Glock found incomprehensible – 'as though in purpose and ideals they inhabited the same universe!'[56] Keller would have countered that with Berg's reported comment to Gershwin ('music is music') and with his own view that it was Gershwin's essential originality that deserved the label 'genius', while Webern's passive nature and 'almost infantile, lifelong dependence on Schoenberg' confined his status to that of a 'master'. 'Genius can be wrong-headed,' he wrote later, 'but the one dependable negative condition of genius has always been that it will not give in to its environment — that it does not wish to be led.'[57]

~

54 Sharp to Keller, 4 January 1953; Keller to Sharp, 5 January 1953, CULHK.

55 Keller's draft for *Music Review* does not survive: quotations are from the revised version he produced for *Monthly Musical Record*: 'Gershwin's Mastery and the Possibility of an Exact Critical Tool'. Both articles remained unpublished, because of length and the Gershwin estate's refusal to permit quotation of music examples from *Porgy and Bess*. Schoenberg's comment about K.478 appeared in 'Brahms the Progressive' (*Style and Idea* (New York: Philosophical Library,1950), 95–6). According to a letter from Keller to Erwin Stein of 8 January 1953, Britten had difficulties with the same passage in performance. Keller concluded, 'I will have to write an article about this place.'

56 Glock, *Notes in Advance*, 103.

57 'Not a Genius', *Spectator* 242/7853 (13 January 1979): 22.

Discussion of music criticism and attempts at its reform gathered pace in Britain during the 1950s, mirroring earlier battles over the criticism of English literature. Donald Mitchell made a thought-provoking contribution to the debate in his 1955 essay 'Criticism: A State of Emergency', where he followed F.R. Leavis in asserting the vital importance of criticism to the relationship between artist and audience, and the necessity of its defence in the face of an over-valuation of historical scholarship. The difficulty of making artistic judgments in the bewildering world of modernism, thought Mitchell, made 'the musicologist's concrete and verifiable achievements' all the more attractive to young writers on music:

> When one realises that the 'authenticity' of musicology functions as a kind of substitute for the value judgments that critics have given up making, it is easy to see why so many talents who might have become critics turn instead to historical, textual or pre-classical studies. . . . [But] only a revival of positive critical judgments can redress the ill-balance of a situation where we permit our own culture to rattle itself to pieces while we impeccably re-assemble fragments of the past.[58]

Musicology in the 1950s was beginning to benefit from institutional support as it became an established subject in British universities. The Faculty of Music at Cambridge was set up in 1947, and Oxford's first music undergraduates began their studies in 1950. History dominated their curricula, and a similar historical focus and interest in 'pre-classical' music was very visible in the schedules of the BBC's new Third Programme. The BBC of the inter-war years had been notable for its adventurous programming of new music, but by 1950 things had changed. Now early music seems to have provided an alternative source of novelty for an institution that was becoming increasingly unsure of how to deal with contemporary composition.

Mitchell's article drew attention to the potentially damaging role of 'public institutions whose *imprimateur* in itself seems to constitute a value judgement'.

> Criticism is by-passed, and the act of dissemination accrues to itself the character of a discrimination, regardless of the actual value of the commodity. The better the institution's intentions, the more 'authoritative' and 'impartial' its reputation, the greater is the danger of passive acceptance of its arbitrary standards.

So great was the level of public funding now flowing into music that the artistic judgements of the institutions channelling it were indeed highly influential. The musical judgement of the BBC in particular was under intense scrutiny. Before the war it had effectively wrested the musical leadership of Britain from the conservatoires, a situation symbolically confirmed by the Ullswater Report of 1936,

---

58 *Tempo* 37 (Autumn 1955): 6–11. Mitchell cited Leavis's 'The Responsible Critic', *Scrutiny* XIX/3 (Spring 1953).

which gave strong support to the BBC's music policy in the face of determined opposition. After 1945 its greatly increased broadcasting hours, rising licence-fee revenue and monopoly in radio further strengthened the BBC's power over music in Britain. It was therefore inevitable that the artistic judgements underlying the deployment of these vast resources were subject to questioning by the representatives of the music profession. The 1950s saw an intense battle over the judgements of the BBC's score-reading panel, as the Corporation tried to show its standards were not 'arbitrary'.[59] During these years the BBC took a step back from any assertion of musical leadership – a situation that changed radically with the appointment of William Glock at the end of the decade. Glock's declaration to the 1962 Pilkington Committee that he wanted to give listeners 'what they will like tomorrow' sounded very like the Corporation's pre-war statement to the Ullswater Committee – when it had claimed to provide 'a service somewhat ahead of what the public would demand were it possible for such demand to be made articulate and intelligible'.[60] In between these two bold declarations, the more cautious tone of the 1950s is well exemplified by the policy statement Maurice Johnstone made to colleagues on taking up the post of Head of Music Programmes in 1953: 'We must do our utmost to destroy finally the impression that we . . . are the arbiters of the musical destiny of Great Britain.'[61]

> There's all the difference in the psychic world between the need to communicate and the need to communicate something true.

As has been seen, Keller could be a fierce critic of the BBC and in 1952 had publicly questioned the judgement of its reading panel after hearing it had rejected Mátyás Seiber's *Ulysses* and Humphrey Searle's *Poem for 22 Strings*. In the same way that he had opposed *The Times*'s policy of anonymous music criticism, he challenged the unaccountable mystery that shrouded the BBC's decisions: 'Since we do not know what happens behind the scenes of the B.B.C.'s musical efforts, we, like the people in an autocratic state, have to depend on rumours. We don't know the names of the so-called listeners-in who report on the competence of performances. We don't know the names of that secret society, the Reading Panel.'[62]

But Keller's main efforts during the 1950s were directed at the reform of criticism rather than broadcasting. In this he agreed with Mitchell that the exercise of artistic judgement was essential (or rather, inevitable) – but so was the establishing of objective fact. Also necessary was a clear understanding of what *is* a fact and which facts are relevant to evaluation: for example, while psychology could contribute to an understanding of music history ('by which I mean, not the

---

59 See for example, the public statement by Controller of Music Richard Howgill in *MO* 911 (August 1953): 651.

60 See Glock, *Notes in Advance*, 115, and WAC R4/7/8/1 (Ullswater Committee 1935/Other Written Evidence, paper 16).

61 'Statement on Ideals and Policy', 14 August 1953, WAC R27/223.

62 *MS* IV/3 (June 1952): 448.

chronology of styles but the evolution of techniques'), Keller thought it irrelevant to evaluation (which he insisted should be strictly 'intra-musical'). He also took issue with using the term 'musicology' to cover the 'unscientific' disciplines of history and textual criticism.[63] In 1953 Keller reorganised his 'First Performances' and 'Film Music and Beyond' columns in *The Music Review* into a new tabular format, as an explicit rejection of 'literary' music criticism in favour of an economical presentation of basic information. He assembled a team of contributors (principally Donald Mitchell, Paul Hamburger, Erwin Stein and his pupil Godfrey Winham) among whom he divided his fee, and they all reviewed using the same set of symbols Keller devised. The aim was to 'distinguish as clearly as possible between objective information, technical criticism, appreciation of content and personal reflexes.' The new scheme was introduced by Keller with a quotation from T.S. Eliot:

> . . . any book, any essay, any note in *Notes and Queries*, which produces a fact even of the lowest order about a work of art is a better piece of work than nine-tenths of the most pretentious critical journalism, in journals or in books.[64]

A year before this, the Earl of Harewood had devoted the March 1952 edition of his *Opera* magazine to a forum on the subject of criticism. One of its contributors had been Benjamin Britten, whose strictures on his own critics – 'practically all have been unobservant if not actually inane'– added fuel to the furore over Keller and Mitchell's *Commentary*. At the same time, Harewood's father-in-law Erwin Stein attempted to compose a 'critical charter' (probably intended for *Opera*, but in the end not published), a draft of which he discussed at some length with Keller. Stein's draft has not survived, but part of their subsequent correspondence has:

[January 1952] – to Erwin Stein

Dear Mr. Stein:

CRITICISM

I have thought about your charter; I have also looked up my copious notes on the subject. I think my first impression was right, tho' not intense enough: as it stands, or as I know it, the charter is naive, limited and primitive. It takes into account a few artistic requirements, and that is all. But without considering the chief forces involved in any "critical" situation, constants as well as the main variables, such a manifesto can have no

---

63 See *MR* XV/4 (November 1954): 307–10 and Keller's subsequent correspondence with H.C. Robbins Landon in CULHK.
64 Eliot, 'The Function of Criticism,' in *Selected Essays* (London: Faber, 1951), 33.

more than journalistic value: it is a first step, and first steps have a way of remaining such. To me personally it seems that the way to hell is plastered with first steps. Above all, it is impossible to discuss the ethics of criticism without taking the sociology and psychology of any critical attitude into consideration. By that route, you arrive at the inevitable limitations of a critic's competence, and at the relative value of his prejudices, and it is from there only that you can start telling a critic what to do, when not to judge and so on. To throw out the mere commandment: "Do not judge!" is childish because judgment is a spontaneous artistic function which no one can ever rid himself of, and all you can achieve by it is that your model critics will give hidden and implied judgments which will be twice as dangerous, because thrice as uncontrolled, as our current idiocies. Good God, if life were as simple as your charter has it, the Ten Commandments would at least have had a chance of success, and Christ's wonderful philosophy would have resulted in moral behaviour rather than moralistic murder. Unfortunately, Moses, Christ and you think of what is to be done before they seriously reflect upon who's supposed to be doing it. When I'm up at your office, I always tend to stop myself thinking and to try and agree as much as possible because I know that otherwise a lot of time will be spent on things which need yet a lot more. Letters like the present one are the expression of my uneasy conscience over my hypocritical behaviour. At the same time, it is impossible for me to go into detail now: that would cost me at least 1,500 words, and for those I need, at the present moment, at least 5 guineas. But this I must say: An ethical charter without the strongest possible scientific foundation is unethical because, literally, untruthful – and your charter's scientific foundation is meagre. Since, however, you confine yourself to half-time commonplaces which have been said a hundred times before and will be said a hundred times again without changing any one's mind, I should be inclined to think that your charter will be relatively harmless and may even be useful inside the confines of OPERA.

After this little eruption, I hope you know me well enough not to misunderstand me when I say that the exclusion of Keller from the issue on criticism is very understandable, as understandable in fact, as the exclusion of Stein from the BBC's SCHOENBERG series. "Zu exponiert" – that was almost exactly Isaacs' implication.

<u>Believe me</u>, I'm not offended: I know the course of our worlds, which is why I shall contribute to changing it – without first steps, but with ten different second steps at once.

Stein was much interested. 'Our differences of approach & attitude towards artistic problems are caused by our different natures. You are a fighter, I am conciliatory & try to mediate.' He defended his strictures against making judgements by the way in which 'publicly announced personal opinions become judgements & judgements verdicts':

> The bad thing with it is the attitude of finality which even a preliminary "judgement" assumes. At the risk of being childish I say: do not "judge".
>
> The competence of the critic is of course one of the major points. But – Hugo Wolf was probably competent in musical matters, but was he competent to "judge" Brahms?
>
> You could not have found a better defence for the BBC's attitude. I am quite satisfied that there was no place for me in this "feature". But I would be happy if you could write for good & simple people without feeling that you have to play down. As for first steps, repeat them until they are commonplaces, or these good & simple people dare to tread it before you prepare the 2nd step for them. They do not want to go to Hell, but you must help them.[65]

[January 1952] – to Erwin Stein

Dear Mr. Stein,

[. . .] Yes, our differences of approach are due to differences of character. I do not doubt the validity of the reasons behind your "Do not judge!" What I doubt is the purpose in front of it. Hugo Wolf's incompetence to judge Brahms is exactly the point where the problem of the critic's competence becomes interesting and urgent, the point where a mind like mine starts rather than stops to think and investigate. That a critic should be musical is obvious, as obvious as the reasons why unmusical people tend to become critics.

I do not see why I should write for good and simple people except when I'm paid enough. [. . .] I have new things to say, and the danger of self-corruption looms large when discoverer and popularizer are rolled into one. Besides, good and simple people are dying out: at the end of a culture, simplicity is bad except in the form of the simplest possible complexity. The simple things have been discovered a long time ago; if and when they need repeating, a sufficiently complex mind should do it which isn't burdened by any new discoveries. Such a mind must think of its public; I must think (in my few spare minutes) of creating one. This is not megalomania: my desk is full of new facts waiting to be expounded which, if simplified, would look dangerously like old facts. They have to create a basic receptivity before someone comes

---

65 Stein to Keller, 12 January 1952, CULHK.

along and simplifies them. <u>A priori</u> simplification (beyond the simplest possible communication "to oneself", as it were) is an excuse, on the part of writer and/or reader, for not thinking to the end. In one respect you misunderstand my character: I'm not an educator, but an educer. Perhaps it is for this reason that, when I educate, I take great care not to educate people who shouldn't be educated. My dog has absolute pitch; yet I'm not trying to get him used to a simplified version of the Ninth. Today he doesn't understand the Freudenthema; tomorrow he'd say it's too simple, in fact banal. Even the necessary simplification (to oneself or the ideal audience) creates dangers of misunderstanding; how much more the "advisable" variety! As long as there are people who hate what I say or write at first sight and come to see my point, on their own account, a week or a month or a year later, I know that I'm precisely on the right track. So you see, in my own way, even I go by my market.

Wozzeck: I was interested in your non-reaction, as interested as you were in my reaction to the work. That I am aware how one has to treat the public in this special case you may see from my baby talk in the November 1951 <u>Music Review</u> (THE ECLECTICISM OF "WOZZECK", p. 311 ff). Incidentally, even the famous C major passage comes from Schoenberg (1st mov. of F sharp minor quartet) and also from the <u>Lieder eines fahrenden Gesellen</u>: and this is <u>not</u> a case of thematic reminiscence. Berg, by the way, is among other things a case of premature – i.e. at first seemingly helpful, later obviously harmful – popularization.

After this, Keller began to think of writing a critical manifesto of his own. Rather than go back to Rockliff, he approached a new publisher – André Deutsch, a fellow Viennese émigré of his own age, who had recently set up a new publishing company and was looking for new authors.

29 September 1953 – to André Deutsch

Dear Andre:

I seem to remember – quite wrongly, no doubt – that some time or other you said (in some milk-bar or other) that if I ever felt like changing publishers and so on. Well, I feel like a semi-change (a complete one is impossible: there are too many commitments) and I suggest

CRITICISM

A Musician's Manifesto

50,000 – 60,000 words, about 10 music type exx.; style technical but breezy. 2 parts; I: Classification & theory of possible and impossible types of criticism; II: Practical part: application of principles of criticism developed in Part I; examples from my own work.

There is no question of my doing anything – even half a chapter – on spec.; I can't afford to play around. Besides, you are in a position to make up your mind whether you want my kind of stuff or not.

Forget it if I misremember your remarks.

Greetings

[Hans]

A few months later Keller reported to Sharp that 'I have signed a contract with André Deutsch for a book on criticism.'[66] Sharp was enthusiastic: 'No doubt it will stir up the old brigade and provoke deep discontent – at least I hope so!'[67]

Keller was also stirring up the old brigade at the Critics' Circle. As soon as he was elected himself, he started proposing other younger writers for membership: his early candidates included Donald Mitchell, Charles Stuart and Wilfrid Mellers, who, as Keller told Sharp, 'always forgets his application for election to membership of the CC somewhere: a Freudian slip ("parapraxis" is the word, but I'm reserving that one for <u>Musical Opinion</u>)'.[68] Sharp became president of the Circle in 1954 and sought Keller's help with its reform: 'I am trying to make a last attempt to turn [the Circle] into a real body with real guts in it,' he told Keller, asking him for 'any good constructive ideas that you and/or anyone else can put forward'.[69] Keller had already promised 'to think of some pungent propositions',[70] but more practical action came the following year, when Keller put the Circle's 'guts' to the test.

The event that prompted this was Frank Howes's *Times* review of a concert by the Juilliard Quartet at the International Music Association on 15 November 1955:

> The quartets were Schönberg's third (1927), Webern's Five Movements for String Quartet (1909), and Bartok's sixth quartet (1939), none of which presented any great difficulties to the following of their procedures. Even Schönberg in this quartet is not using a serial technique but has reverted to classical forms with a set of variations for slow movement. But Schönberg is not so much a composer as a source of composing in others, a great musician but a poor composer with no sap in his music.[71]

Keller was particularly irritated, not only by Howes's usual dismissal of Schoenberg, but by his airy confidence that 'none of [these works] presented

66 Keller to Sharp, 11 May 1954, CULHK.
67 Sharp to Keller, 14 May 1954, CULHK.
68 Keller to Sharp, 22 June 1950, CULHK.
69 Sharp to Keller, 14 May 1954, CULHK.
70 Keller to Sharp, 11 May 1954, CULHK.
71 'Modern Chamber Music', *The Times*, 16 November 1955, 3.

any great difficulties to the following of their procedures' – a statement then invalidated by a basic technical error:

16 November 1955 – to the Editor of *The Times*
SCHOENBERG

Sir, – Reviewing the Juilliard Quartet's performance of Schoenberg's third string quartet, your music critic suggests (November 16) that "Schönberg in this quartet is not using a serial technique." In point of fact, the work is written in serial technique from the first note to the last.

I submit that your readers ought to be offered a chance to reconsider your music critic's qualifications for his confident pronouncements on Schoenberg's stature as a composer in the light of this basic blunder. What would they say if a writer informed his readers that Beethoven did not use a key in his fifth symphony, and proceeded to criticize the composer's creative faculties out of existence?

Yours, etc.,

Hans Keller

The Times declined to print this, so Keller wrote again to insist that at least some sort of factual correction of the wrong information was required. When that also failed, he proposed to address the matter in his next article for *The Music Review*. Geoffrey Sharp was sympathetic, agreeing that *The Times*'s behaviour 'shows a nauseating streak of humbug'. However:

> I do not think that MR can usefully interfere in this for 2 main reasons: that by Feb it will be stale news, and that the bulk of MR's readers are in the US and other foreign countries and would have little interest in the behaviour, however unethical, of an English newspaper.[72]

'If you want to pursue this distasteful business,' Sharp advised him, 'you could bring the humbug out into the light of day by sending the correspondence to Matthew Norgate as Hon. General Secretary of the Critics' Circle'. Thus began a long campaign to persuade the Critics' Circle to censure one of its most influential members – indeed one of its former presidents. After consideration by the Circle's Executive Council in January, and its Music Section in March, the Chairman of the Music Section wrote a formal letter to *The Times* in April 1956:

> It is much regretted that, contrary to precedent, The Times did not print the factual correction contained within Mr. Keller's letters of November 16

---

72 Sharp to Keller, 29 November 1955, CULHK.

and 20 – a correction of some musical consequence which, the section felt, would have been of substantial interest to readers of the original notice.[73]

The Times refused again. That was when the real battle started, for Keller wanted the matter to be submitted to the Press Council. Sharp made the formal proposal to do so at the Music Section's meeting on 10 October, but despite the Section's unanimous agreement on the matter of fact, the majority present voted not to take any further action. Keller complained afterwards about all the members who 'came up to me afterwards & "apologized", "privately" expressing their sympathy & agreement (?) with our case – but one couldn't go that far, had to "compromise" . . . I refused to play the good-loser game & resolve the disharmony in jolly good fellowship.'[74]

Meanwhile, Howes continued to provide grist to Keller's mill with more pronouncements on dodecaphony in *The Times*. In January 1956, for example, he published an article on 'Serial Technique: Why it Attracts Composers', which Keller promptly added to his charge-sheet:

11 March 1956 – to Arthur Jacobs, chair of the Music Section, Critics' Circle [extract]

Dear Arthur,

Further to my complaint against The Times, I should be grateful if you could read this letter to the meeting of the Music Section on March 20.

On January 6, 1956, The Times published an article, obviously by Frank Howes, on 'Serial Technique: Why It Attracts Composers', which culminated in three 'chief objections' to twelve-tone technique. Upon careful scrutiny, I have been unable to detect in it a single piece of correct technical information. Perhaps the most damaging statement occurs at the very beginning: "(The) principles (of composition by means of the tone-row) were first enunciated by Schoenberg about 1910 (sic), when they were iconoclastic in intention. . . .", and so forth.

It will be noted that Mr. Howes anticipates the first twelve-tone compositions by more than 10 years and Schoenberg's "enunciation" of serial principles by several decades. Now, while historical ignorance does not always imply musical ignorance, it clearly follows from Mr. Howes' misinformation that he mistakes so-called "free atonality" for twelve-tonality, and that he is under the impression that all those atonal works which Schoenberg wrote before he discovered twelve-tone technique were, in fact, dodecaphonic. The conclusion is absolutely inescapable that Mr. Howes has

---

73 Arthur Jacobs to *The Times*, 18 April 1956, CULHK.
74 Keller to Sharp, 11 October 1956, CULHK.

never attempted as much as a superficial study of twelve-tone technique, and that he has not the very vaguest idea of its operation – a conclusion amply borne out by the rest of his article which, it must be realized, purports to be an authoritative appraisal and critique of serial technique.

Keller confined his criticism of Howes to specific errors of musical fact, which he used to question the validity of Our Music Critic's repeated assertion that Schoenberg was 'not a composer'. There may, however, have been other aspects of Howes's writing which helped make him a particular target for Keller, including his English nationalism and his (highly colourful) descriptions of Vienna as a source of musical 'decadence' – a city with a 'canker eating at its heart', its music 'fleurs du mal. . . dangerous, possibly corrupting', giving off a 'smell of decay', spreading 'like a virus', and so on.[75]

The Times's usual page layout meant that Howes's music criticism often appeared opposite its law reports, of which Keller was also a regular reader and which he very much admired. He began to draft an article explaining why he attached so much importance to *The Times* and – following the model of the lawyers – what form he thought its musical journalism should take:

March 1956 – '*The Times* and Our Times' [extract]
Unpublished draft

The Times newspaper occupies a unique position in European, if not indeed in global journalism. Before the last war, there were perhaps one or two Continental daily journals – the Prager Tagblatt, the Neue Zürcher Zeitung, and possibly the Frankfurter Zeitung – which more or less successfully rivalled The Times' perfectionism, its untiring endeavours to present the truth, the whole and serious truth, and nothing but objective, or at least carefully considered, sense apart from the truth. Since the war, this rivalry has largely ceased, and so far as its reputation goes, The Times reigns supreme. Whether or not it does so with complete justification is another question and a most important one.

By and large, the anonymous and genuinely objective reporting on the news pages remains excellent, even though an artificially "literary" style, a three-quarter-hearted imitation of the idiom of the immediate past, results in a certain sham dignity whose effect is similar, paradoxically enough, to that of the cruder varieties of present-day journalese adopted by the sensational press, against which The Times is anxious to stand out in the strongest possible contrast – an effect of un-genuineness and hence of kitsch. This impression is inevitably intensified on the Arts

---

75 'Decadence in Music: Viennese Tradition', 18 February 1952, 7, and 'Health and Decadence in Modern Music', 15 February 1957, 3.

page, because the style of artistic criticism is to a greater extent subject to artistic evaluation than the language of news reporting and political comment. The anonymous objectivity of factual reportage, moreover, is liable to degenerate into a pretentious pseudo-objectivity and a self-inflated modesty with an ill-concealed capital "M" as soon as events and subjects are reported and commented upon from whose discussion the subjective element can scarcely ever be excluded.

As a result, The Times has come to throw itself into relief, not only against other papers, but also, far more strikingly so, against itself. On the one hand, that is to say, there are its music criticisms, some of which are, as we shall see, ever sagely inaccurate to an extent which make them a far greater cultural menace than is the honest sensationalism of the Daily Glamour's medical report upon Miss Marilyn Monroe's present state of psycho-sexual health. On the other hand, there are the Law Reports. None of the critical points made in the lines preceding apply to these models of serious journalism. Prepared by experts in the field without pseudo-literary pretentions, by barristers in fact, they are unfailingly accurate, intensely informative and always technically competent. In short, they are the greatest journalistic achievement known to my generation, a continuous reassurance and encouragement to those amongst us who value the truth more highly than our own Objectivity, Authority, and imPersonal modesty.

Despite Keller's and Sharp's efforts, the Circle was not persuaded to take any more action. Keller objected that this contravened Rule 1 of its constitution ('to promote the art of criticism and to uphold its integrity')and told the Chairman that 'unless there is a possibility of redress at the Executive Committee or Council level, I wish to resign from the Circle on ethical grounds, Rule 1 having been the sole reason why I ever joined it.'[76] Sharp agreed and also offered his resignation. By this time, however, Donald Mitchell had become Secretary of the Music Section, and he may have been instrumental in persuading Keller and Sharp to remain on board. A new idea was afoot: 'The plan is to submit a memorandum to the Committee for the foundation of a new MUSICOLOGY SECTION'.[77] This is the memorandum as Keller first drafted it:

8 January 1956 – Draft Memorandum for the Formation of a Musicology Section of the Critics' Circle [extract]

Aims

(1) To reinforce the existing contact between musicology and newspaper criticism. The young science of musicology, in itself a brand of criticism,

76 Keller to Norgate, 17 October 1956, CULHK.
77 Keller to Sharp, 20 December 1956, CULHK.

has built up a body of knowledge that must be placed at the service of the musical journalist in the interest of the highest possibly degree of factuality. Conversely, the musicologist (who is inevitably a critic, e.g. a textual critic) must be in touch with the needs of the newspaper critic if his is to become a properly "applied science".

(2) To establish close and constructive contact between musicological criticism and practical music-making. Criticism is potentially the most important bridge between musicology and music, which, once firmly built, would make possible "constructive criticism" par excellence, i.e. a collaboration between artist and critic towards musical truthfulness.

(3) To promote the factual accuracy and musical competence of criticism by musicological means. [. . .]

(4) To facilitate international co-operation between musicological critics.

[. . .] The basic reason for the proposed foundation of the Musicology Section is the newly emerged branch of musicological criticism with its special needs and aims. It is hoped that no formal obstacles will be put in the way of what may prove a major step in the development of music criticism.

The idea was that the new Musicology Section would work alongside the Music Section, with some members belonging to both. In this way, criticism could be enriched by the ideas and scholarship of excellent musicians currently ineligible for membership either through being insufficiently active in musical journalism, or because they were based overseas. Likewise, musicology would be prevented from retreating into an ivory tower. Keller, Sharp and Mitchell approached some of those they thought might be interested in joining, such as Paul Hamburger, David Drew, Gerald Abraham, Robert Donington, Arthur Dickinson and Edward Dent. Potential overseas members included H.C. Robbins Landon, Dika Newlin, René Leibowitz, Erwin Ratz and Rudolph Reti. Keller's memorandum was agreed, and submitted to the Critics' Circle's Executive Committee, appended by an impressive list of musicological names. But there was not much enthusiasm from the Executive, which kept postponing any decision. 'The matter is becoming stale,' Keller complained to Mitchell after a whole year of procrastination. Though he was never one to give up, on this occasion even he could see that he was getting nowhere.

As the 1950s wore on, Keller was increasingly struck by similarities between the disputes taking place on either side of Schoenberg. The progressives who rejected

Schoenberg as too traditional seemed now to be adopting some of the same arguments as his older opponents – and further, Keller thought, were setting out to do precisely what those older opponents had wrongly accused Schoenberg himself of doing: making technique an end in itself:

Dodecaphoneys [extract]
MR XVI/4 (November 1955): 323–9

With the ever-widening influence of serial technique, a powerful social group is in the process of formation in the musical world, composed of an astounding variety of personalities, talents and occupations which, nevertheless, evince sufficiently essential common characteristics to deserve a common name, if not indeed a flag and a national anthem based on a row of twelve notes of which only seven are exposed, the other five being clearly implied by the vacancies on the stave. For, as a matter of confusing fact, both diatonicists and twelve-toners belong to the group, whence it will not be altogether easy to compose the seven-note *cum* twelve-note anthem. [...]

Further confusion results from the circumstance that the dodecaphoneys (as we shall call the group) show a very fluid social structure, at any rate for the moment. You may be a homophoney to-day and a dodecaphoney tomorrow, at least for an hour or two. It partly depends on what the world expects from you at any given moment, whether it be the world of advanced musicography or Baden-Baden or Donaueschingen or the Universal Edition or *The Musical Times* or even the commonest of musical senses as expressed by the critical brotherhood of daily ignorance. For another part, it is, on the contrary, a matter of conscience. Schönberg's technique seems to have come to stay, and every self-respecting conscience has to take up an attitude towards it ("Stellung nehmen" is the favourite expression of the German cultural twaddlers). [...]

Every acute dodecaphoney knows that a great deal depends upon geography. Say he writes a certain work which exposes the twelve notes within the narrow space of a half hour movement. The question now arises whether the music is in strict twelve-tone technique or not. This is where geography comes in. If the work is to be performed on the Continent it will tend to be in the very strictest twelve-tone technique, and dodecaphoney critics and composers alike will admire its method and savour every finesse in the treatment of its highly segmental row, even though they may not be able to hear, as in the case of the prize-crowned Peragallo fiddle Concerto, that it has the greatest difficulty in getting itself out of G minor. If, on the other hand, the selfsame piece is to be played on this island, the great and individual freedom with which it employs the twelve-tone technique will immediately be evident, and dodecaphoney critics and composers alike will drop their ear-trumpets in sheer amazement at the *human* warmth which, *via* the above-mentioned G minor triad, radiates through this creative application of Schönberg's inhuman technique. If the composer happens to be British-born, the general public will presently learn all about the specifically English contribution to twelve-tonery; nevertheless, a few paragraphs further down, it will all be shown to derive from the *human* Berg and, if the dodecaphoney article in question is published in one of our more learned journals, the first three notes of the basic set of Berg's fiddle Concerto will be fervently recalled, for though the dodecaphoneys I am thinking of at the moment don't know a G minor triad when they hear one, they know it when they see one, and are delighted to meet and re-meet it in what they know is the tone-row of the Berg Concerto because the composer said so. It is, in fact, they who are basically responsible for making a Berg out of an admittedly major molehill. [. . .]

We [also] have to consider the sub-group of the critical composers, inasmuch as they have not been dealt with by Dr. Adorno himself. They are the widely first-performed people for whom serialism means exactly the opposite of what it means; who urgently need electronic noises in order to be able not to express what they don't want to express; for whom the Universal Edition has now started a special dodecaphoney journal, *die Reihe* ("The Series"), edited by Herbert Eimert with the assistance of Karlheinz Stockhausen; for whom Schönberg is a poor beginning, an old fogey, a detestable expressionist, an illogical fool, nay, a madman who dared to write impressive twelve-tone sonata forms although twelve-tone sonata forms are obviously unwritable; and who think that Webern, an end if ever there was one, was but a beginning. I do not deny the genuine talent of men like Pierre Boulez or Luigi Nono (who, not without complex psychological significance, has recently become Schönberg's posthumous son-in-law); what I am here concerned with is their dodecaphoney aspect, which is (1) what they say, (2) what they propose to do, and (3) what, alas, they do if and when they succeed in realizing their intentions. In one respect, they are absolutely identical with the critics they most detest: instead of listening and understanding, they criticize. Having postulated "the twelve-tonal misunderstanding that the tone-row can carry traditional forms", they don't acknowledge the existence of the sonata structures of major masters – Schönberg and Skalkottas – or of minor masters, such as Mátyás Seiber or Alban Berg. Deep in mathematical thought, they do not as much as suspect that they may be involved in a pitiable *petitio principia*, that the extended, developing, polythematic integration that is a twelve-tonal sonata movement is only a "traditional form" inasmuch as it shows these selfsame characteristics, and that you might just as well say that it is impossible for the spirit of *homo sapiens* to carry the traditional form of an ape. [. . .] The new dodecaphoneys have taken over not only the old objections to dodecaphony, but are in fact trying their best to realize the intentions that were wrongly ascribed to Schönberg. Technique is replacing content, the means becomes, not only an end in itself, but also the very creative beginning, and every little bit of nothing is subjected to an all-embracing systematization and organization, if organ is the word. Teeth clatter out of terror at the possibility of something slipping through in the end, of something being *expressed*, and as a counter measure, white magic is invoked and every available number of entities is serialized and proportionalized, including the buttons on the jacket of the composing anti-creator and the note-like traces left on his staves by those flies who, strolling over them, suffer traumatic neuroses because they feel that what is here taking place is an attack on life itself. However, we are not flies, and we shall survive it. Where music ceases not only to develop, but to be comprehensible in exclusively acoustic terms, where the ear is no longer, as Schönberg put it, the musician's sole brain, the musician ceases to be interested. At the same time, the paradoxical necessity arises for the intensest talents among these dodecaphoneys to become the absurdist fanatics for totally "prestabilized orders", because the stronger your creative need, the stronger must be your exertions to do something against it. [. . .] What, however, should make us think is the fact that there is a market for organized nothings. Our musical crisis, which has so often been said to be "over" by anti- and post-dodecaphonic dodecaphoneys alike, has created grave social neuroses and psychoses, and there are innumerable musicians and music-respecters who don't know the difference between the phonic and the phoney.

Intense arguments in public and private followed this article, most notably with some of the critics Keller had attacked, including friends like Colin Mason. Mason accused Keller of 'refusing to believe that his ears might be fallible' and of using the same arguments against 'the neo-Webernites' as critics like Howes and Blom had used against Schoenberg:

The only essential difference is that whereas they stop at Berg and refuse to accept the arid mathematical compositions of Schönberg, Hans stops at Schönberg (or at the very last at Webern, that 'end if ever there was one', as he calls him), and refuses to accept the arid mathematical compositions of those who want to go beyond that. Hans is like the old dodecaphoneys even in his reliance exclusively on his ear, the difference being merely that with his acuter ear he can hear links with tradition in Schönberg that they hear only in Berg.[78]

While acknowledging the acuteness of Keller's ear for pitch, Mason thought that 'the keenness of his ear works against his judgment, because of his undue reliance on it, and his seeming inability to conceive of any possible limitations to its keenness.' He then went on to define what he thought those limitations were:

Where his ear seems less sensitive is in its perception of rhythmic and dynamic elements – as is suggested by his resistance to the music of Bartók, in which these elements are particularly important, and his apparent insensitivity to the weakness of Skalkottas' music in this respect. The same insensitivity is the basis of his attack on the 'neo-Webernites', as he calls them, 'the new dodecaphoneys' . . . He seems unable to imagine, for instance, that there might be an ear as sensitive to rhythms, accents and time-values, as his own is to pitch, an ear as capable of following the rotations of a rhythmic series as his own is capable of following a melodic one. So we have the delightful spectacle of Hans lined up with those very old-fashioned island dodecaphoneys whom he attacked in the first sub-section of his article.

The audibility of serial technique was at the heart of the question – and Keller discussed it further in another article, written at the same time as 'Dodecaphoneys' and in which he asserted that 'in one point even the fiercest opponents of dodecaphony are absolutely right: the aesthetic significance of serialism stands and falls with its audibility.'

The Audibility of Serial Technique [extract]
MMR (November 1955): 231–4

The whole problem, then, hinges on the delicate question of audibility. The question is delicate because we are dealing with two variables and no constant, i.e. with the row in question and its mirror forms, and with the ear hearing them or not hearing them; and because the latter variable immediately introduces a personal element into any truthful discussion of the subject. Now it would be relatively easy, if tactless, for me to say to the critic of serialism: 'We hear what you don't hear and there's an end to it all.' But there isn't; while my statement would certainly be true on many occasions, it would not even begin to solve the problem. On the contrary, by implying that it is all a matter of the better ear, such a

78 Colin Mason, 'Dodecaphoneys', *MR* XVII/1 (February 1956): 90–94.

challenge would confuse the issue still further. It is not just the acuity of the ear but, below all, the kind of ear that counts. What is needed for serial technique is a contrapuntal ear: the audibility of serial technique is a function of the listener's contrapuntal understanding. Gluck could never have understood Schönberg, but Bach could. I am introducing these two names in order to indicate that the audibility of serial devices does not *primarily* depend on the listener's historical stage or development, on keeping abreast with the times. Secondarily, however, it does: we are living in a transition to a contrapuntal age which, worse luck, has come too soon, inasmuch as the development of harmony and homophony has not yet been exhausted.

In his 'Dodecaphoneys' article, Keller had stated that 'The supreme vice of our age is hearsay: we are content to say "there must be" and incapable of independently enquiring whether *there is*.' Arguing against this, Mason insisted that it was essential sometimes to accept that 'there must be', even if one cannot yet hear it, in order to make progress. His view was that the 'neo-Webernites' were simply ahead of Keller, and if he would only 'let himself sometimes say "there must be", he might even one day catch them up, as I believe he suddenly caught up with Schönberg once'. But Keller remained suspicious of any idea of musical 'progress' that involved accepting structures that could only be comprehended on the page, not through the ear. Writing to Mason later, he explained that his main concern was: 'Auralism v. visualism. It is this critical question which I feel very strongly about. What you regard . . . as "facts", I regard as dangerously phoney.'[79]

In this context, it is important to recall the extent to which music was politicised after the Second World War – and the significance of extreme modernism as a symbol of 'freedom'. For institutions and governments, the new serialism's internationalism, anti-romanticism and incomprehensibility to most people was a demonstration of music's emancipation from the controlling and conservative policies of both the Nazi past and the Soviet present. In Britain, this was felt less strongly than in Germany, where the moral trauma of the past was acute, and where the American occupying forces on the front line of the Cold War had been financing the new centre of the avant garde at the annual international summer school in Darmstadt.

One demonstration of the polarising of attitudes to serialism was the stunned reaction to Stravinsky's adoption of it after Schoenberg's death, the psychological significance of which Keller was not slow to point out – though he hotly denied that his own admiration of a work like *In Memoriam Dylan Thomas* ('Strawinsky's greatest and most perfect since the *Mass*') had anything to do with the fact that it was serial: 'I have never said, suggested or implied that serial technique has made

---

79 Keller to Mason, 3 December 1956, CULHK.

a better composer of Stravinsky, and I have never used idiom, style or technique as a criterion for the evaluation of any work of any composer.'[80]

Towards a Psychology of Stravinsky's Genius
Listener 56/1444 (29 November 1956): 897, reprinted in *HKSMM*, 45–8.

In his penetrating though often fallacious *Philosophie der Neuen Musik*, Theodor W. Adorno plays off Schoenberg against Stravinsky, whom he calls a death-mask of the past. Professor Adorno usually knows what he is talking about, but his talk is not always equal to his knowledge, chiefly because it is not inspired by that respect for a great genius without which the truest observation on him lacks perspective.

The fact remains that Stravinsky's creative character in general, and his attitude to the past in particular, has proved a headache to most musicians and critics, for the simple reason that we have never encountered this kind of great composer before. All good composers start out from the past; most bad composers remain stuck in it; but Stravinsky is the first great creator who speaks through it. [. . .]

Ordinary artistic development always starts with identification: while the composer's own creative ego is still weak, he identifies himself with his teachers and with older masters and proceeds to imitate them. As his originality grows, these father figures recede or are absorbed by his conscience and, if nothing drastic happens (such as the Bach crisis in Mozart's life), his creative 'love relations' with the music of other composers amount to no more than sporadic flirtations resulting in, say, variations on another composer's theme, which will be children of 'object love' rather than of identification.

Alone among geniuses, with the possible exception of Picasso, Stravinsky has actually developed his capacity for identification together with the unfolding of his intense originality. At the same time, as his commentary on *Pulcinella* indicates, his creative mind also employs a good deal of highly aggressive 'object love': he makes the aggressive best of both love worlds, though identification remains the basic 'dynamic force'. No previous

---

80　See 'Rhythm: Gershwin and Stravinsky'. Keller was reacting here to a remark by Anthony Milner in his essay 'The Lunatic Fringe Combed', that 'Stravinsky's adoption of serial techniques earned him the ecstatic eulogies of two London critics who had previously been lukewarm in their appreciation. One of these has recently hailed Mozart as an unconscious serialist,' *MT* 97/1364 (October 1956): 516–18. 'Mozart as an unconscious serialist' refers to Keller's *Tempo* essay 'Strict Serial Technique in Classical Music'. Keller published a serial analysis of *In Memoriam Dylan Thomas* in *Tempo* 35 (Spring 1955): 13–20.

composer has shown any desire to compose his way 'into the very essence of a being'. [. . .]

The *Symphony of Psalms* [. . .] is a spotless and gigantic masterpiece, profoundly expressive in its very suppression of expressionism, its in-turned, self-castigating aggression. Identifications with the past span a wide field, stretching back into the archaic, and when the opening four-part fugue of the second movement (with the answer in the dominant) raises its voice through what we might call the life-mask of Bach, we realise that the term 'neo-classicism' is just not good enough. The severe limitations that Stravinsky's identifications impose upon his intense imagination are precisely what he wants. His urge towards formal stringency and simplicity goes beyond the requirements of unity and clarity: he does not discipline his inspiration; rather he is more lavishly inspired by self-discipline than any other composer. Again, his love, this time his artistic self-love or self-respect, is unlike the usual artist's: again it is vehemently ambivalent, combined with, perhaps even outweighed by, aggression turned inward. [. . .]

After Schonberg's death, and too late for Professor Adorno to revise his theory about the antithesis of Stravinsky's and Schoenberg's attitudes, Stravinsky embarked on his serial period, which has now culminated in his first twelve-tone music – the three middle movements of the *Canticum Sacrum* (1955), whose first and fifth movements, moreover, mirror each other in self-restrictive retrograde motion. My own little hypothesis, on the other hand, here seems to receive its final confirmation. The 'identification with the lost object' (Freud, *Mourning and Melancholia*, 1916) is no news to the psychoanalyst, who will see in the previous ambivalent relation between the two musical leaders of our time an ideal foundation for Stravinsky's 'introjection' of Schoenberg's method: by way of creative mourning, Stravinsky identified with Schoenberg's serialism as soon as it had become a thing of the past. In justice to Professor Adorno, we must remind ourselves that his 'death mask of the past' now assumes a new significance, but we must continue to reject the negative valuation implied in, or insinuated by, his formulation.

For the rest, great geniuses are few and far between, and we cannot afford to miss them when they come.

Sketches done by Milein Cosman during a Royal Festival Hall concert on 16 January 1955 (CULHK).

Functional Analysis

From HANS KELLER

50 WILLOW ROAD LONDON N W 3

HAMpstead 9114

Dr Roger Fiske,
BBC,
Broadcasting House,
W I.   28.4.56

Dear Dr Fiske:

<u>XYZ: THE UNITY OF CONTRASTING THEMES</u>

Under this title ("XYZ" stands for the work to be analysed), I propose an hour's broadcast, wordless throughout, which would attempt to analyse a work or movement of your own choice according to my method of analysis as demonstrated in the recent <u>Mozart Companion</u> and <u>The Music Review</u> for February and May (<u>K.503: The Unity of Contrasting Themes and Movements</u>). With a ten minutes' interval in the middle, this experiment would not, I think, prove too exhausting for Third Programme listeners.

At the end of Part I of the last-mentioned study (MR, February '56, p.58), I have pointed out that "the ultimate aim of the present method of analysis is to get at the heart of the music by dispensing with verbal accounts altogether." I think I have meanwhile arrived at a stage where such a demonstration would easily be possible.

The best analytic object, probably, would be a very well known classical movement. In the case of an orchestral movement, I should need (a) records and (b) a pianist, preferably Paul Hamburger, who is familiar with my method. In the case of, say, a string quartet, a "live" body of players would be very welcome: they could do both the exposition of sections, themes etc. and the actual analysing.

Not a word need be spoken, though the announcer may perhaps have to say an introductory word or two; in addition, an introduction in THE LISTENER and/or the RADIO TIMES would be useful, but nowise indispensable. For the rest, the sections played and repeated, the analytic extracts and outlines demonstrated, and the placing and length of pauses between the various "exhibits" would make the trend of the analysis quite clear. Every problematic or surprising point would be demonstrated twice over, and time would be allowed for the listener to become conscious of his objections which – so far as they could be foreseen – would be taken into account in what one might call the "modified recapitulation" of the first demonstration.

Like music itself, my method is more easily "played" than described.

Yours sincerely,

Hans Keller

The radical idea proposed in this letter – the analysis of music in sound alone – is the innovation for which Keller is best remembered. For Keller himself it was of enormous symbolic importance, asserting as it did the unique nature of musical thought. When he later wrote of music that 'there is no art that produces as much comfort for the mind feeling and thinking it, and as much discomfort for the mind thinking about it,' he was speaking from the heart.[1]

It was probably the experience of making his first BBC broadcast (a *Music Magazine* talk on the contrasting personalties of Mozart and Haydn in February 1956) that prompted Keller to consider radio as a solution to the problem of writing about music. Naturally he had used many music examples in his talk to explain his points to his listeners, and he was struck by how much more more direct this was on radio than in print, since listeners needed neither technical terms nor score-reading ability to understand what he was getting at. Keller began to wonder to what extent they needed words at all.

His letter to Fiske focused more on the manner than the matter of his proposed programme – since its wordlessness was what made it particularly radiogenic – and Fiske was referred to two recent articles to discover in detail what Keller's new method of analysis actually was. Although 'functional analysis' (as Keller later called it) eventually came to be synonymous with 'wordless analysis', it did not start out that way. He himself identified as his first functional analysis the substantial study of Mozart's chamber music he wrote in 1955 for *The Mozart Companion*. Immediately afterwards, he applied the same methods to the study of a single work, Mozart's Piano Concerto K.503, for the Mozart bicentenary issue of *The Music Review*. Here Keller described his new method – and what had prompted it:

---

1 'Towards a Theory of Music', *Listener* 83/2150 (11 June 1970): 795–6, reprinted in *EOM*, 121–5.

The Unity of Contrasting Themes and Movements [extract]
MR XVII/1 (February 1956): 48–58 and XVII/2 (May 1956): 120–29

Tautology is the greatest insult to the dignity of human thought. Yet most so-called "analytical" writings about music, from the humble programme-noter who has absolutely nothing up his record-sleeve to the great Tovey who may or may not have withheld a lot, boil down to mere tautological description. I maintain that if you want to open your mouth or typewriter in order to enlarge upon music, you must have a special excuse. Mere "sensitivity", receptivity, and literacy will not do, for it will merely land you in describing the musical listener's own *perception* of the music, as distinct from promoting his *understanding* – whereupon, to be sure, he will consider you "an excellent critic". [. . .]

The analysis which here follows is based on the tenet that a great work can be *demonstrated* to grow from an all-embracing basic idea, and that the essential if never-asked questions of why contrasting motifs and themes belong together, why a particular second subject necessarily belongs to a particular first, why a contrasting middle section belongs to its principal section, why a slow movement belongs to a first movement, and so forth, must be answered if an "analysis" is to deserve its name. During my work on Mozart's chamber music as well as in the course of previous analyses, I have developed, first a method of analysis, and then, on a purely practical basis, a theory of unity, which I hope to formulate in full in a book on criticism. Frankly, I am in no hurry to systematize my abstractions: practice should precede theory. That, at the same time, I continuously demand theoretical justification from myself goes without saying. But basically, my method is as intuitive passively as the creative process is actively, and from the reader I require nothing but an unprejudiced musician's *ear* which, as Schönberg has said, is the musician's sole brain. My analysis, then, aims at ascertaining the *latent* elements of the unity of *manifest* contrasts. [. . .]

The ultimate aim of the present method of analysis is to get at the heart of the music by dispensing with verbal accounts altogether. As soon as the principles of unity implied in the method are accepted, it will be possible to analyse unities simply by way of music examples (or, in lectures, by playing), with hardly a word in between.

Keller had long been concerned with thematic integration, so what he was doing here was not a complete departure. But despite his disclaimers about being 'in no hurry to systematize my abstractions', these writings do show a new interest in creating a theoretical structure around his insights, and it is significant that he now intended his book for Deutsch to put forward 'a theory of unity'. It is also notable that Keller's writing at this time concerned itself particularly with the music of the classical period, rather than the contemporary works with which his regular review columns generally dealt. This was partly due to the topicality of the Mozart bicentenary, but also because this kind of thinking required a particularly intimate knowledge of the works concerned. As Keller often said, 'far from analyzing for the purpose of comprehension, what one analyzes is one's own, instinctive musical understanding. If this has not taken place, analysis is of no avail.'[2] This could only happen with a work so utterly familiar that every detail is, as he put it, 'soundingly in your head'. He insisted that his starting point was emotional rather than intellectual – but he was well aware that his critics were determined to believe he was driven by pre-determined theories, creating (as Eric Blom put it) 'an unbridgeable gap between his approach to music and sensitive experience of it'.[3]

Trying to counter this misunderstanding, Keller described how he worked:

Mozart's Chamber Music [extract]
The Mozart Companion, 92–4, 115–16

My method is essentially naive. [. . .] I listen inwardly to contrasts until their unity emerges, and without any theoretical preconceptions. Usually, since I know all these works very well, my self-analytic reaction is immediate, and its formulation amounts to no more than a rationalization of spontaneous emotions, sifted, to be sure, by my technical knowledge. I shall not put anything into words or symbols that has not been felt on the one hand, and – alas, privately – substantiated in theory on the other. I must ask the reader for one more favour – to keep the harmonic aspect of any passage or motif in mind throughout its discussion. Many of my observations on thematic unity will stand with the harmony of the melodic entity analysed, but it would be cumbersome to add harmonic riders in every single instance, though where necessary or convenient I shall do so. There will also be occasions when I shall regard essential rhythmic relations as self-evident. I hope nobody will think that I am 'picking out any old notes' to suit my purposes before he has satisfied himself about the harmonic and rhythmic implications of my analysis. [. . .] Finally, with a few exceptions, my music examples are not so much examples as references: it is not they that ought to be studied, but the passages and sections and tonal contexts to which they direct the reader's attention.

[. . .]

2 Keller to Thomas Szasz, 21 October 1981, CULHK.
3 *M&L* 37/3 (July 1956): 285–9.

One gradually begins to realize what Mozart meant when he recalled those beautiful moments of inner creation where the whole work sounded 'like a picture', simultaneously; what Schoenberg meant when he talked of 'the unity of musical space'. The oneness, the simultaneity is the inner reality, the Kantian thing-in-itself, the Schopenhauerian will, the Freudian unconscious (which is essentially timeless), while temporal succession is its necessary appearance, the Schopenhauerian idea, the Freudian conscious. Thus experienced, *variety is the necessary means of expressing a unity* that would otherwise remain unexpressed, as indeed it remains silent in monotony, which cheats time of its purpose.

The Mozart Companion was edited by Donald Mitchell and the ebullient American musicologist H.C. Robbins Landon – who was another factor drawing Keller back to his core repertoire. Landon had settled in Europe after the war to pursue his interest in Haydn, and Keller and Mitchell got to know him early in their *Music Survey* days, when Landon was embarking on his major study of Haydn's symphonies. Landon was doubtless delighted to meet in Keller someone who valued Haydn as highly as he did and was keen to draw him into his own work (one of his many proposals was that they should write a book on Haydn's quartets together). Landon's 850-page study of Haydn's symphonies was published in 1955 and its appearance was a landmark in Haydn scholarship.[4] Such a vast enterprise naturally drew on others for some of its details and Keller was one of those to whom Landon turned for help. As the manuscript neared completion in 1953, Landon, who had already been 'bombarding' Keller with queries by telegram as he rushed to finish the work, now asked if he would translate it into German and, as Landon put it, 'footnote-around (sounds obscene doesn't it?) in my book'. In the end, the German edition did not go ahead, but Landon still wanted Keller to go over his work: 'Even if you don't translate it, would you read it through with a red pencil and make comments? I should hate to have my opus go into the world without the benefit of your comments and objections.'[5]

At the same time, Landon told Keller how frustrated he was, throughout his studies of the eighteenth century, by the 'dismal lack of decent Mozart literature'. Having admired Keller's contributions on Mozart in *The Music Review*, Landon urged him: 'Keller, leave your Britten and twelve-tone and help us out with Mozart.' He suggested a series of studies of different parts of Mozart's work ('piano concerti, symphonies and operas one after the other, and as soon as possible'), but Keller was sceptical: 'If and when a publisher wants it and pays for it.'[6] Happily, the Mozart bicentenary provided an occasion when publishers were willing to pay for new work on Mozart, and Landon and Mitchell secured a contract from Rockliff for their *Mozart Companion*.

4 *The Symphonies of Joseph Haydn* (London: Universal Edition and Rockliff, 1955).
5 Landon to Keller, 26 June 1953, CULHK.
6 Keller to Landon, 6 July 1953, CULHK.

Landon was an enthusiastic correspondent and keenly interested in Keller's analytical methods. After he had seen his Haydn symphonies book safely into press, he was eager to discuss questions of unity and structure in Mozart. On 25 January 1955, for example, he asked Keller about the finale of the E flat Symphony No. 39, criticising the tutti that follows the initial statement of the theme:

> What one hears, no matter what any brilliant conductor does, is the doodle-doodle of the fiddles . . . I suppose you can say that this first tutti is a derivative of the 2nd violin part, but I think it's more a paper derivative than a conscious musical tie up on M's part. . . . I don't feel that [this] particular tutti contributes anything to the formal, melodic or aesthetic construction of the finale.[7]

24 February 1955 – to H.C. Robbins Landon

Dear Robbie:

K.543.

When Haydn develops a concentrated monothematic structure, you are perfectly aware of what he is up to, but in K543's finale you don't show the same degree of insight. You might just as well criticize the doodle-doodle of a good doodle-doodle coda, but there you are no doubt alive to its function, i.e. relaxation. The problem for Mozart was to offer sufficient relief before the tense monothematic concentration reveals itself in the second subject and to give a firm foundation to the highly compressed & equally tense modulation to the Wechseldominante.[8] You are worrying about the lack of thematicism in the tutti; but Mozart was worrying about how to make it a-thematic (relief stage of monothematic build-up) without making it un-thematic. The unconventional rhythmic structure of the modulation to the Wechseldominante w'd, moreover, be impossible without a conventional, firmly established sequential model. The problem, then, is – relative neutrality from the thematic point of view, i.e. integration without thematic work.

No, I don't say that the tutti is a derivative of the 2nd vln part, for not every old doodle-doodle derives from any old doodle-doodle; nor am I ever interested in paper analysis: in fact, I'm incapable of it. The integration must be heard, and you will hear it via your Urlinie-consciousness;

7 Landon to Keller, 25 January 1955, CULHK.
8 'secondary dominant'.

the theme's antecedent

and the doodle-doodle

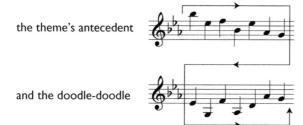

fulfil one of those subtle Mozartian complementary relationships which are based on an underlying antecedent–consequent construction. The 'consequent' function of the doodle-doodle is in itself highly charged with potential energy, which becomes actual as soon as this "consequent" turns out to be an "antecedent", i.e. the model for the modulation. Thus Mozart combines momentary relief with forthcoming tension (Ruhe vor dem Sturm)[9] – the surest proof of formal mastery. Had he started any unconventional "funny business" as early as the doodle-doodle, it w'd immediately have become "A Musical Joke", whose study I recommend from my present point of view. I therefore consider that you are absolutely wrong in your criticism of K.543.

Nor do I agree about 334/III, but I sh'dn't like to write about it without the score, & the Kitzbuehel Lending Library does not seem to be interested in Mozart.

Ever,

Hans

'I hope you are going to do a piece on Mozart's unconscious thematic consequents for your bit for the Mozart Handbook,' replied Landon; 'this seems to me to be a brilliant and as far as I can see entirely original theory of yours.'[10]

6 March 1955 – to H.C. Robbins Landon [extract]

Dear Robbie:

Many thanks for yours of the 2nd. Glad you agree about doodle-doodle. I in my turn agree ab't hns in bars 21 ff.[11] I think you attach too much importance to the difference between unconscious and conscious

---

9 'calm before the storm'.

10 Landon to Keller, 2 March 1955. Keller did introduce in his chapter 'the creative principle of reversed and postponed antecedents and consequents'.

11 Landon had written that 'the horns in bars 21ff are generally played too prominently, which lends a sort of da-da-da-da character to the tutti.'

processes in composition. Of course, the distinction is most important psychologically, but hardly musically: what is cs [conscious] in one composer (e.g. Beethoven) is ucs in another (e.g. Mozart), and identical processes may be unconscious and conscious in the same composer upon different occasions (Britten). I may deal with those section consequents in the book if & when they 'come in': my main analytical approach will be "unity" – a very conventional term which, however, covers almost wholly uncharted territory: why does a particular 2nd subject belong to a particular first? Why is the slow movement theme "of" this particular work? Why does the finale "follow"? etc. We've heard enough about "the contrasting 2nd subject" and so forth: the contrast is obvious to everybody – it is the unity that remains to be analysed. Reti has made a good if undisciplined beginning. This is the secret of the sonata – i.e. of extended polythematic integration. I'm afraid there will be quite a few music exx. "The consequentation", incidentally, is not "very often harmonic as well as melodic": it always is, tho' the strength of the harmonic factor may vary.

When *The Mozart Companion* was completed, Landon told Keller that 'of all the articles, the only ones which will be a source of delight to men in 2000 years will be your own and [Mitchell's] preface.'[12] Some of the critics agreed: Andrew Porter, for example, thought that 'the most exciting chapter of all is Hans Keller's.'[13] But there was also considerable opposition from some of Keller's old sparring partners. Dyneley Hussey deplored 'the current tendency towards a severe and anatomical dissection of music', and Eric Blom devoted two *Observer* articles as well as his *Music & Letters* review to an emotional attack on Keller's new method: 'If anybody ever succeeds in making me hate Mozart's music, it will be Hans Keller's boast to have done so.'[14]

A more satisfactory response came two months later in a letter from America. Keller had acknowledged in *The Mozart Companion* the 'stimulating incentives' he had found in Rudolph Reti's book *The Thematic Process of Music*,[15] alongside his debts to Schenker, Schoenberg and – most importantly – Oskar Adler, whose 'uniquely organic and motif-conscious way of playing taught me more about the

---

12 Landon to Keller, 27 November 1955, CULHK.

13 *London Musical Events*, May 1956, 29–30.

14 Hussey, 'The Mozart Companion', *MT* 97/1361 (July 1956): 358–9; Blom, 'The New Approach', *Observer*, 8 April 1956, 10; 'Tethered Fancy', *Observer*, 15 April 1956, 14; 'The Mozart Companion', *M&L* XXXVII/3 (July 1956): 285–9.

15 New York: Macmillan, 1951. Though Keller was of the opinion that Reti's approach 'exaggerates the melodic aspect', he still thought that this book 'with all its serious defects is a milestone in the history of analysis'. He hoped that Reti's second book (then still in manuscript but published posthumously as *Tonality–Atonality–Pantonality* (Westport, CT: Greenwood Press, 1978)) would correct the imbalance in his approach, but when he saw it he was bitterly disappointed. (See *MR* XVIII/2 (May 1957): 156–60 and *Tempo* 50 (Winter 1959): 30–31.)

essentials of chamber-musical forms and textures than any analytical teacher could possibly have done'. When Reti read Keller's work in June 1956 ('a bit late, but with much interest') he wrote him a warmly appreciative letter, thanking him 'for the whole spirit and direction of your writings.'

> Musicology so far has been pursued in several separate, almost independent provinces; history of music, musical theory and musical aesthetics. In the treatment of all of these there seems to have been little connection with the actual process of musical creation. . . . But in your own approach I see the endeavor to delve into the very compositional process, that previous research has almost invariably neglected. Also, with great pleasure I see a similar endeavor emerging in the writings and discussions of some other younger musicians in several countries. This makes me very happy. . . .
>
> It seems to me that today we are again entering a period of "creative musicology". Such periods are to be found repeatedly in music history. In fact, almost invariably when style and expression underwent decisive changes, these changes were accompanied by a complete reassessment of the theoretical concept.
>
> Now if, as it seems, the number of these students of a new discipline increases, they should not remain isolated, different as their opinions and interests may be with regard to single questions, but should meet to discuss their problems and exchange their opinions, in fact, almost unite as a "group". Then, perhaps, the long prevailing deplorable gap between music and thought on music could gradually be bridged. For these new methods of investigation would not only feed from that process of musical creation, but might in turn, to a certain degree, also nourish compositional movements. Thus the confusion which so often prevails today in all matters concerned with contemporary music could perhaps be somewhat cleared away. At the same time a better understanding of our great musical past would, I think, become more general.
>
> With this I shall conclude. I am aware that all I have said is hardly more than a scant indication. But if you, with your dynamic approach, and some of your friends would like to use some of the hints here advanced, I do not doubt that fruitful consequences would result. In the meantime heartiest greetings and good wishes.[16]

15 July 1956 – to Rudolph Reti

Dear Dr. Reti:

Many thanks for your kind letter with which, in principle, I entirely agree. If I don't take up your idea of a group it is simply for reasons of personal

---

16 Reti to Keller, 27 June 1956, CULHK.

character: emotionally I am quite gregarious, but intellectually I am basically a recluse who does not profit by discussion – except more or less accidentally, e.g. when teaching. This does not mean that I deem myself cleverer than everybody else, but when somebody has something important to say and is able to say it clearly, he will write it (as you have done) and I will read it and profit by it or not, as the case may be. Whenever I am drawn into a discussion, I find that from my own point of view it is a waste of time.

Nor, frankly, do I think that one could "nourish compositional movements" in any essential way: if they aren't nourished by individual creative needs, the food won't be much good anyway. But this is a minor point.

Please do not think that I regard your idea as worthless; only, I am not the man for it, and what you call my "dynamic approach" only functions when it serves individual expression. In a group, moreover, one has, inevitably, to make intellectual or artistic concessions – of which, again, I am characterologically incapable. I do hope you understand.

My mother asks me to convey her kindest regards to you; she used to play under you in Vienna; at that time she was called Grete Jonasz. Also I have a vague recollection of my father* (who died in '38) telling me that you once played an opera of yours (?) at our house in Vienna (XIX (Döbling), Nusswaldgasse 13). And do I remember correctly that you were music critic for the evening paper <u>Telegraf</u> (or its predecessor, <u>Der Abend</u>)?[17] I was a small boy then.

Yours sincerely,

[Hans Keller]

* Dr. Fritz Keller

'I understand your point of view very well,' replied Reti:

I, who have always borne a strong antipathy towards groups and cliques, should be the last to try to persuade anyone towards such things. But every once in a while the eternal optimist seems to come alive in me (just as it did some thirty years ago when I conceived the idea of the I.S.C.M.). At those moments I indulge in Utopean schemes, with the thought that the blind might be made to see.[18]

They did not correspond any further, for Reti died shortly afterwards. 'I must confess that had I known that he would die so soon,' wrote Keller, 'I should

---

17 Reti was music critic of *Das Echo* from 1930 until he left for America in 1938.
18 The manuscript of this letter is lost, but Keller quoted this paragraph in his obituary for Reti in *MR* XVIII/2 (May 1957): 156–60.

not so easily have foregone the pleasure of further contact, of comparing notes about our intense common analytic concern – the simple question of how things hang together.'

~

Keller's proposal to the BBC was received with considerable interest. It took time to become a reality, however, partly because Keller was involved in so many other projects that it was hard to find the requisite time to write the score. One large task then claiming his attention was the editing and translation of the memoirs of the great violinist and pedagogue Carl Flesch.[19] Among the problems with this was Keller's insistence that Flesch's characterisation of Bronisław Huberman could not be allowed to stand without comment. Back in 1952, when the publisher first asked him to read the manuscript sent by Flesch's son, Carl Franz, Keller had diagnosed a form of group self-contempt in Flesch's negative attitude to Huberman, and he refused to edit the book unless he was allowed to include a substantial footnote on the matter. He insisted that this was not simply a matter of his disagreeing with Flesch, but of his fear of readers discounting Flesch's perceptive accounts of *other* violinists if they were put off by an unreasonable dismissal of Huberman.

27 October 1952 – Reader's Report on Carl Flesch, *Lebenserinnerungen* [extract]

In one respect, however, the question of cutting and editing assumes ethical importance, i.e. where the author's neurotic antisemitism (he is, of course, a Jew) comes into play. [. . .] At one point, these prejudices even intrude upon his artistic and technical judgment: the description of Bronislav Huberman's art (incidentally, and significantly, the only name which is wrongly spelt throughout, tho' Flesch must have seen it hundreds of times!) does not only fall short of all the other characterizations – most of them quite outstanding – of the great violinists Flesch has known, but actually borders on the incompetent. In addition, Huberman's efforts for Pan-Europe, Zionism, and his Open Letter to Furtwängler, one of the most inspiring documents of integrity which our time has produced, where Huberman states his reasons for his refusing Furtwängler's invitation to play in (early) Nazi Germany, are simply branded as "self-advertisement", based, in the case of the

---

19 *The Memoirs of Carl Flesch* (London: Rockliff, 1957).

Open Letter, on no more than "a difference of opinion" in matters of "Weltanschauung"! All this does Huberman the gravest injustice, for in point of fact he was one of the few musicians (indeed a supreme artist) whose extra-artistic conscience was strong enough to make him fight for a United Europe; nor does Flesch mention that Huberman's Zionism, which according to this book was based on his business sense, made him found (together with Toscanini) the Palestine Orchestra under considerable personal and material sacrifices. There is no doubt that Flesch's hostility to Eastern Jews (he was one himself) powerfully contributed to this distorted picture of a typical Eastern Jew; besides, Huberman was a difficult person and had most colleagues (Flesch's most distinguished friends among them) against him. (Furtwängler himself is, *mutatis mutandis*, a similar case.) For Flesch's own sake, then, the entire section on Huberman would have to be rectified by an informed editorial note (or possibly in a translator's preface), for readers who knew Huberman's art and ethics might otherwise come to regard Flesch's portraits of other violinists with entirely unjustified suspicion. Opposite violinistic characters like Rosé and Heifetz are delineated with the same penetrating insight, and the playing of Joachim (of which I happen to have an idea from a very old record) is described with downright miraculous empathy plus objectivity.

Keller was initially reassured such a note could be included, but the exact form it would take was not properly discussed until shortly before publication, when Flesch's son saw what Keller proposed to include and refused to accept its 'inordinate length' and polemical style. According to C.F. Flesch's own account,

> Keller threatened to abandon the (almost completed) work and to issue a statement to the press explaining his reasons. I told him to go ahead – I could not, in my wildest dreams, have thought up a better publicity ploy. Eventually, and after long and heated arguments, we arrived at a compromise: Keller was to give his views in an appendix immediately followed by a reply from me. . . . But what really crowned it all was the fact that Keller, after reading my reply in draft, considered it not sufficiently effective. So he helped me to improve it and state a better case – Hans Keller in a nutshell.[20]

~

20 C.F. Flesch, *'And Do You Also Play the Violin?'* (London: Toccata, 1990), 131.

In the end, Keller could only find the time to think properly about 'The Unity of Contrasting Themes' by taking the score of the chosen work (Mozart's D minor quartet K.421) and a sheaf of manuscript paper on his annual skiing holiday the following March. At the end of the month, the first three sections of his analysis arrived on Roger Fiske's desk:

30 March 1957 – to Roger Fiske
WAC, Keller Contributor File I

Dear Dr Fiske:

I have been back for over a week, but I wanted to check these first 3 sections of my wordless talk against the Authentic Edition and try them out on a few musicians before passing them on to you.

Section (I) is a record of K.421's 1st movement. Section (II) shows the unity of its 2 subjects, between which my score moves to and fro. First, the unity of the respective accompanimental rhythms is demonstrated (the 2nd subject's being a strict diminution of the 1st's); the basic thematic relations follow. You will note that the recapitulation of the 2nd sub. is introduced before its exposition, not only because of the tonic key, but because it is altogether more closely related to the first sub. than the expository F major version; besides, it is the recapitulation which the listener remembers best from Section (I). Eventually, the exposition of the second subject is included in the demonstration, forming, at the same time, the (relative major) link with, and showing the derivation of, the slow movement, a record of which (Section III) follows without a break. So much for the first movement and its basic connection with the second: I hope to deal with all four within a reasonable time. There will be a pause between the andante & the minuet, i.e. before the return to the tonic.

Title: THE UNITY OF CONTRASTING THEMES. Sub-title: 'An Experiment in Functional Analysis' – this being the name I have recently given to my analytic method (see current issue of TEMPO).[21] "Experiment" is not strictly true: my score is really post-experimental,

---

21 'A Slip of Mozart's: its Analytic Significance', *Tempo* 42 (Winter 1956–57): 12–15, reprinted in *EOM*, 139–43. 'I must find a name for it before my critics do,' wrote Keller, rejecting Reti's suggestion of 'Process-analysis' as too American. He wanted the name to counter the idea that his method was one of 'dissection': 'What *is* dissection is the traditional form of "analysis" – "first subject, bridge passage, second subject, closing section" and so forth. This kind of investigation is essentially *anatomical*. My own method, on the other hand is essentially *physiological*: it attempts to elucidate the *functions* of the living organism that is a musical work of art. Accordingly, I propose to call my method *functional analysis.*'

for I have played every single point to a pupil and/or colleague in order to see whether the demonstration is clear enough.

50–100 words for the announcer will follow. If the RT can give me a bit of space, so much the better, but I don't really need it. On the other hand, a LISTENER article for those who are interested in wider implications would probably be useful; if there is nothing very newsworthy in that particular week, I'm sure Gerald Abraham will allow me to write about functional analysis. In any case, the listener will be told that this acoustic analysis ought to be more easily comprehensible than the actual music; if it isn't, I have failed. After all, I'm merely trying to make the implicit explicit.

The demonstration is not, of course, identical with that given in THE MOZART COMPANION: there, I tried to solve the most difficult questions, whereas in the present context I want to solve the most important ones. For instance, I haven't said anything there about the rhythmic unity between the 1st mvt's 1st & 2nd subjects (see my first "round" in Section II).

We can discuss at a later stage whether I should or shouldn't participate in the actual playing (violin or viola); in any case, I want, of course, to supervise rehearsals.

If necessary, I can complete the score very soon.

I am eager to hear what you think of it.

Yours sincerely,

Hans Keller

Fiske was fascinated and full of questions:

If a classical work is the better for a relationship between its two themes, it must conversely be the worse if no such relationship can be shown. Or has the thing got nothing to do with values? I feel a desire to rush home and work out the proportion of cases in which the subjects can be related in Dussek piano sonatas and Beethoven piano sonatas; if you are right, it ought to be higher in the latter.

Another thought that assails me is that early Haydn symphonies and quartets often use the same theme for the opening subject and the allegedly contrasted one in the dominant. Does this make them better or worse? Does the relationship, to have its maximum musical effect, need to be sub-conscious?[22]

---

22 Fiske to Keller, 2 April 1957, WAC Keller Contributor File 1.

11 April 1957 – to Roger Fiske [extract]
WAC, Keller Contributor File 1

Dear Dr. Fiske:

Thank you for your letters of April 2 and 4. Unity is a condition, not a criterion of value. The criterion is the widest possible variety on the basis of absolute unity. There is no classical work whose absolute unity cannot be demonstrated by functional analysis, as long as it is good music.

No doubt Dussek is more monotonous than Beethoven. Functional analysis does not suggest that 10 repetitions of the 'Harry Lime' tune are superior to the Choral Symphony.

A monothematic sonata movement is not, as such, better or worse than a polythematic one. The thematic dimension is not the only one in which variety can be achieved. Much great Haydn is more monothematic than much great Mozart, but it is also, proportionately, more diversified in respect of key schemes and harmonic structures. Neither is better than the other.

So far, so easy. Your question about unconsciousness ('sub-consciousness' is not, psychologically speaking, a legitimate term) is far more difficult, the answer far more complex. For one thing, it depends on the character of the composer: much that Mozart could not have achieved consciously, Beethoven could not have achieved unconsciously. But there certainly has to be a minimum of unconsciousness, if only because consciously, you can't think of everything. Also, consciously you tend to overdo unity at the expense of possible variety. Even a great master like Brahms was guilty of over-thematicism in his most exclusively conscious moments, don't you think? The theory of functional analysis is by no means complete, but at the present stage I suspect that a genius's variety is in any case based on a far-reaching repression (and consequent unconsciousness) of the underlying unity, tho' there are considerable individual differences; the background unity may or may not have been conscious to begin with.

> *Great music diversifies a unity; mere good music unites diverse elements.*

I hope you won't take offence at my abrupt style; I'm trying to get a lot into a few words. I certainly do not consider any of your questions "far from intelligent"; on the contrary, it might be a good idea to deal with them at some greater length in the LISTENER article, if & when it comes. Incidentally, to return the compliment, you must think me terribly naïve if you are under the impression that for me, mere thematicism is bliss! Variety is bliss – but in order to analyse it, you have to analyse the underlying unity, the <u>tertium comparationis</u>, whereupon the variety explains itself. Please let me know whether any doubts remain – or whether, perhaps, I have created some new ones!

[. . .]

Thank you for your interest, business apart.

Yours sincerely,

Hans Keller

The broadcast went out on the BBC Third Programme on the evening of Saturday, 7 September 1957. Keller was unhappy with the under-rehearsed performance by the Aeolian Quartet, but the programme was a success nonetheless. There was some gratifying fan mail from musicians and the BBC's listener research report was encouraging, showing the majority of the sample audience 'very much interested in this broadcast':

> They thought the idea original and ingenious, even revolutionary. It had many
> fascinating possibilities, particularly as a form of radio technique. . . . There
> were a large number of requests for a repetition of the broadcast and for sim-
> ilar treatment of more familiar and symphonic works, 'to prove the theory'
> added some.[23]

'Wordless FA has proved a very considerable success,' Keller told Geoffrey Sharp happily. 'It's being repeated on the Third; I've been commissioned to write a new analytic score; and the BBC is talking of future ones too – as if it had become a permanent institution.'[24] The programme was also aired in Germany, as part of a showcase 'Third Programme Evening' put out by Norddeutscher Rundfunk in Hamburg. Rolf Liebermann, NDR's Head of Music, was fascinated when he heard it: he broadcast Keller's next score as soon as it was available and commissioned from him a series of Haydn analyses to mark the 150th anniversary in 1959 of Haydn's death.[25] The Incorporated Society of Musicians engaged the Aeolian Quartet to perform the K.421 analysis again at its 60th annual conference in December 1957 and William Glock published its score in his journal. Walter Legge of EMI approached Keller with the idea of producing Functional Analysis gramophone records, while Universal Edition and Augener asked him about publishing scores.[26]

Amid all this keen interest, there was one notable lack of reaction: apart from Colin Mason in *The Guardian*, the British newspaper critics ignored Functional

---

23   WAC R9/6/69.
24   Keller to Sharp, 10 October 1957, CULHK.
25   Keller was surprised and touched that Liebermann should do this 'despite his knowledge of all I've written about his music!' (Keller to Hansjörg Pauli, 23 December 1957, CULHK). Keller thought Liebermann 'a real dodecaphoney talent' (*MR* XVI/4 (November 1955): 324–7).
26   The Haydn quartets Keller analysed for NDR were Op. 50, No. 5; Op. 20, No. 1, and Op. 76, No. 2, broadcast in January 1959. The K.421 analysis was published in *The Score* 22 (February 1958): 56–64. The recording and publishing options were not pursued by Keller, who felt at this stage that 'time is on my side'. (See Keller to Fiske, 18 December 1957, and to Pauli, 23 December 1957.)

The opening of Hans Keller's Functional Analysis No. 6: Haydn String Quartet in E flat, Op. 20, No. 1 (CULHK Add Mus 9371/17).

Analysis completely. 'Interesting, incidentally, the critics' (I mean dailies') complete silence ab't FA No. 1 and (so far as I know) No. 2, except for Colin,' wrote Keller to Donald Mitchell after his second score was broadcast. He had probably been expecting something from Blom at least. 'Not that I'm complaining (heaven help me when they do start on it), but considering the effect the method has had, my colleagues' form of revenge seems primitive, even for them.'[27]

Naturally Keller was keen 'to utilize the prevailing atmosphere and to satisfy the requests for "more" as soon as possible'. After hearing the Mozart, many listeners asked for an analysis of a Beethoven quartet next: 'The impression seems to have been that Beethoven would prove a harder nut for FA than Mozart,' said Keller – though of course he thought they were wrong. 'The truth is, of course, exactly the reverse: Beethoven's thematic background unities are usually nearer the foreground than Mozart's, because his conscious intentions were more thematic anyway. But his contrasts often happen within a far narrower space than Mozart's: perhaps this is the reason why people think that they are, as such, greater.'[28] All the requests for Beethoven put Keller in something of a quandary, because his own intentions for FA's next step had been very different: 'the melodic and rhythmic style of George Gershwin'. But 'if everybody wants structural unity in Beethoven, I don't for the moment want to do stylistic unity in Gershwin,' he wrote to Fiske. 'What do you think? I'm in two minds about it, all the more so since I am burning to demonstrate the potential range of functional analysis . . . which again drives me towards the Gershwin idea.'[29]

Another factor driving Keller towards Gershwin was that 1957 marked the 20th anniversary of Gershwin's death, an ideal occasion for a reassessment of his music. In Keller's opinion, Gershwin's early death had 'changed the imminent course of film-musical history: where Gershwin musicals would have created a new art form, Gershwin imitations turned Hollywood into what we understand by Hollywood'. Analysing the various creative tensions in Gershwin's music, Keller found that 'the consistent contradictions between a suppressed sentimental background and a cheerfully anti-sentimental (though nowise unemotional) foreground were among the most frequent and the most original. Tragically enough, the light-music industry could not tolerate many a Gershwin song in its original creative form and proceeded to reduce it as far as possible to its sentimental background.'[30]

27 Keller to Mitchell, 7 March 1958, CULHK. Mason's review ('Music Better than Words for Analysing Music', *Manchester Guardian*, 9 September 1957, 4) was enthusiastic – if not very perceptive, according to Keller: 'The relations he finds wholly convincing are less close than the ones he doesn't. He always commits the same mistake: where a relation shown consists of a complex of elements, he picks out one element and finds it strange.' Keller to Fiske, 17 September 1957 (WAC Keller Contributor File 1).

28 'Wordless Functional Analysis: the First Year'. *MR* XIX/3 (August 1958): 192–200.

29 Keller to Fiske, 13 September 1957, WAC Keller Contributor File 1.

30 'George Gershwin (1898–1937) or "Music in Music" (Alban Berg)', unpublished manuscript [1957], CULHK.

Keller thought that Gershwin's 'unsentimental attitude towards the most sentimental of forms, that of the American popular song, must have had a powerful root in his early environment'. Accordingly, his eye was caught by the passages about Gershwin's early musical influences in David Ewen's new biography, specifically Gershwin's first hearing of Dvorak's *Humoresque*, Op. 101, No. 7, and Anton Rubinstein's *Melody in F*, Op. 3, No. 1.[31] 'It is possible to trace these small-form models, the Rubinstein and the Dvorák, right through Gershwin's development,' wrote Keller, 'positively in that their structural outlines and the spontaneity of their melodic invention are remembered in virtually every Gershwin song, but also negatively in that Gershwin reacted against their pandering to sentimentality.'

It was the 'positive' part of this influence that Keller wanted to explore in his proposed Functional Analysis:

2 July 1957 – Keller to Fiske [extract]
WAC Keller Contributor File I

Dear Roger,

[. . .] With undue haste (in view of this year's 20th anniversary of Gershwin's death), I suggest a very different application of functional analysis, this time to The Melodic and Rhythmic Style of George Gershwin (d.1937).

"However, the most significant of George's musical adventures came in his tenth year. He was playing ball outside P.S. 25 when, through the open window, he heard the strains of Dvorák's Humoresque played on a violin. . . . 'It was, to me [Gershwin], a flashing revelation of beauty.'" (David Ewen, A Journey to Greatness, 1956.)

After a very brief introduction quoting from this passage, the Humoresque would be played, whereupon my score would expound its rhythmic and melodic influence, including the diatonic assimilation of the tonal penta-scale. I sh'd not confine myself to Gershwin's "serious" works, but sh'd devote much attention to the masterpieces that are his songs for various musicals. Perhaps you'd like to have a look at my article on Rhythm: Gershwin & Stravinsky in the forthcoming issue of THE SCORE (out any day now, I'd think) in order to get a more concrete picture of at least some of the things it would be all about – though I must stress that my score would parallel the relevant observations in my article as little as, if not less than, the Mozart programme parallels my analysis of the D minor quartet in the Mozart Companion.

I should need a pianist, possibly a singer, and gramophone records.

---

31 Ewen, *A Journey to Greatness* (London: W.H. Allen, 1956), 30.

The powers that be are invited to regard my proposal as an adjustment to the new TP policy.[32]

Finally, I must thank you once again for your most understanding & helpful attitude during the recording session. It is a pure pleasure to work with a musician: there aren't many about in our musical world.

Yours,

Hans

Meanwhile, the 'negative' part of Gershwin's response to his early models – his reaction against their sentimentality – was what Keller wanted to explore in another programme on Gershwin he had already suggested to the BBC's Controller of Music.

27 April 1957 – to Richard Howgill
WAC Keller Contributor File I

Dear Mr Howgill,

July 11 will see the 20th anniversary of George Gershwin's death. I think it is a mistake to concentrate on the "respectable" Gershwin on such occasions – as Hilversum recently did in a memorial programme which included the 'American in Paris' and Piano C'to. Gershwin was, above all, a great master of small forms.

I should like to arrange a programme of his popular songs for the attention of the serious musician – without watered-down harmonies (and rhythms) and sentimentalized tempi, and if possible (tho' not necessarily) for the Third.

The frequent harmonic adulterations are well-known, but that, for instance,

There's a some-bo-dy I'm long-ing to see

is supposed to have strongly rhythmic scherzando character will come as a surprise to most. In this respect, a record called "Gershwin playing Gershwin" (obtainable at the US Information Service) proves an ear-opener.

Yours sincerely,

Hans Keller

---

32 Keller refers here to the BBC's major review of its radio services in 1956–57, as a result of which the Third Programme's broadcasting hours had been cut in order to make way for 'less elitist' programming.

This programme was not intended to be an analysis, but simply a recital of songs, performed 'without watered-down harmonies and sentimentalized tempi', by performers who apparently included Britten and Pears.[33] The BBC considered the idea, but kept wanting to recast it as a talk. Keller pleaded in vain, 'It's a recital, for the simple reason that there's nothing to say, except, "That's how it really goes".' He insisted there was no need for words: 'Truthful interpretations of well-known and well-distorted Gershwin songs, with some of his lesser known or hardly known masterpieces in between, would, I think be enormously effective in themselves.'[34] What Keller was seeking to create in the mind of the listener was the kind of 'ear-opening' encounter he had recently experienced himself when he first heard the recording of Gershwin playing 'Someone to Watch Over Me' – a song normally 'played and sung as if it were Isolde's hit tune' by other performers, 'whereas Gershwin meant it to be highly rhythmical, in fact <u>scherzando</u> (<u>doppio movimento</u> in relation to the usual <u>tempo</u> of its performance)'.[35]

Unfortunately neither Howgill nor the producer to whom he delegated the programme, Horace Dann, listened to the recording Keller recommended, so it was hard for them to appreciate his point and separate Gershwin's songs from the 'Hollywood' versions they already knew. Although Dann had several conversations with Keller and went through the motions with the US Information Service, an internal memo to his colleague Maurice Johnstone shows his real thoughts:

> The lyrics being the drivelling doggerel they are and the accompaniments being as commercial as the Anglo-American alliance in Charing Cross Road can be, I suggest that Hans Keller's idea is not a Music Division Programmes exercise at all.
>
> "Gershwin playing Gershwin" has no bearing on the case at all, although I have tried to obtain the recording. A play-back would be a waste of time.[36]

It was also hard to get serious articles about Gershwin into print. Glock had accepted Keller's piece contrasting Gershwin's and Stravinsky's rhythm, but Geoffrey Sharp, despite his interest in *Porgy and Bess*, proved less accommodating when Keller wanted to discuss the revival of *Lady Be Good* which toured the country in 1956–57. Keller heard this production at the Golders Green Hippodrome in May 1956 and was so impressed, both by the work itself and by Sonnie Hale's performance, that he returned to the theatre again and again, just as he had done with Peter Pears in *Così fan tutte* and *Peter Grimes* a decade earlier.

---

33 See Horace Dann to Maurice Johnstone, 1 November 1957, WAC Keller Contributor File 1. 'Even on the shattering hypothesis of an acceptance from this exclusive duo,' wrote Dann, there were too many problems for the programme to be viable: 'The accompaniments, I presumed, would be realized by Britten, if so, Chappell might prove to be very thorny.'

34 Keller to Fiske, 5 October 1957, WAC Keller Contributor File 1.

35 Compare, for example, Frank Sinatra's 1945 version (https://www.youtube.com/watch?v=E07b0SbWWFc) with the Gershwin recording Keller heard (https://www.youtube.com/watch?v=B4QDsbucFxQ, accessed 11.11.17).

36 Dann to Johnstone, 1 November 1957, WAC Keller Contributor File 1.

But Sharp didn't want a review of a Gershwin musical, nor did he want the anniversary article on Gershwin films that Keller gave him the following year. 'I'm sorry, but I think you will not be surprised,' he wrote. 'Time may show you to be right and me wrong; but meanwhile I shall continue to regard him as Kitsch and to use MR space for things which I think more worth it.'[37] Keller argued his case hotly: 'It is true that most critics share your opinion, but the vast majority of, by now, three generations of musicians share mine. On the basis of such evidence alone you would agree, when faced with any other controversial issue, that time has shown me to be right, whereas in the case of Gershwin you keep waiting – for what?'[38]

When Sonnie Hale died two years later, Keller recalled with regret that unappreciated performance of *Lady Be Good*:

Sonnie Hale
MR XX/3–4 (August–November 1959): 289.

The death of Sonnie Hale (John Robert Hale-Monro) on 9th June at the age of 57 has removed, amongst other things, a musician from the contemporary scene whose art I would gladly exchange for that of most of our "serious" performers. I use the word "contemporary" ideally rather than literally, for in Hale's heyday I was a small child, nowhere near England. And of late, as W. MacQueen-Pope wrote in *The Daily Telegraph*, "the West End ignored him, methods and tastes had changed". To me, however, the change of methods and tastes is of little interest, except where a bad method changes into a good one. Nor do I regard the merely fashionable as contemporary; the term should apply to all real art of our age – the one age for whose history mere chronology is of no significance whatever.

I heard and saw Sonnie Hale in a single production to which, however, I repeatedly returned. It was at the Golders Green Hippodrome a few years back. The show was George Gershwin's *Lady be Good*, a work of genius which at the moment is likewise ignored by the West End because "methods and tastes have changed". It will return, but Hale unfortunately won't. Outstanding as was the light-comedy aspect of his performance, what was really unique was his musical interpretation, his rich yet absolutely relevant imagination, his sense of rhythm, of phrasing and motivic characterization, of re-creative variation. Together with Donald Mitchell, I tried at the time to get this production into one of our major

---

37 Sharp to Keller, 16 February 1957, CULHK.
38 Keller to Sharp, 5 March 1957, CULHK.

European Festivals.[39] For a while matters seemed hopeful, but there are other great performances which one ought to make more generally accessible before it is too late: Julius Patzak's interpretation of the title role in Hans Pfitzner's *Palestrina*, for instance, or his overwhelming performance in Franz Schmidt's oratorio *Das Buch mit den sieben Siegeln*. If any reader wonders why I throw Gershwin, Pfitzner and Schmidt, Sonnie Hale and Patzak under one hat, that is his – a snob's – funeral. For myself, I can think of no better epitaph for Sonnie Hale than, *mutatis mutandis*, Schönberg's for Gershwin.

"An artist is to me like an apple tree. When the time comes, whether it wants or not, it bursts into bloom and starts to produce apples. And as an apple tree neither knows nor asks about the value experts of the market will attribute to its product, so a real composer does not ask whether his products will please the experts of serious arts. He only feels he has to say something and says it."[40]

Keller's attempt to bring Gershwin's songs into the realm of 'serious' music recalls the shifting musical boundaries of the time – and Keller's response. Horace Dann's assertion that a Gershwin song recital was 'not a Music Division Programmes exercise' reflects the structural divide within the BBC of the 1950s between 'music' and 'light music'. This was not to last much longer, as the concept of 'light music' began to fade in the face of the new 'popular music', a phenomenon that, at least as far as the BBC was concerned, lay outside the realm of Music altogether.[41] In another direction, boundaries were also shifting as a result of the rapid advance of the early music revival. In one way this was an exciting rolling-back of the frontiers of the canon, but it also threw up new boundaries between musicians as the growing interest in historically-informed performance separated periods and styles. Added to these developments was the music of other cultures, which recording and broadcasting were making increasingly available. Benjamin Britten's long tour of the Far East in 1955–56 led to a deep engagement with other ways of musical thinking, and Keller was confronted with the result when he went to the premiere of Britten's ballet *The Prince of the Pagodas* in January 1957.

---

39 The Holland Festival in 1957 (see Keller to Mitchell, 1 January 1957, CULHK).

40 In *George Gershwin*, ed. Merle Armitage (New York: Longmans, Green and Co., 1938), 97–8.

41 'Light Music' was a department within Music Division, but the new 'Popular Music' department created in 1963 was placed outside, in General Division.

Keller's attitude to all this could appear quixotic at times, but was actually quite consistent. To him style had nothing to do with value and he was always suspicious of conventional categorisations. As a consequence, some of his boundary-crossing juxtapositions (from Britten and Mozart to Gershwin and Webern) made him seem startlingly radical, but at the same time the depth of his roots in his own Austro-German symphonic heritage put considerable restraint on the enlarging of his musical horizons. Such was the power of that profound early experience in Vienna's Neubaugasse that it framed Keller's understanding of everything he encountered afterwards in the turbulent post-war world. He was, however, very aware of this limitation – hence his self-injunction not to write about music he didn't understand. In the face of so much change he was intensely suspicious of superficiality and refused to take anything on trust (to 'let himself sometimes say "there must be"', as Colin Mason was urging him to do in their 'dodecaphoneys' row) because, he thought, to do so was to risk letting go of musical meaning.

Keller went to *The Prince of the Pagodas* in his role as London correspondent for the Swiss daily the *Basler Nachrichten* (for which he had been writing since 1949), and his review there is his only article devoted to this particular work of Britten's. He singled out the gamelan-influenced Pagoda Land scene (Act II, scene 2) as the one weak spot in the work – where Britten 'forgets his *Weithörigkeit* and plays around with a stylistically out-of-place little Balinese song brought back from his world tour, which he then guiltily tries to build into the broader context with inappropriate percussion'.[42] Keller was not alone in finding this scene a problem: many other critics thought the same. Donald Mitchell agreed at the time that 'this Oriental interlude is wildly out of stylistic place,' but later put such reactions down to culture shock – an indication, he thought, of 'how novel the experience was that Britten's gamelan offered and how sharp was its impact'.[43]

During his long trip East, before and after his time in Bali, Britten had spent some weeks in India. One of the musicians he heard there was Ravi Shankar, who gave him and Pears a private performance in a small studio of All-India Radio (where Shankar was director of music) – 'our first real taste of Indian music, & it was tremendously fascinating'.[44] Shortly after this Shankar embarked on his first tour of Europe, performing in London in the autumn of 1956. Marion, Countess of Harewood (Erwin Stein's daughter and a close friend of Britten) met Shankar during this visit, and asked him to play to a select group of musicians in her home on his next trip to London the following year. The aim of this intimate setting was to promote a better understanding of his music than was possible in the concert hall, as she explained to Keller when she invited him to be present: 'He wants to play, and explain what he is playing, as he believes Indian music need not remain so exotic a thing to English musicians as it is at present.'[45]

---

42 *Basler Nachrichten*, 8 January 1957.
43 See Mitchell, 'The Prince of the Pagodas', *MT* 98/1368 (February 1957): 91, and *Benjamin Britten: 'Death in Venice'*, ed. Donald Mitchell (Cambridge: Cambridge University Press, 1987), 207, n. 16.
44 Britten to Mary Potter, 23 December 1955, in *Letters from a Life* (London: Boydell, 2008) vol. 4, 374.
45 Countess of Harewood to Keller, 9 May [1957], CULHK.

11 May 1957 – to the Countess of Harewood

Dear Lady Harewood:

Many thanks for your invitation which, with great personal regret, I am unable to accept. For one thing, judging from past experiences, I should find it physically impossible to stand a performance of Indian music; for another, even if my prognosis is too pessimistic, I have strong reasons against superficially widening one's artistic horizon.

I can understand that Ravi Shankar wants to explain what he is playing. However, music explains itself, and I don't believe in explanations of explanations: I have seen their effects. True analysis is another matter: it explains your own experience to you and can – as I shall show in a forthcoming experimental broadcast – always be achieved without words, just by playing, at any rate in principle.

Ravi Shankar may make his music seem less exotic, but he cannot succeed in making its experience less exoteric, tho' the listener may come to cheat himself into believing that it has become esoteric. Width of information instead of depth of knowledge – this is the danger of our time, which even its greatest living musical genius has not been able to escape altogether: hear the only bad scene in The Prince of the Pagodas.

With renewed thanks,

[Hans Keller]

Erwin Stein was surprised at the way Keller 'seemed to reject the business so passionately' and suspected some kind of ideological reason lay behind it.

11 May 1957 – to Erwin Stein

Dear Erwin:

Your description, "religion", for my aversion to Indian music is, if I may say so, fantastic. I am reverting to it because I want to object to the automatic special pleading it implies.

No belief is involved in my attitude, no theoretical preference, no evaluation. The comparison with the "historical" Mozart performances is irrelevant: one attitude is based on understanding, the other on the certainty of non-comprehension.

There is one thing worse than being narrow-minded, and that is not knowing the limitations of one's mind – the over-riding danger at a late cultural stage.

You mentioned your "interest" in Ravi Shankar. I don't think a true artistic experience can be interesting. It should be compelling. "Interest" is a symptom of sterility in the historical air.

~

At the beginning of 1956, Keller again redesigned his regular columns in *The Music Review*, abandoning the tabular reviews and reverting to prose. For his film column he retained the title 'Film Music and Beyond' he had been using since 1950, but for his writing on new music he changed 'First Performances' into 'The New In Review', 'in order to ensure its continued substance & not to depend on the arbitrary circumstance of some First (English/Concert/Broadcast) Performance'.[46] Sharp commissioned additional specific articles and reviews from Keller, but in these two regular columns seems to have been happy for Keller to choose his own subjects – that is, until Keller chose Gershwin's films. The row over that unprecedented rejection and the ensuing hiatus in his 'Film Music and Beyond' column marked the beginning of the end of Keller's film writing. It left him without a regular outlet on film, since he had recently terminated the parallel film music column he had been writing in *The Musical Times*, after its editor, Martin Cooper, inflicted savage cuts (after proof stage) on his analysis of Alan Rawsthorne's score for the documentary *The Drawings of Leonardo da Vinci* – in Keller's view not only Rawsthorne's best film score, but a significant contribution to modern sonata thought, 'teem[ing] with unconventional and intensely imaginative exploitations of conventional schemes and devices'.[47]

Keller revived the 'Film Music and Beyond' column briefly two years later – stung into action by the Academy Award conferred on Malcolm Arnold for *Bridge on the River Kwai*, whose 'virtually illiterate' score, Keller said, made the Oscar into a mark of shame upon such a gifted composer.[48] The revived column did not last, for the newer medium of television was now claiming Keller's attention – as will shortly be seen. Keller's last 'Film Music and Beyond' article before the Gershwin row with Sharp had been a particularly pointed one. He had previously noted with approval British film's 'noble tradition of shedding all background music in such places as hospitals (*White Corridors*), police stations (*The Blue Lamp*), or any similar stores of naturalistic problems.'[49] Naturalism, which Keller defined as 'the art of remaining inartistic yet expressive', and at which the understated British excelled,

---

46 Keller to Sharp, 20 November 1955, CULHK.
47 'Rawsthorne's "Leonardo"', *MT* 97/1355 (January 1956): 29. The original uncut version is preserved in Keller's archive, and Keller recycled his analysis in *MR* XVII/1 (February 1956): 95–6.
48 'Malcolm Arnold Oscarred', *MR* XIX/2 (May 1958): 150–51.
49 'Film Music and Beyond', *MR* XVII/3 (August 1956): 254–5.

'will always be able to say more, rather than less, without music'. Sometimes the avoidance of music was a moral imperative, as in the case of *Yield to the Night* (starring Diana Dors as a young woman awaiting execution for murder), which Keller reviewed under the title 'No Music'.[50]

Film Music and Beyond : No Music
MR XVII/4 (November 1956): 337, reprinted in *HKFM*, 205

This feature has always conscientiously recorded those rare and remarkable instances of music-less sound tracks which respect alike the ethics of naturalism, the craft of the film, and the art of music; as we have indicated at the end of our last *Film Music* article, they are not quite so rare in this understating country. The latest example, again a British one, is perhaps so far the most important one ethically. It is a tendentious film, supra-politically so, and members of the House of Lords were invited to see it (though few availed themselves of the opportunity) before they arrived at a vote which, owing to the Parliament Act, is still *sub judice*, so that whatever the final outcome of the issue, the picture will remain intensely topical for some time after the appearance of the present lines. The issue is, of course, that of the death penalty, and the film, *Yield to the Night*, reports without fuss upon the degrading influence of this institution upon all whom it enlists in its service. It is not the only aspect of the problem, nor indeed the most important, but degradation being a matter of the emotions, it lends itself well to faithful dramatization. Now, to denature this almost photographic account of the prison staff's emotions, moral and instinctive, by an admixture of background music, would not only have been unwise, but downright immoral. The whole point of the film is that the discovery of truth needs more imagination than the assimilation of fiction and that, conversely, the kind of sadistic thoughtlessness that goes by the name of "realism" produces the most pitiable of all manifestations of the human mind – fiction without imagination. Owing to the absence of music, then, the truth establishes its anti-fictional emotive power. More of a document than most documentaries, this feature film thus defines the antithesis between imagination and the imaginary.

---

50 The sound-track of this film is not entirely devoid of music: what is important is that the scenes in the prison cell have no music. Furthermore, most of the rest of the music (in the flashback scenes) is diegetic – for which the director, J. Lee Thompson, had to fight against the studio music director: 'Studios like to use their own orchestra and write the music themselves. I had quite a battle to use the jazz music we did.' (Quoted in Steve Chibnall, *J. Lee Thompson* (Manchester: Manchester University Press, 2000), 101, n. 30.)

Yield to the Night was released in June 1956, just as Sidney Silverman's bill to abolish capital punishment successfully passed its third reading in the House of Commons. As in 1948, when the Lords had rejected Silverman's previous attempt to suspend the death penalty, the question of capital punishment in 1956 was suspended between an abolitionist House of Commons and a House of Lords that remained in favour of hanging (hence the special screening of *Yield to the Night* for their lordships). The Lords' power of veto over legislation passed by the Commons had been ended by the 1911 Parliament Act, but they could still delay it. When Keller wrote his review, the legislation was still *sub judice* in the sense that the government was considering whether to exercise its right to force Silverman's bill through the Lords. In the end, ministers shied away from such drastic action, in favour of an attempt at compromise legislation.

In 1948 public opinion had still been against abolition, so the Lords could fairly claim to be protecting the will of the people against a quixotic House of Commons. Since then, attitudes had shifted as a result of a series of dramatic and controversial murder cases, most prominently those of Derek Bentley (executed in 1952 for a killing carried out by another man), Timothy Evans (whose 1950 conviction was undermined when his neighbour, John Christie, was exposed as a serial killer in 1953) and Ruth Ellis in 1955 (whose story was uncannily similar to that of the fictional protagonist in *Yield to the Night*).[51] All three cases aroused considerable public sympathy and raised important legal questions over – respectively – the doctrine of 'common purpose', the reliability of the courts, and the potential defences of provocation and diminished responsibility.

The National Campaign for the Abolition of Capital Punishment (NCACP) was formed after Ellis's execution, organising a massive campaign in support of Silverman's bill. Keller, for whom the ethical, legal and psychological questions involved were of intense concern, threw himself into this effort. According to Peggy Duff, NCACP's Secretary and Treasurer, no other person in the country managed to collect so many signatures for the petition; writing to congratulate Keller on 2 January 1956, she told him 'You hold the record and nobody looks like wresting it from you.' The composer Michael Graubart has given a telling anecdote of Keller's campaigning methods:

> I encountered Hans in the foyer after an SPNM concert. He rushed up to me, brandishing a piece of paper, and demanded: '*Which* of those pieces did you like?' Tentatively, I told him which I had thought to be the only good piece in the programme. '*I entirely* agree!' he almost shouted; 'In that case, you will *certainly* want to sign this petition!' The petition? Support

51 The similarities led many to believe that the film was actually based on Ellis's case, but in fact the book from which it was adapted had been published before Ellis had fired her fatal shot (Joan Henry, *Yield to the Night* (London: Gollancz, 1954)).

for Sidney Silverman's bill to abolish capital punishment! I was furious. Why should taste in music go with views on social and political ethics? Hans, of course, for whom truth and beauty, art and life were one, would have known why. But the main reason why I was angry was because he was right: I was about to extract another copy of the same petition from my pocket to ask him to sign![52]

Keller's attempt to persuade Eric Blom to sign was more orthodox:

13 January 1956 – to Eric Blom

Dear Mr Blom,

Many thanks for your letter. Capital punishment: I think you misunderstand my motives. I am not moved by pity for the murderer. My reasons are (a) idealistic, (b) ethical, and (c) practical. (a) I believe that thou shalt not kill, not even a killer. (b) Human justice being fallible, any irreparable punishment is <u>ipso facto</u> evil. The execution of Timothy Evans for a murder committed by John Christie is a case in point. (c) It has been statistically shown, beyond reasonable doubt, that capital punishment is no deterrent whatsoever. All but two European countries have abolished it. Their murder rates have either remained static or actually decreased – the reason being that certain psychopaths are attracted to murder by the prospect of the death penalty. This is a psychiatric fact which every policeman will confirm: almost every murder elicits an astonishing number of wrong confessions. In this country in the last century, capital punishment existed for over 200 offences which did not increase when it was abolished. Finally, it is a criminological fact that most murderers are not professional criminals and do not repeat their crimes. Of those who do or would, most are insane and wouldn't be hanged anyway, and of the remaining number some could be cured and others used for urgently needed psychiatric investigations. Your argument is only 'fair' to those who wouldn't repeat their crime anyway. The constitutional criminal is quite incapable of realizing that he will be caught – otherwise he would occupy himself differently. All this only by way of explanation. I don't think it's much use arguing: deep-rooted prejudices are usually involved on either side – certainly on mine. But I assure you that I wasn't sorry when those who tortured me and killed others were executed. Emotionally, I was in fact relieved. But ethically and rationally, I was still against it; in fact, I won an Evening Standard competition on what to do with Hitler & Co.[53] [. . .]

All good wishes,

Yours

[Hans Keller]

The government's compromise legislation became law in the Homicide Act of March 1957, which divided murder for the first time into capital and non-capital offences, established the partial defences of provocation and diminished responsibility, and abolished the doctrine of 'constructive malice'. Problems with the practical application of the new Act became apparent almost immediately. Most notoriously, the very next execution case – that of John Vickers, convicted for an accidental killing in the course of a burglary – brought into question whether constructive malice had actually been abolished at all.

One of the elements of NCACP's campaign was 'to give people already opposed to capital punishment an opportunity for expressing their conscience':

> We shall suggest, for instance, that abolitionists may think fit to abstain from going to any entertainment or party on the eve of an execution, and may wish to attend a place of worship or assembly (and we shall arrange for such places to be open for the purpose).[54]

So when Vickers was hanged at Durham prison in July 1957 there were many such expressions of conscience. A letter in the *Evening Standard* on 26 July noted that 'several prominent politicians attended a silent prayer meeting at the Friends' House, Euston, and a short service at St. Paul's Cathedral'. Evidently disapproving of this, the writer (Mr S. Harrison) went on to wonder 'how many of these individuals attended the funeral service of the old lady?' (Vickers's victim).

31 July 1957 – to the editor of the Evening Standard

'CONSTRUCTIVE MALICE'?

I attended the silent meeting at the Friends' House when John Vickers was hanged, and I think I can tell Mr. Harrison why I did not attend the funeral service of the old lady whom Vickers killed. It was because we,

53 At the beginning of April 1945 – with the end of the war in sight but before Hitler's suicide – the *Evening Standard* invited readers to submit answers to the question 'What shall we do with Hitler?' Thousands of letters were received of which a few were published. Keller won a guinea for his published reply, advising 'Subject him and as many of his collaborators and followers as possible to extensive and intensive psychological research.'

54 Victor Gollancz, *Spectator* 6635 (26 August 1955): 276–7.

the community, were responsible for the premeditated killing of Vickers, whereas we were not responsible for the unpremeditated killing of the old lady. The meeting was an expression of guilt: we were all guilty of constructive malice.

Hans Keller, Willow Road, N.W.3

~

In the autumn of 1958 Milein Cosman made her first appearance on television, and she and Keller acquired a television set. Straight away Keller began a lively 'Television Music' column in the journal *Musical Opinion*. It was not quite 'The Need for Competent Television Music Criticism', as Keller was sensitive to the fact that this was a very different medium, of which as yet he knew little. He proceeded cautiously at first, aware that 'I have much to learn about the new medium,' in which he could already see that music was playing a much smaller role than in either film or radio: 'television is not primarily a means of musical communication; music will always take second or third place.'[55]

One thing that stands out from Keller's early 'Television Music' articles is his interest in this new medium as a potential tool for teaching, enabling useful technical close-ups, the simultaneous seeing and hearing of music examples, and 'a strong and immediate impression of a creative artist's personality' – something he thought could be of considerable value in breaking down barriers between contemporary composers and their audiences (he noted Schoenberg's own interest in television's pedagogical use).[56] Keller was also unusual among 'highbrow' commentators for showing as much interest in ITV as in the BBC – indeed his first television column urged 'Lowbrows of the world, unite!' against the 'pathological snobbery' of those who automatically dismissed anything produced by the commercial network.

Keller's interest in television as a medium for teaching was a result not only of his own teaching activities, but also of Cosman's involvement in teaching on television. His interest in ITV might also have owed something to the fact that the series she devised and presented was broadcast not by the BBC but as part of Associated-Rediffusion's pioneering schools service. Associated-Rediffusion

---

55 *MO* 82/976 (January 1959): 247. Keller's 'Television Music' column is reproduced complete in *HKFM*.

56 See *MO* 82/976 (January 1959): 247, 82/977 (February 1959): 319, and 'The Raised Lowbrow', *MR* XIX/3 (August 1958): 226–8, in which Keller gives a detailed reaction to an early television recital. When Humphrey Searle invited Schoenberg in 1951 to record a lecture for the BBC, Schoenberg initially assumed this meant on television, where he could make better use of music examples (see Schoenberg to Searle, 25 May 1951, published in *MS* IV/3: 470–71).

was the first ITV network to reach the airwaves after the 1954 Television Act broke the BBC's monopoly, beginning its London weekday service in September 1955. The following year it announced the appointment of Boris Ford (supported by an educational advisory committee) to design daily programming for schools, to be launched the following April – thus pipping at the post the BBC, whose schools television service had been years in the planning but was not due to start before the autumn. ('We are going to shock auntie by showing her how fast things can be done if you try.'[57]) Ford was keen to stress the public-service intent of their new service, designed to 'stimulate the imagination of the young', focusing particularly on 'the 14–15 age group':

> Mr Ford, the new head of School Broadcasting, told a news conference that he had watched 'very little' television. 'We have got to introduce into the programmes an element of participation,' he said. 'They must combat all forms of passive watching. I hope a great amount of our work will show children grappling with problems.' The curriculum would include current affairs, science, and historical geography. 'The programmes will be extremely lively and experimental. One of the first aspects of the programmes will be to teach people to look and see. I think our population is largely visually illiterate.'[58]

Keller was very interested:

28 December 1956 – to Boris Ford

Dear Boris:

ITV for schools

I was struck by two of your remarks as quoted by the GUARDIAN this morning, to the effect that the programmes must combat passive watching, and that they will be experimental.

I am impressed by this approach, and although I don't know much about TV and loathe what I know, I should be delighted if it were possible for me to join your educational advisory committee which, I gather, will be expanding. The dangers of passivity are even greater in music than in any other cultural sphere, and in the course of my own educational activities I was often struck by the possibilities which TV, properly handled, might offer towards making musical education what it once was, i.e. development of activity as distinct from discomania. [. . .]

Speaking both as a musician and as a psychoanalytic worker, I sh'd say that 14–15 is an ideal age so far as musical stimulation is concerned.

57 *Guardian,* 29 December 1956, 4.
58 *Ibid.,* 28 December 1956, 1.

This offer did not come to anything, as Sir John Wolfenden, the committee's chairman, was reluctant to add to its twenty-four members, and music was not one of the subjects planned for his opening season.[59] 'Looking and seeing' was top of the list, however, and it must have been not long afterwards that Milein Cosman was approached by Fernau Hall, the Canadian-born dance critic who had been appointed Education Officer at Associated-Rediffusion. Cosman was already friendly with Hall, who admired her work and had included her drawings in some of his books.[60] 'He said have you got an idea for a course for the schools?' remembered Cosman; 'and I said yes, of course I have, and it was on drawing. And so I did a course of nine talks on drawing for ITV.'[61] Her series *Black and White* was broadcast every Friday from 3 October until 12 December 1958, and showed Cosman in combination with a variety of other artists, exploring a wide range of techniques and applications of drawing. In the first programme, for example, she was seen making a drawing 'for its own sake', before introducing the architect Frederick Gibberd showing his drawings for London airport and the sculptor Benno Schotz explaining the 'surprising ways' he used drawings as the basis for sculpture.[62]

For both Cosman and Keller, teaching had long been a useful source of income, but for Keller it was also a vocation. By the late 1950s, his growing reputation meant he was inundated with requests for personal tuition from performers, composers and scholars. Young musicians found him exceptionally encouraging, perhaps surprisingly so considering his pugnacious public manner. Here, for example, is a letter to Dori Furth (the 'talented young cellist' he had mentioned to Roger Fiske), who had just come second to the Jamaican pianist Audrey Cooper in the Royal Overseas League's 'Festival of Commonwealth Youth' competition. Keller put his finger in the gentlest way on the reason why she had lost to Cooper's 'natural freedom of declamation' and 'instinctive understanding of structure':[63]

28 March 1958 – to Dori Furth

Dear Dori:

Congratulations!

I think that the adjudication was just, if somewhat less than articulate. At the same time, I (like Malcolm) "have no hesitation" in declaring that you were, if I may say so, the potential first: there is no doubt that as far

---

59 See Ford to Keller, 3 January 1957, CULHK, and *TV Times*, 8 March 1957, 31.
60 *Modern English Ballet* and *An Anatomy of Ballet* (London: Melrose, [1950] and 1953 respectively).
61 Milein Cosman, interviewed by Daniel Snowman, 1997. (https://www.iwm.org.uk/collections/item/object/80024350, accessed 23 March 2018).
62 *TV Times* 12/152 (26 September 1958): 34.
63 See also *MR* XIX/2 (May 1958): 137–8, where Keller commended both performers, as well as the judge Malcolm Arnold's 'exceptionally realistic critical attitude'.

as your talent is concerned, you are superior to Audrey Cooper both in musicianship and as a musical personality.

"Potentially" is the word. It isn't a question of what went wrong, and Malcolm Arnold is the last to think that it is. You only need a step or two in the direction of greater freedom of declamation, of sharper characterization, of "big-line" phrasing, in order to be able to give a really outstanding performance. It is difficult, but by no means impossible, to pin down such things. If the phrasing of the Fauré theme had been as wide-spun on the forte level as it was when played softly, Arnold wouldn't even have been struck by the "wonderful dynamic range"; instead he'd have been overwhelmed by what the range is there for – by wholeness and conviction. As it was, the forte statements were too "beautiful", with almost the same accents, the same vibrato, on every single note, so that the halved values didn't lead on to the next bar: it didn't "sweep" at these junctures.

The rubati, too, were too calculated, too "good", i.e. student-like; this was especially striking at one point in the Francoeur. Rather have a little accidental friction with the accompanist in the rit. I'm thinking of, than measure it out beforehand so precisely that all spontaneity and, again, the "sweep" is lost.

I would not make these criticisms if you were not so very near the real thing, which even few first-rate musicians rarely achieve. Which is just another way of saying that as it stood, the performance was already most impressive – and I did observe naive reactions.

Yours,

[Hans]

Another pupil, the young Swiss musicologist Hansjörg Pauli, was also warned by Keller of the dangers of being too careful:

17 March 1957 – to Hansjörg Pauli

Dear Mr Pauli,

In view of your replies to I/3, 4, & II/I[64] as well as parts of other reactions, I have formed a preliminary impression of what may be your chief weakness, or Kinderkrankheit if you like. This impression may be absolutely wrong, in which case you will not find it difficult to disregard it, but if it happens to be right, you may find it helpful to take it into

---

64 This refers to specific analytical questions set by Keller (details no longer extant).

account at the earliest possible opportunity. It seems to me you tend to be too much of a perfectionist. Alles muss stimmen; you'd rather sacrifice a discovery than contradict yourself – and thus the sacrifice of the discovery becomes unconscious: you sometimes don't make the discovery you would have made but for psychological reasons. This attitude also has its repercussions on your happily & basically aural approach: you don't give yourself sufficient aural freedom, which is to say that in proportion, you think too much and dream too little aurally. Trying to make it all fit, you sometimes concentrate on incidentals and miss essentials: at times you behave like a composer whose music is too good – who has a first-rate technique and doesn't want to risk anything. I need not tell you that it is easier to be consistent superficially than to contradict oneself profoundly, and that such contradictions are more valuable inasmuch as at least one of the contradictory thoughts is right.

I cannot give you any illustrations, for I should have to tell you what I want you to discover, but in any case I'm either right or wrong; if I'm right, you don't need any concrete examples, and if I'm wrong, just forget it. It is only for brevity's sake that I have given my tentative view rather apodeictically.

I/3: I cannot accede to your request: you are too good for me to make it too easy for you. I call "basic shapes" what you call "basic shapes". But there is one misunderstanding: for the time being, I want you to analyse the trio separately, and my question regarding 71f. is put within the trio's own terms of reference. For the rest, your diagram does not contain the whole truth, nor indeed always the most important part of it. Your analysis is not sufficiently sub-thematic (pre-serial) on the one hand, and there is no formal surface analysis on the other. My question about bar 34f. (cello) rolls the two issues into one. From the sub-thematic point of view, I should like you to reconsider it with reference to the first two rhythmic motifs which I have marked in your diagram, and to which you have, in fact, already reduced this juncture – but not completely enough, nor with sufficient precision. From the formal point of view, you haven't told me yet where we have got at this point. In fact, I should like you to map out a conventional analysis too: what is the rhythmic structure of [the] theme of the movement, and what is the latter's form?

Further stuff anon.

Greetings.

Yours,

[Hans Keller]

Keller's teaching relationship with Pauli was conducted almost entirely by letter, so their surviving correspondence shows his methods in a little more detail than most. The twenty-five-year-old Pauli lived in Winterthur (north of Zürich), where he wrote music criticism for the *Neues Winterthurer Tagblatt* and taught at the Winterthur Konservatorium. Frustrated by his rather conservative musical education, he asked Keller to teach him 'the analysis of contemporary works' by correspondence: 'I figured it like that: You set the task; as soon as I have worked it out I send you the solution and name all the problems which I have been unable to solve; you mark the mistakes and show me the lacks in my work. And so on!'[65]

Keller agreed, but warned Pauli that in his opinion contemporary music should not be studied in isolation: 'I don't teach analysis in historical compartments – only on the basis of classical methods, which insure the student against a non-aural "paper" approach, our time's greatest danger in both composition and analysis'.[66] Pauli therefore found himself analysing classical string quartets and various nineteenth-century works alongside the Stravinsky and Schoenberg he was initially keen to study. Some of Keller's tasks were nevertheless very topical, such as the one he set a few months prior to their first meeting in person, at the 1957 ISCM Festival, held that year in Zürich:

18 March 1957 – to Hansjörg Pauli [extract]

Lesson No.2, 3rd instalment

(6) At the ISCM Festival in Zuerich, Matyas Seiber's Concert Piece (Konzertstueck) for violin and piano – in my opinion his best work – for violin and piano – will be performed; it has been published by Schott's. If you can get hold of a score,

  (a) describe the peculiarities of

   (i) the row &

   (ii) its utilization, and

  (b) demonstrate any technical or stylistic influences that make themselves felt in the work.

Keller also drew Pauli into his own work:

19 September 1957 – to Hansjörg Pauli [extract]

Dear Hansjörg,

I have been in touch with the MUSIC REVIEW, and the editor seems very interested in your doing a "pure" (i.e. wordless) application of

---

65 Pauli to Keller, 3 November 1956, CULHK.
66 Keller to Pauli, 18 November 1956, CULHK.

FA for his journal; the only thing he's worried about is the cost of music engraving, so we shall keep that in mind and won't actually write a score (as I did for the BBC), but the shortest possible analytic exposition for musical purposes. I have invited him to make suggestions for a short work or single movement. Here they are: Tragic Overture, Eulenspiegel, Beethoven op. 133, Wolf Italian Serenade. I think the last-mentioned work might be a very good idea from our own instructional point of view, but leave the choice to you: as I have just explained to the editor, I should like you to choose the work which you feel you do – or might come to – understand best. I shall be in Donaueschingen, where we can talk over procedural questions; nevertheless, you can, if you like, start right away. Subject to your agreement, I should like you to rediscover the principles and technique of FA for yourself, since this seems the only way in which one can make sure that it is based on musical experience. In other words, I don't for the moment, want to molest you with the theory of it, nor indeed with too many characteristics of the method, some of which may be personal. The basic aim is obvious to you anyway: the audible background unity of contrasting themes and motifs, to be expressed without words, simply via notes. I shall explain further as we go along, and shall point out the theoretical implications of what you are doing when you have done it: this, I think, is the correct approach to theory. [. . .]

Best,

H

Another young musicologist who approached Keller for lessons at this time was Alan Walker, who became his pupil at the beginning of 1958. He was then a doctoral student at Durham University, but lived in Harrow so could have lessons with Keller in person. He went on Saturday afternoons to Keller's house in Willow Road, where they would have long discussions, 'some of them lasting more than three hours':

Although I generally prepared specific scores for the next lesson, they often served merely as the starting-point for further wide-ranging conversations the following week. The range of topics was vast, but I now see that it was fundamental. What kind of language is music? What, if anything, does music express? Is musical talent inherited or is it acquired? What is the difference between talent and genius? What is the nature of absolute pitch? What are the requirements for a good musical memory? What can we learn from infant prodigies? And so on and so forth.

In those days Hans was a pacer; he liked to teach on the move. At the commencement of each lesson he used to position himself in a rocking-chair and rock back and forth while he talked. And when the conversation grew complicated, the rocking would become agitated, at which point he would propel himself at high velocity out of his chair and onto the carpet, and start pacing. From chair, to settee, to fireplace, and back to the chair, he would zig-zag across the room in an endless journey, describing circles both literal and metaphorical around me. Meanwhile, I sat in an armchair, immobile. The point having been made, the conclusion drawn, he would once more settle into his rocking-chair until the next idea sparked his imagination and prompted another perambulation.[67]

Composers too came to Keller for help and support. Even when they were not formal pupils, they still found that a discussion with Keller could unlock all sorts of problems. Mátyás Seiber, who was a good friend in the late 1950s, explained to Keller as follows why he found their conversations so valuable:

I find that you are one of the few persons with whom it is worth while discussing things: it is always stimulating and challenging what you say. I find that for me there are 2 types of persons: I might call them "freezers" and "openers". In the presence of some people I feel I just freeze up completely, I can't think what to say, I feel uncomfortable and if I force myself to say anything it probably comes out awkwardly & stupidly. With you, I feel I "open up", I speak freely, without inhibitions, and I feel I can say just what I want. Which is very nice, and very rare. When we talk (and battle) I feel there is not only an intellect opposite me, but also a heart underneath. In other words, that you are a real Mensch, which is, after all, the most important thing.[68]

Benjamin Frankel agreed that it was Keller's emotional response to music, beneath his formidable intellect, that made him such a help – as he told Keller in 1957, 'my regard for your intellectual grasp of all these questions arises from my belief that you love music and <u>what it can do</u> in the same way that I do myself.'

At this time, Frankel had recently left London for Switzerland, where he was struggling with the writing of his fifth string quartet (Op.43, later dedicated to Keller):

I badly need your help, Hans, in discussing how one may arrive, without <u>undue</u> self-consciousness, at the tonal possibilities of the serial technique without "cheating". For I am completely certain that tonality for me is the truth, however much it needs to be qualified by the inclusion of all the hard thinking and experiment of the last fifty years.

Having avoided serial technique hitherto, he explained how he now felt an 'urgent need for a strict discipline', but was finding it 'extremely difficult to work with the 12 notes and still "honestly" avoid the atonal consequences'.

---

67 Walker, review of *EOM* etc., *Canadian University Music Review* 17/2 (Jan 1997): 118–28.
68 Seiber to Keller [undated], CULHK.

Not that there is anything so disastrously bad about atonality as such. But (1) I don't really like it – certainly I am not convinced that it is a complete musical language in itself and (2) it seems to lead (or at any rate to lead <u>me</u>) into the very subjectivism that I most consciously need to avoid. . . . It will be no help to me if I succeed in producing a work or two of coldly objective and hideously unmusical sound in the effort to avoid my own sense of over-romantic subjectivism. . . . The "sound" of Schoenberg, though I find it of the greatest imaginative and emotional depth, seems to me (in my immod-esty) the very thing that I need to leave behind. And, most dangerous heresy of all, I am not altogether convinced that the discipline of the single tone row will necessarily produce the much vaunted unity.[69]

12 September 1957 – to Benjamin Frankel

My dear Ben,

Forgive me for my belated reply; now it was my turn to have dental trouble. In fact, I was quite ill, complete with a temperature which slowed down my work to somewhere near zero, and as a result I am behind with everything. The thought of the most urgent rush jobs alone makes me quite sick; for instance, my publisher wants me to get through the proofs of the Carl Flesch Memoirs (which I have translated & edited) within a matter of 11 days, and that's only one job among several. But there is at least the success (or so it seems to me) of the first demonstration of my wordless 'functional analysis' (Third Programme, last Saturday) to cheer me up. So much, then, for your learned practitioner's own mental balance. [. . .]

Very glad you have been working at your quartet. Naturally, so long as you want to get out of it by the back door, twelve-tonality won't seem "complete" to you. I don't say this critically, it's simply a fact. Berg, for instance, was none the worse for building a back door rather like the front gate of a palace garden. The only important thing is to know whether one knows what one wants. I'm not altogether happy about your fear of romanticism, subjectivism, and so forth. If, by character, you are an out-and-out suppressionist like Strawinsky, well and good. But – if I may abbreviate – you hate him anyway, which shows that you don't love your own anti-romanticism all that much either. Nor, of course, do you love your romanticism, which is why you react against Schoenberg and, by way of projection, narrow down his emotional range (which actually is at least as wide as Beethoven's, and I mean it) to what you want to deny yourself. Just apply to Uncle Hans, he's got a wrong answer to everything.

69 Frankel to Keller, 4 September 1957.

Seriously, tho', conflicts aren't overcome by denial, and discipline is only successful when it makes them into a means of expression (i.e. of creating tension) rather than the quasi-pathological end you dread. The very conflict between your serialism and your tonal urges will, I think, open up new fields of expression and will thus create its own technique. In its essence, the conflict is typical of the mature artist.

But if there is to be any point in the back door at all, it ought itself to be built along strictly functional lines, otherwise one soon needs a side door in order to be able to avoid the back door too. In a word, poly-serialism has to be approached with caution. The row underlies the basic idea, and if you have two rows, you still have to have an expressed or implied basic idea which underlies them both, so things are getting more difficult on the one hand while seeming to get easier on the other. Practical compositorial experience does not show that single-row technique is not combinable with tonal organization; on the other hand, I readily admit that there are minds (Berg, Skalkottas) which, paradoxically, unify more easily with two or even more rows than with one. We'll talk about it.

In reading the cello pieces I found them even more valuable from the point of view of invention and texture ("Satz") than I had thought, while on the other hand the serial technique appeared more primitive and not always absolutely necessary.

Let's meet in town* or in Rodmell, as you prefer, but give me another week or so until I have caught up with the most urgent tasks.

Much love to you both,

Ever,

[Hans]

* If so, in Hampstead, of course.

~

The success of Functional Analysis on the radio brought more potential pupils and commissions and the end of the decade saw Keller busier than ever. Reactions to the broadcast of his second analytical score in March 1958 (Beethoven's Op. 95 was chosen, not Gershwin) were again 'very gratifying' and the BBC decided to invest in an orchestral score next. Fiske's colleagues were keen on a Mozart concerto, and 'there was also a strong feeling we should try and scrape up the money to have [Clifford] Curzon if he's interested'.[70] Unfortunately Curzon was taking a sabbatical year in 1958, so FA No. 3 went ahead with Dennis Matthews, and Curzon was invited to choose another work for the following year. Curzon had been an admirer of Keller's analytical method since hearing the first FA, after which he wrote, 'I felt I was participating in some strange creative act – a beautiful and somewhat terrifying experience.'[71] On his return from sabbatical, he chose Beethoven's Fourth Concerto for their work together. Keller was ecstatic:

7 April 1959 – to Roger Fiske [extract]
WAC Keller Contributor File I

Dear Roger,

[…] FA No. 8. I am happier than I can say. Curzon's insight is fantastic, as is his ability to do what he wants to do. This is the kind of collaboration I've been dreaming of ever since No. 1. I suppose it's platitudinous to say that there is all the difference in the world between a first-rate artist and a great one, but one is human enough to rediscover the fact when one's own work is involved. Whatever Pope[72] is like, this will be by far the best FA perf ever.

There are a few more corrigenda – not important enough to bother either Pope or the copyist with them (most of them self-evident, & most of them in the piano part anyway).

Yours sincerely,

Hans

Curzon was also delighted with their collaboration: 'I shall await your score eagerly, and I shall probably plague you horribly nearer the time,' he told Keller. 'By the way, Schnabel once asked me whether I thought bar 102 of the 1st mov. was a premonition of bars 47/8 of the slow mov.'[73]

2 April 1959 – to Clifford Curzon

Dear Clifford,

Many thanks. Schnabel's question raises a problem about which I have thought a great deal – not only in the case of this c'to, but in many similar

---

70 Fiske to Keller, 20 March 1958, WAC Keller Contributor File 1.
71 Curzon to Keller, 12 December 1957, CULHK. Curzon evidently heard the second broadcast of FA No. 1 (on 11 December 1957).
72 The conductor Stanley Pope.
73 Curzon to Keller, 31 March 1959, CULHK.

instances. So far as functional analysis is concerned, I always ruthlessly exclude relations of this kind, even though they would be very effective – superficially so. But FA is concerned with background unity of contrasts, not with foreground resemblances whose structural significance is, to me, doubtful. I shd even go so far as to say that if one had drawn Beethoven's attention to the passages you mention, or Mozart's to the E flat 4tet's I/23 as compared with IV/21ff., they wdnt have been at all pleased. On the highest level, these things seem to me a step in the wrong direction – away from the greatest possible variety (on the basis of an all-embracing unity). I have never yet discussed this problem in public because I am bound to be misunderstood – to appear to "criticize" Beeth or Mozart. But I do sometimes mention it in teaching – when these "slips" happen to young composers on a lower level. (Cyclic structure is an altogether different proposition.) In my opinion, both Schnabel & you were right. But I shd say "recollection" instead of premonition and, anyway, it's psychological, not structural. As for your "idiom", I shd again agree, but narrow it down to the composer's, not just the time's. In all humility, and just because I can't think of a more sharply defining word, I shd call such resemblances mannerisms on the highest plane. I am talking abt the resemblances (which aren't expressive of anything), not of each relevant passage taken by itself (which is, of course).

Forgive my hasty ramblings; as Pascal said, I have no time at the moment for a short letter, so do accept a long one instead. Greatly looking forward to tonight (BBC tv); I'll write abt it too, since, believe it or not, I am tv critic for that rag 'Musical Opinion'.[74]

FA no.8: the suggestion that you cd, at any point in any respect "make a fool of yourself" is so profoundly ridiculous that, for once, words fail me (outside the artists' room). Meanwhile, you will have received the score & seen that it's all perfectly straightbackward.

Happier abt this collaboration than I can say.

Ever,

[Hans]

As Curzon was rehearsing the analysis, he found Keller's score beginning to merge with the Beethoven concerto in his memory and he disentangled them with difficulty. According to Alan Walker, 'Keller interpreted this episode as the best compliment that could possibly be offered to his scores'.[75]

---

74 Curzon gave a performance of Schumann's *Kinderszenen* in BBC television's 'Celebrity Recital' series that night. See *MO* 82/4 (May 1958): 539.
75 *HKSym*, 396.

Another person who had shown considerable interest in Functional Analysis from its beginning was William Glock. As well as publishing Keller's first score in his journal, he invited him to teach at Dartington in 1958, for which he commissioned a new analytical score. He also wanted Keller to teach 'a class in analysis (of classics) for our young Boulezerie',[76] but when they met to discuss it Keller had a better idea:

23 December 1957 – to Hansjörg Pauli [extract]

Dear Hansjörg,

By way of atonement for not yet having tackled your sketch for the FA of the Italian Serenade I have bought you the current issue of the Score – a very shabby Xmas present in any case! [. . .]

In August at Dartington, there will be 1 or 2 further FA's – played by whatever string quartet they are going to employ for concerts there, or by an ad hoc group of performers.

I shall be teaching at Dartington (Summer School) myself. I was invited to do a fortnight's tough analysis for our young dodecaphoney composers, but I thought (a) that a fortnight was not enough; (b) that it would be partly a fight and therefore not very fruitful; (c) that inasmuch as those people were really interested, they could get quite a lot out of my written analyses anyway; (c) that I had something far more important in mind in which (d) the purposes of this suggestion c'd at least partly be incorporated. . . . . . .

To cut a long story short, I shall be giving a practical 4 weeks' course in the interpretation of (virtually all) Haydn Quartets, linked up, of course, with analysis, and with a few quartets by other composers (at the students' choice) thrown in. The end of each week will be "public", i.e. open to other students (e.g. composers) who wish to listen. I'm very happy that altho' I was invited to do one thing, they agreed within 5 minutes to let me do another; in fact, I seem to have complete freedom (touch wood again).

Keller sent Glock a detailed list of suggested repertoire for the student quartets. Each was to choose one Haydn work ('any quartet from Op. 9 onwards except the 'Seven Words') and one by another composer. Keller gave the students free choice (asking only for a day's notice of the chosen works so he could bring the right scores), but nevertheless supplied detailed advice on what might be best for different levels of performer. He encouraged students to consider

76 Diary, 13 December 1957, BLWG MS Mus.978.

Mendelssohn in particular 'for reasons of both outstanding quality and general neglect' and also asked that 'any player who possesses both a violin and viola' should bring both instruments: 'as occasion arises, he will be asked to play both.' While acknowledging that many string teachers were now advising their pupils to specialise (on the grounds that swapping instruments was harmful to their intonation), Keller declared that view to be 'anti-musical, neurotic nonsense, typical of this obsessional "specialist" age.'[77]

Glock began to worry that the standard of string-playing at Dartington might not be sufficiently high for Keller's scheme and proposed a dilution:

> On thinking once more of the usual standard of string playing at the Summer School, I really think it might be better to devote three days a week to your course in Interpretation and then take two classes, for composers as well as others, in analysis. The chamber music situation will not be improved by the fact that I have been unable to arrange for this year a Master-class for cellists.[78]

Keller preferred to keep the focus on the string quartet, which he considered to be in a state of crisis. He set out the 'basic motive' for his course in the following draft for the Summer School's prospectus:

HAYDN'S STRING QUARTETS: A COURSE IN INTERPRETATION

The crisis of chamber music has become acute. True chamber music is written for the player; you cannot fully understand a string quartet without playing it, unless you are the composer. Yet chamber music has been pushed out of the chamber into concert hall, recording and radio studios, while in the chamber itself, wireless and gramophone occupy the places previously reserved for music stands. Composers, all but the greatest, have forgotten what the string quartet — once the highest form of instrumental music — really sounds like; and so have players, all but the most fortunately educated or stimulated.

Symptomatically enough, most of Haydn's many masterpieces for string quartet are virtually unknown nowadays, even though they tower above all his other great works and have never been surpassed as quartets. The present course is intended as a basic contribution towards the survival of chamber music. While the accent will be on spontaneity, it is hoped that the analysis of interpretation and that of composition will prove inseparable.

Hans Keller

---

77 For details see Keller's (undated) notes to Glock in CULHK, and his article 'The Interpretation of the Haydn Quartets,' *Score* XXIV (November 1958): 14–35.
78 Glock to Keller, 16 January 1958, CULHK.

A few months later, Glock asked, 'Cd you please include in your Haydn scheme a talk, which cd be given twice (to two different lots of students, in the theatre)? Please let me know what you think.'[79]

11 May 1958 – to William Glock

Dear Glock,

Thank you for your letter of May 2. Meanwhile, it appears that I shall be writing yet another article on Dartington – for that rag, MUSIC & MUSICIANS.

As for the note on the back of your envelope, I think I fully appreciate your reasons for asking me to include a talk in my Haydn scheme, but frankly, I do not wish to do so, because this would go right against my whole scheme, indeed my whole educational outlook and practice. I am most anxious to proceed strictly inductively, from concrete musical thought and experience towards the more general and conceptual conclusions. I am absolutely sick of the effect on my pupils of talks and the like, including good talks – and including my own talks or general verbal instruction. I cannot stress too strongly that there is something very basically wrong here with our whole musical culture, and that, if musical intelligence does not in the first place draw upon spontaneity – even wrong spontaneity, or rather spontaneity below right and wrong – the result tends to be sterile intellectualism which may look 'right', but which hasn't even enough blood to be wrong.

I hope I am not proving difficult. I can't go against that which makes me musical. Quite factually, I even hope that you are the first to understand.

Yours,

[Hans Keller]

P.S. I shall always be happy to answer particular questions – collectively or individually – arising out of our concrete studies. This kind of approach I have found genuinely fruitful.

Keller's first visit to Dartington turned out highly successful and – since he evidently enjoyed the experience as much as did his students – the Summer School became an annual feature of his calendar from then on. Students were enthralled by his passionate and provocative presence and many beat a path to his

79 Note on back of envelope, Glock to Keller, 2 May 1958, CULHK.

door seeking advice and personal tuition, or gathered round him on the lawn for hours of intense debate. One who remembered his arrival vividly was the twenty-six-year-old pianist Susan Bradshaw:

> I first met Hans at Dartington Summer School in 1958 and was, predict-ably, bowled over by the sheer exuberance of the man – by his bound-less enthusiasm for every one of his consuming passions, and his interest in anybody and everybody who shared them. People came alive in his presence; he took every encounter, every question, as if it were the most important issue of the moment, and would talk all day – even into the early hours of the next morning – in order to resolve it. He was the only person I ever met to whom everything (particularly, of course, musical things) really *mattered*.[80]

'With his seemingly unquenchable intellectual energy, he forced us to question everything,' said Bradshaw, who later told Glock that 'but for him, I for one should never have considered the possibility of writing or talking about music – and I'm sure there must be others who could say the same.'[81] Others did say the

Hans Keller surrounded by students at the Dartington Summer School in 1958. Lying in front of him is Susan Bradshaw. (Photo: Catherine Scudamore)

80 *HKSym*, 377–8.
81 Bradshaw to Glock, 17 March 1988, BLWG MS Mus.949.

same: 'he taught a whole generation of us,' according to the composer Hugh Wood (twenty-five when he met Keller at Dartington that year), 'only a lucky few of us formally, the rest by this process of friendly, undogmatic osmosis of a remarkable personality into one's own.'[82] As for Glock himself: 'After Hans's classes at Dartington in 1958 I rarely listened to the Haydn string quartets without being reminded of some of his golden sayings'.[83] He asked Keller to write an article on his Haydn coaching for *The Score*, the result being the marvellously broad-ranging 'The Interpretation of the Haydn Quartets'. Keller in turn admired Glock's piano-playing, and one of the highlights of his first visit to Dartington was Glock's performance with George Malcolm of Mozart's Sonata for two pianos: 'That Mozart interpretation was one of those rare occasions where, whatever happens, the performance thrills you literally throughout.'[84]

Both at the Summer School and over the next few months, Glock and Keller had long discussions on the future of the School and on music education in general. Keller felt strongly 'how wrong, how inflated teaching has become in our uncertain age,' and how anxious and dependent were the pupils it produced. In his view, 'the teacher's religious goal must be to make himself unnecessary, and if a grown musician calls himself an "XYZ pupil", we have conclusive evidence that somewhere both he and Mr. XYZ have failed in their common task.'[85] For Glock a major impetus was his dissatisfaction with the general run of music teaching in Britain. He had published in *The Score* some severe criticism of British conservatoires by younger musicians, most notably Anthony Milner on 'Teaching in the Musical Academies' (the experience of which Milner said left most students 'in an intellectual and aesthetic poverty of which few become aware') and Peter Maxwell Davies on 'The Young British Composer' (asserting that British musical diplomas were of such little value that 'one is always mildly surprised upon meeting a knowledgeable musician who has one').[86]

Milner and Davies both picked out British nationalism as a major source of the problem. Davies blamed some individuals for 'aspiring to carry on a nonexistent "national" tradition', while Milner questioned institutional staffing policies:

> It is remarkable that in the general exodus of eminent composers, players and teachers from Europe prior to 1939, none of them came to English academies. Were any invited? Did some offer their services and were refused? Such questions may be unnecessary, but they are continually asked and are not answered. If the academic authorities had been willing and swift in their offers we might yet have had a Bartók or a Schönberg teaching among us

82 *HKSym*, 398.
83 *Ibid.*, 379.
84 'Dartington Summer School,' *MO* 82/10 (October 1958): 15–16.
85 'The Interpretation of the Haydn Quartets' (see note 77).
86 Milner, 'Teaching in the Musical Academies', *Score* III (June 1950): 20–24. Davies, 'The Young British Composer', *Score* XV (March 1956): 84–5.

and giving us the benefit of a master's genius in contact with the main stream of musical culture.[87]

This would have accorded with the personal views of Glock, who was highly critical of what he called 'insular attitudes' – partly as a result of the discouragement he had received as a young man from Herbert Howells and Ralph Vaughan Williams when he wanted to study with Schnabel in Berlin – they were, he said, 'adamant that there was no need whatever to look abroad for a teacher'.[88] With the help of Edward Dent, he had managed to go nevertheless and all his life remained convinced of the crucial importance of that experience and the 'European outlook' it gave him. As a result, he was determined that his Summer School students should have the benefit of teaching by great musicians from other countries – despite the fact that 'this leavening from abroad aroused much wrath'. According to Peter Cox (Arts Administrator of the Dartington Hall Trust), the Summer School was known as 'Glock's Circus' by some senior members of the London conservatoires, and 'little was done to encourage their best students to attend'. Susan Bradshaw, who spent five years at the Royal Academy, agreed: 'I doubt if you could possibly imagine the self-satisfied isolation of the music colleges in the 1950s. . . . We were certainly never told about Dartington, and it was only as a result of a chance encounter with Priaulx [Rainier] that I found myself there.'[89]

In his mission to open students' eyes to the wider world, Glock was astonishingly successful. The roll-call of world-famous composers and performers he managed to persuade to come to a rather spartan boarding school in Dorset, and later a less spartan but still remote corner of Devon, is remarkable – especially when it is remembered that the Summer School ran on the very tightest of financial shoestrings. 'I suppose only Olivier Messiaen and Pierre Boulez were lacking, to make it an incomparable galaxy of teachers,' Glock reflected. Actually Boulez had agreed to teach in 1957 but pulled out under pressure to complete his Third Piano Sonata for its Darmstadt premiere. Still, 1957 was not short of stardust, that being the year that Stravinsky honoured Dartington with a fortnight's visit.

'It was a truly mind-blowing experience in every way,' recalled Bradshaw, who came to Dartington regularly from 1954. 'I still remember the heady excitement of trying to savour everything on offer in the action-packed days.' Not all the foreign stars quite lived up to expectations: 'Nono's classes were rescued by Max, who padded out his translations to

> Questions are never stupid;
> only answers are.

---

87 In this context it should be noted that Wellesz and Gal were employed by universities, not conservatoires.

88 Glock, *Notes in Advance* (Oxford: Oxford University Press, 1991), 19.

89 Cox, *The Arts at Dartington* (Dartington: Cox, 2005), 96. Bradshaw to Glock, 17 March 1988, BLWG MS Mus.949.

cover a noticeable lack of prepared substance,'[90] and Bradshaw was very disappointed by Aaron Copland, who gave the main composition class in 1958, the
year of Keller's first visit. Keller agreed, having sat in on one of Copland's classes
after hearing repeated complaints from students: 'I must admit that what I wit-
nessed was distinctly depressing.' One problem was that Copland had struggled
with the serial idiom in which many of the students were writing – watching this,
however, Keller did not conclude that the class had necessarily to be taken by a
serial composer: 'it is my considered submission that even an ultra-conservative
like William Alwyn would have done far better with the serialists than our distinguished American guest. (I once had a serial pupil who had studied with Alwyn:
my suggestion is strictly empirical.)'[91]

Keller took an intense interest in all aspects of the Summer School and immediately started planning what he would do there the following year. Since 1959
was the 150th anniversary of Mendelssohn's birth as well as Haydn's death, he
thought a course on the quartets of both composers would be ideal – 'a very
convenient coincidence from the string quartet's point of view, for the great
Mendelssohn quartets are perhaps the only absolutely natural and masterly works
of the *genre* in the entire romantic era.'[92] They had, however, sunk almost into
oblivion, and Keller had considerable difficulty getting hold of enough scores and
parts to run the course. He was also writing a new Functional Analysis, this time
of Mozart's A minor Piano Sonata, for the pianists Susan Bradshaw and Susan
McGaw. As he embarked on this, Keller had the idea of scoring it for different
forces from the original work. 'Upon reflection, I have decided to write the analysis for piano quintet', he wrote to the Dartington Quartet's cellist, asking if they
would play it: 'the single-timbre texture of the work thus gives me an opportunity
to differentiate and articulate by way of scoring as never before.'[93]

The Dartington Quartet had been formed specifically for Keller's first visit
in 1958: Glock persuaded the three string teachers at the Dartington Arts Centre
(later Dartington College) to 'get hold of a fourth' to perform Keller's 'Lark'
Quartet FA and broadcast it for the BBC.[94] Violinist Peter Carter therefore joined
Colin Sauer, Keith Lovell and Alexander Kok a couple of weeks before the scheduled performance. They had not heard any of Keller's previous analyses and, as
Carter remembers, were initially at a loss to understand what he was doing:

> On the first morning of the summer school we had arranged to meet to look
> at Hans' manuscript and had to work hard to dissuade him from coming
> to the beginning of the rehearsal – we had not yet played a note of music

---

90 Peter Maxwell Davies (who had studied in Rome with Petrassi) was acting as translator for Nono.
    Bradshaw to Glock, 17 March 1988, BLWG MS Mus.949.
91 *MO* 82/10 (October 1958): 15–16.
92 'The Interpretation of the Haydn Quartets', 34–5.
93 Keller to Alexander Kok, 28 May 1959. In the end, this version was abandoned because Keller
    feared overloading the Dartington Quartet (see draft letter to Kok, 3 June 1959, on reverse of letter
    to Glock of the same date, CULHK). The piano version is published in *EOM* as well as *HKFA*.
94 Glock to Keller, 30 March 1958, CULHK.

together and felt we needed at least to have spent a few minutes looking at his work before he should discover our frailties. What luck! We were help-less with laughter for most of the session. It would have been extremely embarrassing had he been there.[95]

Luckily this changed when Keller arrived – 'needless to say Hans soon convinced us of the value of his ideas and also of his incredible knowledge of the quartet repertoire.' Keller became a valued mentor and friend to the quartet, crucial to the process of their establishment as a permanent ensemble. They continued to go to him for coaching sessions for years – as Carter now says, 'Most of what I know about music came from him.'[96]

As well as the Haydn and Mendelssohn classes and functional analysis perfor-mances, Keller led a 'professional discussion group for composers' at the 1959 Summer School. This he also wrote up afterwards for *The Score* in an extended article that Glock published in two parts under the title 'Principles of Composition'. For the eight sessions at Dartington, Keller chose 'eight standpoints from which the burning central questions of musical creation in our time might be approached: *Pre-composition, Purity and Consistency of Style, Audibility, Rhythm, Form, Contemporaneity, Writing for, against and beyond the Instruments,* and *Teaching*

L to R: Paul Hamburger, Hans Keller, Susan McGaw, Hugh Wood and Helen Marshall at Dartington. (Photo: Catherine Scudamore)

95 Carter to authors, 5 January 2018, by email.
96 Carter, oral communication, 9 January 2018.

of Composition' – all questions which had emerged from his prior discussions with the composers who were to take part and with Luigi Nono, who was teaching the main composition class that year. Keller's *Score* article followed the same structure, giving his personal response to the issues raised in the (rather tense) public sessions. (Keller described the atmosphere in the group as 'one of chronic "complex-readiness"',[97] in which he needed 'constantly to interpret the different views to each other'.) Although Keller described his article as 'my personal views', he also wished it to be understood that 'without arrogance, I claim objective validity for them, which means that they are either right or wrong – never a matter of opinion. This is indeed part of the contemporary crisis – that fact has become "a matter of opinion".' Here is an extract from the section on 'Purity and Consistency of Style':

Principles of Composition [extract]
Score 26 (January 1960): 35–45 and 27 (July 1960): 9–21, reprinted in *EOM*, 212–32

The term 'style' here is used in the sense of 'method of composition'. Why, then, don't I say 'method of composition' instead? For two reasons. First, because we do not speak of the polyphonic method of composition and the homophonic method of composition. Secondly, because when our leading, 'advanced' composer-teachers speak of the necessity of 'purity of style', they always mean 'method' – for instance when they object to tonal procedures within serial technique. In short, I am using the word 'style' technically, not aesthetically. For the aesthetic meaning of the term, for that which makes a 'personal style', I am simply using the word *character*.

The concept of 'purity of style', a very modern one, has a disastrous effect on growing talents, on pregnant minds groping for expression. It is, of course, again an obsessional symptom, another effect of the fear-inspiring break-up of tonality. The music of the greatest composers has always evinced the greatest stylistic impurities; in fact, in our musical culture, there seems to be only one composer of genius who has a pure style – Gluck; and the purity of his style seems to be the only thing that is wrong with his music. Nevertheless, there is a grain of truth in the demand for purity – which again makes the compulsive illusion around it all the more dangerous. It is obviously easier to work with one method than with two; it is extremely difficult to work with two methods which have little in common. But if you succeed, you can express all the more. We all know those fugal expositions in homophonic movements whose

---

97 Keller's translation of Jung's term *Komplexbereitschaft*, which he explained to *Score* readers as 'the psychological situation which arises when a complex is being touched by an external stimulus'.

sole *raison d'être* is an inability to start or go on. But we also know the last movements of Mozart's G major String Quartet K.387 and of the *Jupiter* Symphony. We all know those twelve-tonal works where tonal passages are thrown in whose sole *raison d'être* is to give the listener, if not the composer, a break. But we also know Schoenberg's *Ode to Napoleon* and his String Trio – or do we? Not a word has yet been said about the Trio's recapitulated A major passage, a tonal eruption which is all the more decisive for Schoenberg's use of a note (D♯) that isn't tonal to the key. He would not be Schoenberg if he did not imply extensive functional harmony within this compressed space (see Ex. I). The D♯ assumes the significance of a leading-note to the dominant and thus confirms the tonic *qua* tonic, placing the passage (as Tovey would have said) not merely 'on' the key, but 'in' it. Why, then, don't the *avant-couriers* who praise the piece as one of Schoenberg's greatest (rightly so, but for the wrong, i.e. stylistic reasons) take note of this outbreak of tonality, though they are the first to object to such crass stylistic impurity when it occurs elsewhere? Is it possible that they don't hear the key, just because it is not driven home by way of a cadence *à la Ode to Napoleon*? Or are they vicariously ashamed of it? Or is it simply that they feel how profoundly the tonal passage fits into the atonal context, but cannot see why?

I can't either, but do let us be honest. Let us stand by our artistic experience and wait for analytic enlightenment. [. . .]

The crux of the matter is character. It is the character of invention that unifies styles; and the greater the composer, the more characteristic his invention. Even though we cannot yet show how Ex. I fits, we are able to say, not merely that the phrase could only be Schoenberg, but also – at the risk of seeming to beg the question – that it is characteristic of this particular work. Further we cannot go for the

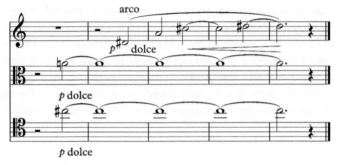

Ex. 1 Schoenberg String Trio, bars 52-56

time being; for the serial 'sense' of the passage is a symptom of its
fitness, not a cause.

Until this point neither Keller nor Glock had held any full-time post in any institution, though Glock was now fifty and Keller approaching forty. It was suggested
to Glock that it was time to move into the mainstream in March 1958 when the
directorship of the Guildhall School of Music fell vacant. 'The whole thing seems
v. fantastic,' was his initial reaction to the idea that he should be a candidate, 'but
if it came off there would be the most wonderful opportunities.'[98] The following month an even more 'fantastic' suggestion was made to him by the BBC's
Controller of Music, Richard Howgill:

> Howgill says I ought to think of taking over his job, in a year's time. ?? It wd
> be far more influential than the GSM, but less 'musical'.[99]

This threw Glock into 'a state of some turmoil, suddenly confronted with the possible choice between two major tasks and two very different futures, neither of
which I would have dreamed of a few weeks earlier.'[100] It was made all the more
difficult by the extremely slow speed at which both institutions moved, so that
discussions continued sporadically with both throughout the rest of 1958. Another
difficulty was Glock's attachment to the Dartington Summer School, which he
was very loath to give up. He realised that major institutions like the BBC and
the Guildhall were unlikely to want his divided attention, but the thought of relin-
quishing Dartington brought a 'bitter aspect' to the decision had to make.

The possibility that Glock might leave Dartington therefore formed the background to the conversations he and Keller were having about future plans for the
Summer School. Keller's first visit had made him keenly aware of the importance
of what was happening there, and he was full of ideas for its development. When
Glock consulted him on what to do should he have to leave, Keller was not slow to
offer his own services. Glock had, however, already been considering the conductor and pianist Peter Gellhorn (then Chorus Master at Glyndebourne and running
the conducting class at Dartington) as a possible successor, which made things
a little awkward for Keller – Gellhorn was a friend whose musicianship he held
in high esteem. They had met while interned together on the Isle of Man, where
Keller had been immediately impressed, describing Gellhorn in a letter home as a
'consummate musician' and 'profound human being'.[101]

98 Diary, 11 March 1958, BLWG, MS Mus.979.
99 *Ibid.*, 11 April 1958.
100 *Notes in Advance*, 98.
101 Keller to Grete Keller, 8 January 1941, CULHK.

It was all hypothetical until Glock knew whether he would be offered one of the proposed posts, and on what terms. As autumn drew on towards winter, interest from the BBC seemed to dry up, while the Guildhall held its first round of interviews on 23 December. Glock's spirits sank when he walked in and saw Frank Howes on the panel – only days beforehand he had dismissed in print as 'nonsense' Howes's review of Stravinsky's *Agon*. During the interview Howes apparently said not a word about this, or anything else, 'but I heard afterwards that he (naturally) did his best to make sure that I shouldn't be chosen.'[102]

Keller – a veteran of many battles with Howes – wrote to wish him luck, and to carry on their discussions about the 1959 Summer School, to which Glock had just invited Karlheinz Stockhausen:[103]

21 December 1958 – to William Glock
BLWG MS Mus.954.

Dear William,

Good luck, all my best wishes for Tues; shall be praying to whoever is the saint of musical education. A pupil of mine (form & FA) who teaches at the Guildhall[104] tells me that in effect, there is no musical directorate at present.

Dartington 4tet, new dvpt.: the cellist rang me. C'd I teach them. C'd I come to Dartgtn occasionally, "on a strictly professional basis", to coach them. C'd they do more FA's at the next Summer School. C'd I quickly coach them in a Casella trio (this was the only question to which I said 'no'), etc., etc.; very keen indeed. I suggested, as vaguely as possible, that plans for the SS were in fact in the making; that I would no doubt be able to use the 4tet; and that he might ring you. However, he is positively frightened of you & wants to wait until the official negotiations in Jan. Meanwhile, I am having lunch with him on Tues and shall try my best to de-frighten him. As you know, he is a problem child (psychologically speaking), possibly far more talented than he has so far been able to appear.

At our last meeting, I suppressed two criticisms. Upon reflection, it was less than realistic of me to do so.

(1) Re Gellhorn taking charge of the SS. Since I mentioned myself, I did not feel like criticizing anybody else. It does seem to me, however, that he is not sufficiently in touch with new music.

---

102   Diary, 23 December 1958, BLWG MS Mus.979. See 'Mr. Stravinsky's 50 years: Retrospect', *The Times*, 11 December 1958, 3, and 'Stravinsky Conducts', *NS* LVI/1449 (20 December 1958): 881.

103   Stockhausen declined, pleading pressure of work in Cologne. Stockhausen to Glock, 29 December 1958, BLWG MS Mus.956.

104   Probably Alan Walker.

(2) Stockhausen. Since you probably know my views, I did not feel like recapitulating. I am aware of Strawinsky's current switch from Boulez to Stockhausen. I think it will be just as temporary as the "Boulez period" (I predicted the end of the latter). The fact is, in my respectful submission, that Str is trying his admirable best to go with the youngsters & not to make the GOM's usual mistakes. In the circumstances, however, it is impossible for his motives to be strictly and purely musical. If what he told me abt my writings is true, it wd follow that he completely agrees with me abt what music is (sound alone).[105] All this, however, is slightly beside the point; I am merely cross-examining the leading witness for Stockhausen's defence, as it were. My immediate point is that what Susan suggests* would amount to analysis of something which isn't (yet?) part of the recipient's musical experience: analysis before, rather than after the event. This is phoney, and all my analytic endeavours are directed against it. I am not asking you to change your mind, and I personally shall certainly find Stockhausen's presence very interesting indeed. But it might be as well to be clearly conscious of its possible dangers (which do not, at any rate theoretically, exclude hopes). For the rest, some time I'd like to show you a few things in 'Counterpoints' which cannot possibly have anything to do with aural experience – quite a few things, in fact. I have not yet found any (potential) apologist for Stockhausen who has contested my demonstration.[106]

I shall write the prospectus par as soon as I have yr reply to my last letter.

Do you happen to know a man called Page (Prof. of Music at Victoria, New Zealand)? He's here for a year & wants to study with me (form & FA). Additional pupils are becoming a problem, & I like to know something abt them before I take them on. Phps you've come across this man. He sounds interesting: he says he's got a bad conscience about his teaching.

---

105 Keller had met Stravinsky a couple of weeks earlier, at a party given by Faber & Faber in the composer's honour. According to Keller's account (twenty-four years later), Stravinsky had flattered him with 'hypocritical enthusiasm'. According to Donald Mitchell's (even later) account, Keller had been no less flattering to Stravinsky, whispering into 'the astonished composer's ear "I think you're a very great genius".' (Keller, 'Words About Music', *LRB* IV/24 (30 December 1982): 15–16; 'Donald Mitchell Remembers Hans Keller', *LRB* IX/15 (3 September 1987): 8–11.)

106 Keller first heard Stockhausen's *Kontrapunkte* (under the composer's direction) at the 1956 ISCM Festival in Stockholm, where he listened to it four times and examined the score – finding 'more and more details which, as Stockhausen's own performance showed, cannot be realized in sound. How, then, can one avoid the suspicion that this music has not been aurally conceived, that it is not music in the physically accepted sense?' ('The Thirtieth Festival of the ISCM', BBC Third Programme, 19 July 1956, script in CULHK.)

In the usual haste,

Yours ever,

Hans

Do let me know abt Tues, if you have a second to spare!

* re Stockhausen

Somewhat to his surprise, Glock got through the first round of Guildhall interviews. As the selection process went on he gradually realised he was considered a significant contender and that interest in him was mounting. Meanwhile the opposite seemed to be happening at the BBC and by January 1959 Glock was assuming they had dropped him – 'a grandiose idea that had alas come to nothing' – so he concentrated his efforts on the Guildhall, where he was down to the last three candidates. Then, unexpectedly, the BBC was back in touch and on the very morning of Glock's final Guildhall interview he received a call to say the Governors would be making their decision at three o'clock the following Thursday – and that Glock would have the recommendation of the Director-General. 'Nothing is definite yet,' he told Keller. 'It will be settled on Thursday, so please cross your fingers at about 3 p.m. that afternoon.'[107] When the day came Keller decided not to wait for 3 pm: instead he went out earlier and sent a telegram.

5 February 1959 – telegram to William Glock
BL MS Mus.954

PROPHETIC CONGRATULATIONS = HANS +

He was right. A new era had begun.

---

107   Glock to Keller, 2 February 1959, CULHK.

The BBC

The appointment of William Glock as Controller of Music at the BBC was a stunning surprise – at the time, the record producer and impresario Walter Legge likened it to the thought of Luther becoming Pope. The subsequent appointment of Hans Keller to join the staff of Music Division was also highly controversial: 'Over my dead body!' the BBC's Head of Music Programmes is said to have declared. Over the following decades, the two appointments became no less contentious as they receded into history, and 'the Glock–Keller regime' (or 'the Glock/Keller dodecaphonic nuclear winter' as Fritz Spiegl once colourfully dubbed it) was soon the stuff of myth.[1]

The reasons why the BBC should have made such a major change in its music policy at this point were complex and by no means entirely musical. Although its role in the war had left it in a powerful position after 1945, the BBC's confident postwar expansion received a horrible shock only a decade later with the loss of its broadcasting monopoly in television. By then it was clear that television was going to become the dominant medium and radio entered something of an existential crisis – symbolised institutionally by the BBC's 1956–57 Working Party on the Future of Sound Broadcasting and the resulting cuts to the airtime of the Third Programme. Music, being one thing that radio indubitably did better than television, was now vital to the survival of radio as a medium – and thus to the future interests of the BBC, to justify its remaining monopoly and prevent further incursions by the commercial sector into broadcasting.

There was therefore strong support within the BBC's management for a Controller of Music who would seize the initiative and do something radical – and Glock soon realised he had powerful support. Even before his arrival, when he met Director-General Sir Ian Jacob and senior colleagues over lunch at Broadcasting House just after his appointment was announced, he could detect the appetite for change. At the lunch Glock was seated between Director of Sound Broadcasting Lindsay Wellington and his deputy Richard Marriott, who had chaired the recent Working Party. Marriott was an independent-minded

---

1 See Glock, *Notes in Advance* (Oxford: Oxford University Press, 1991), 99; *Music Survey*, preface to collected edition (London: Faber:1981); *Independent*, 19 September 1995, 10.

man, unafraid to think radically, and in talking to him, Glock was pleased to discover that 'he seemed all too willing to wake things up, I thought; and it may be that "they" are actually pleased to have an outsider who will want to stir a little.' This impression was confirmed when Glock took up his post in May and started to work with Marriott: 'He seems full of energetic intentions, and will welcome changes in the music policy. i.e., there's a v. strong set of allies over at Broadcasting House, and the thing is to MOVE.'[2]

In the circumstances, it might seem surprising that Glock was originally identified for the job by his predecessor, but it was without doubt Richard Howgill who made the choice. Howgill had been looking for the right man to follow him for a long time – ever since 1952, when he himself had been appointed Controller of Music with a clear brief to find his successor.[3] As can be inferred from the time it took, his task was not an easy one. Indeed it can be said that the BBC had been in search of musical leadership for even longer than that, having never completely recovered from the disruption of the war (which put an end to the BBC Symphony Orchestra's initial golden age) and the loss of Edward Clark and Adrian Boult on either side of that great cataclysm.[4] During the 1930s Boult (in the dual role of Director of the Music Department and Chief Conductor of the newly-formed Symphony Orchestra), together with Clark (an imaginative programme builder with a rare understanding of modern music and the continental scene), had pursued a remarkably progressive and cosmopolitan music policy, enabling the fledgling Corporation to establish itself astonishingly rapidly as the most important musical force in the country. Decades later, Glock was still lost in admiration of what they had achieved: 'Many times I sat in my office in Yalding House looking through the *Radio Times* of the 1930s and saying to myself, I'll never reach that.'[5]

Before Howgill, the post-war recovery of BBC music had been much hampered by disrupted leadership. Boult's successors in the Director of Music post had come and gone with unsettling rapidity (including two deaths in office), while his successor as Chief Conductor, Malcolm Sargent, had neither Boult's catholic repertoire nor his commitment to broadcasting. Meanwhile, the expansion of radio after the war meant the pressures on the department were mounting – particularly from the high-quality demands of the Third Programme. In 1952 the decision was made to upgrade the Music Department to a Division with its own Controller and to appoint to run it an experienced senior administrator who had been on the Corporation's staff since its foundation (Howgill), who could be relied on to get things onto an even footing.

2 Diary entries 25 February and 21 May 1959, BLWG MS Mus.980. 'Broadcasting House' in this context means 'senior management' (Music Division was in Yalding House).
3 See minutes of the Board of Governors, 13 November 1952, WAC R1/20/1.
4 Clark left in 1936 and Boult in 1950 (having already given up the Director of Music post during the war) – in neither case entirely willingly.
5 Glock, interviewed by Frank Gillard in 1983, WAC R143/51/1.

As soon as he took up the post, Howgill had combed the musical world for a deputy he could train to succeed him. At first he worked on the assumption that 'a considerable knowledge of the BBC and its workings is a necessary concomitant,' so his initial plan was to offer the preferred candidate the post of Head of Music Programmes with a view to succeeding Howgill as Controller after a year or so of working under him. Unfortunately, it proved impossible to persuade anyone of the calibre required to relinquish their current role for the lesser post, and Howgill was forced to find someone from the BBC's existing staff for the Head of Music Programmes role. There was a need to act quickly, to avoid imperilling some major projects, so Howgill brought down from Manchester Maurice Johnstone, Director of Music for the BBC's North Region. He knew Johnstone would not be the man to succeed him, but he had been successful in Manchester and had the skills and experience needed in the short term. 'He has only some of the qualities ideal for the job,' Howgill told Wellington, 'but amongst them is very wide programme experience both in the BBC and outside and the drive to carry through important projects quickly.'[6]

One quality that was lacking was an understanding of contemporary music – but that did not seem so much of a problem at the beginning of the 1950s as it did by the end of the decade. When considering the reputation for conservatism of the 1950s BBC, it is important to remember that Howgill's tenure as Controller (1952–59) was a period of rapid change in contemporary composition and its reception in Britain. It is instructive to compare, for example, the twentieth-century music performed at Glock's 1952 Summer School with his programmes at Dartington in 1959. The 1952 School offered only one post-war work, Alan Rawsthorne's *A Canticle of Man* (written for the occasion), whereas the 1959 School featured several very recent works including premieres. If one takes the Summer School as one possible marker of modernism in Britain, it seems that contemporary music in 1952 was still Bartók, Hindemith and Stravinsky (not a note from the Second Viennese School), whereas 1959 heard works by Milton Babbitt, Pierre Boulez, Alexander Goehr, Hans Werner Henze, Elisabeth Lutyens, Luigi Nono and Stefan Wolpe – with Schoenberg and Berg now part of the programme.

What is perhaps most surprising in Howgill's choice of Glock as his successor is that he should have picked someone with so little institutional experience. After thirty years with the BBC, during which he had seen it grow from a tiny enterprise into a huge national bureaucracy, no one knew better than Howgill how complex the job of running Music Division now was. Part of the answer to this conundrum may lie in Howgill's observation of Glock's involvement with the music committee of the Institute of Contemporary Arts (the British section of the ISCM), which Glock joined in 1953, taking over as chairman the following year. When he arrived, it was – and had been for some time – crippled by the most appalling strife, which in 1953 was going from bad to worse, culminating in embarrassing scenes at that year's ISCM Festival in Oslo and an acrimonious court case in

---

6 Howgill to Wellington, 2 February 1953, BBC WAC L1/1509/1.

1955 between Edward Clark and Benjamin Frankel that split musical London. Glock's handling of this situation, and the speed at which he got the committee functioning again, brought in new members (including Keller),[7] repaired relations with the ISCM and the BBC, and transformed the ICA into a real force in London concert life, was superb. Quite apart from musical considerations, Howgill must have thought that this was someone who could get things done. Howgill's respect for Glock's musical judgement is also shown by his decision to hand over control of the programming of their joint ICA/BBC concerts – something the ICA had been seeking in vain for years (the BBC having insisted hitherto that every work should go through its own score-reading panel, as well as the ICA's). The most radical product of that decision was the visit of Pierre Boulez and players from the Domaine Musical to give a live broadcast on 6 May 1957 of works by Nono, Stockhausen, Webern and Boulez himself. Although there had been a couple of works by these composers broadcast before, this was the first time that the BBC had devoted a whole concert to the continental avant garde, not featuring any British composers, performed by a foreign ensemble and broadcast at peak time. Howgill had to force it through Music Division in the teeth of determined opposition from all but one of his colleagues.[8]

As this shows, Maurice Johnstone was by no means the only conservative in the Music Division of the 1950s. He was, however, the leader of the *derrière garde*, with whom, Glock realised very quickly after he took up his post in May 1959, 'a battle royal seemed inevitable'. When Keller arrived, he too identified Johnstone as the biggest obstacle to a progressive musical policy, telling Glock 'the only strong personality on the other side is Maurice.'[9] Swords were finally unsheathed in the autumn of that year over the planning of the 1960 Proms. To Johnstone's dismay, Glock announced that he would take personal charge of Proms planning – a major change from the procedure established after the death of Henry Wood in 1944, when the Proms had been deliberately 'depersonalised' and the planning entrusted to a committee. Although a new personality for the Proms had arrived in 1947 in the person of Malcolm Sargent, he did not control the planning and repertoire as Wood had done for so long. None of the postwar Directors of Music took charge either – indeed for a dozen years the bulk of Proms planning was not done by anyone in Music Division, but contracted out annually to a former member of staff, Julian Herbage. Glock was astounded that such a prominent part of the BBC's output had been left so long in this semi-detached state, but when he sought to make the concerts a central part of his new strategy, 'I was denounced to the Director of Sound Broadcasting as a Hitler intent on destroying the very foundation of BBC music policy.'

7 'I'm in the ICA executive & programme committee now & having rows with Glock,' Keller to Sharp, 21 November 1957, CULHK.
8 See Glock, *Notes in Advance*, 100, and diary entry 17 April 1959, BLGA MS Mus.980. Harry Croft-Jackson was the only one to support Howgill.
9 Glock, *Notes in Advance*, 101; Keller to Glock, 24 October 1959, CULHK.

Arguments broke out on several fronts as it became clear Glock was deter-mined to take a much more active role in the details of musical planning than the self-effacing Howgill had done. He was also bent on a wholesale reorganisation of Music Division that would naturally ruffle feathers. But it was perhaps his cos-mopolitanism that provoked the strongest objections, from musicians outside as well as inside the BBC. The Composers' Guild noted with alarm the rise in broad-casts of foreign contemporary music during Glock's first year – in the Proms particularly 'the proportion of foreign works had gone up considerably.'[10] As for performers, one telling early battle Glock lost was over his attempt to include the Italian conductor Nino Sanzogno in the 1960 Proms. This row made waves well beyond Music Division, and Lindsay Wellington received complaints from Sir Thomas Armstrong, Director of the Royal Academy of Music, and Lady Jessie Wood (who kept a keen eye on what the BBC was doing with her beloved Sir Henry's legacy). The reason for their outrage was not strictly musical: it was that Sanzogno was not British.[11]

It is tempting to dismiss all the flags and patriotic singing of the Last Night of the Proms as having nothing to do with music, but – as successive BBC plan-ners have discovered to their cost – this tradition became an indelible part of the Proms's post-war identity. The increasingly patriotic tone that developed after 1945 is another indication of the strength of the 'English musical renaissance' narrative at that time. Although Wood's *Sea Songs* had long been a regular fix-ture, it was not until the 1950s that Sargent cemented the Last Night ritual as a celebration of all things British – and television broadcasting from 1953 set it in stone. As David Cannadine has remarked, it seems odd that this patriotic ceremony should have become established during the 1950s ('in many people's minds, the leitmotif of those years was not so much "hope and glory" but rather "decline and fall"') – but that was precisely the point: music was one place where, it was strongly felt, a period of national glory was just beginning.[12]

In 1959 Sargent was still Chief Conductor of the Proms, but had recently been replaced at the helm of the BBC Symphony Orchestra by the Viennese-born Rudolf Schwarz – an appointment that roused the same sort of criticism that had greeted Karl Rankl at Covent Garden ten years before.[13] Concerns were even raised in Parliament during Schwarz's first season about 'the continued employ-ment of foreign conductors in the very few official posts in this country'.[14] The fact that both Rankl and Schwarz were now British citizens was ignored by the protestors, but taken up by Keller, who sent a letter to the *News Chronicle* objecting to 'the tendentious prominence' given to the claim that only 'British born' musicians should be appointed to conduct British orchestras. 'I felt for a moment I was back under Hitler rule,' he wrote, quoting the legal entitlement

---

10 Guild Executive Committee minutes, 18 July 1960, WAC R27/760/1.

11 See WAC R30/2345/10.

12 Cannadine, 'Last Night Fever,' *LRB* 29/17 (6 September 2007): 21–4.

13 See *The Times*, 6 January 1949, 2.

14 26 February 1958, Hansard, vol. 583 c.351.

of a naturalised citizen to the same status as one born in the country. 'So far as I am aware, the provisions of the British Nationality and Status of Aliens Act, 1914 . . . make no reservations about conductors.'[15]

~

It was unlikely to have gone unnoticed that the first new member of staff to join Music Division after Glock's arrival was of foreign birth. But this may actually have been the least of the reasons why the appointment of Hans Keller was, as Glock put it, 'the most controversial decision'. Keller was still a contentious figure and, since he was now very well known, his appointment could not fail to make waves. He had also on many occasions published trenchant criticism of the BBC which, in an institution that valued – and contractually enforced – public loyalty, was a serious matter. 'After what *Music Survey* has done to us?' was apparently the reason for Maurice Johnstone's cry of 'over my dead body!' to the Appointments Board after Keller's interview – though Keller's fervent advocacy of Schoenberg would also have been a factor, if Glock's description of Johnstone's musical tastes is accurate: 'in 1959 [he] still dismissed the works of the Second Viennese School in a spirit of almost moral indignation.'[16]

Unlike the wave of new staff who arrived in Music Division after Glock's 1960 reorganisation (who came in on new short-term contracts), Keller applied for a pre-existing permanent post – that of Roger Fiske, Music Talks Producer (who had produced all the Functional Analysis programmes). Keller's application is dated 15 April 1959 – before Glock had taken up his own post – and it is not clear whether the initiative was his or Glock's. Three weeks earlier, Glock had noted Fiske's resignation in his diary ('it will be v. important to find someone better in his place') and since the diary also records a visit from 'Hans and Milein' four days later, it is possible that they discussed Keller's applying for the post. However Glock recorded only that 'Hans and I worked most of the evening at the Henze article,' after which they seem not to have met again until the actual Appointment Board in June.[17] Keller told Nicholas Kenyon years later that he and Glock had been having one of their periodic tiffs over Schoenberg at the time of his application and were briefly 'not on speaking terms' – possibly confirmed by a letter surviving from June 1959 in which Keller told Bobby Kok that he couldn't finalise their Dartington plans because 'I haven't seen William for months.' Nevertheless once

15 'Too many foreigners conducting?', *News Chronicle*, 18 September 1956, 4; Keller to editor, 18 September 1956, CULHK.
16 Glock, *Notes in Advance*, 101–2.
17 Diary entries 26 and 30 March 1959, BLWG MS Mus.980. The 'Henze article' was Hansjörg Pauli, 'Hans Werner Henze's Italian Music', *Score* 25 (June 1959): 26–37.

Glock had taken up his post in May he did recommend Keller to Third Programme Controller Howard Newby, arranging for them to meet over lunch. This evidently went well: Keller's impression of Newby was 'very favourable' and although Newby's thoughts on that occasion are not recorded, his later opinion was unequivocal: 'If I had to answer the question, "Have you ever met anyone whom you think was a genius," I would say "Yes", and it would be Hans Keller.'[18]

Joining the BBC marked a major turning-point in Keller's life – and although he never said so, it was a moment of considerable emotional significance, which may explain his reluctance to contemplate leaving the Corporation in later years when the atmosphere changed. For Keller, who had felt like an embattled outsider all his working life, the BBC represented a measure of acceptance by the British musical establishment that he had not enjoyed before. 'I am now . . . a genuine civil servant, in fact, however improbable,' he told Benjamin Frankel, adding, 'I find my job eminently satisfying; the BBC isn't changing me; I'm changing the BBC.' Frankel expressed himself 'happy and gratified to read on all sides (at long last) the evidence not only of your influence but your (relative) acceptance. Very soon Howes and Shawe-Taylor will write something approving and then you will be in trouble.'[19] Joining the BBC also represented, for the first time in Keller's life, financial independence and security. For much of their life together so far, Milein Cosman had been earning as much if not more than he was, and they were also helped financially by Keller's mother and sister.

But there was a much deeper emotional aspect to this turning point in Keller's life, springing from the double bereavement that hit him and his sister in May and June 1959. Their mother, to whom Keller had been extremely close, fell seriously ill and died on 19 May. Only a few weeks later (in the same week as Keller's BBC interview) his sister's husband, Roy Franey – who had saved Keller's life by securing the British visa that freed him from detention in Austria – also died. There are very few hints of any of this in Keller's correspondence of the time: a brief comment in a letter of 7 July to Susan Bradshaw and Susan McGaw that 'life has been rather trying' seems to have been as much as he could bear to put in writing.

Keller kept himself frantically busy that summer, no doubt partly a result of all this – and it was probably a help. He received the BBC's job offer the day before he went to Dartington for four weeks' teaching and, despite being told he could name his own date for starting the job, elected to do so the minute he was back in London. He also took on a significant extra task at this time – a new departure for him: his first step into original composition. This was incidental music for a radio play by the poet and fellow Viennese émigré Erich Fried. Like Keller, Fried had left Vienna in 1938 in his late teens and settled in London, but unlike Keller he remained writing exclusively in German for the rest of his life, despite a mastery of English that

18 Keller to Kenyon, [December 1981]; Keller to Kok, 18 June 1959; Glock to Keller, 27 May 1959; Keller to Glock, 30 May 1959; Newby, interviewed by Humphrey Carpenter, quoted in *The Envy of the World* (London: Weidenfeld & Nicolson, 1996), 204.
19 Keller to Frankel, 28 February 1960; Frankel to Keller, 19 January 1960, CULHK.

led to his becoming a major translator of English literature into German. The play for which Keller wrote the music was *Izanagi und Izanami*, based on the ancient Japanese myth of the sibling creator gods, and Fried's text focused on the episode of the grief-stricken Izanagi's journey to the underworld after Izanami's death (parallels with Orpheus) to tell its story of love and loss. Keller's delicate score was written for a chamber ensemble of string quartet and piano (mostly playing a single line), with a *Sprechstimme* chorus and tenor and bass soloists.

Keller's manuscript records that he composed the music in 'Autumn 1959' – a little later than Fried would have liked, judging from the letter Keller sent him from Dartington that summer:

23 August 1959 – to Erich Fried

Lieber Erich!

Willst Du mich denn mit Deinem Dichten

noch vor der Tat zugrunde richten?

Die Seele schweigt es red't der Mund,

und tut den Bochern Weisheit kund.

Muss Tag und Nacht hier unterrichten,

da soll ich noch in Toenen dichten?

Im Anfang ist das Wort, am End' der Ton,

der wird noch fertig vor der Produktion;

er schwingt sich auf das Tonband gar,

ganz ohne vorbezahltes Honorar.

Sei ruhig, bleib' ruhig, mein Fried,

ich kraechz' Dir noch einen mieses Lied.

Inzwischen viele, viele Gruesse.

P.S. Mit weichem "S" schreibt man die Schmuese.[20]

H

20 'Do you wish then to destroy me with your poetry / even before the deed? / The soul is silent, it is the mouth that speaks, / and provides wisdom to the young. / If I must teach here day and night, / should I still make poetry in sound? / In the beginning is the word, in the end the sound, / which is ready even before it is produced; / Indeed it leaps onto the tape / without any prior payment. / Be calm, stay calm, my Fried, / I'll still croak you out a lousy song. / In the meantime many, many greetings. / P.S. One writes the shmoozing with a soft "S".'

Fried was then working for the BBC's German service, but this play was commissioned by the Hamburg-based Norddeutscher Rundfunk for broadcast in March 1960. After the recording, Fried told Keller that NDR considered the music 'excellent and far above anything they normally got in this sphere' and Keller was particularly pleased to hear that the players had described the music as 'written by a colleague' (i.e. a chamber musician).[21] He was encouraged by this success – 'which is not to say that I now think of myself as an immortal composer,' he wrote to Benjamin Frankel. 'But I do feel I have some little bit to say – perhaps even to teach thru composing: chiefly honesty in all dimensions.'[22] Shortly afterwards, NDR commissioned another score from him, for a radio production of Nelly Sachs's mystical Holocaust play *Eli*. This had its first broadcast in 1961 and was repeated on the Sudwest Rundfunk in 1962, before being translated and adapted for the BBC, where it went out twice on the Third Programme in 1963. It was to become the best-known play by Sachs, who won the Nobel prize for Literature in 1966.[23]

~

Keller took up his BBC post on 1 September 1959. Glock was then in Manchester, but there was a note from him asking Keller to bring what he could remember about the organisation of NDR to their meeting the following day. Meanwhile Keller spent his first day sorting out practicalities with the BBC's Establishment Office. In both his and Glock's case, their extensive outside interests were an issue. Keller had to accept some curbs on his writing – his 'Television Music' column for *Musical Opinion* had to go, for example, since his BBC contract forbad him to write or speak in public about broadcasting. But Functional Analysis was another matter: 'I said at the interview that I shouldn't step down from FA in any way.' He was, however, alive to the possible conflict of interest and urged Roger Fiske to record the long-delayed 'Lark' analysis before Fiske's retirement, so as not to have to do it himself. 'Just imagine I got your job and the first thing I did was to record FA No. 4 for 17 hours on end,' he wrote. 'The BBC wouldn't remember that this score was commissioned 1½ years ago and that the transmission was more than a year late. I'd be out by the back door in no time, and there is no espresso bar in Great Portland Street either.'[24]

Glock eventually had to give up *The Score* (Keller tried in vain to persuade Donald Mitchell to take over the editorship), but he fought hard to keep running

---

21 Reported by Keller to Glock, 6 February 1960, CULHK.

22 Keller to Frankel, 28 February 1960, CULHK.

23 Extracts from the manuscript of Keller's music for *Eli* are published in *HKSym*, 402–5.

24 Keller to Fiske, 9 July 1959, WAC Dartington String Quartet file 1.

William Glock and Hans Keller in conversation at Dartington.
(Photo: Catherine Scudamore)

the Dartington Summer School, arguing successfully to Lindsay Wellington that it was vital to his BBC work:

> I know from long experience of the Summer School how much stimulation one derives from practical music-making and from having the opportunity to meet leading composers and executants and confront oneself with their ideas more thoroughly than can be done over the luncheon table in London. So long as you wish to have me as C. Mus, I shall insist on not going to sleep; and the Summer School would be an effective insurance against that ever happening.[25]

At the end of Keller's first day at the BBC he wrote a long letter to Glock – evidently Dartington, rather than broadcasting, was still at the forefront of his mind:

1 September 1959 – to William Glock

Dear William,

I remember everything I ever knew abt the organization of the NDR, but, of course, I don't know everything; in fact, I only got a little glimpse here and there. Report tomorrow.

The rest of my letter is in bad ternary form: sections I and III are on the same subject, but have nothing to do with each other, and section II is a contrast which, if subjected to FA, would not evince any unity with the principal section.

I. FA No. 9a. I shd have loved to react to your reactions, but I did not understand them. Don't take this as a glib phrase: I really didn't, which circumstance worried me quite a lot. (1) "Shift to the things that aren't Mozart." I asked the others present what you might have meant by that. Everything is Mozart tho' there are compressions, reductions, isolations, repetitions. Did you mean those? [John] Carewe thought you simply meant the transitions from the movements into the analytic interludes – the fact that something happened in between. I can't quite believe that. You seemed a little annoyed by my exclamation, "prejudice", but I meant it far more factually than (I think) you thought: one expects things to go on one way, and they go on another. But this kind of shock is functional; it is part of the analytic composition – in exactly the same way as functional "surprises" are part of a creative composition. Then there was your very mystifying "diffusion". I asked David [Drew] what you might have meant by that. He had studied the analysis and reacted

---

25 Glock to Wellington, 24 September 1959, WAC L2/84/1. Keller to Mitchell, 10 September 1961, CULHK.

in exactly the opposite direction: "extreme compression". However, I think he understood you – better than I, because he hadn't written the analysis. What he said was that on first acquaintance, it was the sharp analytic articulations that struck one, whereas the "continuity" bits in between (my formulation) were so unobtrusively com-posed that one's attention was not actively excited. I myself would add that wherever you get a comparatively large chunk of more or less pure quotation, every note in it refers (often in more than one dimension) to its analytic surroundings, and the cadential links are equally functional: they couldn't be any other. My first FA was comparatively diffuse; if I had written FA No. 9 in the same style, expressing everything it does express as it stands, the whole thing would have taken 1½ hours (I mean this quite seriously). "Transition from form into no form". This misunderstanding seems to me to be linked with that about "diffusion". The analysis has a very definite form but, of course, my cutting the ground under the feet of the piece's manifest form (there is a point to my metaphor) may create the impression of formlessness. May I finally say that every analytic transition in this FA has at least two (sometimes more) analytic meanings which I refuse to separate because I don't want to re-intellectualize what I have succeeded in de-intellectualizing. I am leading analysis back into musical experience, from which it should never have been divorced. The main "prejudice" which I shall have to overcome is the traditional approach to analysis, which is basically intellectual. Needless to add, my analyses are intellectually controlled and controllable at the reception end, but basically they function by way of intuition, as musical thought. I am not alone in regarding this as the most important step yet taken by analysis and criticism. I myself have not said so before, because it sounds megalomaniac; in fact, when, just having written it, I read this phrase now, I find it highly irritating. But I must ask myself, "Am I convinced of it or not?", and if I am, I must stand by it, at least privately.

II. S.S. 1959 was a definite and definable improvement on 1958. But the central gap remains. (I apologize once more for raising the question in unsuitable circumstances.) I tried my best to fill it, regardless of material considerations; thus, I refused 5 private lessons because I was more urgently needed elsewhere. But the whole thing has to be organized, and one man is not enough. On the other hand, manpower in this particular respect is very scarce indeed. In short, I think that you ought to come into it too. Can you give a valid reason why your talent should be confined to your present activities at the S.S., invaluable as these are?

Which brings me to a new idea. I have been thinking a great deal about (a) teaching, (b) people who enlist a team of teachers [. . .] and (c) the element of truth in this wrong-headed attitude: every given (good) teacher tends to concentrate on certain aspects at the expense of others. My new suggestion is <u>team teaching</u>. A master class in piano chamber music taken by yourself and myself together. You survey the whole interpretative field from the piano, I from the strings. Chamber-music-making by chamber-teaching. It wd be a complex task; a certain amount of tolerance, quick give-and-take, and instantaneous adjustment would be necessary – but hardly more than when one actually plays together. The experiment is only possible with very few teachers and on a very high level of artistic competence and imagination. But I suggest it would be likely to succeed between you and me. An entirely new approach to teaching, accentuating the advantages of the "model" and eliminating the disadvantages. Unforeseeable consequences – or rather, foreseeable in my wildest dreams, which are my fondest. Of course, we shouldn't do it all <u>ex abrupto</u>; certain basic points wd be discussed in advance. Think of it! Even if we failed, we shd succeed in starting something. Absolute failure is – artistically and psychologically – impossible. And, by the way, it wd certainly be an unprecedented draw. I can see your sceptical face. Cut. Re-take.

III. FA & the BBC. Not so private. You will, in due course, see my letter to the Establishment, and Hetley will discuss it with you. Some time ago you were kind enough to say that I, like you, was incorruptible. I am not even corruptible by amiable arrangements, which is the one danger I can foresee. As I said in my letter to the Establishment, all I want is complete impartiality. I would object as violently to favouritism as to neglect. What I fear is neglect as a means of publicly denying favouritism. This, frankly, isn't good enough. Genuine impartiality has no uneasy conscience. If "n FA's per year" is an objective requirement, then n FA's per year it shall be, not n minus one. You will remember that I immediately raised the question of FA when we first discussed the possibility of my joining the Corporation. I raised it again at the interview, in reply to a question by Newby. I raised it again in my letter to the Establishment, and again when I talked to Hetley this morning. At the end of the interview, I said that I had a heavy sense of responsibility. Perhaps you are the only one in the Corporation who has been in close touch with this side of my character – at the S.S. You may be the only one who can concretely foresee that; how I shall put my whole mind and heart into the BBC job; I am constitutionally incapable of any other attitude, once I have decided that a job is worth while. [. . .]

I have written this letter in great haste, almost in my last free hour. I may not be able to read thru' it carefully before catching the last post. Please edit in yr mind while reading it. And don't fear that you will receive this kind of thing every other day – tho' a lot more may have to be said abt the Summer School. [. . .]

Yours ever,

Hans

~

The post of Music Talks Producer meant that, for the first time since his *Music Survey* days, Keller was in a position to commission work from other musicians and writers, and he seized the initiative with gusto. Unsurprisingly, he sought to diminish the role of critics in favour of hearing musicians themselves talk – and some of his proposals (like his aborted 'The Artist Replies', a forum to criticise critics) certainly echoed *Music Survey*'s defensive work. But the days of battling with Howes and Blom were now past – and this was another way in which 1959 marked a turning-point, as the old critics made way for a new generation. Eric Blom died that year, as did the doyen of British music critics, Ernest Newman. They had stayed at the helm of *The Observer* and *The Sunday Times* until the end, preserving the values and style of another age. Blom's penultimate column, published only three weeks before he died, was another attack on 'the new criticism', in which Keller (though not mentioned by name) was clearly the principal target.[26]

Frank Howes was very much alive in 1959, but the following year he retired from *The Times* after thirty-seven years. Keller's last attack on his criticism was not on their usual Schoenbergian battleground, but in defence of Tchaikovsky – responding to Howes's 1959 article 'Tchaikovsky with the Right Inhibitions' ('the Right Inhibitions' being those of 'the English public schools').[27]

The New in Review [extract]
MR XX/2 (May 1959): 159–62.

Tchaikovsky has been on the black list ever since our recent Tchaikovsky Festival (so called). *The Times*' contribution to this event was to give Tchaikovsky's E minor Symphony the nick-name of "The Insufferable". Stupid as we musicians are, we shall look to it that Tchaikovsky's music will survive Mr. Howes' revelations, but meanwhile

26 'The New Criticism', *Observer,* 29 March 1959, 12, referring to Keller's 'Strict Serial Technique', in *Tempo* 37 (September 1955): 12–24.

27 *The Times*, 23 January 1959, 13. 'Tchaikovsky was not a product of the English public schools and did not suffer from the English inhibitions of self-pity,' wrote Howes. 'But if he is played with some of these inhibitions, the music appears without the lather and reveals some of its otherwise submerged merits.'

a lot of harm can be done by this kind of writing, especially in the case of a composer whose very popularity inhibits serious studies of his music. Instead of telling us that "there is . . . . a certain amount of inexpugnable claptrap in the three symphonies (4 to 6)", Mr. Howes might, for once, have studied their structures. So much claptrap is there in the finale of the great Fourth, for instance, that, to the best of my knowledge, nobody has yet discovered its highly original form. In the text-books, it is described as "a set of free variations upon a Russian folk-song, *In the fields there stood a birch-tree*". This is utter rubbish. The fourth movement is not a variation form at all, but one of Tchaikovsky's revolutionary sonata forms, whose significance for the development of composition remains to be traced. (Latest effect: Shostakovich!) As in the first movement of the same Symphony (of which more below), a decisive contrasting stage, here the second-subject theme, is anticipated by the middle section of the preceding stage, *i.e.* the first subject: after a mere eight bars of the first subject in the tonic (F) major, which has been the key of the scherzo, Tchaikovsky jumps upon us with the folk-song in A minor which, after the first subject has been resumed, turns into the second subject. It is a stressedly simple tune which confines itself to the first five notes of the diatonic scale, like the 'Joy' theme from Beethoven's Ninth. At the second subject stage, it is treated as an *ostinato* climax in B flat (the subdominant) minor, the key of the slow movement; and in the recapitulation it returns, modified, in D minor, the tonic's relative minor: compare the recapitulation of the opening movement. The Symphony's motto theme finally returns between the end of the recapitulation and the coda, as it does in the opening movement – an ideal spot indeed for such a free insertion: it is the structural juncture where, in the first movement of a classical concerto, the cadenza unfolds. [. . .]

Tchaikovsky's profoundly individual contribution to the development of symphonic thought can be outlined in a word or two – it is the creation and integration of new and violent contrasts. The usual sonata procedure is based on the tension between the first subject in the tonic and the contrasting second subject in a related key which pulls you away from the tonic, prototypically the dominant. Now, Tchaikovsky not only increases the contrasts between the themes on the one hand and the keys or harmonic regions on the other, but he introduces a new kind of contrast altogether – that *between* the thematic and the harmonic contrasts: the two no longer coincide. In embryo, a precedent can be found in a composer much admired by Tchaikovsky – Mozart, whose G minor Quintet evinces a thematic second subject which harmonically belongs to the first, and, conversely an harmonic second subject which thematically belongs to the first.

The first movement of Tchaikovsky's Fourth is perhaps the most outstanding example of his symphonic revolution and may well be his greatest symphonic achievement altogether, as well as being one of the greatest structures of his century. It is by far the longest and the most complex movement in the work, and it must have been the puzzling wealth of its ideas, keys, developments and interrelations that was responsible for the rather mild success of the Symphony, at its first performance in Moscow. "The public received your Symphony very well", Mme. Von Meck wrote kindly, "especially the scherzo".

Not even the formal function of the introductory, basic motto theme has ever yet been recognized. Fundamentally, the purpose is structural definition: the reappearances of the theme help to define the outlines of what would otherwise be too novel, too bewildering a sonata arch. Thus, the motto recurs as a transition from the exposition to the development section and again at the climax of the development itself, as well as by way of lead-back to the recapitulation. Eventually, it goes to form the transition to the coda, wherein it then appears in imitation. But now for the contrasting contrasts themselves, developed within this framework at the highest level of inspiration. The second subject, it must be noted, is not in the main contrasting key, which is B major, but in A flat minor. B major appears, to begin with, as a 'middle-section key' of this second subject, which then returns to A flat minor; and by the time the proper second key in command, B major, has established itself, the second subject proper is over and we have entered the enormously expanded closing section of the exposition. As in the case of the Mozart Quintet, then, the *thematic* second subject precedes the *harmonic* second subject. (The latter's B major, incidentally, has to be understood as C flat major, i.e. the relative major of the second subject's A flat minor, which in its turn is the tonic minor of the home key's (F minor's) relative major: the contrasting keys are, at the same time, closely interlinked.)

A similar surprise awaits us in the recapitulation, which we have already compared to that of the finale: the first subject now appears, not in the tonic, but in D minor! So indeed does the second subject, until the tonic major emerges in the middle of it – in the same place where the chief contrasting key had appeared in the exposition, whose harmonic scheme is thus retained. The home mode, F *minor*, however, is saved up for the coda. As a result, the climactic restatement of the first subject with which the movement ends, assumes the tense significance of a first complete recapitulation: long as the movement is, one is almost shocked that it is already over. [. . .]

"Critics misinform the public and delay comprehension." When Stravinsky said this, he was thinking of Schönberg, Webern, Berg and himself, not of Tchaikovsky. The catholic breadth of the achievements of my senior colleagues is not yet fully appreciated.

A collection of the writings of Ernest Newman was published after his death, including the whole of his famous dispute with George Bernard Shaw over Richard Strauss.[28] Reviewing it, Keller used the Newman–Shaw controversy to illustrate what he called 'the headlong collision between the artistic and the critical mind'. While Newman represented the critical mind, Shaw was an artist, which Keller said explained why Shaw was 'ready to extend what he called "artistic good faith", and what I prefer to call a credit account of trust, to any creator who had proved himself a master of genius'.[29] It was the critical mind's attempts at balance and objectivity that caused the problem, as Keller explained in a fascinating article for the last issue of *The Score* on an undervalued work of Beethoven:

New Music: Beethoven's Choral Fantasy [extract]
Score 28 (January 1961): 38–46, reprinted in *EOM*, 40–47.

It is an uphill job, of course, this striving for the 'balanced' point of view, but nowadays it is not so difficult as it used to be. We have all become critics, a 'critical attitude' has become something of a criterion of competence. Everybody has become interested in critical views, with the exception of a tiny group in our midst, the composers themselves. They still stubbornly refuse to write for critics. They are, in fact, more interested in saying something than in not making mistakes. Like everybody who talks to you, they count on your goodwill. But goodwill is not 'balanced'. It is prejudiced, it takes something for granted. This is the fundamental difference between the critic and the artist: the critic wants to be unprejudiced; the artist wants prejudice. Every artist only addresses himself to those who are biased in his favour. He wishes to be understood, and if he has made himself as clear as possible to those who are willing to understand, he is satisfied.

As part of his effort to shift the bias of public discourse in favour of the artist, Keller took great pains to help young composers and performers speak on the radio. There were many who, like Susan Bradshaw, would 'never have considered the possibility of writing or talking about music' had it not been for Keller, who not only showed them how to do it, but convinced them of the importance of having their voices heard.

'Sometimes the least articulate people are the most articulate when they finally get round to saying something,' Keller told his colleagues, explaining why 'the

28 *Testament of Music*, ed. Herbert Van Thal (London: Puttnam, 1962).
29 'Newman: scholar and journalist', *Sunday Times*, 13 January 1963, 29.

thoughtless "professional" radio attitude – take the most articulate speakers, the best broadcasters first – is to be discouraged.' He spent endless time helping new voices onto the air: as the composer Alexander Goehr wrote after his own first talk, 'it's rare to find anyone in life who will take this much trouble with the work of another.'[30] Keller's method was not to rewrite contributors' talks, but to take his radio speakers through an intense process of editing and questioning, helping them think through what they had written. 'For these blasted five pounds, or whatever I got paid,' recalled Goehr, 'he made me work. I mean I perhaps had to write that five times before he was satisfied.'[31] It was exhausting, but produced lasting results, as Robin Holloway, another young composer coached through his first broadcast by Keller, also found: '[it] was a lesson, efficacious and unforgettable, which opened up . . . a potential for writing about music that I have followed ever since'.[32]

The overwhelming impression one receives from Keller's voluminous correspondence during his early months at the BBC is of phenomenal energy and a clearly stated purpose. Reminders that 'talking time is limited' and 'my stringent policy is to accept only talks which deal with burning problems' appeared repeatedly in his letters and memos, the concise style of which added even more to the sense of urgency and excitement. No one, inside or outside the BBC, could be in any doubt that things had changed.

7 September 1959 – to all members of Third Programme Music Meeting [extract]
WAC R51/889/1

Generally speaking, I can already see that our music talks policy is not sufficiently alert. We are riding, passively, on waves of interesting suggestions, the most interesting of which are taken up. So far, so competent. We need more than competence. Most suggestions are interesting, and an unfortunate number is most interesting. Here lies the danger. Talking time is limited; it is our overriding duty to find the most important people, spheres of interest, subjects, at the risk of dropping many a most interesting suggestion. This is not to say that we should push the potential broadcaster into a passive role. On the contrary, mutual activity is the solution. Once we know whom and what we want – what our culture wants – there is plenty of room for suggestions, for free activity on the part of the broadcasters. But we must show enough knowledge and imagination to teach them what to teach us.

---

30 Goehr to Keller, 17 November 1959, CULHK.
31 Goehr, oral communication, 28 November 1996.
32 Robin Holloway, 'Keller's Causes', *LRB*, 3 August 1995, 10.

One example is Keller's correspondence with Charles Mackerras over his series 'Style in Orchestration':[33]

6 October 1959 – to Charles Mackerras

Dear Charles,

I have submitted your fascinating plan to the Third Programme Music Meeting and, on the whole, the reception was favourable. In order finally to clinch it, however, I think it would be a good idea for you to detail the project in writing, so that it can be studied at leisure. One point in particular is still quite vague – the length of the 2 programmes (including the length of the scripts). Are you still thinking in terms of a 45–50' script cum illustrations for either programme (see your letter of September 11)? This is not a critical question; for the moment, I just want to know. I hope you won't think me bureaucratic; I have to 'sell' what amounts to a major undertaking to the Third Programme, and they must be in full possession of the facts as you want them, so please write an up-to-date exposé, and be as concrete as possible.

So much for the business side. I now want to return to an artistic and ethical point which I made in the course of our conversation, and about which I feel very strongly. I think any attempt to throw either Beethoven's or Schumann's suggested miscalculations into relief (let alone exaggerate them) would be quite wrong: it would amount to a journalistic rather than a musical approach. The first duty is to realize (in both senses of the word) the original intentions; the second, to define Mahlerization in terms of improvement, clarification, rather than in terms of correction. An apparent miscalculation by a Beethoven or even a Schumann often has more textural point behind it than a less problematic, 'correct' calculation by a lesser man* – and I could give you plenty of very concrete examples where I proved my own criticisms (as well as other people's, e.g. Tovey's) wrong. Finally we must never forget that Mahler 'improved' Beethoven's F minor Quartet by way of a string-orchestral version – but then, you are, of course, fully aware that he was quite capable of going too far.

I hope you won't feel that I'm interfering. There's de-bunking in the air – a realistic reaction to the romantic approach when it is controlled by the credit account one has to extend to genius, but usually it isn't. To treat Beethoven's or Schumann's miscalculations as if they were Michael Tippett's is not realistic. No doubt you agree; so why have I written

33 Two concerts and two forty-five-minute illustrated talks, broadcast on 19, 20, 28 and 29 September 1961.

what must be the longest letter yet from this office? Let me know by return of post.

Yours ever,

(Hans Keller)

*Not to speak of the problem of <u>orchestration and creative character</u>: note how Schoenberg and Strawinsky rally to the defence of Schumann's instrumentations!

2 November 1959 – to Charles Mackerras

Dear Charles,

Many thanks for your letter of October 16. All has been approved, and the plan is to record in Manchester with the Northern Orchestra.

There is only one point, one qualification, which I want to make as strongly as I possibly can – praying, at the same time, that I won't seem dictatorial. I cannot accept the suggestion that Mendelssohn is one of the "lesser composers whose music <u>depends</u> almost entirely on their excellence as orchestrators". I'm absolutely convinced that Mendelssohn is a great master who, for topical reasons, is underestimated at the present stage of musical history. I implore you to have a look, say, at the string quartets, or the two string quintets for that matter; you will then see that it will be impossible for you to maintain your position. Last summer, I started a Mendelssohn renaissance at the Summer School of Music at Dartington; it has been entirely successful, although Mendelssohn's orchestration did not come in anywhere. As for the Mendelssohn music you know, what about the Midsummer Night's Dream Overture or the fiddle concerto?

It's easier to explode when one dictates than when one writes. For a second I thought I'd better re-dictate the letter and put it all in a more diplomatic form; but then, I do think that between musicians there ought to be ruthless frankness about music. But because I felt guilty about opposing your opinion on Mendelssohn so violently, I thought it my duty to consult the Controller of Music on this point, and I must add that I have his full support. Artistically speaking, of course, I don't feel guilty at all because what I'm doing is defending a creator. I wouldn't ever dream of telling a broadcaster not to praise a composer whom I happened to dislike or think little of. In order to reach some common position, may I finally say that as a matter of musical principle one has to give the composer the benefit

of substantial doubt. So, while this letter may, superficially, seem
to be intolerant, I'm really pleading for tolerance, and against your
intolerance of Mendelssohn.

As you know, I am profoundly enthusiastic about your projected
programmes, all the more so since I have the greatest and most detailed
admiration for your musicianship. So, while you may be annoyed at my
passionate plea for Mendelssohn's art, it has been my passionate plea for
Mackerras's art which has made this project possible.

Yours sincerely

(Hans Keller).

Keller's search for the best speaker for each particular project meant that he
did not hesitate to look abroad where necessary. When Josef Rufer's catalogue
of Schoenberg's works was published, for example, Keller proposed to travel to
Paris to record René Leibowitz talking 'on, or rather around, this important book'
and conducting live illustrations with his own ensemble. 'I have convinced the
Third Programme', he told Leibowitz, 'that your musicianship and knowledge of
Schoenberg – the man and his music – makes you the only available speaker on
the subject'.[34] Needless to say, when important foreign musicians visited London,
Keller made sure to ask them to speak – and the more eminent they were, the
harder he pressed them:

31 October 1959 – to Igor Stravinsky

Dear Mr. Stravinsky,

You may have heard that I am now in charge of music talks – trying to
revolutionize them as far as possible. Critics out, musicians in. Twaddle
out, substance in – new, essential substance, wherever possible.

I don't care whether a talk takes one minute or one hour, except that I
prefer a substantial one-minute talk to the usual, extended superfluities. I
am not asking you whether you have anything to say, because I know you
have. But I am imploring you to say it. It won't cost you any time. You
won't need any preparation. So far as I'm concerned, you can walk into a
studio, talk freely for five minutes, and walk out again. I would then edit
the tape to your satisfaction.

I don't wish to sound arrogant, or to appear to be lecturing you, but
it seems to me that as a great composer, it is your duty to open your

---

34 Keller to Leibowitz, 28 October 1959, CULHK. Leibowitz's programme was broadcast on 12
February 1961.

mouth before you leave these shores again. Do you see what I mean? Don't be cross if you don't.

Kindest regards,

Yours,

Hans Keller

A similar appeal went to Benjamin Britten: 'You know that *pace* Stravinsky, I regard you as the greatest composer alive. I therefore consider it my absolute duty to try and get something out of you, however pessimistic I may feel about my own attempt.'[35] Britten was a notoriously reluctant speaker, but he found it hard to turn Keller down:

> The trouble is that if anyone else but you had asked me to take part in this discussion the answer would have been an immediate and firm "no". It is respect, affection and gratitude (for your prompt and stimulating help over the Schubert grace-note) which makes me hesitate.[36]

The 'Schubert grace-note' is a telling little incident, to which Keller refers in the article below on 'Britten as Interpreter'. This piece is one of several responses Keller made to the speech given by Britten in America on 31 July 1964, 'On Receiving the First Aspen Award'. The award of this valuable new prize – intended to honour 'the individual anywhere in the world judged to have made the greatest contribution to the humanities' – was widely reported, and Britten's lengthy acceptance speech was published by Faber (where Donald Mitchell was now in charge of music publications). It drew much attention – Neville Cardus even hailed it as 'one of the wisest, acutest, most simply eloquent and friendly utterances on music I have come upon in a lifetime'.[37] Britten was then at the height of his fame, after the near-universal acclaim that had greeted the *War Requiem* in 1962 and the lavish celebrations of his 50th birthday the following year. Donald Mitchell at Faber published a *Tribute to Benjamin Britten on his Fiftieth Birthday* (edited by Anthony Gishford and including a fascinating essay by Keller on 'Key Characteristics'). Thinking back to the *Commentary* they had produced a decade earlier, Keller and Mitchell might have reflected on the difference in the reception now accorded the composer and a new book in his honour. This 1963 *Tribute* really was the 'bouquet for Britten' from his friends that Eric Blom had accused the *Commentary* of being, but this time no one complained.[38]

The most famous part of Britten's 'Aspen Award' speech is probably his statement that 'the loudspeaker is the principal enemy of music,' with which Keller

---

35 Keller to Britten, 10 September 1959, WAC Britten Artist File 2.
36 Britten to Keller, 19 September 1959, WAC Britten Artist File 2.
37 'Britten's Humanity', *Guardian*, 3 December 1964, 8.
38 Keller's comment on this may be the title (though not the content) of another birthday essay: 'How Great is Britten? *or* Why I am Right', *M&M* XII (November 1963): 12–13.

took issue on radio's behalf in an essay written for the first concert series of the European Broadcasting Union.[39] Another of Britten's points – that society should provide the artist with 'a secure living and a pension' – Keller addressed in his *Music Review* column 'Today's Tomorrow': 'The system would work splendidly with a Mozart or Britten; it would be the death sentence on a Beethoven or Schönberg,' he wrote, adding that 'Britten makes the time-honoured creator's mistake of thinking only of one type of creative character – his own.'[40] In 'Britten as Interpreter', Keller considered Britten's statement that 'What is important in the Arts is *not* the scientific part, the analysable part of music, but the something which emerges from it but transcends it, which cannot be analysed because it is not *in* it, but *of* it.'

Britten as Interpreter [extract]
Audio Record Review (January 1965): 9

In the Schubert song cycles with Peter Pears, Britten has brought the art of accompanying – not, heaven forbid, to perfection, but to a stage of complex, improvisatory interplay between the singer and himself, a state of re-creative *ensemble* previously only reached by the greatest string quartets at their best, i.e. in private. For Britten and Pears, as for a good string quartet, the other person is always right.

'Though I have worked very hard at the *Winterreise* in the last five years,' said Britten in his recent speech, 'On Receiving the First Aspen Award', 'every time I come back to it I am amazed not only by the extraordinary mastery of it . . . but by the renewal of the magic: each time, the mystery remains'. The 'magic' for Britten is that which is not analysable (I think it is); which is not *in* the music, but *of* it. 'It is the quality which cannot be acquired by simply the exercise of a technique or a system: it is something to do with personality, with gift, with spirit', something that he continuously searches out as a performer, that expresses itself in 'the innumerable small variants of rhythm and phrasing which make up the performer's contribution'. As opposed to, say, a Toscanini, Britten believes that at each performance, the player should 'make modifications. The composer expects him to; he would be foolish if he did not.'

After one of my wordless functional analyses had been performed at an Aldeburgh Festival, a worthy lady got up and asked me whether I didn't think that my analytic score detracted from the poetry of the Mozart quartet I had been analysing. For once, I didn't quite know what to

---

39 Published in the programme of the opening concert of the season (which Britten conducted) on 27 November 1967. (Part-reproduced in Garnham, 'Hans Keller, Benjamin Britten and the First International Concert of the European Broadcasting Union', https://www.ebu.ch/files/live/sites/ebu/files/Projects/Radio/Euroradio%2050th/Doc_50th_years_radio_programme_no_BBC.pdf.)

40 *MR* 26/1 (February 1965): 51–3.

answer, since it wasn't really up to me to say anything – at which moment Britten got up and said, with astonishing aggressiveness, 'For me, it adds to the poetry.' Well, if I may ungratefully say so, he can't have it both ways; my analysis was much concerned with the 'magic'.

Another little incident which I relevantly remember is being rung, at half an hour's notice or so, before one of Pears's and Britten's gramophone recordings, and being collected in a car and rushed to the scene of the last rehearsal – in order to discuss the phrasing of a single motif. The interpretative problem was real enough – but if we didn't analyse at that stage, what was it we were doing?

Yet we all know what Britten means by unanalysable magic; and what I am leading up to is a brief clarification of his – and any other – interpretative genius. In all valid performances, it is the instinctive understanding, the feeling of the magic, that comes first. Analysis cannot replace it; but it does make one aware of the logic of one's emotional experience. In all genuinely musical analysis, that is to say, we confine ourselves to clarifying our own spontaneous experiences as well as each other's; whereas all intellectual analysis without emotional basis is sham.

As a conductor, when he has to address a performing body, Britten shows his clear analytic mind. His instructions, sparse as his textures, are never expressed in his own terms, always through his addressees': he talks through the players' musical and technical experience, clarifying it for them. That is why orchestral players, the most critical of conductors' critics, invariably take to him: he speaks their language before they have thought of the words. At the same time, his musical phrasings and characterizations are, unmistakably, his own. His Mozart G minor Symphony, for instance, is the most characteristic since Furtwängler's, of which he probably disapproves; and through their consistent character, the two interpretations are equally overwhelming. As for Mendelssohn, he re-raises him to the stature he lost through the reactions to his so-called over-estimation. (For my part, I can't see how a genius can ever be overestimated.) It is here that characterization is all-important, for if Mendelssohn is played too smoothly, he sounds too good to be good: perhaps part of Britten's enthusiasm for Mendelssohn is due to the facility with which both of them are blessed and cursed, and which so readily hides their deeper meanings, because the listener is hardly ever *shocked* into attention.

[. . .]

There are few good conductors amongst composers; at the same time, the best do tend to be amongst them. If their creative psychology grants them a selfless insight into other people's work (which happens but rarely), mastery of the art of stick-waggling follows more or less as a matter of creatively inspired course. Composers do, after all, know how music is made.

Britten was very interested in Functional Analysis and commissioned Keller to analyse Mozart's K.590 quartet for the 1961 Aldeburgh Festival. The analysis was performed by the Dartington String Quartet, who also gave the first performance of Keller's analysis of Britten's own Second Quartet, with Britten present to hear it. Peter Carter recalls talking to Britten before the performance – 'I remember Ben saying, I'm not sure I want to know what my subconscious is doing!'[41] – a statement that recalls Britten's reaction to the analysis of his music in Keller and Mitchell's *Commentary*: 'He said it made him feel like a small and harmless rabbit being cut up by a lot of grubby school-boys when he'd *much* rather be frisking about in the fields.'[42] Afterwards though, he told Keller he had recognised in the analysis his own 'pre-compositional thought', partly conscious and partly unconscious; he also later wrote that the Mozart analysis he had commissioned from Keller had influenced his own writing of cadenzas for a Mozart piano concerto.[43] Keller was delighted by Britten's instinctive understanding of what he was trying to do: 'I watched his face when my Mozart analysis was performed at Aldeburgh, and saw from his multiple grins, often two or three a second, that he got every single point.'[44]

> All music analysis is defence. Bad analysis: defence against emotional inability to cope with the work. Good analysis: defence against the literally overpowering experience of living through the creative act without creating anything.

As might be expected, Keller by no means confined himself to matters strictly musical at the BBC. He was intensely interested in all aspects of broadcasting and institutional life and not shy of putting forward his opinion. 'In pursuit of his high concepts he does not hesitate to propose improvements in our institutions, sometimes in a way which is unflattering but stimulating,' wrote Maurice Johnstone

41 Peter Carter, oral communication, 9 January 2018.
42 Imogen Holst, diary entry 19 December 1952, quoted in *Imogen Holst: A Life in Music*, ed. Christopher Grogan (Woodbridge: Boydell, 2007), 183–4.
43 See Britten's note for the programme book of the 1967 Aldeburgh Festival, 36.
44 'From the Third Programme to Radio 3', *M&M* (December 1984): 15.

in Keller's first staff report. 'We can take it, I hope.'[45] By this time, Keller and Johnstone were on surprisingly good terms – according to Keller, Johnstone took him out for lunch to tell him he had been mistaken about him. It was a common pattern: most of those who knew Keller only through his aggressive public writings were surprised by how congenial they found him when they met him in person. His warm and witty personality (and clear and efficient administration) made him a very popular colleague at the BBC.

Keller's many suggestions included talks on non-musical subjects in which he was interested. One early proposal was prompted by the complex legal issues raised in the trial of Guenther Podola, a German-born photographer and petty thief sentenced to death on 24 September 1959 for the shooting of a policeman. Podola had sustained a head injury during his arrest and afterwards claimed to have no memory of the alleged crime. The court was therefore faced with a defendant who could not plead either guilty or not guilty, and could not instruct his defence lawyers. Two consultant neurologists supporting the diagnosis of amnesia were called by the defence, while a consultant psychiatrist and the prison medical officer appeared for the Crown to state that in their opinion the loss of memory was feigned.

25 September 1959 – to J.D.F. Green, Controller, Talks

Unfortunately, your meetings clash with M.P.O.'s,[46] and next week I shall have to combine the two; I may have to be late, but I shall definitely turn up in order to report on Arthur Jacobs' item in <u>Comment</u> (September 24); I agree with the producer that it was a good talk.

And now let me step outside my field for an extended moment.

<u>Podola, criminal responsibility, McNaughten Rules</u>

Apropos of these items in your Minutes and Agenda, a possible follow-up occurs to me which would be of great interest to legal audiences as well as to the 'general' (Third Programme) public: a discussion between (one) British and (one) Continental lawyer on the respective merits of different legal systems (criminal <u>and</u> civil law – perhaps with the accent on the former, because it's simpler).

'Unfitness to plead' might be a topical starting-point. So far as I am aware, the concept is unknown on the Continent. This is one of the many respects in which British justice is superior. On the other hand, the frequent assertion that 'British justice is the best in the world' is meaningless; there is no 'best' system, and all British lawyers whom I have

---

45 Initial report, 1 December 1959, WAC L1/1907/1.
46 Music Programme Organiser, Harry Croft-Jackson.

cross-examined on this statement have evinced an almost total ignorance of foreign systems and procedures – except for some slight knowledge of American law, which is post-British, and French criminal procedure, which is notoriously bad.

In both criminal and civil respects, certain Continental systems (perhaps especially those deriving more directly from Roman Law) may in fact be argued to 'score' in quite a few points. For the purpose of brevity, I am confining my three random examples to criminal law and procedure:

(1)   The concept of witnesses "for" the prosecution and "for" the defence seems grotesque to any Austrian lawyer, who would say that a trial was not a football match. Witnesses, he would hold, are 'for' the truth, and should be summoned by, and responsible to, the Court alone. The fight between expert witnesses (Podola!) horrifies him; in Austria, experts are employed by the Court, and when their evidence is contradictory, additional experts are called upon – say, by application to the Vienna University – to help towards unravelling the contradictions. The idea that witnesses should be paid by one of the contesting parties is incomprehensible.

(2)   Equally incomprehensible to an Austrian or German lawyer is the possibility of an 'express' (3-minute) trial in the case of a Guilty plea (Heath). Austrian and German law attaches far less significance to (a) a Guilty plea itself, which is regarded as a piece of evidence that has to be considered in the total context of the <u>facts established at the trial</u> in the presence of the jury, and under full cross-examination (as distinct from police investigation and the lower courts); and (b) to the omniscience of defending Counsel, who in this country may wrongly advise a defendant to plead Guilty.

One or the other of these points assumes real significance in more complicated cases, such as that of Evans, whose eventual Guilty plea would have been regarded with suspicion by an Austrian court. His trial would have dragged on for months. Every available piece of evidence would have been searched out in an attempt to secure an objective picture of what actually happened; and in the course of the trial certain essential facts would have come to light – for instance, that some considerable time after the murder, Evans bought a teddy bear for the murdered child.

(3)   Increase of punishment on appeal – again an impossible thought from the standpoint of most Continental systems. Continental lawyers I have talked to fail to understand the British fear of frivolous appeals;

they say that their appeal courts cope without difficulty, and that the overriding principle must, after all, be that of justice: it is unjust, they maintain, to frighten off a potential appellant who might have genuine grounds for appeal.

I apologise for this very hasty communication. I am writing from my office, without reference to the notes I have made on the subject over the years.

My memo's slant is, of course, artificial: I could address the opposite kind of memo to C.T. Norddeutscher Rundfunk!

Despite Keller's obvious talent for all aspects of talks production, Glock was thinking of moving him to a different post almost from the moment he arrived – having decided that the revitalisation of Music Division needed Keller's understanding of chamber music more than his talent for words. One of the problems with the staffing structure Glock had inherited lay in the balance of power within the Corporation between 'planning' and 'supply', which gave final editorial control over what was broadcast to the network controllers, to whom the 'supply' departments (including Music) submitted their programmes. The raising of Music from a department to a division had in theory put the Controller of Music on the same level as the network controllers, but the staffing of Music Division still reflected the importance attached to the character of the networks over purely musical considerations. Glock sought to change this by dispensing with the posts of Third Programme Music Organiser and Home Service Music Organiser and grouping his producers instead according to musical genre.

An early draft of his new proposals has Keller's name attached to both 'chamber music' and 'orchestral and choral' – the latter marked 'for 20th-century repertory' until David Drew could be recruited. Setting out his ideas to his senior colleagues, Glock wrote:

> The outstanding advantages of the new scheme are (1) that it represents a realistic classification: chamber music will be planned by chamber-musicians, orchestral music by experts in the orchestral field; (2) that, therefore, planning will be more purposive and rely much less than now on passive acceptance of suggestions from outside; (3) that, with the inclusion of Keller and later on of Drew, there will be a more balanced, imaginative and enterprising choice of repertory than at present; and (4) that the Home Service programmes will be strengthened, and the Third's brought more closely in touch with all that is vital in the musical world today, by having two teams which are occupied with both.[47]

Glock wanted his new scheme to be up and running by November 1959 (in time to plan programmes for the second quarter of 1960), but was persuaded to

---

47 Glock to Wellington and others, 8 September 1959, WAC R49/981/1.

wait until Maurice Johnstone's retirement: 'M[arriott] & S[tanding] both think that the scheme will get off to a bad start if Johnstone is there.'[48] Johnstone's retirement was brought forward six months, after which Glock himself assumed his duties. 'The purpose of this is to place C.Mus. himself as close as possible in the organisation to those who build and produce programmes or are concerned in any direct way with the implementation of music policy.'[49] Eric Warr was retained as Assistant Head of Music Programmes, 'to provide a senior person of long BBC experience at C.Music's elbow', but the direction of music policy was clearly going to be Glock's.

'But, if we want a new era in broadcast music, it is vital for C.Mus. to be able to delegate with confidence.' Three new Chief Assistant posts were therefore created, at a higher grade than the old network liaison posts. Harry Croft-Jackson became Chief Assistant, Music Programme Organisation (an expansion of his previous role). The other two were 'output and planner-liaison' posts, each running a small team of producers and liaising with both the Home Service and the Third Programme. Leonard Isaacs, a senior member of Music Division with over twenty years' experience, was made Chief Assistant, Orchestral and Choral. The other post – Chief Assistant, Chamber Music and Recitals – was internally advertised. This time it is clear that Glock intended the job for Keller, but as a newcomer to the staff Keller could not be appointed without due process.[50]

Keller took up his new post on 25 April 1960, and his team of producers included Peter Gould, David Stone, Allan Giles and two new members of staff: Leo Black from Universal Edition and the early music specialist Basil Lam. Two more new recruits were David Drew and Alexander Goehr, both assigned to Leonard Isaacs's orchestral section. Keller was heavily involved in the recruitment of all the new staff and Glock relied very much on his judgement: 'Clearly the person whose reactions he trusted most was Hans,' said Black, who recalled Keller scouting for new talent on Glock's behalf from the moment he arrived. Goehr's recollection is similar: 'Surely it was Hans who recruited most of the others.'[51]

By this time, Glock's most significant chamber music initiative was already under way, in the shape of the Thursday Invitation Concerts. 'The avowed purpose of this series', it was announced in December 1959, 'is to change the whole concept and standard of chamber music concerts in London,' by presenting imaginative combinations of works from radically different periods and styles. To this end, a single concert might require two or three different ensembles to perform, something unaffordable outside radio.[52] Alongside this high-profile series, Keller worked to change the representation of chamber music on radio so that instead of isolated works, listeners could become aware of a whole tradition, rooted in

---

48 Diary entry, 16 September 1959, BLGA MS Mus.980.
49 M.F. Standing to Wellington, 28 December 1959, WAC R49/981/1.
50 Hetley to Galbraith, 24 March 1960, WAC L1/1907/1.
51 Oral communications from Black, 4 August 1995, and Goehr, 28 November 1996.
52 See *The Times*, 10 December 1959, 4.

*Hans Keller with the Dartington Quartet in 1960. L to R: Michael Evans (who replaced
Bobby Kok as cellist at the end of 1959), Colin Sauer, Hans Keller, Keith Lovell, Peter Carter.
(Photo: Catherine Scudamore)*

Haydn and extending to the present day. It was 'the highpoint of his achievement,'
thought Goehr, recalling how much he and everybody learned from Keller's
efforts: 'suddenly you heard it all and the presentation was terrific.' It was also
'one of the occasions where he and William Glock were working hand in hand,
because William also had very sophisticated views, especially about Haydn.'[53]
    A fundamental part of this new drive had to be a new standard of perfor-
mance, both to avoid unfamiliar works being killed by bad performances and
to preserve as a living tradition the Viennese classics at the heart of the repertoire. Keller's profound understanding of this music and his ability to inspire
young performers was crucial. His commitment to the highest standards meant
extensive coaching of ensembles, and the BBC's management warned him to be
careful of conflicts of interest: 'I told him it was unwise,' wrote the Controller of
Programme Organisation, 'even though entirely innocent, that he should be seen
to give time to coaching musicians whom his section subsequently employed.'[54]
One source of this worry may have been Keller's close relationship with ensembles like the Dartington Quartet, who did get a lot of dates at that time. 'Other
people used to get a couple of broadcasts a year, but we got a couple a month',

53 Goehr, oral communication, 28 November 1996.
54 M.F. Standing, 14 September 1961, WAC L1/1907/1.

remembered Peter Carter, explaining that this was because Keller had 'taught us how to play Schoenberg and Berg'.[55] According to Leo Black, coaching was a feature of all Keller's chamber music production, not just when his own students were involved – 'it was an unquenchable enthusiasm for the truth, the musical truth, as he perceived it.' Even the greatest stars were not exempt: 'he treated everybody as an equal, including people who were supposed to be up there.'[56] Discussions might continue after the broadcast, and Keller often sent a detailed reaction to the performers if he thought it would be helpful. The following example was written to the Allegri Quartet after their performance of Haydn's Op. 77, No. 1, and Beethoven's Op. 74 quartets in the Thursday Invitation Concert broadcast on 26 January 1961.

1 February 1961 – to the Allegri Quartet
BL MS Mus.954

Dear Allegris,

I was greatly impressed by much of your performance at the last Thursday Invitation Concert, and if I offer a few criticisms, it is, as usual, as a musician rather than a BBC official.

1. The march character of the Haydn's principal theme seems to me repressed rather than open; in other words, the alla Marcia of your accompaniment pulled the background against which the theme is composed into the foreground.

2. What do such sforzandos as those in bars 21–22 of the adagio mean? The answer, in my opinion, lies in a Jewish counter-question: how would one play these phrases if there were no sforzandos? In other words, a complete de-accentuation of what follows the sforzandos seems to me to be required. Conversely, in the ensuing semiquaver phrase, the beauty of Eli's last couple of semiquavers was diminished by his accents on the preceding slurred couples.

3. I failed to understand the relation between minuet and trio. While the minuet had no real presto character, the trio's tempo was exaggerated to the point of incomprehensibility.

4. The finale I thought absolutely brilliant; I became terribly cross with the critic who objected to its performance and whose review did not display much knowledge of either violin technique or indeed quartet playing. Eli's performance was quite outstanding, and to

---

55 Carter, oral communication, 9 January 2018.
56 Black, oral communication, 4 August 1995.

notice the occasional semi-slip in such circumstances seems to me to be beneath contempt. Congratulations, also, to Jimmy on those very uncomfortable (but not uncomfortable-sounding) semiquavers.

5.   Another tempo relation which I did not understand was that between the introduction and the body of the first Beethoven movement.

6.   The adagio could have been a great performance if all the bars containing two quavers and two semiquavers on the last beat hadn't been slightly unrhythmical: the two semiquavers were consistently too fast. A more isolated disturbance occurred before the second return of the theme where, in the espressivo passage, the semiquaver up-beats were hardly distinguishable from the quaver up-beats.

7.   In the scherzo the fortissimo after the double bar marks the main accent of the phrase; if you play a long, and hence inevitably accented, A flat in the preceding bar, the ensuing climax of the phrase is undermined.

8.   The spiccato in the third variation of the last movement did not really work over the home receiver (I rushed home in the interval in order to hear it there). It was a relief to hear the détaché in the coda. The preceding viola solo, though very beautiful, could have been done with more freedom, more declamation. In my submission, the sforzato three bars before the end of variation 5 is another of those which serve to de-accent: this time it is the preceding high B flat whose accentuation ought to be, but wasn't, avoided. As for variation 6, I would shyly suggest that it is UN POCO piu vivace.

I hope I am not getting things out of proportion: I'm dictating at top speed and, needless to say, I concentrated on my doubts without going into any detail about my great appreciation of your performance.

Yours ever,

(Hans Keller)

> *Inner authority increases with the weakening need to exercise it.*

Keller's chamber music post meant that, for the first time in his life, he was institutionally responsible for managing the work of other people. As time wore on, he developed a deep suspicion of 'management' – and a bad conscience about his own earlier enjoyment of it. He recalled those early days in the polemic against 'the myth of management' he wrote fifteen years later:

Things began to dawn on me as Chief Assistant, Chamber Music and Recitals, after the initial flush of excitement had subsided over having got the job I had put in for, and over now being in a position of musical 'leadership': at that time, I still thought that was something to be proud of, a heavy responsibility for better broadcasting, for more musical broadcasting, which one had to meet, whatever the cost. . . .

Programme x was a wonderful idea, series y a still better one, programme balance z the only logical solution to the problem of duplications and clashes of works. My staff – at that time, shame upon me, I still thought in terms of 'my' staff – had to be persuaded of our obligation to do just these things, and if, looking sideways, one spotted unhappinesses on the way, personal frustrations, neglected artistic urges, that could not be helped.[57]

A short diary fragment from this time survives in Keller's archive, displaying a certain amount of private impatience with some of his colleagues. Nevertheless he was by all accounts a very popular boss – 'a joy to work for' according to Leo Black.

18–21 September 1961 – diary fragment

Monday 18 September: Start 9.15

Listeners' enquiries. – 1st 4ter Offers (most of the day). Weekly HS [Home Service] planning: Extract stage. RT publicity. Preparation for TPMM [Third Programme Music Meeting]. Conferences with [Alan] Walker (presentation of Beethoven 4tet series) & [Peter] Gould (weekly planning, TICs [Thursday Invitation Concerts]). Cleared urgent in-tray, started unurgent one. ½ hour lunch interval.

Gould crisis: what with the Haydn piano series for the Offers and the TIC problems, he can't face the week's HS planning, especially since Projected Arrangements didn't arrive in time. He was on the point of resigning from his newly created job (in charge of Recitals) when I decided to treat him as a patient (he is also developing a cold) & plan twice over – into his Schedule as well as mine. For the moment, then, my task is doubled instead of halved; but he'll recover. Just imagine he had got my job: he w'dn't have lasted a month.[58] Cards from CMus: new ideas for TICs.

Left at 6.

57 *1975*, 20–21.

58 Two years later Peter Gould did get the job of Chief Assistant, Chamber Music and Recitals – and lasted many years before being promoted to Head of Music Programmes Radio.

<u>Tuesday 19 September</u>: <u>Start 9.30</u>

Producers' enquiries; Artists Committee delegation; listeners' enquiries; <u>1st 4ter Offers</u>. In-tray; correspondence.

Curzon–Cox crisis. Copy of Clifford's letter to David (pages of it): Cox made a mess of (a) the Edinburgh contract and (b) Clifford's offer to record the solo Schubert in the studio without extra payment. Clifford, after weeks, is still very cross with David.

<u>Lunch with Malcolm Williamson</u>: re his organ piece for February TIC & the possibility of his giving organ & pno recitals, including Ives' organ variations on 'God Save the King'.

<u>Rubinstein crisis</u>: [Paul] Huband rang me: we still don't know whether he is prepared to have his Leeds recital relayed. Asked Clare [Lawson Dick] (in the chair today) at HS meeting for the deadline and rang Huband from the meeting. 1st 4ter Offers continued after the meeting; prep. for tomorrow's TPMM then unurgent intray.

<u>Left at 6.30</u>; took 1 hr's intray home

(Evening: lesson to AW [Alan Walker]).

<u>Wednesday 20 September</u>: <u>Start 9.25</u>

<u>Offers</u>: last stage. Intray.

Took offers along to TPMM, where chief point of discussion was my suggestion to do something towards a greater number of live recitals. Newby, always nervous when there is any implication of a desirable change in planning procedure, contradicted himself by 'not being sold on live broadcasts' on the one hand and eventually stating that 'we were all agreed that live recitals were desirable' on the other. I was asked to (re-)discuss with MBM [Music Booking Manager] the possibility [of] open pencillings and did in fact persuade him to accept such a formulation as 'pre-rec. or preferably live between January and March' for a pencilling from Offers. This is one step forward; much more c'd be done if planning procedures were ever open to criticism. The only constitutional possibility I can see here is for CMus to talk to CTP and, if he is unsuccessful, go one step higher. But he will never have the time to acquaint himself fully with the situation & proceed. The <u>Gould crisis</u> (see Mon) continues time-robbingly; he is in a neurotic state which, however, produces one or two good ideas for changes in MPO [Music Programme Organisation] procedure. More if & when it comes to something.

<u>Left at 6.15</u> after clearing up weekly planning mess-up by Gould and prep. for tomorrow.

Thursday 21 September

First TIC of the season at Glasgow, looked after by myself. Left home at 7.20 – unable to get on a later plane. Then fog delay at London Airport. Prep. for tonight & portable intray during wait. I hope Peter hasn't timed Part II too closely: 50' for 45' of music. He has billed the Scriabin Sonata wrongly: 'Op. 64, No. 7' – but it's the 7th Sonata, Op. 64! – Further intray in plane.

~

Despite Keller's success at running chamber music, Glock soon had him on the move again. The 'new resourcefulness' (as Glock described it) in chamber music was very palpable, but the orchestral side of Music Division was not developing at the same rate. The more complex world of orchestral music was understandably harder to change, but Glock felt Keller would probably get better results than Isaacs, so asked them to swap posts in January 1962. The results were as he hoped:

> [Keller] continues to pour out a flood of ideas and criticisms which certainly prevent any slumber in the department. Last January he moved over from chamber music to orchestral, and in the half-year since then his influence has led to livelier and more substantial programmes from the regions, and to a more energetic attempt to bring Yalding House closer to the actual music-making going on in the studios and in public concerts.[59]

'It may be that his most important function for the moment is to <u>reform</u>,' reflected Glock, now considering the possibility of moving Keller to television next: 'I'm sure he would have a great contribution to make and would be a first-rate help to me in making use of the new opportunities that will arise.'

The 'new opportunities' to which Glock was referring were those opened up by the Pilkington Committee on Broadcasting, whose report was published on 27 June 1962. For the BBC it was (in the words of a former Director-General) 'a splendid vindication' – indeed 'almost embarrassingly so', a former senior controller confessed – so the BBC was anticipating a bright future.[60] Although the Conservative government that had commissioned Pilkington failed to implement some of his principal recommendations (most notably the revision of the

---

59 Glock, annual report on Keller's work, 12 August 1962, WAC L1/1907/1.
60 William Haley to Hugh Greene, 26 June 1962, and Basil Nicolls to Greene, 9 July 1962, WAC R4/4/16/1.

relationship between the Independent Television Authority and its contracting companies), it did authorise the BBC to launch a second television service (BBC2), introduce colour television and expand considerably the hours of its radio services.

Earlier that year, Keller had made his own first appearance on television, on the late-night arts programme *Monitor*. The programme was 'an enquiry into the music of our day from Jazz to Schoenberg', and Keller appeared alongside Aaron Copland, Michael Tippett and Deryck Cooke, with Colin Davis and the London Symphony Orchestra providing musical illustration.[61] As *Monitor*'s editor and presenter Huw Wheldon told Keller afterwards, 'Our programme seems to have gone over like an absolute bomb,' and Keller was the star of the show: 'You seem to have made a great impression on everybody ("Who is this chap Keller?"). You certainly make an impression on me!'[62] Fan mail started arriving for Keller, most of which, Wheldon noted after Keller's second *Monitor* appearance, seemed to be 'from young (presumably) women!'. (Keller replied, 'Next time, don't forget to remind me to address myself to senile men with particular care.')[63] Keller's second television appearance was judged by the *Sunday Times* to be 'the most enjoyable *Monitor* of the season: a delightful dust-up concerning the greatness of Gershwin, championed by that singular and engaging character, Hans Keller.'[64]

Keller thoroughly enjoyed the chance to defend Gershwin on television, since his attempts to get him taken seriously had still not borne fruit. He had tried again shortly after his arrival on the Corporation's staff, when a copy of *The Music Review* landed on Third Programme Controller Howard Newby's desk, with this note on the cover:

November 1959 – to Howard Newby

Howard: please read 3 lines on p. 289 & return to my office.

Question: <u>what does the Third Programme listener know abt Gershwin?</u>

May I have your answer, which can only consist of one word, by return of internal post?

HK

The one-word answer was presumably 'nothing', for not a note of Gershwin had yet been broadcast on the Third. 'P. 289' referred Newby to Keller's obituary for Sonnie Hale, and the three lines Keller underlined for him were about the greatness of *Lady be Good*, a performance of which Keller now proposed for the Third.

61 'Do My Ears Deceive Me?', broadcast 11 February 1962.
62 Wheldon to Keller, 13 February 1962, CULHK.
63 Wheldon to Keller [undated] and Keller to Wheldon, 26 November 1962, CULHK.
64 Maurice Wiggin, 'Laughter before tears', *Sunday Times*, 4 November 1962, 39.

But Newby remained unconvinced, even though Keller persuaded Glock and most of Music Division to support him.

Three years later, the success of Keller's television programme encouraged him to try again:

15 November 1962 – to William Glock
WAC R27/1026/1

At the last Third Programme Committee, H. Talks (S) drew attention to my recent 'Monitor' programme on Gershwin, which, he thought, was highly successful, in that I 'crushed the opposition'. Since he dramatized the event, I decided to dramatize it still further, saying that while I had evidently convinced five million people, I had yet failed to convince C.T.P. [Newby], who hadn't even been watching; and that the time had come for him to re-inspect his prejudices. CTP replied that if I succeeded in persuading C.Mus to include Gershwin in a Thursday Invitation Concert, he would consider further ventures (meaning, no doubt, the originally projected Gershwin musical.)

Would you kindly consider the idea at this morning's TIC meeting? Lamar Crowson, who has long been wanting to play some Gershwin at a TIC, could be invited to do a group of Preludes and Gershwin's own piano arrangements of some of his best songs; it would, of course, be easy to find room for him elsewhere in the programme.

A copy of this goes to [Harry Croft-Jackson] who, almost three years ago, was one of the originators of the 'Gershwin on Third Programme' idea; at that time, it had the full support of Music Division, including your own.

[16] November 1962 – to William Glock
WAC R27/1026/1

I gather that the idea went down at yesterday's meeting. On an issue of this kind (which is not without its mythical aspects), it is essential that musical realism should be conscientiously retained. Towards this purpose, may I submit these factual questions:–

(1) Which of the preludes and/or piano arrangements were known to any of those who rejected the idea?

(2) What, in hard musical words, were the reasons for rejection?

(3) Why did you support a major Gershwin operation for Third Programme three years ago but do not feel like accepting a comparatively minor one now?

> (4) Why is jazz in a TIC – as you once said – possible, and Gershwin impossible?
>
> I think my questions deserve an answer <u>sine ira</u>. [. . .]

For all Keller's determined arguing, he failed again to move Gershwin out of the category of 'light music', and was left to fume that 'pre-occupation with style at the expense of substance is the curse of the age.' He began to think that it might actually be harder to achieve a proper appreciation of a figure like Gershwin than of Schoenberg: 'where Schoenberg has to face incomprehension, Gershwin has to suffer misunderstanding – a fate worse than death because resurrection is proportionately postponed.'[65] He noted that when he challenged those who dismissed Gershwin as trash to sing a Gershwin tune, they 'promptly sing a tune by somebody else' – a significant confusion, said Keller, since it showed that 'they hear Gershwin's music in terms of its imitations; the language is vaguely perceived, the substance neglected.'[66] Somehow, the culture surrounding the music was preventing the music itself being heard.

Keller reflected again on the distancing effect of modern 'culture' while reviewing the English translation of Schoenberg's letters that Faber & Faber brought out in 1964:

The Music and the Man [extract]
Sunday Times, 25 October 1964, 47

> The word "culture" was not used in anything like its modern sense before the beginning of the nineteenth century. Just imagine: it's bad enough that Mozart didn't know he was writing sonata forms, first and second subjects, developments and recapitulations, but not even our own Handel (pardon my possessive pronoun, but I'm at least as unmistakable a Briton as he was) ever knew that he was an essential part of our culture. Why did we become culture-conscious? What, in fact, is culture? What motives lie behind the reasons for the creation of the term?
>
> Culture is the loss of immediate understanding which places us at one or more removes from what we are supposed to understand. Without culture, there's something. Within a culture, there is something about something; and when a culture reaches one of its peaks, you can easily get something about something about something, like an article about Schoenberg's letters, many of which are about his music about which nobody knows much. Thousands will read the article; not so thousands will read the book; and about twenty-three will follow it up by listening to the music.

65 'Gershwin's Genius,' *MT* 103/1437 (November 1962): 763–4.
66 'Five Misunderstandings about Gershwin,' *Listener* 1798 (12 September 1963): 402.

If you don't like my Concise Philosophy of Culture imagine those eighteenth-century faces reading about Handel's or Mozart's letters in advance of the music. Well, there we are. We have a culture; we can't get out of it; so we'd better make the best of it.

Schoenberg has been dead for thirteen years. The chief benefit he derived from his death was that his major works were more or less immediately proclaimed contemporary classics. One of the least unknown among them, though by no means the earliest – "Erwartung" – is now fifty-five years old, as old as "The Magic Flute" was when Wagner started writing the music for "Lohengrin." You see what one regards as "contemporary" when one is cultured, so there is a real point in reading Schoenberg on "Erwartung," whether you know the monodrama or not: –

> In "Erwartung" the greatest difficulty is this:

> > It is essential for the woman to be seen always *in the forest*, so that people realise that she is *afraid of it*!! For the whole drama *can* be understood as a nightmare. But for that very reason it must be a *real* forest and not merely a 'conventional' one, for one may loathe the latter, but one can't be afraid of it.

There is more here than meets the eye – more even, perhaps, than met the combined eyes of the otherwise perceptive, bilingual translators.[67] In Schoenberg's original, the "conventional" wood is a "sachlich," matter-of-fact one – an allusion, this, to the style of *Neue Sachlichkeit* ("New Factuality"), which apparently made him shudder but not scared (as I would have translated the concluding joke). One can just see what Schoenberg would have thought of the successors to *Neue Sachlichkeit* – those abstract woods that aren't even recognisable as woods.

For if one thing clearly emerges from this imposing collection of letters, it is that he was an incorruptibly concrete thinker. Of course, if we didn't have a culture, we would know that from his music anyway. As it is, the following type of statement is still capable of producing surprise: "I do not compose principles, but music." "The method of composing with twelve tones was not introduced by me as a style to be used exclusively, but as an attempt at replacing the functional qualities of tonal harmony." "It is true that the Ode [to Napoleon] at the end sounds like E flat. I don't

---

67 Eithne Wilkins and Ernest Kaiser: Keller discussed their 'meticulous' translation in more detail in *The Music Review* ('Today's Tomorrow,' *MR* XXVI/1 (February 1965): 51–2): 'as one reads the translation, one feels like listening to a recording of a highly individual string player whose tone, though still identifiable, is continuously off mike.' See also 'Schoenberg: problems of translation', *Books and Bookmen*, July, August and September 1974.

know why I did it. Maybe I was wrong, but at present you cannot make me feel this." And most significant –

> I can't utter too many warnings against over-rating these analyses, since after all they only lead to what I have always been dead against: seeing how it is *done*, whereas I have always helped people to see what it *is*! I have repeatedly tried to make Wiesengrund understand this, and also Berg and Webern. But they won't believe me. I can't say it often enough: my works are twelve-note *compositions*, not *twelve-note* compositions.

No wonder this instinctive composer, whom intellectuals miscalled an intellectual just because he had an intellect, wanted to get himself out of the culture they had got him into. Towards the end of his life, he wrote to Hans Rosbaud: "But there is nothing I long for more intensely (if for anything) than to be taken for a better sort of Tchaikovsky – for heaven's sake: a bit better, but really that's all. Or if anything more, then that people should know my tunes and whistle them."

> *In this late stage in our civilisation, knowledge is being replaced, gradually and insidiously, by knowledge about knowledge.*

Although Glock had initially been keen for Keller to try his hand at television, by the middle of 1963 he had changed his mind, deciding it was 'very important that he should stay instead at Yalding House, to make sure that there is a constant ferment of ideas and criticisms, of the greatest value to anyone genuinely concerned with doing his best for music and for the BBC.'[68] Part of the reason may have been Glock's relative lack of interest in television – Lionel Salter, in charge of television music when Glock arrived, complained of having 'no backing, no support whatever from Glock'.[69] But added to this would have been anxiety about the large extension of radio broadcasting hours that had been awarded by Pilkington. Although BBC2 television would open up new opportunities, radio continued to be the main medium for music, and the mid-1960s saw the unveiling of two new services. The Music Programme (providing 'good music all day') was launched in three phases during 1964–65, after which Radio 1 began broadcasting popular music in 1967.

68 Glock, annual report on Keller, 19 June 1963, L1/1907/1.
69 Oral communication, 10 January 1996.

Radio 1 was not the concern of Music Division. The Music Programme, on the other hand, posed a huge new challenge – and by no means an entirely welcome one. Glock was seriously concerned that it would deteriorate into mere 'wallpaper', with listeners treating its continuous music simply as background, while 'the almost inexhaustible invention needed to maintain a standard of compelling interest' would be impossible to maintain.[70] Keller, on the other hand, was sanguine at first:

8 January 1965 – to the editor of *The New Statesman* [extract]
published in *NS* LXIX/1765 (8 January 1965): 41

Speaking as one who is constitutionally incapable of background listening, I would yet point out that [. . .] we do not yet know enough about musical perception and cognition. A musician personally known to me once went to sleep in the course of a boring piece, and was afterwards able to put considerable stretches of it down on paper with a surprising degree of accuracy – a feat of which he would have been quite incapable had he remained awake.

There is a considerable body of leading opinion according to which background listening is positively recommendable in cases where there are resistances to the music in question. People who assimilate a musical language pre-consciously may thus learn to absorb the musical substance more readily.

One early decision to which Glock was particularly opposed was the placing of the Music Programme under the overall direction of the Home Service. This was intended to keep it firmly in the 'middle brow' range, neither too intellectual nor too 'musical' in a specialist sense. Music talks were strictly limited ('it is intended to broadcast music, not to teach musicology', wrote Ronald Lewin, Head of the Home Service) and its repertoire was confined to 'generally acceptable "good music"'. Laying down his main principles to Music Division colleagues at the outset of its planning, Lewin stressed how important it was that the Music Programme should 'never become or appear to be becoming too esoteric, too avant-garde, too experimental'. Listeners during the day could not be expected to pay too much attention: 'we should recognise that the greater part of the time we shall be providing background music.'[71]

A new Chief Assistant post was created within the Home Service to co-ordinate the planning of the Music Programme. Keller applied for this in March 1962 and though he was interviewed (and declared 'a very strong candidate') it is perhaps unsurprising that he was not given the job. What he might have done with it is

70 Glock, *Notes in Advance*, 129.
71 Lewin to Glock, Keller and others, 17 September 1962, WAC R27/1029/1.

indicated by papers from a short period he spent in temporary charge of it at the beginning of 1965, as the Programme approached the implementation of its final phase.

12 January 1965 – to William Glock
WAC R27/818/2

THE FACELESS MUSIC PROGRAMME

At the last Direction Meeting, you asked me to particularize my criticisms. Sunday is supposed to be the new Programme's most important day. Yet, on January 10th, there was no substantial and consistently characteristic music between 9.30 a.m. and 2.40 p.m. That this space happens to fall between my two programmes is not to be taken as an implied criticism of their departments: each of the programmes within these 5 hrs 10' could have found its rightful place somewhere. What was wrong was the construction of the day as a whole. So long as the overall editorship is not approached, in the first place, as a continuously imaginative task, we shall be open to the criticism we get: I have not yet seen or heard a single word of enthusiasm from the musical world for the actual Programme, though individual items as well as the sheer idea of it have been praised. Our uncertain attitude inevitably arouses heterogeneous criticism; if we had a face, even those who disliked it would acknowledge its existence and seriously discuss its character.

In the circumstances, remarks to the effect that 'we shall improve the Programme' seem to me beside the basic point. I don't say that we shan't; on the contrary, the Programme is easily improvable. But we still need an all-comprehensive imagination at the production end, which cannot fail to catch the listener's own imagination. The only characteristic Programme at the moment – little as I like some of it – is the Third.

Nothing is as easily lost amongst administrative necessities, jolly good fellowship, and utilitarian realism as artistic integrity; but I cannot believe that we are really prepared to see it sink.

Hans Keller

Michael Tippett was another critic of the Music Programme's lack of imagination: 'I think it has not yet found the way imaginatively through to the much greater variety of music and of listeners than it appears to know of,' he wrote in *The Listener*.[72] 'I never feel it much in touch with the new, more democratic

---

72 Tippett, 'The BBC's duty to society', *Listener* 1900 (26 August 1965): 302.

society growing up around us.' He asked Glock whether new patterns could not be found 'that would help to break away from the division of the Music Programme into neat little concerts?'[73] Music broadcasting on television he also found frustratingly derivative; just as radio was stuck in imitation of the concert hall, 'television music so often merely apes sound radio.' He outlined in his *Listener* article what he would do if he were in charge:

> I'd try to get under the skin of the musical Establishment as fast as may be. I would throw the classical concertos overboard – and all that security. I'd jump bang into the middle of the modern confusion where the ear and the age are to be renewed – and all that jazz. I'd play Charles Ives; bring to the screen the dazzling performance of Seiber-Dankworth as recently given at the Bath Festival; . . . top up perhaps with a fizzing display of *Rhapsody in Blue*. Then turn Wilfred Mellers into a television personality to add music to either end of that spectrum.

Glock took the point about trying to get away from the concert model, and he and Keller used to meet at the weekend with a small group of musicians to plan longer stretches of music in a more innovative way. Keller had some particularly radical ideas for provoking the Music Programme's background-listeners to pay attention:

26 January 1965 – to Lindsay Wellington, Richard Marriott and William Glock
BBC WAC R34/1034/2

> It is my considered opinion, which is supported by Act.Ch.M.P.,[74] that we should place a "Beatles" programme at the opening stage of the complete Music Programme. There is substantial musical opinion, my own included, in favour of the Beatles – or, at any rate, of some of their tunes. I am fully aware of the fact that such an operation would be felt to be controversial both amongst musicians and amongst the wider music-loving public. But it is this very circumstance which I want to utilise, raising a genuinely "live" issue on the one hand and, on the other, trying to establish a bridge, however temporary, between our musical world's two hostile camps. Nobody will feel indifferent about this programme: we cannot go wrong.
>
> The chief Music Critic of The Times is one of the Beatles' supporters, and whatever shape the programme takes, I should like to see him included in it. The speech part of it ought to be confined to a minimum – while at the same time being pungent enough clearly to

---

73 Glock, *Notes in Advance*, 129.
74 This is a joke: Keller was Acting Chief Assistant Music Programme at the time.

raise the issue and start what might develop into a vital controversy. Time is short; for the moment I should be most grateful if my idea were accepted in principle; details can be worked out later (or rather sooner) without difficulty. In lectures up and down the country, in which I have analysed, to audiences which expected a purist exposition of contemporary music, various Beatle tunes, I have come to the definite conclusion that there is not a single member of our music-loving public who is not spontaneously interested in this problem – positively or negatively or, more often both.

I should be happy to take full responsibility for the success of this programme from the broadcasting point of view, though it will, of course, produce some violent reactions.

At the moment we have, of course, some money to spare within the current fiscal year; if that should not prove enough, the programme could easily be managed with gramophone records.

We are now passing through a week in which our thoughts circle round the ideas and decisions of a man whose unconventional realism has produced some of the major achievements of this century. As an act of fruitful piety, it might be a good idea to follow his example within our own field of action.[75]

Hans Keller

Acting Chief Assistant, Music Programme

[P.S.] One might even talk to the Beatles about music – for once in their own pseudo-flippant language (tho' for this purpose, the Times critic w'd be unsuitable).

The *Times* critic Keller referred to was not Frank Howes, but his successor William Mann, who had raised eyebrows by hailing Lennon and McCartney as 'the outstanding English composers of 1963'. Wilfrid Mellers too was showing interest in the Beatles, controversially featuring them in the music curriculum he was devising for the new University of York.[76] None of the lectures Keller gave on the Beatles survives (Keller generally lectured without script or notes), but a few details of what interested him about them can be found in an unpublished piece he wrote for *The Observer* in 1968:

75 Winston Churchill had died on 24 January 1965 and was lying in state at Westminster Hall until his funeral on 30 January.

76 See Mann, 'What Songs the Beatles Sang', *The Times*, 27 December 1963, 4; Mellers, *Twilight of the Gods* (London: Faber, 1973); John Paynter, 'Renewal and Revelation: Wilfrid Mellers at York', *Popular Music* 13/2 (May 1994): 201–4.

The Beatles – the Music [extract]

Take the use of modes. It is true that, say, in 'A Hard Day's Night' and, still more so, in 'Can't buy Me Love', McCartney employs modality a little conventionally – at any rate for the sophisticated listener, who's heard it all before even though the composer may not have [. . .] But then listen to his 'I Am the Walrus' of last year, one of the most original recent songs, in which Indian sounds are, for once, functionally combined with 'advanced' noises and recording devices. The end bit, the final babble, avails itself of the most elementary of materials for the purpose of novel invention: over and over again, the Dorian mode slowly ascends on its way to the fade – in a context which makes you expect a diatonic conclusion, with F sharp as the leading note. Each time, therefore, you receive an invigorating jolt as the scale goes beyond the expected tonic G and points to A as the real tonic – whereupon you remind yourself instinctively that the piece had previously established itself in A major anyway. That's what I mean by meaningful contradictions of expectations.

As for chords, McCartney rediscovers their freshness for us because he himself never lost it in the first place. For him, a chord's a key unless you do something about it. By the sparsest of means, he lets us expect one key and replaces it by another. 'I am the Walrus' pretends B major before it lands in A, and the opening of 'Strawberry Fields Forever' is an equally simple but yet more inspired example of what, in 'serious' music, the analyst would call 'progressive tonality' – from E to A in the printed music, from F to B flat on the record.

Or could there be anything more rudimentary harmonically than a perfect cadence on the one hand and an interrupted cadence on the other? But by letting you actually savour the perfect cadence before he introduces the submediant chord in the bar preceding the coda of 'I Want to Hold Your Hand', McCartney lets you have the surprising best of both cadences – gratification suspended, rather than merely interrupted by inhibition. Nor is the effect wilful: the sweeping, melismatic melody tells you that not all is over when the tonic chord is reached at the beginning of the bar – that the end of the phrase is yet to come.

Again, is there anything more outworn than a plagal cadence? But by making the D major chord the dominant of G at the end of 'Lucy in the Sky with Diamonds', McCartney even turns the last stage of the journey home, to A major, into a surprise event.

Melodically and rhythmically, too, the material is no sooner presented than it is contradicted: it is the responsive phrases which, in countless tunes, contract and so produce tense asymmetry. 'Strawberry Fields Forever', a mine of creative wealth in every respect I'm trying to define, offers perhaps the most imaginative examples of compressed responses, above all with the 6/8-bars intervening in the 4/4-bar scheme, and the single 3/4-bar replacing the expected 4/4 one just before the end.

Formally, I'd like to hark back to 'She Loves You', which everybody, including the Beatles, tends to be snooty about nowadays. It remains their prototypical masterpiece, the inspiration of such later, great numbers as 'Help'. In this early song, contradiction of expectation overwhelms you right from the start: the chorus explodes in the wrong place – at the beginning! Thematic economy and integration reach their climax in the contrasting theme, where in the sentence, 'She says she loves you and you know that can't be bad' the opening phrase is interjected as the opening words recur in a musically unsuspected context.

When I first heard that tune in the very early sixties, I felt I wanted to acquaint our musical world with what was happening. I remember a public lecture in which I analysed the piece in minute detail. The reaction was no more than amused: 'Keller is at it again!', I could hear them say. If I had then been asked to write the present article, I'd have taken my hat off to the asker. Now, with respect, I leave it on: it seems the inescapable fate of criticism to be prophetic after the event.

The Beatles are the most important event in popular music since Gershwin. He was a genius; McCartney, musically the most talented of the four, is not. But his is an intense gift, such as respectable composers could be proud of.

A few notes on Beatle songs survive in Keller's archive, among which is the thought that the Beatles were 'not the modern folk music [but] the modern chamber music'. Just as the string quartet had been distorted by its translation from the chamber to the concert hall, so also had been the Beatles by their move out of the pubs and clubs of Liverpool.

~

After the success of Keller's first appearances on television, his voice appeared more frequently on radio, in a variety of interviews and discussions with prominent musicians and artists of the day. By his own account, however, some of his most stimulating broadcast conversations were not with cultural figures but with footballers. The first of these took place on 17 April 1964 on the Home Service – and was 'on a higher level of thought, substance and, may I say, honesty, than many a public discussion on more serious subjects in which I have taken part,' said Keller, who was delighted by 'Phil Woosnam's quiet intellectualism, Danny

Blanchflower's not so quiet roving imagination [and] Jimmy Greaves's sharp wit and acute self-perception'.[77] Greaves and Blanchflower were both members of a particularly strong Tottenham Hotspur side, whose matches Keller had started attending in 1963 – reawakening in him a love of the game that had been dormant since his teenage years as a supporter of Hakoah and player in the Kritzendorfer Sportklub.

Spurs Supporter [extract]
NS LXVI/1707 (29 November 1963): 802

I did not expect to become a fan again as an adult, but when I went to see Spurs on a few occasions, I realised that I had never seen such an unstereotyped side in my life. For many football enthusiasts, it is shocking to identify oneself with a good side, cowardly almost. Well, knowing all about supporting a weak side, I find it most illuminating to watch a good one. What is unique about Spurs is the combination of necessarily uneven genius (Greaves), mastery (Brown, Blanchflower, White), exceptional talent (Norman, Jones) and mutual understanding – a combination that produces ever-creative moves. Mackay, who resists classification, is the only power player I have ever seen with a sovereign technique, and with a hypnotic spirit which contributed to the victory over Atletico Madrid last season, even though he wasn't playing: Dyson, though playing a very different role, palpably identified himself with the absent hero. Bobby Smith's skill is consistently underestimated by the more neurotic supporters because he 'plays it a bit tough'. Marchi, now again in the League side, has been the most collected, uncharacteristic reserve player in the history of the game. As for the regular full-backs, paradoxically enough the recent 4–2–4 approach (in practice not all that different from some of the Thirties' 3–5–2 variations) proved more fruitful in attack than in sheer defence; but I cannot see those intrinsic defensive shortcomings about which I read almost every week. 'You can send this Tottenham team anywhere in the world with pride. Why can't the England eleven play like this?' asked Leo Horn, the Dutch international referee, after Rotterdam. Anywhere in the world except England.

Ever since Tottenham made the double, they have been up against what J. C. Flugel called the 'Polycrates complex', which makes us regard everybody who is immaculately successful as presuming above his station.[78] Hardly had the Spurs reached the top than they were considered over it; and this season they are alleged to be more over

---

77 'Soccer from the Stars', *RT* 163/2109 (9 April 1964), 53.
78 Spurs had won both the FA Cup and the League Championship in the 1960–61 season. See pp. 111–12 for the Polycrates complex.

it than ever before. The possibility of a plateau is not accepted; on the contrary, the team which, five months ago, was the first to bring major international honours to this country is suddenly and mysteriously ageing.

This was the first of over eighty articles on football Keller wrote over the next twenty years for the *New Statesman*, *The Listener*, *The Spectator* and the *Sunday Times*. Although he was not the first music critic to write on sport (Neville Cardus was famous as a cricket correspondent), Keller's idiosyncratic combination of interests (not to mention his intellectualism and Austrian accent) awoke the satirists – and 'Hans Killer, Professor of Soccer Hooliganism at the University of Schoenberg' became a regular in the pages of *Private Eye*: 'Not sinz extra time was plied in ze Cup Final Newcastle v. Leyton Orient in 1925 hes sech fantaschiches contrapuntal howz-your-onkel been heard as for ze newes elbum von de Turds "Sergent Major Hatterji und His Lonely Bend of Dhobi Vallahs".'[79]

According to Leo Black, accompanying Keller to soccer matches was almost as popular a BBC social activity in the 1960s as debating with him in the pub after work:

> An extraordinary variety of people used to share with him the fortnightly journey across London to White Hart Lane. I did so a couple of times, and recall mostly his courting arrest trying to get a better view of the game: he kept shinning a few feet up on the standards that held the footlights. Your friendly local bobby was then torn between wanting to watch the match himself and needing to keep an eye on the eccentric gentleman.[80]

When the World Cup was played at Wembley in 1966, Keller persuaded his colleagues in Music Division to mark the occasion with a special programme, broadcast the day before the final. It was announced on air as follows:

World Cup Music

It is not generally known that Edward Elgar was a football enthusiast, in fact, a Wolves fan. On March 12th 1898 he set a phrase from a newspaper report on a Wolves match to music.[81]

And it is this little recitative that forms the basis of the seventeen miniature variations we are now going to hear. They have been written by musicians on the staff of the BBC for the eve of the World Cup – and,

---

79 'Diatonic Appogiaturas in Ze Music of Ze Turds', *Private Eye* 161 (16 February 1968), 8; 'What's RIGHT with Britain', *Private Eye* 163 (15 March 1968), 7.

80 Leo Black, 'Hans Keller', in *HKKC*, xix–xx.

81 Keller would have come across the story of Elgar and football in the memoirs of Dora Penny (later Mrs Richard Powell), to whom the little football phrase was originally sent: *Edward Elgar: Memories of a Variation* (London: Oxford University Press, 1937), 4–5.

as a bridge between what some people think are hostile camps: the Music Programme and the Sports Service. The instrumentation is that of Schoenberg's *Pierrot lunaire* ensemble played today by the Vesuvius Ensemble – William Bennett (flute and piccolo), Thea King (clarinet and bass-clarinet), Kenneth Sillito (violin and viola), Charles Tunnell (cello) and Susan Bradshaw (piano). But at half time there will be a short interlude for organ. The reciter and singer is Neilson Taylor (baritone) who, as Jeff Taylor, was a distinguished centre-forward not long ago. He played alongside Johnny Haynes. Some of the link passages between the variations have been composed, others are being improvised by the players. All the variations are receiving their first performance and most of them their last.

Variation on a Soccer Theme by Elgar

LIONEL SALTER – ENIGMATIC VARIATION

TIM SOUSTER – FOUR UNDER THE BAR

LEO WURMSER – VARIATION HONGROISE

Now a BOOGIE WOOGIE – ALAN WALKER

MARTIN DALBY calls his CALCIO

Then GOAL-MOUTH SCRAMBLE – DAVID STONE

SEBASTIAN FORBES – GREAVES GROUND

Half Time – HARRY CROFT-JACKSON plays his variation at the organ

ROBERT SIMPSON'S Variation – INFRINGEMENT

ALEXANDER GOEHR – FORWARD WATFORD TOWN

Now INJURY TIME – JOHN MANDUELL

COLD SHOWER – DUNCAN DRUCE

ERIC ROSEBERRY – THE BALL THAT GOT AWAY

HANS KELLER – A POCKET PASSACAGLIA, FOR REFEREE, SPECTATORS, AND PIANO TRIO

DAVID COX IS BORED BY THE GAME

And finally THRENODY – DERYCK COOKE

Keller followed the World Cup matches closely and throughout the competition wrote lively reports for the *New Statesman*, beginning with a wry look at the special issue of commemorative stamps brought out for the occasion – and their unwitting portrayal of violations of football rules, such as 'on the [1/3d stamp] what must be an Argentinian (blue and white stripes) climbs onto an opponent's shoulder in order to head: a straightforward foul (Law 12, clause g).'[82] His final piece was not a celebration of England's victory, but a serious exposition of his fears of what the England manager Alf Ramsey's emphasis on teamwork at the expense of individual genius might do for the future of the game.

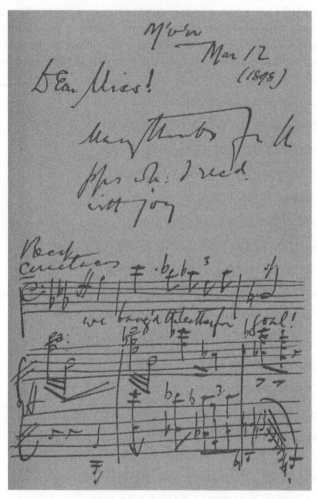

Edward Elgar's letter to Dora Penny containing his setting of 'we banged the leather for goal' to a recitative from Caractacus, *which formed the basis of the* Football Variations *by Keller and his BBC colleagues.*

---

82 'World Cup News', *NS* LXXII/1843 (8 July 1966): 62.

Hans Keller's Pocket Passacaglia for referee, spectators and piano trio, *1966 (CULHK Add MS 9371/8).*

The World Bows to Ipswich [extract]
NS LXXII/1847 (5 August 1966): 207

I haven't been doing badly with my predictions; but then I took great care to predict not only everything possible, but also the impossible – which has happened. What I said in that memorable article on July 8 was that "If Ipswich could win the League Cup the other year, there is no reason why we shouldn't win the World Cup."[83] The connection is more causal than I suspected. Ramsey has done it twice over, and two flukes are no fluke. He did most of it without class forwards. In Ipswich, with the exception of Crawford, he didn't have them. In Wembley, with the exception of Bobby Charlton, the part-time defender, he didn't want 'em: Greaves and Eastham were on the touch-line on Saturday, Haynes and Osgood forgotten. He is said to have adjusted his method to our lack of great players. Rubbish. He adjusted his selection to his highly successful power play. It isn't even true to say that he scrapped wingers because we haven't got any. Charlton excels equally in all forward positions, and Greaves, likewise, is a superb winger, though defensively a wash-out. Anyhow, why should Ramsey worry about geniuses if he can win Leagues and World Cups without them, and might have lost with them? Football is played to win. If we are interested in victory depending on individual talent and not, primarily, on mechanical team drill and defensive stamina, we have to ask how far it was the Ramsey method that won the cup – and, inasmuch as it was, how it can be led back to an imaginative game, where specific talent, far from being at a disadvantage, is irreplaceable.

The supreme importance of individual, as opposed to group, achievement is one of the many parallels that emerged between Keller's writing on football and music. Another was his insistence on the unique knowledge of the insider: 'In order really to understand a string quartet, you have to be, or have been, a quartet player. In order to really understand a football match, you have to have been a footballer.'[84] The difference, of course, was that most people watching football would have played it, a point made by Keller at a 1973 conference on 'Sport, Art and Aesthetics', according to Leo Black: 'He pointed out that at a string-quartet concert in the Royal Festival Hall perhaps ten per cent of the audience would ever have played quartets . . . At White Hart Lane perhaps ten per cent of the crowd *wouldn't* ever have played football.'[85]

83 *Ibid.*
84 Foreword to Keller's unpublished book on football, CULHK.
85 Black, 'Hans Keller' in *HKKC*, xx. See also 'Sport and Art: the Concept of Mastery', *Listener* 82/2104 (24 July 1969): 121, reprinted in *EOM*, 26–8.

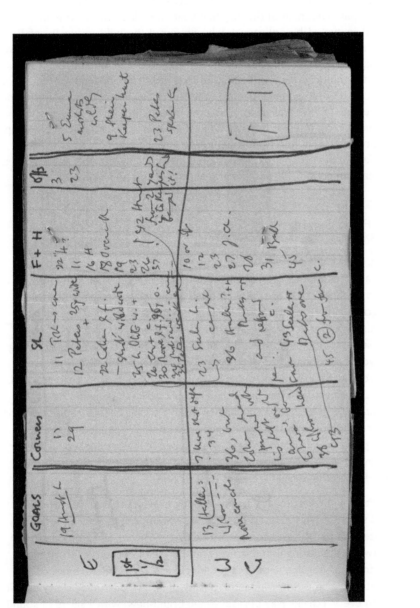

Hans Keller's notes on the first half of the 1966 World Cup final (CULHK).

Despite the way in which football had in this sense stayed closer to its roots, Keller resisted any incursion into the arts of sporting values – the problems of which were brought home to him very sharply a few weeks after the World Cup final, when he went to judge the second Leeds International Piano Competition. He was deputy chairman of the jury that year and Glock was chairman, but they were both outvoted by colleagues who preferred the wild virtuosity of Rafael Orozco to the imaginative poetry of Victoria Postnikova. 'I was confronted with the embarrassing task of appearing on the platform and announcing a decision based, I was quite certain, on a dreadful lack of artistic judgement,' said Glock, who thought Orozco's performance of the Brahms D minor concerto profoundly misconceived. 'Keller was even more convinced that a shameful error had been made, and for five minutes before we faced the public I had to use every scrap of persuasion to prevent him from resigning.'[86]

Baulked of his resignation, Keller aired the problem of 'sport penetrating art' in musical competitions in another article for the *New Statesman*:

The Piano Cup [extract]
NS LXXIII/1856 (7 October 1966): 527–8

Yes, you've guessed it. I was one of the minority on the jury who voted for another winner. [. . .] My admiration for Rafael Orozco, the full-blooded Spaniard (not so full-blooded in the final), was equal to the majority's. In Chopin's F sharp minor Polonaise in the first round, his natural gypsy musicality – every fibre a musician, every second fibre an artist – exploded unmistakeably and indeed unexpectedly: the preceding Haydn E flat Sonata had given no inkling, not even to those who came to vote him the winner. And Liszt's *Gnomenreigen*, sharply characterised, became almost a better piece than it is. At no later stage did he disappoint, even though one had to make a willing allowance for a certain degree of interpretative re-composition – if you happened to know the piece he was playing: otherwise, I suppose, everything would have sounded quite convincing. I wish him well, with every first prize in the world into the bargain – except for this one.

That he came first meant that somebody else had to come second, and since this was Victoria Postnikova, who moreover shared second prize with her Russian compatriot Semyon Kruchin, all common ground between the distinguished majority and myself vanished. With intensely restrained intensity, with breath-taking poise between extremes of contrasting emotion, with an originality of insight that made every phrase, even every Tchaikovsky phrase, sound brand-new, with a sense of sound and sonority, a range of colour, that owed nothing to sound effects and

86 Glock, *Notes in Advance*, 162.

everything to well-defined, yet spontaneous, sound sense-making – in short, with continuous inspiration and mastery, this 22-year-old girl gave performance after performance which showed where music came from: that it was neither entertainment nor duty, but an urgent communication inexpressible by any other means, so urgent as to be, for those who had ears to see, a matter of life or death. At this point, the verdict of the jury became perverse: Miss Postnikova is a supreme artist who composes while she plays, and damn all competitions and second prizes. Well, not altogether. Let's be fair to Leeds. We helped great talents even though we may have failed in the face of genius; but then, genius can help itself.

What our partial failure threw into relief was the inartistic side of artistic competitions. Nobody in the world except ourselves thinks that we have the best football team in the world – but we did win the World Cup, unbeaten. I think virtually nobody in the Leeds Town Hall, with the exception of the majority of the jury, thought that Postnikova was second-best, but she emerged beaten – and not, after all, democratically: the people had not been asked. Beaten? Does one beat, is one beaten in art? Does one play *against* people? Should one try to play 'better' than others, or does one, if one is a real artist, simply play differently?

Eight years later, when he founded a new international string quartet competition for the European Broadcasting Union, Keller determined that 'in an attempt to attain the highest possible degree of musical realism, there will be no pre-determined prizes.'

Keller's involvement with the European Broadcasting Union – initially chairing the planning of its new International Concert Seasons, followed by additional series devoted to contemporary music and chamber music – began in 1965.[87] This was just one among many extra responsibilities that he took on alongside his official job at the BBC, not to mention his own broadcasting, writing and teaching. Glock began to be anxious lest 'he might be overdoing it a little' even before Keller took on the EBU role. But there was clearly no need to worry, as Glock reported two years later:

He is undoubtedly one of the finest musicians living in the country. . . . There are no signs whatsoever that his energy or inventiveness are giving out, as

87 See Garnham, 'The First International Concert Season of the European Broadcasting Union', *MT* 158/1940 (November 2017): 7–17.

might happen with a smaller man in face of the incessant demands imposed by a job such as his. . . . Like Boulez, he evidently 'sleeps fast'.[88]

Awarding a 'personal grade' salary bonus at the beginning of 1968, Frank Gillard, Director of Radio, told Keller that 'I hope this award will show you how highly we regard your work and that in the future it will be an encouragement to you.'[89]

24 January 1968 – to Frank Gillard

My dear Frank,

Your task is comparatively easy: you probably write a standard letter. But my up-gradings have not yet been quite frequent enough for me to devise a standard answer.

It might be argued that if I need the encouragement, I don't deserve the award. But if I don't need the encouragement, why award me? New vistas open up for BBC economy. Meanwhile, my sincere thanks!

Yours,

Hans

Indeed, no encouragement was ever needed. Keller had arrived with his own mission and, from the start declared himself 'extremely happy' at the BBC. Twenty years later he described his first decade there as 'paradise' – not only because of 'my elementally artistic collaboration with William Glock which out-balanced our differences', but because of the way in which 'the people in charge in the Sixties proved capable of accommodating, indeed desirously provoking, individual thought'.[90] Keller's constant ranging beyond his own job, his uncom-promising standards and his relentless questioning of everything the BBC was doing seemed to be warmly welcomed at that time. Glock was not the only one who thought that one of Keller's most important functions was 'to reform': Frank Gillard also recalled that 'one of the things I felt strongly about from time to time in my BBC days was that Keller ought to be turned loose to shake up everybody from religious broadcasting to light entertainment.' Leo Black thought that the ideal job for Keller would have been 'Questioner, Programmes, Radio'.[91]

This was in tune with the times, and there was a strong sense in the BBC of the 1960s that its purpose as an institution was to question rather than reflect

---

88 See Glock, annual reports on Keller's work, 5 May 1964 and 7 March 1966, WAC L1/1907/1.
89 Gillard to Keller, 9 January 1968, WAC L1/1907/1.
90 'Fare Better BBC', *Spectator* 242/7876 (30 June 1979): 29–30.
91 Gillard to Keller, 7 October 1972, WAC L1/1907/3. Black, *Music in the Glock Era and After* (London: Plumbago, 2010), 59.

established opinion, led by Director-General Hugh Greene who believed it a veritable 'duty' to be 'ahead of public opinion rather than always to wait upon it'.[92] Years later, Keller reflected on the importance of this doctrine in a letter praising 'Hugh Greene's BBC' sent to the editor of *The Listener* in October 1980. The letter was never published – in itself a sign of the way things had changed since the period it described:

> For the purpose [of being ahead of public opinion], individual thinkers, minds of 'sincerity and vision' (Greene's words), anti-collectivists, downright dissidents were appointed to important posts and quickly promoted to a level of considerable managerial responsibility: 'corporate loyalty', a much-used managerial phrase nowadays, would have been a dirty word, had anybody dreamt of using it.

> In fact, one almost felt that [Greene] admired one in proportion as one disagreed with him – and one's sense of responsibility was, of course, strengthened by what I would describe as his imaginative trust in one's disloyalty, which was expected to be constructive, to replace current policy with plans and methods that would enable one, and one's staff, 'to be ahead of public opinion'.

> To work in the BBC in his decade was, as a result, sheer paradise, and one knew it at the time – when I coined the phrase 'the good young days' because I knew that once they were past, they would be recognised as the best old days ever – never ageing, ever new. And, sure enough, the ensuing decade regressed to the respectable public service impure and simple – which, at the start of the next decade, seems itself imperilled.

92 Greene, *The Conscience of the Programme Director* (London: BBC, 1965), 9.

The Time of My Life

Dear Jock,

Though we shall meet again, I feel the urge to thank you for your
quite exceptional attitude towards me – all the more exceptional since
you were in on my second, rather than my first decade, and while I
consider the BBC's attitude towards me in my first decade outstandingly
appreciative and realistic, prompting lasting and quite overwhelming
gratitude, I coolly and amiably regard the second decade's managerial
attitude as disgraceful – a chronic, albeit civilized, witch-hunt.

This is the opening of a letter Keller wrote in 1979 on his retirement from the
BBC, to his long-suffering personnel officer, Assistant Head of Radio Personnel
Jock Beesley. It is one of hundreds of letters and memoranda between the two
men during Keller's difficult second decade with the Corporation. By all accounts
Keller and Beesley got on famously at a personal level – and both even rather
enjoyed the intellectual challenge of the intricate legal and procedural questions
thrown up by Keller's various disputes with his employer. Keller's personnel files
in the BBC's archives are enormous – but the excessive paperwork dates exclusively from the 1970s. 'I'd win a handsome bet if you accepted it,' wrote Keller
in 1979 to the then Managing Director of Radio (who had laid the blame for
their disputes on Keller's 'dissenting personality') 'to find me a single example of
Kellerian dissent in the BBC between 1959 and 1969.'[1] He would have won the
bet, as the 'Kellerian dissent' that so infuriated the management of the 1970s is
conspicuous by its absence from the files of the 1960s.

'Did I change personality at the turn of the decade, or did we?' asked Keller,
secure in his own mind that it was 'we', the Corporation, whose nature had
altered so abruptly. The turning point, as he saw it, was the publication on 10
July 1969 of *Broadcasting in the Seventies*, the document in which the BBC
outlined its plans for a radical restructuring of radio, including the abolition of
the Third Programme and the streamlining of the networks, with Radios 1, 2,

---

1 Keller to Aubrey Singer, 5 January 1979, CULHK.

3 and 4 programmed generically as 'pop', 'light', 'classical' and 'talk'. For so slight a document – it ran to only thirteen pages – it provoked an extraordinary storm of protest. (Keller later dubbed it 'a major exhibit in the evidence of the decline of the West'.[2]) The story of *Broadcasting in the Seventies* and Keller's personal involvement in the controversy that followed has been told in detail elsewhere,[3] but in short, what ruined Keller's relationship with the Corporation's senior management was first that he was the major instigator of a public protest by the BBC's own producers, and second – and probably more significant – that he refused ever to give up the argument.

In one sense, the battle Keller fought in the 1970s had been lost even before he arrived at the BBC in 1959, for the arguments used to axe the Third were the same as those that had led to the cutting of its hours in 1957. And the shift from mixed to generic programming had also been heralded years before – as *Broadcasting in the Seventies* pointed out: 'Already BBC radio has moved in this direction, first with the Music Programme, then with the all-pop Radio One.'

Nevertheless, *Broadcasting in the Seventies* did mark a turning-point and there are good reasons why it appeared to Keller and others at the time that the BBC had suffered 'an abrupt change of corporate personality'.[4] First was the relative secrecy in which the plans had been prepared. The unprecedented revolt by the BBC's producers was provoked in part by the simple fact that they had not been consulted – a genuine shock to those used to working under Hugh Greene's anti-authoritarian rule. Greene himself was now on his way out. The appointment of Charles Hill as Chairman of the Governors in 1967 had heralded a new managerial style and one sign of the changing times was that the small group responsible for *Broadcasting in the Seventies* was (as the document itself stated) 'assisted by McKinsey & Co.' rather than by the BBC's own staff.

But the main reason why *Broadcasting in the Seventies* was seen as so important was because it signalled so clearly the final abandonment of the high ideals of public education and cultural patronage expressed first by Reith and then even more strongly by William Haley after 1945. The ending of the Third Programme – a service 'conceived in war as an act of faith', as a BBC staff member once movingly described it[5] – was a profoundly symbolic act, made all the more significant by the prosaic language of *Broadcasting in the Seventies'* failure to convey any understanding of what was being lost. In its conclusion, summing up the losses and gains of the proposed new policy, the only reference to the demise of Haley's extravagant ambition to 'enable the intelligent public to hear the best that has been thought or said or composed in all the world' was that 'a few may regret a shift of emphasis in Radio Three in the evening.' Apart from a couple of paragraphs

2 'The BBC', *Spectator* 243/7888 (15 September 1979): 18–20.

3 See Asa Briggs, *History of Broadcasting in the United Kingdom* vol.5: *Competition* (Oxford: Oxford University Press, 1995), 719–810, and *HKBBC*, 149–73.

4 Keller, 'Fare Better, BBC', *Spectator* 242/7876 (30 June 1979): 29–30.

5 Unsigned undated memorandum to the Director of Sound Broadcasting, written at the time of Marriott's review, WAC R34/1022/3.

on the cuts to be made in the high cost of music broadcasting, the arts were mentioned nowhere in the document, nor did it betray any sense that radio might be important to the cultural life of the nation. Cultural broadcasting was described simply as 'programmes for minorities' and the purpose of radio as 'a continuous supplier of music and information'. In stark contrast to the open and undirected nature of Haley's original vision for the Third ('let it remember always that it is an experiment, even an adventure'), the policy of *Broadcasting in the Seventies* was that 'ends must be tailored to means.'

There was no room in all this for a 'Questioner, Programmes, Radio'. Indeed William Glock, who had used Keller's questioning mind to such remarkable effect to open up and reform music broadcasting at the beginning of the decade, was now advising him to leave. Glock's position as Controller meant he had clear sight of the direction in which the BBC's priorities were shifting, with increasing resources directed to television – and, in radio, towards a new network of local radio stations with which the BBC hoped to counter the commercial radio that was almost certain to follow the election of a Conservative government.[6] Money needed to be saved elsewhere and the high cost of the Third Programme made it an obvious target. Replacing live music with a greater use of recordings was another way in which the BBC could cut its costs, and for the first time it questioned explicitly its role as music patron: 'The licence income is supposed simply to finance broadcasting,' stated *Broadcasting in the Seventies*. 'How far should it sustain a level of musical patronage beyond the immediate needs of broadcasting?'

It was therefore announced that the BBC would seek to disband or secure alternative funding for several of its house orchestras and negotiate with the unions a large increase in 'needletime' (its use of gramophone records). The future of the BBC Scottish Symphony Orchestra, the Northern Dance Orchestra, the London Studio Players, the BBC Chorus, the Concert Orchestra, the Welsh Orchestra, the Northern Ireland Orchestra and the BBC Training Orchestra were all now in doubt, and although negotiations were opened with the Arts Council for possible reprieve, it was obvious that the creative opportunities available to Keller as Chief Assistant, Orchestral and Choral, were rapidly shrinking. Glock could see nothing but frustration ahead for Keller and seems to have warned him some months before the publication of *Broadcasting in the Seventies*, when they met for Keller's routine annual review.

Keller was no fan of the Corporation's hierarchical staff assessment process (in which heads of department reported annually on those below them, via a written report followed by a formal interview), and in later years he refused to cooperate with it. This was to be the last occasion on which he and Glock went through the process in full, and they had a frank discussion about Glock's suggestion that it might be time to move on. In his written report Glock acknowledged

---

6 The Conservatives under Edward Heath were elected in June 1970 with commercial local radio as part of their manifesto. The resulting Sound Broadcasting Act became law in the summer of 1972 and the first independent radio stations began broadcasting the following year.

the force of Keller's 'passionate' concern for the BBC, but added 'I doubt if any-one of his intellectual ability can be fully satisfied as Chief Assistant (Orchestral and Choral).'[7]

21 January 1969 – to William Glock
BLWG MS Mus.954

Dear William,

Just because of my poor opinion of our reporting system, I want you to know how much I appreciate, not just the fact that your report was very favourable, but your insight into my situation – despite your not having been in touch with me to any extent: thank you.

On the other hand, I am shocked (if I may be playfully dramatic) at your view of what 'bright' chaps ought to do – not because it's wrong, but because it's schematic and treats two variables (the personality & the corporation) as constants. You know I like extreme examples. Just imagine William walking up to Kant one day & saying, 'That's enough of Königsberg now; you ought to get moving. If you stay here much longer, you'll get stale.'

The brightest brightness, brighter even than Omo,[8] is inside us. If our environment makes it grey instead of our whitening it —— well, my pity is limited.

Thank you again.

Yours,

Hans

Keller had now been Chief Assistant, Orchestral and Choral for eight years. He had taken on additional responsibilities – most notably the EBU concerts, which were widely applauded – but compared with the rapid promotions of his early years with the BBC, his career seems to have stalled. Most striking, perhaps, was that he had not been moved in the 1967 reorganisation of Music Division prompted by the retirement of two senior figures, Gerald Abraham and Eric Warr. Warr's post was allowed to lapse and Abraham's Assistant Controller job went to Lionel Salter. Salter said later that 'Hans was initially very chagrined, because he had wanted to take that job over, and I think that he felt that Glock had let him down on this.' However, 'the upper management – I'm not talking about Glock, but people above him – were very suspicious of Hans. . . . He was regarded as a hot-head.'[9]

7 Glock, report on Keller, 20 January 1969, WAC L1/1907/1.
8 'Omo' was a brand of washing powder, whose slogan was 'Omo adds Brightness'.
9 Salter, oral communication, 10 January 1996.

There is no evidence on file of Keller wanting the Assistant Controller position in 1967, but he had made an unsuccessful application for it back in March 1962, when the post was first created. His application form shows that the upper management's suspicion was already established – and that Keller was aware of it:

> My qualifications are known – as is a myth of slight mischievousness which tends to surround me in the minds of some of my colleagues in Broadcasting House who do not know me personally. At one or two removes, controlled exuberance, employed for the purpose of relaxed administration, is easily misunderstood. Given a chance, I shall be happy to destroy the myth.[10]

The idea of Keller moving to television may also have been revived in 1967. Again there is no application on file, but Keller later described himself and the record-producer John Culshaw (who came to BBC television from Decca) as rivals for the job. Reviewing Culshaw's memoirs later, Keller recalled him 'beating me to it at the post, where the two of us had been short-listed without having put in for the job'.[11] So *Broadcasting in the Seventies* may not have been the only reason why Glock advised Keller to leave in 1969. Despite what had been a successful first decade with the Corporation, there was now no way out in any interesting direction from the shrinking post in which Keller was now stuck.

The main source of the 'myth of mischievousness' that dogged Keller even in the early 1960s was probably 'The Strange Case of Piotr Zak', broadcast in 1961:

5 June 1961 – *Mobile* by Piotr Zak

> Piotr Zak is one of the youngest and most controversial figures in contemporary music. He is of Polish extraction, and now lives in Germany. The strong influence of Kagel, Stockhausen and John Cage can be felt in his music, which he will not allow to be published, because he considers his scores as private instructions to the professional performer, which has certain renaissance parallels. 'Mobile' takes its name from the aerial sculptures of the American John Calder. It consists of an electronic tape, against which two percussion players play music written down, but giving scope for improvisation. The tape exploits the full range of the aural spectrum, controlled by strictly measurable quantities – frequency ratios, velocity graphs and decibel indexes. [. . .] The soloists CLAUDE TESSIER and ANTON SCHMIDT are coming to this country specially for the performance: they have already given the work in Europe.

---

10 Application form, 22 March 1962, WAC L1/1907/1.
11 'Football and Music', *LRB* IV/2 (February 1982): 23.

This was the press release that Keller had written to accompany the broadcast of an unknown work he had inserted at the last minute into a recorded Third Programme concert in which Bruno Maderna was conducting works by Petrassi, Webern, Nono and Mozart. It was in fact a hoax – or, as Keller insisted, a serious experiment. Zak, Tessier and Schmidt did not exist, and neither did the accompanying tape with its velocity graphs and decibel indexes. What was broadcast was simply Keller and Susan Bradshaw bashing about at random in a studio full of percussion instruments. 'I wanted to pose a problem,' explained Keller afterwards, in a broadcast discussion with Donald Mitchell and *Times* critic Jeremy Noble, both of whom had reviewed the 'work' in the press – 'How far would this kind of thing be taken seriously?'[12]

William Glock was not amused. While Keller insisted that the programme was a serious illustration of the crisis of communication in contemporary music – at no previous time in history could senseless noise ever have been mistaken for music – Glock feared it had done real damage to his attempt to widen the audience for modernism. From the beginning of Glock's serious engagement with the avant garde (around 1953, when he joined the ICA committee and the Summer School moved to Dartington), he had been convinced that music stood at a threshold. What was to come was unknown, so experimentation was legitimate and should be heard – as he had said in his first recorded statement to the ICA committee in 1953. According to the minutes:

> Mr Glock stressed that it was important for the Committee to define its attitude towards contemporary music. This was the beginning of a musical era, and there were two ways of contributing to music: first, the classical way, through the composer's own personal and imaginative needs, and secondly, the experimental way – certain groups of young composers were trying out certain ideas, and whatever the outcome they would make definite contributions to music which should be heard and discussed. . . . As far as the writing of music was concerned, it was progress rather than quality that was important.[13]

To Keller, on the other hand, music could never be other than a personal communication, dependent for its meaning on the individual character of its creator and on common terms of reference between composer and audience. It was the erosion of these common terms of reference – the background expectations which the composer evokes and then contradicts – that was the cause of the modern crisis of communication. 'Musical meaning', according to Keller, 'depends for its sheer existence on the clearly implied conflict between that which you hear and that which is being contradicted by what you hear. It is this tension, varying in intensity according to the structural juncture a composition has reached, between

---

12 'The Strange Case of Piotr Zak', Third Programme, 13 August 1961.
13 Minutes of the ICA meeting on 24 November 1953, copy in WAC R27/157/2.

what the composer does and what he makes you feel he was expected to do that constitutes musical logic.'[14]

~

In 1963 Glock went to Paris, where he heard a 'masterly and stirring' performance of *Wozzeck* at the Paris Opera, conducted by Pierre Boulez. This was the first time Glock had heard Boulez conduct a full orchestra – and he immediately invited him to London, to give four concerts with the BBC Symphony Orchestra the following year, including the first British performance of *Le Soleil des Eaux*. This series got off to an uncertain start – Boulez's first concert (an afternoon Sunday Symphony Concert in Worthing Assembly Hall) was not an ideal programme for him, and he felt 'like a waiter who keeps dropping the plates' accompanying Vladimir Ashkenazy in Chopin's Second Piano Concerto. But in his chosen repertoire of Webern, Stravinsky and Debussy 'he achieved marvels,' according to Glock. 'Especially in Webern, one felt as though the music were being imaginatively unfolded for the first time, so finely calculated were all the individual intensities and timbres and their connexion one with another.'[15]

In Boulez's readings of Debussy, what Glock called 'the magical interaction between composer and conductor' was even more intense, and he described a later performance of the *Trois Nocturnes* as bringing 'tears to the eyes with its unique combination of exactitude and an almost unbearable delicacy and sensuality of sound'. Keller, whose lack of response to Debussy and indeed to most French music was another difference between himself and Glock, was more interested to hear 'the impact of Boulez's mind on Schoenberg, and of Schoenberg's mind on Boulez' in the third concert of the series, which included Schoenberg's Four Orchestral Songs: 'their artistic personalities could hardly be more different.'[16]

After this visit, Boulez became the creative centre of Glock's work in his later BBC years, his legendary ear and exacting standards rekindling hopes of restoring the BBC Symphony Orchestra to something like its pre-war glory, despite Glock's failure to persuade the BBC's management to undertake a serious upgrading of the orchestra's pay. The government's 1966 pay freeze and subsequent economic constraints prevented the increases Glock saw as essential for the recruitment and retention of the best players – even before the arrival of the men from McKinsey. But the excitement of planning programmes with Boulez and the exhilarating sound he was able to draw from the players was considerable compensation – 'in working with him I nearly always felt elated, or (by my standards) prodigiously awake.'[17]

14 'Towards a Theory of Music', *Listener* 83/2150 (11 June 1970): 795–6, reprinted in *EOM*, 121–5.
15 Glock, *Notes in Advance* (Oxford: Oxford University Press, 1991), 134.
16 *RT* 162/2103 (27 February 1964): 6.
17 *Notes in Advance*, 138.

This was not something that Keller could really share. For all his admiration of Boulez's remarkable ear, he rarely enjoyed his performances of symphonic music – conscious of the lack of 'a musical *Gestalt*' and 'depressed by the crystal-clear audibility of subordinate parts or accompanimental figures that shouldn't really be heard all that obtrusively'.[18] Keller said and wrote little about his doubts, however, mindful of his own lack of sympathy with the French aesthetic. But after what he considered a 'disastrous' performance by Boulez of Schoenberg's *Moses und Aron* in December 1974, and further depressed by the collective enthusiasm by which he had been surrounded on the night, he gave considerable thought to how it was that a musician like Boulez could commit what he saw as such misunderstandings, and what, despite its brilliance, he found lacking in Boulez's own music.

1975 – The Crisis of Communication [extract]
1975, 200–202

Boulez is without identifiable harmonic backgrounds. Single combinations of notes, to be sure, he writes with great skill and persuasion: one would not deny him *chordal* backgrounds. What his music lacks is any sense of harmonic *movement*, with the result that from a vertical point of view, we are often presented with a catalogue of sonorities rather than a continuous evolution of vertical tensions and distensions.

I wouldn't make such a noise about this disability, were it not for the fact that in two ways, it is patently symptomatic of the harmonic chaos with which the composer of the late twentieth century is confronted, and its effects on him. In the first place, that is, it forces him to turn his back on the dynamic, kinetic function of harmony, to do things instead of moving harmonically in order to hold the attention – and Boulez is a veritable virtuoso, unequalled among contemporaneous practitioners, in doing things instead: there are catalogues and catalogues in this world, and some of them, very few, make you turn their pages despite the absence of cogent continuity. Even over extended stretches – and some of them might strike us as being too extended for structural comfort – Boulez is able to prevent us from leaving the hall. While he does not make us wonder about the consequences he is going to take, he does make us curious as to what is going to happen next, and never mind why: when you hear a fascinating sound, you want to hear another one. Many react like Boulez; few interest us in their reactions.

But in the second place, Boulez exposes the mortal danger, the paralysing effect of renouncing harmony that can in any way be regarded as functional, and so generates its own rhythm – which indeed used to be called 'harmonic rhythm' in tonal music. We can hardly assume that with his wonderful ear which penetrates, in rehearsal, the finesses of

18 *1975*, 202.

vertical combinations of sounds as easily as all other aspects of music in performance, Boulez was born without a sense of harmony. It is far more likely, I suggest, that he let this sense atrophy, because he didn't need it, didn't want it – because he needed, in fact, to deny harmonic reality.

The audible result of this atrophy is downright sensational, and must be obvious to any natural musician and music lover, even though he be totally out of touch with contemporary musical developments [. . .] : Boulez cannot phrase – it is as simple as that.

[. . .] His conducting of Bach, Beethoven or Wagner is absolutely identical: with all the precision and translucence he achieves, with all his so-called rhythm which is really metre, he does not bring about a single well-shaped phrase – the reason being that he ignores the harmonic implications of any structure he is dealing with, to the extent of utterly disregarding harmonic rhythm and hence all characteristic rhythm in tonal music.

Susan Bradshaw had played in that 1974 *Moses und Aron* performance. She rang Keller in his office next day, similarly depressed by the experience, and by the inexplicable enthusiasm of the rest of the performers. Bradshaw had studied with Boulez in Paris, and she and Richard Rodney Bennett had recently translated into English his 1963 book *Penser la musique aujourd'hui* (*Boulez On Music Today*) – which Faber & Faber brought out in paperback shortly after the *Moses und Aron* performance. Reading this, Keller started thinking about the parallels between Boulez's words and his music:

Boulez on Music Today [extract]
Unpublished draft

I [call] these ruminations 'studies', rather than a book. My reasons are two. First, there's the author's own inscription: 'These studies were written in Darmstadt for Darmstadt'. [. . .] Secondly, and more importantly – he's right: the three chapters are no more than studies – etudes in thought, as it were. Or, if they are more, they are concert studies, but they certainly don't amount to a consecutive, extended argument.

Thus, Boulez's creative character is mirrored, consistently and, yes, impressively so, in his reflective character: his music does not show any consistent forward drive either, no unambiguous diagonal impulse – and this is not meant critically. The music has to be heard for what it shows, not for what it doesn't. What I call diagonal power – prototypically, what happens in tonal, diatonic music – is the energy produced by harmonic tensions (basically, of course, by the bass), which urges towards melodic resolutions: a diagonal can, as it were, be drawn from a given point in the bass to the end of the melody.

In large-scale logical thought, similarly, the energy engendered by apparent frictions between basic premises drives upwards, towards resolutions on the immediately perceptible surface level of the verbal edifice. No such drives for Boulez! No foreseeing, no anticipating the end at the beginning; mere continuity from point to point is extremely slim, and in no way dependent on a basic idea <u>perceptibly</u> dominating the entire thought-structure, be it conceptual or musical. The way Boulez' mind naturally works is in terms of creating a catalogue of ideas – which are not, of course, disconnected or unrelated to an overall plan (catalogue entries never are), but which merely <u>lead</u> from one to the next, rather than <u>forcing</u> the recipient to proceed in one particular direction, or else not at all. His catalogues could, therefore, conceivably be arranged in a different order, and the individual ideas would make equal sense – as would, indeed, their arrangement. [. . .]

Both in his approach to musical language and to verbal language, Boulez is heedless of the laws that govern comprehensibility: I submit that all understanding stands or falls with the percipient's ability to refer to his past experience – whether this is confirmed or contradicted by what is to be understood. But Boulez's understanding of the past is so fragmentary, his hostility towards past and past-consciousness so emotional, that he feels compelled to erect a whole system of musical and verbal thought in which notes and words are invested with meanings they have never carried before – nor do they definedly contradict the meanings they have carried before: hence the confusion. It is a hopeful confusion, however, because there is, at the same time, this continual yearning for clarification.

~

By the time of *Broadcasting in the Seventies*, William Glock was due to retire from the BBC, having passed its statutory retirement age of sixty the previous year. Given his advice to Keller, one might have thought he would have been happy to leave the BBC himself before the gathering storm clouds could do their worst. But Glock remained at the helm of Music Division throughout the row over *Broadcasting in the Seventies* and its uncomfortable aftermath. The reason was Boulez – for in 1968 the coincidence of two unexpected operatic events had opened up one last revitalising opportunity for Glock before he retired. Colin Davis, Chief Conductor of the BBC Symphony Orchestra, was invited in 1968 to take over at Covent Garden when Georg Solti's contract expired in 1971. At the same time the Paris *événements* caused the collapse of the grand reform plans at the Paris Opéra, with which Boulez was deeply involved. Glock seized the opportunity to

Hans Keller's Fare Better and Better *for implied piano and string quartet. Composed for the retirement of William Glock in December 1972 (CULHK Add Mus 9371/26).*

persuade Boulez to succeed Davis at the BBC and 'reform London's musical life' instead. Boulez would agree only if Glock were still there for his first season, so Glock stayed on until the end of 1972, 'exhilarated' but also 'somewhat conscience-stricken at distracting him from his work as a composer'. In fact, Boulez took on the New York Philharmonic as well – and Keller wondered whether 'his intense re-creative activities may be indicative of a creative crisis.'[19]

It was therefore Glock, rather than his successor, who was faced with the task of reorganising Music Division to fit the demands of the new Radio 3. Unlike the musically driven structure he had designed on his arrival, the Music Division that emerged in 1971 was heavily overshadowed by *Broadcasting in the Seventies*, to the extent that it is unclear how far the result accorded with Glock's wishes, or with those of his senior colleagues in Broadcasting House. One factor seems to have been the matter of who did and who did not sign a certain infamous letter to *The Times* of 14 February 1970 – the letter that marked the climax of months of internal battling by the BBC's production staff against the changes proposed in *Broadcasting in the Seventies*. The protest had been led by a group of six: Hans Keller, Robert Simpson and Deryck Cooke from Music, Lord Archie Gordon (Talks), Hallam Tennyson (Drama) and Leslie Stokes (who with George Barnes and Etienne Amyot was one of the original triumvirate who ran the Third Programme at its opening). These six had co-ordinated very effectively the fury of their colleagues, but were still unable to wrest more than minor concessions from a management determined that there should be no alternative to the plans they had announced. After the details of the new schedules were presented in the *Listener* in January 1970 and Director-General Charles Curran refused the six leaders' request to meet the BBC Governors – 'the dissentient group's views were well-known to the Board'[20] – Keller and his colleagues felt they had no option but to make known to the public the nature and extent of their opposition to the direction the BBC was taking.

'Our letter had been prepared in surreptitious haste,' recalled Stokes, who only just made it out of Broadcasting House in time with the precious piece of paper, on which were gathered as many signatures as they could get without attracting attention. 'When I was in Printing House Square, delivering the letter, another of the group of six instigators was called into the office of one of our "superiors", who had caught wind of it'.[21] 134 producers had managed to sign, and this initial letter was followed by more multi-signature letters to *The Times* from producers in the regional centres and the Association of Broadcasting Staff, plus former members of staff and many famous names from the arts and academia. What to do with rebels in such numbers was a problem, so Ian Trethowan, Managing Director

19 Glock, *Notes in Advance*, 140. Keller, 'Boulez', in *Sunday Times* '1000 Makers of the Twentieth Century', 15 June 1969.
20 See: *Listener* 83/2129 (15 January 1970): 81–4. Minutes of the Board of Management, 16 February 1970, WAC R2/23/1.
21 Unpublished letter to *The Times*, 16 August [1980], CULHK.

Radio, concentrated on the six leaders, writing a mild warning to the rest. Keller recalled (in print) his own meeting with Trethowan:

> The leaders of the rebellion were individually summoned before radio's boss: "If this were the Gas Board", he made a show of containing himself in my presence, "you'd be sacked tomorrow". "Sack me then, I don't want any favours", was my amiable reply. He didn't. Why not? The reader shouldn't find the real answer difficult.[22]

After this, the six initiated no more multi-signature letters to the press, but they were not about to give up the internal argument. Though the Third Programme was no more, they tried to mitigate the effects of the new policy in any way they could. They remained together, became known as 'the Group', expanded their numbers and took upon themselves the role of unofficial watchdog of the new schedules. They were still operating at the time of the Annan Committee on the Future of Broadcasting (1974–77), whose final report noted that of all the evidence it had received, 'the strongest criticism of generic programming came from a group of BBC Radio producers'.[23]

Although the Group tried to be constructive in its criticism, and was responsible for some useful practical initiatives, it was seen by the management as a toxic influence, perpetuating a damaging division among the Corporation's staff. Robert Ponsonby, who arrived to take over from Glock as Controller of Music nearly three years after the letter to *The Times*, couldn't believe the strength of feeling still persisting:

> I can remember walking down a corridor in my first few months with Ian Trethowan, and people walking ahead and Ian [pointing them out,] saying, 'Gould – he didn't sign the letter; Keller did' . . . The pain and poison lasted a very long time.[24]

It is therefore hardly surprising that the two main Chief Assistants in Music Division, one of whom had led the protest while the other had kept out of it, received very different treatment in the restructuring that followed.[25] Their posts of Chief Assistant (Orchestral and Choral) and Chief Assistant (Chamber Music

---

22 'From the Third Programme to Radio 3', *M&M* (December 1984): 15.
23 *Report of the Committee on the Future of Broadcasting* (Cmnd. 6753, 1977), 83, para. 8.12.
24 Robert Ponsonby, oral communication, 14 July 1995.
25 There were two other Music Division staff at Chief Assistant level in 1970 (Light Music Section having now been abolished): Harry Croft-Jackson (Music Programmes Organisation) and Brian Trowell (Opera). They had both signed the *Times* letter and both left the BBC at this point (Croft-Jackson retired and Trowell went into academia). After he left, Trowell continued his criticism of *Broadcasting in the Seventies* and on 14 April 1972 gave a lecture on the subject to the Royal Musical Association. Keller arranged for Trowell's lecture to be followed by a live debate on Radio 3, but Controller Stephen Hearst put a stop to the broadcast after hearing Trowell's RMA lecture; see Hearst to Keller, 14 April 1972 and Trowell, 'Music and Broadcasting,' *Music and Musicians* 20/10 (June 1972): 34–43.

and Recitals) were abolished and the two production groups were brought together into one unit. To manage the new united group Maurice Johnstone's old post of Head of Music Programmes was resurrected and given to Peter Gould. Keller was given the function of 'correlating and developing the repertoires and performance standards of the Regional symphony orchestras' (what was left of them).[26]

Keller's reaction to this was characteristic. He did not leave, he does not appear to have complained – indeed he even put a positive spin on the move, telling regional musicians that it was partly 'because he felt so strongly about the necessity to develop the regional orchestras within a more realistic and respectful organisational context that he had been appointed to his present job'.[27] He took the job seriously – as ever – but he did it in his own way, added to it a great deal of other work he had not been invited to do, and continued doggedly to push the BBC in the direction he thought it should go.

But it was an uncomfortable situation, and those above him in the Corporation's hierarchy seem to have avoided trying to manage Keller after his sidelining, or to define his new role very closely, so that a gulf quickly opened between his 'official' post and what he was actually doing. The initial job description drawn up for the post of 'Chief Assistant, Regional Symphony Orchestras' (C.A.R.S.O.) was extremely brief, and there appears to have been little clarification thereafter. Nor was there much taking stock: Glock avoided writing any reports on Keller for three years after *Broadcasting in the Seventies*, and when an exasperated Jock Beesley finally managed to extract something from him (a single report covering 1970, 1971 and 1972), Glock pleaded 'it is difficult to write a straightforward report on Keller, because his worth and his activities cannot be adequately related to any known job or post in the BBC.' He reported that the Regional Orchestras post was working well – but was clearly not enough to occupy Keller:

> I would not pretend that his new functions, plus his role as chief activator of the E.B.U. concert seasons (the latest prospectus is the best I have seen), come anywhere near to exhausting his intellectual energy. Much is left for writing, arguing, dictating of memos on a truly remarkable scale, and the defending of causes that are of passionate concern to him. When, one day, he leaves the BBC Music Division it will almost certainly become too comfortable for a while. It won't be so much a matter of programmes as of a general undertow of thought and criticism of which everyone is aware, and which is invaluable in helping to keep the place alive and more self-questioning than might otherwise be the case.[28]

Howard Newby added his own appreciation of 'Mr Keller's highly individual contribution to broadcasting' but added that the extra work Keller was doing

26 There is a parallel here with Glock's sidelining of Maurice Johnstone in 1959 – one of his early drafts for the restructuring of Music Division has Johnstone 'perhaps co-ordinating regional programmes'. 'Proposed re-organisation of Music staff', 8 September 1959, WAC R49/981/1.

27 Minutes of the BBC Welsh Orchestral Committee, 13 June 1972, WAC R172/9/3.

28 Glock, annual report, 18 May 1972, WAC L1/1907/1.

beyond his job description 'is a reproach to us organisationally. It should be regularised.'[29]

Newby's principal concern was Keller's co-ordination of daytime music talks. The Music Talks Producer (now Robert Layton) traditionally provided talks only for the evening Third Programme; when the daytime Music Programme went on air it was unclear who should be responsible for what happened in its concert intervals. An informal practice grew up of music producers arranging talks themselves for the concerts they produced, but the lack of editorial control (and the increasing number of on-air staff contributions) began to be a problem. Keller had retained a keen interest in talks from his own talks-producing days and was full of ideas for the imaginative combination of words and music. Since most of the intervals to be filled were in orchestral concerts (thus falling within his section) it was natural for him to take charge of their co-ordination. When Radio 3 arrived, the daytime/evening split continued, with Robert Layton's activities confined to the evening and Keller in clear but unofficial charge of the daytime, in which there were now several hundred music talks a year.

The longer the situation remained unresolved, the more it became infected by the rancour over *Broadcasting in the Seventies*, since the balance of music and talk on Radio 3 was now a hot political issue. Just how highly charged things had become can be seen, for example, in the wording of Peter Gould's description of the problem to incoming Controller Robert Ponsonby: 'Come Broadcasting in the Seventies,' he wrote, 'dissident elements decided to infiltrate daytime music broadcasting on Radio 3 with talks on music in the intervals of two-part programmes.'[30] While it is not true that daytime talks had only started after *Broadcasting in the Seventies*, it is true that their number had greatly increased, and it began to be suggested that Keller was putting the department under strain as a result of his enthusiasm for talk.

Related to this issue was that of 'staff contributions' – broadcasting by music producers themselves. The BBC was keen not to be seen to take work away from outside experts, and concerns about the number of appearances by music producers on air were raised in 1966 and regularly thereafter.[31] The increase was caused by the pressure for output following the launch of the Music Programme, and the difficulty of finding enough good external speakers compared with the talent available in house at the time. Keller was not the only frequent broadcaster (Deryck Cooke, Robert Simpson and Basil Lam were also regular contributors), but it was partly to curb the number of his broadcasts that a rule was introduced stipulating that 'no member of staff should undertake more than six broadcasts of more than five minutes in length in any one year'.[32] Keller continually overstepped these limits, and by the early 1970s could do so in a single broadcast, since Radio 3 was

29 Newby, annual report, 22 May 1972, WAC L1/1907/1.
30 Gould to Ponsonby, 19 December 1972, WAC L1/1907/3.
31 See Standing to Glock, 20 September 1966, WAC R34/1034/2.
32 Salter to Beesley, 19 August 1970, WAC L1/1907/3. Keller's recollection was that 'William's directive was 'six – not a magic number – up to eight' – see note dated 15 February 1973, WAC L1/1907/3.

now transmitting some of the hour-long lectures he was giving at music festivals around the country – such as 'Originality and Influence' at the 1971 Aldeburgh Festival and 'The String Quartet at its Greatest' at the Cheltenham Festival the same year. BBC managers were divided between their admiration for Keller as a speaker – 'I listened to [him] absolutely spellbound' admitted Radio 3 Controller Stephen Hearst – and frustration – 'How presumptuous can he be allowed to be?'[33]

Keller's insistence that the limits were not his responsibility since he didn't initiate his own broadcasts – 'I did what I was asked to do if I was interested, but am quite happy if I am not asked to do anything' – cut no ice and the arguments rumbled on for years without solution. The issue of the co-ordination of daytime talks, on the other hand, exploded in spectacular fashion on 17 June 1972 over a single phrase in a twenty-minute talk given by the avant-garde composer Cornelius Cardew, broadcast in the interval of a Monday afternoon concert at the Aldeburgh Festival. Cardew had been invited to discuss Stockhausen's *Refrain* (performed in the second half of the concert), of which he had given the first performance in 1959. Since then, however, Cardew had become disenchanted with Stockhausen and in recent months had been converted to the Maoist ideology that would shortly lead to his withdrawal from avant-garde music altogether. For the moment, however, he and his Scratch Orchestra were still scheduled to perform at the Proms on 24 August 1972 the first two paragraphs of his setting of Confucius: *The Great Learning* – its texts specially re-translated by Cardew to reflect his new political thinking (though in the end the BBC insisted that the Maoist slogans be removed, lest they set off demonstrations in the Albert Hall).[34]

Two days before its broadcast, the first half of Cardew's talk on *Refrain* was published in *The Listener* under the title 'Stockhausen Serves Imperialism', causing much controversy in the correspondence columns. Robin Maconie and Peter Britton sought to defend Stockhausen and Victor Schonfield supported Cardew – while Colin Matthews called a plague on both their houses: 'what the two of them have in common is music of blinding irrelevance to any social order, past, present or future.'[35] According to *Radio Times*, Cardew's subsequent Radio 3 talk was expected to 'look at "Refrain" in relation to other German music of this century'. But Cardew, hurriedly writing the rest of his talk the day before the recording, changed his mind: 'I experienced a real dislike for contributing to the already proliferous documentation of the work. I decided to tackle the subject from a wider viewpoint' – which meant a four-page exposition of Marxist theory.[36] Even this would probably not have done more than raise eyebrows in its context: the real problem came in his conclusion:

---

33 Hearst, oral communication, 4 November 1996; and Salter to Glock, 28 January 1972, WAC L1/1907/3.

34 See Tim Souster, 'The Great Learning', *Listener* 2264 (17 August 1972): 218, and Newby to Trethowan, 24 August 1972, WAC R101/302/1.

35 'Stockhausen serves Imperialism', *Listener* 2255 (15 June 1972): 809, reprinted in Cardew, *Stockhausen Serves Imperialism* (London: Latimer, 1974).

36 Note written by Cardew on the script of his talk preserved in WAC.

I've exposed the true character of the piece as part of the superstructure of imperialism. I've shown that it promotes a mystical world outlook which is an ally of imperialism and an enemy of the working and oppressed people of the world. If in the light of all this it still retains any shred of attractiveness, compare it with other manifestations of imperialism today: the British army in Ireland, the mass of unemployed, for example. Here at least the brutal character of imperialism is evident. Any beauty that may be detected in Refrain is merely cosmetic, not even skin-deep.

It was the words 'the British army in Ireland' that lit the blue touchpaper as Director-General Charles Curran listened on his car radio in Aldeburgh. It was the peak of the Troubles, ten weeks after the British government had suspended the parliament in Stormont, imposing direct rule for the first time in fifty years. Nearly 500 people died in 1972, the bloodiest year of the conflict. Cardew's talk was broadcast the day after the death of John Johnson, from injuries inflicted on Bloody Sunday five months before. The next day three British soldiers were killed by an IRA bomb in County Down.[37] This explains why these few words at the end of a Monday afternoon Radio 3 interval talk were so incendiary.

Because of the last-minute nature of the broadcast, Keller had not seen the complete script. Elaine Padmore, the producer who recorded it (three days before transmission) had asked him to review an earlier section, but he had not read the rest of the talk, so failed to notice the reference to Ireland. It was a disaster – as one of Keller's colleagues at the time recalled, 'he was very nearly sacked for that.'[38] Howard Newby conducted a formal disciplinary investigation – 'a sterile, time-robbing, Kafka-like operation,' thought Keller, who of course argued that the unresolved issue of who was supposed to be in charge of daytime talks was at least partly responsible for the debacle: 'I put it to Mr. Newby that the "organisational defects" to which he refers, and which in my submission were at the root of the trouble under discussion, were his responsibility.'[39]

This was not the only disciplinary process that Keller went through in that summer of 1972. Little over a week after the Cardew broadcast, another serious issue erupted. 'I have just become aware,' wrote Newby to Glock, 'that C.A.R.S.O. has been conducting meetings with the orchestral committees of the BBC Welsh Orchestra, the BBC Northern Symphony Orchestra, and the BBC Scottish Symphony Orchestra [and] that these meetings have discussed matters of high managerial policy.'

At the time when we are conducting delicate negotiations with the Union it passes my comprehension how C.A.R.S.O. could conduct discussions of this nature and have them formally minuted. He has considerably irritated the

37 http://cain.ulst.ac.uk/othelem/chron/ch72.htm (accessed 30 March 2018).
38 Stephen Plaistow, oral communication, 27 July 1995.
39 Keller, 'Amendments to D.P.R.'s Record of Interview on July 19', WAC L1/1907/3.

Musicians' Union, harmed our relations with them, and postponed indefinitely the enlarging of the Welsh Orchestra. He must be stopped from discussing managerial issues of this importance with orchestral committees and formally reprimanded.[40]

Newby had just seen the minutes of a meeting that Keller had held a fortnight earlier with the BBC Welsh Orchestral Committee, and had been dismayed to read in them a direct quotation from a memo written to Keller by Newby's predecessor as Director of Programmes, Radio, Gerard Mansell. The issue was the augmentation of the orchestra's string section, and the minutes quoted Mansell's memo reassuring Keller that, one way or another, the BBC would find the money.[41] The trouble was that the reassurance Keller quoted was eight months old, and there had been many changes since then of which he was unaware. Negotiations with the Arts Council and the Musicians' Union over the orchestra's funding were now at a delicate stage, and the Mansell memo (which, courtesy of the minutes, quickly leaked) contradicted the BBC's more recent statements that there was no chance of internal money becoming available.

It seems extraordinary that someone of Keller's experience should not have foreseen the possible consequences of giving reassurances about money to regional orchestras after *Broadcasting in the Seventies*. That he did not shows how isolated he now was from the real decision-making and how far his conception of his responsibilities differed from that of the management. He insisted that the crisis was 'due to my being kept totally uninformed about negotiations then in progress', asking why he had been told so little, given how long and hard he had been campaigning for the orchestra's augmentation. 'The BBC Welsh Orchestra has been, for some considerable time, an orchestra in distress,' he insisted; 'the string augmentation is an absolute priority not only from the artistic point of view, but also from that of sheer humanity.' He refused to accept the financial argument: 'In my submission, the money can be made available without undue difficulty: my saving experiment was conducted in order to show this fact to be true, and it has done so.'[42]

Yet another dispute was over Keller's secretarial staffing. He was one of very few senior staff to have more than one secretary, and it was now decided that this was not justified by his job description. Keller and his secretaries started keeping detailed logs of their work, and had little difficulty showing themselves to be more than fully occupied. The question was, of course, what they were occupied with. Most of Keller's senior colleagues would have been more than happy to see his productivity decline. 'The mere cost of the secretarial effort [caused by] Hans would have gone into thousands of pounds,' remembered Radio 3 Controller

---

40 Newby to Glock, 28 June 1972, WAC L1/1907/3.
41 Minutes of the Welsh Orchestral Committee, 13 June 1972, WAC R172/9/3.
42 Keller to Newby and others, 2 February 1973, and to Glock and Newby, 16 August 1972, WAC L1/1907/3.

Stephen Hearst, 'because the memos had to be answered, and they were addressed with copies to everybody, and he'd pronounce on everything!'[43]

It must have seemed, during that summer of 1972 – as the disciplinary processes dragged on and Keller was temporarily banned both from overseeing talks and from visiting the Regions – that the battles would never end. Certainly Jock Beesley seems to have thought so, and he began to seek a way to achieve an amicable divorce. One potential solution lay in the 'constant war of attrition' over Keller's appearances on air. He was in such demand as a radio speaker that it would not be difficult to guarantee him a freelance income at least as big as his current salary. If he could be persuaded to leave the administrative staff, thought Beesley, all the problems would go away. Keller would be free to broadcast as often as he liked and Music Division would be free of a demanding presence that was no longer in tune with the times.

> Keller's repertoire is so wide that it would be difficult to control it in normal circumstances. Given a man of his temperament it is well nigh impossible. . . . He is a gifted musicologist, a witty and erudite speaker on the air, a lecturer who is in constant demand and, strangely enough, something of an authority on Football.
>
> Even with a possible re-drafting of S.I.211 it will always be difficult to bring Keller's contributions within the regulations. The difficulty of control will continue. These facts are allied to Hans Keller's own temperament. It is unlikely that he will ever be a serious contender for a Managerial post. His capacity for argument and indeed mischief, is considerable. Advancing years and perhaps a degree of frustration will aggravate the situation and there would be considerable advantages if he could at this stage be persuaded to a free-lance engagement.
>
> In financial terms Hans Keller would probably be better off and certainly we would have to gear his BBC remuneration and work to ensure he suffered no diminution in salary. . . . As Keller is practically at the top of the league this is unlikely to be difficult.[44]

What would be difficult, however, would be persuading Keller even to contemplate the idea. Beesley probably knew before he tried that he would never succeed.

On the evening of Monday, 2 October 1972, Keller left Yalding House with his colleague Julian Hogg, after working late. Hogg recalls that a senior BBC official

---

43 Hearst, oral communication, 4 November 1996.
44 Beesley to George Tree, Head of Personnel and Administration, Radio, 7 August 1972, WAC L1/1907/1.

was due to be interviewed on the news that night – Keller wanted to watch it, but it was now so late that he would not be able to get home to Hampstead in time. Hogg was then renting a flat round the corner in Great Portland Street, so invited Keller to watch the interview there. Quite what the interview was about is now forgotten, but what Hogg does remember clearly is what happened when he switched channels afterwards:

> It was a discussion programme. There was one man standing in the middle
> of a circle of accusers firing hostile questions at him, and he was answering
> them so calmly and rationally. Hans was transfixed.[45]

The programme was part of a BBC2 series called *Controversy* – 'in which scientists discuss controversial topics among themselves and with an invited audience'[46] – and the man being grilled was the American psychiatrist Thomas Szasz, Professor of Psychiatry at the State University of New York. A Jewish émigré from Budapest who had left Hungary at the age of eighteen in 1938, Szasz had become a controversial figure in psychiatric circles after the publication of his 1961 book *The Myth of Mental Illness* – which was the subject of the BBC2 programme Keller and Hogg stumbled across in 1972. Szasz contended that the concept of mental illness is more metaphor than disease and that in dealing with the problems of their patients, psychiatrists are not in reality concerned with illness and treatments: 'In actual practice they deal with personal, social, and ethical problems in living.'[47] The medicalization of these problems and their consequent removal from the spheres of ethics, law and personal responsibility was, in Szasz's view, dehumanizing and dangerous:

> *All truth distorts what we think is the truth.*

> In the past, fundamental false truths were religious in nature. Today, they are
> mainly medical in nature. . . . Many persons categorized as mentally ill are
> not sick, and depriving them of liberty and responsibility on the grounds of a
> nonexistent disease is a grave violation of basic human rights.[48]

After this broadcast Keller began to explore Szasz's writings and became very interested in his ideas, which had much in common with the individualism in his own thinking. But on the night when he first saw him on television, according to Hogg, it was not Szasz's ideas, so much as his courage under fire that struck such a chord with Keller: 'I sensed a sort of empathy.'

Keller quickly got in touch with Szasz and invited him to give a series of three talks for Radio 3, on 'Why Mental Illness is a Metaphor', 'Why Suicide should

45 Hogg, oral communication, 8 November 2017.
46 *Listener* 2267 (22 June 1972): 839.
47 *The Myth of Mental Illness* (London: Secker & Warburg, 1962), 296.
48 'Fifty Years After *The Myth of Mental Illness*', *The Psychiatrist* 35/5 (2011): 179–82.

be considered a Basic Human Right' and 'Why all Anti-drug Laws should be Repealed'. The first two were broadcast and repeated, but the third was suppressed by Stephen Hearst, who thought Szasz 'an original but immensely questionable thinker', urging Keller to 'spread the expert's net wider' and consider 'Rycroft, Jacques Lacan or Bruno Bettelheim' instead.[49] Szasz was nevertheless grateful to Keller for giving him the opportunity to be heard, and afterwards regularly sent him copies of his books and articles, which Keller read with keen interest. Keller responded with a few of his own writings (such as his wide-ranging 1971 piece on 'Music and Psychopathology'[50]), but what Szasz called his own musical illiteracy prevented any real discussion between them of Keller's core work.

There was much they could share, nevertheless – including some of the ethical questions arising from Keller's recent professional preoccupations:

29 April 1975 – to Thomas Szasz

Dear Professor Szasz,

Many thanks for your excellent paper on <u>The Moral Physician</u>. An important aspect of lying is what is called 'hiding the truth' when practised by the controlled, and 'confidentiality' and 'discretion' when practised by those in control. We know the concept of the 'white lie', but have not yet discovered the need to exonerate concealment by claiming 'white confidentiality' and 'white discretion'.

Kindest regards,

Yours sincerely,

(Hans Keller)

As Keller and Szasz delved into each other's ideas – and public battles – they discovered a close affinity, as Keller explained to John Crammer, of the Institute of Psychiatry at King's College:

6 February 1978 – to John Crammer

Dear John,

Like you I hugely enjoyed our dinner and, in particular, meeting you. My intellect was proportionately dismayed by your letter, even as my emotions appreciated your attitude. Two conclusions [. . .] seem to emerge:–

49 Hearst to Keller, 13 March 1974, CULHK.
50 *History of Medicine* III/2 (Summer 1971): 3–7, reprinted in *EOM*, 29–34.

(1) You need an essay of over 1500 words in order to demonstrate (as you think) to a psychiatrist that Szasz isn't worth talking about.

(2) You clinch your argument about what you call his continual 'intemperate language' by describing his argument as 'dishonest', 'journalistic', 'demagogic', 'mediaeval', and 'pre-scientific' – three of these five concepts being metaphors, and three identical with Szasz's own ideas about any psychiatry that goes beyond responding to an adult patient's request for help or advice in the problems of living. It remains to be remembered that the scientific world applied four of your metaphors to Freud when psychoanalysis first appeared upon the scene. [...]

You asked me why I was 'championing' Szasz. There is no championing. I speak with his a priori agreement (he and I have discussed the situation) when I say that intellectual loners that we are, we have been drawn together (an unprecedented event in our respective lives, as he pointed out) by a number of insights, independently achieved, which produced our 'elective affinity', as we both call it. Some of them you may have seen in my book. One of them you didn't – and since you say that 'the issues are, of course, what should be proper standards of kindness and care', I had better define it by way of leave-taking. Each of us thinks that there is far too much ill-motivated, irrational kindness in this world, and far too little rational respect and justice – with which civilization stands or falls. 'The proper standards of kindness' are not a public issue, but a personal problem. The public issue can never be anything else but human duties and human rights. I agree with Szasz's submissions on human rights, and he agrees with mine on the primacy of human duties: the issue of human rights arises secondarily, when something has gone wrong, as when you tolerate compulsory treatment.

Kindest regards,

Yours,

(Hans Keller)

Despite all they had in common, Keller was not uncritical of Szasz. One of their biggest areas of disagreement – which first emerged when Keller reviewed Szasz's 1977 book *Karl Kraus and the Soul Doctors* – was over Freud:

Freud and anti-Freud [extract]
Spectator, 28 May 1977, 19

When the common intellectual reader dislikes a thinker, he accuses him of repeating himself — Freud ever since *The Interpretation of Dreams*, Szasz ever since *The Myth of Mental Illness*. When the common intellectual likes a thinker, however, he blames him for not repeating himself —for developing his views far beyond what the reader had come to cherish. The idiot has a point, of course, both ways. If Freud had died after *The Interpretation of Dreams*, the job he alone could do would have been done; yet, what he discovered later dated the dream book. If Szasz had died after *The Myth*, the job would have been done, but the crusader against crusades, especially creeping crusades, against 'the ostensibly, value-neutral languages of the "sciences"', would never have fully emerged.

> This attempt to . . . deny valuation is, for obvious reasons, especially important and dangerous in psychology, psychiatry, psychoanalysis, and the so-called social sciences. Indeed, one could go so far as to say that the specialised languages of these disciplines serve virtually no other purpose than to conceal valuation behind an ostensibly scientific and therefore nonvaluational semantic screen.

This book's 'noble rhetorician' is Kraus, the unerring critic of concealed linguistic devaluation; its 'base rhetorician' is Freud, the practitioner of the craft: the white-and-black story develops as simply as that, like a Western – of which Szasz may well be inordinately fond, if I know anything about his naivety, whose devastating charm is proportionate to the intellectual intensity behind it, and its ethical integrity too.

Matters moral, however, are not as simple as that – even though Szasz is right in intimating that they are simpler than the common intellectual's obscurantism would make them appear. [. . .] In trying to establish an ethical polarity between Kraus and Freud, Szasz overrates Kraus the artist as generously as he gravely underestimates Freud the discoverer. But in the two central purposes of his book, he succeeds with his characteristic independence of thought and observation. For one thing, that is, he destroys the psychoanalytic myth about the Freud–Kraus relationship, while for another, he establishes Kraus as a penetrating critic of the psychiatric and psychoanalytic devaluation of ultimate human values – or, to pinch psychoanalysis's own magic term, of 'reality'. [. . .]

The trouble is that the Westerner won't solve the story – that Freud was not only greater as a discoverer than Kraus was as an artist, but, in my view, greater as an artist too. Szasz accepts a critic's verdict that Kraus's style is 'the most brilliant in modern German literature,' but compared to the style of Freud, the recipient of the Goethe prize for Literature in 1930, it well nigh vanishes into insignificance. Freud's style could not have been beautiful without being dignified and indeed truthful; that, at the same time, he 'pointed the way to the theory and practice of psychoanalytic character assassination' is a fact which Szasz demonstrates with unyielding logic. Do read him.

Although he felt Szasz was underrating Freud's achievement, Keller was nevertheless taken with some of his criticisms of psychoanalysis – most notably the idea that it had repressed the concept of power, a repression Szasz considered to be currently much more dangerous than that of infantile sexuality.[51] But Keller was still dissatisfied with the picture of Freud that emerged in Szasz's next book, of which Szasz sent him an advance copy the following year:

31 March 1978 – to Thomas Szasz [extract]

Dear Tom,

Many thanks for yours of March 21. It isn't me to whom you have to apologise for your (or anybody else's) unconscious, but yourself – which brings me straight to The <u>Myth of Psychotherapy</u>: I have not only received it, but read it carefully. As expected, it is outstanding, including its outstanding flaws: genuine psychoanalytic discoveries are being attacked without a shred of counter-evidence, and the proper place for your Freud-baiting would seem to be a diary rather than a book. Climaxes of unintentional comedy are reached on several occasions, as when Freud is being blamed for being proud of being a Jew, while Jung is being placed above him ethically, his disgraceful anti-Semitic opportunism at the time of Hitler's advent being simply ignored.

All of which is not to say that the insights your new book offers far, far outweigh the preoccupations which marred the Kraus book. You agreed with me at the time, and no doubt you will agree again, and then proceed as before. If I remember aright, your case then was, that it was all "in a good cause", even though you are no doubt the first to say (or if not the first, a close second) that there is no such thing as the good evil you allow yourself to commit.

Szasz insisted that his arguments about Freud and his work were offered in good faith – and he questioned Keller's description of Jung's 'anti-Semitic opportunism'.

51 See *1975*, 11.

3 May 1978 – to Thomas Szasz

Dear Tom,

> 'Berühmten Leuten wird gemeiniglich
> viel Böses nachgesagt, gleichviel, ob aus
> wahrhaftigem Grunde oder nicht.'[52]

> E.T.A. Hoffmann, Signor Formica

> 'With Tom Szasz, it's a bit of both, which
> makes his all too spontaneous aggression
> none the less tragic – and all the more tragic
> for resulting in underestimation of his own
> monumental achievement.'

> From Hans Keller's charitably
> unwritten diary

Profound apologies for my belated reply to your letters of March 29 and April 11: I have hardly had any personal dictation time in recent weeks, having been at a conference in Stockholm, with business correspondence piling up.

[. . .] I am not condemning your criticisms of Freud in toto, but I object to (a) an underestimation of his achievement, and (b) to what I would describe, with my notorious tactlessness, as creeping character assassination.

Which brings me to Jung. I did not allude to his assuming the editorship of a German psychiatric journal in 1938, but to his first editorial – in which, by sheer chronological coincidence, he first discovered that what was wrong with psychoanalysis was that it was Jewish: this is what I am describing as 'public anti-Semitic opportunism'. Many years ago, in a public controversy with the Jungians, I went into this editorial in some hating detail.

But ultimately, whatever their respective virtues and vices, the prime requirement is a natural assessment of the stature of their respective discoveries: again, it is a matter of seeing things in proportion. Even you might agree that Freud's was not a particularly arrogant personality; at the same time, I think he made one of the most arrogant remarks ever formulated by a genius – which, it so happens, clearly establishes the proportions as I see them. Since the remark was made in private, you may not know it. He was once asked whether he did not admit that Jung, although basing himself on Freud's discoveries, had come to see a little further. 'The louse on the head of a giant sees further than the giant.'

---

52 'Much ill is commonly ascribed to famous people, regardless of whether or not it is true.'

I would not dream of denying the importance of religion and anti-Semitism in the history of psychoanalysis, but (as Szasz is the first to show) motivation is one thing, its evaluation another (and, in my opinion, a priori unjustifiable), and its results are a third thing, legitimately subject to evaluation. In any case, it seems to me that you are confusing Freud's attitude towards Judaism, which was ambivalent, and his attitude towards Jewishness, which wasn't. [. . .]

Your piece on Prescription for Control is magnificent.

Kindest regards,

Yours ever,

(Hans Keller)

~

On 23 September 1973 Keller and Cosman set off together on what was to be a most significant trip. Keller had been invited to visit Vienna, to speak at a pan-European congress organised by the Viennese IMZ International Centre for Music and Media, in celebration of 'Fifty Years of Music on Radio'.

19 September 1973 – Telex to Dr Gerhard Rindauer, IMZ

Here is the summary of my lecture, which will be freely delivered, without a script and without notes. It will fall into seven sections, each of them about four minutes long.

(1) The radio man's conscience: as a public servant who is in a largely, or wholly, monopolistic position, and whom the public keeps alive, he has to have a double loyalty – to his radio organisation on the one hand, and to the public on the other. If, in addition, his is a cultural area, there is a third loyalty – to the art, or science, or religion in question. Inevitably, that is to say, conflicts will ensue – not between his conscience and other forces in his mind, but within his conscience. The way he resolves these conflicting loyalties will show his ethical and intellectual maturity: in any case, he will have to remain alive to the need for self-criticism and, hence, for a constant critique of radio. "I am wonderful", or "We are wonderful" may be good enough for a clothing manufacturer, but not for a radio man.

(2) The basic critical question is what harm radio can do,
notwithstanding its readily demonstrable usefulness: "What would be
better without radio?" is the logical approach to this question.

(3) The answer need not be altogether academic, because there are
people who virtually live without radio, and highly cultured, creative
people to boot. If one knows them closely, one is struck, <u>ceteris
paribus</u>, by their better capacity for concentration, their absolute
single-mindedness when they listen, say, to a concert: they are not
used to hearing great music while doing their income tax.

(4) The conditions of instinctive concentration are the next step in
our investigation: spontaneous, instinctive concentration is the
<u>conditio sine qua non</u> of any successful artistic communication. And
the basic condition is the equally instinctive awareness of a unique,
unrepeatable experience – an awareness which both radio and the
gramophone (about which M. Aubert will be talking this afternoon)
tend to weaken and even obliterate.

(5) As a result – if I may remain within the area within which I am
professionally competent – a generation of musicians and music-
lovers has grown up which, on the whole, is no longer capable of the
type of exclusive concentration and instinctive memorising which,
a generation or two ago, was the order of the day, at any rate the
musical day. In my own boyhood, I knew a composer in this city who,
when one discussed music with him, whether it was a Bach Cantata,
a Haydn or late-Beethoven Quartet, or a Bruckner Symphony,
would walk to the piano and play the passage under discussion in an
instant piano arrangement, note-perfect. This was Franz Schmidt –
and, admittedly, his exceptional musicality might be regarded as an
extreme case. The fact remains that nowadays, equally exceptional
musicalities, if they have grown up with the radio, are quite incapable
of comparable feats.

(6) Amongst lesser musicalities, the dangers of radio have proved all but
mortal – and this even goes for professional musicians, the quality
of whose listening has degenerated to an extent which makes it
impossible for them to listen without doing something else at the
same time in order to fully to occupy their attention. One of the
greatest living performers, who happens to be a close friend of mine,
is not even always prepared to listen to himself: he practises certain
passages of great music while watching a football match on television,
with the sound turned off.[53]

---

53 Norbert Brainin (leader of the Amadeus Quartet).

(7) "With the sound turned off": this possibly gives us the clue, I think,
for turning my message of qualified despair into one of equally
qualified hope. If we can bring ourselves to learn and practise the
art of not listening to the radio, of turning it off, of regarding the
listening experience as something which has to be approached in
the same spirit as one's attendance at a concert, or indeed one's
own performance of a great piece of music: if one thus makes the
art of not listening promote the art of listening, radio can become
a cultural force of unprecedented potency. This is a matter not
only for the individual listener, but also for us radio people and
our consciences: it is up to us to construct programmes in a way
which turns background listening into a very difficult task, counters
the degeneration of the quality of listening and, perhaps, even
promotes further developments of the listening faculty.

Kindest regards,

HK

It was a major conference and Keller and Cosman stayed a whole week in
Vienna – the city that Keller had deliberately avoided for nearly thirty years after
he left in 1938. This was not the first time he had returned: that was in October
1967, when his EBU work had forced him back there briefly for a planning meeting. Cosman was with him on that occasion too, having travelled from Düsseldorf
(her pre-war home, where her parents had returned in 1949 and her mother still
lived) to meet Keller as he flew to Vienna from another meeting in Copenhagen –
her diary records her 'waiting in the hotel for H' and then 'out to Döbling'. Thus
Keller saw for the first time the site of his childhood home, burned down in 1945
when the Russian army entered the city. All that was left from his own time was
the fir tree planted when his sister was born.

That 1967 visit was only a brief one; Keller's return in September 1973,
however, was to become a deliberate act of remembrance. He seems to have
decided to take the opportunity of this visit for a mental as well as physical
return, and write a full account of the nine months between his nineteenth
birthday – the day the Nazis entered Austria – and his escape to London. To this
end, he and Cosman went to look at some of the places where it had all happened. They went back again to Döbling, to see again the site of Keller's family
home in Nusswaldgasse, where Keller remarked that the fir tree 'looked the
same in 1973 as it did in 1938'. They went to Leopoldstadt, the former Jewish
ghetto – 'that's a weird feeling indeed – to walk around there, identify places,
and realise at the same time that the vast majority of the former population has
meanwhile died in the gas chambers.' The Jewish Community Centre where
Keller had been arrested on 9 November 1938 was somewhere in Leopoldstadt,
though Keller found he had 'repressed the road'. The building in which he

had been imprisoned, the primary school in the Karajangasse, he found still standing, and the Prinz-Eugen-Palais adjoining the Belvedere Park, where he and other emigrating Jews were beaten up while queueing for their passport documents, was just round the corner from their hotel. 'The contrast between Milein's delight at the visual aspect of the Belvedere and the palace, and my vivid recollection of what used to happen to me on the pavement there (and how I used to look forward to reaching the relative safety of the entrance), was quite striking, and appreciated by both of us.'[54]

All the arguments at the BBC over the controlling of Keller's broadcasts (which, ironically, had now reached a climax[55]) seemed to fade into irrelevance in the face of the forty-five-minute talk he gave when he came back from that 1973 visit to Vienna. It was broadcast in the Radio 4 series *The Time of My Life*, a series which asked speakers to recount a particularly important event in their past. Keller recorded it ten weeks after his return from Vienna and its first broadcast went out on 3 February 1974. It was called, simply, 'Vienna, 1938'.[56]

For his BBC colleagues and for most of his friends, this was the first time they had ever heard Keller talk about what had happened to him under the Nazis. They were stunned – more than anything else by the 'astonishingly objective, balanced and humane' way in which Keller reported such terrible events, as Robert Ponsonby wrote to him afterwards, adding, 'It is good that you are with us.'[57]

9 April 1974 – to Robert Ponsonby

Dear Robert,

Many thanks for your kind note on The Time of My Life [. . .]

Ultimately, the two subjects on which you wrote to me [his escape and the objectivity of his report] are not unconnected: the 1938 events gave me a chance to escape into reality – as I shall show in a forthcoming large-scale piece (without reference to the BBC of course). They also taught me something else about which one cannot talk in public, and about which I have not yet, in fact, talked to anybody except Milein: the need for genuine, dispassionate fearlessness, as distinct from "courage"

---

54 All quotations taken from Keller to Leslie Stokes, 7 March 1974, CULHK.

55 On 5 February 1974 Keller announced that he would refuse all future requests to broadcast until his retirement, once current commitments were completed. It was not quite the end of his appearances on radio, but during his last five years with the BBC he recorded only two interval talks and a single lecture.

56 A recording of the broadcast is in the British Library sound archive and the full text is reproduced in *1975* and *HKI*.

57 Ponsonby to Keller, 2 April 1974, CULHK. Ponsonby had missed the actual broadcast, so was responding to the publication of an abridged version in *The Listener* 91/2348 (28 March 1974): 397.

that passionately overcomes fear. Nevertheless, I do honestly think that your praise is exaggerated.

Yours ever,

(Hans Keller)

Some colleagues couldn't write – Leslie Stokes, for example, found himself wordless, and rang Keller after a month to tell him why. 'I was much moved by your telephone call last night, and hence, perhaps, uncharacteristically monosyllabic,' Keller wrote to him the next day. 'I have received well over two hundred letters in response to this broadcast, but your reasons for not writing were still weightier than the motives which prompted people to write.'[58]

Letters from listeners poured in – 'in my rich BBC experience I had never known of any such audience reaction' – but despite the numbers, Keller gave every one a deeply thought individual response:

'It is . . . important that we be reminded of the inhumanity of violence directed by one human being against another . . .'

> What you say is important, but the most important conclusion is that human beings, all human beings, are only too ready to try and control each other, interfere with each other, declare each other valueless, evil, sick – as soon as they surrender their individual consciences, however bizarre, to a collective ideal, however "commonsense".

'. . . I felt that the message of your talk was that too much viciousness is allowed in society today without being adequately checked . . .'

> My 'message'? Yes and no. Viciousness as such is not the prime danger. [. . .] It is pseudo-'goodness' that is the perpetual danger, i.e. the primitive part of the human conscience, the very 'checking' agency. In the history of mankind, more people have been harmed and destroyed by consciences and conscientiousness than anything else.

'I thought it was one of the most powerful and brilliantly quiet and moving pieces of autobiography I have read . . .'

> Just as music is the purest and most affecting art because it doesn't depend on extraneous experience, so an absence of moralising principles is the purest and most effective ethic, for the same reason.

Erna Gál, a Viennese émigré herself (sister of the composer Hans Gál) wrote to say 'how much I admire your courage and determination to state the facts after so many years'[59]:

---

58 Keller to Stokes, 7 March 1974, CULHK.
59 Gál to Keller, 3 February 1974, CULHK.

26 February 1974 – to Erna Gál

Dear Erna Gal,

Many thanks for your letter of February 3. I have received over two hundred letters, and the rate of reply is proportionately slow. Also, you don't give your address: I am sending this note care of your brother.

You are mistaken if you think that I might not remember you: I have always been struck by your strong personality and incisive intelligence, and I think I remember all our casual encounters.

I might say, it is very nice to be admired for one's "courage and determination", but you know as well as I do that for our type of people, i.e. artists and/or thinkers, such courage is a matter of course, nothing to write home about, otherwise we would have no right to belong to the world of thought. For what is the risk which this kind of courage entails? Psychological discomfort, nothing else. And without unreserved preparedness (consciously unreserved at any rate!), there is no artistic or intellectual life, and if people try it nevertheless without heeding this sole commandment, the invariable result is trash. No discovery, artistic, scientific, or philosophical, and however minute, has been made without this "courage and determination", and I didn't even report a discovery! I just reported.

Kindest regards,

Yours sincerely,

(Hans Keller)

Composer William Alwyn wrote of his 'admiration that you should have endured beating and humiliations with apparently so little bitterness remaining. . . . Should I have endured with equal fortitude? A question I have often asked myself with diminishing confidence.'[60]

8 March 1974 – to William Alwyn

Dear Bill,

Many thanks for your kind words of February 4, and apologies for my belated reply: I have received well over two hundred letters. I am most grateful for <u>Daphne</u>, which I shall read as soon as possible.[61] You raise two points of central interest to me:–

---

60 Alwyn to Keller, 4 February 1974, CULHK.
61 Alwyn had sent Keller his poem *Daphne, or The Pursuit of Beauty* (Southwold: Southwold Press, 1972), describing it as 'my artistic credo'.

(1) All bitterness is infantile, because it is out of touch with reality: it treats the past as if it were the present. Lack of bitterness, therefore, is nothing to write home about: I would merely regard it as a basic condition of mental health.

(2) Would you have "endured with equal fortitude"? Yes, we find it so difficult to understand the human mind because we tend to underestimate its capacity for both cowardice and courage – depending on the circumstances.

Yours ever,

(Hans Keller)

There was one detail in Keller's broadcast that seemed to strike many of his listeners particularly forcibly: his description of the point at which he had given up all hope of surviving, and the resolve that he had made in that moment:

The Time of My Life : Vienna 1938 [extract]

[. . .] Now, to give a full description of the events of those days of imprisonment would be repetitive and boring; suffice it to say that more often than not, when something frightening was in store for us, we were told of it beforehand, so that we could fully savour our anxiety for hours before the event. As a result, when, on the sixth day, we were told: 'Tomorrow, at 6 a.m., you will be castrated, and at 8 o'clock you will be executed', we believed it. By that time, mind you, most of us were beyond the will to survive – almost too tired to be capable of fear. Nevertheless, at one moment during that night, the thought flicked through my mind: 'If, by any remote chance, I should succeed in getting out of here, and dying in a bed, I swear to myself that I'll never again be in a bad mood, whatever the circumstances of my life or death.' I'll come back to that one later.

[. . .]

I've mentioned the thought which flashed through my mind at the very stage when, rationally, I had given up all hope – that if, against all realistic expectations, I was going to survive, I would never again be in a bad mood. This one, surprisingly, still works. Whenever there is motivation for a bad mood, it is enough for me to remind myself of this thought, and the attendant emotion comes back with it, the result being a grateful elation about being alive.

Many expressed their admiration for this resolve and the 'immense control' it must have taken to maintain it for so many years:

13 March – to Eluned Ellis [extract]

Dear Mrs Ellis,

[. . .] I want to take you up on one point if I may: "How wonderful to resolve never to be in a bad mood and to have the immense control to abide by this". In my talk, I tried my best to make clear that it wasn't a question of "control" at all, but merely of conjuring up the emotion that went with this promise. [. . .] Speaking for myself, if I may, I'd be very unhappy if I had to control myself in order to do something I wanted to do, because that would mean that the wish to do it was not sufficiently strong to make control superfluous – so why do it? [. . .] The worst danger is, in fact, the gratification which people get out of self-control as such: to return to my talk, it is, psychologically, quite easily possible that some of the people who committed acts of violence had to control themselves very severely in order to do so.

One of the letter-writers Keller felt had best understood what he was saying was the literary critic Frank Kermode, who had written to him on the day of the broadcast:

Your programme about the severer matriculation that replaced your academic initiation has just ended, and I find myself unable to think of anything else. . . . What I have to understand is why your experience awoke echoes in me – I seemed to possess a horrible familiarity with them, though nothing of the same degree of disgustingness ever happened to me – I filled out, with my own fears, the understatements of your talk. I suppose it must be that the school bully, the military sadist, and perhaps oneself in certain moments are, though insignificant in comparison, and relatively powerless, continuous in intention with your interrogators and guards.[62]

19 February 1974 – to Frank Kermode [extract]

Dear Professor Kermode,

I have received over 200 letters, and it was impossible for me to read them all at once. Yours, which I have only just read – I am replying within seconds – is by far the profoundest I have seen, in direct line with Kafka's Penal Colony, if I may so put it. "Perhaps oneself in certain moments" is the crucial phrase, for which I admire your letter most – except that you are not being altogether fair on your "self", "one's id" would be a more realistic description, and your "self" deserves, in fact, every conceivable compliment for being prepared to face it. If all selves were, the problem would

---

62 Kermode to Keller, 3 February 1974, CULHK.

evaporate – a problem which is not aggression (that's below good or evil), but self-preoccupation, which renders one's own aggression unrecognisable, harmful and indeed sadistic, even on the most civilised levels.

It isn't only a matter of the school bully and the military sadist – nor of physical action alone: most organised groups with "authorities" in authority are guilty, and words are used, less to explain than to overpower.

In general, though, Keller was depressed by the way that most of the letters he received expressed 'one or other type of moral satisfaction at being able to be horrified at the past.' Everyone seemed desperate to get themselves 'out of the present, out of the need to do something here and now'. Yet, as he had said to Kermode, 'if there is any lesson to be drawn from any crime against humanity, it is that its sources, inevitably, are actively around us all the time, and within us too, otherwise it could not possibly have happened.'[63]

Keller found one contemporary example of 'collectively approved sadism' in the high-profile case of Dolours and Marian Price, two sisters recently jailed for their part in the Old Bailey bombing of March 1973. The sisters were then on hunger strike, as part of their campaign to be transferred to a prison in Northern Ireland (where IRA prisoners then had Special Category Status). At the time, government policy was to force-feed hunger strikers, an experience described by the Price sisters as torture and which they endured for 200 days.

16 May 1974 – to the Editor of *The Listener*
Listener 2355 (16 May 1974): 636

SIR: A few months ago, when I described my experiences in a Nazi prison in *The Time of My Life* (Radio 4, partly printed in the *Listener* of 28 March), I received hundreds of letters of appreciation: in my rich BBC experience I had never known of any such audience reaction. *In toto*, it saddened me: the past is morality's dreamland, where nothing need be, can be done. 'Wait,' I said to my friends (and indeed to my correspondents), 'until we are confronted with a piece of contemporary sadism, duly rationalised, authorised and legalised, and we shall see whether the Nazis – the corruption and degeneration of individual conscience – have taught us anything.'

The current issue is simple: to call it complex is to try and get out of it until it is safely in the past, when it will disclose its glorious simplicity. I ask every MP in the country, and above all the Home Secretary: 1. Is the forcible feeding now practised torture? Yes or no? 2. Is torture contemptible, in any circumstances, whatever its purpose? Yes or no? 3. Since suicide is no longer a crime in this country, what is it that is being forcibly prevented? 3. If you do not want to, or cannot answer, these

63 *1975*, 49–50.

questions, can you explain, in a few simple words, what, in general, you are alive for, and why, in particular, you are politicians?

Invariably, collectively approved sadism is moralised out of recognition in the most moral 'humane' quarters. I have seen doctors in favour of forcible feeding describe the victim as 'the patient'. A patient, may I remind them monosyllabically, is sick and wants to be cured.

HANS KELLER

Another *Listener* correspondent related this to a different example of contemporary, rationalised sadism: forced electro-convulsive therapy (ECT). Keller took this up eagerly, quoting extensively from Szasz's recent book *The Ethics of Psychoanalysis*, after which Szasz himself entered the debate. Keller told Szasz this correspondence 'is doing some good; I think it is the first public debate on the subject in this country.'[64]

An abridged reprint of Keller's *Time of My Life* talk had been published in *The Listener* on 28 March 1974. The day after it appeared, Keller had a telephone call from Paul Betts, editor of *The Observer*'s colour section, who wanted to commission a follow-up article. Keller decided to use this opportunity to pull his readers out of the past and into the present, and concentrate on the collective regression that tends to happen in any paternalistic group setting, enabling human beings to harm each other with a clear conscience. As his correspondence with Betts shows, Keller's post-*Broadcasting in the Seventies* experiences in the BBC provided plenty of fuel for a new (Szasz-inspired) concept of 'the myth of management'.

1 April 1974 – to Paul Betts

Dear Mr. Betts,

Further to our telephone conversation of March 29, it would be nice if you could confirm the commission in writing. You will have my copy in good time – but may I say now, in order to avoid any future disappointments, that easy as I am, I can be depended upon to prove the most difficult customer alive if and when editorial changes are considered (as one of your predecessors may be able to confirm).

I have decided to devote the analytic part to what it all means to us today and tomorrow: I'm fed up with people wallowing moralistically in the past's sadism while continuing, in most of our modern institutions and organisations, a para-military, regressive, paternalistic approach which is the surest guarantee of achieving a good conscience by harming people,

---

64 John Gould, letter to the editor, *Listener* 2357 (30 May 1974): 699; Keller, *Listener* 2358 (6 June 1974): 728; Szasz, *Listener* 2365 (25 July 1974): 115; Keller to Szasz, 8 August 1974, CULHK.

or having them harmed. Collective fantasies rule from top "management" (whatever that mythological term may mean, and I have been in three "managerial" jobs without discovering the reality behind it) right down to the secretarial level, where, regardless of what is or isn't being done, offices are expected to be permanently "manned" (by women) as if they were forts or ships engaged in battle; from the sado-masochistic concept of our being "fully stretched", or wanting others to be, to our chronic preoccupation with what others (colleagues, rivals, subordinates, bosses) should be doing instead of what they are doing, regardless of whether they meet the requirements of their customers or clients, or the real needs of production and output, or of a guiding philosophy ("policy").

What it all meant to me, then, was an escape from the extreme forms, hence visible to the naked eye, of a collective paranoia (complete with delusions of grandeur and persecution) which, less obtrusively, still dominates our group life, political, organisational and institutional, and whose pathology remains undiscovered just because it is collective. Yet, how easy life becomes, collective life included, once it is discovered that one actually needn't hate anybody! All hatred, alas, is blind or blinding, and therefore harmful intellectually even where it happens to be morally harmless – and that, of course, goes for self-hatred too. In my experience, only artists and thinkers (not all of them!) have been able to keep themselves outside the psychotic mess, to remain unsoiled by real or psychological blood. In short, I consider I escaped into reality; I hope so, anyway.

I trust you approve; you had better let me know immediately if you don't. As you can see, thought has, inevitably, begun to flow.

Yours sincerely,

[Hans Keller]

Escape into Reality [extract]
Unpublished draft[65]

'Investigate what is, not what pleases', Goethe says somewhere. [. . .]

When, months ago, I first told the story of my escape from Hitlerite Austria over the radio, the effect, the 'success' of the broadcast was explosive. I got hundreds of letters, all full of conscience about the human condition, full of admiration for the way I had behaved, which was precisely the way you'd have behaved, [and] for the style of the report – which was styleless, because it was facts and facts only.

65 Despite Keller's warning about editorial changes, Betts did attempt to alter the article, whereupon Keller withdrew it.

I don't want to offend anybody, and I apologize to the few people to whom I have not yet replied, but I must remind everybody that none of the 70,000 refugees in 1938 and 1939, most of whom had a similar story to tell, commanded a comparable audience, or any audience to speak of, when it would have mattered – at the time. On the contrary, a British consulate official in Vienna treated us like dirt. World Problem No.1 was not crimes against humanity, but Nazi expansion, in the propaganda fight against which the crimes against humanity came in handy. Nobody would have declared war on the Germans because they killed off the Jews.

But now we investigate what <u>was</u>, and it pleases – moralistically. We wallow in the past's sadism in order not to have to cope with the present's – our own. I am retelling the story, or rather summarizing it, on one condition – that we draw the moral – and not about what one ought to have done either: that's what those letters were about. No, I shall talk about what <u>is</u>, and what to do about it. [. . .]

It is an empirical fact that in any civilization, though there may not be more good people than bad people, there are certainly immeasurably more who don't want to torture and gas anybody than those who do. It follows that the really bad people shouldn't be a problem: they should not be able to gain the upper hand, especially not in peace-time, when collective regression and the resultant moralization of the killing of innocent people cannot take place – though the spotlessly clean conscience with which many decent people favour capital punishment should, perhaps warn us that not even in peace-time is it possible to render killing immoral in any circumstances. [. . .]

Humanity's evils, then, are not the work of evil people who, alone, wouldn't have a chance; it's the good person like you and me who, in <u>any</u> paternalistic context, in any group, institution, organization, political party etc. as we know them is readily prepared to surrender his individual conscience to the common bad. A whole system of self-deceiving double-talk has, for the purpose, developed in all civilizations.

'Discretion', for instance, when used in the service of institutional aims, of a party conscience, means lying. 'Confidentiality' means keeping things secret from those below, the relative infants, and from those outside the group, in order to ensure power. Most strikingly, 'responsibility' means the abandonment of responsibility: the more 'responsible' your job, the more you are asked to silence your personal sense of responsibility, and replace it by what the people on top of you think is good for you and everybody else. As a result, when we say that a man has 'grown into' his senior job, we cover up for the fact that he has shrunk into it. A German general had little chance left to show humanity; a German soldier had, and some did.

Beyond Broadcasting

If there is any point in an anniversary at all (victimization by over-exposure apart), it is a momentary pause: we stop at the traffic lights to reflect, for a moment, upon where we are going. Or rather, we know where we're going, or think we know, but we think about what it means – perhaps even about what it means to have got that far.

I shall try briefly to assess Schoenberg's significance in four dimensions – the historical, musical, aesthetic, and philosophical, in order to show where his work and influence are going, and where we must needs go with him if his music affects us at all; if it doesn't, we can't do worse than read articles about him.

So far as musical history is concerned, Schoenberg finished it, what there was of it: when Bach's sons, arguing strictly historically, deemed their father out of date and hence of no further value, they had struck the first powerful blow at history – or else Bach himself had done, just by being late, yet a genius.

But Schoenberg's blow came from the other side of time: he came early – so early, in fact, that it was mortal. There was no question of tonality being exhausted when he (and his music) felt it was, and when his pupils were made to feel that it was. Not even Berg ever quite recovered. In fact, there's no question yet of tonality being exhausted: geniuses like Britten and Shostakovich successfully do as if nothing had happened. Well, almost nothing: they do play around with the twelve notes, a little. Yet the time between now and Schoenberg's break-up of tonality is the same as that between the completion of *Lohengrin* and that of Mozart's second great string quartet – the D minor. That's musical history for you – or chronology, anyway.

Schoenberg's premature arrival (a great composer's occupational hazard which Bach escaped) was the strongest single cause of the decline of a general musical language, and the development of several, simultaneous languages. Thus, what used to happen successively is now happening simultaneously – or sometimes even the wrong way round, anti-historically: what Shostakovich wrote yesterday sounds earlier than what Schoenberg wrote more than half a century ago. At the traffic lights, then, we find that wherever we are going, we can't use the main road any more – a disadvantage so far as speed is concerned, an advantage in that we can choose and see things we couldn't have seen otherwise.

Musically, this means that the composer and player and listener can please themselves more than ever before. Paradoxically, at the very time when the contemporary choice is unprecedentedly wide, many people want to escape into the past – that part of it which is still part of history, where there was still a main road. But for the present and future, and indeed for the anti-historical past in the future (say, the next work by John Tavener), Schoenberg has opened up an unprecedented variety of styles and kinds of music, of which twelve-tone music is but one. At the present moment, in particular, there happen to be quite a few composers and listeners who are more fascinated by Schoenberg's so-called 'free atonal' works (Five Orchestral Pieces; *Erwartung*; *Pierrot lunaire*) than by his 'classical' twelve-tone music, such as the Third String Quartet or that 'art of fugue' of dodecaphony, the Orchestral Variations – while the later twelve-tone music, such as the Violin Concerto, is definably 'in' again. At the traffic lights however, we realise that music is music (as Alban Berg once said to George Gershwin who was surprised that Berg liked his songs); that during the twentieth-century crisis there has been too much preoccupation with styles anyway, and too little with ideas – which is what Schoenberg himself said in his book, *Style and Idea*.

But whatever his styles, whatever his revolutionary ideas, Schoenberg remained an ultra-conservative all his creative life in two well-definable respects. First, he believed in music as communication, and only in that – in music saying something, as all the great composers in the past had done. The idea of sound effects, of mere stimulation instead of communication, was abhorrent to him: he saw instrumentation, however novel, as a means of communication, not as an end in itself, nor as a main attraction. Once, in class, he was asked to define 'good music'. 'When you transcribe something for the zither,' he rejoined, 'and it still sounds like good music then it's good music.' At the traffic lights, the moment has come to remind ourselves of the many deaf alleys ahead, and circular roads too – the many ways of getting round composition, round saying something, whether by leaving the invention of meaning to the player or listener, or by writing deliberate nonsense or anti-sense which even fails in poking fun at anything, because there is no fun without meaning.

The other respect in which Schoenberg was a conservative is yet more striking in an age which, at least musically, is overwhelmingly secular: if asked what it was that music had to say, he would unhesitatingly have replied that it – great music, anyway – was concerned with those higher truths which, otherwise, were only obtainable by religious or other metaphysical revelations. He did, in fact, keep his own music on an other-worldly level throughout his creative development – not only in such overtly religious works as *Jacob's Ladder*, the opera *Moses and Aron*, the *Kol Nidre* for speaker, mixed chorus and orchestra, or his very last piece, an unfinished psalm with his own text, but also in much of the purely instrumental music, quite especially in the string quartets, the string trio, and the violin phantasy, with the result that he achieved moments of serenity denied to most other twentieth-century music, especially the more 'advanced' kind.

At the traffic lights, then, Schoenberg compels us to think not only about where we are going but, more fundamentally, about why we are going where we are going. I am sure that he would be (or is?) happy to know that amongst our hundredth-birthday presents, there's one which simply consists of the promise to think about the purpose of music – creatively, re-creatively, and receptively.

At the Schoenberg Centennial Conference, McMaster University, 1974.
L to R: Hans Keller, Richard Hoffmann, Valerie Tryon and Milton Babbitt.

This is Keller's abridged version of the ninety-minute illustrated talk he recorded for broadcast by the Canadian Broadcasting Corporation in 1974 – one of the many lectures, broadcasts and articles he produced for the Schoenberg centenary celebrations that year. For the BBC he gave four public lectures on Schoenberg's quartets, broadcast at weekly intervals during September, the month of the composer's birth. Speaking as usual without script or notes, he took his listeners through an analysis of each of the four quartets in turn, illustrations provided by the Dartington Quartet sitting alongside him. 'I was amazed by the informality of it,' says Peter Carter, who remembers hanging on Keller's every word because he was not entirely sure what was coming next. And yet everything went immaculately to time: at the end of the hour, 'we looked up and there was the second hand coming up to the dot.'[1]

There were many more invitations to lecture on Schoenberg that year and Keller travelled widely to do so. Until 1974 he had left Europe only once: to speak at a conference on 'communication in action' at the University of Natal in 1970, which he found a disturbing experience – 'intellectual anticipation of racial discrimination is one thing, emotional experience another, especially if you have been here before'[2] – though the opportunity to make a public stand about it 'eased the trauma considerably'. Even more disturbing was his first trip behind the iron curtain (judging a string quartet competition in Prague in 1975): this time 'there was no possibility of protest: whenever you urgently felt like it, you were being told, by seasoned dissidents, that you were going to get someone into trouble.' Keller described that as 'hell – for that is the place from which you can't, morally, escape, and *in* which you can't act right, whichever way you try'.[3] Keller's first trip across the Atlantic was prompted by an invitation to speak at the Schoenberg centenary events organised by his former pupil and BBC colleague Alan Walker, now professor of music at McMaster University in Hamilton, Ontario. Schoenberg was also the catalyst for his first visit to Israel, to speak at the centenary symposium held as part of the 1974 Israel Festival.

It was a time of political volatility in the wake of the Yom Kippur War and the resignation of Prime Minister Golda Meir, succeeded in the summer of 1974 by Yitzhak Rabin. For Keller at a personal level, the timing of this first visit to Israel was of considerable emotional significance, coming as it did just after he had revisited the events of 1938: 'Israel is an elemental experience – the answer to extermination.'[4] It was the first of four visits Keller made to Jerusalem, prompting a great deal of thought and writing. Delegates to the 1974 Schoenberg festivities were housed at Mishkenot Sha'ananim (Dwellings of Serenity), restored the previous year as a residence for visiting artists, musicians and writers. Josef Tal,

1 Carter, oral communication, 9 January 2018. Keller's thinking for these lectures formed the basis for his article 'Schoenberg: the Future of Symphonic Thought', *Perspectives of New Music* X111/1 (Fall–Winter 1974): 3–20, reprinted in *EOM*, 179–91.

2 'Views', *Listener* 2156 (23 July 1970): 105.

3 *1975*, 52.

4 'Next year in Jerusalem', *Guardian*, 25 November 1976, 14.

the Israeli composer with whom Keller became very friendly (and for whose opera *Der Turm* he later wrote the libretto), arranged for Keller and Cosman to be offered residencies at Mishkenot Sha'ananim for the summers of 1977 and 1979, 'to think and write in inspiring surroundings, as peaceful as they are warful'.[5]

This intense writing-time was just what Keller was looking for. The period between 'The Time of my Life' and his retirement from the BBC in 1979 was a very productive one for him as a writer – scarcely surprising, given his diminished opportunities within the Corporation. It also saw a change in the way he was writing as, for the first time in his life, this master of the aphorism took to extended forms, producing four books within three years, each written very rapidly over a few weeks. Keller's style of writing had been gradually loosening for years as his audience broadened, making longer forms easier, but he also seems have become conscious in the early 1970s that the time had come for a more substantial publication. In 1974, with the help of his former BBC secretary, Pauline Beesley, he reviewed his vast bibliography and began to discuss a book of selected essays with the publisher Heineman. The publication of old material was always less interesting to Keller than the writing of something new, however, and this project was soon overtaken. The first of the books he now produced – and the only one published in his lifetime – was *1975 (1984 minus 9)*. This was really a collection of long essays, of which the first was a reprint of Keller's 'Time of my Life' talk – included not as a period piece but as the moral touchstone for the whole book's reflection on 'the state of things we'd reached in 1975 in areas of life I know'.

Thinkers of the World, Disunite! [extract]
1975, 9–10, 22

'1975' is, of course, meant symbolically rather than merely chronologically: less than a decade to go until 1984, less than a spiritual decade.

When I first read George Orwell's book, I hated it as much as you may come to hate mine. And I hated it with what I thought was good reason. I remember having a violent argument about it with Margaret Phillips, the educational psychologist, with whom I was then collaborating; although not an educationist, I had a less pessimistic view than she about the possibilities of disasters open to humankind. I felt that my attitude of mild optimism – I never went as far as conceiving of the possibility of an end to wars – was well fortified by the results of psychoanalytic research. Man, I suggested, could not live on hate alone, rather blatantly disregarding the possible implications of Chapter I below [Vienna, 1938].

What I have meanwhile learnt, not only about lovelessness, but about pure evil perpetrated with, in fact by, the best and easiest of consciences,

5 *Ibid.*

has made me change my mind – gradually, yet radically in the end. There is, in short, no limit to the degree to which man can cheat himself into believing that he is good and full of love and concern and respect – especially for those he wants to control; after he has accomplished the major task of self-deceit, the successful cheating of others is a minor matter. [...]

I have learnt about one ultimate value without which there are no human beings to speak of, and one ultimate vice with which there are no human beings to speak of. The ultimate value is the independence of individual conscience, while the ultimate vice is its cession, capitulation, loving surrender, arrested development, collective envelopment. There is no collective wisdom; there is only unacknowledged, collective stupidity. Man has lived for quite some time now and still hasn't discovered, once and for all, that a group doesn't think.

The book went on to examine different 'closed societies' in turn, including Keller's experiences in communist Prague, and at the 1975 Congress of the International Psycho-analytical Association, where he had been appalled to discover that 'what had promised to be the twentieth century's leading method of safeguarding the individual psyche . . . has led to the formation of a secret, moralising, soul-destroying society . . . which allows less intellectual and ethical freedom than do the dogmata of the most fanatical creed.' Keller also included a chapter on football, inspired by a conversation with a Viennese taxi driver about the terrible effect of England's victory in the 1966 World Cup: 'You and your "team spirit"!' the driver had exclaimed; 'It's had a disastrous influence. No more room for *persons*, for talent, for the finer arts of the game.' Keller couldn't have agreed more.

The longest chapter examined 'Music, 1975' – and here Keller's railing against closed societies came to an abrupt halt. For the musical society in which he was living in 1975 was the reverse of closed – 'but it used to be, before the disintegration of tonality, the ageing of key, the loss of the Western world's common musical language. And here we encounter a fundamental paradox: in life, closed societies produce de-individualisation. But closed artistic societies produce, on the contrary, a flowering of individual achievement.' This brought Keller back to Schoenberg, and the 'crisis of communication' he had caused, which, for the first time, had let unmusical people into music's 'secret society', gaining entry because 'so few musical musicians understood what Schoenberg was on about.' The worst consequence of this was the problem it caused genuine musicians – such as 'when good new music is being played by unmusical performers, to the satisfaction of the unmusical majority of listeners (professionals included), and leaving the musical minority helpless and guilty: "I can't understand this." Of course you can't, if it's played like that.'[6]

---

6 Keller to Andrew Porter, 5 July 1982, CULHK

To drive home his point about the disintegration of understanding in the new 'open' society, compared with the 'closed' one it had replaced, Keller gave as an example to his *1975* readers the one Schoenberg work they might have thought they *did* understand:

The Crisis of Communication: the Schoenberg trauma [extract]
1975, 152–3

When *Transfigured Night* first burst upon the scene, professional and public reactions were, in fact, hostile. A Viennese concert society refused its first performance because of one chord – 'that is, one *single* uncatalogued dissonance', as Schoenberg puts it in his afore-quoted essay,[7] the chord being B flat–A flat–E flat–G flat–C–E flat. Nor is it good enough for us just to sneer. This was the last-ditch defence of the West's closed musical society, and there was more musicality in that act of incomprehension of Schoenberg's harmonic foreground than there is in the kind of contemporary enjoyment of *Transfigured Night* which remains unaware of the harmonic adventure, the extreme tensions between foreground and background, in this first symphonic poem for chamber ensemble. If, thus, the enjoying ear misses frictions of essential structural significance, it fails to understand the very passages which the work's first audiences found incomprehensible, but it fails for the opposite reason: where they were too much taken aback to understand, the conventional contemporary ear, alienated from real musical understanding altogether, is not taken aback far enough!

I don't like talking in generalities, and the mention of a single chord won't suffice. If the reader wishes to test his own ear to see whether he is the victim of bogus appreciation, of our time's degeneration of musical understanding, he can easily do so. Gramophone records abound, and here is a selection of passages in *Transfigured Night* which, if we are at all in touch with the tensions between the work's foreground and background, we cannot but be pulled up by; pain as well as pleasure is a function of understanding:

Bars 64 ff.; bars 79–80; bars 124 ff.; bars 144 ff.; bars 153 ff., with their complex counterpoint of a theme played against its inversion; and bars 310 ff. And this, let us remember, is the music to the accompaniment of which children nowadays do their homework and grown-ups their income tax.

---

7 'Criteria for the Evaluation of Music', in *Style and Idea* (London: Faber, 1975), 131.

As soon as he had finished *1975*, Keller turned his mind to his long-standing intention to write a book on criticism. The one he had offered to André Deutsch in 1953 had never been written, either in its original form or as an exposition of the 'theory of unity' underlying functional analysis. Now Keller was much concerned with criticism's essential role in all 'phoney professions', as he called them – a phoney profession being one that 'creates grave problems which it then fails to solve'. Keller included in this category many professions in which he had been involved himself: viola player, musicologist, broadcaster, editor, psychoanalyst and teacher. The book was written during a three-week holiday with Cosman in Tenerife in the autumn of 1976. Their skiing holidays of old had been replaced by holidays in the sun, which he and Cosman devoted to writing and drawing (and the occasional swim): 'In such surroundings, with no interruptions and the sun to stimulate, I write 3,000 words a day.'[8]

The offer of a two-month residency at Mishkenot Sha'ananim the following year was a welcome opportunity for more uninterrupted writing. Even before he embarked on *Criticism* in Tenerife, Keller had decided on the subject of the book he would write in Jerusalem – provoked by reading what a previous recipient of a Mishkenot residency had written: Saul Bellow's *To Jerusalem and Back*.

> The older people grow, the more they resemble themselves.

'[It] hit me just at the right moment,' he wrote, reviewing it in *The Guardian* just before setting off for Tenerife. 'It is being accorded a place of honour in an intellectual life rich in anti-models. I know now what and how not to write in Jerusalem.' Amid the many things Keller disliked about Bellow's book, what annoyed him most was its dismissal of the Mendelssohn Violin Concerto as 'all this silvery whickering'. 'My mind is made up. The book I shall write at the Mishkenot Sha'ananim will be on the Mendelssohn Violin Concerto, arguably the greatest of them all.' By the time Keller flew home, however, he had completed not one, but two books, having decided on the plane over to Jerusalem to write (for publication) a detailed diary of his time there. He wrote extensively in it every day – it was the first time he had succeeded in keeping a diary for longer than a few days. It was also, he wrote as he started it, 'the first time in my life that I do something, intellectually, which I hadn't carefully mapped out and indeed specifically thought out'.

～

One thing Keller admired about the state of Israel was that it had, so early in its history, effectively abolished the death penalty, since when its only execution had been that of Adolf Eichmann for Nazi war crimes. The year after his first visit, however, controversy erupted over the repatriation of the bodies of two members of the Zionist paramilitary 'Stern Gang' executed in 1944 for the assassination in Cairo of the British Resident Minister Lord Moyne. As part of a prisoner exchange agreement in 1975, their bodies were returned to Israel by the Egyptians, after which they lay in state and were re-buried on Mount Herzl with full military honours. Yigal Allon, Israel's Deputy Prime Minister, represented the government at the burial and afterwards defended what had been done, following a protest from the British Foreign Secretary, James Callaghan.

14 July 1975 – to Yigal Allon

Dear Deputy Prime Minister,

I have let the conflicting emotions surrounding the funeral of Eliyahu Hakim and Eliyahu Beth Zure die down before addressing this letter to you; I want to divest it of any trace of topicality or political debate. Mine are a conscious Jew's reflections on ultimate human values, and on Jewry's commitment to them. [. . .]

My practical and intellectual involvement in the State of Israel is of long standing, but last year, it received powerful reinforcement when your Festival invited me to participate in its Schoenberg symposium; I was deeply impressed by the high degree of individualism which Israel's society has retained in circumstances which readily make for collective regression.

Ceteris paribus, the more highly developed a society's individualistic tendencies, the higher are its ethical standards. In fact, the reason why I – who is not alone in having learnt to be suspicious of national pride – allow myself to be proud to be a Jew is, simply, our ethical history. To my mind, the circumstances of this funeral have done harm to our moral dignity – and your reply to James Callaghan's message of June 26 does nothing to dispel my anxiety. The very fact that your letter (which the Embassy of Israel has put at my disposal) is not easily comprehensible seems to indicate that no clear justification has been found for what, to the outside world, must appear an act of homage.

What, for instance, is 'the attitude of the Government of Israel towards assassination as a political instrument'? What indeed does 'assassination as a political instrument' mean? There is a difference between killing, say, Hitler and killing an innocent man, which can hardly be glossed over by both acts being covered by the same term. You undoubtedly know the Jewish joke about a young soldier, marching out of step with his platoon, with his mother observing: 'My boy is the only one who is marching in step'. In traumatic national situations, there always is a terrible danger that a group within a nation is convinced of being absolutely in step with rectitude, while the rest of the world considers it out of step. South Africa is an outstanding example: the only people who feel that apartheid is fully justified are South Africans. I would suggest to you, sir, that the only people who did not notice anything amiss with this funeral are Israelis. A little more than your letter is needed to prove why the rest of the world is wrong.

Again, what is this 'act of grace' which you think Mr Callaghan does not understand? An act of grace is a privilege, a concession, that cannot be claimed as right – and, in particular, an act of mercy or clemency. On what precise grounds have you based this act? How do you wish the rest of the world to understand these grounds? What, precisely, was pardonable in this 'assassination'? How, from any conceivable ethical standpoint which can be accepted as Jewish (religious, secular, traditional) can you defend this 'effort of national reconciliation' which seems to deny the ultimate value of human life itself? For the duration of this historical (though, I hope, not historic) episode, my pride in being a Jew remains gravely muted; I don't know how much 'national reconciliation' you have achieved through this act, but is it not time that you examined the views of Jewish dissidents? As a member of the Government of Israel (of all governments) should know, disagreement can be more realistic, and more dignified, than the fear of disunity.

Yours sincerely

Hans Keller

Keller and Cosman's first residency at Mishkenot Sha'ananim was from April to June 1977, so they were able to observe at first hand the seismic shift in Israeli politics that took place in May that year:

17–19 May – diary extract

May 17: Today was election day, with 22 parties fighting for seats in the Knesset (Parliament), appealing to the 2.2 million who are expected to vote. The result will be an old story, a story outlived maybe, by the time these lines are in print. [. . .] The main opposition party is, of course, the right-wing Likud – the militant 'Revisionists' as they then called themselves, with whom I went to school and had one argument after another – rightly so, as it turned out, for they developed into the pre-1948 Jewish terrorists. Their leader, Vladimir Jabotinsky, my boyhood's pet aversion, now has one of Jerusalem's most beautiful streets named after him. [. . .]

May 18: Well, well, I'm not so sure any longer that the election result will be a mouldy story by the time my diary is read. I don't dream much, but all night I dreamt of the Likud and my school days with them – under the influence of my diary entry, I thought. I also dreamt, and told my wife that I dreamt, that they would win the election. It was a little bit of a waking dream – enough of the waking variety to shape itself into a question, almost an ironical question: what would happen if, against all expectations, the Likud won the election?

In two visits to Israel during which, of professional necessity, we met plenty of people, we never encountered anybody who gave the Likud the slightest chance of a victory at any future election – and three years ago, we only met one person who actually voted for them. [. . .] In short, in the circles in which we move, in which most of my readers would move, the new government party is hardly represented. Is this a verdict on them or on 'us' I wonder? [. . .]

There are perfectly honourable motives to be found in the contemporary right-winger's soul – honourable on the highest level of humanism: the waves of justifiable hostility against government control, government spending, government philosophies for all. From inflation to mental health movements, the evil results of 'socially responsible' governmental good-doing have struck ever more thinking people, and it cannot be an accident that two of the most independent (if not indeed the most progressive) thinkers of our time are – let's face it bluntly – capitalist: the Nobel-prized economist Milton Friedman, and the anti-psychiatric professor of psychiatry, Thomas Szasz.

Both are Jews too – which brings us back, maybe, to the Likud: if, following the reflections of the new right as well as the traditional ideals of Jewish individualism, they are going to emerge as an anti-collective force against the old, at times senile, left, a force for individual dignity widening the area of individual self-determination, much may be forgiven. But with their past, they are guilty until and unless proved innocent – though 'guilty with mitigating circumstances' is, in politics, the most likely of the more favourable prospects.

Keller gave his diary the anti-Bellow title 'To Jerusalem and Forward', under which heading it was published in *The New Review* in the autumn of 1977.[9] Readers liked it and Keller was encouraged 'to overcome my lifelong aversion against diaries and start a regular one'. Within days, this London diary was over-taken by more historic events in Jerusalem:

---

9 The original intention was that the full diary should be published in three sections, but only the first two appeared: *The New Review* IV/43 (October 1977): 13–24 and IV/45–6 (December 1977 – January 1978): 43–55. The complete text is published in *HKJD*.

13–19 November 1977 – diary extract

November 13. Today's news is Begin's official invitation to Sadat to address the Knesset (parliament) in Jerusalem. Let me stick my neck out: the waves of pacific emotions now emanating from both sides, whether real or hypocritical or – most likely – a bit of both, are bound to have as palpable an effect as have the more usual waves of aggression, an effect that will be overestimated by the world's doves and underestimated by its hawks. That is the human problem: man, let alone woman, loves peace as much as war – though not, mind you, as effectively, because war is psychologically easier, capable of having it both ways: internal peace (collective self-love) is combined with externalised aggression.

November 14. Still about Begin. Anti-Israeli non-Jews and pro-Israeli, socialist Jews alike call him a Fascist. A fascist is somebody in favour of dictatorship; if he isn't, the description turns into rhetorical gas – the oxygen, indeed the ozone of politics. I reject most of Begin's policies, but have to accept that as a matter of sheer fact, he has proved himself an unreserved, enthusiastic adherent of parliamentary democracy, in which he has figured as a responsible leader of the opposition. Not everybody one rejects is everything one rejects.

November 19. [. . .] Psychologically, the present diary is the outcome, one outcome, of my Israel diary. Why is it I have to start a couple of days before one of the most sensational events in Israel's history – one which was utterly unforeseeable on the day I started this diary, and one which now dominates the political and indeed humanistic thoughts and feelings, of the world – president Sadat's visit to Israel? He arrived there tonight at 6 o'clock, at the end of the Sabbath. [. . .]

A historic event in all conscience – more historic than any other, in that it is utterly unprecedented: never in the history of the world has the head of a state that declares itself at war with another paid it a friendly, peace-seeking visit.

Israel's explosively friendly reaction does not only do them honour, but forms a clarifying contrast to the reactions of the other, hostile side – hostile, that is, not just to Israel, but now also to Sadat. Syria's official behaviour, above all, unmasks the ethics, if 'ethics' is the word, of the hostile part of the Arab world: those 'balanced' people who see equal right on either side are, as from now, demonstrably wrong, for there is violent imbalance between the morals of the two sides. Syria, that is, have declared a <u>day of mourning</u> (no misprint), with flags at half-mast. A day of mourning – not because anybody has died, but because two hostile governments have decided to suspend hostility, at least for a moment, in order to save life! They're mourning the threatening saving of life on

הפסטיבל הישראלי 1978

מיסודו של א. צ. פרופס

התזמורת הפילהרמונית הישראלית

מנצח: אליהו ענבל

Misha Maisky sketched by Milein Cosman during the 1978 Israel Festival (CULHK).

either side: inhumanity seems to be reserved for humanity, compared to which the higher mammals appear, in such a situation, as humaneness animalified. They couldn't understand what the Syrians were on about – nor would it be their lack of intelligence that would produce their lack of understanding.

In the summer of 1978 Keller paid a shorter visit to Israel for a World Congress on Jewish Music, in which he gave a lecture entitled 'To what extent can music by a composer of the diaspora represent Jewish ideas or traditions'.[10] Returning the following year for his second Mishkenot Sha'ananim residency, he reflected on the way in which contemporary Zionism seemed now to involve 'the abandonment of the Diaspora' – and with it, he thought, a vital cultural blessing: 'the blessing of being persecuted, a foreigner everywhere, dependent on oneself alone, not exposed to the risk of deindividualization, of hiding behind, and posing in front of one's national identity'.

In an unpublished review of a 1982 book by Chaim Raphael, *Springs of Jewish Life* (whose 'all-pervasive sentimentality' he had found intensely irritating), Keller addressed again the question of the Diaspora, and the importance of persecution to the formation of Jewish identity. He decided to 'take Jewish genius as representative of "the springs of Jewish life" (if any), in the hope that they will thus appear under a magnifying glass', and therefore examined 'the three Jewish geniuses without whom our century would be unrecognisable', Freud, Einstein and Schoenberg. His starting point was two famous statements by Einstein: on the one hand his description of 'three outstandingly Jewish ideals' ('knowledge for its own sake; an almost fanatical love of justice; desire for personal independence') and on the other, his statement that he owed his personal sense of his own Jewish identity 'more to Gentiles than to Jews'. 'Were the Jewish springs of Einstein's life, then, to be found in the minds of Gentiles?' asked Keller. 'The ironical form of the question doesn't rob it of its rhetorical element, i.e. the possibility of an affirmative answer.'

It was 'Jewry's unparalleled and unrivalled role as scapegoat', thought Keller, that had produced Einstein's three ideals ('the ineluctable consequence of a prolonged state of moralistic persecution') and he wondered to what extent they could survive the loss of that role. With the establishment of a Jewish state 'the trauma of persecution has been replaced with the trauma of its removal,' he wrote. 'Not for long, therefore, was Israel able to tolerate the love of the world: with the help of Freud's "repetition compulsion" on the one hand and, on the same hand, Begin [. . .] she acknowledges the world's "persecution", which she has provoked, with a paranoid sigh of relief.' Keller also feared that the desire for personal independence was being replaced by a desire for *collective* independence, defined as national security, which risked eroding the other two ideals that Einstein had identified.

---

10 This 'meaningless title', according to Keller, was imposed on him by the Congress organisers. At the end of his talk he inverted it and asked his audience 'to what extent can the Jew in Israel free himself of his national preoccupations'. Transcript, CULHK.

Chaim Raphael had asserted that the security of Israel was 'by far and away the most potent link' between all Jews worldwide; Keller countered that 'equally potent, for me and my fellow Jews in as well as outside Israel, is our "almost fanatical love of justice" for any Arabs whom our state may be treating unjustly: if Einstein's love of justice were as widely in evidence as it used to be in the Diaspora, the problem of the Middle East would not be insoluble.'[11]

~

At the BBC meanwhile, its senior management probably felt that Keller's own 'repetition compulsion' was at work in his unceasing questioning of their policies, so the 'witch-hunt' he felt he faced was partly of his own making. In particular, the issue of the public discussion of broadcasting by BBC staff was raised again and again by Keller pushing the boundaries of the regulations requiring staff to seek official permission for anything they said. In 1972, for example, he defended the publication of his personal 'philosophy of radio' on the basis of a private comment by Director-General Charles Curran ('[if] you're speaking for yourself, I have no objection') two years earlier. (That, countered Jock Beesley, 'was no more than an obiter dictum and certainly not a ratio descendi.'[12]) In 1973, during the proceedings of the Senate Watergate Committee, Keller was reprimanded again for a letter to *The Listener* criticising the BBC's television coverage of the hearings – which, he said, had clearly implied guilt in a case still *sub judice*: 'It should not be necessary to point out that the victims of miscarriages of criminal justice come, exclusively, from one category of people – those gravely or universally suspected.'[13] This letter caused ructions at the highest level of the Corporation, but Keller pointed out that authorisation had never been required before for writing in the BBC's *own* publications, forcing the management to clarify its regulations. They were clarified again in 1976 to add a rider that 'staff cannot assume that de facto permission exists because the substance of the article has been published on a previous occasion.' That was prompted by the publication in *The Spectator* of a paper Keller gave to the Canadian Broadcasting Corporation's conference on 'Radio in the Eighties'. 'I note your point,' he wrote to Beesley after yet another reprimand, 'but wish to emphasise that it wasn't only "the substance of the

> I am of course making a
> mountain out of a molehill.
> But the decline of truthfulness
> always starts with molehills.

---

11 'Jewish Ideals and Jewish Selves', unpublished review for the *LRB*, CULHK.
12 'Views', *Listener* 88/2267 (7 September 1972): 293. Beesley to Newby, 14 September 1972, WAC L1/1907/1.
13 'Trial by Television', *Listener* 2312 (19 July 1973): 89.

article" which had been published on a previous occasion (in <u>Ariel</u>), but the entire piece (by CBC) – and that it had, in fact, been written at the instigation of the BBC, for the purpose of publication.'[14]

The following month began the longest of Keller's many disputes over his publications, when he submitted the manuscript of his book *1975* for approval. There was little in it about the BBC or broadcasting, but Keller's discussion in its preface of the evils of 'management' made much (if general) reference to his own experience (while still describing the Corporation as 'a magnificent employer'). Delays at the BBC (whose instruction to delete the preface was apparently lost in the post), as well as at the publisher, meant that the arguments were still going on well into 1977, when the Annan Report on the Future of Broadcasting added fuel to the fire. Paragraph 28.8 in its chapter on 'Industrial Relations' was unequivocal:

> We were disturbed at the extent of the restrictions which the BBC in par-
> ticular find it necessary to impose upon their staff. For example, we were
> surprised to find that the BBC did not allow their staff to publish anything
> or speak in public about broadcasting generally, without seeking the BBC's
> permission. We consider this an unnecessary restriction which in law would
> most likely be held against public policy. Nor should the restrictions con-
> tinue to operate during the time when a person under contract, having been
> made redundant, receives his redundancy pay. The BBC have made a move
> to reduce the number of staff bound by restrictions and that is to the good.
> But we would go further and restore rights to individuals which they should
> never have been asked to surrender.[15]

'I have very good reason to believe,' wrote Keller to Beesley, 'that what the Committee was concerned with, and about, was the BBC's attitude towards my own writings on broadcasting.'[16] This put the Corporation – which until that point had been insisting that if *1975* were published unedited, Keller 'cannot expect to remain in the Corporation' – into a quandary. Any industrial tribunal would force it not only to justify its action on the technical breach, but also to declare why permission could not have been given in the first place – which, as Beesley was only too aware, would 'give Keller and others an excellent forum for what could prove unwelcome publicity.'[17]

Despite the general nature of Keller's preface to *1975*, the BBC feared that others would 'take the generalisations as insinuations', as Beesley put it, and use them 'to undermine C.Mus.'s authority in particular and BBC Management

---

14 'Broadcasting: In the 'Eighties', *Spectator* 237/7724 (10 July 1976): 29. Keller to Beesley 21 July 1976, WAC L1/1907/1.

15 *Report of the Committee on the Future of Broadcasting*, (Cmnd. 6753, 1977), 436. Keller wrote an Open Letter to the Director-General on the subject: *Spectator* 240/7812 (25 March 1978): 27.

16 Keller to Beesley, 21 April 1977, WAC L1/1907/1.

17 Beesley to Douglas Muggeridge, 24 March 1977, WAC L1/1907/1.

in general'.[18] 'C.Mus.' was now Robert Ponsonby, Glock having retired in December 1972 with a knighthood and widespread acclaim for his revitalisation of BBC music. It must have been hard for Ponsonby to follow such conspicuous success – as he said himself, Glock 'occupied a position of unique standing and his sheer authority was redoubtable'[19] – and it was doubly hard in the rebellious post-*Broadcasting in the Seventies* atmosphere. Triply hard was having the arch-rebel Hans Keller under him, sidelined yet determinedly active, wielding a formidable musical authority and a huge public profile – and, moreover, very popular with younger staff. What to do with him was one of Ponsonby's first problems. 'I have given a great deal of thought to the question of Hans Keller's role within the Division,' he wrote to Newby just after his arrival, stressing the importance of finding Keller something substantial:

> The alternative is to leave him in a position of isolation, allocating to him a variety of insignificant responsibilities, including Regional orchestral programme correlation, foreign tapes, chamber music, etc. etc. This would be very unsatisfactory as he would not have enough to do, would not want to do what he had to do, and would, as so often in the past, extend his influence unofficially in various directions, thus irritating and embarrassing certain of his colleagues![20]

Many ideas were discussed – including letting Keller back into talks – before Peter Gould came up with the proposal of 'a general supervisory role in the field of new music'.[21] There were anxieties here – Gould worried about 'drawbacks due to personal taste' and Ponsonby thought Keller's musical instincts too conservative (his own view being that 'contemporary music has to find its own new format').[22] But in the end that did not matter, since Keller's approach to the role of 'Chief Assistant, New Music' (C.A.N.M.)[23] was not ideological, but eminently practical.

A major part of Keller's new job was to deal with the constant stream of unsolicited scores the BBC received from composers and publishers, and their assessment by 'the Panel'. At that time, there were about fifty living British composers the BBC designated 'Panel free' – a status some had fought for years to obtain – whose works producers were free to programme without further scrutiny. All other new scores were formally assessed, initially by three readers, each providing a written report on the basis of which a final decision was made by the BBC's New Music Committee. Difficult cases (of which there were an increasing number, given the stylistic diversity of the times) might be referred for further readings.

---

18 Beesley to Muggeridge, 2 September 1976, WAC L1/1907/1.
19 Ponsonby, *Musical Heroes* (London: Giles de la Mare, 2009), 115.
20 Ponsonby to Newby, 9 January 1973, WAC L1/1907/3.
21 Gould to Ponsonby, 13 February 1973, WAC L1/1907/3.
22 Ponsonby, oral communication, 14 July 1995.
23 'We ought to adopt as our motto CAVE CANM.' Ponsonby to Newby and Beesley, 30 July 1976, WAC L1/1907/3.

By 1973, practice was not matching theory (if it ever had). As David Cox (then chairing New Music Committee) explained to Ponsonby after his arrival, 'there is often the feeling of the whole thing being a sterile exercise,' as composers waited for months if not years for decisions and the committee spent ages deliberating over contradictory reports. It was feared some Panel readers might 'make capital' of their BBC employment, while others provided incompetent reports on works written in an idiom they did not understand. Some of the recommended scores were impossible to broadcast, leading Cox to wonder if score-reading might better be an internal matter – especially since producers were sometimes ignoring the whole Panel process anyway – while the backlog of scores 'accepted' but not broadcast grew.[24]

Keller's first decision was to take personal responsibility:

8 May 1973 – to M.G. Brewer, Senior Assistant, Music Services
WAC R27/1030/1

Re: REPLIES TO COMPOSERS

I am trying my best to replace cold standard replies by individual letters. In the circumstances, with your agreement, I propose to take over all replies to composers: even when they are unhappy they can then write directly to the man responsible – and one possible source of friction or irritation will have been removed. I think it is wrong for us to hide behind you and use you as a clerk.

Let me know what you think.

Initially the Composers' Guild thought this a bad idea, fearing that some composers might 'take advantage' of Keller's openness, and endless arguments would ensue.[25] In fact, the reverse was the case, and Keller was able to show that rejections were accepted much more easily if accompanied by a detailed reaction to the score in question. Reforming the internal bureaucracy took rather longer, but this is how Keller reported his progress after two years:

15 October 1975 – to Howard Newby
WAC R27/1030/1

Dear Howard,

Thank you for your note of October 6. Our methods vis-à-vis new scores have been radically revised. I have abolished New Music Committee,

---

24 Cox to Ponsonby, 17 January 1973, WAC R27/1030/1.
25 Anthony Hedges to Keller, 30 August 1973, WAC R27/1061/1.

as well as the rigid panel system: after inspecting new scores, I decide on whether to submit them to "maxi-" or "mini-" panels. Those which seem to me likely to elicit a clear and unproblematic decision (positive or negative) are submitted to the smallest possible panel, i.e. one outside reader and myself, whereas problematic scores go to large panels, from three outside readers upwards; there are graded variations, according to the complexity of the score in question. The new method, initiated in 1973, has proved eminently successful; disappointed composers can have their scores re-read by an entirely different panel within a short space of time. Quite generally, in fact, our notorious time lag has been abolished: the longest a composer has to wait for a decision (re-readings excepted) is two months, and decisions within 36 hours are by no means unknown – whereas previously, it quite often took years until a decision was arrived at. (This may sound unbelievable, but Clerk, New Music and I have had to work up a backlog stretching back in one instance to 1945, i.e. 8 years before she was born.) The Composers' Guild of Great Britain is highly appreciative of our new methods, and there is constant liaison between them and us.

The aim, you appreciate, is to extend the benefit of the doubt to its maximum; in fact, when a senior member of the Department takes full responsibility for the quality of a new score, I do not even show it to the panel, but accept it as a matter of principle. Where there is strong panel disagreement, I either ask for further readings (including myself amongst the readers) or, upon personal inspection, decide on an acceptance, despite the conflict of opinion. There are two types of acceptances – one outright, the other "if offered": controversial scores tend to land in the latter category, which means that if the work in question is offered to us, by a performer or conductor, within the context of a programme which we wish to record, we try our best to place it. There is a small percentage of works which I reject outright, without showing them to any panel: they are of the wholly illiterate variety, though I must add that when I see an illiterate score with a creative spark in it, I do pass it on to a mini-panel, despite its lack of mastery or professionalism. Quite seriously, my negative model is the system we operated before I joined the Corporation, when one of the minor masterpieces of our time, Mátyás Seiber's "Ulysses" Cantata, was rejected by a highly competent panel which was not, however, competent to read this particular score: I choose my panel readers according to the style of the work in question, and when I invite people to join our panels, I give preference to leading composers. By now, my panel reservoir is highly distinguished: all members are leading musicians, either composers and/or established interpreters of contemporary music, and/or teachers. While we maintain strict anonymity, you may be interested in the present list, in alphabetical order:

Richard Arnell
Susan Bradshaw
John Carewe
Edward Downes
Norman Del Mar
John Lambert
John Ogdon
Edmund Rubbra
Hugh Wood

The Composers' Guild of Great Britain agrees with the principle of anonymity: their own members would be subjected to a lot of harassment if the names of the panel readers were disclosed. Upon certain occasions, in critical situations, I do, however, disclose my own participation in the reading process, and give the composer my own detailed view of the score in question.

Standard replies (acceptances or rejections) have, in fact, been largely abandoned: whenever I see the need for a personal letter (i.e. for specification and substantiation), I write it. Virtually all our reactions are dictated and typed within hours of the panels' decisions.

Lists of acceptances (outright and "if offered"), as well as lists of rejections, are regularly circulated amongst producers, both basic and regional. They help a great deal in trying to get accepted works placed, and together with Dr. Simpson, we have initiated an unending series of concerts (Now and Then) in which we try to place, at least, all accepted chamber works, together with works from the established repertoire. (Orchestral works are, of course, a special – financial – problem.) [. . .]

Foreign scores are treated with less caution: our prime responsibility is towards British scores. We do not, in fact, submit foreign scores to panels: I read them myself and decide on the basis of two criteria – outstanding quality and demonstrable historical significance (even if the quality is 'instanding': prototypically John Cage).

Yours ever,

(Hans Keller)

Ponsonby must have been relieved the new post had worked out so well, reporting to Newby that 'Keller has filled it to admiration . . . relations with composers and publishers are exceptionally good'.[26]

26 Ponsonby, annual report on Keller, 19 December 1974, WAC L1/1907/1.

The hardest part of the job was getting accepted works into programmes. Keller supported to the hilt the 'essential' principle of producers' independence, but continued to press on them the importance of allowing accepted works to be heard. 'The purely psychological fact remains,' he warned his colleagues, 'that unless one is careful, one is inevitably prejudiced against a "mere" panel acceptance, and prefers one's own discoveries, even when one or the other panel acceptance happens to be objectively preferable.'[27] Keller found 'the most helpful region so far as performances of accepted works are concerned' to be Scotland – 'it may not be altogether accidental that the Head of Music there is a distinguished composer himself.'[28] Overall, though, progress was depressingly slow, and Keller concluded after five years that his New Music post had been 'the most unsuccessful part of my BBC life'.[29] For although it was indubitably the case that relations between composers and the BBC had been enormously improved and a chronic grievance removed, all that ultimately mattered was what was actually heard, and it was not enough. 'Our central responsibility', he wrote on his retirement, 'is the kind of patronage that the 18th century provided through its aristocracy. I am not, you understand, talking about neglected talent in the first place, but about talent which, without us, would never get the chance of being neglected.'[30]

But to young composers in particular, Keller's openness and responsiveness made an enormous – to some life-changing – difference. Judith Bingham, for example, was in her early twenties when she first sent her scores to the BBC and received a long letter from Keller in return. 'He had a startling effect on me, because up to that time no-one had ever taken me seriously, including myself I think.' The correspondence continued 'with me sending him scores and him writing back in a very friendly way' until Bingham moved to London in 1974 and asked Keller for lessons. The experience was 'totally different' from any teaching she had ever received before:

> [He] would do something that was much more like psycho-analysis: he would say 'How do you feel about this piece?', and I would start talking about it. And then gradually, in a rather cunning, backdoor way, we'd get round to how things might be improved. . . . He was brilliant: an 'anti-teacher' teacher! He was a very paternal, totally selfless and altruistic person. And now, looking back, knowing all about what it's like in the music world, I can see how kind he was to me. I often wish he was still alive, so I could thank him. Because he died before I could ever really say 'I now realize what you did – and how selfless it was.' But he did have a really radical effect on me.[31]

---

27 Keller to all producers, 27 January 1974, WAC R27/1030/1.
28 Keller to Ponsonby, 12 August 1974, WAC R27/1030/1. Martin Dalby was Head of Music in Scotland at that time.
29 Keller to Ernest Warburton, 28 January 1979, WAC R27/1030/1.
30 Keller to Ernest Warburton, 9 January 1979, WAC R27/1030/1.
31 Bingham interviewed by Mark Doran, 'Composer in Interview', *Tempo* 58/230 (October 2004): 20–36.

What would have pleased her 'anti-teacher teacher' most was the moment when Bingham tentatively suggested – shortly after dedicating her *Pictured Within* to Keller – that the time had come to discontinue her lessons. His ultimate aim as a teacher was to make himself unnecessary, and he constantly impressed on his pupils the vital importance of developing their own independent artistic conscience. This was particularly valuable for those tonal composers who felt out of step with contemporary trends – like Elizabeth Brusa, who met Keller at Dartington in 1978 and who describes herself as 'living like a fish out of water' in those days:

> I just felt I could not compose in an 'Avant-garde' way and was very worried about it. I tried to become 'more modern' and I was just uselessly complicating my harmonies.

Over the next seven years she had sixty lessons with Keller, who gave her the confidence to write in her own way. 'Hans had a capacity of understanding the thoughts behind a musical work even if he had never seen it before,' she recalls. 'He once told me "You know everything already. I am only here to clear up your ideas."'[32]

6 April 1982 – to Elizabeth Brusa [extract]

Dear Elizabeth,

I was delighted to have your letter of March 21st – though I am depressed to see you react to reactions to an enormous extent. If you were composing commercial music, that would indeed be a realistic course of mental action, but once you have decided to say something, you can only rely on two types of judgment – your own and, in exceptional well-definable circumstances, the judgment of a listener of whose total competence you have conclusive proof, and whose insight, at the time of judgment, is superior to your own. In other words, there is not the remotest justification to "feel mixed up about other people's reactions", if only for the simple reason that absolutely nothing positive has ever been composed without eliciting negative reactions.

The development of a clear-eared, independent conscience is just as important as the development of one's sheer creativity, and everything I have told you has been said with a view to developing your musical conscience and make you independent, contemptuous even, of other people's views. True composition is not an experiment one tries on other people, but a communication addressed to them in the clearest

---

32 Brusa to authors, 3 June 2018.

possible manner. Only one's own, realistic conscience can tell one whether the lack of clarity to which negative reactions are due is one's own or the reactor's. I am very glad, anyhow, that the performance went well enough for RAI television to have recorded it: it will be interesting to watch reactions to its transmission – without considering them judgments!

'Genius! You know it all yourself, specifically, so why do you invite reactions?' Keller asked critic and composer Bayan Northcott, who had requested some lessons, but had just put his finger precisely on the places in his latest score where Keller felt slight transitional weakness. 'The proposition of a lesson is preposterous; we shall discuss it at length, from musician to musician, without imposing the implication upon the situation that I know better.'[33] Keller enjoyed discussions with Northcott – 'each time we meet, run into each other, you make at the very least one observation of striking originality & insight' – and a few years later suggested an epistolary discussion for eventual publication. Keller was intrigued to know how Northcott the critic related to Northcott the composer: 'as you probably know, I am heavily preoccupied with our time's thinking about music, at the expense of thinking music.' They also discussed 'mad music' – the musical version of the Freudian free association method Keller sometimes recommended to his students as a way of getting them out of the 'analytical compulsion neurosis' to which he felt the teaching of composition had degenerated. Northcott was doubtful, though did concede that he had in the past experienced occasions when 'time off on a bit of "mad music" might well have saved perplexity and effort'. He tried it, and reported the results to Keller, concluding 'I am not so far convinced that I need the method that much.' 'Nobody needs it,' replied Keller, 'but there is no question that everybody derives stimulation from it; in fact your report tends to show that you do, too. I think you are judging very cleverly at what specific junctures it might come in handy.' He thought the method, even where it did not offer direct help, could still teach a composer 'a great deal about the instinctive and reactively instinctive musical behaviour of one's mind, and such knowledge is bound to prove helpful in certain (very certain) creative situations'. Nevertheless there were probably some composers, he added, 'the intensification of whose inhibitions could prove more fruitful than their removal'.[34]

'As it happens,' wrote Northcott, 'your latest reply arrives just as I am about to embark upon the development section of a slow sonata movement' – and he thought he could foresee a place 'which could well involve recourse to "mad music" in the composing'. He suggested sending Keller a rough draft of his exposition 'from which you may care to draw your own conclusions as to the

33 Keller to Northcott, 23 July 1979 and 2 December 1982.
34 Keller and Northcott never published their epistolary conversation, which began on 30 March 1984 (and is preserved in CULHK), but a description of Keller's 'mad music' method can be found in 'Epilogue/Prologue: Criticism and Analysis', *MA* I/1 (March 1982): 3–31.

expectations it raises (for the contradicting)'. But at this point, Keller drew back: 'my reaction could only hamper the further course of the composition; the expectations it raises and proceeds to contradict are part and parcel of it, and should not be influenced by an outside ear.' They stopped their correspondence at this point, and Northcott completed the movement he mentioned (the first movement of his Sextet Op. 5) a few months later, sending it only then to Keller, who admired 'the double feeling of (a) satisfaction and (b) expectation' it aroused. As so often, when praising or criticising contemporary music, Keller cited the great composers of the past, in this case a similar double feeling 'in highly comparable structural circumstances in the first movement of Mozart's Clarinet Trio' – and (when he attended the first performance of the complete work the following year) the contrast between Northcott's combination of rondo and double variation form in his second movement with Haydn's very different use of the same combination.[35]

Keller never let his composer friends forget what they owed to their talent. As Hugh Wood remembered, 'His care for one's better – or at least one's creative – self, as a naturally self-appointed and ever-vigilant super-ego, never let up.'

7 February 1977 – to Hugh Wood

Dear Hugh,

I write on an enormously important matter – practically, personally, artistically: reverse the order of the adverbs if you want to think in terms of priority. Rightly or wrongly, it had been assumed that you would be writing the quartet for the June 13 concert, which has therefore firmly (internationally) been planned. Speaking for myself, I was under the impression that you had accepted the commission, but now I gather that you never replied to the Arts Council's letter (of last November). Still speaking personally, I think it would be an unmixed disaster if you did not creatively respond to this invitation, which one has tried one's utmost to make possible.

I gather, both from yourself and from what Francis Routh tells me you told him, that you have very little time because you have to keep alive, and that you are busy both with Cambridge and with a BBC talk. While I appreciate these difficulties, the quartet will contribute towards their solution too: £400 await you, and I take it that you would receive half this fee immediately upon acceptance of the commission. We have talked about work – and getting out of any particular piece of work – before, and I appreciate that our respective attitudes towards these problems are

35 See Keller to Northcott, 25 October 1984, CULHK, and 'Two-and-a-half Major Events', *M&M*, July 1985.

different – especially towards the problem of pressure of time. But I do think that when we last discussed this central area of one's life, you did at least give me a little point.

Today, I want to make this very point a little more emphatically: without wanting to sound patronising – in fact, out of sheer respect and admiration – I simply wish to say that you owe it to your talent to respond to this commission which, after all, is a direct result of the very high esteem in which your work is held by some of us. Since my own role in bringing this invitation about is by no means negligible, I feel justified, both musically and morally, in imploring you not to walk past one of the main purposes of what you are around for, whatever the psychological cost. For it is only psychological cost that is the problem here: with respect, the financial aspect is solvable. We might remind ourselves that Mozart did not even reject Titus.

Yours ever,

Hans

'The immediate appeal to the highest court is typical,' recalled Wood of Keller's reference to Mozart's *Titus*, as was Keller's 'constant solicitude for one's own work'.[36] 'Who knows, the whole crisis may turn into something good,' wrote Keller when he had resigned himself to the fact that Wood was not going to meet the deadline; 'it usually & eventually does with substantial people, & especially creative people. Beethoven wanted to commit suicide because he was going deaf – but the crisis turned into one of mankind's ultimate creative blessings, however much of a personal curse it may have continued to be.'[37]

This commission was probably particularly close to Keller's heart not only because of his admiration for Wood, but because it was for a string quartet (Wood's third, completed the following year). This was the form that Keller was desperate to preserve as a living tradition, in whose concentrated instrumental colour '*texture itself turns into structure*, whence the logic of the music becomes all-pervasive, turning all its sounds into sense.'[38] A fundamental part of his campaign was the fullest possible understanding of the masterpieces of the past. In Mozart's chamber music it was his string quintets that Keller most admired – 'the greatest and most original symphonic structures of Mozart' – and in Beethoven's the 'ultimate metaphysical discoveries' of his late quartets. Haydn, however, was the alpha and omega of the string quartet, in whose '45 profound and profoundly different, absolutely flawless, consistently original

---

36 *HKSym*, 400.
37 Keller to Wood, 23 March and 25 April 1977, CULHK.
38 'Why This Piece Is about *Billy Budd*', *Listener* 88/2270 (28 September 1972): 419, reprinted in *EOM*, 198–200.

master quartets' were to be found the seeds of all that was to come. 'From any naturally musical point of view, every string player ought to know the 45 as well as every responsible pianist knows the "48",' yet Keller found 'string players all over the place who mention the great Haydn symphonies and his great quartets in the same breath, unaware of the immeasurably weightier and subtler substance any of the master quartets evinces when heard next to a comparable master symphony.'[39]

In 1974, when he was designing a new annual string quartet competition for the EBU – and trying (as ever) to make it serve musical ends (rather than turn into the spectator sport he felt most music competitions had become) – Keller devised a new challenge for the finalists: to rehearse before the judges a Haydn quartet chosen at random. The rules required each quartet 'to work at, show *musical – i.e. not technical* – knowledge of one of the 45 masterpieces of Haydn contained in List 3':

> The working period of each such session will be 45 minutes and the piece will be chosen by the jury, which will give the quartets at least one hour's notice of it, the purpose of this study session being twofold: to establish the ensemble's basic literacy as well as its understanding of the essential improvisatory nature of all characteristic string-quartet playing.[40]

Representing Britain in the competition was the young Chilingirian Quartet, formed three years earlier by Levon Chilingirian, who had first encountered Keller in the late 1960s as a student at Dartington. He and his new quartet played music examples for Keller's lectures there in the 1970s and began to go to him for regular coaching.

The EBU competition was to be held in Stockholm in November 1974. Keller met the quartet in July for a coaching session in which they first worked on Haydn and then listened together to a late-evening broadcast on Radio 3 of the Chilingirians playing Haydn's Op. 42 and Beethoven's Op. 130 (on which Keller was writing a book and had given four magnificent broadcast lectures the previous year[41]). The session finished on a low note, since the quartet were dissatisfied with their performance of the Beethoven. Keller, as he went to bed that night, was more worried by the realisation of how little time there was before the EBU competition to work with them on Haydn, given their respective schedules. Among other things, he was very busy with the Schoenberg centenary, for which he would be in Israel in August and Canada in October.

---

39 *HKH*, 5
40 From the published rules for the 1978 EBU String Quartet Competition (CULHK).
41 Recordings of Keller's lectures on Op. 130 are available in the British Library's sound archive. Keller's book on the work remained unpublished: an incomplete manuscript is preserved in CULHK.

11 July 1974 – to Levon Chilingirian

Dear Levon,

I was depressed last night – not because of Op. 130 (whose good
aspect you didn't notice any more in the end, when everything seems
to have been declared disastrous), but because we only got through
less than 1½ Haydns. I thought to myself that while a few words (if they
stimulate what you want to do, anyway) can change your approach out of
recognition and make it strikingly meaningful, we won't meet again until
September – and then it will be Schoenberg, not Haydn. Thinking further,
of the possible (if intermittent) frustration of my experience as a mere
listener in Stockholm, where I might have to realize that one warning
syllable here and there would have produced a wholly different picture,
I decided, at 0007 precisely, to act realistically, if unconventionally: that's
what life usually is about, and art always. I shall devote about ½-hour
per day (not, perhaps, every day) to one of the forty-five, sending you
notes about what to avoid, and what might be overlooked on superficial
acquaintance – all based on wide, specific coaching experience. Of
course, the things we discussed last night I shall not reiterate, nor will
I say anything (I hope) which you can be expected to glean, anyhow.
Needless to add, no fee, or gratitude, or indeed acknowledgment will be
involved: these things don't play any role in real art. When one player
takes up an idea from another in the course of playing a string quartet, he
doesn't say "thank you very much" either.

Op. 9, No. 4.

First movement: The "Boccherini tempo" (my term)[42] should not induce
one, on the one hand, to split the music into half-bars – nor, on the other
hand, to play it too fast by way of over-compensation. The beginning is
mysterious, contained, slowly developing, especially in view of the double
start (bar 7). The gravest danger in the movement is an unintended
accent on the semiquaver upbeat in bar 2 and all corresponding
places: the motif plays a dominating role, not only here, but also in the
development. The danger is heightened when three instruments answer
one (bar 3). If this phrase and its reply is thought of as a contrasting
variation (but still very much a variation) of the end of the first phrase
(middle of bar 2) and its echo in the second violin, the interpretation is
bound to be logical. The more de-accentuation on the upbeat, the better.
There is a danger of an unconscious quickening of pace when the second

---

42 Keller defined this as 'the kind of weighty tempo character, that is, which induces the somnolent,
quasi-orchestral lower-part player, even though he may not be slow-witted, to mistake half a bar
for a whole one during rest- or also minim-time'. *HKH*, 20.

violin has the triplets – and, on the other hand, of an insufficiently light flow where the first has the demisemiquavers (second subject). In the recapitulation, there is an almost historic wrong accent – in bar 29 after the double bar, on the syncopation (first and second violins). It remains to be said that the opening cello quavers have to contribute to the mystery, and that accompaniments tend to be too loud unless one does something about them.

Minuet: The contrast between forte and piano is all-important, and the resumption of the forte in bar 5 ought to be a revelation – or a declamation, anyhow, without the lower three producing dotted minims like sausages. The Trio is evidently intended as a Trio with a difference: Haydn could have put the second-violin part into the viola, and the first violin's lower line into the second violin. Instead, he wants, not only unanimity of colour but, on the other hand, the friction produced by the double-stoppings – or rather, the overcoming of that friction: a discreet virtuoso approach is recommended, with the listener being aware that the first fiddle is doing quite something. Inevitably, therefore, the Trio will be a little slower that the principal section.

Adagio: Need I say more? But it is not only the adagio which is often forgotten. The piano, too, tends to evaporate by bar 11. Outstanding wrong accents in all four instruments will easily be found in bars 45 and 46 – on the complete triplet preceded by 2/3 of a triplet. Immediately afterwards, the most frequent disturbing feature is over-articulation, lack of blend, and lack of pianissimo (I know it doesn't say so) in the accompanimental triplets in the lower three instruments.

Finale: Even though this is the simplest movement, it is usually the worst played. The reasons are two, or two halves of one: the music tends to be split up into half-bars, thus never assuming real presto character. It's got to be jolly fast to make sense, and the fastness has to be in the phrasing and shading. Even dynamic shadings are readily ignored, and a utility mezzoforte easily dominates everything. Except in performances which I have coached, I have not yet heard the opening played piano on a single occasion – as if one couldn't be decisive on the piano level! For the rest, as so often in Haydn, staccato dots on quavers preceding a couple of slurred quavers in compound time (10 bars from the end, etc.) don't mean explosive staccatos, but are simply intended to remind the player (and copyist) that the note is separate, not part of the slur. In fact, you won't find any such groups without a dot on the single note, which would seem to prove my case.

Yours,

Hans Keller

In his second letter, Keller discussed Op. 42, 'because your playing of it is fresh in my mind' after the broadcast they had listened to together. After that he moved on to Op. 20, the first of which, as Levon Chilingirian recalls, turned out to be the quartet they were actually given at the competition in the autumn:

> Each of the four finalists taking part had to pick a brown envelope which contained the score and parts of a lesser-known Haydn Quartet. We went away and rehearsed for an hour and then came back and continued work in front of the judging panel. Our brown envelope contained Op. 20 No. 1![43]

16 July 1974 – to Levon Chilingirian

Dear Levon,

The opening movements of the first, second, and fifth quartets of Op. 20 are still in "Boccherini tempo". In the case of the E flat, this means, again, the danger of a superabundance of accents, of a split-up into half-bars. There are other dangers of mis-accentuation too: the 3-semiquaver upbeat will receive an accent unless one strenuously avoids it (a) because a first note is always in danger of an accent anyway, and (b) because two instruments play the figure, so that any subtly wrong approach is automatically doubled. Perhaps the gravest danger of an accent in the middle of the bar is in the second subject.

Minuet: Need I say less? No mature Haydn quartet ever is a minuet, and the 1-2-3 is still a danger that lurks behind your interpretations of these movements. To all intents and purposes, bars 5 and 6, for instance, are a 6/4 bar. In fact, the first main accent is not reached until the middle of the sentence (bar 4), up to which the interpretation ought to urge: the relaxation in the piano consequent will re-establish (or rather, establish for the first time!) temporal balance. I would go so far as to suggest that in this way, the opening period can be played so freely that the basic tempo is not reached until after the double bar: this shows one the fallacy of thinking of a tempo first, and of structure and phrasing afterwards. For the rest, you will note that my point about the first main accent is stressed by the unprecedented absence of slurs in the lower instruments from bar 3 to bar 4.

The spirit of the slow movement can be approached by way of a better-known movement which it has influenced, again an A flat movement in an E flat quartet – Mozart's, of course, where Haydn's 3/8 is replaced by 6/8. Haydn's 3/8 need not in fact be taken all that literally either, except

---

43 Oral communication, 26 October 2016.

where it is stressed by sforzatos, whose very presence shows, on the most superficial level, how he wants the texture to flow when they aren't there: remember our conversation. Mezza voce, incidentally, does not mean the affected, or else lifeless piano one usually hears, but the kind of repressed, contained tone which is only possible in a string quartet. The blend (as distinct from balance) must of course be treated with extreme caution in a movement of this kind, where the most infinitesimal lack of blend easily shows up. (It is this Haydn movement, and also the Mozart one, which are marvellous tests for the compatability of the actual instruments.)

Two crucial points of phrasing arise in the Finale. One is the viola's and cello's restatement of the opening, whose forte means forte <u>level</u>, not an inadvertently accented upbeat; indeed, the main beat of the structure is not reached until the next bar – and this, of course, goes for the opening phrase itself too.

Secondly, there are the syncopations. It is surprising how may players who manage the most complex modern rhythms with superficial ease are unable to realize this texture naturally. Everybody must hear everybody; as the greatest quartet player I knew once said, "The other person is always right". When the passage finally flows, you yourself will have a chance to shape your line without anxiety – and, incidentally, the whole quartet will be prepared for the Coda of the first movement of the "Fifths" Quartet (Op. 76 No. 2).

Yours,

Hans Keller

The letters continued to flow throughout the following months. 'It was a summer of letters,' recalls Chilingirian: 'As the letters poured in, we would work on them whenever we had time; they were like a series of footnotes to our own work on the quartets.' After the competition, they continued their sessions with Keller: 'He had an uncanny ability to predict what we would get right (and to know when we knew we had got it right) and an equal ability to predict what we would get wrong,' says Chilingirian, 'and woe betide you if you thought something had gone really well and it hadn't – he would blast away at you!' This was hard to take at times, especially when Keller criticised a performance others had praised, but they knew his close attention was a compliment, an indication of what they could achieve.

In common with all those Keller coached – and indeed any performer in whom he was interested – the Chilingirians found their concerts were often followed by a letter from Keller discussing their performance, usually in great detail, sometimes even accompanied by marked-up scores. ('They were BBC Library scores,' says Chilingirian, 'so I had to rub out all the comments before I sent them back!')

Here is an extract (the section on the first two movements) from the long letter Keller sent after hearing them play Beethoven's Op. 74 ten years later:

17 August 1984 – to Levon Chilingirian [extract]

Dear Levon,

[. . .] Your musical personality is, at the moment, very close to my mind, because I heard you play outstandingly the other night. To the Fricker I won't react, since I don't know the work, but your performance in the "Harp" was so impressive that I shall allow myself a few criticisms of the less impressive moments.

The very beginning I didn't understand. You seem to have placed the phrase's main accent on the Eb – a misinterpretation which you did not repeat in bars 3–4, where the main accent rightly ensued on the Db.

As for the <u>Allegro</u>, the viola over-played its principal part in bars 31 ff. Nor was the <u>forte–piano</u> contrast sufficiently heeded in bars 43 ff – a relative neglect of <u>piano</u> which made itself felt later on too.

Though you yourself were not to blame, the tempo got unmotivatedly faster with the semiquavers in bar 53 – an inconsistency which recurred in the repeat. What you were to blame for was your accent on the upbeating triplet in bar 57; no doubt it happened under the influence of the <u>crescendo</u>, which <u>can</u> be realized while the upbeat phrase retains its shape. The <u>crescendo</u> in bar 66 was one of the many that were not sufficiently realized – as was the <u>piano</u> five bars from the end of the exposition (in the repeat, too).

The viola's <u>pianissimo</u> in the second bar of the development did not materialize as a sufficient contrast to the preceding <u>forte</u>, and the balance before bar 100 was, frankly, a mess. In the successive, upward-aiming <u>pizzicatos</u>, continuity was not sufficiently listened to, and the ensuing <u>crescendo</u> in bars 136 ff needed more power. In the <u>pizzicatos</u> before bar 160, there was another rushing contradiction of your basic tempo character, and the upbeating triplet in bar 183 paralleled the one I have mentioned. There was little trace of the piano at the beginning of bar 192, or of the ensuing <u>diminuendo</u> in 198.

I am convinced that Beethoven meant the first two of your semiquavers after the barline and at the half-bar in 221 ff to be <u>legato</u>; have you any information which contradicts my conviction?

Your last rush happened in bar 245, and your last lacking contrast in 250, as against the ensuing <u>forte</u> in 254 ff.

The opening tempo of the <u>Adagio</u> had no adagio character at all and, significantly enough, it promptly slowed down both at bar 15 and again at bar 25. But at bar 40, we got faster again, and at bar 49, your all-important <u>legato</u> was missing. In bars 51, 52 and 53, there was no logical displacement of accent: <u>both</u> the <u>sforzatos</u> and the first beats were stressed. At bar 61, you led back into a real adagio tempo, which was sustained throughout the <u>cantabile</u>. The <u>piano</u> in bar 80 was amongst the neglected soft dynamics, and in bar 83, there was an illogical <u>legato</u> from the A♭ to the G. Before and at 110, the contrast between <u>pianissimo</u>, <u>forte</u>, and <u>fortissimo</u> was not sufficiently realized. At 121, there was another illogical <u>legato</u> linking the octave C. At 135, there was another neglected <u>crescendo</u>, and while the <u>glissando</u> in 141 was illogical, the one in 145 was absolutely to the point. At 149, you fortunately, by way of conclusion, led back into a proper adagio character.

[. . .]

But let me reiterate: from you it was one of the profoundest performances I have heard in recent times – far superior, I would guarantee, to the first performance of the work. Renewed congratulations! You realize that I w'dn't have dreamt of thus criticizing a mediocre performance, or even a tolerable one.

All the best until we meet again!

Kindest regards,

Yours ever,

Hans

One who shared Keller's view of Haydn's quartets – almost to the extent that it was scarcely possible to say more in the face of such comprehensive mastery ('it's all there') – was Benjamin Britten, whom Keller reminded more than once of his promise in 1947 to 'write a string quartet for you'. 'Are you fully aware that a 4tet written with the little and neighbouring toe of your left foot while you are asleep and dreaming of tooth-ache w'd be immeasurably better than ANY 4tet written between 1960 and 1980?' he asked Britten in 1968, stressing how desperately the form needed his genius: 'The greatest of all instrumental combinations is in the worst possible state.' 'I will (& do) think alot about that St. Quart.,' Britten assured him, 'but I'm now mad about Haydn's, & need we add to them?'[44]

---

44 Keller to Britten, 21 March, BPF; Britten to Keller, 11 April 1968, in the collection of Christopher Wintle. Keller's correspondence with Britten is reproduced complete in *BB2013*.

14 April 1968 – to Benjamin Britten
Postcard, BPF

I know what you mean about the Haydn 4tets – the beginning & the
end, & so many of them, all different! [. . .] Nevertheless, Mozart allowed
himself to add to them (and virtually said so) – tho', let's face it, his are
not only fewer, but more alike (Not so the 5tets.) 'Need we really add
to them?' Not before the addition is made. But afterwards, wise after the
event, we recognize the need: that's what great creation is about.

Love & speedy recovery,

Hans

Britten was then just out of hospital and – not for the last time – Keller suggested
that the quiet and introspection of convalescence was ideal for quartet-writing. 'No
deadlines, no practical problems, no extra-musical considerations, no collaborators –
nothing but you, the music, and the player-listener,' he wrote in 1974, as Britten was
recovering from his major heart operation. 'The literature needs you, and so do its
players: might not one convalescence help another?'[45]

It was not until the beginning of 1975, the year before his death, that Britten
finally began to write his Third Quartet. A year later, he sent a note to Keller asking if he might dedicate it to him. Keller was overcome:

20 January 1976 – Telegram to Benjamin Britten
BPF

ONE OF THE FEW MOST SUBSTANTIALLY HAPPY MOMENTS IN MY LIFE
I SHALL NOT BE ABLE TO SLEEP WHICH WILL BE A GOOD THING

LOVE HANS

Poring over the score, Keller found the first movement to be an extraordinarily
creative answer to the point he had made to Britten all those years ago about the
heart of sonata form being 'the contrast between statement and development'.

Benjamin Britten [extract]
M&M (September 1984): 10, reprinted in *BB2013*, 174–6

The Third Quartet [. . .] is conclusive proof of what we might call
the sonata side of Britten's creative character: so original is the first

---

45 Keller to Britten, 30 January 1974, BPF.

movement's sonata structure that, as has been said, it is not recognised as a sonata build-up by perceptive critics: so far as I am aware, I (its dedicatee) was the first to draw attention to the movement's allegiance to sonata form.

And paradoxically again, it is Britten's monothematicism which produces the most original sonata innovation in the Third Quartet's first movement; one might almost call it revolutionary, in that it certainly hadn't happened ever before in the course of the Austro-German symphonic tradition. His monothematic creativity, that is, enables him to use the self-same thematic material which had expressed the utmost instability and tension (in the development, of course) for the purpose of expressing, in the course of the coda, their straight opposite, to wit, extreme stability and relaxation.

The creative position is crystal-clear: only a mind instinctively capable of using one and the same theme towards expressing the most contrasting emotions, moods and atmospheres, could have been capable of this type of thematic economy, this mode of extremely contrasting variation. While an instinctive ability to express the contrasts of a complete piece of music through a single theme will always come in handy when polythematic structures are attempted, an instinctive ability to invent contrasting themes will not help you in your monothematic endeavours.

The reason, this, why Haydn ranks as one of the outstanding innovators within the area of sonata form, whereas Mozart, whose capacity to invent contrasting themes was unprecedented and unsurpassed, did nothing towards the development of the form: most later sonata geniuses continued from Haydn, while literally none of them continued from Mozart. Intriguingly, in most other respects, Britten's creative character resembles Mozart's rather than Haydn's, but so far as his fruitful monothematicism is concerned, he continued where Haydn left off – and indeed, every night, he took a Haydn quartet with him to bed.

~

Unlike the 1950s, when Keller had refused to attend Marion Harewood's evening with Ravi Shankar, the music of other cultures was now everywhere. Glock had introduced it to the Proms in 1971, bringing the sitar-player Imrat Khan into one of his late-evening Roundhouse Proms, and Ponsonby continued the trend, with Indonesian gamelan music in the 1979 Proms and the Thai Classical Music Group of Srinakharinwirot University in 1981 – a performance in which Keller's old friend Donald Mitchell was much involved. Earlier that year, Mitchell had presented two hour-long Radio 3 programmes on the Thai Classical Music Group; when they came to the Proms he not only wrote the programme notes and introduced the television relay, but actually took part in the performance.

'I approached the event with maximal humility,' wrote Keller afterwards, 'as a guilt-laden cultural foreigner who had not grown up with the music's terms of spontaneous reference', which did not stop him describing it as rhythmically and melodically 'primitive'. Donald Mitchell reproached him for 'critical criteria quite inappropriate to non-Western music', but Keller insisted he was not making judgments – only observations: 'are you suggesting that I misheard one or other factual detail?'[46]

Metrical Rhythms [extract]
Listener 2725 (3 September 1981): 251

Melodically, though we had to cope with a scale of seven equidistant notes whose relation to our own diatonic scale forced us to refocus our attention on unfamiliar intervals, it soon became apparent that the music suffered from a double lack of differentiating development.

For one thing, pitch differentiation was, to put it mildly, crude: pitches which, emerging from different instruments, were treated as identical, weren't really – but to the players' ears, such distonation didn't seem to matter. For another thing, a certain type of scale and its conjunct motions pushed all other possible combinations of notes into the background or ignored them altogether; if we felt the individual notes in terms of their relation to our nearest semitone, what obtruded, predictably in due course, was a close relative, a veritable twin, of our own folkloristic tonal pentatonic scale in its third mode – or, comprehensibly speaking, sundry approximate transpositions of the piano's black keys starting on F sharp. Admittedly, the 'gapped' notes did occur – but invariably in a subordinate position, i.e. ornamentally.

Rhythmically, elementary simplicity was maintained through a preference for, indeed often the exclusive use of, equal note-values – with, again, a proportionately high (sometimes maximal) rate of predictability: the ultimate climax consisted of what we would call an extended series of percussive semiquavers with equally percussive quaver 'accompaniment' (the crochet equalling, metronomically speaking, 60). Excitement was here engendered by a gradual accelerando which, though not very successfully executed, prompted the audience to overburden the quaver

46 See Mitchell, *Cradles of the New* (London: Faber, 1995), 247.

accompaniment by way of handclapping. The primary effect of the music, then, was hypnotic rather than revelatory; increase or decrease of speed or volume and the co-ordinated interplay of colours tended to enhance stimulation rather than convey meaning.

Keller found that 'the Western rest of the evening' (Birtwistle's *For O, for O, the Hobby Horse is Forgot* and the organ version of Messiaen's *L'Ascension*) shared this 'predilection for equal values, for pulse, metre' and he reflected on the way 'our century is celebrating an unprecedented festival of equal values, a protracted sacrificial orgy: rhythmic invention is being sacrificed to metric patterns.' His next Proms review ranged widely over the question of rhythm, linking the 'festival of equal values' in contemporary composition to the decline of improvisatory performance (in the context of a recent performance by Ida Haendel, a violinist prized by him for her individuality and spontaneity, and the Proms performance of the symphonic poem *Persephone Dream* by his former pupil Jonathan Harvey).

Spontaneity [extract]
Listener 2726 (10 September 1981): 283

The decline of improvisation is the gravest current danger to the art of performance, which thus threatens to degenerate into a mere craft whose mastery, readily recognisable, is duly mistaken for art. And just as rhythm is the loser here, so that we need an Ida Haendel to remind us of both rhythm's unrepeatability and its proportionately complex, ambivalent relation to its underlying metre (which *is* repetition), the over-concern with pre-composition among our age's composers, with theories, systems, methods, plans and schemes, has reduced the element of spontaneity in the very act of creation, of sheer musical invention, to an extent which, again, endangers music's life-blood – rhythmic shape, character, and contrast.

Jonathan Harvey's *Persephone Dream* was introduced by a Pre-Prom Talk, wherein the composer described his orchestral piece as a 'river' – which turned out to be an ideal metaphor. The effortless flow of the music, the natural changes of its harmonies and colours and its equally unforced cohesion, produced an experience of utter artlessness, of a natural event indeed, untroubled by human interference. So far, so good – but no further. For in order to turn music into concrete meaning, we have to allow human beings to float and swim in the river, sometimes maybe even against the stream.

In which case, there will be tangible entities in that river, well-defined and contrasting, perhaps even bumping into each other – yet all part of, affected by, the stream. It is not mere pitches, but rhythmic shapes,

characters, sharp rhythmic articulations and definitions I am talking
about – that which, before the rhythmless tone-row – not Schoenberg's,
but Webern's – came in, was simply known as musical ideas.
Hearteningly enough, Schoenberg himself was incapable of inventing
an abstract row: he had to abstract it from a tune that, invariably, had
occurred to him in the first place.

Harvey, too, thinks dodecaphonically, almost instinctively so – and by
now, his spontaneous, concrete, rhythmical fancy may well have vastly
developed: *Persephone* is close on ten years old. As his former teacher
who could not think more highly of his musical imagination, I humbly
suggest to him that, in any case, he won't ever regret plunging into the
river and showing us – quite naturally, of course – what he can do in
and about it. Where he jumps in we come in – as addressees, not mere
empathisers.

Keller's review elicited a lengthy and thoughtful response from Harvey, who
wrote that 'Yes, I agree basically,' but asked 'is there a new and important aesthetic in lack of argument, in "empathy" between composer and audience as
opposed to what you call the composer "addressing the audience"?'

There may be a danger in your emphasis on well-defined entities, contrasted
and clashing. It's the danger that the baby of transcendence will be thrown
out with the bathwater of wish-washy weak form. What you refer to may
be applied to the period 1650–1950 most convincingly. Palestrina deliberately de-emphasised his lines. So did Beethoven in some of the late quartet
slow movements, so did Mahler at the end of Das Lied, and there are many
other exceptions: but I would call these passages transcendental, and they
are exceptions to the prevailing language of contrasts & gestures of the tonal
period. I think what is struggling to be born now is a new sense of the transcendental. . . . I am doing a lot of research into what transcendence actually
is, and one of the points of this has been an increased sensitivity to individu-
ation, of how people and objects are unique. This is where the future lies, in
my aesthetic![47]

'Oh God,' wrote Keller on this letter, circling the words 'in my aesthetic',
and he instantly wrote a long letter back to Harvey, telling him that 'dependence
on what you call "an aesthetic" is symptomatic of an anti-creative attitude; . . . I
would put it to you that insofar as musical aesthetics can be formulated at all,
any formulation that proves creatively valid can only be arrived at a posteriori,
after the creative event.'[48] That letter, which Keller felt on reflection was too

---

47 Harvey to Keller, 27 September 1981, CULHK.
48 Keller to Harvey, undated and unposted, CULHK.

dictatorial, was never posted, but he was prompted to return to the subject when Harvey wrote to him about a new project:

> Having just read your <u>Operatic Music and Britten</u> in David Herbert's book, I'm inspired to plague you with some thoughts of my own! It really is a fascinating argument you propound, and touches exactly and uncannily on my own problems. I enclose a (rather sketchy & hasty) scenario for an opera that has been growing for 10 years or so.'[49]

17 February 1983 – to Jonathan Harvey

Dear Jonathan,

Abject apologies for my delayed response to your interesting letter of January 21st, for which there are psychological as well as eminently real practical reasons [. . .].

As for the psychological delay, a long letter in reply to your last was never posted, because on reflection, it seemed to me that the ex-teacher was too much in evidence – the worst crime I know of. But your letter had aroused my aggression, which was proportionate to the imbalance between your exceptional (potentially enormous, and actually still very rich) imagination and invention and your fallacious theorizing which threatens to intervene. In particular, perhaps in response to my remarks on what I call the Contemporary Festival of Equal Values (if I made my point in these terms), I remember a gravely faulty reference to late Beethoven, which remained blissfully ignorant, or else heedless, of his harmonic rhythm, both in the background and in the foreground; without their harmonic aspects, the late Beethoven's rhythms cannot be discussed at all. In fact, within the diatonic era, so long as the master in question is capable of distinct, and at the same time complex harmonic implications, his equal values (if any) cannot, in any circumstances, be compared to the equal values of the post-diatonic era, when by the nature of things, harmonic rhythm cannot be as clearly and unambiguously defined, implied, and hence contradicted, as it used to be: the Festival of Equal Values is a function of the twentieth century, and, of harmonic necessity, of that century alone – whereas, to put it aphoristically, the equal values of former times are not, or need not be, equal.

---

49 Harvey to Keller, 21 January 1983, CULHK. Keller's article in *The Operas of Benjamin Britten*, ed. Herbert (London: Hamish Hamilton, 1979) is reprinted in *BB2013*, 147–69.

Well then, now that I have both unburdened my soul and warned you sufficiently, I might send you that letter after all – if and when I come across it. Meanwhile, there is the important, truly creative subject of your last letter, about which I feel far shier while I am, of course, fascinated by the links between your creativity and my chapter in David Herbert's book, I find it very difficult, at this stage, to answer questions which depend, to a decisive degree, on the direction your own creative thought is going to take. At the moment, that is to say, and without knowing the tiniest, concrete fragment of the <u>musical</u> side of your plans, I find a convincing rhetorical element in every single question you put to me: boringly, perhaps, my answers are just one yes after another. It's possible, however, that I've read the scenario too hastily, and hence too superficially, and that a rereading will produce more specific thoughts. In the meantime, please bear with me: I'll get down to it as soon as possible. Your plans sound very spontaneous and, proportionately, exciting: it is when your creative thoughts are interrupted or even modified by theoretical preoccupations that the ex-teacher feels like saying, "Dr. Harvey, stand in the corner, get on with it and stop babbling about it: <u>all</u> babbling has to <u>succeed</u> your invention if it is to mean anything creative at all. Otherwise, inevitably, its function is, exclusively, anti-creative.

I shall write again, then – and thank you for what you say about my chapter: by now, you must know very well what it means to be understood.

All the best!

Yours ever,

[Hans]

Keller also wrote about 'our time's rhythm(lessness)' to Hugh Wood, whom he considered 'one of the very few who have remained unaffected by what, invariably, proves a malignant disease'.[50] 'I agree with the underlying issue: that the all-important thing must be rhythm,' said Wood, but he thought Harvey's piece did show considerable rhythmic invention 'and I am left envying the plasticity of movement and the free formation of climax to which this rich rhythmic vocabulary can give rise.' He complained that 'I myself can't keep things afloat like that – my ideas are always, alas, so four-square,' and feared that 'I can only formulate rhythmic cliché, in everyone else's eyes (ears, I mean, & unspoken thoughts) inside a metre.'[51]

50 Keller to Wood, 16 September 1981, CULHK.
51 Wood to Keller, 28 October 1981, CULHK.

3 November 1981 – to Hugh Wood [extract]

Dear Hugh,

[…] Most unfair, however, you are on your own creativity: it is demonstrably wrong to say that you can "only formulate rhythmic cliché". I know you add "in everyone else's ears", but the very fact that you consider them worth quoting shows that this nonsense has affected you. Worst of all, you add "inside a metre", as if extra-metrical (as distinct from anti-metrical) rhythm could exist. The very fact that you talk about "this rich rhythmic vocabulary" proves that conceptually, you have no idea what rhythm is, however well you know it musically. For there is no such thing as a rhythmic (as opposed to metric) vocabulary; it is from the well-defined contradictions of vocabulary that rhythm arises, just as a great Haydn or Mozart minuet arises from the well-defined contradiction of the minuet. It's downright fascinating to observe that our age's rhythmic crisis has produced this autobiographical confusion in your conceptual thought. […]

The most comprehensive proof of our rhythmic crisis is the – altog. modern – separation, isolation of the notion: at pre-critical stages, rhythmlessness just didn't exist. Rhythm was (is) an inseparable aspect of all music that meant (means) anything; its seeming opposite, harmony, doesn't exist without harmonic rhythm.

Kindest, rhythmic regards,

Yours ever,

Hans

They revived this discussion after the premiere of Wood's Symphony in 1982 – 'A real sym,' declared Keller, 'the 1st in ages: genuine, sym'ic thought, even tho' it doesn't altog escape 2 contemp. symptoms – (a) my Festival of Equal Values at the expense of rhythmic characterization (the A & O of music), & (b) the quotation compulsion, which started with our age's insecurity (Schbg II): one of your quotations replaces thinking music with thinking about music.' Although Wood was relieved at Keller's positive reaction ('I've been waiting for it for months, thinking a) has he heard it? b) has he missed it? c) has he heard it, but doesn't like it?'), the reference to the Festival of Equal Values ('if it's what I think it means') reawakened his worries about his 'lack of really adventurous rhythmic invention'. He also confessed himself 'guilty again' of the quotation compulsion, but insisted that 'they're absolutely and purely private in their connotations – like the Mendelssohn quote in the Enigma Var. or – forgive me – Schoenberg II itself.'[52]

---

52 Keller to Wood, 9 January; Wood to Keller, 25 January 1983, CULHK.

3 February 1983 – to Hugh Wood

Dear Hugh,

Many thanks for yours of January 25th. Yes, you're right about the Festival of Equal Values, nor can I accept your confession ("lack of really adventurous rhythmic invention"); in fact, I remember strongly objecting to this, or a similar formulation when we last discussed the matter two yards from the French door of our living room. If you "admit" to this lack, I congratulate you, for the simple reason that people who've got "adventurous rhythmic invention" haven't got any invention, anyway.

What I am saying is that invention produces an idea, not a facet of an idea. And it is demonstrable beyond any doubt that you have a wealth of invention – some of which, I suspect, is being marginally standardized on its way to notation. I would go so far as to say that hearing you play your music, some of it, might well enable one to renotate it more truthfully. In short, there is much that is so intensely alive rhythmically that one can realistically diagnose some artificiality, or inhibition, and/or harmonic and/ or structural preoccupation whenever this intensity is absent.

And so to the quotation compulsion. People who quote for the reasons you adduce don't even deserve one's contempt. The most interesting musico-psychological source is, of course, our age's insecurity, which makes the compulsion virtually universal; about that aspect I believe I have written in 1975, including Schoenberg, of course.[53]

But the source you are drawing attention to made me mention the matter in the first place: inasmuch as something, anything, is "absolutely and purely private in its connotations" its place is a diary and not a symphony, for throwing light on keeping something dark is a pastime which reaches, or should reach, its climax at the age of four. Don't worry, your quotations don't fall into the category into which you push them – nor, of course, do Elgar's or Schoenberg's. At the same time, these examples are highly relevant: the insecurity had started. (The self-quotations known as "cyclic structure" are merely special cases, which take the insecurity back to Beethoven 5 and 9.)

The long and the short of it is that symphonic meaning, if it is new and therefore necessary, will inevitably be universal – at any rate, within its culture, That doesn't exclude, but, on the contrary, necessitates private connotations whose apparent subjectivity follows from the composer's having discovered something in himself which his listeners hadn't yet discovered in themselves: his communication, if understood, leads to

53　*1975*, 224–9.

self-discovery. At the same time, there may, of course, be "absolutely and purely private" associations (rather than connotations), whose presence does not, however, detract from the universality of the communication, of which your Elgar and Schoenberg instances are outstanding examples: their musical sense is not only utterly complete, but the surrounding music's meaning would lose if robbed of their context – while on the other hand, absolutely nothing is added to one's musical experience, to one's self-discovery, when one is told "why" Schoenberg quoted that tune. In other words, the "absolutely and purely private" associations are, from a musical point of view, a mere means towards the end of a selfless self-discovery. So far as my understanding went, the second Magic Flute quotation did not meet these conditions, and won't if it is curtailed and made more distant, unless something is going to happen, contextually too, which I can't forehear; that, of course, is easily possible.

It is a thorough pleasure thus to criticize your work locally, because one is thinking on the basis of a total experience of often crystal-clear, weighty, significance; rarer and rarer are the occasions when one hears substantial music, for even when a great deal is to be said in its favour from an intra-musical point of view, the substance is only too often lacking, or else so thin that half the duration would have sufficed, or again so old that one has known it since Dittersdorf, and never mind Haydn.

In one dimension, and one dimension only, most of the most gifted composers of our age have achieved mastery, and that's the dimension of cheating, including self-deceit, which even a Ligeti indulges in without his musical conscience bothering him at all. But a symphony, like a string quartet, can't cheat, and so far as my inadequate insight into yours is concerned, I can say with confidence that even its uncertainties are meaningful, in that they draw attention to contexts in which we all experience them, and usually repress them by means of superimposed, phoney clarity.

It so happens that this particular dictation session is over, and that its end coincides with the end of one of this letter's clearly planned chapters. No matter: the next chapter will inevitably follow – though it might, of course, happen orally. In any case, I can be depended upon not to forget – for the experience of your symphony was deep enough to conjure up my thoughts about it whenever it is recalled. I apologize for what, in the intellectual circumstances, is the brutal brevity of this letter.

Yours ever,

[Hans]

~

Although Keller's immersion in everything musical going on around him was complete, he still found time for extra-musical pursuits. In particular, his interest in football continued as keen as ever – indeed it became a substantial source of income in his later years, not only from writing and broadcasting about it, but from betting on it. He was a master gambler, as his letters to his BBC colleague and fellow football enthusiast Julian Hogg show:

Undated – to Julian Hogg

<u>Julian</u>

I'm refining my system: unfavourable odds are accepted so long as a draw is likely.

This week, the worst offs are on Luton (a) agst Grimsby (h). Last year, I'd have ignored the match in view of Grimsby's relegation fight. This year, I'd have ignored it for the additional reason of the odds. Now, I'm including it because of G's relegation fight, which is likely to result in a draw. Chelsea v Spurs & B'ham v MU are the other two – safe bets with undramatic odds, which depend on the Luton draw. I'd think that at least 50% of such bets will succeed, which is enough.

BUT it's possible that you didn't get the point of my question – tho' you probably did. If, in anticipation, you viewed the Ipswich game in the same light as the Celtic game (as you said you did, & as I did), your criticism of the choice of the Celtic game loses its force, unless you are arguing against the choice of any such game (as distinct from 2 or 3 of them, which w'd indeed be irrational): what happened at Ipswich (a pretty close parallel altog, in view of Swansea's position) has a sufficient statistical incidence to make the choice reasonable on the daring level – since, for other reasons, all daring choices that week were (and indeed proved) equally unlikely. <u>The only alternative I considered – you'll be amused to hear this confession</u> – was Spurs, in view of their 0 home draws 3 home wins (as opposed to the surrounding teams' including all the higher-placed ones), but WBA's 2 away draws & 0 away wins didn't make it any better, but worse than the Celtic game: only Leeds & Notts County were worse than they. (Nor indeed do I curse myself too much: WBA – did you see them on Sun? – were luckier than Aberdeen w'd have had to be to win, especially in the Ardiles-less ½ ! The manager was happy with the Spurs performance!)

In short, in the same circumstances, I'll do it again. They do actually obtain next week – <u>but without any Ipswich or Celtic game.</u>

Undated – to Julian Hogg

Well, well. This is getting very serious – rational, high-class investment, so far as I can see. The '3 awys' bet was <u>16–1</u>; <u>I put most money on it & prepaid tax.</u> (Wolves v Ips: 0–2; Cambridge v. W Ham: 1–2; Wrexham v Blackburn: 0–1.) Very soon now, the statistical sample will be valid, don't you think? Whenceforth one ought to put, say £10 or £20 on a bet: what is the answer to the question, why not? Subtle question: at what stage do I advise another person to go with me – behaving like an unpaid stockbroker, as it were?

One thing I discovered: compared to my forecasts, the newspapers' (Sunday Times, Sunday Express) are incompetent; what are these people being paid for? Does anybody check? And football journalism is all they're doing! Which brings me back to – so much for professionalism. [. . .]

Keller did share his system with David Ellis, Head of BBC Music in Manchester, a fellow football enthusiast who had expressed interest in 'the Keller system for amassing a small fortune – or even a large one – using three aways or draws':[54]

25 October 1980 – to David Ellis [extract]

Dear David,

[. . .] Your reference to my 'draws' indicates that you are not aware of what, precisely, I am doing: why should you be? But since I have now won ten out of eleven weeks, and in view of your own, deep footballing knowledge, I feel the duty to tell you of my system, in case you are in need of supplementary earnings. In the Long List, I select three matches each of which will, one can confidently predict, be either an away win or a draw. The matches have to be very carefully chosen; it takes me hours each week to select them – and I strongly recommend particular attention to the Scottish League, which evinces more away wins than the English League.

I then place eight bets to cover all possible permutations (combinations): x,x,x; 2,2,2; x,2,2; x,2,x; x,x,2; 2,x,x; 2,x,2; 2,2,x. I lose seven bets and win one – on what, in fact, is on odds. If, however, special odds are offered on three away wins and/or three draws, and either of these results ensues, I win immeasurably more – on highly favourable against odds. This has happened once so far.

---

54 Ellis to Keller, 9 October 1980, CULHK.

If you are interested in my particular selection, don't hesitate to let me know – but you may think that your selections would be even better than mine, and that you would have won eleven out of eleven.

Yours ever,

[Hans]

Another colleague, Leo Black, recalled that 'some of his bets were bizarrely specific,' including such gems as 'the first goal to come in the first five minutes of the first half, by a header'. The reactions of the betting-shop managers, according to Black, 'went through a recurring cycle – initial disbelief, happiness to accept this fool's money, growing alarm as he kept winning' – leading eventually to Keller being banned from all his regular bookmakers.[55]

Keller reached the BBC's retirement age of sixty on 11 March 1979 – a date long earmarked by Robert Ponsonby 'for the closing of BBC ranks'.[56] But before the management had had a chance to breathe its sigh of relief, Keller was back in his office next day, and continued there until his departure for Jerusalem in May, working steadily through a pile of self-imposed handover work. 'People shouldn't expect that my retirement means that I have suddenly lost all my interest in music broadcasting,' he told his successor Stephen Plaistow – indeed even after he stopped coming to Broadcasting House he continued to write

> *What really interests me is whether God had any choice in the creation of the world.*

to his colleagues, advising, praising and admonishing them. He was never the first to let a correspondence lapse and his huge circle of friends found his letters invariably thought-provoking. This, for example, was his reply to music producer Helen Cooke's ecstatic letter announcing she was at long last expecting a child:

Undated – to Helen Cooke

Dear Helen,

My criminal neglect of your elating letter has not been unmotivated: little is in this world, except for Kant's Critique of Pure Reason,

---

55 *HKKC*, xix.
56 Ponsonby to Hearst, 8 March 1978, WAC L1/1907/3.

which is so totally reasoned that motives, if any, can no longer be diagnosed.

For once, I just did not know what to say – in reply to one particular passage: 'I find myself wishing I believed in God, so that I c'd thank someone. I know you do, so c'd you tell him. . . . .'

What are you talking about? I thought you believed in God, & I didn't? In fact, I don't believe in anything: belief is not part of my psychic apparatus. Knowledge and ignorance are. I know – thru' music – about metaphysical reality, & there's no doubt that other people (wrongly) call it God, some of them, while yet others call something 'God' that just isn't there, and it's they who have conversations with Him and thank Him on your behalf; if they talk to Him, they are respected, pious members of our community, but if He talks to them they are schizophrenics.

No matter, I, we are terribly happy with you, both of you, about having shown the world, once again (and the world still isn't listening), that creation is not subject to criticism, but, on the contrary, the one human activity beyond Best and Evil.

It's time we met again – tho' for the moment, you may not be as mobile, externally, as you are within.

All the best to the three of you, meanwhile.

love

Hans

Naturally, Keller took full advantage of finally being free to discuss broadcasting in the press, and he started with an open farewell – or rather 'Fare Better' – to the BBC in *The Spectator*.[57] There was plenty of call for such public discussion in the year after his retirement, when the BBC's music policy hit the headlines in no uncertain terms. The orchestral cuts threatened in *Broadcasting in the Seventies* had not so far materialised, the government having made the maintenance of employment levels for musicians part of the 1971 licence fee deal. But they were back on the agenda with a vengeance in 1980: raging inflation had wiped out the short-term licence fee increases granted by the outgoing Labour administration, the boost from the take-up of television was falling off, and the incoming Conservative government, elected with an agenda of financial control and anti-union rhetoric, was hardly likely either to increase the licence fee or insist on the preservation of musicians' jobs.

Five orchestras were scheduled to be axed, including the BBC Scottish Symphony Orchestra, whose enterprising policies Keller had particularly admired.

57 20 June 1979, 29–30.

The Musicians' Union called a strike, causing the cancellation of Prom concerts for the first time since the V2 bombing in 1944. Then the composer and producer Robert Simpson resigned very publicly from the Corporation after thirty years. 'I can no longer work for the BBC without a profound sense of betrayal of most of the values I and many others believe in, and its management includes elements whose authority I cannot accept without shame,' he wrote to the *The Times*. 'It is now necessary for me to be able to say what I wish to whom I wish when I wish, without the shackles imposed by that all too sinister phrase "corporate loyalty".'[58] Keller watched the ensuing debate for three weeks before joining the fray, then wrote both to Simpson and to *The Times* from the Dartington Summer School – where Peter Maxwell Davies (who had just taken over the directorship of the School from Glock) was circulating Simpson's *Times* letter 'with explosive enthusiasm'.[59]

'I gave 20 years of my life and its central loves to the BBC,' wrote Keller in his own letter to *The Times*, a paean to radio's vital role as patron, 'without which important new music and important new musicians just don't happen: music without mass appeal depends on a mass medium for its survival.'[60] He went into more detail in an article for the *London Review of Books*, trying to show among other things that there might actually be artistically fruitful ways of saving money:

Music on Radio and Television [extract]
LRB II/15 (7–20 August 1980): 7–8

Artistically, the decline of live broadcasting is a catastrophe: by now, live broadcasts are confined to concerts and recitals in front of an audience; live studio work is virtually dead – or, one would hope, temporarily dead-alive. The catastrophe comprises two tragedies: on the one hand, faked performances (which recordings inevitably are) are replacing artistic events, with the result that while a mistake is assuming disproportionate importance, the *condition sine qua non* of a truly musical performance, spontaneous risk-taking, is vanishing from the interpretative scene:

> There is far too much emotional distress in the intellectual world, and far too little intellectual distress.

what is art without the taking of risks? On the other hand, such novel programme-building as could not, at this stage, attract an audience to a concert hall has been largely abandoned, which means that the radiogenic concert *par excellence*, the concert which needs a studio in order to

---

58 *The Times*, 18 July 1980, 15.
59 Keller to Simpson, 11 August 1980, CULHK.
60 *The Times*, 15 August 1980, 11.

escape a depressingly empty (and expensive) concert hall, has become a thing of the past – and, the far-eared amongst us realise, the future. The amount of money which would be saved if studio recordings with their attendant editing sessions were, to a large extent, abandoned would prove downright sensational: energy, material and manpower could be drastically reduced. [. . .]

Let us turn to what is the most topical evil of them all – the BBC's projected orchestral cuts. [. . .] The demonstrably disastrous effects which the demise of the Scottish Symphony Orchestra would or will have are not remotely realised. They are simply ignored by BBC management – at any rate, so far as, again, the radiogenic part of a staff orchestra's work is concerned. And once again, it is a matter of unconventional, culturally necessary programme-building: there are countless types of radio programmes for which there is no public replacement, countless important, new or unfamiliar works which only staff orchestras can take on because, as yet, they cannot feasibly be included in the repertoire of a public orchestra. [. . .]

The development of players and, quite especially, soloists and conductors is an equally essential, equally irreplaceable function: the BBC Scottish Symphony Orchestra itself has bred, almost given birth to, some of our most distinguished conductors. That the management of a radio organisation should remain unaware of the central part which radio orchestras play in the life, the survival, of our musical civilisation is all the more frightening since the more developed sister organisations – the German ones, for instance – are fully alive to the crucial significance of staff orchestras.

Robert Simpson made more waves the following year, with the publication of his polemic *The Proms and Natural Justice*,[61] which questioned the wisdom of entrusting 'the awesome responsibilities' of the Proms 'to one person (till death or retirement).'

No matter how gifted and imaginative, how evangelistic for worthy causes, how inspired is one man, his idiosyncrasies and prejudices will feed themselves over a long period, try as he may to eliminate them. This is not a plea for another committee. Artistic conceptions are best from a single mind, prejudices and all.

Simpson's solution was simple: a strict limit (five years) on the length of time each planner of the Proms could serve.

---

61 (London: Toccata, 1981)

Although he tried to make clear that 'this little book is in no sense an attack on William Glock,' it was inevitably taken as such, since Simpson had focused his analysis entirely on Glock's period in charge. He recalled Glock's 1959 'coup' in taking over Proms planning and discussed the ensuing fourteen seasons with reference to lists of composers unrepresented, or barely represented, during that time. Robert Ponsonby, on the other hand, was not directly implicated, as Simpson felt it would have been 'neither fair nor altogether realistic' to have listed his omissions in comparison, he having been in charge for less than half Glock's time by this date. This, Keller thought, was 'a grave error', reminding Simpson that 'Glock, with all his quirks, was an outstanding instinctive musician, and many of his Prom programmes, whatever their quirks, bear witness to his musical imagination, which produced a downright revolution in programme planning.' Concentrating on one man had also weakened Simpson's argument: 'strictly logically, the fact that you have these two totally dissimilar planning types at your disposal is a heaven-send.'[62]

It was during the public discussion over Simpson's book that the myth of 'the Glock–Keller regime' came into being. It was composer Carey Blyton (nephew of Enid) who first used the term and described what this 'regime' had allegedly done:

> In 1959, when William Glock became Controller of Music, with Hans Keller as his Chief Assistant, New Music, the BBC Music Division began a rigorous championing of the more extreme forms of avant-garde music to the virtual exclusion of any new music which had an immediate appeal. ('Schoenberg is the One, True God, and Pierre Boulez is His Prophet' became the faith that all had to live by, whether composer or BBC producer.) . . . Heaven knows, there is a tremendous backlog of attractive and interesting music available, written during the 'Black Years' of the Glock–Keller regime, but never heard by most music-lovers because never broadcast.[63]

The chairman of the Composers' Guild, Derek Bourgeois – despite being himself one of the unrepresented composers listed by Simpson – came to the defence, pointing out that there was 'no such regime in the BBC. Hans Keller was not appointed Chief Assistant New Music until 1972, *after* the retirement of Sir William Glock.' He also paid tribute to Keller's work on behalf of British composers of all styles, for which the Guild had honoured him with a special award.[64]

15 October 1981 – to the Editor of *The Listener*
Listener 2731 (15 October 1981): 439

SIR: I am deeply grateful to the Composers' Guild of Great Britain for replacing Carey Blyton's detailed fiction about my BBC work (Letters,

---

62 Keller to Simpson, 28 October 1981, CULHK.
63 *Listener* 2727 (19 September 1981): 305.
64 *Ibid.* 2730 (8 October 1981): 405.

17 September) with equally detailed fact (Letters, 8 October). My own role apart, however, two facts remain to be clarified.

(1) The solitary fact in Mr Blyton's letter is that he wants his opera to be broadcast. In my 20 years at the BBC, new operatic scores always received special treatment: studio productions of new operas being difficult and expensive, the question of acceptance or rejection was always left to the person in charge of opera production, and the original rejection of Mr Blyton's opera had as much to do with Robert Ponsonby or Sir William Glock or any radio policy as THE LISTENER'S rejection of an article has with the BBC's Director-General.

(2) The Composers' Guild is right in suggesting that Sir William Glock and I 'disagreed quite a bit about contemporary music'. What we unreservedly agreed about, however, was the idiocy of evaluating in terms of schools or groups (Mr Blyton's 'avant-garde music', 'music of Continental origin', 'Second Viennese School', 'British composers'); I have never heard Sir William talk about anything but individual works, individual composers. As for Schoenberg being 'the One, True God', Sir William's own attitude towards Schoenberg's music is distinctly ambivalent – but unlike Mr Blyton, he doesn't reject what he dislikes.

A profound musician and imaginative programme-builder, William Glock has his prejudices and makes his mistakes like the rest of us, but by now the fact is demonstrable that, like Sir Henry Wood, he has been responsible for a downright historic reinvigoration of our musical life. In my wide experience the only musicians who would question the factual accuracy of this observation are some of those composers of whose music Sir William doesn't think as highly as they do.

Hans Keller

Nevertheless, the myth of the 'Glock–Keller regime', together with the 'black-list' of proscribed tonal British composers to which Glock allegedly forced his producers to adhere (no trace of which has yet emerged from the archives), took root and remained remarkably persistent. The reasons for this are complex, but have much to do with the high hopes engendered by the powerful narrative of national musical renaissance prevalent after the war, together with the expectations raised by the state subsidy of music instituted at that time – expectations dashed for many by the rapid technological and social changes that followed. While all the arts were publicly funded as never before, the mechanisation of music left the composer in a weaker economic position, as public interest became ever more fixated on performance (the dominant saleable commodity now being recordings rather than sheet music). Composers were also competing for listeners' attention with the vast repertoire of newly available music of the past (now with its own distinct performance practices) as well as the unprecedented phenomenon of a powerful popular music industry that was both an expression and an engine of profound social change.[65]

Glock kept his distance from the public arguments in 1981, reserving his defence for the autobiography he published ten years later. He and Keller were in touch after the *Listener* debate (discussing Keller's proposed lecture on 'Musical Education: its Mortal Dangers' for the Bath Festival, which Glock was now running), and Glock gave him a brief private reaction to the Proms controversy:

> I never do see <u>The Listener</u> nowadays, though one or two friends have phoned about the literature on the Proms that it has been printing. Nothing on earth would make me wade through all that. The choice between one set of second, third, fourth or fifth-rate composers and another seems to me a subject of striking triviality; and who was it who first brought the BBC regional orchestras into the Proms? Far more important to me was something that I believe you yourself said: that I looked back on each season's programmes as though someone else had planned them; far more important, too, even than (if possible) a strong and imaginative choice of 20th C music, was the panorama, as a whole, and the wealth of great works that I passionately wanted to include. I don't really have to tell you any of this.[66]

27 October 1981 – to William Glock

Dear William,

Many thanks for yours of October 22nd – and, for heaven's sake, don't think that the present note needs a reply; on the contrary, it is one to both the questions you raise and problem you imply.

Problem first. As you rightly suggest there was no need to spell out your views on the Prom controversy, but I do think that you ought to write to Bob, who (a) respects and even admires you deeply, not withstanding all ambivalence and (b) will therefore feel deeply wounded if you don't: I know for a fact that he is anxiously awaiting your reaction.

Nor indeed is his a weak case, despite the central relevance of your remarks. We must not forget that statistically speaking, the incidence of Wood and Glock within a shortish span is an extremely unlikely event: it happened to happen, but we can't possibly accept it as a basis for the planning of Prom-planning. Far more likely is an uninterrupted succession of Ponsonbys: what entitles them to be in charge "until death or retirement"? [. . .] The burden of proof is really on the other side:

---

65 See David Wright, 'Concerts for coteries, or music for all?', *MT* 149/4666 (Autumn 2008): 3–34 for a detailed discussion of Glock's programme planning and the myths that surround it.
66 Glock to Keller, 22 October 1981, CULHK.

how, without a Wood or Glock, can the present approach be justified? Anyhow, now it's for me to say that there really is no need for me to spell out this obviousity: I should think that notwithstanding incidental disagreements and essential differences in the evaluation of greatness, it ought to be easily possible for you to send Bob an encouraging note; after all, his last silly chapter apart, he ruthlessly kept evaluation out of it altogether, and what he deems good or bad, first- or fifth-rate, does not play any role in his argument. But your rhetorical question about the regional staff orchestras is very relevant indeed: you might pull Bob's leg while you are about it.

As for <u>Musical Education: Its Mortal Dangers</u>, with great respect, I disagree with your second thoughts: I would, on the contrary, prefer a festival audience, since I tend to talk in terms of the audience's own experience. At a festival, I could, very fruitfully, argue on the basis of the concerts surrounding my lecture, their position in a context of our musical world's educational set-up. The performers, all of whom I expect to be interesting, would be examined, on the one hand, as recipients and rejectors of musical education, and, on the other, as potential educators.

There would, undoubtedly, be an opportunity to work in the disastrous influence of the gramophone record – above all as a promoter of arrested development. Both creatively and re-creatively, arrested development is, in fact, the worst and most characteristic symptom of our time, affecting as it even does, with very few exceptions, outstanding talents.

Your questions about myself I shall try to answer as briefly and selectively as possible. Your guesses are right, and both as a writer and as a teacher, I am chronically snowed under. Three books (<u>1975</u> apart) are finished, and musical journalism I am trying to confine to an essential minimum (<u>The Listener</u>, <u>The Musical Times</u>, the <u>London Review of Books</u>. . . .). You will probably have heard about my Visiting Professorship in Canada and my stint at Princeton; the former I enjoyed moderately, the latter hugely. From now on, I am confining institutional teaching to activities or jobs which don't involve any waste of time on non-talents. Thus, I am in ultimate, dictatorial charge of all string quartets at the Menuhin School, where one encounters an astonishing amount of talent – and is, at last, in a position to guide developments from the outset, rather than having to undo what has gone wrong, chiefly as a result of the aforementioned education. And as I write, I am being invited to start a string-quartet masterclass at the Guildhall School of Music – an invitation which I shall probably accept; if talent turns out to be inadequate there, it should still be possible to run away, so long as I don't commit myself contractually for too long a period. Privately, and rather ironically, it seems that I'm coaching, and preparing for concerts, more pianists than string players! You will have noticed that the Leeds jury, on the other hand, confined itself to pianists.

Your report on your health does not make depressing reading: the awareness of, and spirit behind, total recovery is palpable.[67] For the rest, I agree that sometime soon, an oral exchange would prove highly fruitful. Do you ever listen to the radio nowadays? In <u>The Listener</u> and (equally unsuccessfully) in <u>The Musical Times</u>, I am regularly trying my best from the outside. [. . .]

All the very best from both to both,

Yours ever,

[Hans]

~

Keller's primary activity in retirement was teaching – and for the first time he was doing it institutionally. Much had changed in British music education while he had been at the BBC – especially within the rapidly expanding university sector, into which some of Keller's old critical colleagues had already moved. Donald Mitchell, for example, became in 1971 the inaugural Professor of Music at the University of Sussex, an institution founded in the early 1960s as the first of a new generation of 'plate glass' universities. The University of York, founded two years after Sussex, had actually been the first of these new universities to start teaching music – the work of Wilfrid Mellers, originally appointed in 1964 to teach English, but soon the author of a lively curriculum for music and its first professor. The University of London established its new faculty of music at King's College in 1964 with Thurston Dart in the chair, eager to reform music teaching after a frustrating time at Cambridge. His course made a defiant move away from traditional technical exercises – 'Abandon counterpoint all ye who enter here' was apparently pasted over the faculty entrance – and introduced a more critical approach to the history of music and historically-informed performance practice. As music established itself in the universities, it rapidly fragmented into different specialisms, and by the time of Keller's retirement the University of London was becoming the centre of a new American-inspired study of theory and analysis. Keller became involved in this after Christopher Wintle approached him in September 1980, asking him to speak in the series of seminars he was organising at Goldsmiths' College.

---

67 Glock had just been in hospital.

> *The teaching of trust is as important as the teaching of doubt.*

Keller had taught at Goldsmiths' before, a postgraduate course in Aesthetics and Criticism in 1973–74, at which time Wintle had been spending a year as a visiting fellow at Princeton. (When Keller went to lecture at Princeton himself he was pleasantly surprised to find that 'both students & professors knew my writings better than I do.'[68]) By 1982 Keller was teaching regularly at Goldsmiths where, says Wintle, he was 'a charismatic and sometimes overwhelming' presence.[69] Wintle and his colleagues at Goldsmiths' and at King's College (where in 1982 Arnold Whittall was appointed the first Professor of Music Theory and Analysis in a British university) were in the process of founding a new journal, *Music Analysis* – the first British journal to specialise in this discipline. It was launched in March 1982 and two years later the same group mounted the first British music analysis conference.[70] Keller was invited to write the opening essay for the journal, as well as to join its Advisory Board. His association with *Music Analysis* was not entirely comfortable, however, as his empirical approach was out of step with the theory-dominated times and he was suspicious of the new status of analysis as a separate discipline. Replying to a circular from editor Jonathan Dunsby asking Advisory Board members for feedback ('confidentially if necessary'), his opinion was blunt:

9 June 1983 – to Jonathan Dunsby

Dear Jonathan,

I hope my reaction to your circular of April 7th is not too late. What is wrong with the current issue is, simply, that you won't find me three substantial contemporary composers who show the remotest interest in it, whereas I can find you ten who say they don't understand a word of it. Let us, for heaven's sake remain in touch with genuine (a) musicality and (b) creativity; outside these areas, there is no place for musical analysis, whereas one of our most gifted young composers considers the current issue a positive insult to the creative imagination. I disagree with him, but I know (a) what he means and (b) that he should not be led thus to misunderstand.

---

68 Keller to Northcott, 27 February 1980, CULHK.
69 Wintle's memories of Keller at Goldsmiths' are preserved in CULHK.
70 This was held at King's College on 27–30 September 1984, and featured a performance of Keller's Functional Analysis of Mozart's G minor Quintet.

An area of enormous educational importance is the analysis of performance, of interpretation, of the relation between the score and its realization: why don't you make a concerted effort to develop a discipline which, institutionally, has not even been born yet?

I certainly don't wish my reactions to be kept confidential; on the contrary, I want an answer from everybody responsible to the questions I am raising, explicitly and implicitly.

Kindest regards,

Yours ever,

[Hans]

Wintle asked why Keller had cited composers' reactions rather than those of other analysts: 'aren't analysts a breed apart?'[71]

26 April 1984 – to Christopher Wintle

Dear Christopher,

Many thanks for your letter of April 15th. Let me immediately descend upon the most important point: "But aren't analysts a breed apart?" Certainly not; in fact analysis goes wrong whenever its authors consider themselves a breed apart. [. . .] The only analytic truths worth capturing are those which clarify both the recipient's and the composer's own experience. You say, "I only wish we had more articles that students could profitably turn to." I don't. In fact, I wish there were still fewer – by which I mean that my analytic teaching, at both institutions, is strictly confined to the students' own experience of the music in question; ultimately, it therefore invariably results in self-analysis, which is the only type of analysis creatively worth undertaking. [. . .]

And now, to your own most important point – Erwin Ratz. I know all his writings – and, in fact, knew him very well: in my teens, I met him every week.[72] So far as I am aware, everything he wrote deserves translation: he is a real analytic insider. I say this although we had a passionate disagreement – about the proper finale of Op. 130: he plunged for the Fugue, whereas in my submission Beethoven's preference, his <u>creative</u> preference, for the second finale is demonstrable. As a listener to string quartets, Ratz was, in fact, an outsider (though he knew more about

---

71 Wintle to Keller, 15 April 1984, CULHK.
72 Ratz had also been a regular attender at the Adler–Schmidt quartet sessions in the Neubaugasse.

quartet texture than Brahms). Had he not been, he would have realized that apart from everything else, the Fugue fails as a quartet texture – which can otherwise only be said about certain movements of the Op. 18 set. At the same time, this set does contain a single textural masterpiece – the Scherzo (as violently opposed to the first movement) of the C minor.

Lastly, the only other "German or Austrian analyst" worth translating is Adorno; has the whole of Schenker yet been translated? If not, he is, of course, another.

Kindest regards,

Yours ever

[Hans]

'The Americans have control over Schenker translation,' replied Wintle,[73] agreeing that 'we should do more for Adorno'. The second issue of *Music Analysis* had already included a translation of Adorno's 'Zum Probleme der musikalischen Analyse', which Wintle had found 'brilliant and fascinating: I should be very curious to know what you thought of it.'

13 December 1983 – to Christopher Wintle [extract]

Dear Christopher,

[. . .] "Brilliant and fascinating": yes indeed, that's one side of Adorno, but not his only side. The other is his intellectualizing obsessional neurosis, of which there are traces in this article too – and which, it seems to me, deafened Schoenberg to his stature as a musician. Have you heard or seen any of his compositions? Amazingly enough, he confines his compulsions to his verbal thought; there is no trace of them in his music – unless you want to consider his surprisingly free dodecaphony a compulsive attempt to imitate Schoenberg's own primacy of musical instinct.

Pursuing his point about the 'enormous educational importance' of the analysis of performance, Keller suggested to Dunsby that they commission a performer to write for the journal, on the grounds that 'an analyst who has proved himself as a meaningful interpreter deserves a credit account of trust.'[74]

73 Wintle to Keller, 5 December 1983. Ernst Oster's landmark translation of *Der freie Satz* had been published five years earlier (Longman: New York, 1979). Until this point, Schenker studies had been dominated by Schenker's own students who had emigrated to America before the war. The next wave of translation involved scholars from both sides of the Atlantic, beginning with William Drabkin and Ian Bent's English edition of *Das Meisterwerk in der Musik* (Cambridge: Cambridge University Press, 1994–97).

74 Letter to the editor, *MA* I/2 (July 1982): 229.

27 February 1984 – to Jonathan Dunsby [extract]

Dear Jonathan,

[. . .] I hope you agree with me when I say that John Ogdon is so outstanding and articulate a musician that it would be difficult to find more than half a dozen people of his musical calibre in this country; his psychiatric difficulties, of which you may have heard, have not in any way interfered with his musical development: I heard him but recently. Now, I happen to know that he would be terribly interested to write about Liszt's "Faust" and "Dante" Symphonies, and I would urgently suggest to you that you write to him immediately, telling him that you heard from me about his current, conceptual musical preoccupations, and invite him to write a major piece on the subject; I may say that when I was in charge of new music at the BBC, and engaged him as an outside assessor, his reports on new scores stood out among the rest, although the latter were highly gifted musicians' analyses too. The only reports I remember which were on John's level were Matyas Seiber's.

If one faces a new possibility, you may agree that the only logical approach is to ask oneself what one would risk if one tried it. What sort of risk would your commissioning John entail? For once, you will get a piece which, whatever its shortcomings, will not contain an unmusical, or extra-musical, or musically irrelevant word. It may well turn out to be on the naïve side, but so what? Haven't we had enough pseudo-sophistication? And think of the real musicians who will suddenly crowd round the issue in question!

By now, Keller was deeply involved in the institutional teaching of performance. Since September 1981, he had been teaching at the Yehudi Menuhin School, one of five specialist institutions set up in the 1960s for school-age children – another innovation in British music education. Menuhin asked him to take charge of all the students' quartet-playing, and Keller was delighted at the opportunity to guide young musicians from the beginning of their chamber musical lives. Soon afterwards, he was invited to coach quartets at the Guildhall School of Music: 'I am in nineteen minds,' he wrote to Peter Norris (Director of Music at the Menuhin School) 'and have postponed my final decision: we might discuss. Above all, is there not a danger of one's contradicting the more regular teaching staff, some of whom are, after all, regular quartet coaches?'.[75] Despite these reservations, he joined the staff in October that year, not only coaching quartets but also teaching the general musicianship course with composer Buxton Orr. He made his acceptance of the Guildhall post conditional on not having anything to do with examinations, telling its principal John Hosier that 'in no circumstances must any of the works in whose analysis I shall be involved be chosen as a "set work", nor can I possibly agree to any of the activities we shall be engaged

75 Keller to Norris 18 May 1982, CULHK.

on leading to any kind of eventual exam.'[76] He also argued hotly against the idea that young musicians could benefit from competitions: 'if an essentially inartistic and anti-musical enterprise exerts an <u>irreplaceable</u> favourable influence on a youngster's musical development, there's something wrong with his education.'[77]

But exams and competitions were not the whole problem. As his experience of institutional teaching broadened, Keller's anxiety about it deepened. He was working with some wonderfully gifted students and yet, again and again, he was struck by the way in which much in their playing was, as he put it, 'horrifyingly infantile'.[78] He thought a lot – 'protractedly, frantically, worriedly' – about this problem and its possible causes and towards the end of 1982 thought he had found the answer. He immediately addressed formal letters to John Hosier and Yehudi Menuhin:

11 December 1982 – to John Hosier [extract]

Dear John,

I write on a matter of the utmost, elemental and elementary importance, compared to which any problem you and/or the Menuhin School may have had to face at any stage must needs be considered secondary. [...]

For years, I have been wondering, helplessly groping. [...] Why were all young musicians, so-called, whom I taught, coached, and/or advised, why were even the most outstanding talents amongst them so immature musically, so downright infantile in many cases, that I have been unable to resist the feeling that at the age of 9 or 10, my musical pals and I had reached a higher and deeper degree of insight, especially interpretative insight, than I have encountered in many a supremely gifted 16-, 17-, or 18-year-old? And why was even his sight-reading so abysmally pre-musical, as if he had never before seen a note of the composer whose music he was reading?

It was only the other week when, in an analytic session, I carefully and cautiously introduced specific and concrete cross-references to helpfully selected works with which, I fondly thought, the students in question would be intimately familiar (since I confined myself to great masterpieces from their own instrumental literature), that the traumatic answer came to me in a flash: <u>the contemporary music student doesn't know any music</u>; the instrumentalist does not even know his own literature. Thus a fiddler will tell you he knows one or two Mozart sonatas, one or two Beethoven sonatas, one or two Haydn or Mozart or Beethoven quartets....

We cannot escape the conclusion that he has spent the most important years of his childhood and adolescence in artificial isolation

76 Keller to Hosier, 11 August 1982, CULHK.
77 Keller to Norris, 29 November 1982, CULHK.
78 Keller to Norris, 19 November 1982, CULHK.

from music – even when involved in the learning of his instrument. For a naturally musical child who has just played his first Mozart or Beethoven sonata will only know one overwhelming desire – to know them all, play them all, become an inhabitant, a native if possible, of this spellbinding musical world.

Instead of spontaneously <u>learning music</u>, however, the contemporary child, the contemporary youngster has artificially <u>learnt about it</u>: instead of encountering a quick <u>leggiero</u> passage in a masterpiece whose imagined phrasing would induce him to acquire the necessary <u>spiccato</u> technique for its realisation, he has spent meaningless hours, days, weeks on musicless <u>spiccato</u> exercises which, unphrasingly, he transfers, applies to that selfsame masterpiece if and when, years too late, he at last encounters it.

The separation between music and technique is, in fact, one of the traceable sources of contemporary ignorance and its inevitable consequence, which is musical infantilism. The typical contemporary student, that is, devotes a considerable proportion of what he wrongly regards as his musical time to unmusical, anti-musical or, at the very least, extra-musical practice. The centre of realistic and hence normal instrumental development would be practical – i.e. playing – <u>study</u>, which is the natural reaction to artistic curiosity, for there is no such curiosity without the acutely felt need to get to experience, know, & to be able to play, great music. All too readily, indeed with the teacher's connivance, this natural centre of early musical life is replaced with the artificial, neurotic (obsessional), and musically thoughtless centre of <u>practice</u> – often to the extent of truly musical <u>studies</u> by Kreutzer or Rode yielding to Sefcik-like <u>exercises</u>. [. . .]

It is important to recognise a central source [of contemporary ignorance] – the absence of internal motivation (as distinct from such external motivations as exams, or concerts, or, worst of all, competitions): conversely, the thirst for knowledge which, in the world of musical music, is inseparable from the thirst for experience, for musical excitement, is the only genuine ultimate source of genuinely musical knowledge, and it is this thirst which, whatever the other educational needs, has to be reawakened if the meaningful performance of music is to survive; yes, the situation is as critical as that.

For a start, I invite you to let me know whether you accept my facts – whether you agree that the contemporary music student doesn't know any music (though pianists seem to be slightly less gravely diseased than string players), in which case you will also kindly let me know whether you agree that this state of affairs is untenable. When I talk of ill-health and disease I do not wish to be understood too metaphorically: an individual will not easily survive without adequate liquid and food; he will,

in fact, fall ill. Our youngsters' musical life finds itself at precisely such a
stage of dehydration and starvation.

Yours ever,

[Hans]

23 December 1982 – to Yehudi Menuhin [extract]

Dear Yehudi,

[. . .] You are my ideal addressee: I am reminding you of Yehudi Menuhin
at the age of 16. Though you are older than I am, I remember your
then phrasing crystal-clearly; I have given proof of the precision of such
recollections. I'm not now talking about the boy's unique violinistic
talent, but about the stage of musical development he had reached: he
had, let's face it, grown up musically, had developed a sharply defined
musical personality, and couldn't have done so if he hadn't known any
music. Arrested development is a symptom of our own age – which,
nevertheless, throws up the occasional outstanding and even great player.
At the age of 14, Anne-Sophie Mutter, though still under the influence
of phrasings from outside sources upon which she had projected her
musical conscience, already evinced comprehensive familiarity with music,
with how music goes, which she could not conceivably have attained without
substantial, deep, and continual musical experiences (I prefer the specifying
plural). Music had become her life.

> *Music should be taught as
> religion was taught in a less
> secular age – as the life-giving
> centre of life, and also as
> revealer of a level of life of
> which, without it, we'd know
> nothing.*

The ultimate question, and the ultimate answer, is motivation. It is fascinating
to observe how in our own time, the transitive verb "to motivate" has
imperceptibly changed its connotation. Time was, that is to say, when
something motivated me to act in a certain manner, and that "something"
was well inside me. Nowadays, however, it is somebody who motivates
a person to act in a certain manner, and that "somebody" is well outside
the motivated person. [. . .]

The reason why, uncharacteristically, I am treating this matter in extenso
is that all too easily, it might come to be regarded as just another
problem, one of the many we teachers have to cope with, anyway. No,
it is the most fundamental problem of them all and, musically speaking,
a matter of life or death; it is, moreover, the dead-alive we have to face.
The other day, Peter Norris made a very wise observation when, in the
present context, he drew attention to the fact that a generation or so

ago, we tended to blame instrumentalists for only knowing their own repertoire; nowadays, they don't even know that. Music must cease to be a subject and, instead, become a reason for existence.

Yours ever,

[Hans]

~

'Teaching has made me more radical than ever before,' wrote Keller to Susan Bradshaw (who was also teaching at Goldsmiths')[79] – indeed his reforming zeal seemed only to increase with age. He was happiest with his young pupils at the Menuhin School, where, he apparently told Menuhin, he had found 'a quality for which he had waited all his life'.[80]

But time was running out. And Keller had long known that it was. For twenty years he had been suffering from an undiagnosed 'muscular complaint' – or that is what he called it on the rare occasions when he was forced to refer to it. It had first manifested itself in the early 1960s as a weakness down one side, putting an end to his violin-playing, skiing and typing. According to Milein Cosman, Keller refused the tests his doctor wanted to carry out (including lumbar puncture) because he feared side effects affecting the brain. Having made that decision, he ignored his symptoms until August 1978, when he arrived home from Jerusalem (the Congress on Jewish Music) in excruciating pain. How he got through the conference and the journey can only be imagined. It was Sunday evening, so a frantic Cosman rang George Stroh, Keller's old schoolfriend from Vienna and a medical man (child psychiatrist), who came straight round with a stock of industrial-strength painkillers:

8 August 1978 – to George Stroh

Dear George,

The time has come to test a well-analysed analyst's reality-principle. I am in a state of wellnigh uncontrollable euphoria, owing to your medication and, much more so, your advice freely to experiment with it. I must say that old grump Schopenhauer did have a very substantial point: it isn't easy to find anything as acutely and chronically pleasurable in life as freedom from pain – hours of exaltation, until you're quite exhausted from sheer joy!

Well, imagine I had consulted someone in Harley Street. On the one hand, he'd have been incapable of such unconventional advice – while on the other hand, had he given it, I'd have considered his likely fee (attached)

79 Keller to Bradshaw, 11 November 1983, CULHK.
80 Recollection signed by Menuhin found in Keller's archive, CULHK.

dirt cheap. Now, will you make it impossible for me to behave in a normal, realistic way – to pay, with beautiful simplicity, for professional services rendered? Is even a psychoanalyst incapable of venturing anywhere near what everyone (except for him!) would describe as sheer reality?

You will say, of course, it isn't. 'Mei Moritzl is', der einzie, der im Schriff geht.'[81]

Yours,

Hans

Stroh's painkillers enabled Keller to carry on as if nothing was happening until September the following year, when Stroh himself fell ill and died unexpectedly at the age of only sixty. On the recommendation of one of their neighbours, Cosman turned to Dr Donald Rau, whom she had never met, but who knew her close friend, the artist Marie-Louise von Motesiczky. He came to their house in Frognal Gardens to examine Keller – and, he says, the diagnosis was immediately clear: motor neurone disease. Rau suggested referral to a neurologist for confirmation, but Keller refused. 'He seemed to accept what was happening to him,' remembers Rau, 'and just wanted to get on with life and make the best of it with the least possible fuss.'[82]

Eventually, friends began to suspect that something was wrong. But Keller deflected all enquiries: 'His emphatic "Fine!" and immediate embarkation upon an

Milein Cosman and Hans Keller after his retirement, in the garden of 3 Frognal Gardens, where they lived from 1967.

81 'My little Moritz is the only one who marches in step.'
82 Donald Rau, oral communication, 14 June 2018.

enthralling musical discussion indicated in no uncertain manner that the subject of his health was not on the agenda.'[83] He carried on regardless with all his teaching commitments, and his literary flow continued unabated. Julian Hogg became his amanuensis and with his help Keller kept up his writing and his vast correspondence. There were many offers and enquiries from publishers eager for his work, and the 1980s also saw a growing interest in collecting and republishing his past writings. Faber reissued *Music Survey* in 1981, and pressed Keller repeatedly for the manuscript of *Criticism*. Oxford University Press was interested in *The Mendelssohn Violin Concerto* and Faber, Dent and Cambridge University Press all sought to publish collections of his essays. To Keller, however, 'things which haven't yet been written are more important, more urgent, than things that have,'[84] and instead of returning to his old manuscripts he dictated to Hogg a new book on *The Great Haydn Quartets: Their Interpretation* for Dent, which he intended to follow with a book on Mozart. Although this Haydn book was the product of a lifetime's thought, it was no mere repetition – indeed it was while writing it that Keller made 'a crucial discovery: there isn't a single compositorial innovation between Haydn and our own time (all of Beethoven's included) that can't be traced back to Haydn.' Writing about this to Alexander Goehr, Keller told him 'I would even include atonality and, needless to add, serialism. But I would exclude all innovations which are not part of musical reality' – by 'musical reality', he explained, he meant 'music as heard thought'.[85] While writing this book, Keller was also helping H.C. Robbins Landon with a new edition of the quartets for Doblinger – as ever, he remained concerned not only to express his own thoughts, but to help others express theirs. In fact, one of his very last projects was to plan with Martin Anderson of Toccata Press a book of conversations to preserve Reginald Goodall's thoughts on Wagner.

Keller still gave the occasional radio talk, his last being on Britten's quartets in June 1984, by which time speaking was becoming an effort (the producer had to speed up the tape for transmission). In the summer of 1985, his former pupil, the clarinettist Anton Weinberg, recorded an interview for Channel 4's television documentary *The Keller Instinct*, by which time Keller was desperately frail. But he continued to work, resuming his teaching at the start of the new term in September, recording in October the first of the planned series of discussions with Goodall for Anderson's projected book, and dictating to Julian Hogg right up until the last day of that month:

31 October 1985 – to Alfred Brendel

Dear Alfred,

What did Solti say in defence of his slow movement? Amazing how much sense you (as opposed to him) made of it! The outer movements received the greatest performance I have ever heard.[86]

83 Robert Matthew-Walker, *HKKC*, xiii.
84 'Epilogue/Prologue: Criticism and Analysis', *MA* I/1 (March 1982): 9–31.
85 Keller to Goehr, 13 December 1984, CULHK.
86 This refers to Brendel's performance of Beethoven's Fifth Piano Concerto (conducted by Solti) at the Royal Festival Hall on 27 October 1985, broadcast on Radio 3.

As for your Mozart article, from your subsequent reflections it is quite clear that you consider the Busoni quote as naïve as I do; Mozart let himself be inspired by whatever he wrote for.[87] After all, he was an outstanding pianist too – though you are quite right in suggesting that the first movement of the A minor sonata is a piece for symphony orchestra. Most outstanding composers for the piano implied something else when they wrote for the instrument: the "vocal scene with a dramatic middle section" and the "wind divertimento" are marvellous interpretations. The rest of the article is outstanding, too; I would add important character traits to your juxtaposition of Haydn and Mozart: Mozart was a starter, Haydn a developer. For Mozart the wealth of unified melodic inventions was as important as harmonic adventure was to Haydn. It has to be admitted, though, that when Mozart addressed something to Haydn, he assumed, pro tempore, his friend's creative character traits. In short, what, for Mozart, was melodic wealth, was harmonic wealth for Haydn. As a result, Haydn's sonata forms tend to have three development sections, not one: the other two occur between the first and second subjects in both the exposition and the recapitulation. Do we still agree? We might discuss the question in the course of your next visit. [. . .]

Yours ever,

31 October 1985 – to Yehudi Menuhin

Dear Yehudi,

Many thanks for your letter of October 25th. I am delighted the Paris Concours went well.

When, at the latest, may I decide about April 30th? My muscular complaint may prevent me from going, though in principle, I should be delighted to take on the job.[88]

May I say that your recent and not so recent performances (recordings) have convinced me that yours is the very deepest insight into the music you play? It gives me much satisfaction to have such a friend, even though we meet but rarely. In our musical world, it doesn't happen often that

---

87 Brendel, 'A Mozart Player Gives Himself Advice', in *Music Sounded Out* (London: Robson, 1990). The 'naïve' Busoni quote was, 'Unmistakably, Mozart takes singing as his starting point.'
88 A masterclass at the Congress of the European String Teachers' Association in Copenhagen.

two understanders meet whose comprehension evinces utter harmony. Long may our friendship last.

Yours ever,

The letters from this last dictation session were never signed. Hogg typed them on 4 November, and put them in the post back to Keller as usual. By the time they arrived in Frognal Gardens, however, it was too late. Cosman phoned Hogg in his BBC office on 6 November, with the news that Keller had died at 11 o'clock that morning. It was his regular day for teaching his Menuhin School pupils, she said, and even the night before he had still been determined to carry on.

Martin Anderson also remembers the call he received from Cosman that day: 'Der Hans ist gestorben' – she told him afterwards she hadn't realised she had spoken in German. She asked him to ring Robert Simpson and *The Times* 'in that order'. Later, Anderson went down to the South Bank, knowing there was to be a London Sinfonietta concert that evening at the Queen Elizabeth Hall, where many of Keller's friends and colleagues were likely to be gathered. Sure enough, there were Susan Bradshaw, Bayan Northcott and many others. 'I felt like the angel of death.'[89]

By an extraordinary chance – so extraordinary that it seems scarcely credible it was not designed – the very last piece of music played on Radio 3 on the day Hans Keller died was the quartet dedicated to him by the dying Benjamin Britten. It was a scheduled studio concert given by the Medici String Quartet in Manchester and they cannot possibly have known. Switching on the radio at home in Clapham after his return from the South Bank, Martin Anderson couldn't believe his ears. As the music played, he rang Radio 3 continuity, trying to persuade them to change their closing announcement: 'That was Britten's Third Quartet, dedicated to Hans Keller, who died today.'

It was shortly before midnight, and the announcer on duty felt he couldn't make such a statement without official confirmation. Bayan Northcott, also listening at home after the Sinfonietta concert and marvelling at the fitness of Britten's Third Quartet being played at this moment, wrote sadly in his diary afterwards, 'How cruel there should be no announcement of the death of its dedicatee.'[90]

Even so, the BBC could scarcely have offered Keller a better tribute than a performance of this quartet – especially since the work the Medicis had paired with the Britten that night was Beethoven's Op. 135.

89 Anderson, oral communication, 14 June 2018. Bayan Northcott recorded in his diary being met by Anderson in the foyer as he arrived for the Sinfonietta's Boulez concert. 'How arid *Domaines* sounded after that.'

90 Quoted by Northcott in an email to the authors, 18 June 2018.

Music proves the reality of another world, & w'dn't make sense without it.

~

When I lectured on [Britten's Third Quartet] at Snape the other month I analysed the heavily charged end, or non-end, against the harmonic background of the traditional interrupted cadence, and ventured that the only possible verbal translation of these last, unfinal notes was, 'This is not the end.'

~

As for Op. 135, it isn't the same 'period' as the Last Quartets at all. In fact, Beethoven survived his Last Quartets characteristically: Op. 135, the last before he died, is a First, the beginning of an entirely new style, the Sixth Period, approximately, whose development he did not live to hear with his deaf, clairvoyant ears – the beginning of a future we shall never hear.

Hans Keller by Milein Cosman.

Index

Page numbers in **bold** relate to illustrations.

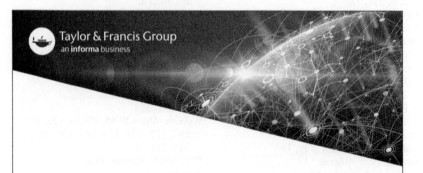